OLD
PEOPLE
IN
THREE
INDUSTRIAL
SOCIETIES

OLD PEOPLE IN THREE INDUSTRIAL SOCIETIES

Ethel Shanas ∗ *Peter Townsend*

Dorothy Wedderburn ∗ *Henning Friis*

Poul Milhøj ∗ *Jan Stehouwer*

AldineTransaction
A Division of Transaction Publishers
New Brunswick (U.S.A.) and London (U.K.)

First paperback printing 2007
Copyright © 1968 by Transaction Publishers.

All rights reserved under International and Pan-American Copyright
Conventions. No part of this book may be reproduced or transmitted in any form
or by any means, electronic or mechanical, including photocopy, recording, or
any information storage and retrieval system, without prior permission in writing
from the publisher. All inquiries should be addressed to AldineTransaction, A
Division of Transaction Publishers, Rutgers—The State University, 35 Berrue
Circle, Piscataway, New Jersey 08854-8042. www.transactionpub.com

This book is printed on acid-free paper that meets the American National
Standard for Permanence of Paper for Printed Library Materials.

Library of Congress Catalog Number: 2007060653
ISBN: 978-0-202-30950-7
Printed in the United States of America

Library of Congress Cataloging-in-Publication Data

Old people in three industrial societies / Ethel Shanas—[et. al]
    p. cm.
  Originally published: New York : Arno Press, 1980.
  Includes bibliographical references and index.
  ISBN 978-0-202-30950-7 (alk. paper)
    1. Older people—United States. 2. Older people—Great Britain.
  3. Older people—Denmark. I. Shanas, Ethel.

HQ1064.U5O4 2007
305.260973—dc22   2007060653

Preface

This volume presents the findings of a cross-national survey of living conditions and behavior of elderly people in Denmark, Britain, and the United States.

The idea for this research project developed out of discussions held under the auspices of the Social Research Committee of the International Gerontological Association, which was established in 1956 with a branch for Europe and a branch for the United States. At a research conference in Copenhagen conducted by the European branch in October, 1956, under the chairmanship of Mr. Henning Friis, a number of suggestions for comparative research were discussed. The background papers and research proposals were later published in the report on *Cross National Research on Old Age* (Ann Arbor, Michigan: Division of Gerontology, University of Michigan, 1958).

With the assistance of the United Nations Technical Assistance Administration and of the Attivitá Assistenziali Italiane e Internazionali, the European Committee organized a special meeting of experts in Assisi, Italy, in September, 1959, to discuss the details of a program of research with the object of submitting an application to a research foundation or agency for financial assistance. A survey to pilot a possible future cross-national survey of old people had been carried out in England earlier that year with financial support from the Gulbenkian Foundation.*

Finally, an international research seminar, organized by the American branch of the Committee under a grant from the United States National Institute of Mental Health, was held in Berkeley in August, 1960, and carried the discussion further. An agreement was reached among three of the present investigators, Henning Friis, Ethel Shanas, and Peter

---

* Peter Townsend and Brian Rees, *The Personal, Family, and Social Circumstances of Old People: Report of a Survey to Pilot a Future Cross-National Survey* (London, England: London School of Economics, 1959).

Townsend, who took the initiative and decided to attempt to undertake coordinated national sample surveys in Denmark, the United States, and Britain.

Further detailed planning for this research was made possible through a travel grant from the Ford Foundation to the American investigator, Ethel Shanas, to visit both Denmark and Britain in January and February, 1961. The assistance of Mr. Stacey Widdicombe, Program Associate of the Foundation, is gratefully acknowledged.

Because of the great interest shown by the United States National Institute of Mental Health in developing international research in the field of gerontology, in the winter 1960–61 applications were made to the Institute for grants for the financing of the surveys in each country and for the regular cooperation among the investigators. The applications were received in a very positive spirit by the National Institute of Mental Health, which awarded its first grants for the surveys in the summer of 1961. Very substantial grants have been awarded during the years 1961–66, first by the National Institute of Mental Health (grant numbers: for Denmark, M 5509; for Great Britain, M 05511; for the United States, M 5630) and later by the Community Health Services Division of the Bureau of State Services of the United States Public Health Service (grant numbers: for Denmark, CH 00052; for Great Britain, CH 00053; for the United States, CH 00054). We owe more than we can adequately summarize here to the farsightedness, generosity, and trust of the agencies of the Public Health Service. The cooperation and assistance of Philip Sapir, Louis A. Wienckowski, and Evelyn Flook of these agencies are gratefully acknowledged.

The detailed preparation of the surveys began in spring, 1961. Interviewing was undertaken in 1962; in Denmark, mid-April–early June; in Britain, mid-May–July; in the United States, mid-May–August.

The scale of the inquiry in each individual country alone was such that a full-scale research team was required. In addition, much work was involved in coordinating and planning on an international basis. The following bodies and persons were involved in each of the three countries. The Danish part of the survey was undertaken by the Danish National Institute of Social Research. Under the general overview of its Director, Mr. Henning Friis, the study was in its first years directed by Mr. Poul Milhøj, at that time Program Director in the Institute. He was assisted by Mr. Jan Stehouwer, then Research Associate at the Institute, now Lecturer in sociology at the University of Aarhus, and Mr. Frede Østergaard, Research Associate at the Institute. After the appointment of Mr. Milhøj as Professor at the Copenhagen School of Economics and Business Administration in April, 1963, Mr. Henning Friis took on the over-all management of the survey. He was aided by Mr. Erling Jørgensen, Program Director, who has been responsible for the analysis of the material on old people's financial resources and expenditures, assisted by Mr. Østergaard. Professor Poul Milhøj, assisted by Mr. Ole Asmussen, continued to be in charge of the analysis of the material on work and retirement. Mr. Jan Stehouwer has been responsible for the material on health and welfare, living arrangements, family relationships, and contacts.

Mr. Finn Madsen designed the Danish sample. Mr. Ove Per Henningsen assisted in adapting the punch card material for electronic computers.

The British part of the survey was organized from the London School of Economics and Political Science, of the University of London, and the Department of Applied Economics, of the University of Cambridge, under the joint direction of Mr. Peter Townsend, then a lecturer in Social Administration at the School, and Mrs. Dorothy Wedderburn, then Senior Research Officer in the Department. The work began in late 1961. The Government Social Survey agreed to undertake the responsibility for interviewing elderly persons throughout Britain; and from the start Mr. Louis Moss, the Director of the Survey, and his staff played a major part in developing a viable program and working out the questionnaire and the method of analysis. In particular, Miss Amelia Harris and Mrs. Myra Woolf contributed enormously, through their ingenuity, patience, and technical expertise, to the plans that took shape during a series of meetings between the research teams working in the three countries. Mr. Douglas Stewart and Mr. Ronald Blunden also played an important role at certain key stages. While the Government Social Survey cannot be held responsible for the interpretations made of the data in these pages, the fact that the Survey was responsible for collecting and sifting the British data in the first place must not be forgotten

The British government must also be thanked for making the work possible. Permission had to be sought for the services of the Social Survey to be used and, as is usual in these matters, this depended to some extent on the support of the principal government representatives of the subjects under study (in this case the Ministers of Health, Housing and Local Government, and Labour, the Minister of Pensions, and the Chairman of the National Assistance Board).

In the later stages of the research, further tabulating help was given by the Computer Units of the Universities of London and of Essex; and though Mrs. Wedderburn's work on income and assets continued to be based on the Department of Applied Economics, the remaining part of the work, under Professor Townsend, was based on the Department of Sociology in the new University of Essex, Colchester. Mrs. Sylvia Tunstall, Research Assistant in the Department, has been responsible for a large part of the analysis and has contributed much of value to these pages. Miss Sheila Benson, Research Assistant working primarily on a parallel study of the elderly in institutions, and Mr. Jeremy Tunstall, Research Officer in independent charge of a supplementary study of the isolated elderly, also helped the program of research at various stages.* Among those who contributed to the development of the research were Mr. Brian Rees, Dr. Royston Lambert, Mrs. Gay Boehm, Mr. Gurmukh Singh,

---

* See Sheila Benson and Peter Townsend, *The Elderly in Institutions* (London: Routledge and Kegan Paul [forthcoming]); J. Tunstall, *Old and Alone: A Sociological Study of Old People* (London: Routledge and Kegan Paul, 1966).

Mrs. Daphne Partos, Mrs. Wendy Morgan, Miss Katy Pringle, and Miss Deborah Paige. Among those who helped greatly by commenting on drafts and providing additional information were Mrs. Ida Merriam, Miss Lenore Epstein, and their colleagues in the Division of Research and Statistics of the Social Security Administration of the Department of Health, Education, and Welfare in the United States, as well as Professor Brian Abel-Smith, Professor Richard M. Titmuss, Mr. Brian Reddaway, Mr. Ted Marmor, and Mr. Tony Lynes.

The American part of the survey was undertaken at the University of Chicago by Miss Ethel Shanas. The American investigator is particularly indebted to D. Gale Johnson, Dean of the Division of Social Sciences, Philip M. Hauser of the Department of Sociology, and Robert D. Hess of the Committee on Human Development, for their generous support and scholarly criticism.

Interviewing on this program was done by the staff of the National Opinion Research Center. Peter H. Rossi, Director, and Richard D. Jaffe, Associate Director, of that agency were extremely helpful during this phase of the work. The complex tasks of data processing were carried forward by Frederic J. Meier of the Graduate School of Business. Margaret G. Reid, Professor Emeritus of Economics, helped design the questions on financial resources and assisted in the interpretation and evaluation of the American findings on the income of the aged. Alice W. Chandler of the Committee on Human Development was responsible for the administrative details of program operation. Esther G. Silverman supervised the coding of the original schedules, the preparation of the tables, and the supplying of United States data to the European investigators.

The planning of the surveys and the analysis of the data have been a most interesting exercise in international research cooperation, which has been carried out by means of fourteen meetings and hundreds of letters. This cooperation has been based on great frankness in discussions regarding procedure, together with the desire of each of the national groups to understand problems affecting other participants.

Henning Friis
Poul Milhøj
Ethel Shanas
Jan Stehouwer
Peter Townsend
Dorothy Wedderburn

Contents

1 : Old People in Three Industrial Societies: An Introduction

Old age is a universal phenomenon. With varying degrees of probability, individuals survive childhood, grow to maturity, and become old, in all societies. But are the experiences and problems of old age the same in different countries? This book describes and analyzes the condition of persons aged 65 and over in three industrial societies: Denmark, Britain, and the United States. It therefore provides an early example of the results in the social sciences of systematic comparative research. It considers the capacity of older persons for self-care, their role in the family network, and their ability and opportunity to provide for themselves in old age. The book begins with an account of the physical capacities of older people and their attitudes toward their health, and goes on to explore the dependence of the elderly on the medical and welfare services, their family relationships, their work experience, their attitudes toward work and retirement, and their financial resources.

The findings reported here result from the concerted effort of investigators from different disciplines in each of the three countries. In this introductory chapter we shall first explain why we undertook this study of the elderly. Second, we shall consider the general theoretical positions in social gerontology relevant to our investigation and the implications of these theories for social policy. Third, we shall outline some of the hypotheses that guided our research and then present a few salient facts about the situation of the elderly in Denmark, Britain, and the United States at the time we began our study. Finally, we shall discuss some of the problems of comparative research as we confronted them and also the methods that we employed in the present cross-national study of older people.

Why This Study Was Made

The number of persons aged 65 and over in the population of Western countries has been increasing steadily since the Industrial Revolution. Within the last half century all Western countries have experienced a marked increase in their older populations not only absolutely but also in proportion to their total populations. In 1900 persons over 65 formed 6.6 per cent, 4.7 per cent, and 4.1 per cent, respectively, of the populations of Denmark, Britain, and the United States; by 1960 and 1961, however, they comprised 10.6 per cent, 11.7 per cent, and 9.2 per cent of each country's population.[1] Concomitant with this rise in the number of older people have come even greater urbanization of Western countries, and structural changes in the economy which have had important implications for the employment opportunities available for older men. Western societies in the last few decades have become aware not only of the presence of more older people, but of older people as having problems: as persons who need health care, as persons who need financial assistance, as persons who need special housing, and as persons many of whom are widowed, unmarried, and socially isolated.

During the past 15 years there have been an increasing number of studies of old people. These studies vary in their design and in their emphasis. Many are concerned with special populations among the aged: the sick, or the destitute, or those who come to the attention of service agencies. Others have been concerned with specifically local populations. While the findings from such research may be pertinent for the special groups studied, it is difficult to draw general conclusions of national or cross-national applicability from them. As a result, research in depth suffers from a lack of basic knowledge about the aged in general and certain popular assumptions or myths are perpetuated in the public mind. The following are the kinds of assumptions frequently made:

1. Most old people are in poor health.
2. Most old people are physically isolated from their families.
3. Most old people want to continue to work.
4. Most old people are living in poverty.

To the extent that these assumptions are generally accepted they have serious implications for social policy. The elderly tend to be treated in policy as a monolithic homogeneous group, rather than as a heterogeneous section of the population with diverse needs, with the result that programs for the elderly may offer too little flexibility and choice to those they are designed to serve.

In the present study the investigators therefore wished to provide fundamental information about the life situation of old people in the three countries studied to allow certain hypotheses about the role of the aged in Western societies to be tested. The information would provide a basis also for social policy. It was felt that the data secured in the surveys would give a balanced and varied picture of the state of the elderly so that the above generalizations could be revised and the magnitude and nature of elderly groups with particular difficulties could be described. In the area of social theory, the investigators felt that certain phenomena associated with aging, such as declining physical capacity, were universal, but that the reactions of older people to declining physical capacity varied from country to country. It was hypothesized that the conditions and conduct of older people would change with advancing age in all three countries because of the differing cultural and socio-structural situations in which old people lived. The specific hypotheses investigated in this study are spelled out later in this chapter.

The Basic Theories of Social Gerontology: Integration versus Segregation

The basic preoccupation of social gerontology as it has emerged within the last two decades may be categorized as being concerned with integration versus segregation. Are old people integrated into society or are they separated from it? This is perhaps not only the most important theoretical question in social gerontology today but also the key question affecting all social policies concerning the aged. Specifically, should old people be integrated into society by new forms of employment and social activities, or should they be removed gently from the main streams and the cross-currents of ordinary life? Do they prefer to live in the midst of the larger society or in retirement communities (such as groups of bungalows and residential institutions)? The answers given to these questions and others like them could make a very great difference in how governments interpret the needs of old people and go about meeting them.

A number of theories have been developed, based on the themes of segregation or integration. In general, they are theories of segregation, and take several different forms. The first group of theories is concerned with historical changes in the relationships, roles, and the attitudes of the elderly. It is postulated that while the elderly used to be integrated into the family and society, they are now increasingly segregated. The second group of theories is concerned with individual aging during the life-span—involving patterns of socialization and engagement and disengagement. It is postulated that an increasing degree of segregation is the normal experience in the final phase of the individual life cycle. The third group of theories is concerned with relationships between the aged and the young, particularly within the family, and with the present attitudes and roles of the elderly. In these formulations, it is usually stated that, whatever happened in the past, in modern society the elderly are segregated from the young.

HISTORICAL CHANGES IN RELATIONSHIPS

Early sociological theory alleged the disintegrating effects of industrialization on settled rural communities and extended families. Just as the family unit was said to have diminished in size, so also the functions of the family were said to have diminished in number and importance. In consequence the elderly were assumed to be losing their function and to be largely isolated. As old people grew in number during the twentieth century, social theory continued to stress the shift from the extended family to the nuclear or immediate family, the looser ties of social life, and the isolation of the aged. Parsons, for example, writes of the "structural isolation from kinship, occupational, and community ties" as the reason for political agitation in the 1940's to help old people. "By comparison with other societies the United States assumes an extreme position in the isolation of old age from participation in the most important social structures and interests."[2]

Really good information on the family life of older people in the past is lacking. What information is available does not, in general, support the theories that suggest that old people in the family have been isolated as a result of industrialization. Evidence for pre-industrial periods suggest that three-generation households were rare in the past in both the United States and Great Britain and that a large number of old people lived alone in towns and villages alike.[3] Again evidence in this century from pre-industrial societies shows that in many of them there are pauper aged who are given minimum consideration rather than maximum respect, and who tend to be isolated or, at the most, to lead a fitful social existence.[4] There are also infirm aged, variously referred to as the "over-aged," the "useless stage," the "sleeping period," the "age-grade of the dying," and the "already dead," who tend to be regarded as "living liabilities" and who in many societies are neglected and in some even abandoned.[5]

In the attempts of previous theory to account for the changes in the life of the aged in industrial as compared with pre-industrial societies, two points of fundamental importance have not been dealt with. First, old people tend to be rare in pre-industrial but not in industrial societies; second, in both pre-industrial and industrial societies a differentiation is made between relatively active and relatively infirm old age which has apparently been ignored by family theorists.[6] Moreover, in describing the role of the aged, far too much reliance has been placed on scattered and wholly inadequate information. As better base-line data become available for a number of societies, changes in the situation of the aged can be measured more rigorously and systematically.

INDIVIDUAL AGING AND DISENGAGEMENT

The second approach to segregation and integration in old age focuses on *individual* adjustment and participation. Throughout human history it has been evident that as some people get older their activities shrink in number and range. Old people are more likely to be infirm and therefore unable to travel about easily. They are also more likely to be poor and to lack the resources which make participation possible. Some theorists, however, have gone further in explaining the limitation of activity in old age. René König and others have used the concept of "desocialization," in contrast to the concept of "socialization" in childhood and adolescence, for the social and psychological changes in old age. Cumming and Henry have developed the concept of "disengagement."[7] The Cumming and Henry theory is one of the most interesting theories currently being debated in social gerontology. These investigators postulate that, independent of ill-health and poverty, "normal aging is a mutual withdrawal or 'disengagement' between the aging person and others in the social system."[8] As Cumming and Henry see it, the psychological and social processes of individual development and senescence form a curve of activity. In the last stages of life the curve descends steadily to the point of death. The individual organism "prepares" for death by disengaging from activity and the collective social organism prepares him for the last stage of life by withdrawing its integrating pressures. Disengagement theory suggests an "ultimate biological basis for reduction of interest or involvement in the environment."[9] Whether disengagement is initiated by society or by the aging person, in the end the old person plays fewer roles and his relationships have changed their quality. Disengagement then reflects a triple withdrawal—a loss of roles, a limitation of social contacts and relationships, and a much smaller commitment to social norms and values.

The disengagement theory has led to considerable controversy, especially since many of its critics suppose it condones a policy of indifference towards the social problems of the aged. The evidence for the disengagement theory is that many old people do experience a loss of roles: whether through the death of a spouse, the departure of adult children, or through retirement from paid employment. Further, there tends to be a corresponding dissociation from group membership in old age. Some studies indicate a decline with age in membership in voluntary associations and formal organizations generally.[10] Other studies refer to the reduction, through retirement and death, in the circle of "acquaintances" and "friends," but they do not define those terms very clearly or measure their numbers.

The positive evidence for disengagement is incomplete, even within the severely limited terms in which the theory has been expressed. There are a number of alternative arguments to disengagement theory. While old people lose some of the central relationships in the family, such as those with a spouse and with siblings, there is little or no evidence of a decline in contacts with children. Some weakening of emotional ties with children and other relatives is occasionally hypothesized but it has not been successfully demonstrated.[11] Insufficient attention may have been given to forms of compensation, replacement, and substitution when there are losses of roles and relationships in old age as at other times of life. Widowed people remarry or join their married children, or develop more intensive relationships with one or more of their children. They begin to spend more time with the neighbors. *Extensive* social interaction may be gradually replaced by *intensive* local social interaction, involving fewer people. Loss of roles may heighten the subjective importance, and increase the effectiveness of execution, of those roles that remain.

The difficulty of correctly interpreting losses of role in old age should be stressed. Roles can be embryonic as well as mature. They can vary in scope and importance. In terms of ego-satisfaction they may be replaceable or irreplaceable. For any individual his roles are a continually evolving constellation which is never fixed, but which adapts to the changing social and physical environment as well as to his changing capacities. The dual fluidity of roles—that is, variation in each role and variation in the *combination* of different roles actually performed daily by individuals—is often overlooked.

There is little evidence that old people take the initiative in "disengaging" and there is a good deal of evidence to suggest that they dislike loss of roles and relationships. Not everyone reaches a high plateau of involvement and activity in middle life from which there is a gradual fall in later life. Many individuals never reach a high plateau; they cannot be said to have become "engaged," or to have reached more than the foothills of social integration. Even when disengagement appears to be gradual, as when an elderly housewife gives up first the shopping, then the heavy cleaning and washing, and only last of all the cooking, there is evidence of marked unwillingness to surrender these functions. Even very old women retain important roles as housewives, mothers, and grandmothers.

INTERGENERATIONAL RELATIONSHIPS AND SOCIAL ISOLATION

The third approach to segregation theory is least developed. It tends to be linked with the historical approach which seeks to explain the disintegration of the extended family over time. Thus after writing of the steady decline in patriarchal sentiment in Germany and the emergence of new relationships between family members, Baumert refers to the "increasing tendency towards exclusion of aging parents from the families of their married children" and "the trend towards a separation of the young and old."[12] Of America, Nimkoff writes:

> In 1900, in an era still agricultural, the aged were generally persons of considerable power in the family because they controlled property and occupations, and they were greatly respected for their knowledge and ability. Since then, with the growth of our industrial society, property and jobs have moved away from family control. Increased physical mobility separates the aged more often from their children and other kin.[13]

In Australia, Hutchinson finds it the case that:

> For the mass of older people increasing age carries with it a decreasing association with the younger generations. In the . . . social scene the conjugal family is the sole unit of intimate relationships. With the withering of this unit the surviving members must, on the whole, expect to continue their lives as individuals.[14]

This approach to the separation of generations culminates in a series of generalizations about *existing* relationships. For example, Ruth Benedict writes of "our atomistic American families" and of "our great cities where each family is strange to all others" in a paper which makes no mention of wider kinship ties.[15] Ralph Linton remarks of city relationships: "The average city dweller recognizes his extended ties of relationship only in the sending of Christmas cards and in the occasional practice of hospitality of visiting kin."[16]

But do old people lose touch with their married children and lead an isolated life? Are the bonds of kinship of little or no consequence, especially in urban areas? And do the old mix predominantly with their peers rather than with the younger generation? Several studies disclose that a minority of the elderly population are in fact isolated from kin. Many of them are old people who have no children. Some have few contacts with friends and neighbors, or with voluntary associations. Yet they often have reasonably high morale and are not lonely. Moreover, the information given in these studies is rarely detailed enough or sufficiently relevant to national populations to allow the clear formulation of conclusions.

On the other hand, in Europe and America there is accumulating evidence from local and regional studies, and even from certain national studies which were directed primarily at obtaining data on other subjects, that inter-generational contacts within the family are often frequent and emotionally close.[17] While there appears to have been a trend in some countries for old people to live apart from their children in separate dwellings, there is considerable evidence of their living near their children and exchanging services every day—"intimacy at a distance" is the phrase coined by Rosenmayr and Köckeis.[18]

The General Approach

We sought to obtain a rich body of data which would help to show to what degree old people, in different ways, are integrated in industrial society. This meant exploring their physical capacities, their relationships with relatives and others, the roles they perform whether in employment or at home, the incomes they depend on, the services they receive, and some of the attitudes they have toward, for example, retirement or isolation. We realized that our investigation could not be exhaustive; in particular it was not aimed at those under the age of 65, nor did it follow the elderly from year to year. But at the most general level we felt that it would help to answer questions of urgent relevance to the development both of social gerontology and social policy.

Some of these questions are:

1. What is the general level of physical functioning of older people?
2. What are the sources of social support for older people, and, in particular, what is the role of the family in later life?
3. Why do people retire; what are their attitudes towards retirement?
4. What are the sources and levels of income of old people?
5. What services may be necessary to maintain older people in their own homes in the face of their declining physical capacity?
6. How do levels of physical capacity, occupation, income, and social integration differ between people in certain broad age groups over the age of 65?

7. How do levels of physical capacity, social and family integration, and attitudes towards retirement differ between older people of different social class and socioeconomic status?
8. How many older people lead isolated lives, and what are the main characteristics of these persons?

Having posed the general questions, we then sought to develop and test hypotheses about old people which could draw on descriptive correlations between variables such as age, incapacity, social interaction, social class, and income. These hypotheses were focused on the general areas of physical capacity of the aged, the role of old people in the family and in their social relationships, employment and retirement among the elderly, and the economic situation of the aged. We set them out below in their original crude form to show what were the starting points of our inquiry.

INTEGRATION AND CAPACITY

One crucial factor in the social participation of old people is their health, or, more precisely, their level of functional capacity. Some persons with a serious disease or handicap may be able to participate in social life to an equal extent with a person who is healthy. For our purposes, therefore, it was appropriate to consider not so much the number and kinds of ailments from which old persons suffer, but the physical and social consequences of such ailments. To what extent are old people able to get about, look after their persons, and manage a household? In exploring the answers to these questions we developed an index of incapacity which we used to measure physical functioning.

In the general areas of capacity the following simple hypotheses were formulated at the start of the investigation:

1. The level of physical capacity declines gradually with age.
2. The level of physical capacity varies according to sex and marital status.
3. If an old person has children, the more infirm he is, the more likely he is to live with or near an adult child.
4. Attitudes towards health are determined to a considerable extent by prevailing social values.
5. The kinds of social services required by old people depend not only on their levels of capacity, but also on their relationships with their family and kin.

As may be seen, our hypotheses correlated age, capacity, and family structure. The old person, and the problems that arise from limited physical capacity, do not exist in a social vacuum.

INTEGRATION AND FAMILY RELATIONSHIPS

Old people are knitted into the social structure through the relationships they have with their relatives, friends, and acquaintances, and through the roles they perform in these relationships. Because we felt that the family life of old people was of crucial importance in understanding their role in contemporary society, many data were collected on family structure, the numbers of children of old people, the physical proximity of relatives to the old person, and the frequency of contact among family members.

In the general area of family relationships the following major hypotheses were among those formulated:

1. If an old person has children he is likely to live with or near at least one child.
2. More daughters than sons are in close contact with old people.
3. When the family of the old person is standardized according to size, there is little difference between persons of different social classes in the frequency of their contacts with relatives.
4. More women than men are socially isolated, but more are also in close contact with relatives.
5. Isolated persons are not always "desolated" persons (that is, those who have recently lost a spouse or other close relative).
6. Loneliness is correlated with desolation rather than isolation.
7. The kind of public services required by older people depends on whether or not children exist and live nearby.

In the following discussion of the family life of old people, these and many additional hypotheses are explored and considered within the limits of the available data.

INTEGRATION AND WORK

Old people, particularly old men, are also knitted into the social structure through their participation in the work force. Work not only serves as a source of income but also is purposeful activity. Work serves to organize the day and to provide the worker with something to do. For some the work situation can be the center of social life as well as the context within which individual existence can be "justified." For others it is merely a mechanical activity drawing them away from social relationships which are more meaningful and satisfying. But even for the latter persons the change of status and additional number of hours of leisure brought by retirement may bring serious problems of adjustment.

In the area of employment and retirement we particularly looked for evidence that:

1. Those in occupations in which the hours and conditions of work are inflexible have less desire to remain at work than those in other situations.
2. There is no close correlation between physical capacity and the length of time in retirement.
3. There is a correlation between the physical capacity of the retired worker and his desire for a job.

4. Attitudes of workers toward retirement depend on the relationship between employment income and income after retirement.
5. Retired men in the three countries with the same occupational background will enjoy the same things in retirement.

Not all of these hypotheses could be formulated in a way that was entirely satisfactory for data collection. Attitudes toward work and retirement can be explored in a wide variety of ways and are not easy to interpret out of their cultural contexts.

INTEGRATION AND INCOME

Old people also participate in social life according to their differential ability to purchase the necessities of existence as well as other consumer goods. We were interested in the income levels of old people not only within the aged population itself, but also as these income levels relate to the income levels of younger adults and to the income level that the individual old person might have had in the past. In the analysis, the income of old people is analyzed by income units: married couples, unmarried men, and unmarried women. For different types of income units the range of income around the median is compared, country by country.

Among the hypotheses originally formulated were:

1. With increasing age, there is a marked shift in the sources and level of income.
2. In every country, single and unmarried old women are the poorest group among the aged.
3. Living arrangements with children are independent of income level.

The hypotheses listed above as they relate to integration of the elderly and their health, family and social relationships, occupation, and income have been expressed here in their simplest forms. The chapters that follow will give somewhat more complex statements of these and other hypotheses, and the evidence for their verification or disavowal will be presented in a detailed fashion.

The Elderly in Denmark, Britain, and the United States: A Brief Description

Denmark, Britain, and the United States, the three countries participating in this research, vary greatly in the size of their populations. At the time this study was made (1962) Denmark had 5 million people, Great Britain 53 million, and the United States 186 million. Despite differences in size, all three countries are highly industrialized, with industrial production dominated by large firms. Denmark still has a substantial proportion of its total labor force engaged in agriculture—16 per cent, compared with 5 per cent in Britain and about 7 per cent in the United States. All three countries are among those nations with high *per capita* real incomes.

It appears in fact that the standards of living in Denmark and in Britain are remarkably close, while the average in the United States is higher than either of them.

As may be expected in industrialized countries with high standards of living, all three countries have substantial numbers of people over 65. As stated earlier 10.6 per cent of the total population in Denmark, 11.7 per cent in Britain, and 9.2 per cent in the United States are aged 65 and over. Britain has a significantly higher proportion of older women than the other two countries. Fourteen per cent of all women are over 65, compared with 12 per cent of all women in Denmark and 10 per cent in the United States. The age distribution of the population over 65 is quite similar in all three countries. As Table I-1 shows, slightly more than one-third of the elderly population in each country is under 70 years of age. Roughly one-twentieth of the elderly population is over 85 years of age.

Table I-1: AGE DISTRIBUTION OF THE ELDERLY POPULATION, 1962
(Percentage Distribution)

Age	DENMARK			BRITAIN			UNITED STATES		
	Men	Women	All	Men	Women	All	Men	Women	All
65–69	27	37	37.3	39.7	34.5	36.4	37.5	35.2	36.2
70–74	28	28	27.9	27.9	27.6	27.8	29.3	28.6	28.9
75–79	19	19	19.4	18.6	20.2	19.6	18.9	19.3	19.1
80–84	11	11	10.4	9.5	11.7	10.8	9.5	10.7	10.1
85+	5	5	5.0	4.3	6.1	5.4	4.9	6.3	5.7

Source: Statistical Yearbook for Denmark, 1962 (Copenhagen: Det Statistiske Departement 1963), Table 12, p. 33.

Great Britain, the General Register Office, *The Registrar-General's Quarterly Return for England and Wales, Quarter ended 30th September, 1962* (London: HMSO, 1962). *Quarterly Return of the Registrar-General, Scotland, Quarter ended 30th December, 1962* (London: HMSO, 1963).

U.S. Bureau of the Census, Current Population Reports, *Population Estimates, Estimates of the Population of the United States by Age, Color and Sex, July 1, 1950 to 1962*, Series P-25, No. 265 (May, 1963) (Washington, D.C.: U.S. GPO, 1963), Table 1, p. 11.

In all three countries the average new born girl can be expected to live to about age 74, the average new born boy to between 67 (in the United States) and 70 years (in Denmark). In all three countries women who reach the age of 65 have a longer expectation of life than men; the difference between the sexes in this regard is more pronounced in Britain and the United States, less pronounced in Denmark.

Partly as a consequence of differential mortality rates, but also because men are generally older than their wives, the populations of each sex

Table I-2: LIFE EXPECTANCY AT BIRTH AND AT AGE 65, 1960

Country	Men	Women
Expectancy at birth		
Denmark[a]	70.4	73.8
Britain[b]	68.1	74.0
United States[c]	67.0	73.6
Expectancy at age 65		
Denmark[a]	13.8	15.1
Britain[b]	12.0	15.2
United States[c]	13.0	16.1

[a] *Statistical Yearbook for Denmark, 1962* (Copenhagen: Det Statistiske Departement, 1963), Table 34, p. 60. Expectancy at birth, based on registrations of the years 1956–60.

[b] General Register Office, *The Registrar-General's Quarterly Return . . . June, 1963* (London: HMSO, 1963). Based on the deaths registered in England and Wales in the years 1960, 1961, 1962. There is a full discussion of the production of life tables in *The Registrar-General's Decennial Supplement for England and Wales 1957* (London: HMSO, 1957).

[c] Life Expectancy, 1900–1975, *Health, Education, and Welfare Trends, 1963* (Washington, D.C.: U.S. GPO, 1964), p. 13. Expectancy at birth, based on registrations of the year 1961.

differ markedly according to marital status. In each country also, while most old men are usually married, most old women are either widowed or have never married. The proportion of widows in each case is two or three times the proportion of widowers. Compared with the United States, Britain has a high proportion of old women who have never married.

Table I-3: MARITAL STATUS OF THE ELDERLY POPULATION, 1960 (*Percentage Distribution*)

Marital Status	DENMARK			BRITAIN			UNITED STATES		
	Men	Women	All	Men	Women	All	Men	Women	All
Single	7.6	15.2	11.8	7.6	15.6	12.5	7.1	8.4	7.8
Married	67.0	37.9	51.2	70.3	34.3	48.0	71.1	36.3	52.0
Separated							1.3	0.9	1.0
Widowed	23.1	43.4	34.0	21.9	49.8	39.1	18.8	52.9	37.5
Divorced	2.3	3.5	3.0	0.3	0.4	0.3	1.6	1.5	1.6

Source: *Statistical Yearbook for Denmark, 1962* (Copenhagen: Det Statistiske Departement, 1963), Table 12, p. 33.

General Register Office, *Census, 1961*, England and Wales, Age, Marital Condition and General Tables (London: HMSO, 1965).

U.S. Bureau of the Census, *U.S. Census of Population, Part I, United States Summary, Detailed Characteristics*, Table 176 (Washington, D.C.: U.S. GPO, 1963).

Official statistics show that about the same proportion of older men in each country were at work or seeking work—34 per cent in Denmark, 31 per cent in Britain, and 30 per cent in the United States. Denmark and the United States differ from Britain in the proportion of the older male work force employed in agriculture—31 and 19 per cent respectively, compared with 9 per cent in Britain. A much smaller proportion of women than men were in employment. The three social security systems vary somewhat in their general provisions, as is explained in some detail in Chapter 12. Here it is necessary only to point out that the age at which men may receive full social security pensions is 65 in Britain and in the United States and 67 in Denmark. This variation in benefit age is undoubtedly one cause for the differences between Denmark and the other two countries in the proportion of men still employed at age 65.

Even a cursory description of the elderly populations of the three countries reveals some striking similarities. In life-expectations and distributions according to age, marital status, and employment status, the populations are broadly alike. There are, it is true, important differences in social structure between the three countries, the United States being far more heterogeneous in terms of race and religion than either Denmark or Britain. Yet the marked basic similarities in the composition of the older population of the three countries would seem to offer special advantages for comparative research. Close analysis of the conditions, behavior, and reactions of the three populations would help to reveal what changes in the life-situation of old people are the result of age, and what are the result of differences in cultural milieu and expectations.

Problems of Comparative Research

In recent years there have been an increasing number of comparative studies of various social phenomena.[19] To dismiss the growth in such comparative studies as a "fad," or as a result of the ease of communication among scientists in different countries, is to ignore the basic problem to which comparative studies give attention. Comparative studies in the social sciences try to establish general laws about social life which are independent of cultural settings, or, alternatively, to indicate how the differing social behavior of specific populations is the result of differences in given cultural settings. The interest in comparative studies arises from a major question: to what extent can a hypothesis about social life be considered proved by a study made within a single culture? Where the phenomena under investigation occur in all societies—as, do for example, child-rearing practices, marriage, adult socialization, and aging—the serious investigator must be increasingly concerned with whether what he has found to be true in one society is a phenomenon that occurs under a given set of circumstances in all societies or whether it is relevant for that society only.

Many investigators have recognized the need for cross-national research and proceeded to make such studies. Unfortunately, much of what appears under this general rubric must be regarded as trivial. Many cross-national studies are based on population samples quite different in kind. Schedules for use in surveys have been developed by an investigator in one country, and translated literally for use in another country. Often too little consideration is given to the general problem of whether questions meaningful in one country are really meaningful in another. Still other studies use secondary analyses of data gathered in different ways and for different purposes.[20] In the present investigation we tried to avoid some of the errors of other cross-national investigations of social phenomena by employing comparable samples and sampling methods, comparable methods of interviewing, comparable questionnaires, and similar methods of data analysis and tabulation. So far as we are aware, such a degree of collaboration and control has not been reached previously in such investigations.

Methods of the Present Study

The findings in this book are based on structured interviews with national samples of approximately 2,500 persons in each country, aged 65 and over, and living in private households in Denmark, Britain, and the United States. The sampling method used in each country is that of "area-probability sampling," a method which gives each older person in the population an equal chance of being located and thus participating in the research. Interviewing was undertaken in approximately the same season in 1962: in Denmark from mid-April to early July, in Britain from mid-May to July, and in the United States from mid-May to August.

No study can be better than its basic data. In this instance, the basic data are the answers of old people to a series of questions. The questionnaires used in the study were developed jointly by the research teams from the three countries, meeting together at a series of conferences. Most of the questions in each of the three national questionnaires are comparable in content and often in wording. No attempt has been made to force exact similarities in wording, however, or to translate questions literally. Differences in national style, in ways of talking and approach, are reflected in each national questionnaire. People are "dizzy" in the United States, "giddy" in Britain, and "svimmel" in Denmark. "Giddy" is not commonly used in the United States, just as "svimmel" is not used outside Denmark. In each questionnaire some questions were added to satisfy purely national interest but usually at the end of sections of the questionnaire so that the cross-national questions were comparable in sequence. The results of these special investigations will appear in national publications.

In order to ensure a high degree of comparability in each country, all concepts and variables were defined in the same way, both in the questionnaires and in the tabulations. As far as possible, interviewers in each country received the same instructions and training. The research teams meeting together discussed coding of all "open" questions and adopted standardized coding methods. The same procedure was followed in planning tabulations. The importance of some analyses, however, became apparent only when second and third drafts of chapters had already been circulated, and, in certain instances, additional tabulations to furnish these analyses were not possible for all three countries.

This necessarily high degree of comparability, as well as the concerted actions of all those engaged in the study, were obtained through 14 meetings, each of several days' or weeks' duration, and the exchange of hundreds of letters. This procedure is time-consuming and expensive. It presupposes great frankness in discussion, as well as a desire on the part of each of the national groups to understand the preoccupations of other participants. Of course, it has not been possible to meet all national wishes, and compromises have been necessary regarding study content and details. The continual access to national experiences, however, has served greatly to enrich the analysis and interpretation of the findings.

There are certain problems involving comparability that could not be entirely overcome. The research was limited to those old people in private households, and if there are marked differences in characteristics between them and old people in institutions in the three countries, then this would, of course, affect the findings. In the three countries, however, there are only small differences in the proportion of elderly in institutions (see Chapters 2 and 4). Further, it is our belief that in each country similar kinds of old people are found in institutions—those who are infirm and who lack family members or family substitutes to help them.

In each country, too, there were some persons in the sample who could not be reached by the interviewers or who refused to be interviewed. Although some information was collected about non-respondents, it may be that the latter differ from country to country in certain characteristics. The effect of such differences, if they exist, cannot be completely evaluated. The total effect of non-response on the survey results is discussed in the methodological appendices. When illustrations of individual circumstances are given in the text the reader should note that fictitious names and other devices have been used to prevent identification.

In this brief introduction we have tried to explain why and how we chose to study old people in our three countries. We turn now to a consideration of our findings. What is the level of physical functioning of old people, how do they use community services, what is their relationship with family and friends, and what is their economic position? It is to the exploration of these questions and their theoretical implications that we address ourselves in the chapters that follow.

NOTES

1 Data for Denmark from *Statistical Yearbook for Denmark, 1903.* Population as of January 1, 1962, *Statistical Yearbook for Denmark, 1962* (Copenhagen: Det Statistiske Departement, 1963), p. 32. Data for Britain from Great Britain, *Annual Abstract of Statistics,* No. 89 (London: Her Majesty's Stationery Office, 1961), Tables 7 and 8, pp. 7, 8. United States data from U.S. Department of Health, Education, and Welfare, *Health, Education, and Welfare Trends, 1963* (Washington, D.C.: U.S. GPO, 1964), p. 3.

2 Talcott Parsons, *Essays in Sociological Theory* (New York: The Free Press of Glencoe, 1964; rev. paperback ed.), p. 102.

3 In 1703 in New York, for example, only 4 per cent of household units "could be considered three-generational" and during the early phases of industrialization, the New York State Census of 1865 indicated that only 3 per cent of households contained three generations. Eugene A. Friedmann, "The Impact of Aging on the Social Structure," in Clark Tibbitts, ed., *Handbook of Social Gerontology* (Chicago: University of Chicago Press, 1960), pp. 120–144. In villages and urban areas in medieval Britain elderly parents tended to remain in their own households, separate from their married children. J. C. Russell, *British Medieval Population* (Albuquerque, N.M.: University of New Mexico Press, 1948), quoted in Friedmann, *loc. cit.*, p. 131. See also the evidence marshaled by Laslett for seventeenth-century England. The number of households with grandchildren never reached one in ten. Peter Laslett, *The World We Have Lost* (London: Methuen, 1965), pp. 90–98.

4 Leo W. Simmons, "Aging in Preindustrial Societies," in Clark Tibbitts, ed., *op. cit.*, pp. 62–91; see also William H. Harlan and J. Singh, "Social Status and Attitudes of Old Men in an Indian Village," a paper read at the Sixth International Congress of Gerontology, Copenhagen, Denmark, August, 1963.

5 Of 39 tribes on which definite information could be obtained, neglect and abandonment were customary in 18. Leo W. Simmons, *The Role of the Aged in Primitive Society* (New Haven, Conn.: Yale University Press, 1945).

6 L. W. Simmons, "Aging in Preindustrial Societies," *loc. cit.*

7 Elaine Cumming and William E. Henry, *Growing Old* (New York: Basic Books, Inc., 1961).

8 Elaine Cumming, "Further Thoughts on the Theory of Disengagement," *International Social Science Journal*, XV, 3 (1963), 377.

9 *Ibid.*, p. 379.

10 For example, C. R. Wright and H. H. Hyman, "Voluntary Association Memberships of American Adults: Evidence from National Sample Surveys," *American Sociological Review*, XXIII (1958), 284–294.

11 For example, Rosow calls attention to the importance of investigating the quality of familial relationships. Irving Rosow, *Housing and Social Integration of the Aged*. Final report of a study submitted to the Cleveland Welfare Federation and The Ford Foundation (Cleveland: Western Reserve University, 1964), pp. 20–22.

12 Gerhard Baumert, "Changes in the Family and the Position of Older Persons in Germany," in Clark Tibbitts and Wilma Donahue, eds., *Social and Psychological Aspects of Aging* (New York: Columbia University Press, 1963), pp. 415–425.

13 M. F. Nimkoff, "Changing Family Relationships of Older People in the United States During the Last Fifty Years," in Clark Tibbitts and Wilma Donahue, eds., *loc. cit.*, pp. 405–414.

14 B. Hutchinson, *Old People in a Modern Australian Community* (Victoria: Melbourne University Press, 1954).

15 Ruth Benedict, "The Family: Genus Americanum," in Ruth Nanda Anshen, ed., *The Family, Its Function and Destiny*, 2nd ed. (New York: Harper & Row, 1959).

16 Ralph Linton, "The Natural History of the Family," in R. N. Anshen, ed., *loc. cit.*

17 For example, see Peter Townsend, *The Family Life of Old People* (London: Routledge and Kegan Paul, 1957); Henning Friis and Erik Manniche, *Enlige Aeldre* (Copenhagen: Danish National Institute of Social Research, Teknisk Forlag, 1961); and Ethel Shanas and Gordon F. Streib, eds., *Social Structure and the Family: Generational Relationships* (Englewood Cliffs, N.J.: Prentice-Hall, Inc., 1965).

18 Leopold Rosenmayr and Eva Köckeis, "Propositions for a Sociological Theory of Aging and the Family," *International Social Science Journal*, XV, No. 3 (1963), 410–426.

19 A number of them are listed in Bruce M. Russett and Hayward R. Alker, Karl W. Deutsch, Harold D. Lasswell, eds., *World Handbook of Political and Social Indicators* (New Haven, Conn., and London: Yale University Press, 1964). See also, for example, Richard L. Merritt and Stein Rokkan, eds., *Comparing Nations* (New Haven, Conn., and London: Yale University Press, 1966) and Gabriel A. Almond and James S. Coleman, eds., *The Politics of Developing Areas* (Princeton, N. J.: Princeton University Press, 1960).

20 See, for example, the discussions in Stein Rokkan, "Introduction, The Use of Sample Surveys in Comparative Research," *International Social Science Journal*, XVI, No. 1 (1964); Clodwig Kapferer, "The Use of Sample Surveys by OECD," *International Social Science Journal*, XVI, No. 1 (1964); Robert E. Mitchell, "Survey Materials collected in the Developing Countries: sampling, measurement, and interviewing obstacles to intra- and inter-national comparisons," *International Social Science Journal*, XVII, No. 4 (1965).

2 : *Health and Incapacity in Later Life*

In most Western countries old age is associated with illness. The person who is old is thought to be sick. This belief is widely accepted both by those who are active in providing medical care for the elderly and by the public at large. The fact is, however, that although widespread pathology exists among the elderly population, old age and illness are not synonymous. There is no such disease as "old age." Some old people function well, others function poorly. Some old people are severely restricted in their mobility, others are able to maintain themselves in the ordinary activities of daily living. The variation among the elderly in their physical health and in their degree of impairment is enormous.

One can speculate why old age has come to be synonymous with sickness. It can be argued that we only notice old people when they are ill and enfeebled. Perhaps the best explanation for the common public association of old age and illness has been succinctly stated by a study group of the United States Institutes of Health:

> Many prevailing ideas and facts about aging and the aged come from studies of the sick and the institutionalized. Because of the nature of the studies and of the population studied, the dominant theme has been one of *decline*.[1]

As the work of this study group demonstrates, old age is not a period of marked physical decline for all old people without exception. Some persons of very advanced age perform as well as younger persons. Nevertheless, widespread pathology does exist among the older population. Overall the elderly are not as well as the young and the middle-aged; old people are more impaired physically and less mobile than middle-aged people. Furthermore, at some point in his life span, if a person lives long enough, chronic conditions, some severe and some minor, begin to affect his ability to function efficiently. Such conditions are more noticeable among those of advanced ages, particularly those over 75, than among those under 75.

The present discussion of the health of old people in Denmark, Britain, and the United States considers the health needs of the elderly in each country while at the same time emphasizing the variability in the health status of old people. We first develop estimates of the health status of old people in each country. We then explore, in turn, the factors associated with poor health and physical incapacity in old age and the relationships between age and health, the theme of the present chapter; the importance of subjective attitudes in the health and functioning of the elderly, the theme of the next chapter; and finally, we make some assessment of the health services required by old people.

Specifically in this chapter we focus on three topics: the development of estimates of health status, the differences between the incapacitated and the well aged, and the over-all relationship between health and age. To begin with, while certain indices of the health status of the elderly are available in reports of sickness and mortality in all three countries— Britain, Denmark, and the United States—there is no estimate of health of the elderly based on the concept of function, that is, the ability of the elderly to maintain themselves. Accordingly, the estimates given in this chapter are primarily related to this concept. Such estimates include the proportions of institutionalized and bedfast old people in each country, the differences in physical mobility among the elderly living outside institutions, and an over-all ranking of the incapacity of the elderly, using a common scale for each country. The second topic considered in this chapter is the difference between the incapacitated and the well aged. Incapacity among the aged is associated with certain demographic and social characteristics, among them advanced age, widowhood, and poverty. Our third general theme in this chapter is the over-all relationship between health and age. Here we consider briefly the effect that persons of advanced age have upon the use of health facilities. We then analyze some of the pertinent similarities and differences in the health of the elderly in the three countries.

In Denmark, Britain, and the United States more people than ever before are living to advanced ages. Since the turn of the century each country has experienced a marked increase in the proportion of its population aged 65 and over. In 1901, one of every 15 persons in Denmark, and one of every 25 persons in Britain and the United States, was 65 years of age or more. By 1960, however, one of every 9 persons in Denmark, one of every 8 in Britain, and one of every 11 in the United States, was 65 years or over. In each of these countries in 1960 the average man who reached the age of 65 could expect to live to about 78, the average woman, to about 80.[2]

The Health Status of the Elderly: General Estimates

Is the physical functioning of old people similar, or does it differ, in Denmark, Britain, and the United States? To understand the health needs of the aged, one must first measure the health status of old people. As long as all persons over 65 are viewed as sick, infirm, and incapacitated, rational planning for a program of health care and services is impossible. Obviously not all old people require health services to an equal degree. The frailest persons among the elderly make the greatest demands for health care. Many of these frail persons are institutionalized; others are being cared for at home. The over-all questions, then, must first be: What is the proportion of old people who are institutionalized? What is the proportion of old persons living at home who are bedfast and housebound? And finally, what is the proportion of old persons living at home who are ambulatory without limitation? For our purposes, we define as "ambulatory without limitation" those old people who are able to go outdoors without difficulty. Later, we shall further refine our measurement of health status by the use of a scale to determine the degree of incapacity of the elderly living at home.

THE INSTITUTIONALIZED

In this study a person who lives in group quarters (such as a long-term chronic disease or mental hospital, a nursing home, a residential home, a rehabilitation center, or a center for the retarded) is considered a resident of an institution. The proportion of old people actually resident in institutions and not living at home at any one time is difficult to determine. Some among the elderly who are in short-term hospitals have been in the hospital for long periods, 30 to 60 days or more. According to our definition, however, these persons are living at home. This categorization is based on the assumption, sometimes unfounded, that the old person in a general hospital is there for only a temporary period and that he will ultimately return to his home. A more rigid categorization than this common one, however, would probably include these long-stay patients in general hospitals among the institutionalized. (A further discussion of the institutionalized and their special needs is given in Chapter 4.)

In each country only a small proportion of old people live in institutions. If we employ the definition spelled out earlier, the estimated proportion of all old people in institutions in the three countries ranges from a high of 5.3 per cent in Denmark to a low of 3.6 per cent in Britain and 3.7 per cent in the United States.[3]

Traditionally, Denmark has placed greater emphasis on institutional living for the elderly than either Britain or the United States; however, although Denmark has roughly one and one-half times the proportion of old people in institutions than either Britain or the United States, the variation between the three countries in the proportions of their older population in institutions is far less than had been expected.

Most of the elderly who live in institutions are frail and sick. More than half of those in institutions in both Britain and the United States (2 and 2.3 per cent of the total elderly population, respectively) are in hospitals and nursing homes and therefore can be assumed, with some few exceptions, to be either bedfast or otherwise in need of nursing care. In Denmark,

Table II–1: PERSONS AGED 65 AND OVER RESIDENT IN INSTITUTIONS[a]

Country and Type of Accommodation	Number	Per Cent
Denmark		
Long-term hospitals	2,400	0.5
Mental hospitals	2,000	0.4
Chronic disease and tuberculosis hospitals	400	0.1
Nursing homes	4,600	0.9
Residential homes	19,400	3.8
Other institutions	300	0.1
Total	26,700[b]	5.3
Britain		
Hospitals other than psychiatric	121,219	2.0[e]
Psychiatric hospitals	59,282	0.9
Residential homes	96,510	1.6
Total long-stay and short-stay	277,011[c]	4.5
Approximate total long-stay		3.6
United States		
Long-term hospitals	215,202	1.3
Mental hospitals	177,840	1.1
Chronic disease and tuberculosis hospitals	37,362	0.2
Nursing homes	172,779	1.0
Private	144,922	0.9
Public	27,857	0.1
Residential homes	215,174	1.3
Private	185,066	1.1
Public	30,108	0.2
Other institutions	6,805	[f]
Total	609,960[d]	3.7

[a] An extremely detailed report of this institutional population is given in Chapter 4. See particularly Table IV–5.

[b] Census figures of 1960 published in *Statistiske Eferretninger*, No. 45 (Copenhagen: Statens Trykningskontor, 1964).

[c] General Register Office, *Census 1961*, England and Wales, Age, Marital Condition and General Tables (London: HMSO, 1965).

[d] U.S. Bureau of the Census, *United States Census of the Population: 1960. Subject Reports. Inmates of Institutions*, Final Report PC(2)=8A (Washington, D.C.: U.S. GPO, 1963), Tables 3, 5, 6, 7, pp. 3–7.

[e] Based on hospital census, therefore includes all aged patients in short-stay hospitals on day of census.

[f] Less than one-tenth of one per cent.

one-third of those in institutions (1.7 per cent of the total elderly) are believed to be bedfast and non-ambulatory.[4]

Institutionalization among the elderly is associated with advanced age. In each country, a higher proportion of very old persons (those over 75) than of younger persons (those under 75) live in institutions. The over-all reports, country by country, are very similar. In England and Wales in 1961 less than 3 per cent of all men and women aged 65 to 74 were in all types of institutions (including general hospitals), compared to almost 8 per cent of persons aged 75 and over. In the United States 2 per cent of all persons aged 65 to 75, compared to 7 per cent of persons aged 75 years and more, are in institutions.[5] In Denmark, less than 2 per cent of those aged 65 to 70 are in institutions, compared to almost 8 per cent of those over 70.

Although at most only from 4 to 6 per cent of the total elderly are institutionalized, nevertheless a substantial number of those who are most frail and in need of care *are* institutionalized and are thus not represented in the interviews. For this reason, the findings of the present survey, based as they are on interviews with old people living outside institutions, should not be interpreted as reporting the situation of the total elderly population. Later in this chapter, when we consider the relationship between health and age, we shall have occasion to discuss further the institutionalized population and its effect on the results of our survey.

THE BEDFAST, THE HOUSEBOUND, AND THE AMBULATORY

The proportion of all old people who are either bedfast or housebound and living at home in each of the three countries is greater than the proportion of all old people in each country resident in institutions. In Denmark and in the United States about twice as many old people, and in Britain about four times as many old people as live in institutions of all kinds are bedfast and housebound at home. Fourteen of every hundred old people living at home in Britain (13 per cent of the total elderly population), 10 of every hundred at home in Denmark (9 per cent of the total elderly population), and 8 of every hundred at home in the United States (8 per cent of the total elderly population) are bedfast and housebound. Among the elderly living at home, Britain has one and three-fourths as high a proportion of bedfast and housebound persons as the United States, and almost one and one-half times as high a proportion of such persons as Denmark. The lowest proportion of ambulatory old persons living at home is found in Britain, where there are 86 such persons out of every hundred elderly; the highest proportion of ambulatory old persons is found in the United States—92 of every hundred persons.[6]

These estimates of the elderly at home as bedfast, housebound, and ambulatory do not give a completely satisfactory description of the mobility of the aged. It is not enough for the old person to be neither in bed nor housebound. To be mobile, he must also be able to go outdoors without trouble or difficulty. As long as going outdoors is difficult or fraught with hazards—if the old person is afraid of falling, for example—old people will go outdoors alone only rarely or not at all. In a sense, although these old people may be ambulatory, they become prisoners of their fears of being hurt or incapacitated and are thus immobilized.

Estimates of the mobility of the total elderly population living at home are available for the interviewed sample only. As such, these estimates slightly overstate the proportion of old people living at home who are completely mobile. The United States has the highest proportion of mobile old persons, 89 of every hundred, and Denmark, the lowest, 78 of every hundred.[7] Although Britain has a higher proportion of bedfast and housebound old people than Denmark, the Danes are somewhat less likely than the British to report that they can go outdoors without any difficulty.

Table II-2: MOBILITY OF THE NON-INSTITUTIONAL POPULATION, AGED 65 AND OVER (*Percentage Distribution*)

Degree of Mobility	DENMARK			BRITAIN			UNITED STATES		
	Men	Women	All	Men	Women	All	Men	Women	All
Total sample located[a]									
Bedfast	2	2	2	2	3	3	2	3	2
Housebound	6	9	8	5	15	11	4	8	6
Ambulatory	92	89	90	93	82	86	95	89	92
Total	100	100	100	100	100	100	100	100	100
N=	1,354	1,559	2,913	1,195	1,812	3,007	1,220	1,519	2,739
Sample interviewed only									
Bedfast	1	1	1	1	1	1	*	1	*
Housebound	4	9	7	4	13	10	3	7	5
Ambulatory	95	91	93	95	85	89	97	92	95
Can go outdoors with difficulty	11	17	14	6	9	8	4	7	6
Can go outdoors without difficulty	84	73	78	89	77	82	93	86	89
Total	100	100	100	100	100	100	100	100	100
N=[b]	1,145	1,301	2,446	1,004	1,496	2,500	1,081	1,361	2,442

[a] The proportion of bedfast respondents is based on all bedfast persons located; interviews with proxy respondents were taken for all bedfast persons who could not be interviewed. The proportions for housebound and ambulatory respondents are estimated from their proportions in the sample interviewed and from background data on non-respondents secured by the interviewers in the United States and Denmark.

[b] The percentages of eligible respondents who answered this question are: Denmark, 100; Britain, 99.9; United States, 100. In subsequent tables, where 98 per cent or more of all eligible respondents have answered a question, detailed information on non-response will not be given in footnotes.

* Less than one per cent.

There are marked differences in the mobility of older men and older women. Older women are more likely to be housebound than older men; they are also more likely to report difficulties in getting about. In each country, roughly 10 per cent more women than men report that they have difficulty in going outdoors.

What it is like to be bedfast or housebound in old age, or ambulatory but unable to go outdoors without difficulty, cannot be determined from statistics. Some illustrative cases may convey the feelings of the older person who is bedfast or housebound.

Miss Burns is bedfast. She was interviewed sitting in a wheelchair. Miss Burns is a spinster of 81 living in a West Coast American city. She says of herself: "I have a heart condition and arthritis. I'm crippled and can't work. I'm all crippled up with arthritis."

Miss Burns was a practical nurse, but she gave this work up forty years ago because of poor health. She then tried to support herself by dressmaking. In 1935, when she was 54 years old, she stopped working completely. She lives now on money she receives from public assistance. She makes her home with an elderly couple, Mr. and Mrs. Wagner (aged 78 and 66). She pays the Wagners forty dollars a month for her room and an additional sum for her care. Although Miss Burns is totally disabled, she describes her health as "fair, for my age." Miss Burns sees a doctor only when he is sent for and last saw a doctor over a year before she was interviewed. When asked, "How often does the doctor visit you?" Miss Burns said: "About once a year. I treat myself." Despite her ailments, Miss Burns says that she is never lonely and never alone.

Miss Roberts is housebound. She too is a spinster, aged 80. When Miss Roberts was asked what kept her in the house she said: "I'm too old. I can't get up and down stairs. I only go out when my nephew takes me in the car." Miss Roberts is very frail. She fell last week and often feels as though she is going to fall. The interviewer described her as "feeble."

Miss Roberts was a clerk in a dress shop. She stopped work completely in 1936, when she was 55 years old. Miss Roberts lives on the proceeds of her investments. She shares an apartment with her brother, who is 77. She and her brother pay 120 dollars a month for their apartment. Miss Roberts says her health is "poor." She last saw a doctor three months before she was interviewed. Like Miss Burns, Miss Roberts too says that she is never lonely and seldom alone.

As is apparent from the descriptions of Miss Burns and Miss Roberts, the over-all categories of bedfast and housebound cover old people with a variety of impairments. Some of the housebound—for example, Miss Roberts—are almost as restricted in their activity as the bedfast. In all three countries, however, most old people are classified as ambulatory. This too may describe a broad group of persons. In one instance, to be ambulatory may mean complete freedom from impairment, whereas in another instance, as the case of Mrs. Carpenter illustrates, to be ambulatory may mean to have only extremely limited mobility.

Mrs. Carpenter is an 86-year-old widow. Although Mrs. Carpenter is ambulatory and able to get about, she is blind and hard of hearing. As a result, she can do nothing without help. Money is not a problem for Mrs. Carpenter. She and her husband, who were childless, had their own business, which she operated alone after his death. She retired in 1949, because "I could not see my customers." Mrs. Carpenter says her health is good for her age. She is seldom alone, since her paid companion and housekeeper accompanies her everywhere. She says: "I have never allowed myself to get lonely."

How Sick Are Older People?

The discussion to now has been concerned with crude measures of the health status of the elderly: the proportion in institutions, the proportions bedfast, housebound, restricted in ambulation, and mobile. While these measures are useful indicators of broad categories of health among the elderly, a more precise measure of how well old people function is needed.

The rationale behind this interest has been summarized by a World Health Organization study group. This group states: ". . . health in the elderly is best measured in terms of function . . . degree of fitness rather than extent of pathology may be used as a measure of the amount of services the aged will require from the community."[8] In taking the position that function rather than pathology is of primary interest in old age, the study group accepts the fact that most old people exhibit signs of pathology upon physical examination. The study group also assumes—as has been documented here—that most old people living at home are mobile. It is as though when people become old they accommodate to chronic disease and physical discomfort. The old person tends to ignore the symptoms of disease and to continue with his activities as though these symptoms did not exist. Complaints that at one time would have been considered important enough to be called to a doctor's attention, are often believed to be inevitable in old age and thus remain unremarked and untreated.

A succinct description of the health of any person, young or old, is difficult to achieve. A person's health may be evaluated by a physician in a physical examination, it may be evaluated by how the person says he feels, and it may be evaluated by how the person behaves. In the instance of a physician's examination, the doctor describes the health of his patient on the basis of the presence or absence of certain conditions. At first sight this method of separating the healthy from the sick seems a totally objective one. Numerous studies have shown, however, that the assessment by different physicians of the degree of pathology of the same patient may vary greatly. An alternative measure of individual health is how a person feels. The subjective feelings of the individual are often better indices of of how he will function than are the results of a physician's examination. Many people who are clinically sick continue to act as though they were quite well. On the other hand, every medical practitioner can report in detail on a patient who insists that she is sick and behaves as though she were sick, although all medical findings are essentially negative. The state of a person's health can also be measured by his behavior. Can he walk about without discomfort? Does he have to stay in bed most of the day? If one measures health in terms of behavior, the judgment about the state of health can be made either by the subject person himself or by an observer.[9]

Each of these methods for defining who is sick and who is well—the physician's examination, the person's subjective judgment, and the observation of behavior—is useful for a particular purpose. If one wants to know how many people in a given population have suffered cerebral-vascular accidents (strokes), detailed physical examinations of individuals are necessary. One cannot depend on respondents to report or even to know whether or not they have had a stroke. If, on the other hand, one wants to know how many people have impairments that are likely to be an aftermath of a stroke, it is possible to secure an estimate of such impairments by asking individuals a series of questions in this general area.

AN INDEX OF INCAPACITY

In the present research the functioning of old people is measured by an index of incapacity.

Over-all indices of the health of old people have been used in a number of American studies of the aged in the community. Kutner and his associates in a study of old people in New York developed a Physical Health Index, based on the amount of time the old person was confined to bed, social and economic deprivations due to ill health, numbers of illnesses, and seriousness of reported diseases. Shanas in her 1957 survey of the health of older people used an index derived from numbers of illnesses, seriousness of reported diseases, and time spent in bed or wheelchair. Beyer, in his studies of the housing of the elderly, used an index of health status that combined numbers of illnesses, seriousness of reported diseases, time spent in bed or a wheelchair, help received in activities because of health needs, and a count of how many activities were abandoned because of poor health.[10]

The present index differs from those used earlier in its concentration on physical functioning. In many ways the index is similar to that developed by Drs. Sidney Katz and Austin Chinn and their associates in their study of a group of old people with fractured hips. Katz and Chinn categorized these ill people on a scale of daily function and ultimately developed a graded scale based on whether or not the old person could perform adequately in bathing, dressing, toilet activities, transferring (moving from bed to chair, et cetera), continence, and feeding.[11] It should be stressed, however, that Katz and Chinn were studying a group of hospitalized persons, not persons in the general population.

The index of incapacity in the present survey is primarily derived from the work of Peter Townsend in Great Britain. Investigating old people living at home, Townsend was impressed "that the presence of a particular disease does not necessarily indicate for any given person the inhibition of activity which results from it."[12] He decided that the most useful approach to the measurement of incapacity was one that attempted to score the consequences of disease or injury, and he began by developing a scoring system for those activities that an old person living alone would have "to perform and the faculties he would have to employ to maintain life, assuming he received no assistance."[13] The activities necessary for self-care in the Townsend scale included personal care, sensory abilities (that is, the ability to see, hear, and speak), and the ability to perform certain physical tasks necessary in maintaining an independent household.

THE INDEX OF INCAPACITY OF THE CROSS-NATIONAL STUDY

The index of incapacity used for cross-national comparisons in the present study focuses on the ability of the old person to perform those minimal tasks which make him independent of others for personal care. The cross-national index of incapacity reduces the number of items in the Townsend index. It includes no measure of sensory impairment and, since the conditions of life in each country may vary greatly, no measures of the ability of the old person to maintain himself while living alone.

The index requires an answer to six questions from the old person: (1) Can he go out-of-doors? (2) Can he walk up and down stairs? (3) Can he get about the house? (4) Can he wash and bathe himself? (5) Can he dress himself and put on shoes? And finally (6) Can he cut his own toenails? The old person is asked whether he can do each of these tasks without difficulty and without assistance, with some difficulty but still without the help of another person, and finally, with difficulty and only with the help of another person. To function as a member of the community, every person, young or old, needs to be able to leave the house and encompass at least a little of the life outside his immediate surroundings. To experience freedom of movement, he must be able to move around his home and, if need be, to walk stairs. To take care of himself on the most personal level, he must be able to perform certain elementary tasks: to wash, to dress himself, and to cut his toenails. The inability to perform any one of the six tasks in the index without assistance from another person is an incapacitating handicap to an old person. Being unable to cut one's own toenails and the resulting foot problems may be just as great a handicap to the elderly person's daily functioning as a sensory impairment or the symptoms of a chronic disease.

INCAPACITY SCORES

Scores on the index of incapacity may range from zero to 12. The ability to perform a task without any restriction is assigned a score of zero, the ability to perform a task only with difficulty is assigned a score of one, and complete inability to perform a task is assigned a score of two. A score as high as seven or more means that a person can do all of the six listed tasks only with difficulty and at least one task not at all, or that he can do some of these tasks with difficulty, and some, not at all.

The range of incapacity scores for older people living at home in the three countries is given in Table II–3. In each country more than half of all ambulatory and housebound old persons living at home have zero scores on this index. These persons are able to function without limitation as measured by our scale. An additional quarter of the elderly have scores of one or two—that is, they may have some difficulty with one or two items composing the index or they may be completely unable to do one item. More than three-quarters of the elderly, then, have only minimal incapacity as measured by this index. At the other extreme, the proportion of ambulatory and housebound old people seriously incapacitated, those with index scores of seven or more, is 5 of every hundred in Denmark, 6 of every hundred in Britain, and 4 of every hundred in the United States.

Old people in the United States living at home report less incapacity than old people in either Britain or Denmark. A higher proportion of the

Table II–3: INCAPACITY FOR SELF-CARE, NON-INSTITUTIONAL POPULATION AGED 65 AND OVER[a] (*Percentage Distribution*)

Index Score	DENMARK			BRITAIN			UNITED STATES		
	Men	Women	All	Men	Women	All	Men	Women	All
0	58	48	53	65	48	55	68	58	63
1–2	26	27	26	22	25	24	21	23	22
3–4	7	13	10	7	12	10	6	9	7
5–6	5	6	6	3	7	5	4	3	4
7 or more	4	6	5	3	8	6	1	6	4
Total	100	100	100	100	100	100	100	100	100
N=	1,130	1,286	2,416	985	1,462	2,447	1,080	1,352	2,432

[a] Excludes bedfast persons.

American aged have incapacity scores of zero or one and two. How are we to account for this difference in incapacity scores among the three countries, and the apparent greater agility of the American aged? We will approach this problem in two ways: through further analysis of the component parts of the index of incapacity and through an analysis of changes in incapacity scores with age.

COMPONENT PARTS OF THE INDEX OF INCAPACITY

The ability of old people to function in each of the six areas covered by the index of incapacity varies considerably. Some people are able to walk about the house but they cannot go outdoors without help; others can

Table II–4: PROPORTION OF PERSONS AGED 65 AND OVER REPORTING DIFFICULTY WITH COMMON PHYSICAL TASKS[a]

Task	Per Cent with Difficulty								
	DENMARK			BRITAIN			UNITED STATES		
	Men	Women	All	Men	Women	All	Men	Women	All
Walking stairs	31	41	37	19	33	27	24	35	30
Getting about the house	6	9	7	4	8	7	4	8	6
Washing, bathing	8	10	9	8	19	15	7	13	10
Dressing, putting on shoes	12	11	12	8	11	10	7	9	8
Cutting toenails	23	31	27	25	39	33	15	22	19
N=	1,139	1,292	2,431	994	1,475	2,469	1,080	1,352	2,432

[a] Excludes bedfast persons.

dress themselves but need help in washing, bathing, and in cutting their toenails. We have already considered the performance of old people in one component area of the index, the ability to go outdoors. Let us now analyze what people say they can do in walking up and down stairs, getting about the house, washing and bathing, dressing and putting on shoes, and in cutting their own toenails.

The most difficult of these five tasks for the average old person is walking up and down stairs. From a fourth (27 per cent in Great Britain) to a third (37 per cent in Denmark) of all old people say that they have trouble or difficulty with stairs. A substantial number of all people say that they cannot walk up and down stairs at all. The proportion of such persons is 5 of every hundred in Denmark, 6 of every hundred in Britain, and 7 of every hundred in the United States. The reasons why these old people cannot use stairs vary. Some are disabled, others suffer from shortness of breath, some become dizzy.

> Mr. Simpson, for example, is one of that 7 per cent of all old people in the United States who are unable to walk up or down stairs. He is 71 years old. He told the interviewer: "In January, 1957, I woke up and couldn't move. I tried to turn over and couldn't. Couldn't do a thing for a while but sit in this chair." When he describes walking stairs, he says: "I'm awful slow. I sort of pull up."

Many old people in all three countries live in walk-up flats and apartments. The high proportion of otherwise ambulatory old people who find stairs difficult to negotiate, and the proportion who cannot walk stairs at all, are indications that some among the elderly may be ill-housed on this basis alone. They are living where they have to walk up and down stairs, but they need either ground-level housing or housing with ramps or elevators.

Three parts of the index deal with items of personal care: washing and bathing, dressing and putting on shoes, and cutting toenails. The most difficult of these three items for old people in every country is cutting their own toenails. Difficulties in care of the feet are two or three times as common among old people as difficulties in washing or bathing or in dressing. From a fifth (19 per cent in the United States) to a third (33 per cent in Britain) of all respondents said that they had difficulty in cutting their toenails. The reasons why old people are unable to cut their toenails vary: some are crippled by rheumatism, some have poor eyesight, some find it impossible to cut the hard nails which develop with age. It might be expected that these same physical changes would affect old people in all three countries equally. This is not the case, however, since the proportions of old people who were absolutely unable to cut their toenails varied from 15 of every hundred in Denmark and 18 of every hundred in Britain to 9 of every hundred in the United States.

These reported differences between old people in Denmark and Great Britain, on the one hand, and in the United States, on the other, suggest that perhaps the availability of social services may create an awareness of needs. In both Denmark and Britain chiropody services for the elderly are available under state health insurance plans. The old person in these countries who has problems in caring for his feet may simply not accept this difficult task. In the United States, with its different organization of health and medical care, old people who might well need a chiropodist for the care of their feet but who are either unable or unwilling to pay for such care may continue to do what they can by themselves or with the help of children and relatives. These Americans may be less likely than either Danes or British in comparable circumstances to say that they are absolutely unable to take care of their own feet.

In Denmark, Britain, and the United States, the overwhelming majority of old people live not in institutions but at home. From 9 to 14 per cent of old people living at home are housebound or bedfast. About half of all old people living at home, however, report no limitation in their capacity for getting about or in their capacity for personal care. More than three-fourths of all old people living at home report only minimal limitations in their capacities for self-care. While these findings on the level of function among the aged are encouraging, they should not be allowed to obscure other, less optimistic findings: a substantial group of older people, small perhaps in terms of over-all proportions but large in term of numbers, find it difficult and sometimes impossible to perform the common physical tasks related to their mobility and their personal care.

Characteristics of the Incapacitated and the Well Aged

Old people living in the community differ in the extent of their incapacity. Some function well; others are seriously handicapped.

> Mr. Robinson has the maximum score, 12, on the index of incapacity. Mr. Robinson is 71 years old and housebound. He describes his health as poor, and he further says that his health is worse than the health of other people. He told the interviewer: "I'm in worse shape than any man I know." Mr. Robinson is afraid of falling so he stays in the house. "I don't get dizzy. No, I don't have no warning. I feel it. My ankles give way." Mr. Robinson needs help to walk up stairs, to get around the house, to wash, dress, and cut his toenails. When the interviewer asked Mr. Robinson whether he can wash himself, he said: "I give up trying."

> Mr. Connelly, in contrast, has a score of zero on the index of incapacity. Mr. Connelly is a 78-year-old farmer. He says that his health is good, better than that of most people his age. He works 72 hours a week on his farm. Mr. Connelly said: "I enjoy working more than anything I could mention."

Not all the severely handicapped among the aged are like Mr. Robinson nor are all the able-bodied like Mr. Connelly. Are there some general characteristics, however, which serve to distinguish severely incapacitated old people from their contemporaries? Do the incapacitated aged differ significantly from the well aged in more than their incapacity scores?

Higher indices of incapacity among the elderly are associated with advanced age. Persons who are restricted in mobility and unable to take care of their personal needs are more likely to be found among the oldest people in the community. In both Britain and the United States, as the scores on the incapacity scale rise, the proportion of those aged 80 or more at each score level rises concomitantly. In Denmark, in contrast, persons aged 80 and over are roughly one-fourth of those in each group with more than minimal impairments.

In all three countries, the very old, those over 80, include both high proportions of women and of the single and widowed. Once a relationship was established between age and incapacity, it was expected that these two characteristics would be associated with high incapacity scores. Eight of every ten persons with incapacity scores of seven or more in Britain and in the United States are women. Seven of every ten persons with scores of seven or more in Britain and six of every ten in the United States are unmarried. In Denmark the very old, those over 80, are found in almost equal proportions in each of the various categories of incapacity, from minimal to extreme. As a result, in that country the proportions of women and of the unmarried among those with the highest incapacity scores are substantially lower than the reports for Britain and the United States.

Table II–5: INCAPACITY SCORES OF OLD PEOPLE BY AGE, SEX, AND MARITAL STATUS[a]

Age, Sex, and Marital Status	0–2	3–4	5–6	7 or More	All Persons
Per cent of persons over 80[b]					
Denmark	10	24	26	22	13
Britain	11	23	30	37	15
United States	12	20	25	32	14
Per cent women					
Denmark	50	67	62	59	53
Britain	55	70	77	82	59
United States	53	63	60	83	56
Per cent married					
Denmark	57	46	48	53	55
Britain	52	41	31	33	48
United States	57	46	71	38	55
Number of cases					
Denmark	1,908	248	134	121	2,411
Britain	1,926	244	130	147	2,469
United States	2,066	183	92	91	2,432

[a] Excludes bedfast persons.

[b] Thirteen women in the United States gave their age as "over 65." They have been included with those under 80 in this table.

Old persons with high incapacity scores are more likely than other old people to have sensory impairments. In all three countries a rise in incapacity scores is associated with a rise in the proportion of persons who are blind or almost blind. A marked rise in incapacity scores is also associated with self-reports of giddiness—the tendency of people to lose their balance and to feel as though they were going to fall. The loss of a sense of balance is very common among the elderly. Those old people who feel they are likely to fall seriously restrict their movements. Usually they will not go outdoors alone, and often they will not move about the house any more than is absolutely essential but sit quietly in a chair. Among the most incapacitated group, 40 per cent in Denmark, 45 per cent in Britain, and 54 per cent in the United States said that they had been giddy during the previous week.[14]

Table II–6: INCAPACITY SCORES OF OLD PEOPLE BY SENSORY IMPAIRMENTS[a]

Sensory Impairments	0–2	3–4	5–6	7 or More	All Persons
Blind or nearly so					
Denmark (%)	1	5	10	10	3
N=	1,908	251	136	121	2,341
Britain (%)	3	7	5	9	4
N=	1,894	241	130	144	2,429
United States (%)	4	13	16	25	6
N=	2,055	182	90	90	2,417
Giddy in past week					
Denmark (%)	12	29	38	40	17
N=	1,877	247	135	121	2,396
Britain (%)	9	25	28	45	13
N=	1,919	243	130	146	2,460
United States (%)	11	38	37	54	16
N=	2,046	181	89	91	2,407

[a] Excludes bedfast persons.

Persons with high incapacity scores are more likely than other old people to have had a recent illness severe enough for them to stay in bed, and to have had some recent contact with a physician. The proportion of ambulatory and housebound old people who said that they had been ill in bed during the last year ranges from 26 per cent in the United States to 32 per cent in Denmark, or roughly from one-fourth to one-third of all elderly. The most likely of all old people to have been ill in bed during the last year, however, are the most incapacitated old people as measured by the index. In each country more than half of these very incapacitated old people had spent some time in bed during the past year. The proportion of old people who saw a doctor within the last month ranges from 22 per cent in Denmark to 34 per cent in Britain. Recent contacts with doctors, like reported illness, are more frequent among those old people with incapacity scores above the minimal level. In Denmark and the United States almost half, and in Britain more than half, of the seriously incapacitated old people had seen a doctor within the past month.

Table II–7: INCAPACITY SCORES OF OLD PEOPLE BY ILLNESS AND USE
OF DOCTORS[a]

Illness and Use of Doctors	0–2	3–4	5–6	7 or More	All Persons
Ill in bed in past year					
Denmark (%)	28	47	48	53	32
N=[b]	1,908	251	136	121	2,415
Britain (%)	26	37	43	56	30
N=[b]	1,926	244	130	147	2,446
United States (%)	23	44	42	53	26
N=[b]	2,066	183	92	91	2,432
Saw doctor within past month					
Denmark (%)	18	31	34	43	22
N=[c]	1,813	242	132	115	2,315
Britain (%)	29	48	57	57	34
N=[c]	1,909	244	130	146	2,450
United States (%)	27	45	43	48	30
N=[c]	2,038	179	92	91	2,400

[a] Excludes bedfast persons.

[b] The percentages of eligible respondents who answered this question are: Denmark, 100; Britain, 99.9; United States, 100.

[c] The percentages of eligible respondents who answered this question are: Denmark, total 95.2; Britain, total 99.2; United States, total 98.7.

We have shown that old people with the highest incapacity scores are more likely than those with low scores to be over 80, unmarried, and women. They are also more likely than those with low scores to have been ill in bed during the previous year and to have recently seen a doctor. Let us now consider the relationship between high incapacity scores in old age and social class and income levels. In the present study we have used occupation as an index of social class. Men and single women are classified by their own occupations, married and widowed women by the occupation of their husbands. In Chapters 4 and 8 we will discuss the validity and reliability of this classification in some detail. At this stage, we simply present the relationship between the old person's social class and his incapacity scores.

In the United States, but not in either Britain or Denmark, there appears to be a high correlation between social class and incapacity scores. The proportion of persons with white collar backgrounds at each score level declines as incapacity scores increase; the proportion of persons with backgrounds in agriculture rises as incapacity scores increase. Can it be that a rural background is associated with incapacity? This may be the case in the United States, but it does not seem to hold for either Britain or Denmark. In neither of these countries does there appear to be a relationship between a white collar background and lessened incapacity.

Table II–8:   INCAPACITY SCORES OF OLD PEOPLE BY SOCIAL CLASS[a]
(*Percentage Distribution*)

Social Class	0–2	3–4	5–6	7 or More
Denmark				
White collar	36	31	34	34
Blue collar and service workers	41	41	36	40
Agricultural workers	23	27	30	26
Total	100	100	100	100
Britain				
White collar	29	20	28	29
Blue collar and service workers	67	77	68	67
Agricultural workers	4	3	4	4
Total	100	100	100	100
United States				
White collar	31	25	20	14
Blue collar and service workers	49	50	46	52
Agricultural workers	20	26	34	34
Total	100	100	100	100
Number of cases[b]				
Denmark	1,885	249	134	116
Britain	1,845	230	125	142
United States	1,989	175	90	85

[a] Excludes bedfast persons.

[b] The percentages of eligible respondents who answered this question are: Denmark, 98.1; Britain, 94.9; United States, 96.2.

Further, in the United States old people with the highest incapacity scores are more likely than other old people to be poor. With each rise in incapacity scores, there is an associated rise in the proportion of old people with the lowest incomes. Half of all old people with the highest incapacity scores are found among the aged with the lowest incomes. Comparable data relating incapacity to income level are available only for the aged in Denmark. Income levels among the aged in that country (as will be shown in Chapters 12 and 13) do not vary as much as they do in the United States. In Denmark we find no marked relationship between low income and incapacity. Persons with the lowest incomes comprise from a fourth to a third of old people with various degrees of incapacity.

In all three countries, Denmark, Britain, and the United States, there are differences in the characteristics of those aged who have minimal incapacity and those who are severely incapacitated. In each country, the severely incapacitated are more likely to be older and to include a disproportionate share of women and unmarried persons. The data for the United States point up the relationships between incapacity and social class, and between incapacity and poverty in old age, in that country. Persons with agricultural backgrounds form a disproportionate share of the severely incapacitated. Persons with the lowest incomes also form a disproportionate share of those who are severely incapacitated.

Table II-9: INCAPACITY SCORES OF OLD PEOPLE AND INCOME LEVEL[a]

In Lowest Income Quartile	0–2	3–4	5–6	7 or More
Denmark (%)	24	33	27	29
United States (%)	23	32	42	47
Number of cases				
Denmark[b]	1,637	215	116	120
United States[c]	1,884	168	86	85

[a] Excludes bedfast persons.

[b] Excluded from the quartile distribution because of unknown income amounts were 110 married couples, 71 single women, 37 single men, and 71 married women.

[c] Forty-nine married couples, 7 unmarried men, and 67 unmarried women with income did not report the amount of income and are excluded from the quartile distribution. Also excluded are 64 married couples where the wife was interviewed but the man either was under 65 years of age or was not interviewed because of illness, deafness, or language problems.

The more incapacitated the old person is, the more likely he is to report sensory impairments, an illness that has kept him in bed, or a recent doctor visit. The relation of high incapacity scores among the aged to reported sensory impairments, illness, and the use of doctors suggests that the index of incapacity, although designed to measure functioning among old people, also may be an indicator of the use of medical care among the aged. Those old persons who, for whatever reason, have complaints about their functioning are more likely than other persons to spend time in bed and to see doctors. The old person who feels that he is functioning well, irrespective of clinical pathology, tends on the whole to behave as though he were well. He is unlikely to stay in bed, and he is unlikely to visit the doctor.[15]

Age and Health

A major interest of the present survey is the change that occurs in the functioning of people by age cohorts, beginning with age 65. The age span from 65 to 100 covers 35 years, as great a time span as that between age 15 and age 50. Although there are pronounced variations in the functioning of older persons within each specific age group, generally those persons who are younger—that is, in their 60s or early 70s—would be expected to be less incapacitated than those aged 80 or more. We would also anticipate that those persons who are younger would report fewer sensory impairments than the very old and, furthermore, that these younger aged would have different patterns in their use of medical care. We shall now turn to a consideration of some of the direct relationships between age and health pointed up by the survey.

INCAPACITY AND SENSORY IMPAIRMENTS

If the population aged 65 and older living at home is divided first into men and women and then into five-year cohorts beginning with those aged 65 to 69, the various persons classified together on the basis of calendar age alone are found to differ markedly from one another. Some are "young" for their years; others are more deteriorated than their calendar age would warrant. On the whole, however, there are gross differences between age cohorts in their ability to function as measured by the index of incapacity.

Table II–10: INCAPACITY FOR SELF-CARE BY AGE AND SEX, NON-INSTITUTIONAL POPULATION AGED 65 AND OVER[a] (*Percentage Distribution*)

Age Group and Index Score	DENMARK			BRITAIN			UNITED STATES		
	Men	Women	All	Men	Women	All	Men	Women	All
65–69									
0	65	58	61	77	66	71	71	68	69
1–2	23	27	25	18	18	18	19	20	19
3–6	9	12	11	5	12	9	9	9	9
7 or more	3	3	3	*	4	2	1	4	3
Total	100	100	100	100	100	100	100	100	100
N=	443	485	928	386	494	880	405	506	911
70–74									
0	60	51	55	66	48	55	72	59	65
1–2	24	28	26	21	29	26	20	24	22
3–6	10	17	14	9	16	14	8	13	10
7 or more	6	4	5	3	6	5	1	4	2
Total	100	100	100	100	100	100	100	100	100
N=	311	393	704	281	432	719	347	420	767
75–79									
0	55	39	46	59	40	47	69	50	58
1–2	27	27	27	24	24	24	18	28	24
3–6	14	25	19	15	25	21	11	15	14
7 or more	4	10	7	2	11	8	2	7	4
Total	100	100	100	100	100	100	100	100	100
N=	223	249	472	198	287	485	182	225	407
80 and over									
0	25	39	32	35	24	27	53	39	45
1–2	25	33	28	35	30	32	29	28	28
3–6	39	22	31	21	29	26	14	20	18
7 or more	11	6	9	9	17	15	4	12	9
Total	100	100	100	100	100	100	100	100	100
N=b	153	159	312	120	249	369	146	188	334

[a] Excludes bedfast persons.

[b] The percentages of eligible respondents, 80 and over, who answered this question are: Denmark, total 98.7, men 98.7, women 98.7; Britain, total 97.4, men 97.6, women 97.3; United States, total 100.

* Less than one per cent.

Younger persons have fewer incapacities than older persons. In all three countries, persons aged 65 to 69, both men and women, are functioning quite well as measured by the index of incapacity. From six to seven of every ten persons in this age group report that they have no difficulties whatsoever in going out-of-doors, walking stairs, washing and bathing, dressing and putting on shoes, and in cutting their toenails. Beginning with the cohort aged 70 to 74 in Denmark and in Great Britain, and that aged 75 to 79 in the United States, there is a change in physical capacity among the elderly. The proportion of persons who experience difficulty with common physical tasks rises with each advance in age. There is an increase among old people who report minimal difficulties—trouble in doing at least one of the tasks that make up the index—as well as an increase in the numbers of old people who report serious difficulties in functioning. The very old in the United States report less incapacity than the very old in either Denmark or Britain. In the age cohort 80 and over, only two of every ten men and four of every ten women in Denmark, three of every ten men and two of every ten women in Britain, but five of every ten men and four of every ten women in the United States report no incapacity.

An analysis of the impairments of the very old, those aged 80 and over, points up the special needs of these old people who still live at home. In all three countries from a third to a half of these very old people have difficulty with stairs. A substantial proportion have trouble in washing, bathing, and dressing themselves. Half of these very old people in Denmark and Britain, compared to about a third in the United States, have difficulty in cutting their toenails.

Each item, going outdoors, walking stairs, getting about the house, washing and bathing, dressing and putting on shoes, and cutting toenails, has an equal weight in the computation of the index of incapacity. Because there is such a marked difference between very old people, particularly in Britain on the one hand, and very old people in the United States on the other, in the proportion who report difficulties in cutting their toenails, the question may be raised whether this single item of foot care is responsible for the differences in incapacity scores among the very old in the three countries. We have therefore computed two average incapacity scores for men and women in each age group, one score including and the other excluding this item on care of the feet. From these necessarily rough computations it is apparent that whether or not the item on care of the feet is included in the average incapacity score, beginning with the age cohort 75 to 79 and continuing through the age cohort 80 and over, old people in the United States have consistently lower incapacity scores than old people in the two European countries.

At this time we mention this finding with no attempt at explanation. We shall further consider these country-by-country differences later in this chapter.

Sensory impairments, particularly vertigo, are reported by old people in every age cohort. Women more often than men report being giddy, but irrespective of sex, the older the respondent the more likely he is to report some experience with vertigo. At ages 65 to 69, 12 per cent of the Danes,

10 per cent of the British, and 14 per cent of the Americans report that they had some experience of vertigo during the week before their interview. Among those aged 80 and over, however, 26 per cent of the Danes, 22 per cent of the British, and 23 per cent of the Americans report that they experienced vertigo during the past week. Among persons over 80, one in 25 fell as an aftermath of such a seizure.

Table II–11: PROPORTION OF PERSONS AGED 65 AND OVER REPORTING DIFFICULTY WITH COMMON PHYSICAL TASKS, BY AGE AND SEX[a]

| | *Per Cent Reporting Difficulty* | | | | | | | | |
| | DENMARK | | | BRITAIN | | | UNITED STATES | | |
Age and Task	Men	Women	All	Men	Women	All	Men	Women	All
65–69									
Walking stairs	28	34	31	14	23	19	24	27	26
Getting about the house	5	5	5	2	4	3	3	7	6
Washing, bathing	6	6	6	4	10	7	6	8	7
Dressing, putting on shoes	9	8	8	4	6	5	8	8	8
Cutting toenails	16	20	19	13	23	18	13	15	14
N=[b]	444	488	932	387	495	882	405	506	911
70–74									
Walking stairs	30	37	34	18	31	26	21	36	29
Getting about the house	6	8	7	4	6	5	3	7	5
Washing, bathing	8	7	7	8	16	13	4	11	8
Dressing, putting on shoes	15	8	11	9	10	10	7	9	8
Cutting toenails	24	28	26	25	38	33	13	21	17
N=[b]	316	393	709	284	435	719	347	420	767
75–79									
Walking stairs	34	50	42	20	41	33	25	40	33
Getting about the house	5	13	9	4	11	8	4	8	6
Washing, bathing	7	13	10	9	25	18	8	17	13
Dressing, putting on shoes	11	18	15	8	15	12	5	9	7
Cutting toenails	26	41	34	32	49	42	15	28	22
N=[b]	224	249	473	200	289	489	182	225	407
80 and over									
Walking stairs	39	58	49	37	44	42	33	50	42
Getting about the house	7	14	11	14	17	16	9	12	11
Washing, bathing	15	23	19	20	34	30	14	23	19
Dressing, putting on shoes	18	19	18	19	21	20	11	14	13
Cutting toenails	36	54	45	50	61	57	29	38	34
N=[b]	155	161	316	123	256	379	146	188	334

[a] Excludes bedfast persons.

[b] Rates computed on the basis of the number of eligible respondents who answered this question. The base for each rate therefore varies slightly. The number of "no answers" ranged from 0 to 17; in no instance did less than 99 per cent of the respondents answer the question.

Table II-12: AVERAGE INCAPACITY SCORES BY AGE AND SEX OF NON-INSTITUTIONAL POPULATION AGED 65 AND OVER[a]

Average Incapacity Score	MEN					WOMEN					ALL				
	65–69	70–74	75–79	80 and Over	All	65–69	70–74	75–79	80 and Over	All	65–69	70–74	75–79	80 and Over	All
Denmark															
Score	1.0	1.4	1.3	2.2	1.3	1.2	1.5	2.4	3.1	1.7	1.1	1.4	1.9	2.6	1.5
Score minus foot care	0.8	1.0	0.9	1.5	0.9	0.9	1.0	1.7	2.1	1.3	0.8	1.0	1.3	1.8	1.1
Britain															
Score	0.5	0.9	1.2	2.2	1.0	1.1	1.7	2.5	3.4	1.9	0.9	1.4	2.0	3.0	1.6
Score minus foot care	0.3	0.5	0.7	1.5	0.8	0.8	1.1	1.7	2.2	1.4	0.6	0.9	1.3	2.0	1.2
United States															
Score	0.8	0.7	0.9	1.5	0.6	1.0	1.3	1.7	2.4	1.3	0.9	1.0	1.3	2.0	1.1
Score minus foot care	0.6	0.5	0.6	1.0	0.6	0.8	1.0	1.2	1.8	1.1	0.7	0.8	1.0	1.5	0.9
Number of cases[b]															
Denmark	443	311	223	153	1,130	485	393	249	159	1,286	928	704	472	312	2,416
Britain	386	281	198	120	985	494	432	287	249	1,462	880	713	485	369	2,447
United States	405	347	182	146	1,080	506	420	225	188	1,352[b]	911	767	407	334	2,432[b]

[a] Excludes bedfast persons.

[b] Includes 13 women past 65 years of age whose exact age is unknown.

Table II-13: PROPORTION OF PERSONS AGED 65 AND OVER REPORTING GIDDINESS AND FALLS IN PAST WEEK[a]

Reported Giddiness and Falls in Past Week	MEN					WOMEN					ALL				
	65-69	70-74	75-79	80 and Over	All	65-69	70-74	75-79	80 and Over	All	65-69	70-74	75-79	80 and Over	All
Giddy (%)															
Denmark	9	12	19	22	13	15	18	23	31	19	12	15	21	26	17
Britain	9	8	10	14	9	11	14	19	26	16	10	12	16	22	14
United States	12	13	13	17	13	15	14	21	28	17	14	14	18	23	16
Fell (%)															
Denmark	*	*	*	5	1	1	1	2	4	2	1	1	1	4	1
Britain	1	1	2	1	1	1	2	3	4	2	1	2	3	3	2
United States	2	2	2	3	2	2	1	3	4	2	2	2	2	4	2
Number of cases															
Denmark	436	306	221	150	1,113	481	389	248	160	1,278	917	695	469	310	2,391
Britain	386	284	200	121	991	494	433	287	255	1,469	880	717	487	376	2,460
United States	399	343	180	145	1,067	502	415	223	185	1,338[b]	901	758	403	330	2,405[b]

[a] Excludes bedfast persons.

[b] Includes 13 women of unknown age.

* Less than one per cent.

ILLNESS AND MEDICAL CARE

Let us now consider some of the relationships between age and reported illness and the use of medical care. A full statement of the use of health facilities by the elderly is given in Chapter 4. At this time we shall restrict ourselves to a discussion of the effect of age on reported illness and contacts with physicians.

Since persons in their 60s and early 70s are less incapacitated than those of 80 and over, the former might be expected to report fewer illnesses, fewer hospitalizations, and fewer recent contacts with doctors than the latter. There is no clear-cut evidence for all three countries that there is less illness or hospitalization among the younger aged who live at home than among the very old in comparable circumstances. There is evidence in each country, however, that very old people living at home are more likely than the younger aged to have had some recent contact with a doctor.

In the three countries, between 26 and 32 per cent of all ambulatory and housebound old people living at home say that they have been ill in bed during the year. Old people in the United States are less likely than old people in either Denmark or Britain to report such illness. When the patterns of illness by age cohorts for each country are compared, certain differences between the countries are apparent. In Denmark and Britain a higher proportion of those over 80 than of those in the younger age cohorts say that they have been ill at home within the past year. This is particularly true for old women. In the United States, however, the proportions ill at home are almost the same among those over 80 and those aged 65 to 69.

The proportion of all old people who report stays in the hospital during the past year in the three countries varies between 8 and 13 per cent. In Denmark, the highest hospitalization rates are reported by persons aged 80 and over and the lowest by persons aged 65 to 69. In Britain there is no marked relationship between advanced age and increased hospitalization rates, and in the United States the highest hospitalization rates of any age cohort are reported for persons aged 75 to 79. Analysis of the American data further indicates that for this sample of old people still living at home, length of hospital stay is not directly correlated with age. Persons 80 and over, and persons aged 65 to 69, had the same average hospital stays.[16]

When we turn from reports of illness and hospitalization to consideration of recent contacts with doctors, a clear association of the use of doctors and the age of the patient, comparable to the association that exists between advanced age and incapacity, is once more apparent. The older the person, the more likely he is to have seen a doctor recently. In Denmark 19 per cent of all persons aged 65 to 69, contrasted with 27 per cent of those aged 80 and over, saw a doctor within the past month; in Britain 29 per cent of all persons aged 65 to 69, compared with 41 per cent of those 80 and over, saw a doctor within the past month; and in the United States 29 per cent of those aged 65 to 69, compared with 33 per cent of those aged 80 and over, saw a doctor. In every country, old women

Table II-14: REPORTED ILLNESS DURING PAST YEAR OF PERSONS AGED 65 AND OVER, BY AGE AND SEX[a]

Illness in Past Year	MEN					WOMEN					ALL				
	65–69	70–74	75–79	80 and Over	All	65–69	70–74	75–79	80 and Over	All	65–69	70–74	75–79	80 and Over	All
Ill (%)															
Denmark	27	29	30	30	28	34	38	32	42	36	31	34	31	36	32
Britain	27	27	30	31	28	28	30	33	39	32	28	29	32	36	30
United States	25	19	25	23	23	31	23	34	31	29	28	21	30	27	26
Number of cases															
Denmark	443	314	223	155	1,135	487	394	249	161	1,291	930	708	472	316	2,426
Britain	386	281	198	120	985	494	432	287	249	1,462	880	713	485	369	2,447
United States	405	347	182	146	1,080	506	420	225	188	1,352[b]	911	767	407	334	2,432[b]

[a] Excludes bedfast persons.

[b] Includes 13 women of unknown age.

Table II-15: REPORTED PHYSICIAN UTILIZATION BY PERSONS AGED 65 AND OVER, BY AGE AND SEX[a]

Physician Utilization	MEN					WOMEN					ALL				
	65–69	70–74	75–79	80 and Over	All	65–69	70–74	75–79	80 and Over	All	65–69	70–74	75–79	80 and Over	All
Saw doctor within past month (%)															
Denmark	17	18	21	27	19	21	25	24	28	24	19	22	23	27	22
Britain	24	34	33	43	31	34	32	33	30	36	29	33	39	41	34
United States	27	24	32	38	28	32	30	36	29	31	29	27	34	33	30
Saw doctor one year or more ago (%)															
Denmark	48	44	41	40	44	34	32	31	25	32	41	37	36	32	38
Britain	34	35	30	20	32	33	28	25	22	28	33	31	27	22	30
United States	38	43	36	32	38	30	34	28	33	31	33	38	32	33	35
Number of cases															
Denmark	425	301	209	149	1,084	461	381	237	152	1,231	886	682	446	301	2,315
Britain	385	281	199	122	987	493	430	287	253	1,463	878	711	486	375	2,450
United States	398	343	181	146	1,068	499	415	221	184	1,332b	897	758	402	330	2,400b

a Excludes bedfast persons.

b Includes 13 women of unknown age.

were more likely than old men to have seen a doctor, but in both Britain and the United States very old men (those 80 or more) were more likely than very old women to have seen a doctor.

Of equal interest is the group of old people who report that they have not seen a doctor for a year or more. The large number of old people who have not seen doctors is surprising. This group includes roughly one-third of all old people in the three countries studied. In both Denmark and the United States a greater proportion of old people have not seen a doctor for a year or more, than have seen a doctor within the past month. In both Denmark and Britain (but not in the United States) not seeing a doctor for a year or more is inversely related to age: those 65 to 69 are the most likely not to have seen a doctor, while those 80 and over are the least likely not to have seen a doctor.

The pattern of medical usage with advancing age among old people living at home is contradictory. Recent use of doctors is clearly correlated with advances in age, but illness in bed and hospitalization are not. How do we explain these findings?

People 75 years of age still living at home are more impaired than the younger aged. They are more likely than these younger persons to bring their complaints to the attention of physicians. This is apparent from our analysis. Those over 75 and certainly those over 80 still living at home are the least incapacitated among all persons in this age group. The most incapacitated in this age group are resident in institutions. The data suggest that persons in their 60's and early 70's with extensive periods of illness either at home or in the hospital are likely to remain living at home; those over 75 or 80 with comparable periods of extensive illness are likely to be institutionalized. Therefore, our sample does not include many of those over 75 who have been ill in bed or hospitalized during the past year. These persons have been removed from the community, and as a result we find no clear association with advancing age either in the amount of illness reported or in the reports of hospitalization.

The Aged in Three Countries

A number of facts about the health of old people in Denmark, Britain, and the United States have been established in this chapter. Let us summarize them briefly, and then consider the similarities and differences in the health of old people in the three countries.

In all three countries a small proportion of persons over 65, five in every hundred or less, are in institutions. The proportion of institution-alized persons is greatest in Denmark, less in Britain and the United States. The reasons for institutionalization appear to be similar in each country: the physical or mental decrepitude of the old person, the inability or lack of family members to cope with nursing needs and super-vision, and finally, the failure of community services. There are some old people in institutions, particularly in residential homes, who might well be living in the community if housing and community services were organized to meet their needs. The proportion of such persons among the institutionalized is greater in both Denmark and Britain than in the United States.

In each of the three countries more old people are found to be bedfast and housebound at home than are resident in institutions. In Britain, four times as many old people are bedfast and housebound at home as live in institutions; in the United States and Denmark, twice as many. Further, as many people appear to be bedfast at home in each country (about 2 to 3 per cent of the total elderly) as are resident in hospitals and nursing homes in that country. Consequently, those responsible for services to maintain old people in their own homes must consider that if their clientele for basic services is made up only of the bedfast and housebound, it includes from 14 per cent (in Britain) to 8 per cent (in the United States) of all elderly persons living at home.

The proportion of persons living at home who are neither bedfast nor housebound, but who are able to go outdoors only with difficulty, is also greater than the proportion of old people living in institutions. At least twice as many people in Denmark and about one and one-half times as many' people in Britain and the United States as live in institutions of all kinds, are able to go outdoors only with difficulty. These old persons who are limited in mobility are also in need of full programs of community services. While the need of these persons for medical attention and for nursing care may be less than that of the bedfast and the housebound, those limited in mobility and their families need help from the community to continue their present living arrangements. The proportions of people over 65 who are bedfast, housebound, or limited in mobility, who are living at home, and who must be considered in planning a broad program of services, are roughly 24 per cent in Denmark, 21 per cent in Britain, and 14 per cent in the United States.

While substantial groups of old people living at home require assistance from their families and the community, the majority of the elderly in all three countries are able to perform the minimal tasks needed for personal care without difficulty and without assistance from others. It should perhaps be stressed that about half of all noninstitutionalized old people in Denmark and Great Britain, and two-thirds of all old people in the United States, report no functional incapacity.

In each of the three countries the most seriously incapacitated among the aged can be categorically described as old women, either single or widowed. These women in every country are also among the poorest persons in the elderly population.

Incapacity in the elderly increases with age. Active, functioning old people are usually under 75 years of age. The most seriously incapacitated old people are those aged 80 and over. Both the numbers and proportions of very old people in each country are expected to increase, so that in the near future persons over 80 will comprise an even higher proportion than they do now of those aged 65 and more. Should this shift in age composition of the elderly occur as forecast, the proportion of functioning old people is likely to decline below its present level.

In all three countries the very old living at home make the greatest use of physicians. Recent contact with physicians is reported least often in Denmark, most often in Britain. Although the organization of the medical services in the United States differs from that in Denmark and Britain, the American aged were almost as likely as the British and more likely than the Danes to have recently seen a doctor. A full discussion of survey findings about the use of health and welfare services by the aged in the three countries is given in the chapters that follow.

The variations among the health of old people in Denmark, Britain, and the United States are not as great as the differences in the health status of the elderly in any one country. In each country some old people in the community are functioning very well; others are maintaining a precarious balance, continuing to live in the community only with the help of relatives, neighbors, and community services. Nevertheless, there seem to be some over-all country-by-country differences in the health of the aged.

Denmark has the highest proportion of its old people in institutions, the United States and Britain a somewhat lesser proportion of old people in institutions. Old people in the United States are less likely than old people in either Denmark or Britain to be housebound or restricted in their mobility or to report incapacities in functioning. Of the three countries studied, the United States has the highest proportion and Denmark the lowest proportion of old people living at home who are ambulatory. These differences in reported incapacity of the aged in the three countries are particularly marked in the oldest age groups, those over 75. The very old in the United States are more incapacitated than Americans aged 65 to 69, but less incapacitated than their European contemporaries.

What are the reasons for these differences between the American and European aged found in this survey? The differences are not the result of the somewhat different age distribution of the three country samples, since when these age distributions are standardized, the differences in over-all incapacity scores among the countries do not vanish. It may indeed be that the American over 65, or more particularly over 75, is more agile and able-bodied than his European contemporary. Some of this difference in self-reports of incapacity between older Americans and older Danes and Britains, however, undoubtedly results from the feeling of many older Americans that, irrespective of age and infirmity, it is necessary to be active and completely self-sufficient. Old people in the United States, more than old people in Europe, seem to feel that to admit illness or incapacity is somehow psychologically wrong. At this time, we can only mention the fact that such attitudes play a part both in behavior and in reports of incapacity. In the next chapter, however, we shall further explore the relationship between psychological attitudes and reports of health status among the aged in the three countries.

NOTES

1 James E. Birren, Robert N. Butler, Samuel W. Greenhouse, Louis Sokoloff, Marian R. Yarrow, "Ir·roduction to the Study of Human Aging," *Human Aging*, James E. Birren, Robert N. Butler, Samuel W. Greenhouse, Louis Sokoloff, Marian R. Yarrow, eds. (Bethesda, Md.: U.S. Department of Health, Education, and Welfare, Public Health Service, National Institutes of Health, 1963), p. 1.

2 For Denmark see *Statistical Yearbook for Denmark, 1963* (Copenhagen: Det Statistiske Departement, 1963), Table 34, p. 59. For Britain see *The Registrar General's Quarterly Return . . . June, 1963.* Life expectancy is based on deaths registered in England and Wales in the years 1960, 1961, 1962. There is a full discussion of the production of life tables in *The Registrar General's Decennial Supplement for England and Wales 1957* (London: Her Majesty's Stationery Office, 1957). For the United States see U.S. Department of Health, Education, and Welfare, *Health, Education, and Welfare Trends, 1963* (Washington, D.C.: U.S. GPO, 1964), p. 13.

3 There is some evidence from the United States that if long-stay patients in short-stay hospitals are included among the institutionalized, the proportion of institutionalized would rise about one per cent. The United States Social Security Administration in its 1963 survey of the aged reports that roughly 10 per cent of all old people who reported stays in short-term hospitals had hospital stays of more than 30 days. See Dorothy P. Rice, "Health Insurance Coverage of the Aged and Their Hospital Utilization in 1962: Findings of the 1963 Survey of the Aged," *Social Security Bulletin*, XXVII (July, 1964), 24. In the present survey, 11 per cent of the American sample who had been hospitalized reported stays of more than 30 days. Something less than one per cent of the total elderly population, therefore, were resident in short-stay hospitals more than 30 days.

4 "The estimates of the elderly institutionalized population are based on the number of beds (places) in homes for the aged and nursing homes (plejehjem). There are about 800 homes for the aged, with 22,000 inhabitants: 3,400 of those in homes for the aged are placed in the hospital department of the homes, or in other departments for people too sick, too weak or infirm to be able to take care of themselves. At least one-third of the inhabitants in nursing homes are unable to take care of themselves (bedfast, non-ambulatory). The lowest estimate on the proportion of elderly people who are bedfast, chronically ill or non-ambulatory, living in institutions is 1.7 per cent." Jan Stehouwer. Source: Ministry of Social Affairs, *Betaenkning om alderdomshjem og plejehjem* (Copenhagen: Ministry of Social Affairs, 1962), betaenkning nr. 318, pp. 14–15.

5 General Register Office, *Census, 1961*, England and Wales, Age, Marital Condition and General Tables (London: HMSO, 1965), Table 4, pp. 105–106. U.S. Bureau of the Census, *United States Census of the Population: 1960. Subject Reports. Inmates of Institutions*, Final Report PC (2)-8A (Washington, D.C.: U.S. GPO, 1963).

6 In the interviewed sample, Britain has almost 11 per cent of its old people bedfast and housebound, twice as high a proportion as the United States and one and one-half times as high a proportion of such persons as Denmark. Certain old people who were located in the older population living outside institutions could not be interviewed. Some persons were too ill to be interviewed. Using data secured in this way, an assessment was made of the health condition of these old people which is reflected in the distribution "Total sample located" in Table II–2.

7 A somewhat comparable figure is reported for the United States from the National Health Survey. The Survey reports that 14.9 per cent of all noninstitutionalized persons aged 65 and over are unable to carry on their major activity—i.e., working or keeping house. U.S. National Center for Health Statistics, *Bed Disability Among the Chronically Limited, United States, July 1957–June 1961* (Washington, D.C.: U.S. Department of Health, Education, and Welfare, Public Health Service, 1964), p. 15.

8 World Health Organization, *The Public Health Aspects of the Aging of the Population*, Report of an Advisory Group Convened by the Regional Office for Europe (Copenhagen: World Health Organization, 1959), p. 8.

9 An excellent discussion of definitions of health is given in Walt R. Simmons, "The Matrix of Health, Manpower, and Age," in Richard H. Williams, Clark Tibbitts, and

Wilma Donahue, eds., *Processes of Aging* (New York: Atherton Press, 1963), II, 353–354. For an experimental study of different procedures in gathering health statistics, see: U.S. National Health Survey, *Health Interview Responses Compared with Medical Records* (Washington, D.C.: U.S. Department of Health, Education, and Welfare, Public Health Service, 1961).

10 Bernard Kutner, David Fanshel, Alice M. Togo, Thomas S. Langner, *Five Hundred Over Sixty* (New York: Russell Sage Foundation, 1956), pp. 134–139; Ethel Shanas, *The Health of Older People: A Social Survey* (Cambridge, Mass.: Harvard University Press, 1962), pp. 180, 188–189; Glenn H. Beyer and Sylvia G. Wahl, *The Elderly and Their Housing* (Ithaca, N.Y.: Cornell University Agricultural Experiment Station, New York State College of Home Economics, 1963), pp. 40–42, 61.

11 The Staff of the Benjamin Rose Hospital, Cleveland, Ohio, "Multidisciplinary Study of Illness of Aged Persons, I, Methods and Preliminary Results," *Journal of Chronic Diseases*, VII (April, 1958), 332–345; "Multidisciplinary Study of Illness of Aged Persons, II, A New Classification of Functional Status in Activities of Daily Living," *ibid.*, IX (January, 1959), 55–73. See also the index of illness developed for old people living at home by W. Hobson and J. Pemberton, *The Health of the Elderly Living at Home* (London: Butterworth, 1955).

12 Peter Townsend, "Measuring Incapacity for Self-Care," in Williams, Tibbitts, and Donahue, eds., *op. cit.*, II, 272. See also Peter Townsend and Brian Rees, *The Personal, Family, and Social Circumstances of Old People: Report of an Investigation Carried out in England in 1959 to Pilot a Future Cross-National Survey of Old Age* (London: London School of Economics, 1959), and Peter Townsend, "Measuring Incapacity for Self-Care," *The Last Refuge* (London: Routledge & Kegan Paul, 1962), Appendix 2, pp. 464–476.

13 Townsend, "Measuring Incapacity for Self-Care," in Williams, Tibbitts, and Donahue, eds., *op. cit.*, II, 272.

14 Sheldon states that vertigo is not only widespread among old people but also that it is a primary factor in falls among the aged. J. H. Sheldon, *The Social Medicine of Old Age* (London: Oxford University Press, 1948). See also J. H. Sheldon, "Medical-Social Aspects of the Aging Process," in Milton Derber, ed., *The Aged and Society* (Champaign, Ill.: Industrial Relations Research Association, 1950), pp. 229–231.

15 The findings reinforce those reported in an earlier study by Shanas: ". . . heavy users of medical care were more likely to be older than the remainder of the population; they were more likely to be women; they were more likely to be widowed; and, as will be shown, they were far more likely to be indigent," *op. cit.*, p. 44.

16 Hospital rates are given in Chapter 4. The small numbers in the American sample over 80 years of age, and the resulting high sample variance, have undoubtedly distorted these data on admission and length of stay. A study of Spanish-American War veterans with an average age of 86 indicates that one in four were hospitalized during the year. See Arthur H. Richardson, James F. Cummins, Howard E. Freeman, Harold W. Schnaper, and Norman A. Scotch, "Use of Health Resources Among an Advanced Aged Population: A Preliminary Report of the Spanco Study," a paper given at meetings of the American Sociological Association, Montreal, Canada, September 1, 1964.

The proportion of those in the United States who were in the hospital for long periods (more than 30 days) was actually less among those aged 80 and over than among those aged 65 to 69. Again, because of the small numbers in this sample and the resulting high sampling variance, these data should be interpreted cautiously.

3 : The Psychology of Health

Health has its subjective as well as its objective aspects. The physician makes an assessment of the health of a patient based on the presence of pathology; the patient, however, evaluates his health in his own way. The two evaluations, that of the doctor and that of the patient, sometimes agree; sometimes they do not. An individual's assessment of his health in old age, as in youth and in middle age, is based upon various factors, some of which may be quite separate from medically verified conditions. Some old people with major or minor impairments think that they are well; other old people with similar complaints think that they are sick.

This idiosyncratic self-assessment of health can be illustrated by the cases of three old people in the United States. Mrs. Robinson, Mrs. Slayton, and Mrs. Igoe are all widows in their 80s. Mrs. Robinson and Mrs. Slayton are both quite feeble, yet Mrs. Robinson says her health is poor and Mrs. Slayton says her health is good. Mrs. Igoe, on the contrary, seems physically well, yet she says her health is poor.

Mrs. Robinson is 81 years old. She shares a home with two divorced daughters, both in their 50s. She reports difficulty with each of the tasks that make up the index of capacity. She says she often feels as though she is going to fall "flat on my face"; she has difficulty in seeing; she has gall bladder trouble and arthritis. Mrs. Robinson was ill in bed during the last year, and she saw the doctor during the last month. Although Mrs. Robinson says that her health is "poor," on the whole she considers her health to be about the same as the health of other people her age.

Mrs. Slayton is also an 80-year-old widow. She lives alone. She is hard of hearing, badly crippled by arthritis, and reports that she has difficulty in going out of doors, washing and bathing, dressing, and putting on her shoes. She often feels as though she is about to fall. Mrs. Slayton says that she cannot walk stairs at all and that a neighbor has to help her dress. The housework is done by her daughters, who live about ten minutes' distance. Despite her impairments, Mrs. Slayton says that her health is good for her age. She spent no time in bed during the past year and has not seen the doctor for several months. In fact, Mrs. Slayton says that her health is better than the health of most people her age.

Mrs. Igoe is 82 years old, a widow, and like Mrs. Slayton she lives alone. Mrs. Igoe can get about indoors and out. She reports some difficulty in walking stairs, but otherwise reports no physical impairments. She says that she can and does do heavy household tasks like washing windows and cleaning floors. Mrs. Igoe was ill in bed during the past year, and her daughter who lives nearby came in to take care of her. Mrs. Igoe sees the doctor every month. She considers her health to be poor, but about the same as the health of other people her age.

In view of the impairments reported by these three women, Mrs. Robinson, Mrs. Slayton, and Mrs. Igoe, only Mrs. Robinson seems to make a realistic assessment of her health. Mrs. Robinson is obviously in poor health and she describes her health as poor. Mrs. Slayton, too, is in poor health but she says that her health is "good." Mrs. Igoe, on the contrary, seems to be in good health but she says that her health is "poor." Mrs. Robinson is a health realist; Mrs. Slayton, a health optimist; and Mrs. Igoe, a health pessimist.[1]

The problems inherent in interpretation or evaluation of the health status of old people and of the self-assessment that old people make of their health are emphasized in a Soviet study of some 18,000 persons aged 80 and over. In this study old people were examined by physicians who then made an assessment of their health status. At the same time, each old person was asked to describe his own health. In a summary report, the investigator states:

> Fewer people . . . regarded themselves as strong than were given the evaluation "almost well." On the other hand, the doctors classed as "ill" and "very ill" more people than placed themselves in these categories. Some of the old people did not know they were suffering from serious diseases.[2]

From our data we cannot determine why among old persons with apparently the same degree of impairment some say they are sick and others say they are well. We cannot find what are the causes either of health realism, health pessimism, or health optimism. However, we can isolate those factors that are associated with reports either of sickness or of good health, and explore the meaning of such associations. In the present chapter, we shall first investigate the differences in the evaluation of their health by the younger aged (those under 75) and the older aged (those over 75), and by men and women. We shall then consider whether old people in the three countries differ in their health evaluations. Following this discussion of the effects of age, sex, and national style on evaluation of health, we shall demonstrate that there is a direct relationship between physical incapacity as measured by our index of incapacity and health evaluation.

We shall then try to learn something more about the psychological differences between the sick (those persons who consider themselves in poor health) and the well (those persons who feel that their health is fair or good). Self-assessment of health among the elderly may be as closely related to subjective feeling states as to objective measures of incapacity. Finally, we shall investigate whether old people themselves share the common image of the elderly as sick and decrepit or whether they tend to describe the health of other old people in the same fashion as they describe themselves.

Self-Evaluation of Health

The majority of old people in Denmark, Britain, and the United States say that they are in good health for their age. There is no clear-cut relationship among old people in any of the three countries between advances in age and either an increase or a decline in the proportion of old persons who feel that their health is good. In each country, more old men than old women are likely to be optimistic about their health. And, finally, old people in Britain, both men and women, are more likely than old people in either Denmark or the United States to say that their health is good.

EVALUATION OF HEALTH AND AGE AND SEX DIFFERENCES

In all three countries most old people living at home say that their health is good. Only a minority of old people say that their health is poor. The older population includes both 65-year-olds and centenarians. A whole generation lies between these two extremes. It was expected that when all persons over 65 were divided into age cohorts, those in the oldest cohort, 80 and over, would be less likely than those in the younger cohorts to say that their health is good and more likely to say their health is poor. We had some reason to anticipate this finding since on an objective index of incapacity the average person over 80 living at home reports more incapacity than the average person within the 65 to 69 or the 70 to 74 age cohort.

The data, however, show that there is no marked decline with age in the proportion of old people who feel that their health is good. About the same proportion of persons in every age category say their health is good. Indeed, persons over 80 still living at home tend to make more optimistic evaluations of their health than those in the immediately younger age group, that is, those aged 75 to 79. In each country, it is among women aged 75 to 79 that we find the smallest proportion of those who feel that their health is good.

The proportion of old people who feel their health is poor clearly rises with age only among old women in Denmark. Among old men in Denmark, and among both old men and old women in Britain and in the United States, there is no marked increase with age in those who say their health is poor.

Even though the proportion of old people who say their health is good for their age remains stable with advancing age, why is there no rise in the proportion of those who say their health is poor? Can it be that the old person's self-assessment of his health is a poor index of his physical functioning? George Maddox in his study of the self-assessment of health of a group of elderly volunteers in Durham, North Carolina, found that roughly two of every three subjects displayed "a reality orientation" in their subjective evaluation of their health. Among those whose self-

Table III-1: SELF-EVALUATION OF HEALTH OF PERSONS AGED 65 AND OVER, BY AGE AND SEX (Percentage Distribution)

Self-Evaluation of Health	MEN						WOMEN						ALL					
	65–66	67–69	70–74	75–79	80 and Over	All	65–66	67–69	70–74	75–79	80 and Over	All	65–66	67–69	70–74	75–79	80 and Over	All
Denmark																		
Good	52	55	56	55	62	56	55	50	48	46	47	49	53	52	52	51	54	52
Fair	30	31	29	31	22	29	35	33	35	36	33	35	33	32	32	34	28	32
Poor	18	14	15	13	16	15	10	17	17	18	20	16	14	15	16	15	18	16
Total	100	100	100	100	100	100	100	100	100	100	100	100	100	100	100	100	100	100
N=a	184	262	316	225	156	1,143	218	269	396	251	166	1,300	402	531	712	476	322	2,443
Britain																		
Good	61	62	59	61	62	61	57	58	53	48	55	54	59	60	55	54	58	57
Fair	26	30	27	26	25	27	28	29	31	37	30	31	27	29	29	32	28	29
Poor	13	8	14	12	13	12	15	13	16	15	15	15	14	11	16	14	14	14
Total	100	100	100	100	100	100	100	100	100	100	100	100	100	100	100	100	100	100
N=a	164	226	286	201	123	1,000	211	285	436	291	265	1,488	375	511	722	492	388	2,488
United States																		
Good	54	56	59	47	51	55	58	48	51	44	52	51	56	51	54	46	52	52
Fair	28	24	26	34	32	28	27	34	31	34	27	31	28	30	29	34	29	30
Poor	17	20	15	19	17	17	15	18	18	22	21	18	16	19	17	21	19	18
Total	100	100	100	100	100	100	100	100	100	100	100	100	100	100	100	100	100	100
N=a	176	229	346	182	146	1,079	205	303	423	226	191	1,361b	381	532	769	408	337	2,440b

a Detailed information on non-response is not given in this or subsequent tables if 98 per cent or more of all eligible respondents have answered the question.

b Thirteen women of unknown age are included in this distribution.

assessment of health differed from the findings of medical examinations, the optimists as distinct from the pessimists were older, relatively active, male, and had modified their work role.[3]

In our surveys we have no medical assessments of our subjects. An old person's self-assessment of his health, however, correlates highly with his self-reported incapacity. We would argue that there are several valid explanations for why the proportions of those in the survey reporting themselves in good health do not decline markedly with age and why the proportions reporting poor health do not rise with age. One reason may well be, as Maddox demonstrates, that those over 80 who remain in the community, even if frail, are apparently more optimistic about their health than younger persons with an equivalent degree of impairment. Another reason must surely be that the frailest members of the oldest group, those who would be likely to say their health is poor, have already been institutionalized.[4]

Men are more likely than women to say their health is good. This finding was expected, since men report less incapacity than women. This difference in health attitudes between men and women is consistent for all age groups in both Denmark and Britain, except for the years immediately following retirement. In Denmark, as in the United States (but not in Britain, however), in the years just after 65 men are more likely than women to say that their health is poor. Once the age of 70 is reached, however, the general pattern reasserts itself. Men in Denmark and in the United States (as in Britain) are more likely than women to say their health is good, and less likely than women to say their health is poor.

Whether or not an old person says his health is good or poor is related to his degree of incapacity. This will be demonstrated shortly. It is also related to the culture or style of life of the country in which he lives. Let us illustrate: in each country old men report less incapacity than old women and they are more likely than women to say their health is good. It is doubtful whether old men are actually in better health than old women. Statistics on length of life indicate that women outlive men. In Denmark, Britain, and the United States, however, men are the dominant sex. They are expected to be stronger than women, hardier, and less complaining. This cultural pattern is followed throughout the life span and into old age. Consequently, old men in comparison with old women are more likely to say their health is good.

The differences in national style among the three countries are evident in the self-evaluations that old people make of their health. Old people in Britain, both men and women, are generally more optimistic about their health status than old people in either Denmark or the United States. These findings were not anticipated, since the highest scores on the index of incapacity were reported from Britain, and the lowest from the United States. The British character, with its emphasis on "making do" and "keeping a stiff upper lip," is nowhere better illustrated than among the elderly. The physical changes associated with aging are accepted by the British with fewer complaints than are expressed in comparable situations by either the Danes or the Americans.

The American aged, on the other hand, are more likely than either the Danes or the British to report that their health is poor. It may be recalled that Americans in the older age groups (those 75 and over) report substantially less incapacity than the British and somewhat less incapacity than the Danes on almost every question on the incapacity scale. Yet, compared to the Europeans the Americans appear unwilling to accept the physical limitations of age. They appear to be less content with their health and more complaining. We shall try to explain the reasons for these country-by-country differences in health evaluation when we relate these evaluations to mobility and the scores on the index of incapacity.

RELATIONSHIP BETWEEN HEALTH EVALUATION, MOBILITY, AND THE INDEX OF INCAPACITY

The self-evaluation that old people make of their health is highly correlated with their reports of restrictions on mobility, their sensory impairments, and their over-all incapacity scores. In general, if an old person says his health is poor, he has some physical basis for this self-judgment.

In each country, the more mobile the old person is, the more likely he is to say his health is good. The highest proportion of persons who say their health is good is found among those who can go outdoors without restrictions. Roughly six of every ten of these people say that they are in

Table III–2: SELF-EVALUATION OF HEALTH OF PERSONS AGED 65 AND OVER, BY MOBILITY[a] (*Percentage Distribution*)

Self-Evaluation of Health	Housebound Persons	Mobile with Difficulty	Ambulatory Persons
Denmark			
Good	14	18	62
Fair	28	48	30
Poor	58	35	8
Total	100	100	100
N=	162	353	1,913
Britain			
Good	27	33	63
Fair	32	34	29
Poor	42	32	8
Total	100	100	100
N=	240	191	2,026
United States			
Good	16	21	57
Fair	20	27	30
Poor	64	51	13
Total	100	100	100
N=	121	136	2,173

[a] Excludes bedfast persons.

good health. The highest proportion of persons who say their health is poor is found among the housebound. In Denmark and in the United States six of every ten housebound persons, and in Britain four of every ten housebound persons, say their health is poor. Persons whose mobility is restricted but who can still go out are less likely than the housebound to say their health is poor and far less likely than the totally mobile to say their health is good. Obviously, whether an old person thinks he is in good or in poor health is related to his ability to be active and to get about.

In each country, old people with sensory impairments are more likely than other old people to say their health is poor. The two indices of sensory impairments investigated in the survey were vertigo (giddiness) and blindness. What is of special interest is the extent to which reports of vertigo, rather then blindness, are associated with a self-evaluation of "poor" health. In both the United States and Denmark, the blind person is more than twice as likely as his sighted counterpart to say that his health is poor; however, in all three countries the person who reports that he has spells of vertigo is from three to four times as likely as his less handicapped counterpart to say his health is poor.

Table III–3: SELF-EVALUATION OF HEALTH OF PERSONS AGED 65 AND OVER, BY SENSORY IMPAIRMENTS (*Percentage Distribution*)

Self-Evaluation of Health	Persons Blind or Nearly So	All Others	Persons with Vertigo during Last Week[a]	All Others[a]
Denmark				
Good	25	53	25	58
Fair	37	32	44	30
Poor	37	15	32	12
Total	100	100	100	100
N=[b]	67	2,376	399	1,991
Britain				
Good	—	—	28	62
Fair	—	—	39	28
Poor	—	—	33	10
Total	—	—	100	100
N=[b]	—	—	334	2,123
United States				
Good	30	54	19	59
Fair	32	29	32	29
Poor	38	17	48	12
Total	100	100	100	100
N=[b]	146	2,294	376	2,054

[a] Excludes bedfast persons.

[b] British data on blindness were not comparable with that for Denmark and the United States. The percentages of eligible respondents who answered the question on blindness are: Denmark, 100; United States, 99.9. The percentages of eligible respondents who answered the question on vertigo are: Denmark, 97.9; Britain, 99.7; United States, 100.

The old person's self-rating of his health is a guide to his degree of incapacity as measured by our index. For each country and for both sexes, the higher the incapacity score, the greater the proportion of old people who feel their health is poor. Interestingly enough, in all three countries there are a group of health optimists, persons with incapacity scores of 7 or more who think their health is good. The proportion of health optimists ranges from 12 per cent in Denmark to 27 per cent in Britain. Some

Table III–4: SELF-EVALUATION OF HEALTH OF PERSONS AGED 65 AND OVER, BY INCAPACITY SCORES[a] (*Percentage Distribution*)

Self-Evaluation of Health	MEN				WOMEN				ALL			
	0–2	3–4	5–6	7 or More	0–2	3–4	5–6	7 or More	0–2	3–4	5–6	7 or More
Denmark												
Good	64	25	15	b	59	27	15	14	61	27	15	12
Fair	27	39	40	b	33	47	38	26	30	44	39	29
Poor	9	36	44	b	8	26	46	60	8	29	46	59
Total	100	100	100	b	100	100	100	100	100	100	100	100
N=	944	84	52	49	963	167	84	72	1,907	251	136	121
Britain												
Good	66	28	b	b	64	30	37	26	64	29	37	27
Fair	26	44	b	b	29	48	31	28	27	47	32	25
Poor	8	28	b	b	8	22	32	46	8	24	31	49
Total	100	100	b	b	100	100	100	100	100	100	100	100
N=	853	72	30	26	1,069	172	100	120	1,916	244	130	146
United States												
Good	59	15	b	b	58	23	16	12	59	20	20	15
Fair	29	25	b	b	31	31	40	21	30	29	31	18
Poor	12	60	b	b	10	46	44	67	11	51	49	67
Total	100	100	b	b	100	100	100	100	100	100	100	100
N=	959	67	37	15	1,105	116	55	76	2,064	183	92	91

[a] Excludes bedfast persons.

[b] Per cents are not computed when base is less than 50.

proportion of those with only minimal impairments (scores of zero to two on our scale) considered themselves to be in poor health and undoubtedly should be classified as health pessimists. In each country, however, optimism about health among the elderly is more usual than pessimism.

A country-by-country comparison of the relationships of self-ratings of health and reported mobility and incapacity emphasizes once more the cultural differences between the three countries. The majority of people will not say they think their health good when they are housebound or unable to go about alone. Similarly, persons with high incapacity scores, as has been indicated, usually do not say their health is good. On the other hand, we have already remarked on the health optimism of old people in

Britain: these old people, when housebound or restricted in their mobility, are almost twice as likely as either the Danes or the Americans to say their health is good. Further, a substantial proportion of old people in Britain continue to describe their health as "good" in the presence of high incapacity scores. One-fourth of the British with the highest scores on the incapacity scale, twice as great a proportion as either the Danes or the Americans, continue to rate their health as "good."

The greatest contrasts in their self-assessment of health appear between the British and the American aged. Unlike the British, who continue to describe their health as good for their age despite their ailments, the Americans, once they admit to ailments, also begin to complain about their health. Those Americans who have only minimal incapacity (scores of 2 or less) are only slightly more likely than either the British or the Danes to say their health is poor. Once the Americans have incapacity scores as high as three, however, the proportion who rate their health as poor jumps to 51 per cent, compared to 29 per cent for the Danes and 24 per cent for the British. Old people in the United States apparently set such high standards of "wellness" for themselves that any restriction on functioning is interpreted as a sign of poor health.

The Danes appear to follow a middle road between the British and the Americans. In general, the Danes are not as pessimistic in assessing their health as are the Americans, and not as optimistic in the face of incapacity as the British. Once the Danes have incapacity scores of five or more, almost as many Danes as Americans with this degree of incapacity say their health is poor.

The American aged, more than either the Danes or the British, tend to equate sensory impairments with poor health. Such impairments, like limitations on mobility or the inability to perform the simple physical tasks on the index of incapacity, constitute flaws in the image that old people in the United States have of themselves. The great clue to this self-image is physical independence and activity. Old people in the United States, like other Americans, want to be independent, to be able to take care of themselves. Such independence is equated with activity. Once American old people believe that their capacity for physical independence and activity is threatened, they begin to feel that their health is poor. The stress on physical well-being in America is not new. De Tocqueville, in *Democracy in America*, reported that:

> In America the passion for physical well being is not always exclusive, but it is general; and if all do not feel it in the same manner, yet it is felt by all. The effort to satisfy even the least wants of the body and to provide the little conveniences of life is uppermost in every mind. [5]

The reaction of old people in the United States to restrictions on their mobility, sensory impairments, and incapacity, as found in this survey, is in keeping with the analysis that Stanley King has made of illness in American society:

> One might say that illness, is, therefore, a kind of alienation in American society, alienation from a set of expectations that puts particular stress upon

independent achievement. The passivity and dependence involved in illness are also characteristics of behavior which are counter to the activism of American society.[6]

The sociologist Talcott Parsons has considered the role of illness in both Britain and the United States. Our reports of the health assessment of the aged verify his theoretical analysis. In the United States, with its stress on activism, to be ill is "inherently undesirable."[7] The sick person has an obligation to recover, to put himself in the care of those who are qualified to help him. He must continue to be able to achieve, or in the instance of the aged, to remain active. If the old person is not active, he feels he is in "poor health." In Britain, on the contrary, somatic illness is considered to be beyond the responsibility of the individual. It is self-control which is stressed.[8] The elderly in Britain, then, respond to their physical limitations by acceptance and continue to report that their health is good.

The Sick and the Well

Up to now we have discussed the evaluation old people make of their health and the differences in such evaluation between persons of different ages, men and women, and among the aged in the three countries. We have shown that self-rating of health and self-rating of incapacity appear to be directly correlated. We shall now consider the correlation between self-rating of health and certain subjective moods and feelings of the old person. The present analysis will not enable us to determine the separate effects of reported physical incapacity and subjective attitudes on the old person's evaluation of his own health; however, we will indicate whether there are differences in the subjective attitudes of the sick and the well.[9]

In this survey we have asked only a few questions about subjective attitudes. We ask people whether they are lonely, whether time passes slowly for them, and how their health compares with the health of other people their age. The first two questions—those on loneliness and the passage of time—are interrelated, since both deal with the old person's feelings of alienation. Loneliness in the aged individual has been defined as ". . . a vague sense of being alone and . . . dissatisfied about the nature of his actual contacts."[10] Like self-reports of loneliness, the conception of time as moving slowly, as hanging heavy on one's hands, the report of days being endless, also reflect the aged person's sense of detachment from other persons.

Are old people who say their health is poor more likely than old people who say their health is good to report that they are lonely and that time passes slowly? Further, to what extent does the old person's evaluation of his own health affect his evaluation of the health of others? Are those persons who say their health is poor also those who say their health is worse than the health of other people, while those persons who say their health is good think it better than the health of their contemporaries?

If self-evaluation of health is associated with whether or not the old person reports loneliness and alienation, old people can be ranked on a continuum, with ideal types at each end. At one extreme of the continuum is the person who says his health is poor, who is lonely, alienated, and depressed. When asked to evaluate his health, this person says that it is worse than the health of other people. At the other extreme of the continuum is the person who says his health is good, who is never lonely, for whom there is never enough time. This person will say his health is better than the health of most other old people.

There are some old people who personify the ideal types described here.

Mrs. Sawyer, for example, is at one end of the poor-good health continuum. She says her health is poor. She is often lonely and alone, although time rarely passes slowly for her. Mrs. Sawyer is 78 years old. She and her husband live alone—about 60 minutes distance from their only child, a daughter. Mrs. Sawyer reports that she has difficulty with only one item on the index of incapacity, cutting her own toenails. Further, she has not been ill in bed during the past year, although she did see the doctor two months ago. However, Mrs. Sawyer says her health is worse than the health of other people.

Mrs. Lawton is at the other end of the poor-good health continuum from Mrs. Sawyer. Mrs. Lawton says her health is good. She is rarely lonely and never alone. She says: "I suppose everyone has moments of loneliness but I soon get rid of such feelings. I've got too much to do." Mrs. Lawton is 75 years old. She and her husband each have been married before. Between them they have eight children, only one of whom is the offspring of this marriage. The nearest Lawton children live less than 10 minutes' distance, but two Lawton children live more than 60 minutes' distance from their parents. Mrs. Lawton reports no difficulties with any of the items on the index of incapacity, she says she was last sick in bed four or five years ago, and that she has not seen a doctor for three or four years.

Mrs. Lawton thinks her health better than the health of other people her age. As she puts it: "I've got lots better health than the rest of them around here." The interviewer says of Mrs. Lawton: "This 75-year-old even does a couple of big laundries every week for people, just to have something to do."

Not all old people are as consistent in their self-assessment of health and their reported attitudes as either Mrs. Sawyer or Mrs. Lawton. In each country, however, those persons who say their health is poor are more likely than persons who say their health is good to report that they are often lonely. Men in poor health, compared to men in good health, are from four to eight times as likely to say they are often lonely. Women in poor health, compared to women in good health, are from three to eight times as likely to say that they are often lonely. Time passes much more slowly for those in poor health than it does for those who say their health is good. Men in poor health, compared to men in good health, are from six to eight times as likely to say that time often passes slowly for them. Women in poor health, compared to women in good health, are from four to 18 times as likely to say that time often passes slowly.

The question may be raised whether living alone, with its effect on reducing the number of social contacts of old people, is more important than illness in producing reports of loneliness or alienation. Or does self-conception of illness reshape the social environment of the old person more than actual separation from others?[11] Table III–7 reports the

Table III–5: SELF-EVALUATION OF LONELINESS, BY SELF-EVALUATION
OF HEALTH OF PERSONS AGED 65 AND OVER (*Percentage Distribution*)

"*Lonely*"	Self-Evaluation of Health								
	MEN			WOMEN			ALL		
	Good	Fair	Poor	Good	Fair	Poor	Good	Fair	Poor
Denmark									
Often	2	2	8	2	4	15	2	4	12
Sometimes	14	22	29	22	30	39	18	27	34
Never	83	76	63	77	65	46	80	70	53
Total	100	100	100	100	100	100	100	100	100
N=	634	333	170	638	450	210	1,272	783	380
Britain									
Often	2	5	16	5	9	17	4	8	16
Sometimes	10	18	29	21	30	33	16	26	32
Never	88	76	55	74	61	49	80	67	51
Total	100	100	100	100	100	100	100	100	100
N=	601	271	122	800	460	218	1,401	731	340
United States									
Often	4	9	19	4	8	25	4	8	22
Sometimes	25	37	45	40	48	49	33	44	47
Never	71	54	36	56	43	26	63	48	30
Total	100	100	100	100	100	100	100	100	100
N=	583	297	182	682	417	249	1,265	714	431

feelings of loneliness of those in good health and of those in fair and poor health with different sorts of living arrangements. Those who live alone are more likely than those who live with others to report they are often lonely. Yet in each country, when living arrangements are held constant and those in good health living alone are compared with those in fair and poor health living alone, a higher proportion of those in fair and poor health say that they are often lonely. The same finding emerges when those in good health and those in poor health living with others are compared: a substantially higher proportion of those in fair and poor health say that they are often lonely.

It is apparent that irrespective of the old person's living arrangements, self-assessment of health affects feelings of loneliness. The same pattern is demonstrated in the respondents' replies to the question "Does time pass slowly for you?" Old people living alone are more likely than other old people to say that time passes slowly for them. When living arrangements are held constant, however, those in fair or poor health are significantly more likely than those in good health to say that time is passing slowly.

Our findings on the strong relationship between health assessment and feelings of loneliness and alienation on the part of old people confirm in some measure the report of Kay and Roth investigating the psychiatric disorders of old age. They found that living arrangements were less

Table III–6: EVALUATION OF PASSAGE OF TIME, BY SELF-EVALUATION
OF HEALTH OF PERSONS AGED 65 AND OVER (*Percentage Distribution*)

"*Time Passes Slowly*"	Self-Evaluation of Health								
	MEN			WOMEN			ALL		
	Good	Fair	Poor	Good	Fair	Poor	Good	Fair	Poor
Denmark									
Often	2	3	12	1	5	18	1	4	15
Sometimes	8	18	23	10	17	23	9	17	23
Never	91	79	64	89	78	59	90	79	62
Total	100	100	100	100	100	100	100	100	100
N=	636	334	170	636	445	210	1,272	779	380
Britain									
Often	4	12	30	5	10	20	4	11	23
Sometimes	18	29	35	21	34	40	20	33	38
Never	78	59	35	74	55	40	76	56	38
Total	100	100	100	100	100	100	100	100	100
N=	603	268	121	801	461	220	1,404	729	341
United States									
Often	6	16	32	5	14	32	5	15	32
Sometimes	22	28	31	22	33	33	22	31	32
Never	72	56	38	73	53	35	73	54	36
Total	100	100	100	100	100	100	100	100	100
N=	588	300	186	690	419	251	1,278	719	437

important in association with mental illness than the actual physical
disability of the old person. Kay and Roth state:

> Physical disability, including sensory loss, comes out strongly as the most
> important major associated factor, followed by reduction in number of personal
> contacts, poverty, and deviating personality traits. These factors appear to be
> at least as important among mentally disturbed subjects living at home as
> among those admitted to mental hospitals.[12]

To recapitulate, in all three countries, people who think they are sick
are more lonely and alienated than those who think they are well. The
strong relationship between self-judgment of health and the index of
incapacity suggests that perhaps, over-all, it may be the feeling of poor
health that brings with it feelings of loneliness.

Let us now turn to another question: do old people see the health of
other old people as similar to their own? If they are sick, do they see other
old people as sick? If they are well, do they see other old people as well?
Further, are there differences in how persons of different ages, men and
women, and old people in the three countries studied evaluate the health
of their contemporaries?

An old person's self-evaluation of his health determines how he sees the
health of other people. In each country, the majority of persons who

Table III–7: SELF-EVALUATION OF LONELINESS, PERSONS AGED 65 AND OVER, BY LIVING ARRANGEMENTS AND SELF-EVALUATION OF HEALTH (*Percentage Distribution*)

"Lonely"	MEN				WOMEN				ALL			
	Health Good		Health Fair and Poor		Health Good		Health Fair and Poor		Health Good		Health Fair and Poor	
	Living Alone	Living with Other	Living Alone	Living with Others	Living Alone	Living with Others	Living Alone	Living with Others	Living Alone	Living with Others	Living Alone	Living with Others
Denmark												
Often	9	1	11	3	2	2	12	6	5	1	11	4
Sometimes	28	11	47	20	33	15	40	29	31	13	42	24
Never	63	88	42	77	65	83	48	65	64	86	47	71
Total	100	100	100	100	100	100	100	100	100	100	100	100
N=	119	515	76	427	228	410	249	411	347	925	325	838
Britain												
Often	11	1	a	7	11	2	24	7	11	1	25	7
Sometimes	38	7	a	21	38	13	40	28	38	10	38	25
Never	51	92	a	72	51	85	36	65	51	89	37	68
Total	100	100	a	100	100	100	100	100	100	100	100	100
N=	65	535	41	351	260	538	178	500	325	1,073	219	851
United States												
Often	21	2	40	8	8	2	20	12	11	2	26	10
Sometimes	43	23	42	40	48	38	57	45	47	30	53	43
Never	36	75	18	52	43	60	22	43	41	68	21	47
Total	100	100	100	100	100	100	100	100	100	100	100	100
N=	61	522	72	407	192	492	201	465	253	1,014	273	872

a Per cents are not computed when base is less than 50.

Table III–8: SELF-EVALUATION OF PASSAGE OF TIME, PERSONS AGED 65 AND OVER, BY LIVING ARRANGEMENTS AND SELF-EVALUATION OF HEALTH (*Percentage Distribution*)

"Time Passes Slowly"	MEN Health Good Living Alone	MEN Health Good Living with Others	MEN Health Fair and Poor Living Alone	MEN Health Fair and Poor Living with Others	WOMEN Health Good Living Alone	WOMEN Health Good Living with Others	WOMEN Health Fair and Poor Living Alone	WOMEN Health Fair and Poor Living with Others	ALL Health Good Living Alone	ALL Health Good Living with Others	ALL Health Fair and Poor Living Alone	ALL Health Fair and Poor Living with Others
Denmark												
Often	4	1	11	5	1	1	13	6	2	1	13	6
Sometimes	13	7	26	19	15	7	26	15	14	7	26	17
Never	83	92	63	76	84	93	61	79	84	92	62	77
Total	100	100	100	100	100	100	100	100	100	100	100	100
N=	123	513	76	428	228	408	247	408	351	921	323	836
Britain												
Often	2	4	a	17	8	3	17	12	6	4	18	14
Sometimes	35	16	a	32	27	18	44	33	29	17	41	33
Never	63	80	a	51	65	79	38	55	64	79	41	53
Total	100	100	100	100	100	100	100	100	100	100	100	100
N=	65	536	41	349	259	542	178	503	324	1,078	219	852
United States												
Often	15	5	35	20	7	4	25	19	9	4	27	19
Sometimes	38	20	26	29	23	22	35	32	27	21	33	31
Never	47	75	39	51	70	74	40	49	64	75	40	50
Total	100	100	100	100	100	100	100	100	100	100	100	100
N=	61	527	72	414	192	498	201	470	253	1,025	273	884

a Per cents are not computed when base is less than 50.

think their health is poor are convinced that their health is worse then the health of other old people. The majority of persons who think their health is good, on the contrary, are equally convinced that their health is better than the health of other people. Among every 10 old persons who say they are in poor health, 7 Danes, 7 Britons, and 5 Americans say that their health is worse than that of other people their age. Among every 10 persons who say they are in good health, 6 Danes, 8 Britons, and 8

Table III–9: COMPARISON BY PERSONS AGED 65 AND OVER OF THEIR OWN HEALTH WITH HEALTH OF OTHER PEOPLE (*Percentage Distribution*)

Comparison with Health of Other People	Self-Evaluation of Health								
	MEN			WOMEN			ALL		
	Good	Fair	Poor	Good	Fair	Poor	Good	Fair	Poor
Denmark									
Better	62	13	2	62	14	2	62	14	2
Same	38	72	23	37	73	27	38	73	25
Worse	*	14	75	*	12	71	*	13	73
Total	100	100	100	100	100	100	100	100	100
N=ᵃ	631	327	167	634	440	206	1,265	767	373
Britain									
Better	82	29	4	77	27	3	79	28	3
Same	17	61	19	22	60	28	20	60	25
Worse	1	10	77	1	13	69	1	12	72
Total	100	100	100	100	100	100	100	100	100
N=ᵃ	563	226	104	710	381	180	1,273	607	284
United States									
Better	80	48	17	76	37	15	78	42	16
Same	20	47	35	23	56	31	22	52	33
Worse	*	4	48	1	7	54	1	6	51
Total	100	100	100	100	100	100	100	100	100
N=ᵃ	578	294	183	678	409	242	1,256	703	425

* Less than 1 per cent.

ᵃ The percentages of eligible respondents who answered this question are: Denmark, total 98.3, men 98.2, women 98.4; Britain, total 86.6, men 88.9, women 84.9; United States, total 97.6, men 97.6, women 97.6.

Americans say that their health is better than the health of other old people. Apparently, those among the aged who feel they are in poor health are sure that other old people cannot be as sick as they are, while those who feel they are in good health are equally sure that other old people do not share their robust condition.

In each country, persons aged 80 and over are the most likely of all old persons to report that their health is better than the health of others their age. As has been said earlier, those over 80 still living in the community are a population of survivors. Apparently, so many of their con-

Table III-10: COMPARISON OF OWN HEALTH WITH HEALTH OF OTHER PEOPLE, PERSONS AGED 65 AND OVER, BY AGE AND SEX (Percentage Distribution)

Comparison with Health of Other People	MEN						WOMEN						ALL					
	65-66	67-69	70-74	75-79	80 and Over	All	65-66	67-69	70-74	75-79	80 and Over	All	65-66	67-69	70-74	75-79	80 and Over	All
Denmark																		
Better	33	37	40	35	49	39	38	34	33	36	43	36	36	35	36	36	46	37
Same	46	47	45	49	41	46	47	47	52	49	42	48	46	47	49	49	42	47
Worse	20	16	15	15	10	15	15	19	15	15	14	16	17	18	15	15	12	16
Total	100	100	100	100	100	100	100	100	100	100	100	100	100	100	100	100	100	100
N=a	180	261	314	217	154	1,126	216	266	394	243	161	1,280	396	527	708	460	315	2,406
Britain																		
Better	53	63	55	65	67	60	50	53	48	47	63	52	51	58	51	55	64	55
Same	34	27	31	23	25	28	32	32	37	41	27	34	33	30	34	33	26	32
Worse	13	10	14	12	8	12	18	15	15	12	10	14	16	13	15	12	10	13
Total	100	100	100	100	100	100	100	100	100	100	100	100	100	100	100	100	100	100
N=a	145	202	257	178	112	894	190	250	373	241	222	1,276	335	452	630	419	334	2,170
United States																		
Better	56	54	63	59	68	60	45	51	56	52	58	53	50	52	59	55	62	56
Same	34	33	29	28	25	30	40	37	32	33	33	35	38	35	31	31	30	33
Worse	10	14	8	12	6	10	15	12	12	14	9	12	12	13	10	14	8	11
Total	100	100	100	100	100	100	100	100	100	100	100	100	100	100	100	100	100	100
N=a	174	221	340	178	142	1,055	204	296	415	220	185	1,329b	378	517	755	398	327	2,384b

a The percentages of eligible respondents who answered this question are: Denmark, total 98.4, men 98.3, women 98.4; Britain, total 86.8, men 89.0, women 85.3; United States, total 97.6, men 97.6, women 97.6.

b Includes 13 women of unknown age.

temporaries have either died or been institutionalized that those who remain at home see themselves as a particularly strong group. They are convinced that their health is better than the health of others. The general feeling of these persons may be summed up in the comment: "I feel so well . . . it's the other people my age that must be the aged sick!"

In both Britain and the United States, men are more likely than women to say that their health is better than the health of other people their age. Once again, for these two countries, the findings suggest that in old age most men continue to hold to the masculine self-image, to see themselves as sturdy, uncomplaining, and stronger than those around them. In another American study the question is raised whether these health reports by old men correspond with the actual incidence of illness and health complaints among them. In this study, old people were asked to enumerate their illnesses and health complaints. Despite the fact that more men than women thought their health was good, the average number of reported illnesses and health complaints was the same for both men and women, four per person.[13] In Denmark, unlike Britain and the United States, only those men aged 70 to 74 and those 80 and over were more optimistic about their health than women. In general, the Danes are not as prone as the British and the Americans to say their health is better than the health of other people. Instead, both men and women report their health to be about the same as the health of other people their age.

The Psychology of Health

Old people in Denmark, Britain, and the United States share certain common attitudes about their health; they also exhibit differences in health attitudes which may be attributed to national style or character.

Old age is accompanied by a decline in physical fitness and an increasing experience with body aches and pains. Each person makes his own accommodation to his changing body. Some people become preoccupied with their bodily state, and each ache and pain is magnified. It is these persons who become health pessimists and report their health as poor when objective indices suggest their health is fairly good. Other people seem to ignore physical discomfort. It is these persons who are the health optimists, who insist they are well in the face of appalling physical distress or who overemphasize their physical fitness and the extent to which their health is better than the health of other people.

Robert Peck has given one of the best statements of the importance of health in later life. In considering the major developmental tasks that face old people, Peck argues that one of these is the choice between what he calls "body transcendence" and "body preoccupation." The old person must decide whether he is to dominate his body or whether his body is to dominate him. Peck says:

> For people to whom pleasure and comfort mean predominantly physical well-being, this [declining health] may be the gravest, most mortal of insults. There are many such people whose elder years seem to move in a decreasing spiral, centered around their growing preoccupation with the state of their bodies.

> There are other people, however, who suffer just as painful physical unease, yet who enjoy life greatly. . . . In their value system, social and mental sources of pleasure and self-respect may transcend physical comfort, alone.[14]

The health attitudes of old people are influenced by the way each comes to regard his body. The majority of old people seem to have a conception of how well or how sick they are which is consistent, that is, their health attitudes and their answers to questions on physical functioning are in agreement. For some old people, however, their self-evaluations of health do not necessarily correlate with these objective indices of their health status. It is these persons in all three countries who, in their behavior, best represent the theoretical types suggested by Peck's analysis—namely, the "body-transcendent" and the "body-preoccupied."

In all three countries, men are more optimistic than women about their state of health. The old man's optimistic self-evaluation of his health, as has been indicated, is undoubtedly related to psychological rather than physical factors. There is some evidence that in the years immediately after retirement, a time when men are seeking a meaningful new role for themselves, men are less optimistic about their health than women of the same age.

Persons over 80 still living in the community tend to be optimistic about their health. These very old people are a selected population. The most deteriorated among those over 80 are no longer in the community. Although many people over 80 in the community are quite frail, others are active and mobile. Our findings reinforce those of Cumming and Parlegreco in their study of very old people in Kansas City. These investigators say:

> There is some evidence that living to be over 80 . . . is associated with being a member of a biological, and possibly psychological elite. Furthermore, very old people often have a surprisingly high level of social competence and seem able to maintain high spirits. . . .[15]

Like Cumming and Parlegreco, we find a marked difference between persons in their 70's and those 80 or over. Old people in their middle 70's appear to be depressed about their health; those over 80 are optimists.

> Through the interviews of the seventies there runs a thread of pessimism which sometimes borders into irritability and self-pity. . . . Among the eighties there is less complaining and more chirpiness, sometimes a mood of using up the last days of life in tranquility and sometimes a genuine carefree quality.[16]

In all three countries most old people think their health is at least as good or perhaps even better than the health of their contemporaries. Only a small group of people think their health is poor, and worse than the health of others. Those persons who feel their health is poor are far more likely than other persons to express feelings of loneliness and alienation. Whether poor health is responsible for these feelings of alienation and for spontaneous reports of unhappiness cannot be directly determined from the survey data. A possible interpretation of the relationship between reports of poor health and reports of alienation can be found in psychiatric studies of old people. Psychiatrists familiar with the elderly agree that psychic depression is widespread in this age group, even among those living in the community. Overconcern with one's body and associated depressive feelings are common manifestations of such depression.[17] Old people who exhibit the extreme type of body-preoccupation, whether or not they also have physical complaints, may indeed be suffering from psychic depression.

Certain differences in health attitudes among old people in the three countries apparently are the result of differences in national style or mode of behavior. Observers have described the Danes as essentially middle class; the British as patient, polite, and non-complaining; the Americans as active and gregarious. These over-all descriptions obviously do not apply to all Danes without exception, or to all British, or to all Americans. Yet, there is enough truth in them so that they appear likely explanations of certain differences in health attitudes among old people.

Danish old people in good health are more likely to think they resemble their fellows than either the British or the American aged. The Danes are less likely than either the British or the Americans to say that their health is better than that of other old people, and more likely to say it is about the same as the health of others. Danes in poor health, however, are equally as likely as the British to say their health is worse than the health of other people.[18]

The elderly in Britain compared to the Danes or the Americans put the most optimistic interpretation on their impairments and incapacities. Despite the fact that they report more incapacity than old people in either Denmark or the United States, old people in Britain are the most likely of all old people to say their health is good. Furthermore, along with the Americans, but perhaps for different reasons, the majority of old people in Britain report that their health is better than the health of other people.

The American aged are the most likely of all old people to respond to even minimum impairment by saying that their health is poor. Americans of all ages are active people, and any restriction on activity seems to evoke a maximum response from them. Irrespective of health status, the American aged are more likely than either the British or the Danes to say that they are lonely. The majority of Americans, however, like the majority of the British, think their health is better than the health of other people. We may say that the Americans think their health is better than the health of others because they are optimists, the British because it is unbecoming to complain.

The similarities and the differences from country to country in the health attitudes of the aged reinforce the beliefs with which we began this analysis. First, the general response of old people in Western societies to the physical changes of aging are similar: some old people are health realists; others, pessimists; still others, optimists. Second, within each country, national styles of behavior affect the manner and the degree of each such response.

NOTES

1 These terms are adapted from the studies of self-assessment of health made by George L. Maddox and others at Duke University. See George L. Maddox, "Self-Assessment of Health Status, a Longitudinal Study of Selected Elderly Subjects," *Journal of Chronic Diseases*, XVII (1964), 449–60.

2 N. N. Sachuk, "Some General Studies of the State of Health of the Aged," in World Health Organization *Seminar on the Health Protection of the Elderly and the Aged and on the Prevention of Premature Aging*, Kiev, 14–22 May, 1963 (Copenhagen: World Health Organization, 1963; mimeographed), p. 2.

3 Maddox, *op. cit.*, p. 459, p. 458.

4 Peter Townsend reports a number of extremely frail institutionalized old people who continued to describe their health as good. This may be a function of the reference group they were using for self-comparison, or it may simply be a clinging to another status—that of the "well." Self-assessment or evaluation of health seems to have a major role in determining the behavior of the elderly. In a study of mentally disturbed old people the single item most clearly related to the eventual psychiatric diagnosis was the answer to the question "How is your health?" See D. W. Kay and Martin Roth, "Physical Illness and Social Factors in the Psychiatric Disorders of Old Age," *Third World Congress of Psychiatry, Proceedings* (Montreal: McGill University Press, 1961), I, 306.

5 Alexis de Tocqueville, *Democracy in America*, II, The Henry Reeve Text (New York: Alfred A. Knopf, 1948), 128. I am indebted to Donald P. Kent, formerly of the Office of Aging, U.S. Department of Health, Education, and Welfare, for calling my attention to this discussion.

6 Stanley H. King, "Social Psychological Factors in Illness," in Howard E. Freeman, Sol Levine, and Leo G. Reeder, eds., *Handbook of Medical Sociology* (Englewood Cliffs, N.J.: Prentice-Hall, Inc., 1963), p. 112.

7 Talcott Parsons, "Definitions of Health and Illness in the Light of American Values and Social Structure," in E. Gartly Jaco, ed., *Patients, Physicians, and Illness* (New York: The Free Press of Glencoe, 1958), p. 176.

8 *Ibid.*, pp. 184–87.

9 It may be argued that multi-variate analysis is desirable to determine the weight that physical incapacity and subjective attitudes each contribute to the old person's self-evaluation of his health. We do not feel that the data lend themselves to this analysis. Subjective attitudes may not only affect the old person's evaluation of his health, but they may also affect how he replies to the objective questions on incapacity. An old person's statement that he has trouble getting around the house may not be a reliable assessment of his behavior. It may only represent how he felt about this task at the time of the interview. This point has been well taken by Austin B. Chinn, M.D. (personal correspondence). We shall develop this theme further when we discuss the "sick" and the "well" image among the elderly.

  For a brilliant exposition of the use of the multi-variate technique in the analysis of survey data, see James H. Morgan, Martin H. David, Wilbur J. Cohen, and Harvey E. Brazer, *Income and Welfare in the United States* (New York: McGraw-Hill Book Company, Inc., 1962), Appendix E, "Multivariate Analysis," pp. 508–11. An excellent and pertinent discussion of the role of independent and dependent variables in the analysis of health survey data is given by Howard E. Freeman, Sol Levine, and Leo G. Reeder, "Present Status of Medical Sociology," *Handbook of Medical Sociology, op. cit.*, pp. 484–87.

10 *Vita Humana*, VII (1964), 229.

11 Joep M. S. Munnichs, "Loneliness, Isolation and Social Relations in Old Age": Marian Radke Yarrow, among others, has raised this problem in her paper "Appraising Environment," Richard H. Williams, Clark Tibbitts, and Wilma Donahue, eds., *Processes of Aging* (New York: Atherton Press, 1963), I, 201–22.

12 D. W. Kay and Martin Roth, *op. cit.*, p. 307. A comparable result is reported in an American study by Marjorie Fiske Lowenthal, *Lives in Distress* (New York: Basic Books, Inc., 1964). See also Arthur N. Schwartz and Robert W. Kleemeier, "The Effects of Illness and Age Upon Some Aspects of Personality," *Journal of Gerontology*, XX (January, 1965), 85–91.

13 Ethel Shanas, *The Health of Older People: A Social Survey* (Cambridge, Mass.: Harvard University Press, 1962), p. 7.

14 Robert Peck, "Psychological Developments in the Second Half of Life," in John E. Anderson, ed., *Psychological Aspects of Aging* (Washington, D.C.: American Psychological Association, Inc., 1956), p. 47.

15 Elaine Cumming and Mary Lou Parlegreco, "The Very Old," in Elaine Cumming and William E. Henry, *Growing Old: The Process of Disengagement* (New York: Basic Books, Inc., 1961), p. 201.

16 *Ibid.*, p. 202.

17 Ewald W. Busse, "Psychoneurotic Reactions and Defense Mechanisms in the Aged," Paul H. Hoch and Joseph Zubin, eds., *Psychopathology of Aging* (New York: Grune and Stratton, Inc., 1961), pp. 274–84.

18 This finding, with its suggestion of psychic depression among the elderly in poor health, is consistent with other studies of the Danish temperament. Denmark has one of the highest suicide rates in the Western world, 22.4 per 100,000 persons in 1956, compared to 10.8 per 100,000 for the United States (1960 data). See Kirsten Rudfeld, "Suicides in Denmark 1956," *Acta Sociologica*, VI (No. 3), 1962, 207. United States data from U.S. Bureau of the Census, *Statistical Abstract of the United States: 1962* (Washington, D.C.: U.S. GPO, 1962), p. 66. See also Herbert Hendin, *Suicide and Scandinavia* (New York and London: Grune and Stratton, Inc., 1964).

4 : *Medical Services*

The utilization of medical services by the elderly in different countries depends only in part on the frequency, duration, and nature of illness among them. It also depends on the organization and staffing of medical care services, and the attitudes and values of those providing the services as well as of the public in general. Potential users may be deterred by cost, inaccessibility, administrative authoritarianism, professional preference for treating the young rather than the elderly, or popular superstition—to give just five examples. Although the study of utilization of medical services was not the primary purpose of the cross-national survey, nevertheless some information was obtained which suggests interesting lines for further inquiry. When studied in conjunction with data from other sources, it also helps to put into context the previous discussion of the health of the aged in the three countries. Consequently, this chapter more than other chapters will draw on data not collected in the cross-national survey. It will attempt to describe some of the chief differences that appear to exist between the three countries in the use made by old people of doctors and of hospitals, and will suggest some possible explanations for these differences. The next chapter will go on to discuss welfare and community services in relation to the care given by the family.

Over-all Differences in the Organization and Financing of Medical Care

What are the differences between the three countries in the organization and financing of medical care, and how are the aged in particular affected? The United States has a system very different from many industrial countries. Most of its medical care is provided through private arrangements. Physicians are chiefly private practitioners paid on a basis of fee-for-service. They are registered mainly as specialists even though much of their work may resemble that actually undertaken by general physicians in other countries. Many work both inside and outside the hospital.[1] Hospitals are mainly operated by non-profit-making associations and local governments and charge the individual patient for board and services. Patients insure themselves against costs through non-profit organizations and commercial insurance companies. Although most of the civilian population have some type of protection against hospital costs, however, less than half have some form of insurance to cover, even in part, the cost of physicians' services while in the hospital, and very few have protection against the cost of physicians' services at home or in the office (or surgery). The Medicare legislation has now greatly improved the coverage for the elderly. The federal government caters for the medical needs of military personnel, veterans, and (among other minority groups) American Indians and Presidents. Mental and tuberculosis hospitals are operated by state and local governments, and to a small extent by non-profit-making associations, and are financed predominantly by the government. Public welfare recipients can receive medical care from state and local governments, assisted by federal funds.

By contrast, in nearly all European countries, it is characteristic for hospitals to be owned and managed by public authorities, for the costs of medical and hospital treatment to be met by collective taxation or insurance, and for large numbers of medical and nursing personnel to work entirely outside hospitals (and few of them both inside and outside hospitals). In Denmark 95 per cent of the population are covered for medical care by a system of health insurance societies.[2] The great majority of these are subsidized by the state and local authorities. Pensioners without other income than their pension may obtain membership without payment. Members get life-saving drugs free and other drugs for only a proportion of cost. Medical and hospital treatment are free of charge. In the cities doctors are paid by the capitation system, and this, as in Britain, tends to maintain general practice and continuity of medical care.

In Britain all but 2 or 3 per cent of the population make use of the National Health Service. The service is financed mainly from taxation but also from national insurance contributions. Medical and hospital treatment are free of charge. For the period 1951 to 1965 fixed charges were payable for prescriptions, dental treatment, and certain kinds of health aids and appliances, but in 1965 charges for prescriptions were abolished. As in Denmark, considerable emphasis is placed on domiciliary practice by general physicians, and their work is supported by a national home-nursing organization.

Why are the systems of medical care so different? All the chief differences between the United States and Britain and Denmark were apparent in the 1880's and 1890's. From 1806 on, some of the local authorities in Denmark became responsible for hospitals, and since 1870 local authorities have had a duty to provide them. In Britain the vast majority of hospital patients were treated free long before 1948 (when the National Health Service was introduced). Indeed, paying patients never accounted for more than about 5 per cent of all hospital patients.[3] The social and cultural forces that have molded the medical systems of the three countries are not of modern origin.

Among the crucial historical factors are the later development in the

United States than in most of Europe of medical organization and the comparative rarity in the nineteenth century of established philanthropic and consumer organizations. In Britain, general practitioners were discouraged, with certain exceptions, from having close relations with hospitals. Since the population was concentrated in more compact geographical areas, this may have helped to promote domiciliary medical practice. Such practice was further strengthened by the development from medical relief services under the Poor Law of public health services, and particularly clinics, administered by the local authorities. District nursing developed alongside home medical care from 1859 on.[4] In many parts of Europe pre-payment methods of meeting medical costs were sponsored and controlled by consumers. In 1804, long before the British Medical Association was founded, there were about a million members of friendly societies in Britain, and in 1900, seven million.[5] The system of non-profit voluntary health insurance, strongly supported by trade unions, led in other countries as well as in Britain to compulsory health insurance schemes. In the United States there have been some friendly societies and other consumer organizations, but they have been relatively smaller in numbers of members than in most European countries. Pre-payment systems of meeting medical costs have been initiated by the providers of services, and recently by the profit-making insurance organizations.[6]

Since the early 1950's strong pressure has arisen on behalf of the growing number of old people in the American population. It is important to note that whereas in the two European countries occupational health insurance schemes were broadened to cover the whole community, pressure for reform in the United States concentrated on one section of the population only. Government and other research workers demonstrated the inability of many old people to pay for adequate medical care, and in the late 1950's a series of proposals was made primarily for hospital insurance. In 1960 the Kerr-Mills Bill was enacted, a fairly comprehensive health program for a very small section of the aged poor.[7] Opposition to a universal hospital program was led by the American Medical Association, assisted by the private insurance organizations and conservative members of the House Ways and Means Committee (which has over-all responsibility for health insurance legislation). But gradually various authorities lent their support to the case for further legislation and, in the wake of the overwhelming Democratic election victory in 1964, a major Medicare Bill was passed in 1965.[8]

The hospital insurance plan reflects the emphasis laid by reformers on the catastrophic expense of *serious* illness in old age. It pays for the hospitalization of the aged for up to 90 days for any spell of illness and for 100 days of nursing home care following at least three days of hospital care. Nursing at home following treatment is also covered. This part of the Medicare program includes a deductible of 50 dollars for which the patient is responsible. A supplementary medical insurance plan was unexpectedly added to the basic Medicare program by the U.S. Congress. Old people may participate in this program by contributing three dollars a month. The program provides payment of 80 per cent of the costs of physicians' and surgeons' services after the first 50 dollars in any year, no matter where these services are received, and 80 per cent of the costs of nursing at home (up to 100 visits in a calendar year). A variety of other services are also covered. The two plans do not cover expenses for custodial care, drugs for use outside hospital, hearing aids, dentistry and dentures, immunizations and the rental of medical equipment. By European standards, coverage and scope of the enlarged program are limited. The combination of deductibles and co-insurance leaves the aged with more financial barriers to care than would be the case at the present time in the two European countries.

Measures of the Extent and Quality of Care

Can a precise idea be obtained of the present extent and provision of health services in the three countries? Over-all costs, staffing ratios, and

Table IV–1: TOTAL EXPENDITURE (CAPITAL AND CURRENT) ON HEALTH SERVICES AS A PERCENTAGE OF GROSS NATIONAL PRODUCT AND NATIONAL INCOME[a]

Country	Total Expenditure on Health Services	Expenditure on Health Services	
		As Percentage of Gross National Product	As Percentage of National Income
United Kingdom	£956M[b]	3.5	4.3
United States	$30,737M[c]	5.7	7.0

[a] For the United Kingdom, April 1, 1960–March 31, 1961; for the United States, July 1, 1961–June 30, 1962.

[b] *The Times Review of Industry and Technology*, March, 1963, p. vi.

[c] *Social Security Bulletin*, XVI (November, 1963), No. 11, 10.

institutional provisions will be described, so that the data that are restricted solely to the aged can be usefully interpreted. The United States spends considerably higher proportions of its gross national expenditure and national income on health services than does the United Kingdom.[9] These data are given in Table IV–1. Private as well as public expenditure is included.[10]

Exactly comparable data for Denmark are not available, but estimates based on a rather more restricted definition of health services are available for all three countries. Table IV–2 shows the percentage of gross national product spent on selected health services during the period 1953–1961 in nine countries. The United Kingdom spent proportionately less than the

United States but more than Denmark. It should also be noted that the *proportion* spent on health is increasing year by year for every country for which there is information.[11]

Too much must not be read into the differences between countries in the percentages of gross national product devoted to health services. Independent factors may be operating, which reduce the "real" differences in some respects. In some countries medical costs may be exceptionally large, relative to other costs. Again, the internal distribution of expenditures among different services and among different regions or classes may

Table IV–2: ESTIMATED EXPENDITURE ON SELECTED HEALTH SERVICES AS A PERCENTAGE OF GROSS NATIONAL PRODUCT, NINE COUNTRIES (1953–61)[a]

Country	1953	1957	1961
Australia	2.7	3.1	4.1
Canada	2.5	2.9	3.8
New Zealand	3.1	3.2	3.6
UNITED STATES	2.3	3.0	3.5
France	2.2	2.6	3.3
UNITED KINGDOM	2.6	2.7	3.0
Norway	2.2	2.4	2.7
DENMARK	1.9	2.2	2.4
Netherlands	1.7	1.9	2.3

[a] Includes hospital services, physicians' services, and prescribed drugs. Excludes dentists' services, expenditures on public health and for capital purposes.

Source: Special estimates prepared by the Research and Statistics Division, Department of National Health and Welfare, Canada. *Report of the Royal Commission on Health Services*, I (1964), Table 11–27, 482.

vary from country to country. By way of illustrating this vital qualification, Table IV–3 shows one important fact about expenditure in the United States, compared with some other Western countries. There are greater disparities than elsewhere between different types of hospitals. Expenditures on hospitals containing relatively large numbers of old people—including chronic disease and mental—are comparatively small.

In 1960 there was one physician for every 814 persons in Denmark, one for every 939 in Britain, and one for every 770 in the United States. Both Denmark and the United States therefore have relatively larger numbers of physicians than Britain. In Denmark and the United States these ratios have been improving slightly but steadily in recent years, but in Britain the ratio has been more or less static and has now even begun to deteriorate.[12] As Table IV–4 shows, Britain also has relatively fewer nurses than the other two countries. All kinds of nursing personnel, in addition to fully qualified nurses, are included in the figures. By far the highest proportion

Table IV-3:   COST PER BED-DAY OF HOSPITALS OTHER THAN GENERAL
AS A PERCENTAGE OF THE COST PER BED-DAY OF GENERAL HOSPITALS[a]

Type of Hospital	United States[b]	England and Wales[c]	Sweden	Israel	Czecho- slovakia
General	100	100	100	100	100
Chronic disease	26	45	52	61	57
Tuberculosis and other chest diseases	49	84	72	75	81
Mental	19	32	38	33	46

[a] Extracted, except for England and Wales, from B. Abel-Smith, *Paying for Health Services: A Study of the Costs and Sources of Finance in Six Countries*, Public Health Papers, No. 17 (Geneva: World Health Organization, 1963), Table 17, p. 68.

[b] Estimated, and subject to qualifications specified in B. Abel-Smith, *Paying for Health Services*, p. 52. The data were specially compiled for the following years: United States, 1957–58; England and Wales, 1960–61; Sweden, 1956; Israel, 1959–60; Czechoslovakia, 1958.

[c] Based on hospital costing returns for England and Wales for the financial year 1962–63. The figure used for "general" hospitals in the table is the figure of costs for "all acute" hospital beds, excluding London and provincial teaching hospitals.

of nursing personnel who are fully qualified is to be found in Denmark, with Britain coming in a poor third. It is perhaps worth remarking that Denmark does in fact have the largest number of medical and nursing personnel, relative to population, of the Scandinavian countries.[10] It is therefore somewhat surprising that she spends less of her national resources on health services than either the United States or Britain.

Table IV-4:   NUMBERS IN THE POPULATION PER HOSPITAL BED, PHYSICIAN, AND NURSE[a]

Population per	Denmark	Britain	United States
Hospital bed	99[b]	114	108
Physician	814	939	770
Nurse	163[b]	194	178

[a] *Source*: Data extracted from World Health Organization, *Annual Epidemiological and Vital Statistics, 1960* (Geneva: World Health Organization, 1963), and subject to the qualifications set out in that publication. Beds in mental subnormality hospitals have been excluded from the British totals, since accommodation in mental deficiency institutions has been excluded from the scope of "hospitals" in the other two countries. Nurses include fully qualified nurses as well as midwives, nursing assistants, probationers, hospital auxiliaries, etc.

[b] 1959.

These comparative statistics are, of course, extremely general and need to be supplemented by other data.[14] They refer to the whole population and not just the aged. Although the United States has relatively more physicians for its population than either Denmark or Britain, it should be remembered that higher proportions are in non-clinical posts—that is, research, administration, and defense. More important, practitioners are not distributed as evenly according to population. Large areas of the country, and large proportions of the population, are served by fewer medical and nursing personnel than the two European countries. The distribution of health personnel in the three countries varies not only geographically but also as between hospital and outside practice—as noted already. The division between work in a hospital and work in the community is fairly sharp in both Britain and Denmark, and in both countries relatively more personnel than in the United States engage solely in domiciliary practice. The emphasis on domiciliary practice seems to be of some importance to the aged, as will be indicated later.

In one respect the British ratio of physicians to population, compared with the Danish and American ratios, is worse than it appears. In all countries that have been studied so far the elderly population have a much higher rate of medical consultations than younger adults and even than children under 15 years of age, a fact that corresponds with the general assumption that they require more medical treatment and care. It would therefore follow, other things being equal, that countries with the largest proportions of old people in the population would require a larger ratio of physicians to population. In 1960, however, the percentages of the population aged 65 and over in Britain, Denmark, and the United States were, respectively, 11.7, 10.5, and 9.2. Medical resources in Britain are therefore not only slightly sparser than in the other two countries, but, in at least one major respect, have to be stretched out among a population who need them more.

Hospitals and Other Institutions in the Three Countries

What differences are there between the three countries in their use of hospital and other institutional accommodation? As we have shown, the United States and Britain have relatively fewer hospital and nursing home beds than Denmark. But the differences are fairly small. It is difficult to divide all types of hospitals in the three countries into categories so that the ratios for sub-types can be compared. Different countries have adopted slightly different conventions in describing institutions. "General" hospitals in some countries contain a larger proportion of beds for patients suffering from psychiatric disorders than in others. This seems to be true of Denmark, compared with Britain and the United States, though not to a very marked extent. Very few hospitals in the United States are listed as for "chronic diseases" (providing about 30,000 beds) whereas in Britain there are a much larger number (providing 65,000 beds, plus another 20,000 "geriatric" beds), but this does not mean that there are more chronic sick patients in Britain than in the United States. This is

evident if we consider information about nursing homes. They are
relatively few in Britain but relatively numerous in the United States. A
"nursing home" means different things in different countries. Some
American private nursing homes resemble British hospitals for the chronic
sick in size, facilities, and the patients they have; they are excluded from
the calculations about "hospital" beds given above. Others resemble
British residential homes for the aged.[15] It is also important to remember
that "hospitals" for the "sick" are not clearly distinct from "residential
institutions" or "homes" for the "disabled," "infirm," and "aged." Just
as the sick merge with the disabled, so do the institutions created for them

Table IV–5: INMATES OF DIFFERENT TYPES OF INSTITUTIONS (EXCLUDING
CHILDREN'S HOMES AND ORPHANAGES, AND CORRECTIONAL AND PENAL
INSTITUTIONS)

Type of Accommodation	Number (in Thousands)		Per Cent	
	All Ages	Ages 65 and Over	All Ages	Ages 65 and Over
Denmark				
1 General hospitals	23,2[b]	7,6[c]	0.51[c]	1.6
2, 3 Tuberculosis hospitals and sanitoria	1,9[b]	0,4	0.04	0.1
4 Nursing homes	[d]	4,6	[d]	0.9
5 Mental hospitals[a]	10,3[b]	} 2,0	0.23	} 0.4
6 Mental deficiency institutions	8,4[e]		0.18	
7 Homes for the aged	20,5[f]	19,4	0.45	3.8
8 Institutions and schools for blind, deaf and disabled	2,4[f]	0,3	0.05	0.1
Estimated total, health and welfare	66,6	34,3	1.45	7.0
Total "long-stay"	—	26,7	—	5.3
Britain				
1, 2, 3, 4 All hospitals other than psychiatric[a]	303,9	121,2	0.59	2.0
5, 6 Psychiatric hospitals[b]	214,5	59,3	0.42	0.9
7, 8 Homes for the aged and disabled	109,2	96,5	0.21	1.6
Total, health and welfare	627,5	277,0	1.22	4.5
Estimated total "long-stay"	—	220,0	—	3.6
United States				
1 General hospitals[a]	557,0	131,5[b]	0.28	0.8[b]
2 Tuberculosis hospitals/wards	65,0	} 37,4	0.04	} 0.2
3 Chronic hospitals/wards	42,5		0.02	
4 Nursing homes	200,6	172,8	0.11	1.0
5 Mental hospitals	630,0	177,8	0.35	1.1
6 Homes and schools for the mentally handicapped	174,7	4,8	0.10	[c]
7 Homes for the aged and dependant	269,1	215,2	0.15	1.3
8 Homes and schools for the physically handicapped and others	24,3	2,0	0.01	[c]
Estimated total, health and welfare	1,963,0	741,5	1.09	4.6
Estimated total "long-stay"	—	610,0	—	3.7

Table IV-5: NOTES

		All persons	Aged 65 and over
Population 1960 (000's):	Denmark	4,581,0	479,5
	Britain[a]	51,284,0	6,047,0
	United States	179,323,2[b]	16,207,2
	[a]1961		
	[b]Excluding armed forces overseas.		

Denmark:

General Source: *Social Welfare Statistics of the Northern Countries, 1960 (1960/61)*, (Stockholm: Nordisk Statistisk Skriftserie, 1964). Also *Statistiske Eferretninger*, No. 45 (Copenhagen: Statens Trykningskontor, 1964).

[a] Public and private mental hospitals and nursing homes as well as special wards in general hospitals for mental cases.

[b] Average number of patients during the calendar year 1959. Private as well as public hospitals and nursing homes are included.

[c] For 1960 the Census shows that 6,684 in general hospitals were aged 70 or over The numbers aged 65–69 have been estimated.

[d] Included in total for (1) General hospitals.

[e] 1961/62. Excludes 8,698 patients in "supervised family care."

[f] 1960.

Britain:

General Source: General Register Office, *Census 1961*, England and Wales, Age, Marital Condition and General Tables (London: HMSO, 1965), Table 24, pp. 105–106.

[a] Mainly National Health Service hospitals but also including some non-profit-making and proprietary hospitals and nursing homes. The data do not permit sub-classification.

[b] Including mental nursing homes, hospitals, and hostels for the mentally subnormal.

United States:

General Source: U.S. Bureau of the Census, *United States Census of the Population: 1960. Subject Reports. Inmates of Institutions*, Final Report PC(2)=8A (Washington, D.C.: U.S. GPO, 1963), Tables 5, 6, 7, 8. United States Bureau of the Census, *Statistical Abstract of the United States: 1964*, 85th ed. (Washington, D.C.: U.S. GPO, 1964), p. 76. For general hospitals, see *Journal of the American Hospital Association*, Hospitals, Guide Issue, Aug. 1, 1961.

[a] The average number of patients receiving treatment each day in short-term general and special hospitals for 1960. The figure includes patients in federal as well as non-federal short-term general hospitals.

[b] For the two-year period ending June, 1960, persons aged 65 or over accounted for 19.5 per cent of the total days of care in general short-stay hospitals. U.S. National Health Survey, *Hospital Discharges and Length of Stay: Short-stay Hospitals, United States, 1958–60* (Washington, D.C.: U.S. Department of Health, Education, and Welfare, Public Health Service, 1962). The figure does not refer to persons who died during the period and the Department of Health, Education, and Welfare estimates (in a private communication) that it should be increased to 23.6 per cent to allow for the larger number of persons over the age of 65 who died. This latter figure has been used in estimating absolute numbers of persons in hospital on a particular day.

[c] Less than 0.05 per cent.

overlap in their functions and services. Until more detailed cross-national studies of various types of public and private institutions are carried out, there will remain considerable doubt about the exact inferences that can be drawn from existing statistics.[16]

These qualifications should be borne in mind in considering Table IV–5. Roughly similar numbers of patients, proportionate to population, are in all kinds of psychiatric hospitals in the three countries (though in Britain and the United States relatively more patients are in mental illness hospitals and fewer in hospitals or other institutions for the mentally subnormal). In all other kinds of hospitals and nursing homes (taken together) the numbers are again proportionately similar. There is one striking difference. Proportionately between two or three times as many disabled and elderly persons in Denmark as in Britain and the United States are in residential homes. The difference between Britain and Denmark is not explained by the use made in the two countries of special types of housing. Indeed, more use seems to be made of grouped flatlets and houses for pensioners in Denmark than in Britain. And although more persons in Britain than in Denmark live permanently in residential hotels and boarding houses, the numbers of such persons are small and they do not account for more than a small fraction of the difference.

Table IV–5 also shows the difference between Denmark and the other two countries when persons aged 65 and over are considered separately. Relatively more than twice as many old people are in residential homes in Denmark than in either Britain or the United States. This is why the "long-stay" elderly institutional population as a whole is larger in Denmark than in Britain and the United States. But other differences that are suggested by the table may be more apparent than real. For example, the British figures for hospitals other than psychiatric hospitals include all persons in general and "chronic sick" hospitals at the time of the census. The elderly "chronic sick" population in British hospitals may be similar to the "nursing home" population in the other two countries.[17] Further, the proportion of old people who are in psychiatric hospitals and institutions appears to be lower in Denmark than in the United States and Britain, but in Denmark, unlike the latter two countries, patients in mental nursing homes appear to have been counted under the general heading of "nursing homes."

Everywhere a very high proportion of residents and patients are aged 80 and over. In Denmark, Britain, and the United States the proportions of persons aged 80 and over in residential homes are 44 per cent, 53 per cent, and 43 per cent respectively.[18] Table IV–6 shows for both Britain and the United States the proportion of the population who are inmates of institutions at each five-year period beginning with ages 65–69. These proportions rise slowly with age until 80 and over. More than 10 per cent of those over 80 in each country are resident in institutions.

Table IV-6:   PERCENTAGE OF PERSONS WHO ARE INMATES OF
INSTITUTIONS, BY AGE

Type of Accommodation	65–69	70–74	75–79	80 +
Britain[a]				
Psychiatric hospitals[b]	0.8	0.9	1.0	1.3
Residential homes	0.4	0.9	1.9	5.1
Non-psychiatric hospitals (NHS)	0.9	1.3	1.9	3.9
Non-psychiatric hospitals (non-NHS)	0.1	0.1	0.3	1.0
All institutions (including short-stay)	2.1	3.2	5.2	11.3
United States				
Mental hospitals	0.9	1.0	1.2	1.6
Residential homes	0.4	0.8	1.6	4.4
Nursing homes	0.2	0.6	1.3	3.7
T.B. and chronic	0.2	0.2	0.2	0.5
All long-stay institutions	1.7	2.6	4.4	10.1

[a] See Table IV–5 *Britain*, footnote *a*.

[b] See Table IV–5 *Britain*, footnote *b*.

Source: See Table IV–5.

Hospitalization of the Aged

On the basis of the cross-national survey, more of the aged in the United
States than of their counterparts in Denmark and Britain are hospitalized
during a period of a year; 13 per cent of the sample (excluding the bedfast) had been hospitalized for at least one day during the previous twelve
months, compared with less than 11 per cent in Denmark and 8 per cent
in Britain.

Information on length of hospital stay is available only from Britain
and the United States. Of those who had been hospitalized, a much higher
proportion of old people in the United States had stayed for short periods.
Seventy-one per cent had stayed for less than 15 days, compared with 43
per cent in Britain; only 13 per cent had stayed for longer than a month,
compared with 33 per cent in Britain.[19] It is especially interesting to find
that although more of the aged in the United States than in Britain had
been hospitalized in the year, about the same number had stayed in
hospital for more than a month—2.4 per cent of the entire sample, compared with 1.6 per cent in Britain.

Various problems arise in giving accurate figures for hospitalization
from a survey of old people in private households. Some of these same
problems also affect estimates of contact with the doctor outside hospital.
For one thing, a number of people not contacted in household surveys are
in hospital at the time. For another thing, among those who refuse to be
interviewed on health or other grounds, there are probably a large
proportion who are receiving treatment from a doctor, as well as some
who have been in hospital in the last year. Finally, since some of the elderly

admitted to hospital during a year die there, or subsequently in their homes, it is inevitable that the proportions of the elderly population who are admitted to hospital should be understated.[20] Nevertheless these difficulties seem to apply fairly equally to all three countries and do not invalidate comparisons. Indeed, data from other sources tend to provide approximate confirmation of the actual percentages.[21]

Although the proportion of persons who have been in hospital during the previous year rises slightly among the Danes after the age of 70 and slightly among the Americans after the age of 75, the difference between those in their 60's and those in their 80's is not marked, and among British

Table IV-7: PERCENTAGE OF MEN AND WOMEN HOSPITALIZED IN PAST YEAR, BY LENGTH OF STAY (*Percentage Distribution*)

Length of Stay in Days	Britain			United States[a]		
	Men	Women	All	Men	Women	All
1–7	27	16	21	40	38	39
8–14	20	23	22	26	37	32
15–21	14	17	16	13	11	12
22–28	9	10	9	4	5	5
29–42	16	15	16	6	3	5
43–56	5	7	6	3	1	2
More than 56	9	12	11	8	4	6
Total	100	100	100	100	100	100
N=	80	105	185	156	166	322

[a] Information was given by 97.5 per cent of men and by 94.8 per cent of women who were hospitalized.

old people there is no consistent pattern according to age. However, it must again be remembered that the figures refer only to persons in private households who have been in hospital during the previous year. They do not include persons hospitalized who (a) remain in hospital, (b) die, or (c) are transferred to other institutions.

How should the difference between the countries in the rates be interpreted? The fact that the rates tend to be higher, even age for age, among American than among Danish and British old people does not necessarily mean that more of them are seriously ill. Indeed the evidence adduced in Chapter 2 might lead the reader to expect the highest rates of hospitalization to be found among the British old people. More of them are housebound, and more (particularly at the advanced ages) have incapacities of different kinds. Among the Danish and British samples (and even at almost every age), more people than among the American sample reported illness during the previous twelve months, 32 per cent and 30 per cent respectively, compared with 26 per cent.

When the hospitalization rates are compared with the accommodation figures for hospitals and other institutions given earlier, it is evident that hospitals tend to be used more intensively by the aged in the United States. Possibly this is because of the financial impact on the individual; until the present time the scope of health insurance almost never covered care in nursing homes. Possibly it is also because of the different organization of services. To some extent hospitalization may be used in the United States where domiciliary care would be used in the two European

Table IV–8: PROPORTION OF PERSONS OF DIFFERENT AGE HOSPITALIZED DURING THE PREVIOUS YEAR

Age	Per Cent of Each Age Group Hospitalized								
	DENMARK			BRITAIN			UNITED STATES		
	Men	Women	All	Men	Women	All	Men	Women	All
65–69	9	8	9	10	8	9	14	11	12
70–74	11	13	12	6	6	6	13	11	12
75–79	11	11	11	7	7	7	17	18	17
80 and over	13	12	13	9	8	8	15	14	15
All ages	10	11	11	8	7	8	14	13	13
N=									
65–69	445	487	932	387	492	879	404	506	910
70–74	315	394	709	281	431	712	345	420	765
75–79	224	249	473	197	288	485	182	224	406
80 and over	155	161	316	123	255	378	146	187	333
All ages	1,139	1,291	2,430	988	1,466	2,454	1,077	1,350[a]	2,427

[a] Includes 13 women of unknown age.

countries. Otherwise, it is difficult to account for the paradox that in the United States a larger proportion of the aged enter hospital, although a smaller proportion report illness.

Medical Consultation

Three conclusions emerge from our provisional study of medical consultations outside the hospital. First, there is a striking difference between the United States and the two European countries in the proportion of consultations taking place in the home. Second, there is evidence that consultations with old people are slightly more frequent in Britain than in the United States, and more frequent in these two countries than in Denmark. And third, there is evidence that the differences between countries in frequency of consultations is greatest among the most incapacitated groups living at home, such as the bedfast and the housebound. We will consider these matters in turn.

Although a larger proportion of the elderly in the two European countries than in the United States report illness in bed at home during a year, nevertheless in the European countries a strikingly larger proportion of those who report illness are seen at home by the doctor, as shown in Table IV–9.

What is the real meaning of this difference? The explanation that can be given on the basis of our data and other sources is necessarily incomplete and tentative, since the factors contributing to it are extremely

Table IV–9: PROPORTION OF PERSONS AGED 65 AND OVER ILL IN BED AT HOME DURING THE PREVIOUS YEAR WHO WERE VISITED BY A DOCTOR[a]

Country	Percentage of Persons Visited by Doctor		
	MEN	WOMEN	ALL
Denmark	71	70	70
Britain	82	81	81
United States	49	51	50
N=[a]			
Denmark	317	451	768
Britain	269	462	731
United States	244	383	627

[a] The percentages of eligible respondents who answered this question are: Denmark, 97.9; Britain, 97.5; United States, 90.9.

complex. We will consider the relationship between hospitalization and home-visiting in illness. Table IV–10 reveals a number of interesting differences. More of the elderly in the United States than in the two European countries who are not ill in bed at home during a year are nonetheless hospitalized. It should be remembered in interpreting this finding that the hospitalization may in some instances have occurred at a different point in the year from the illness at home. The questions asked in the interviews were not strictly related. The most plausible explanation of the findings, however, would seem to be that the higher proportion of the elderly who are hospitalized in the United States may be attributable in part to persons who stay in the hospital briefly for a check-up or investigation, or for treatment. Some also may have disabilities that are not associated with incapacitating illness. But among those who are ill in bed during a year there are contrasts in the utilization of services. First, slightly more of those in the United States than in Britain and Denmark who are ill in bed at home and are not visited by a doctor go into hospital at some point in the year, as Table IV–10 shows, and we might reasonably suppose that many of these do so during such illness. This would account for some but by no means all of the difference between the United States and the two European countries in the amount of home-visiting during illness.

Second, twice as many old people in the United States as in Britain, and slightly more than in Denmark, who are ill in bed at home, are neither visited by a doctor during that illness nor hospitalized at any point in the year. This might lead us to suppose that fewer old people in the United States than elsewhere consult a doctor when they are ill, but this does not

Table IV–10: PERCENTAGE OF PERSONS WHO WERE ILL IN BED AT HOME DURING THE PREVIOUS YEAR AND WERE VISITED BY A DOCTOR AND, ALSO WHO ENTERED THE HOSPITAL DURING THE YEAR[a]

Characteristic	DENMARK	BRITAIN	UNITED STATES
Ill in bed, visited by doctor			
Hospitalized during year	8	4	4
Not hospitalized	15	20	8
Ill in bed, not visited by doctor			
Hospitalized during year	1	*	3
Not hospitalized	8	5	10
Not ill in bed, not visited by doctor			
Hospitalized during year	1	3	6
Not hospitalized	67	67	69
Total	100	100	100
N=	2,410	2,436	2,420

[a] The percentages of eligible respondents who answered this question are: Denmark, 98.6; Britain, 97.4; United States, 99.1.

* Less than one per cent.

necessarily follow. In the cross-national survey, we could not collect evidence about telephone or office (surgery) consultations, but other sources suggest that more ill old people in the United States than elsewhere either consult their medical practitioner over the phone or visit him at the beginning of, or during, or at the end of their illness. Whether this is desirable or not is another question. The information about rates of medical consultations among the aged suggest that another part, but again not all, of the difference between the United States and Britain in the amount of home-visiting in illness is explained in this way.

Evidence from other studies indicates that consultation rates for persons over 65 in both Britain and the United States are quite similar. A study of 171 doctors in 100 practices in Britain arrived at a consultation rate of 6.2 per person aged 65 or over in 1955–56. In this study indirect contacts with doctors (such as telephone conversations) were excluded and a consultation was defined as "any occasion when a patient attended for medical treatment or advice at the general practitioner's surgery or when the general practitioner visits the patient to give treatment or advice elsewhere."[22] A consultation rate of 6.7 "physician visits" per year for persons aged 65 and over was given on the basis of the United States National Health Survey of 1963–64. (The equivalent figure was 6.8 for 1957–58 and 6.7 for 1958–59.) Consultation, however, was defined differently to include contact with the doctor at hospitals and clinics (0.6 per year), telephone contacts (0.5), and contacts at industrial health units and other places (0.1), as well as at the office (4.3) and in the home (1.1).[23] Only the latter two groups are comparable with the British definition of consultation. According to this more limited definition the United States consultation rate would be 5.4 per year compared with the British figure for an earlier year of 6.2. Outpatient consultations in hospitals are important in both countries. So far as it is possible to compare such statistics as are available, the volume of outpatient attendances is broadly similar in the two countries.[24]

The average old person in Britain, compared with an old person in the United States, is likely to have a larger number of consultations in relation to those given younger adults. If the consultation rate for those aged 15–44 is taken as a base equivalent to 100, the average elderly Briton had a consultation rate of 198 compared with one of 151 for the elderly American.[25] Although the elderly population in Britain reports more illness, it should also be remembered that there are relatively fewer doctors in that country, and a much higher proportion of consultations are at home.

No attempt was made to try to establish the total number of medical consultations during the previous twelve months in the cross-national survey but a question was asked about the most recent contact with a doctor. The result, shown in Table IV–11, tends to support the evidence reported above of the aged having slightly more medical consultations in Britain than in the United States; 34 per cent, compared with 30 per cent, had seen a doctor within the previous month. Both figures are distinctly larger than the Danish figure. Despite having the highest rates of reported illness among the aged in the three countries, the aged in Denmark also had the fewest recent contacts with doctors.[26]

The call made upon doctors by the elderly population increased with age. The percentages of each age-group seeing a doctor in the last month are given in Chapter 2. Women in all three countries, compared with men of the same age, tended to have had more recent contact with their doctors. With the exception of men aged 65–66 and women aged 67–69, more of the elderly in Britain at every age than of the elderly of the other two countries tended to have seen their doctors recently.

Does the extent of integration with family or with society in general affect the pattern of contacts with doctors? Do more of those living with or near their children see their doctors frequently? The numbers interviewed in the three countries were too small to allow all the major variables—age, sex, incapacity, whether ill in bed in the previous year, living arrangements, proximity to children, and last contact with doctor—to be adequately controlled.[27] In Britain and the United States fewer of those who lived at some distance from their children than of those living with or near their children had seen a doctor recently, but the difference was small and did not exist for Denmark. On the other hand, when only those old

Table IV–11: PERCENTAGE OF PERSONS WHO HAD SEEN THEIR DOCTORS
WITHIN DIFFERENT PERIODS (*Percentage Distribution*)

Last Saw Doctor	DENMARK			BRITAIN			UNITED STATES		
	Men	Women	All	Men	Women	All	Men	Women	All
In last month	19	24	22	31	36	34	28	31	30
1–3 months ago	20	26	23	16	16	16	13	16	15
More than 3 months– 1 year	23	24	23	21	20	20	25	26	26
More than a year or never	38	25	32	32	28	29	33	27	30
Total	100	100	100	100	100	100	100	100	100
N=[a]	1,084	1,231	2,315	987	1,464	2,451	1,068	1,332	2,400

[a] The percentages of eligible respondents in the three countries who answered this question are: Denmark, 94.4; Britain, 98.0; United States, 98.3.

people who reported illness in the last year were considered, it emerged that particularly in Britain fewer old persons who lived at some distance from their children than those who lived with or near their children had seen a doctor recently.

Several factors may be operating to produce the findings reported in Table IV–12. The family's role may be chiefly one of discouraging an old person from neglecting an illness or an obvious ailment, and advising that he or she should have an occasional medical check-up, rather than one of insisting on frequent visits to and from the doctor. Once the doctor is in touch with someone who is ill, however, he may be more likely to call frequently at the house if the person is isolated rather than if he lives with or near his family. Further research would be called for to explore all the major social factors influencing the utilization of medical services.

Independent of factors concerned with the social circumstances of patients, it must be remembered that the organization of the medical services in the three countries differs. In Britain and Denmark, the doctors are general practitioners, working from their own homes or surgery premises; only a small minority of these doctors have specialist qualifications, or hold official appointments at hospitals or clinics. In the United States most physicians practice as specialists and there is no clear division between doctors working in hospitals and clinics and those giving treatment at the "office" and in the patient's home. Even though careful studies have been made of consultation rates, this organizational difference is bound to make meaningful comparisons difficult. In one country two brief consultations in two separate places may correspond to one longer consultation in another. The length and value of consultations may vary inversely with their sheer number. And the distribution of consultations among the population may vary according to extent, type, and severity of illness.

Table IV–12: PERCENTAGE OF PERSONS LIVING WITH, NEAR, AND AT A DISTANCE FROM THEIR CHILDREN WHO HAD SEEN THEIR DOCTORS WITHIN DIFFERENT PERIODS

Last Saw Doctor	Persons Sharing Household with Child		Living within 10 Minutes Journey of Child		Living at a Distance of More than 10 Minutes Journey	
	All	Ill in Bed during Last Year	All	Ill in Bed during Last Year	All	Ill in Bed during Last Year
Denmark						
In last week	6	12	8	14	6	10
In last month	13	16	15	21	16	23
One to twelve months	49	61	47	60	46	57
More than a year ago or never	32	11	31	6	32	9
Total	100	100	100	100	100	100
N=a	372	131	606	195	923	318
Britain						
In last week	13	21	14	18	12	18
In last month	21	30	23	34	21	23
One to twelve months	36	44	34	42	38	55
More than a year ago or never	30	6	28	6	29	4
Total	100	100	100	100	100	100
N=a	784	272	435	145	653	187
United States						
In last week	11	b	12	b	9	b
In last month	19	b	22	b	17	b
One to twelve months	42	b	38	b	40	b
More than a year ago or never	27	b	28	b	34	b
Total	100	—	100	—	100	—
N=a	546	—	656	—	769	—

[a] The percentages of eligible respondents in the three countries who answered this question are: Denmark, 95.1; Britain, 99.2; United States, 98.4.
[b] Computations not available.

Costs, Income, and Medical Care

Prima facie support seems to be emerging for the hypothesis that a higher proportion of national medical resources (in terms of personnel as well as costs) is devoted to the aged in Britain than to the aged in the United States, even allowing for differences in the age-structure of the two populations and in morbidity. The evidence for Denmark is rather uneven. A smaller proportion of total national resources than in the other two countries is devoted to medical services. Whether the proportion of medical resources devoted to the aged is smaller must remain conjectural without further evidence. It would seem that relatively more resources are invested in institutional care and relatively fewer in domiciliary care (including care in a clinic or surgery).

Since many of the aged in the United States, unlike their counterparts in Britain and Denmark, had to meet a large part or all of the costs of medical care themselves, at least in 1962, and since the aged tend to be poorer than the younger adult population, a relatively large number of them may have been deterred from seeking medical care. A national survey carried out in 1957 found that fewer than two-fifths of those aged 65 and over were covered by voluntary health insurance; and although nearly all such persons were covered in part or in whole for hospital bills, only a fifth of them were covered in whole or in part for doctors' bills for consultations at home or in the office or surgery.[28] Various studies in the United States, while they are not always as conclusive as might be expected, have shown variation with income in the utilization of health services. In the National Health Survey of 1957–59, physician consultations per year among persons aged 65 and over ranged from 5.4 for those whose family income was under $2,000 to 7.3 for those whose family income was $7,000 or more. Consultations at home, which are included, ranged similarly from 1.4 to 2.5.[29] Moreover, more of the high-income aged may have been persons classified according to the income of children with whom they were living. Some studies have shown that those who have the lowest incomes of all see as much of doctors as middle-income groups, mainly because of various forms of medical assistance that are available to those who are really indigent.

But whether the low-income aged have *less* or the *same* access to physicians, there is no doubt that more of them than among the higher income groups suffer from one or more chronic conditions; and more suffer from multiple chronic conditions and are limited in activity by their condition.[30] In the cross-national survey only slightly more of the old people in the lowest income quartile in the United States than of those in the highest income quartile had seen a doctor within the previous month (32 per cent, compared with 28 per cent). Yet 33 per cent of those in the lowest income quartile, compared with 19 per cent in the highest quartile, had been ill in bed in the previous year. Again, as Table II-9 shows, as many as 47 per cent of old people with severe personal incapacity (scoring 7 or more on the index) were found in the lowest income quartile. These figures suggest that rather fewer of those in the lowest income groups who are ill and infirm than of those in the middle and highest income groups see a doctor frequently. Our data are too few to allow this suggestion to be analyzed fully; more information about current and recent illnesses and about medical consultations would have to be obtained. But, as an extremely detailed survey in the United States concluded:

> . . . the cost of medical care is high for the aged, principally for those requiring hospital care. Many aged persons never recover from the economic effects of a single hospital episode. Unfortunately, the heaviest burden is likely to fall on those with the least resources. Those with insurance are better able to absorb the blow than those without such protection, but even for the insured there is no present guarantee against dependency in old age caused by catastrophic medical expenses.[31]

Medical Care and Social Class

The frequency and number of consultations according to social class are of special interest. On the whole, however, differences between countries were greater than those between classes within any country. But

Table IV–13: PROPORTION OF PERSONS OF DIFFERENT SOCIAL CLASS WHO LAST SAW A DOCTOR WITHIN THE PREVIOUS MONTH

Social Class	DENMARK		BRITAIN		UNITED STATES	
	Men	Women	Men	Women	Men	Women
White collar	21	24	35	34	29	30
Blue collar	17	23	32	38	28	33
Service workers	a	28	b	34	28	33
Agricultural workers	17	23	17	a	28	32
N=b						
White collar	368	442	252	403	296	384
Blue collar	397	356	614	836	447	403
Service workers	28	151	45	92	116	172
Agricultural workers	288	254	59	42	202	290

a Percentages not computed on a base of less than 50.

b The percentages of eligible respondents in the three countries who answered this question are: Denmark, men 94.7, women 93.1; Britain, men 97.6, women 92.8; United States, men 98.2, women 91.7.

this may be attributable to the data; they refer to recent contact, and only give a rough indication of the likely number of consultations over-all. If consultation rates could be built up from more detailed information they would perhaps reveal a clearer pattern. Categorization according to "social class" is also primitive. The classification into "white collar" and "blue collar," which is used in the United States and which was adopted in the cross-national survey for purposes of comparability, is much more general than the occupational classification used by the Registrar-General in Britain and is not so directly related to class or status. Important differences between major sub-groups may be concealed. Further, there are drawbacks in using any classification based on occupations for the aged, both because many of them have long since given up their occupations, and because the majority of them are women who either cannot give their husband's precise occupation as distinct from his broad industrial category or whose husbands have been dead for many years. The class position of these women may have changed in the meantime.

The hospitalization rates for each class form a more consistent pattern. In all three countries more elderly men and women whose occupations had been classified as "white collar"—than whose occupations had been classified as "blue collar"—had spent some period in hospital during the previous twelve months.[32] While the differences between people from "white collar" and people from "blue collar" occupations are small, they tend to be of the same rough order of magnitude in each country.

Table IV–14: PROPORTION OF PERSONS OF DIFFERENT SOCIAL CLASS WHO HAD SPENT SOME PERIOD IN HOSPITAL DURING THE PREVIOUS TWELVE MONTHS[a]

Social Class	DENMARK			BRITAIN			UNITED STATES		
	Men	Women	All	Men	Women	All	Men	Women	All
White collar	13	13	13	11	9	9	18	13	15
Blue collar	9	12	11	7	7	7	14	11	12
Service workers	b	8	8	b	8	6	22	11	15
Agricultural workers	9	7	8	8	b	5	8	17	13
N=									
White collar	388	469	857	252	403	655	300	391	691
Blue collar	411	370	781	615	839	1,454	451	408	859
Service workers	28	154	182	45	92	137	116	175	291
Agricultural workers	309	270	579	59	42	101	203	292	495

[a] The percentage of eligible respondents was more than 98 in each country.

[b] Per cents not computed on base less than 50.

Medical Care of the Housebound

The principal facts are now presented. Some of the differences between the three countries in utilization of doctors and hospitals seem to be due to variation in the health and other characteristics of the elderly populations, but others to the variations in the medical systems. How far is it possible, by studying the data for certain handicapped groups, to allow for the former? The health characteristics of the elderly populations in the three countries have been described in Chapter 2. There are a number of crucial differences. More of the aged are housebound in Britain than in the United States or Denmark. There are slightly more in Britain than in the United States—but not more than in Denmark—who have been ill in bed in the previous year. More women aged 75 and over are incapacitated in Britain than they are elsewhere—though there are certain puzzling features about the incidence of particular disabilities, as for example, giddiness. The life expectancy of women of 65 years of age and over in Britain is increasing faster relative to that of men than it is in the United States or Denmark, with the consequence that there are relatively more older women than older men in Britain than elsewhere. In terms of the general evidence given in Chapter 2, it can be said that the health capacity of the elderly in the United States is somewhat better than that of elderly people in Britain or Denmark.[33] Although the elderly as a whole in Denmark are rather similar in mobility and incapacity to the elderly in Britain, considerably fewer of them are likely to have seen a doctor recently.

Can we standardize for infirmity or state of health? Table IV–15 shows that compared with those who were wholly mobile, more of the housebound and of those who could move about outside only with difficulty had seen their doctors recently. Nevertheless, more people in Britain with limited mobility than in the United States or Denmark had seen a doctor recently. The patterns for Britain and the United States are more similar

Table IV–15: PERCENTAGE OF HOUSEBOUND AND MOBILE PERSONS WHO SAW THEIR DOCTORS WITHIN THE PREVIOUS MONTH[a]

Degree of Mobility	DENMARK	BRITAIN	UNITED STATES
Housebound or mobile with difficulty (%)	37	53	46
N=	496	431	256
Mobile without difficulty (%)	18	30	28
N=	1,833	2,019	2,144

[a] The percentages of eligible respondents in the three countries who answered this question are: Denmark, 95.8; Britain, 99.2; United States, 98.7.

than might be expected, but it is interesting to note that the difference between them in the proportion of recent doctor contacts tends to be more marked for those of limited mobility than for the mobile. Taking the housebound alone, 26 per cent in Britain, compared with 22 per cent in the United States and 17 per cent in Denmark, had seen a doctor within the last week.

Many of the same conclusions apply if we consider the personally incapacitated. Table II–7 shows that in Britain, compared with Denmark and the United States, more old people with moderate or severe incapacity had seen a doctor recently. Again the differences between Britain and the United States are more striking in the instance of those who are moderately or severely incapacitated than of others in the samples. It should be remembered that home-nursing schemes and other auxiliary services, which might be expected to reduce the call made upon the doctor, are available more extensively in Britain and Denmark than in the United States. This makes the differences between Britain and the United States, on the one hand, and the differences between both countries and Denmark, on the other, somewhat difficult to explain.

Medical Care of the Bedfast at Home

Thus far, the bedfast have been excluded from this analysis. There were relatively few in the sample. Information was obtained about 54 persons in Britain, 48 in Denmark, and 55 in the United States (of whom 31, 15, and 10 were interviewed). But these persons were chosen at random and represent around 2 per cent of persons aged 65 or over in each of the three countries, which means that more of the elderly bedfast lived at home than in all long-stay hospitals and nursing homes put together. Their estimated numbers are 124,000, 10,000, and 350,000, respectively. A very large number of severely incapacitated old people other than the bedfast also live at home, as discussed in Chapter 2. For Britain (where a survey was also carried out of older persons in hospitals and other institutions) it can be estimated that less than a quarter of the most incapacitated persons in the British elderly population are living in institutions. They number rather less than 150,000 in a total of over 650,000.[34] Judging from the Danish and United States data reported in Chapter 2, the number of severely incapacitated persons living at home is certain to be at least twice the number living in institutions.

Although the numbers of the bedfast in any non-stratified random sample of an elderly population will be small, this group are worthy of special attention. The reasons why they are able to live at home will be described and discussed in the next chapter. Their utilization of health services, however, will be described here. Rather fewer of the bedfast in Britain (24 per cent) than of those in the United States (35 per cent), and considerably fewer than of those in Denmark (58 per cent), had been overnight in hospital during the previous twelve months. This finding adds to the evidence of hospitals and nursing homes being used somewhat more intensively by the aged in both the United States and Denmark than

Table IV–16: PROPORTION OF BEDFAST PERSONS VISITED AT DIFFERENT INTERVALS BY A DOCTOR (*Percentage Distribution*)

Regularity of Doctor's Visits	DENMARK[b]	BRITAIN	UNITED STATES
Once a week or more	[19]	22	16
Once a month or more	[11]	33	2
Less than once a month	[11]	27	16
Visits only when sent for	[45]	18	66
Not visited	[15]	—	—
Total	100	100	100
N=a	47	51	50

a One person, 3 persons, and 5 persons, respectively, were unclassifiable in the three countries.

b The percentages for Denmark in this and later tables are computed on a basis of less than 50. For purposes of broad comparison the percentages are given in brackets.

in Britain. By contrast, according to the bedfast themselves or those who care for them, considerably more in Britain than in the other two countries are visited at least once a month or more often by their doctors. There appears to be rather more emphasis on "regular" visiting in Britain. In all countries, but particularly in Denmark and the United States, a substantial number of the bedfast are not visited regularly or occasionally by a doctor. Further investigation of this important matter would seem to be necessary.

Only a fifth of the bedfast in Britain, two-fifths in the United States, and practically none in Denmark were taken "regularly" to see a doctor at a clinic or hospital. Some in Britain and the United States were both visited regularly by a doctor and were taken to see him in his office or surgery. When this is taken into account it still remains true that a higher proportion of the bedfast in Britain than in the United States see a physician frequently.

To some extent the relative lack of regular contact with physicians on the part of the bedfast in Denmark is made up by regular contacts with a professional nurse. This is much less true of the bedfast in the United States, as Table IV–17 shows. In fact, all the bedfast in the sample who

Table IV–17: PROPORTION OF BEDFAST PERSONS VISITED AT DIFFERENT INTERVALS BY A NURSE (*Percentage Distribution*)

Regularity of Nurse's Visits	DENMARK[b]	BRITAIN	UNITED STATES
Once a week or more	[45]	31	17
Once a month or more	[2]	4	4
Less than once a month	0	2	—
Not at all	[52]	63	79
Total	100	100	100
N=[a]	40	52	53

[a] Eight persons, 2 persons, and 2 persons, respectively, were unclassifiable in the three countries.

[b] See footnote *b*, Table IV–16.

were visited by a nurse in that country were persons already being visited by a doctor. The total numbers are of course small and are subject to sampling error. But the implication, which needs to be followed by further research, is that the majority of the bedfast in the United States have no frequent contact with either medical or professional nursing services.

Explanations for Differences in Utilization

A number of hypotheses might be put forward to account for the differences in utilization of health services described in this chapter. A general one is that the differences are partly attributable to differences in population structure and morbidity prevalence, but partly to differences in the organization of medical services and differences in national ideologies about health. Let us consider this hypothesis in general terms. Compared with the elderly populations of the other two countries, the elderly population of Britain contains a larger proportion of, first, women, and, second, retired or employed manual or "blue collar" workers (even allowing for the large numbers of agricultural workers in Denmark and the United States). Each of these factors contributes to the higher rates of reported incapacity and therefore the need for relatively more medical services in Britain. Nonetheless, these "structural" factors do not account for more than part of the differences between the countries. The explanation is more complex. When structural factors are allowed for, a number of other variables have to be considered. Prevalence rates in Britain of some chronic conditions, such as bronchitis, are higher. For this reason, too, the need for medical services therefore seems to be greater. But even when rough account is taken of the nature and prevalence of morbidity, differences in utilization clearly remain. We are forced to investigate national values and the effects of medical organization. If we look carefully again at Tables III–1, –2, and –4 and particularly at Table III–3, there is not much evidence of marked differences in attitudes to health between old people in the three countries who are in good physical condition—representing the great majority of the elderly population. Despite the emphasis that is always given by sociologists to the instrumental values of "work," "efficiency," "activity," and "achievement" in explaining characteristics of American society, it would not seem that the aged in general reflect this emphasis to any great extent in the attitudes they take to their health. More of them than of the aged in other countries are pessimistic, according to a number of measures, but the differences are not uniformly significant, and there are hints that more of the elderly may simply be objective or realistic—at least when compared with the elderly in Britain. More of those in Britain than in the United States who are in relatively poor physical condition say they are in good health (to a lesser extent this is also true of those in Denmark).

How can this important difference be explained? First, is it a question of reference groups? Do more of the infirm old people in Britain think they are in good health by reference to their immediate social surroundings? It could be argued that more of the elderly in Britain than in the other two countries are housebound and therefore do not see other old people so much. They might retain a false image of their own good health. Although the evidence of the extent to which old people see their contemporaries in the three countries is not comprehensive, more old people in Britain see a sibling at least once a week or once a month. More of them live in high density areas, and more of them live with or are visited frequently by children—who help to keep them in touch with the society around them.

Second, is it a question of "referred experience"? Have more in Britain experienced very bad health, by contrast with which they interpret their present health as relatively "good"? Or, more generally, have more of them had the experience of caring for relatives or friends in really bad health? It is possible that the origins of the optimism of some infirm persons in Britain may lie here, but morbidity rates and experience in the three countries do not suggest that this can be more than a marginal explanation for the marked differences between the infirm of the three countries in their attitudes to their health.

Third, is it a question of medical organization and care? This chapter has shown that the incapacitated, the bedfast, and housebound tend to be seen more often by doctors in Britain than in the United States. More of them are visited "regularly." It is possible that more of them are reassured and told they are in relatively good health; their fears of deteriorating health may more often be relieved. While this is only one possible contributory explanation it is rather plausible, for otherwise it would seem difficult to explain why roughly similar proportions of active old people, though different proportions of the infirm, take certain attitudes towards their health in the three countries.

Summary

The more general hypothesis considered in this chapter is that differences in utilization of health services are partly attributable to differences in population structure and morbidity prevalence, but partly to differences in the organization and operation of medical services. This is discussed in the preceding section. The more specific hypothesis is that relatively more of the medical resources of Britain and Denmark than of the United States (in terms of expenditure and personnel) are devoted to the aged. Welfare and ancillary health services (such as homemaker or home help and chiropody services) are discussed in the next chapter.

The United States, compared to Britain and Denmark, spends a higher proportion of its gross national product on health services. But since in many Western countries the proportion of national resources devoted to health increases with real national income per head, the over-all statistics remain arguable. Stated very crudely, the two European countries may be spending relatively more of their resources on health than the United States did when it was at a comparable level of national prosperity or at a comparable point of national economic growth. Of course expenditure may be distributed much more inefficiently in one country than in another, as between public and private sectors, hospitals and domiciliary services, or drugs and personal services. In particular, widely different amounts may be spent in two countries on the administration of medical care. We have been unable even to establish whether the higher proportion of national resources devoted to health in the United States than in Britain and Denmark in fact implies that more services are received on average by the individual. Much depends on the price of health goods and services compared with other goods and services in the different countries.

In Britain there are relatively fewer physicians, nurses, and hospital beds than in Denmark and the United States, although, compared with other Western countries, the differences between the three countries are small. Yet there are relatively more old people in Britain, and (judging from the data on incapacity) relatively more of them are incapacitated and infirm. Nonetheless, fewer old people enter hospital during a year than in the other two countries and, on average, the elderly receive slightly more medical consultations. More of them are visited by a doctor when ill in bed at home. More of the housebound and of the bedfast are visited regularly by a doctor. In relation to the average number of medical consultations enjoyed by a young adult, the person aged 65 or over receives substantially more consultations than his counterpart in the United States. Finally, in relation to expenditure on general hospitals, more is spent on chronic disease and mental hospitals and wards than in the United States.

Denmark would appear to be spending a markedly smaller proportion of national resources on medical services, despite having services proportionately as big or bigger. There are relatively fewer physicians than in the United States but slightly more nurses and hospital accommodation. The utilization of health services by the aged in Denmark does not form a consistent pattern. A much larger proportion of old people are hospitalized than in Britain, though not quite as many proportionately as in the United States. Yet, although more Danish than American old people are visited at home when ill, considerably fewer, even among the incapacitated and housebound, see a doctor frequently (as judged by data on the last contact with a doctor) than in either Britain or the United States. The relatively high number of nurses (a substantial proportion of whom work outside hospital) and the greater dependence by the bedfast living at home than in the other two countries on skilled nursing suggest that there is rather more emphasis on treating illness at home.

In the United States there is greater emphasis on, first, hospitalization, second, short stays in hospital, and, third, treatment in a clinic, office, or surgery than in the two European countries. More old people enter hospital in a year and fewer of those who are ill in bed at home are visited by a doctor. In the United States 70 per cent of physicians work as specialists, compared with 30 per cent in Denmark and 21 per cent in England and Wales. While much serious illness may be dealt with through admission to hospitals, the relatively low proportions of bedfast and housebound persons who are visited regularly by a doctor or by a nurse may deserve further inquiry. Generally, the evidence from the survey and elsewhere suggests that the utilization of services may be more unequal with respect to medical condition in the United States than in the two European countries, though over-all rates of physician consultations are much higher than might be expected by those arguing for the introduction of national health insurance or other health service schemes.

The total proportions of old people living in hospitals and nursing homes in the three countries were small (at around 1½ to 2 per cent) and were roughly equal, though more hospital beds appear to be used intensively in the United States and Denmark (in the sense of there being higher turnover rates) than in Britain. But proportionately twice as many old people in Denmark as in the other two countries resided in homes for the aged. This striking difference may merit further investigation.

For all three countries marked increases with age were found in the utilization of doctors, hospital and other institutional services; more old persons from "white collar" than from "blue collar" occupations entered hospital during a year; and, very important, more old people were estimated to be bedfast at home than in all hospitals and nursing homes put together. Quite how they were able to live at home, and what are the implications of this for social policy, will be discussed in the next chapter.

NOTES

1 63 per cent of physicians in the United States, compared with 29 per cent in Denmark and 20 per cent in England and Wales, are specialists, according to the World Health Organization. *Annual Epidemiological and Vital Statistics, 1960* (Geneva: World Health Organization, 1963).

2 "Beretning fra Direktøren for Sygekassevaesenet for arene 1960–61," *Socialt Tidsskrift*, XXXIX (1963), No. 12, 763.

3 Brian Abel-Smith, *The Hospital 1800–1948* (London: Heinemann, 1964).

4 M. Stocks, *A Hundred Years of District Nursing* (London: Allen & Unwin, 1960).

5 Brian Abel-Smith, "Major Patterns of Financing and Organization of Medical Care in Countries other than the United States," *Bulletin of the New York Academy of Medicine*, 1964, p. 545.

6 H. Somers and A. Somers, *Doctors, Patients and Health Insurance* (Washington, D.C.: Brookings Institution, 1961), p. 292.

7 The Bill provided for financial assistance to the medically indigent. Even by September, 1963, only twenty-eight states had established medical assistance programs for the aged under the Act. In 1963 three-fifths of the expenditure on medical assistance for the aged was incurred by only three of the states of the Union. Half of all recipients lived in these states. H. E. Martz, "Medical Care for the Aged under M.A.A. and O.A.A. 1960–63," *Welfare in Review*, II, No. 2 (February, 1964).

8 The majority view of the Senate Sub-Committee on Health of the Elderly, for example, was that "private health insurance is unable to provide the large majority of our 18 million older Americans with adequate hospital protection at reasonable premium cost." Special Committee on Aging, United States Senate, *Blue Cross and Private Health Insurance Coverage of Older Americans* (Washington, D.C.: U.S. GPO, July, 1964).

9 Combined figures for England and Wales and Scotland are not available. Health costs for England and Wales are assumed to be 89 per cent of those for the United Kingdom as a whole and about 91 per cent of those for Britain.

10 For earlier comparative research see Brian Abel-Smith, "Health Expenditure in Seven Countries," *London & Cambridge Bulletin, Times Review of Industry and Technology*, March, 1963; and Brian Abel-Smith, *Paying for Health Services: A Study of the Costs and Sources of Finance in Six Countries*, Public Health Papers, No. 17 (Geneva: World Health Organization, 1963).

11 For the rapid increase in the United States, see also *Social Security Bulletin*, XXVII (October, 1964), 10; Louis S. Reed and Ruth S. Haupt, "National Health Expenditures, 1950–64," *Social Security Bulletin*, XXIX (January, 1966), 2–19.

12 As calculated on the basis of numbers of practitioners given in annual reports of the Ministry of Health. See, for example, *Report of the Ministry of Health for 1963*, Cmnd. 2389 (London: HMSO, 1964), pp. 6 and 62.

13 *Social Welfare Statistics of the Northern Countries, 1960 (1960/61)* (Stockholm: Nordisk Statistisk Skriftserie, 1964), p. 61.

14 Specialist studies have indicated what is involved. "A simple physician-population ratio does not indicate completely the volume of medical services rendered or needed because it does not take into consideration the nature, scope and quality of the physician's services nor the economic, social and physical characteristics of the people being served." Stanislaw Judek, *Medical Manpower in Canada* (Ottawa: Royal Commission on Health Services, 1964), p. 73.

15 "The term 'nursing home' covers a wide range of facilities, some providing medical service and skilled nursing care, others being simply a sheltered home. . . . As a result there has been a problem of definition. . . . At present, however, a definition employed by the Public Health Service in connection with the Hill-Burton program restricts the term 'nursing home' to those 'facilities the purpose of which is to provide skilled nursing care and related medical services for not less than 24 hours a day to individuals admitted because of illness, disease, or physical or mental infirmity, and which provide a community service.' " George Rosen, "Health Programs for an Aging Population," in Clark Tibbitts, ed., *Handbook of Social Gerontology* (Chicago: University of Chicago Press, 1960), p. 538.

16 In a special survey of institutions for the aged and chronically ill in the United States it was found that 48 per cent could be classified as nursing care homes, 30 per cent as personal-care-with-nursing homes, and 22 per cent as homes providing routine personal care only. U.S. National Center for Health Statistics, *Characteristics of Residents in Institutions for the Aged and Chronically Ill, United States, April–June, 1963* (Washington, D.C.: U.S. Department of Health, Education, and Welfare, Public Health Service, 1965), Ser. 12, No. 2, p. 3.

17 It should be remembered that even discounting psychiatric hospitals, only 15 per cent of patients of all ages are in hospitals and nursing homes outside the National Health Service. Some of these are in special hospitals run by voluntary bodies and are paid for from public funds. The number of elderly patients in private proprietary nursing homes is not more than approximately 15,000, or 0.3 per cent of the population aged 65 and over. C. Woodroffe and Peter Townsend, *Nursing Homes in England and Wales— A Study of Public Responsibility* (London: National Corporation for the Care of Old People, 1961).

18 Danish data from Ministry of Labour and Social Affairs, *Alderdomshjemmene og deres beboere* (Copenhagen: Ministry of Labour, 1957), Table 10, p. 12.

19 A national survey of persons aged 65 and over showed that in 1962, 16 per cent of the discharges from short-stay hospitals aged 65 and over had been there for only one to three days, and another 35 per cent for only from four to nine days. D. P. Rice, "Health Insurance Coverage of the Aged and their Hospital Utilization in 1962: Findings of the 1963 Survey of the Aged," *Social Security Bulletin*, XXVII (July, 1964), 24.

20 "A survey based on hospital records indicates that the inclusion of hospitalization received by persons who died during the survey year would result in an increase of one-fourth to one-third in the total volume of hospitalization for persons aged 65 and over." *New Directions in Health, Education and Welfare* (Washington, D.C.: U.S. GPO, 1963), p. 201.

21 For example, in the 1963 Social Security Administration Survey of the Aged it was found that 13.6 per cent of the aged (12.9 per cent of those aged 65–72 and 14.4 per cent of those aged 73 and over) had spent at least one night in the hospital during the year. D. P. Rice, *op. cit.* In the period July, 1960–June, 1962, however, 11.2 per cent of persons aged 65 and over were hospitalized annually. U.S. National Center for Health Statistics, *Persons Hospitalized by Number of Hospital Episodes and Days in a Year, July 1960–June 1962* (Washington, D.C.: U.S. Department of Health, Education, and Welfare, Public Health Service, 1965), Ser. 10, No. 20.

22 W. P. D. Logan and A. A. Cushion, *Morbidity Statistics from General Practice*, Vol. I (London: HMSO, 1958).

23 The British study was based on records kept by doctors. The United States study was based on household interviews. U.S. National Center for Health Statistics, *Volume of Physician Visits by Place of Visit and Type of Service, United States, July 1963–June 1964* (Washington, D.C.: U.S. Department of Health, Education, and Welfare, Public Health Service, 1965), Ser. 10, No. 18. An average consultation rate for the United

States of 7.6 contacts per year for persons aged 65 and over was found in 1957. This figure, based on interviews with older persons only, also includes contacts with doctors by telephone and at clinics. Ethel Shanas, *The Health of Older People: A Social Survey* (Cambridge, Mass.: Harvard University Press, 1962), p. 12.

24 During 1963 there were 30 million outpatient attendances at hospitals in England and Wales. According to the American Medical Association there were 118 million outpatient attendances in the United States that same year. In relationship to population these figures are very similar.

25 Number of home and office consultations only. Based on W. P. D. Logan and A. A. Cushion, *op. cit.*, Tables 4–18; and for the United States, 1957–58 data as given in U.S. National Center for Health Statistics, *Medical Care, Health Status and Family Income, United States* (Washington, D.C.: U.S. Department of Health, Education, and Welfare, Public Health Service, 1964), Ser. 10, No. 9.

26 Other information is not entirely consistent with these results. According to a survey of most medical practitioners in Denmark outside the city of Copenhagen, there was an average consultation rate for people aged 65 and over of 6.7 per year. Since about 10 per cent of this figure refers to consultations by telephone, it would seem that the comparable Danish rate falls only a little short of the British figure of 6.2. R. Fuglsang, *Praksisstatistik 1958–59* (Copenhagen: 1962).

27 Provisional analyses of the data for one country, Britain, were not suggestive—perhaps because the measures of certain variables were too crude, but also because numbers simply did not allow sophisticated treatment. More of the incapacitated of every age had seen a doctor recently, but there was no discernible trend according to their proximity to children. Roughly the same proportions of the incapacitated who lived with, or near, or at a distance from their children had seen a doctor within the last month (53 per cent, 53 per cent, and 52 per cent respectively).

28 E. Shanas, *op. cit.*, pp. 78–79.

29 Counting home and office consultations only, not consultations by telephone and in hospital clinics. U.S. National Center for Health Statistics, *Medical Care, Health Status and Family Income, op. cit.*, p. 26. Technically, it is unfortunate that persons aged 65 and over who were living alone, those who were living in married pairs, and those who were living with relatives and others were all grouped together according to "family" income.

30 *Ibid.*, pp. 52–60.

31 Among unmarried women in the United States more than two-fifths of those incurring hospital costs in 1962 were without health insurance. Twenty-four per cent of those reporting costs reported figures of between $500 and $1000; and a further 17 per cent, more than $1000. E. A. Langford, "Medical Care Costs for the Aged: First Findings of the 1963 Survey of the Aged," *Social Security Bulletin*, XXVII (July, 1964), 3–8. Two findings reported from the United States National Survey are of special interest. First, although those who were aged 65–74 and who had high family incomes had roughly the same number of physician consultations as persons who had low family incomes, nevertheless, those who were aged 75 and over and who had high family incomes had nearly twice as many consultations, on average, as persons of that age with low incomes. Second, while those who had never married tended to have slightly fewer consultations than other persons aged 65 and over, the widowed have roughly the same number of consultations as the married. U.S. National Center for Health Statistics, *Volume of Physician Visits by Place of Visit and Type of Service, op. cit.*, pp. 19–20.

32 Other evidence, at least for the United States, tends to bear this out. "The rates of hospital discharges increase progressively from 152 per 1000 among elderly persons with less than $2000 family income to 209 per 1000 for those living in families with income of $7000 and over." U.S. National Center for Health Statistics, *Medical Care, Health Status and Family Income, op. cit.*, p. 13.

33 One possible explanation for the higher incidence of incapacity among the British elderly population than among the Danish and American populations may be found in different patterns of morbidity, especially of chronic conditions. It would seem that relatively more of the elderly populations of Denmark and America have short terminal illnesses and relatively more of the elderly population of Britain die after having lingering chronic illnesses. For example, while death rates for different forms

of heart disease among the elderly of the former two countries tend to be slightly higher than in Britain, the death rates for bronchitis are dramatically higher in the latter. The rates for men, for example, range from 389 per 100,000 population aged 65–69, to 1,260 per 100,000 aged 85 and over, while for men in Denmark they range only from 14 to 333 and for the United States only from 15 to 41.

34 It was found that 27 per cent of those in institutions had little or no personal incapacity, 20 per cent had moderate and 27 per cent severe incapacity, and another 26 per cent were bedfast. The latter two groups represented about 148,000 in the total population. Although only 7 and 2 per cent respectively of the old people interviewed at home were in these two categories, they represented 539,000 in the total population. The estimates for institutions are based on information from an achieved sample of 2,205 persons aged 65 and over who were living in 128 psychiatric and chronic sick hospitals, nursing homes, and residential homes throughout Britain in 1963. A fuller account of procedures will be found in Peter Townsend and Dorothy Wedderburn, *The Aged in the Welfare State* (London: Bell, 1965).

5 : Welfare Services and the Family

The relationship between the social services and the family is generally regarded as central to all the theoretical disputes about the rise of the "Welfare State"—and provides the theme for this chapter. Does the existence of such services in industrial societies weaken the sense of loyalty and responsibility which many members of the family feel for each other? As the services grow do they supplement or complement the functions of the family, or do they replace them? Are they simply a much more costly way of providing those services which old people need but which are normally performed by the family in any society? Full answers to questions such as these would assist the reformulation of major sociological theory about the changes that have taken place in the family during the process of industrialization in the nineteenth and twentieth centuries. They would also provide a strong theoretical basis for future social policy.

This chapter will briefly describe the development of the welfare and ancillary health services for the aged in the three countries and then go on to discuss utilization and the characteristics of recipients; the role of the family in illness and infirmity; and the evidence for expansion of services.

It could be argued that the growth of the Welfare State in Denmark, Britain, and the United States was largely attributable to concern about the problems of old people as they grew in number and in proportion to the population. In Denmark and Britain the pace, and indeed the widening scope, of social reform were determined by discussions at the turn of the century about poverty among the old. Charles Booth, for example, published a series of books in Britain specifically on old people as well as on poverty during the last years of the nineteenth century.[1] In both countries Acts of Parliament dealing only with old people preceded a number of other measures for social security, and in the United States the main social security scheme grew out of the concern expressed publicly by a series of state commissions on old age, starting with one in Massachusetts in 1910.[2] It is still called "Old Age, Survivors and Disability Insurance."

Welfare Services in Denmark

Public health and welfare services have developed at different rates in the three countries. As early as 1806 it had become the duty of the counties in Denmark to open hospitals, and by 1870 there was a flourishing system of public hospitals.[3] The Old Age Assistance Act of 1891 compelled local authorities, depending on their size, to open homes specifically reserved for the aged, or to collaborate with voluntary organizations or other local authorities to provide them. By 1951 there were residential homes for 12,000 persons, about 3 per cent of the nation's elderly population. By 1955 there were 590 homes, three-fifths of which had been constructed after 1930, and by 1962 about 800.[4] There were then some 22,000 places in homes for the aged, equivalent to about four per cent of persons aged 65 and over. About 4,000 elderly persons, or another one per cent of the population aged 65 and over, were living in nursing homes. Special apartments containing flats for the aged poor were built by charitable foundations in the nineteenth and early part of the twentieth centuries. By 1960 there were nearly 19,000 pensioners' flats accommodating about 24,000 old people, or 4 per cent of the elderly population.[5]

The number of home helps has been growing rapidly. From 1949 local authorities were able to provide a homemaker service for housewives who were temporarily ill or having children, and from the start some old people were among those receiving help. But since such help could only be offered on a temporary basis (usually up to fourteen days) some local authorities began to introduce permanent home-help services as well for the aged. In 1958 a special Act of Parliament introduced a system of state subsidies for such services. The total number of home helps and home-makers rose from 4,730 in 1954 to 6,182 in 1957–58, when there was one per 728 population.[6] But in 1960–61 only 472 of the 1,390 municipalities in the country, covering roughly two-thirds of all disability and old age pensioners, had introduced services which benefited from the 1958 legislation. In 1962 the number of home helps alone was 4,438, serving 14,834 elderly households, or approximately 3 per cent of the elderly population.[7] Beginning in April, 1968, every municipality is required to provide home-help services for the elderly.

The duties of home helps are wide in scope, covering shopping, washing, cleaning, and cooking, and they may also offer personal help with dressing or getting about the house, for example. But nursing duties must be left to a home nurse. Local authorities are compelled to provide home nursing for all patients who do not require hospitalization, irrespective of age. In 1960 there were approximately 1,050 home nurses, or one for every 4,360 population. It would seem that the number of home nurses, relative to the total of all nurses and relative to the population, has fallen in recent years.[8]

Welfare Services in Britain

The social services in Britain also have a fairly long history. Special public provision for the aged dates from the Report of the Poor Law Commission, which in 1834 attempted to secure a classification of institutions within the Poor Law which would allow the aged to "enjoy their indulgences without torment from the boisterous."[9] In practice, they were rarely accommodated separately and not until towards the end of the century did it become common for them to be treated more leniently than other inmates of Poor Law institutions.[10] Even so, belief in the twin principles of economy and deterrence made the Guardians of the poor reluctant to make conditions attractive for destitute persons, whether they were sick or active and old or young. The emergence of infirmaries from the workhouses, and the development of local authority and mental hospitals to accommodate chronic sick patients whom the voluntary hospitals would not take, gradually built up a free hospital service—for the elderly as well as others in the population.[11] The non-contributory Pensions Act of 1906, followed by the National Health Insurance Act of 1911 and the Widows', Orphans' and Old Age Contributory Pensions Act of 1925, further ensured that the great majority of old people had a small income and access to domiciliary medical care as of right. By 1960 there were 3,644 public, voluntary, and private residential institutions and homes in Britain. Nearly 100,000 persons aged 65 and over, or rather less than 2 per cent of the total population of this age, lived in them. Only a tenth of the accommodation was privately owned and managed. Another quarter was owned by religious and voluntary organizations but two-thirds was owned and managed by local authorities. About half of this local-authority accommodation was then in converted and specially built post-war homes, generally for between 20 and 60 residents.[12]

All post-war governments have insisted that "the underlying principle of our services for the old should be this: that the best place for old people is their own homes, with help from the home service if need be."[13] This principle is put into practice partly through community services. The number of households in England and Wales receiving home-help services because of the presence of someone who was old or suffering from chronic sickness increased from about 11,000 in 1951 to 264,725 in 1962, or, expressed as a proportion of those aged 65 and over, from 2.3 per cent to 4.7 per cent. In 1962, there were the equivalent of 25,653 full-time home helps or one per 2,038 population.[14] But while the service is available in all areas, it varies widely in scope. According to the revised ten-year plans of the local authorities for health and welfare published in July, 1964, some areas have three or four times as many home helps per 1,000 population as others. In 1962 there were 10,588 home nurses. Some of these were part-time, however, and the total is equivalent to 7,800 full-time nurses, or one per 6,701 population. These nurses pay more than half their visits to patients aged 65 and over. Recruitment has been flagging, however, and in recent years the elderly population has been growing faster than the service given to them. Home help and home nursing are the two most important domiciliary services for old people, though there are health visiting and meals services affecting small minorities of the elderly population.

The principle of caring for old people at home is also put into practice through special housing. By 1962 about 200,000 one-bedroom dwellings had been built since the war and the annual number approached 30,000. Sheltered housing and "grouped" dwelling schemes have gradually

Table V–1:   RESIDENTIAL CARE, HOME HELP, AND HOME NURSING

Characteristic	DENMARK	BRITAIN	UNITED STATES
Elderly population in non-profit and proprietary residential homes (%)	0.8	0.5	1.1
Elderly population in public residential homes (%)	3.0	1.1	0.2
Elderly population served by public or non-profit home-help service (%)	3.6 [3.1][a]	4.2 [4.7][c]	less than 0.1
Persons in total population per home help (number)	1,045	2,038[d]	46,000
Persons in total population per home nurse (number)	4,360[b]	6,701[d]	—
Elderly population currently visited by home nurse (%)	between 1 and 2	between 1 and 2[e]	less than 0.5[e]

Source: Denmark, *Social Welfare Statistics of the Northern Countries 1960 (1960/61)* (Stockholm: Nordisk Statistisk Skriftserie, 1964); *Statistiske Eftervetninger*, No. 40 (Copenhagen: Statens Trykningskontor, 1963).

Great Britain, General Register Office, *Census, 1961*, England and Wales, Age, Marital Condition and General Tables (London: HMSO, 1965); P. Townsend, *The Last Refuge: A Survey of Residential Institutions and Homes for the Aged in England and Wales* (London: Routledge & Kegan Paul, 1962); *Report of the Ministry of Health for the Year ending 31st December, 1962*, Cmnd. 2062 (London: HMSO, 1963).

United States, U.S. Bureau of the Census, *United States Census of the Population: 1960. Subject Reports. Inmates of Institutions*, Final Report PC (2)–8A (Washington, D.C.: U.S. GPO, 1963); *Directory of Homemaker Services, 1963*, Public Health Service Publication, No. 928 (Washington, D.C.: U.S. GPO, 1964).

[a] The first figure is based on the cross-national survey and the second on the official number of elderly households receiving help in 1962. This number has been expressed as a percentage of the population aged 65 and over.

[b] 1960.

[c] The first figure is based on the cross-national survey and the second on the official number of elderly households receiving help in 1962 for England and Wales only. This has been expressed as a percentage of the population aged 65 and over.

[d] Taking account of "full-time equivalents," England and Wales only.

[e] Estimated on basis of cross-national data on the number of bedfast persons receiving visits from nurses with reference also to national visiting practices. For the United States, see E. Shanas, *The Health of Older People* (Cambridge, Mass.: Harvard University Press, 1962), p. 15.

become more common, though by 1964 only 35,000 old persons, or six per 1,000, benefited. The local authorities plan to increase the number of such dwellings from 35,000 to 113,000 by 1969.[15] In general it is recognized that community services need to be greatly expanded and better co-ordinated.[16]

Welfare Services in the United States

In the United States large-scale public services for the aged were introduced much later than in either Denmark or Britain. Until the mid-1920's the

> only permanent provision for the needy aged in nearly all the States was through the medium of the so-called "almshouse" or "poor farm." Insufficient and unfit food, filth and unhealthful discomfort characterized most of them. Even in institutions with sanitary and physically suitable buildings, it was found that feeble-minded, diseased, and defective inmates were frequently housed with the dependent aged.[17]

A series of measures variously described as "old-age pensions," "old-age assistance," "old-age relief," and "old-age security" were passed by state after state, beginning with Montana in 1923 and covering twenty-eight states by 1935.

> The American States were slow to enact legislation giving aid to the destitute aged. Long before they took action, European countries, industrial as well as non-industrial, had recognized dependency by making provisions for old people.[18]

Private insurance companies were strongly established, and the philosophy of self-help had prevailed. Not until the country was in the midst of a major depression in the mid-1930s was a major social security scheme affecting the aged enacted. Trade union sick clubs and Friendly Societies, which might have given a basis for a more comprehensive system of social insurance, did not exist in large numbers, and the interest of those concerned to do something about the problems of the aged was largely confined to the question of the size and scope of federal grants to the states for "the care of the needy aged."[19]

As health and welfare services grew in the twentieth century the main emphasis was placed on institutional services. There evolved a fragmented public system of free hospitals for mental patients and the majority of those suffering from tuberculosis and other chronic diseases: Veterans Administration hospitals and federal, state, city, and county nursing and residential homes. Some old people also received free care in hospitals run by charitable groups, but most entered general hospitals and non-profit-making and proprietary nursing and residential homes. The costs for their treatment and keep was met through a variety of means—prepaid private insurance, savings, help from relatives, different forms of public assistance, and so on.

Homemaker services began in Philadelphia in 1923 (though similar services have been traced back to 1903).[20] The idea was taken up in many of the states. Housekeepers were introduced temporarily into families where otherwise, because the mother was ill or absent, the children would have had to go into an institution or into foster care. In about 1938 there was a shift of emphasis in homemaker services from families with short-term problems to chronically ill patients, but until the 1960's the rate of growth in such services was infinitesimal. Even by October, 1963, only 3,900 homemakers were employed to care for 9,500 families. Only 1,205 of the latter were families with aged persons—representing about 0.007 of the population aged 65 and over in the United States.[21]

The development of other community services was also slow. As late as 1956, for example, the Commission on Chronic Illness could write that long-term care for patients at home required:

> nursing, dental, social work, nutrition, homemaker, housekeeper, occupational therapy, physical therapy, and other rehabilitative services. *In most communities these services, except nursing, are not yet available.*[22]

Moreover, nursing was organized by different private and charitable agencies and did not cover all areas.[23] As for special forms of housing:

> save for a few tentative explorations in New York State and in scattered other places, there was little activity at the beginning of the decade (1950's) in the construction of housing especially designed for older people who wished to live independently.[24]

Compared with Denmark and Britain, community services for the aged were late in starting.[25]

Nevertheless, in the last fifteen years there has been a remarkable series of developments in the care of the elderly in the United States. National organizations with an interest or program in aging have multiplied. The National Institutes of Health and private foundations began to support research, demonstration, and training projects on an immense scale. The Ford Foundation, for example, contributed "well over $4 million" during the 1950's.[26] In 1955 the Council of State Governments recommended an intricate pattern of interdepartmental and citizens' advisory committee supported by paid staffs at state level.[27] All 50 states put committees to work in preparation for a giant White House Conference on Aging, which was held in 1961, and afterwards almost all of them created planning machinery. A number of hospitals set about organizing home-care programs. More homemaker services were introduced, and a variety of private, voluntary, and municipal bodies began to build low-rent housing. Much of this has depended on federal aid covered by Acts of 1956, 1959, 1961, and 1962. By 1961 nearly 100,000 low-rent public housing facilities had been built—though this number is relatively small, covering less than one per cent of the population aged 65 and over. A variety of fiscal incentives also now exist to encourage the development of special housing for the elderly.

A Different Emphasis on Community Care

The brief historical review given above, when considered in conjunction with the account of medical services provided in the previous chapter, suggests that the three countries have differed widely for generations in their emphasis on "community care," as well as on the degree to which services are publicly managed and organized. Although community services have been far less extensive in Denmark and Britain than their ardent advocates may have supposed, they have played a very important role in the care of the population. In the United States, however, there have been relatively few such services to supplement the rapidly expanding institutional services. The ethnic heterogeneity of the population and, despite many urban concentrations, its relative dispersal over a huge geographical area tended to promote not only local separation from central control but also individual or family separation from local administrative control. As a result a much more loose-knit system of social administration has developed—with the states retaining considerable powers in relation to those of the federal government, the cities and counties themselves being in some respects independent of the states, and the individual family not having the same clearly defined relationship with the local "municipal" authority. In Europe, furthermore, community services have frequently developed as a by-product of health services. They are even sometimes described as "ancillary" health services, and the establishment of a public hospital system or a publicly supported or co-ordinated system of medical practice has tended to open the way—as well as to reveal the need—for corresponding "social" services. Administrative and organizational differences of this kind between the United States and the European countries correspond with different emphasis on certain values. American faith in pioneering self-sufficiency was fiercely expressed in the nineteenth century and is still important today.

UTILIZATION OF COMMUNITY SERVICES

Some indication of the utilization of services in the three countries was given in the previous chapter. While a broadly similar proportion of the elderly (from about 2 to 3 per cent) are living in hospitals and nursing homes in the three countries at any one time, rather more of the elderly in Denmark than in the other two countries are living in residential homes. This is shown in Table V–1. Turning to those services that support the frail aged at home instead of in institutions, there are very marked differences between the European countries and the United States. More old people have home help in Britain than in Denmark (4.2 per cent compared with 3.6 per cent); but since the total number of home helps, relative to population, is larger in Denmark, it would seem either that a much greater part of the British service is directed at the elderly or that it is spread more thinly among a larger number of old people. In Britain there were, in addition to the 4.2 per cent receiving local authority home help in the sample interviewed for the cross-national survey, another 9.0

per cent who depended on privately paid domestic help—making 13.2 per cent altogether. Although information is not available, it is possible that considerably more old people in the United States than in the other two countries pay privately for domestic help.

In Britain and Denmark just under one per cent of the elderly are bed-fast *and* receive regular visits from home nurses. In the United States the number appears to be one third of one per cent (see Chapter 4). But these figures apply only to elderly persons who are bedfast at home at a particular time and do not include ambulant persons who may also be visited; nor do they give any indication of the number of old persons who may be visited in the course of a year. In England and Wales, for example, over fourteen million visits are paid each year to patients aged 65 and over by the district nursing service.[28] There would thus appear to be a fairly marked difference between the two European countries and the United States in the utilization of public and privately paid nurses.

There are other community services in each of the countries which play an important role for some people. There are hostels, clinics, rehabilitation and day centers, visiting services, and clubs. Many of these are of an experimental nature and are modest in scope. In Britain, for example, 7 per cent of the elderly population receive chiropody treatment regularly through the public or voluntary schemes, and another 11 per cent pay privately for such treatment. Over one per cent receive hot meals (though for varying numbers of days per week) which are delivered by voluntary or local authority services. As many as 29 per cent of old people attend clubs of all kinds, and 10 per cent clubs for old people.

CHARACTERISTICS OF BENEFICIARIES

Excepting medical and ancillary health services (such as chiropody) the proportion of the elderly population using various residential and community services is small. But is this proportion increasing? Is the Welfare State supplanting the family? One of the answers to this question can be furnished by finding out the characteristics of the beneficiaries. Do they have relatives available to help? In fact, do they tend to differ from other old people in their social characteristics and relationships as well as in their health? First, the most incapacitated and frail old people in the population are not *all* in institutions. In the previous chapter we found that there were more bedfast old people at home in the three countries than in all kinds of hospitals, nursing homes, and residential homes. Some of them, and other severely incapacitated old people living at home, do not even receive community services.[29] Second, a substantial proportion of old people in residential homes are only slightly or moderately infirm, and some are not infirm at all.[30] This is also true of some receiving community services. So, while there is a general correlation between physical state and receipt of institutional or community services, the two are by no means contiguous.

Social factors play a major role in determining eligibility for various services. Utilization of institutional and community services is closely related to family structure and relationships. This can be demonstrated very clearly indeed for the populations of certain types of institutions and can also be demonstrated, though less dramatically, for those receiving domiciliary services. A vivid representation is given in Table V–2, which shows that the percentage of persons in various types of institution who are single is disproportionately large, in comparison with the percentage in private households. In both Britain and the United States the interesting difference between the populations of psychiatric hospitals and of residential homes in the percentages who are married and widowed should

Table V–2: PERCENTAGE OF INMATES OF DIFFERENT TYPES OF INSTITUTIONS WHO ARE SINGLE, MARRIED, AND WIDOWED (*Percentage Distribution*)

Marital Status	Total Population 65 and Over	TYPE OF INSTITUTION				
		Psychiatric Hospitals	Residential Homes	Non-Psychiatric Hospitals		All Institutions
				NHS	Other	
BRITAIN						
Single	13	44	36	22	32	32
Married[a]	48	23	7	27	14	18
Widowed/ divorced	39	33	57	51	54	50
Total	100	100	100	100	100	100
N=	6,047,000	59,282	96,510	102,975	18,244	277,011[b]
				Nursing Homes	TB and Chronic Disease	
UNITED STATES						
Single	8	33	23	21	25	25
Married[a]	53	32	10	11	25	18
Widowed/ divorced	39	35	66	68	49	57
Total	100	100	100	100	100	100
N=	16,207,417	177,840	215,174	172,779	37,362	603,155

Source: U.S. Bureau of the Census: *United States Census of the Population: 1960. Subject Reports. Inmates of Institutions,* Final Report PC(2)–8A (Washington, D.C.: U.S. GPO, 1963); *U.S. Census of Population, Part I, U.S. Summary, Detailed Characteristics,* Ref. PC(1) ID US, Table 176.

General Register Office, *Census, 1961,* England and Wales, Age, Marital Condition and General Tables (London: HMSO, 1965).

[a] The legally and informally separated are classified as married in the British census and the United States data have been treated in the same way for purposes of comparability.

[b] Note that the British, but not the United States, figures include persons in short-stay hospitals.

also be noted. Persons who have a spouse to care for them would seem to be much less likely to enter a residential home than a psychiatric hospital in old age.

Table V–3 brings out the same fact. Proportionately more single than other persons are in institutions. But the table also shows that for persons of any marital status the proportion rises sharply with age. There is one interesting point of comparison between Britain and the United States. The elderly population of the former contains relatively more persons than the latter who are single, widowed, and aged 80 and over. It would therefore be reasonable to expect more of the total elderly population to be in institutions. But this is not so. The total number in long-stay institutions is 3.6 per cent, compared with 3.7 per cent. Table V–3 reflects one

Table V–3: PERCENTAGE OF SINGLE AND OF ALL PERSONS OF DIFFERENT AGES WHO ARE INMATES OF DIFFERENT TYPES OF INSTITUTIONS

Type of Institutions	Percentage of Single Persons		Percentage of All Persons	
	65–74	75 and Over	65–74	75 and Over
Britain				
Psychiatric hospitals	3.4	3.1	0.8	1.2
Residential homes	2.4	8.1	0.6	3.4
Non-psychiatric hospitals (NHS)	1.8	4.4	1.0	2.8
Non-psychiatric hospitals (other)	0.3	1.5	0.1	0.6
All institutions	7.8	17.2	2.6	8.0
United States				
Psychiatric hospitals	4.4	4.5	1.0	1.4
Residential homes	2.1	6.8	0.6	2.9
Nursing homes	1.3	5.4	0.4	2.4
Tuberculosis and Chronic Disease	[2.8]		0.2	0.3
All long-stay institutions[a]	7.9[b]	16.8[b]	2.1	7.0

Source: See Table V–2.

[a] The U.S. census data do not include persons in short-stay hospitals.

[b] Single persons in TB and Chronic Disease Hospitals are excluded because information about their age is not available.

further important fact. By contrast with the figures for other types of institutions the percentage of single persons who are in psychiatric hospitals does not rise dramatically with age.

The elderly institutional population differs strikingly from the elderly population at home in marital status, but also in other aspects of family status and structure. The basic reason why relatively more single than widowed persons are in institutions is that most of the latter have children; and the reason why more widowed than married persons are in institutions is that the former do not have a husband or wife to give them help and support at home. In general we should therefore expect fewer married or widowed persons with than without children, fewer with several children than with only one child, and fewer with than without surviving brothers and sisters to be in institutions. This expectation is borne out by such data as are available. In Britain a special survey of the elderly in institutions, which was carried out shortly after the cross-national survey, revealed that 33 per cent of those in institutions were single, 26 per cent of those who were married or widowed were childless, 39 per cent of those who had children had one child only, and altogether 40 per cent had no surviving brothers or sisters. These figures compare with 10 per cent, 16 per cent, 26 per cent, and 22 per cent respectively of old persons in private households (based on the sample interviewed in Britain during the cross-national survey).

The hypothesis that the elderly institutionalized population differ significantly from the elderly home population in all major aspects of family structure is therefore confirmed in the instance of Britain. There would appear to be a marked inverse correlation between the number of close relatives (spouse, children, brothers, and sisters) and the likelihood of institutionalization in old age. When incapacity is also taken into account this correlation becomes more marked, but two further variables also seem to be important—the sex of close relatives and *their* incapacity. More people in institutions than outside who have children have sons only, and it seems that a disproportionately large number have close relatives who are in hospital or disabled or ill at home.[31]

In drawing attention to the ways in which institutions "recruit" old people selectively it should not be forgotten that family organization, as well as family structure, is important. There are many persons in institutions who have close relatives, but who, when living at home, did not see so much of them, or live so near them, as other old persons. Other major variables that need to be investigated are personality, the quality of affective relationships, and the "solidarity" of neighbor relations as well as the effectiveness of formal community organization. Social variables interrelate with physical or health variables in explaining institutionalization, and the latter remain important. There are old people in institutions who have several children as well as other relatives, but such old persons tend to be much more incapacitated than the single and the childless. This suggests that old people with children reach a more advanced stage of infirmity than the single and childless before seeking (or being granted) admission to different kinds of institutions.

When people who are receiving public and voluntary services at home are considered, broadly similar conclusions, at least for Britain, can be drawn. Supplementary inquiries show that substantially more of those receiving than not receiving home help and meals service were incapacitated, lived alone, and were childless or, if they had children, lived at some distance from them. In general, there is little evidence here of health and welfare services being "misused" or "undermining" family responsibilities. Rather, it appears that the services reach chiefly those who lack a family or have none within reach.

The Role of the Family

To show that the institutional and domiciliary health and welfare services tend to reach those who in old age lack close relatives or have none available is only a first, though an important, step in the analysis of the relationships of the family and the Welfare State. How big is the family's role? It is possible to imagine a universal disruption of the relationship between, say, the elderly and their adult children, so that the ordinary functions of furnishing care in illness and infirmity are not carried out. How much larger would the social services have to be?

The cross-national survey gives some information on the extent of family activity and the points at which the demand or need for different professional services is beginning to complicate the division of labor within the households and families of which old people are members. Community services must no longer be thought of simply as replacing the services of the family or substituting for them when they cannot exist—though this is one primary role. They must also be increasingly thought of as supplementing or complementing the services of the family. The sources of help in illness and infirmity of the persons in the sample will first be described, and we shall go on to consider the different combinations of professional and family services that are developing.

THE ROLE OF THE FAMILY IN ILLNESS

How far do old people depend for certain services on the family rather than on the Welfare State? Between a quarter and a third of the elderly in the three samples had spent time ill in bed in the year previous to their interview. The spouse and children living in the household or elsewhere were the most important sources of help with the housework at this time, as Table V–4 shows. The differences between the sexes are largely attributable to differences in the proportions who were married. The differences between the three countries are mainly but not entirely attributable to differences in household composition (and, to a lesser extent, to differences in family structure and proximity). In Denmark, for example, a smaller proportion of old people lived with one or more of their children than in the other two countries, but even when allowance is made for household composition rather fewer Danish old people received help from children. Two other conclusions can be drawn from the table. First, in all three countries substantial proportions of old people had relied during illness on help from children and other relatives, and some of them upon friends, who lived elsewhere than in the household. Second, significantly more of the old people in the United States than in Denmark and Britain said they had "no help"—12 per cent compared with 9 per cent and 7 per cent respectively. This may have been because fewer of them were ill enough to need or be offered help, but more likely, it was because they needed help but had neither family nor social services available to supply it. The figures in the table must be interpreted with care. For example, some people had multiple sources of help. And help from certain sources tended to be better and more sustained than from others.

We also asked who provided meals and did the shopping while the old people were ill in bed. The replies followed a similar pattern, except that the proportions helped by the social services were smaller. In Denmark 6 per cent and in Britain only 1.5 per cent of those who had been ill had meals supplied by the social services (defined as including public or non-profit-making organizations providing personal or household services to members of the public). Again, about a quarter of the old people relied on people living elsewhere than in the household, mainly children and other relatives. Again there were more people in the United States saying they had no help.

Table V–4: PERCENTAGE OF PERSONS ILL IN BED LAST YEAR WHO RECEIVE HELP WITH THEIR HOUSEWORK FROM DIFFERENT SOURCES

Source of Help[a]	DENMARK			BRITAIN			UNITED STATES		
	Men	Women	All	Men	Women	All	Men	Women	All
Spouse	67	24	42	59	15	31	69	18	37
Child in household	7	13	11	14	27	22	7	25	18
Child outside household	6	17	12	7	16	13	6	18	15
Others in household	3	5	4	8	10	9	4	9	7
Others outside household[b]	9	17	14	6	17	13	7	14	12
Social services	3	12	8	4	5	4	—	—	—
None	5	11	9	2	10	7	7	15	12
Total	100	100	100	100	100	100	100	100	100
Per cent ill of total sample	28	36	32	28	32	30	23	29	26
N=[c]	323	454	777	271	466	737	243	389	632

[a] This is a priority code except for Britain where multiple answers have been tabulated.

[b] Including private domestic help, as well as relatives, friends, neighbors, and others.

[c] Detailed information on non-response is not given in this or subsequent tables if 98 per cent or more of all eligible respondents have answered the question.

In Britain the numbers depending during illness on private domestic help were approximately equal to those depending on the social services. More detailed information about help from "Others" inside and outside the household also allowed the family's role to be delineated precisely. Half of those listed as receiving help from "Others" were in fact helped by relatives. Altogether 77 per cent of those who had been ill at home relied on a spouse, children, or other relatives for help with housework, 80 per cent for help with shopping, and 82 per cent for help with meals. It seems from interpolating these data that the likely figures for the United States sample are comparable, but that the figures for the Danish sample are slightly smaller.

FAMILY HELP WITH PERSONAL AFFAIRS

We have described the help available to old people in time of illness in bed. From whom do they obtain help ordinarily with personal and household affairs? A multitude of different activities might be investigated, but questions were confined to matters that frequently give difficulty to the elderly—namely, walking outdoors, going up and down stairs, getting about the house, washing, bathing, dressing, and cutting toenails—and to the source of help, when difficulty does arise. Table V–5 shows that of those persons saying they could not even with difficulty bathe themselves (or give themselves a wash-down at a sink), about or rather less than a half in Denmark and in the United States but only one in seven in Britain were able to depend on a spouse. Only a quarter of the British

Table V–5: PERCENTAGE OF PERSONS UNABLE TO BATHE THEMSELVES
EVEN WITH DIFFICULTY WHO RECEIVE HELP IN BATHING FROM
DIFFERENT SOURCES

Source of Help[a]	DENMARK	BRITAIN	UNITED STATES
Spouse	51	15	42
Child in household	15	28	18
Child outside household	8	5	13
Others in household	8	6	10
Others outside household	6	5	13
Social services	8	7	—
None	5	37	4
Total	100	102	100
Per cent of total sample	3	7	3
N=	65	166	71

[a] This is a priority code except for Britain where multiple answers have been tabulated. The number of replies in Britain is 169.

group were married, and a very large proportion (81 per cent) were women. It is of particular interest that from a tenth to a quarter of these incapacitated persons in the three countries were helped by a child, another relative, or someone else living elsewhere than in the household. Small minorities in Denmark and Britain depended on the social services.

Table V–5 also shows that over a third of those in Britain but only small minorities in the other two countries who were unable to bathe themselves said that no one helped them to bathe. Many old people strive obstinately to preserve their independence and will even pretend to their closest relatives and friends that they are able to do things for themselves which in fact are now beyond their capacities. This is particularly true of personal toilet, and relatives will even join them in a kind of conspiracy to preserve the myth of their independence.

Some of the elderly are in a transitional stage between states of independence and dependence and would rather, for some time at least, have nothing done for them—with all the disastrous consequences this implies in terms of deterioration in standards of personal and household cleanliness. So either they try to conceal from their own families the fact that their struggles with a soapy flannel do not really amount to a washdown or they grudgingly accept help without anyone being ready to call it help. Occasionally, so far as bathing is concerned, an old person is ready to be helped, but cannot accept help from the particular relatives who are available (especially if they are of the opposite sex) or would accept only professional help from outside, with the family kept out of the picture.

For the matters investigated, help from sources other than the family was in all three countries of minor importance—with one exception. A large minority said they could not cut their own toenails even with difficulty (16 per cent in Denmark, 18 per cent in Britain, and 9 per cent in the United States), and many of them depended on publicly or privately paid chiropodists rather than on relatives or friends. Table V-6 shows that in the three countries from a quarter to over a half of the old people who were unable to cut their toenails were helped by the social services or by "Others outside the household," including private chiropodists.

Table V-6: PERCENTAGE OF PERSONS UNABLE TO CARE FOR THEIR FEET EVEN WITH DIFFICULTY WHO RECEIVE HELP FROM DIFFERENT SOURCES

Source of Help[a]	DENMARK			BRITAIN			UNITED STATES		
	Men	Women	All	Men	Women	All	Men	Women	All
Spouse	67	13	34	28	8	13	68	14	32
Child in household	8	14	12	17	14	15	8	29	22
Child outside household	4	11	8	5	9	8	5	15	12
Others in household	5	2	3	4	3	3	5	7	6
Others outside household[b]	14	50	36	9	19	18	12	32	25
Private chiropodist	—	—	—	5	15	11	—	—	—
Social services	1	7	5	25	28	27	—	—	—
None	1	2	1	6	6	6	1	3	2
Total	100	100	100	100	101	101	100	100	100
Per cent of total sample	13	18	16	11	22	18	7	11	9
N=[c]	147	232	379	110	326	436	75	149	224

[a] This is a priority code except for Britain where multiple answers have been estimated. The number of replies in Britain is 441.

[b] For Denmark and the United States, "Others outside household" includes private chiropodists.

[c] The percentages of eligible respondents giving information are: Denmark, 95.7; Britain, 99.8; United States, 100.

More of those in the United States and in Denmark than in Britain who were unable to cut their toenails depended on the family for help. Chiropody organized as a public service barely exists in the United States. But an interesting question is posed when the United States figures are compared with the other figures in the table. Do they imply that the family in Denmark and Britain is beginning to surrender one of its functions *because of* the introduction of a public service? This explanation seems unlikely, and a much more complex explanation may be necessary. The proportion of old people receiving any help in the care of their feet in Britain was twice as large as in the United States, and even discounting those helped by the social services the *total* proportion helped by the family was slightly larger. Why should more people in Denmark and Britain than in the United States say they cannot care for their feet? To some extent this is almost certainly due to physical differences, particularly when we bear in mind the poorer mobility of the Danish and British samples as well as the larger proportion in Britain of extreme age. But other factors are probably at work too. We can hypothesize that, prior to the introduction of a public specialist service, standards of care tend to be lower and thresholds of recognized and acknowledged need are lower also. To put it crudely, in addition to those using a new public service who have always felt a need for help because they lack relatives or friends, or because their relatives or friends give help that is inadequate, there are those who, after its introduction, are no longer satisfied with self-management and feel the need either of the service or of help from their families for the first time. Consequently, the general volume of assistance may increase in both family and public sectors.

On the other hand, the evolution of professional skills sometimes results in society recognizing the inferiority of the "equivalent" skills as practiced by the family. Treatment from a professional doctor is preferred to patent family medicines prescribed by Aunt Jane. We are wrong to imagine that this is the *same* service being provided differently. It is an entirely different (and usually more comprehensive) service, displacing one that at best was very rough-and-ready. What seems to be true of medicine seems no less true of professional nursing and chiropody. The evolution of skilled services does not so much *displace* the functions that the family performs as refine and complement them.[32]

FAMILY HELP WITH HOUSEHOLD AFFAIRS

A few questions were also asked in the cross-national survey about household management, preparing meals, making a cup of tea or coffee, and doing light and heavy housework. The total numbers having difficulty in doing heavy housework were large: 53 per cent of the elderly in Denmark, 49 per cent in Britain, and 44 per cent in the United States. The amount of help received from the family and other sources, in comparison with that from the social services, is therefore of particular importance. Altogether at least three-fifths relied on the family in the three countries. This majority relying on the family compares with 6 per cent in Denmark and 9 per cent in Britain receiving help from the social services.[33] An important minority in all three countries, varying between 13 and 15 per cent, had no source of help—even though they did their housework with great difficulty or could not do it at all.

Table V–7: PERCENTAGE OF PERSONS HAVING DIFFICULTY IN DOING HEAVY HOUSEWORK WHO RECEIVE HELP FROM DIFFERENT SOURCES

Source of Help[a]	DENMARK			BRITAIN			UNITED STATES		
	Men	Women	All	Men	Women	All	Men	Women	All
Spouse	63	14	35	37	10	18	48	13	25
Child in household	8	13	11	19	27	25	10	24	19
Child outside household	5	10	8	8	12	11	9	14	12
Others in household	7	4	5	8	7	7	6	10	9
Others outside household[b]	10	27	20	7	12	11	19	22	21
Privately paid domestic help	—	—	—	10	12	11	—	—	—
Social services	4	8	6	9	9	9	—	—	—
None	4	24	15	6	16	13	8	17	14
Total	100	100	100	104	105	105	100	100	100
Per cent of total sample	50	56	53	39	56	49	35	52	44
N=[c]	554	705	1,259	378	822	1,200	356	687	1,043

[a] This is a priority code except for Britain where multiple answers have been tabulated. The number of replies in Britain are: men, 393; women, 867; total, 1,260.

[b] For Denmark and the United States, "Others outside household" includes privately paid domestic help.

[c] The percentages of eligible respondents giving information are: Denmark, 97.1; Britain, 98.9; United States, 96.5.

A fact worthy of note is that after allowing for privately paid domestic help, about a fifth to a third in each of the three countries depended on children, other relatives, and friends living elsewhere than at home to help them. Daughters are most commonly depended upon—as in the case of Mrs. Furneach and Mr. Frys.

Mrs. Furneach is a widow of 86 living alone in a terraced house, with a W.C. in the yard, in an eastern suburb of London. She has kidney trouble, and a district nurse calls on her each week. Her general practitioner visits about once a month, and in the previous 12 months she had a total of 63 nights in hospital. One of her married daughters lives opposite and two others live less than an hour's journey away. "My eldest girl [who is aged 65] does everything for me. She cooks for me, looks after my pension, and shops and washes for me."

Mr. Frys is a widower of 82 living alone in a Copenhagen suburb. He gave up work four years previously because of a stroke and is in poor health. He has bad vision and hearing and takes a nap every afternoon. He does most things in the house with difficulty, and a daughter living a few minutes journey distant and a neighbor help him with his housework. A son also lives fairly near but his third child, a daughter, lives a day's journey away in northern Denmark. Despite the distance, he has seen her as well as the son in the past month. He is very often alone but does not feel lonely.

Sometimes the help of relatives other than children is crucial.

Miss Thirlton is aged 75 and lives alone in a Nottinghamshire town. She has lived at the same address for sixty years. She used to be a machinist hemming scarves. She walks with great difficulty with a stick and, according to our definition, is on the borderline of moderate or severe incapacity. Although she has difficulty in dressing, she said she did not need help. She would have moved to a modern bungalow years before but for her sister, who lives a few houses along in the same road and "pops in two or three times a day" to help her with housework and shopping. Her legs are painful because of varicose veins, and her sister accompanies her regularly to the outpatients' department of a local hospital for treatment. A niece who also lives nearby visits frequently.

A minority of those having difficulty with housework pay privately for domestic help—11 per cent in Britain and probably a similar proportion in the other countries.[34] Those who are able to pay for help in the home do not regard such help as an impediment to family relationships. When individuals possess more money, bigger homes, and more possessions, there are many services that relatives can still perform for each other, even when paid help exists. But old people are usually conscious that their need for services (as well as their capacity to *give* them) is an important factor in maintaining family relations.

Mr. Shirer is aged 67 and lives with his wife in an apartment on the fifth floor of a block in a large city in Michigan. He had a job as a janitor in a telephone company and retired at the age of 58 as a result of a heart condition. He cannot get out on his own and cannot do any "heavy work" in the home but is capable of light activities—such as making a cup of coffee and washing up. His wife looks after him, except that she cannot undertake the heavy housework. They have only one child, a daughter who lives a few minutes journey away. She calls nearly every day but does not do the housework. "She visits. That's enough help. If I asked, she would do more but she doesn't have much time so I hire to have things done around the house." During the interview he said, "Our daughter and son-in-law want us around. They come to get us to go out there. . . . I like the grandchildren to come visit. . . ." He said he couldn't agree that children do not care about their parents. He pointed at a card: "See this verse on the card our daughter sent for Mother's Day. We both cried—it was so beautiful." He also has a sister he and his wife see most days. Mr. Shirer's total income, including social security benefits and an occupational pension, amounts to just under $2,500 a year.

The proportion of old people in all three countries who had difficulty in preparing a meal was smaller than the proportion who had difficulty with housework. For these latter persons, the pattern of help was even more strongly woven by the family. Fewer of the old people were dependent on private domestic help and fewer, in Denmark and Britain, upon the social services. (See Table V–8.) In Denmark only 3 per cent and in

Britain only 4 per cent of the persons saying they had difficulty in preparing meals were in fact helped by the social services. They accounted for only 17 and 12 people respectively in the two samples of 2,442 and 2,500, or 0.7 per cent and 0.5 per cent.

Table V-8: PERCENTAGE OF PERSONS HAVING DIFFICULTY IN PREPARING MEALS WHO RECEIVE HELP FROM DIFFERENT SOURCES

Source of Help[a]	DENMARK	BRITAIN
Spouse	55	39
Child in household	11	30
Child outside household	5	4
Others in household	8	11
Others outside household	8	6
Social services	3	4
None	11	11
Total	100	105
Per cent of total sample	25	11
N=	598	271

[a] This is a priority code for Denmark. In Britain 286 replies have been tabulated.

CARE OF THE BEDFAST

One of the most important functions of the family is in caring for old people not only when they happen to be ill for a short time or when they are infirm but when they are permanently bedfast. In each of the three countries about 2 per cent of the old people in the sample were bedfast. This is a very small minority but it represents more elderly persons than are in all long-stay hospitals and nursing homes. Altogether the estimated numbers of elderly bedfast living at home are: 10,000 in Denmark, 124,000 in Britain, and 350,000 in the United States. Interview records show the lengths to which some families are prepared to go to continue caring for the elderly at home.

Mrs. Silver is a woman aged 70 living with her husband, who is aged 69 and was formerly a roofer, in a city in the United States Midwest. She has had a leg amputated and is in very poor health. She had a stroke a few years ago, which paralyzed the left side of her body, suffers from diabetes, and there is now some question of amputating the foot of her remaining leg. Her husband helps her into a wheelchair, where she spends most of the day. He prepares most meals and does the shopping, though two daughters living a few minutes journey away help with the housework and washing. A nurse comes in twice a week but a doctor only rarely, when called. She is taken to see him at his office by her children every two weeks. Four of her five children live from 11 to 30 minutes journey distant. Two daughters are seen frequently in the week and the other children at least once a month. Her only son paid hospital bills amounting to more than $1,000 when her leg was amputated. Mrs. Silver said she was often lonely, and that time passed very slowly for her.

It was more common to find men being cared for at home by their wives than the reverse. One man of 70 who suffered from disseminated sclerosis and could not move any of his limbs was lifted and washed and fed by his wife. Although the general practitioner called twice a week, he was not visited by personnel from any of the home social services. There were other elderly wives who undertook a severe burden of nursing, but often they gained support from relatives and friends, who did the shopping and cleaning if not personal nursing. One man of 76 in an extreme condition of emaciation was cared for by his 80-year-old wife, but a daughter did the cleaning and a neighbor some of the shopping.

Often a widow or widower was cared for by the children.

Mrs. Pryden is a widow of 76 living in a Midlands town in England with a married daughter and son-in-law in their 40's. Until a year previous she kept house elsewhere for her two sons, but she became ill with lung cancer, had a short spell in the hospital, and stayed with another married daughter, who nursed her, for six months. She is now extremely emaciated and breathes heavily and was moved to join this daughter for the last months of her life. A district nurse and her general practitioner each pay a routine visit once a week but otherwise she receives no social services. She has three sons and four daughters and sees one of the latter, in addition to the daughter at home, every day. Three of the other children visit at least every week and the other two at least once a month. She murmured that she wanted to stay in this home but generally she thought that "there should be more homes for the old where they could have their own rooms and be looked after by experienced staff, and also hospitals for the old and bedridden who live on their own." One interesting fact about Mrs. Pryden is that she said her health was fair for her age.

Sometimes other relatives provided care.

Mrs. Hoyell is a widow of 80 years who has no children and who lives with a niece of 43 and her three children, in a Lancashire town near Manchester. She is bedfast and is very frail and thin. She has had several strokes and speaking is a great effort, because she also suffers from bronchitis. But apart from being visited occasionally by her general practitioner, she is not visited by any representatives of the social services. Her niece "does everything"—shopping, cooking, washing, bathing, and so on. A great niece visits occasionally to attend to her feet. To the interviewer the niece seemed "gentle and devoted."

Mr. Cutright is 90 years old and he lives with his widowed daughter-in-law of 63. She cooks for him and looks after him in every way in an old Victorian house which has an outside W.C. A district nurse visits once a week. Mr. Cutright has been bedfast for two or three years and, to give some relief to his daughter-in-law, he goes into a local hospital for three or four weeks every year. He is also sent to spend some weekends with two children living elsewhere.

Table V–9 gives some indication of the sources of help for the bedfast. Children living in the household were the most important source of help, and husbands or wives the next in importance. The role of children living elsewhere than in the household, particularly in Denmark and the United States, should be noted. It is, of course, difficult to measure in quantitative terms the degree and sources of help given to the bedfast, but in all three countries between 8 in 10 and 9 in 10 depended mainly on

Table V–9: PERCENTAGE OF BEDFAST PERSONS WHO RECEIVE HELP FROM DIFFERENT SOURCES (*Percentage Distribution*)

Source of Help[a]	DENMARK[b]			BRITAIN			UNITED STATES		
	Housework	Shopping	Meals	Housework	Shopping	Meals	Housework	Shopping	Meals
Spouse	[23]	[26]	[27]	17	13	19	25	24	33
Child in household	[34]	[37]	[33]	50	58	50	47	49	45
Child outside household	[16]	[12]	[16]	2	4	6	13	9	11
Relative in household	[2]	[2]	[2]	11	13	13	5	7	4
Relative outside household	[2]	[2]	[2]	—	—	—	4	2	2
Others in household	[2]	[2]	[2]	—	—	—	5	2	5
Neighbors, friends, and others, including paid domestic help	[7]	[5]	[7]	6	6	6	15	15	20
Social services	[9]	[9]	[9]	15	6	7	—	—	—
None	[5]	[5]	[2]	—	—	—	2	4	4
Total	100	100	100	100	100	100	116	111	124
N=[c]	44	43	45	54	54	54	55	55	55

[a] This is a priority code except for the United States where multiple answers have been tabulated. The number of replies in the United States are: housework, 64; shopping, 61; meals, 68.

[b] Percentages of a base of less than 50 are not normally computed in this report but have been calculated and placed in brackets here to indicate how the figures for the Danish bedfast compare with those of the bedfast of the other countries.

[c] There was no information for a further 4 bedfast in Denmark (5 in the case of shopping).

members of their families for personal and household assistance. In Britain and Denmark small minorities received help from the social services and from either neighbors and friends or paid domestic workers. In the United States a slightly larger minority depended on neighbors and friends and paid help.

The Separation of the Generations

Although the important role of the family for the bedfast as well as the infirm and the temporarily ill has been emphasized in this chapter, three qualifications must be made. They will be discussed in turn.

ISOLATION FROM FAMILIES

To begin with, a minority of old people do not have close relationships with any members of their families and are isolated from all of them. Some of the interviews in all three countries showed that the children were dispersed and saw little of the parents, even when help appeared to be needed. The questionnaires were not designed to allow separations and frictions to be explored, and the information gained in the interviews was usually insufficient to provide more than hints of an explanation for non-existent or slender relationship. Still, the divorce or separation of the parents earlier in life, the need for some men to leave homes and families in search of work, and the difficult relationship between children and stepfathers and stepmothers were among the factors that seemed to have accounted for the loosening of family ties.

Mrs. Smith is a widow aged 76 living alone in a small town in Ohio. Her husband had maintained thrashing machines on wheat farms. She is not strong enough to climb stairs or walk the shortest distances and spends her days in a wheelchair. A neighbor and one of her children help to take her about and the neighbor does her heavy housework. But she is able to prepare her own meals and even do light housework. Her eldest daughter lives some 10 to 30 minutes journey distant and last saw her just over a week beforehand; of her four other children three live more than a day's journey away and one more than an hour's drive distant. Two of them had not seen her for more than a year and the other two not during the past month. During the interview she was particularly tense when any question affecting her children was asked.

Mr. Aarhem is a widower aged 78 who lives in a small Danish town with one of his sons, who is divorced. He cannot walk even a few steps and must stay in bed or in a chair. He also has poor sight and hearing, yet has no hearing aid, never sees a nurse, and sees a doctor only when one is sent for. He has four other children, all of whom live within one hour's journey, but he has not seen three of them in the past twelve months.

Second, both family help and social service help are received by some persons.

Mrs. Mylhøj is a widow of 73 living alone in a modern flatlet in Copenhagen. Her husband had been an army captain. She broke a leg not long ago and this has not healed completely. Her sight is poor. She is unsteady on her legs, and although she can walk about indoors cannot venture outside on her own. She has only one child, a married daughter who lives a day's journey distant, but who visits her often and who performs various small services for her. Other relatives also come during the month. She gets up in the morning at 9 A.M. and goes to bed at 9 P.M. The municipal home-help services for pensioners assist her two or three times a week. She often feels lonely and plans to move to a home for the aged.

There would have to be much more detailed investigation of the circumstances of people like Mrs. Mylhøj to find out whether the introduction of a welfare service had led to the *withdrawal* of family help without some compensating increase elsewhere in intra-family exchange (for example, the married daughter being "freed" to give more services, say, to a mother-in-law), or had contributed to a loosening of relationships between the generations and a diminution in strength of affections. What we can say, therefore, on the basis of a survey approach, is limited. But we have already observed that many beneficiaries lack a spouse or children, or brothers or sisters, and now we can observe that many have only one child or one other close relative to depend upon. The welfare services fill some of the gaps in the unskilled or semi-skilled services that are already available. Thus, even when relatives are living at home it may be justified to provide welfare services. For example, a son or husband may be at work in the day and be unable to get meals.

Mrs. Canley, aged 73, has been separated from her husband for many years. She lives in the West Riding with her only child, a bachelor son of 53. He goes to work on weekdays from 8 until 5. She is bedfast. "I feel very useless now. I can't do anything for myself. I had a stroke and my back is paralyzed. I've had a few heart attacks since then, so I'm no good for anything. I can't do anything at all but just lie here. They are long days and I don't like being dependent on other people." A Council home-help calls each day, and meals are delivered by the Women's Voluntary Service on two days of the week. A district nurse also calls each day and a general practitioner about once a month. Mrs. Canley's son pays all household expenses. As he has to be away so much, she feels the need for company. She used to work in a textile factory and later in a school canteen. "I think people visiting would be nice. It's lonely when you are bedfast. They should come and see how you're getting on."

Among the three samples there were many other instances of relatives living at home who were not themselves able to do all that might be needed. There were husbands or wives who were infirm, a sister who was mentally subnormal, a daughter who was a spastic, and even a number of daughters and sons who were themselves of pensionable age. Much the same was true of relatives living near old people who lived alone. There were many relatives who saw old people frequently and gave some and even considerable help and yet who needed supporting help from the social services.

Mrs. Pennyhall is a widow of 75 living alone in a Victorian house in an East Anglian town. She rarely goes out of doors and has not done so for three months during the winter. She had a severe stroke two years ago and for three months went to live with her married daughter, who lives eight minutes walk away.

One of her hands was badly affected by the stroke and now she finds it difficult to wash and dress. Her daughter calls on her twice every day, first to do the shopping and get the coal up before going to work in a local factory, and then between shifts. A district nurse comes once a week and among other things washes Mrs. Pennyhall's feet and cuts her toenails. Meals (which cost ten-pence) are delivered by the Women's Voluntary Service mobile meals service on Tuesdays and Thursdays. She would like to have them more often. Her daughter and a neighbor do the heavy cleaning between them. She receives £1 2s. supplementary national assistance per week and during the winter an additional 5 shillings per week for extra fuel. "My roots are here. If you took me away, I'd be lost."

The examples given suggest some of the ways in which—at least in Denmark and Britain—the Welfare State provides supports for the family and by so doing enables an old person who might otherwise have to enter a residential institution or hospital to go on living at home.

Third, despite the social services substituting for, or complementing, the role of the family in caring for the elderly, the conjunction is not perfect. In all three countries a strong case can be made that new and additional needs and the emergence of national standards of care have outstripped the introduction and expansion of services. There are sub-stantial numbers of old people who are not getting adequate care—by any standards one wishes to apply.

With the benefits of hindsight it would be easy to explain why the intro-duction or expansion of welfare services was justified at a particular time in the history of Denmark, Britain, and the United States, and why some needs that are fully acknowledged by our contemporaries were overlooked by previous generations. Such an interpretation must apply to present services when viewed by future historians. Industrial society is continually evolving, creating new needs and allowing long-standing ones to be more widely recognized, if not fully met. The increasing specialization and social restructuring that is taking place involves the welfare services as much as other social institutions. Having shown that some of the principal welfare services for the aged tend to serve the more isolated sections of the population and therefore complement, rather than compete with or replace, the functions of the family, we need to consider whether there is evidence for further expansion of existing services or for the introduction of new services.

Are some existing services fully developed, or should they grow many times over? It would be difficult, of course, to give a completely reliable answer to this question. The concept of "need" is complex and can be measured in many different ways. Moreover, the cross-national survey was planned to illuminate a very wide area of gerontology and our data on individual services are extremely limited. The services in the three countries vary, and though the research teams added special national questions to the questionnaire the answers are not easy to compare.

Home-Help Services in Denmark and Britain

One approach to the question of need is to find how many people are receiving a particular service, how many would like to have it, and how many appear to qualify for such services. The social and physical characteristics of these three groups could then be compared with the rest of the elderly population. In the British survey those saying they did not have anyone coming in to help with the housework were asked if they needed someone to help them. Nearly 6 per cent said they did, compared with 4 per cent who were already receiving help from the local councils. Of these 6 per cent, three-quarters said at another point in the interview that they had difficulty in doing heavy housework or could not do it all, and a third claimed they had no one to help them at the present time. The majority were moderately or severely incapacitated, over a third were childless, and nearly a third were living alone. In each of these respects they were significantly different from others in the sample who were not receiving help—though they broadly resembled those already getting help.

In the Danish survey 3.6 per cent were found to depend on municipal home help—and again these persons tended to be much more infirm and isolated than others in the elderly population. Information about the numbers of persons feeling the need for help was not obtained in Denmark but data secured by the Danish National Institute of Social Research in 1960 are relevant here. In a study of social isolation among unmarried, widowed, and divorced persons of 67 years of age and over in a low income area of Copenhagen, nearly 500 persons were interviewed, of whom 6 per cent said they were served by municipal home-helps but another 5 per cent felt the need for the service. Other small minorities expressed the wish for other aid, such as friendly visiting and home nursing.[35]

For both Britain and Denmark, therefore, there is prima facie evidence for substantial expansion of the home-help services. Even if some of those saying they feel the need for help do not qualify for it, there is reason for assuming that some other old people who say they do not need help have serious difficulties and ought to be offered it. In the British survey there were a further 5 per cent who could not undertake heavy housework, or could do so only with difficulty, and who said they had no help at all—whether from relatives, friends, Council, or paid domestics. Yet they also said they did not need anyone to help. It is more than likely that some of them, and perhaps others who have insufficient help from family or friends, would qualify for assistance from local councils, if such assistance were offered and if they could be persuaded to accept it. Scrutiny of our interview schedules suggested that many old people were reluctant to admit the need for help. Some were old women who stubbornly tried to discount or overcome infirmity. Some were men who appeared to need help even though they remained active.

Mr. Hood is a widower of 76 who lives alone in a terraced house in a Lancashire cotton town. The front door opens directly into the living room. The grate is full of ash and bits of paper and there is dust everywhere, covering the rickety furniture, ancient radios, old pipes, and odd bits of clothing. The kitchen is an improvised outhouse. The windows are thick with grime and one, which is broken, is boarded up. Mr. Hood is extraordinarily agile and showed the interviewer how he can touch his feet with his palms, keeping his legs straight. He goes for long walks and swims once a week. He has had three wives, from two of whom he separated, and this may partly account for his poor relations with two sons and two daughters born from the three marriages. One of the children is in London but he sees little of the three who live in Oldham. "They were most attached to their mothers." He is frightened only of going into hospital and losing his home. He does not want meals or home-help services. "I'd rather do it myself." But plainly the housework isn't done.

This example suggests something of the diversity of the problems experienced by old people and the diversity of their resources for overcoming their problems. The examples also suggest how difficult it may sometimes be to determine eligibility for help. But any estimate of unmet need made on the basis of the expressed desire for help on the part of old people, in the final analysis, is likely to be much too low. In Britain the home-help service tends to be thinly spread, in the sense that many people receive only two or three hours help a week, and an expansion of the service could be justified for those already receiving it.

THE MOBILE MEALS SERVICE IN BRITAIN

A second example might be given from the British survey. Just over one per cent of the old people, many of whom were incapacitated and lived alone, received a cooked meal at least once a week from the mobile meals services. Another 6 per cent said they would like to have meals delivered in this way; again, when compared with the remainder of the elderly population, significantly more of these respondents were severely incapacitated, living alone, and childless or, if they had children, were separated from those they had. Another one per cent denied they wanted meals delivered to their homes but said they had difficulty in preparing meals and had no one to help them. Again there was evidence for an expansion of service, which detailed investigations had already indicated.[36]

The Development of Community Services

Table V–10 gives some indication for the three countries not only of the percentages and estimated numbers of old people who have difficulty in carrying out certain personal or household tasks, but also the percentages and estimated numbers of those who have such difficulty *and* have no one to help them. For the three countries these and other estimates certainly suggest that home-help services need to be developed for a substantial minority (say one in 10 or more than one in 10) of the population aged 65 and over, and various other community services for smaller (but still significant) minorities. For example, 8 per cent of the total sample in Denmark and 6 in Britain and in the United States had difficulty in doing

Table V–10: PERCENTAGE OF PERSONS HAVING DIFFICULTY WITH SELECTED PERSONAL AND HOUSEHOLD TASKS AND HAVING NO ONE TO HELP OR RECEIVE SOCIAL SERVICES

Personal or Household Task	Total Sample Completely Unable To Do Task (%)			Number in the Population (1,000's)[a]			Total Sample Completely Unable To Do Task or Having Difficulty (%)			Number in the Population (1,000's)[a]		
	Denmark	Britain	United States	Denmark	Britain	United States	Denmark	Britain	United States	Denmark	Britain	United States
Wash and bathe	3	7	3	12,5	390,3	467,9	9	15	10	40,7	856,3	1,559,7
Dress	3	3	2	14,7	145,6	311,9	12	10	8	54,4	594,2	1,247,8
Cut toenails	16	18	9	70,6	1,031,0	1,434,9	28	33	19	126,8	1,933,9	2,964,5
Prepare cup of coffee	5	2	3	24,4	110,7	467,9	13	4	7	58,4	209,7	1,091,4
Prepare meal	16	6	6	73,0	372,8	935,8	27	11	11	122,2	652,4	1,715,6
Light housework	9	3	5	42,3	180,6	779,8	22	7	12	99,6	407,8	1,871,8
Heavy housework	34	34	32	154,9	1,986,3	4,991,0	53	49	44	241,8	2,860,1	6,925,2

Personal or Household Task	Total Sample with Difficulty or Unable To Do Task and Receiving Social Service (%)		Number in the Population (1,000's)[a]		Total Sample Unable To Do Task or Having Difficulty and with No Help (%)			Number in the Population (1,000's)[a]		
	Denmark	Britain	Denmark	Britain	Denmark	Britain	United States	Denmark	Britain	United States
Cut toenails	0.7	4.8	3,4	278,4	0.2	1.1	0.2	1,0	63,5	31,2
Heavy housework	3.3	4.4	14,9	256,3	7.7	6.3	6.0	35,0	365,8	934,3
Help in illness at some period of year										
(i) Meals	2.0	0.4	9,1	26,2	2.8	1.9	2.8	12,7	111,3	430,5
(ii) Housework	2.6	1.3	11,8	78,1	2.8	2.1	3.1	12,5	123,5	482,0

[a] The total population in private households—i.e., total population minus estimated long-stay institutional population—were: Denmark, 452,800; Britain, 5,825,000; United States, 15,597,200. For Britain the total also excludes the boardinghouse population. Population estimates are based on actual rather than rounded percentages.

heavy housework or could not do it at all and had no help. These proportions are broadly similar. In Denmark 3 per cent and in Britain 4 per cent of the total samples had such difficulty *and* were receiving help from the social services. There was also evidence that around 2 or 3 per cent of the elderly need help with meals and housework at some point during the year because they become ill and have no one to depend upon. These preliminary data require to be elaborated in further research. In all three countries, but particularly in the United States, it would seem that there is considerable scope for expansion of services.

Summary

This chapter has sought to relate data collected during the cross-national survey of old people to the theme of the growth of the Welfare State. Its most important theoretical conclusion is that the health and welfare services for the aged, as presently developing, are a necessary concomitant of social organization, and therefore, possibly, of economic growth. The services do not undermine self-help, because they are concentrated overwhelmingly among those who have neither the capacities nor the resources to undertake the relevant functions alone. Nor, broadly, do the services conflict with the interests of the family as a social institution, because either they tend to reach people who lack a family or whose family resources are slender, or they provide specialized services the family is not equipped or qualified to undertake.

But this review of the extent to which the health and welfare services complement the family in its role of caring for the frail aged also reveals certain inefficiencies and shortcomings in the public provisions of all three countries. Each national pattern of services has particular strengths but each has to be greatly elaborated and developed in order to meet the needs of the frail and isolated aged.

NOTES

1 Charles Booth, *Pauperism: A Picture; and the Endowment of Old Age: An Argument* (London: Macmillan, 1892); *The Aged Poor: Condition* (London: Macmillan, 1894); and *Old Age Pensions and the Aged Poor* (London: Macmillan, 1899).
2 Social Security Board, *Social Security in America:* The factual background of the Social Security Act as summarized from Staff Reports, published for the Committee on Economic Security (Washington, D.C.: U.S. GPO, 1937), p. 159.
3 H. C. Burdett, *Hospitals and Asylums of the World* (London: Churchill, 1893), III, 448–457, 662.
4 "Alderdomshjemmene Og Deres Beboere," *Socialt Tidsskrift*, XXXIII (1957), Nos. 4–5, 81–96.
5 *Social Welfare Statistics of the Northern Countries, 1960 (1960/61)* (Stockholm: Nordisk Statistisk Skriftserie, 1964), p. 109.
6 These are the latest figures given in *Social Welfare Statistics of the Northern Countries, 1960 (1960/61), op. cit.,* p. 135. Figures for home helps in 1954 from *Samordnad Nordisk Statistik Rorande Sociallagstiftningen*, No. 4 (Stockholm, 1964), p. 109.

7 Data for 1960–61 from *Social Welfare Statistics of the Northern Countries, 1960 (1960/61)*, *op. cit.*, pp. 135–136, for 1962, from *Statistiske Eftervetninger*, No. 40 (Copenhagen: Statens Trykningskontor, 1963).

8 Data for 1960 from *Social Welfare Statistics for the Northern Countries, 1960 (1960/61)*, *op. cit.*, p. 62. In 1956, 1,275 of the 14,671 nurses in Denmark were home nurses. *Samordnad Nordisk Statistik Rorande Sociallagstiftningen*, No. 4, *op. cit.*

9 *Report from His Majesty's Commissioners for Inquiring into the Administration and Practical Operation of the Poor Laws* (London: Fellowes, 1834), p. 303.

10 Peter Townsend, *The Last Refuge: A Survey of Residential Institutions and Homes for the Aged in England and Wales* (London: Routledge & Kegan Paul, 1962), pp. 24–25.

11 Brian Abel-Smith, *The Hospital 1800–1948* (London: Heinemann, 1964).

12 Peter Townsend, *The Last Refuge*, *op. cit.*, pp. 41, 516.

13 Rt. Hon. Derek Walker-Smith, Minister of Health, in the *Report of the Ninth Conference of the National Old People's Welfare Council* (London: National Old People's Welfare Council, 1958).

14 *Report of the Ministry of Health for the Year ending 31st December, 1962*, Cmnd. 2062 (London: HMSO, 1963).

15 Ministry of Health, *Health and Welfare: The Development of Community Care* (London: HMSO, 1963).

16 *Health and Welfare: The Development of Community Care*, *op. cit.*

17 *Social Security in America*, *op. cit.*, pp. 156–157. A careful statement of the earlier development of the almshouse in one state is to be found in David M. Schneider, *The History of Public Welfare in New York State, 1609–1866* (Chicago: University of Chicago Press, 1938).

18 *Social Security in America*, *op. cit.*, p. 158.

19 Wilbur J. Cohen, *Retirement Policies under Social Security* (Berkeley and Los Angeles: University of California Press, 1957), p. 2.

20 Maud Morlock, *Homemaker Services: History and Bibliography* (Washington, D.C.: U.S. GPO, 1964), p. 1.

21 *Directory of Homemaker Services, 1963*, Public Health Service Publication, No. 928 (Washington, D.C.: U.S. GPO, 1964), Table 5.

22 "Recommendations of the Commission on Chronic Illness on the Care of the Long-Term Patient," in *Studies of the Aged and Aging*, II, Health and Health Services (Washington, D.C.: U.S. GPO, November, 1956), 78. Italics the author's.

23 In her national survey Miss Shanas found that only 24 per cent of persons aged 65 and over said that there was a visiting nurse service in their area (45 per cent said there was not; 31 per cent were uncertain). Ethel Shanas, *The Health of Older People* (Cambridge, Mass.: Harvard University Press, 1962), p. 15.

24 Clark Tibbitts, "Developments in Gerontology over the Past Ten Years," in Ruth E. Albrecht, *Aging in a Changing Society* (Gainesville, Fla.: University of Florida Press, 1962), p. 23.

25 The consequences have been described in a number of research studies. For example, one of the major findings of a study of old people entering the psychiatric wards of a general hospital was that there were virtually no community services that they, or their relatives and friends, could call on for an alternative way of solving their problems. Marjorie Fiske Lowenthal, *Lives in Distress: The Paths of the Elderly to the Psychiatric Ward* (New York: Basic Books, Inc., 1964).

26 Clark Tibbitts, *op. cit.*, p. 16.

27 The Council of State Governments, *The States and their Older Citizens* (Chicago: The Council, 1955).

28 For example, see *Report of the Ministry of Health for the Year ending 31st December, 1962*, *op. cit.* One survey in the United States found that during the four preceding weeks only 0.5 per cent of the elderly sample (an estimated 800,000 persons) reported receiving nursing care at home from a hired nurse or a public health nurse. E. Shanas, *op. cit.*, p. 15.

29 See, for example, M. F. Lowenthal, *op. cit.*; E. Shanas, *op. cit.*; Ian M. Richardson, *Age and Need: A Study of Older People in East Scotland* (Edinburgh: Livingstone, 1964); and Peter Townsend and Dorothy Wedderburn, *The Aged in the Welfare State* (London: Bell, 1965).

30 See, for example, P. Townsend, *The Last Refuge, op. cit.*
31 Peter Townsend, "The Effects of Family Structure on the Likelihood of Admission to an Institution in Old Age: The Application of a General Theory," in Ethel Shanas and Gordon F. Streib, eds., *Social Structure and the Family: Generational Relationships* (Englewood Cliffs, N.J.: Prentice-Hall, Inc., 1965).
32 "Displacing" may be the wrong term. Aunt Jane may continue to offer her remedies for minor ailments. Otherwise it would be difficult to explain the huge volume of self-medication and the big expansion in private pharmaceutical sales even in countries with major public health services. See Richard M. Titmuss, "Sociological and Ethnic Aspects of Therapeutics," in *Drugs in Our Society* (Baltimore, Md.: The Johns Hopkins Press, 1964).
33 In Britain 54 per cent relied on a spouse or upon a child, whether living in the same household or elsewhere, and another 8 per cent on other relatives, making a total of 62 per cent.
34 The figures for Denmark and the United States are thought to be roughly the same but have been included in the category "Others outside the household."
35 Henning Friis and E. Manniche, *Enlige Aeldre*, Socialforskningsinstituttets Publikationer, No. 7 (Copenhagen: Socialforsknings instituttet, 1961), p. 36.
36 See Amelia J. Harris, *Meals on Wheels for Old People* (London: The Government Social Survey, for the National Corporation for the Care of Old People, 1961).

6 : *The Structure of the Family*

Individual aging takes place within the context of the social structure. Its process and its problems can be understood only in relation to that structure, and differences in the experience of aging in different societies can be explained primarily by systematic delineation of the structural differences between those societies. At each stage of the life cycle the individual belongs to certain social sub-groups and associations. He has relationships with members of the family, neighbors, and friends or colleagues at school or at work—whether these relationships are of the type individual-with-individual or of the type individual-with-group. He performs a variety of roles as child, schoolchild, apprentice, employee, craftsman, husband or wife, breadwinner, parent, grandparent, pensioner, patient, and so on. He commands certain resources and benefits according to the over-all distribution of such resources and benefits among the different strata, sub-groups, and individuals of society. And, briefly, he holds certain standards of conduct and value which reflect his relationships, roles, and command over resources and which interrelate with the complex of norms and values governing social organization and action. During the later as much as during the earlier stages of the life cycle, his experiences, activities, and even his attitudes will be shaped by the social structure of which he finds himself part.

Theoretically two forms of aging must be distinguished: aging when the social structure remains constant, and aging when it changes over time. When the social structure remains constant the individual is conditioned at earlier stages of the life cycle to *anticipate* relationships and roles that he will have at later stages, and in old age his activities and attitudes are governed not only by the current complex of relations and roles in which he finds himself placed, but also by the performance of his successors in the roles he himself formerly occupied. When, on the other hand, the social structure changes rapidly, the individual has to modify his picture of his future relationships and roles and he is unlikely to be able to anticipate them so clearly; furthermore, in old age he can remember his own past relationships and roles but he cannot easily compare them with the experiences and activities of his successors.

This general theme of structural change versus structural stability runs through much of the literature on aging.[1] The problem of older men whose skills become redundant and of older men and women who are typified as "out-of-date" and "old-fashioned" are familiar topics in Western society. But the theme of the diversity of the socio-structural situation during the individual life cycle has not been discussed so fully. The extent to which any society can be typified as "stable" from the viewpoint of the individual may have been exaggerated. Even in stable societies sons proceed through different socio-structural situations from those experienced by their fathers. They may grow up in a different birth-order in the sibling group, enter a different job, marry at a different age, and marry someone from a different type of family, have a different number of children and so on. Demographic studies have revealed many important features of population structure but they have not linked up in the way that they might with anthropological studies of kinship systems and communities or with socio-psychological studies of socialization. This chapter contends that the different ways in which the individual is knitted into the social structure have to be delineated more precisely than they have been in the past if good explanatory theories of individual life processes (such as socialization, adjustment, and retirement) and of social deviance (such as delinquency, isolation, and divorce) are to be developed. The argument uses some differentiating variables—such as sex, age, marital status, and number of children—that are commonly used in sociology. But it also goes on to elaborate or suggest others that seem to be important—the composition of "families" of children and sibling-groups according to sex and age, and generational as well as marital and age differences.

In general it is hypothesized that many aspects of an individual's behavior in non-familial as well as familial society are affected by the composition, structure, and organization of the nuclear or immediate and extended families to which he belongs. For example, the character and the quality of the relationship between husband and wife, or between parent and child, will tend to differ according to the number, sex, marital status, and age distribution of the other members of the immediate or extended family. After describing the various ways in which families can be structured, the chapter will go on to describe the family structure of old people in the three countries and try to account for any differences found between them. It will show the effects of differences in family structure on social organization and social action and conclude by showing what implications there are for both theories of aging and theories of changes in family life. The underlying assumption is that the individual old person's place in the family structure is far more important than many theorists have supposed.[2]

Definitions and Principles of Analysis

In theory, the relationships by blood and through marriage that might be traced for any individual are capable of infinite extension. Consanguineous relationships among large sections of a population might be shown to exist, providing descent is traced through several previous generations. But for most practical purposes the "kinship network" can be defined as the aggregate of surviving kin recognized by an individual or by the other members of the nuclear or immediate and extended families to which he belongs. Figure VI–1 shows the initial and some of the alternative stages in the structural development of a kinship network. First of all, single or widowed persons and married couples (A, B, and C) may be found living independently in households of their own but they cannot be treated as families. Many social and psychological studies have analyzed individual characteristics according to marital status but they have rarely gone on to suggest that differences in the results are attributable more to other, consequential, characteristics of family structure than to marital status as such. Marital status is merely a very crude, and perhaps a rather inadequate, indication of family status or structure.

Second, Figure VI–1 also shows some of the forms that the immediate or nuclear family might take (D, E, and F). The immediate family can be defined as one parent or both parents living with their single children in a household. Any two of its members stand in one of the following eight possible relationships to each other: wife/husband; mother/single son; mother/single daughter; father/single son; father/single daughter; single brother/single brother; single brother/single sister; and single sister/single sister. While the children are young this family can be considered to be a "nuclear" family in the sense that it is a nucleus out of which new families can be

Figure VI–1: ELEMENTARY DIFFERENTIATION OF FAMILY STRUCTURE (TYPES OF HOUSEHOLD)

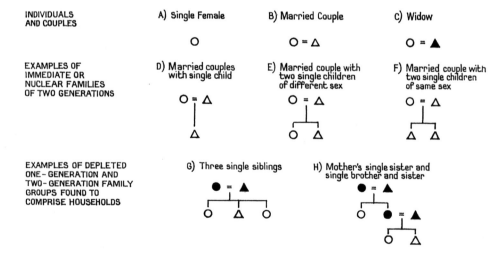

created. But not all the children may marry and set up their own households externally. An elderly couple might be found living with two middle-aged single daughters, or an elderly widow with a single middle-aged son. The term "nuclear" family is not therefore appropriate for every instance of a household containing parent(s) and single children. The term "immediate" is preferred. The family may be an "adult" immediate family or an immediate family of parents and young children. It may also be "depleted" in the sense that some of its original members may have died or have left to marry and start their own families. These terms would appear to be particularly useful in analyzing the family groups to which the elderly belong. Figure VI–1 (G) shows one type of depleted adult immediate family—that of three single siblings. Figure VI–1 (H) also shows one example of a depleted family group of two generations which is sometimes found living as a household.

The network of kin therefore builds up in a variety of ways. Independent of living arrangements and organization, the structure of the network will depend on the numbers, sex, and marital status of an individual's siblings, children, parental and grandparental siblings, and parental siblings' children, and so on; but also on the numbers, sex, and marital status of the relatives of successive generations of affinal kinsmen. The structure kept in being at any single time will be determined by mortality, birth, and marriage rates as they operate selectively. The kinship network is not dispersed uniformly throughout the territory occupied by a society. Some kin within the network form "groups" for certain purposes—whether as households (which are usually immediate families, including denuded and adult immediate families) or as "extended" families. Figure VI–2 gives an illustration of typical organization of a kinship network into different households and wider family groups.

The extended family may be defined as a group of relatives, usually larger in number than the immediate or nuclear family, and generally ranging from three to twenty or more persons, who include at least two individuals standing in a relationship different from that of any two

Figure VI–2: ORGANIZATION OF PART OF A KINSHIP NETWORK INTO TWO
EXTENDED FAMILIES (INCORPORATING IMMEDIATE FAMILIES AND A
MARRIED COUPLE HOUSEHOLD) AND ONE IMMEDIATE FAMILY

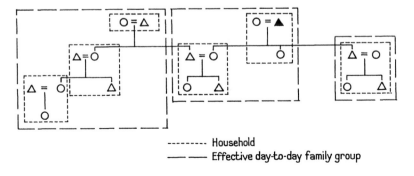

--------- Household
———— Effective day-to-day family group

members of the immediate family, and who share common domestic, social, and economic activities throughout each week. Usually, but not necessarily, the family lives in one household or two or more households in a single locality and usually, but again not necessarily, it consists of three (or four) generations of relatives—grandparents (and great-grand-parents), one or more of the married children (together with children-in-law), and grandchildren. Some extended families, however, may comprise the immediate or nuclear families of two married siblings, for example, when making up more than one household. Like the immediate family occupying a single household, this group of kin serves specific psychological and social functions.[3] Otherwise it would not exist.

Two further aspects of family structure are important and have received too little attention. Within the family the character and quality of individuals' relationships with one another are affected by the difference in their ages and whether they belong to the same or to a different generation. Age differences between siblings, husbands and wives, parents and children, and grandparents and grandchildren can be relatively large or relatively small and can change within one society over long periods of time. One of the most important changes in Western societies during the twentieth century has been in generation structure. Earlier marriage and childbirth, together with smaller families, have contributed to a narrowing of the span in years between the parental and younger generations. The increasing expectation of life, particularly for older women, has also increased the individual's expectation of having a grandparent alive for a considerable part of his lifetime. Figure VI-3 suggests the typical change

Figure VI-3: ILLUSTRATION OF AGE DIFFERENCES BETWEEN SURVIVING RELATIVES ALONG DIRECT LINES OF DESCENT EARLY AND LATE IN THE TWENTIETH CENTURY (BRITAIN)

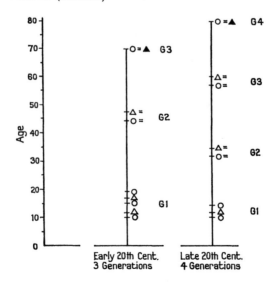

in generation structure that is taking place within the families of individuals in Britain, Denmark, and the United States. Young persons in their teens are increasingly likely to have a surviving great-grandparent and two, or possibly more, surviving grandparents. Some of the implications for future generations as well as for the present generation of old people are discussed below.

The cross-national study was designed to obtain a fairly large body of data on family structure and relationships. Information was collected not only about the marital status, birth-order, whereabouts of and last contact with each child, but also, though more generally, about siblings, grandchildren, and other relatives. Some additional information on matters such as age differences was collected in Britain. The reader should treat what follows as a first attempt cross-nationally to indicate the importance of the analysis of family structure not only to the understanding of the processes of aging but also to the understanding of human growth and development and of social relationships throughout life.

The distribution by marital status of an elderly population is a function of the interplay of different factors; the mortality rates of successive cohorts during different periods of the life-span, marriage and remarriage rates, and the difference in age at marriage between husbands and wives. In Denmark, Britain, and the United States around two-fifths of the population aged 65 and over are widowed, separated, or divorced, as Table VI-1 shows. This fraction has decreased slightly during the last sixty years,[4] but it is nevertheless likely to increase slightly during the rest of the century—for two main reasons. An increasing proportion of the population of this age are aged 75 and over, and relatively more of those over 75 are widowed. Moreover, the proportion of persons aged 75 and over who are widowed is tending to increase because the mortality rates for women aged 75 and over are being reduced more quickly than for men.

Table VI-1: PERCENTAGE OF MEN AND WOMEN, BY MARITAL STATUS[a]
(*Percentage Distribution*)

Marital Status	DENMARK			BRITAIN			UNITED STATES		
	Men	Women	All	Men	Women	All	Men	Women	All
Single	4	10	8	5	14	10	3	6	5
Married	70	42	55	70	34	48	76	38	55
Widowed	24	45	35	25	51	41	17	52	37
Divorced or separated[b]	2	3	2	1	1	1	4	4	4
Total	100	100	100	100	100	100	100	100	100
N=	1,140	1,300	2,440	1,004	1,496	2,500	1,081	1,361	2,442

[a] Detailed information on non-response is not given in this or subsequent tables if 98 per cent or more of eligible respondents have provided information.

[b] Figures for Britain refer to separated only. The divorced (approximately 0.3 per cent) were included with the widowed.

The figures in Table VI–1 differ slightly from those listed in the latest census reports for the three countries but they do show reliably the main differences between the three populations.[5] Britain has the largest proportion of persons aged 65 and over who are single. In the cross-national survey 10 per cent were single, compared with 8 per cent in Denmark and 5 per cent in the United States. As many as 14 per cent of the women were single. The large number of deaths of British males in the 1914–18 war is not, however, the "cause" of the relative excess of spinsters among the British elderly population. The relatively unfavorable ratio of male to female mortality over a long period seems to have been more important, as Figure VI–4 suggests. An increase in the proportions of young women remaining single can be traced to the 1880's and 1890's.[6]

Figure VI–4: EXPECTATION OF LIFE AT THE AGE OF 65

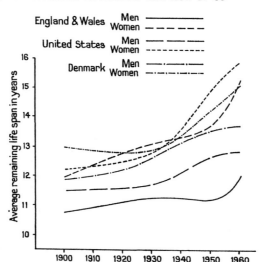

In Denmark the proportion of women who are widowed is relatively small (45 per cent) compared with the United States (52 per cent) and Britain (51 per cent). This is because the excess mortality of older men over older women is not as great in Denmark as in the other two countries —a fact that helps to explain the different ratios of married men to married women and of widowers to widows. But again it should be emphasized that the marital status distribution among a population is determined by many factors, such as the relative mortality at different ages of males and females, and the relative age differences between husbands and wives.

Old people who have no children are more likely to find difficulty in meeting the problems of infirmity and illness. A higher proportion of the aged in Britain than in Denmark and the United States are childless; Table VI–2 shows that in the 1962 survey 23 per cent were without children, compared with 18 per cent in Denmark and in the United

States. This higher proportion can be explained chiefly by the relatively larger number of single persons in Britain, but also by the relatively larger number of the married and widowed in that country having no surviving children. It is not possible to say how many of the childless in all three countries had lost children, but in Britain 3 per cent of those who were married or widowed now had no surviving children whereas another 12 per cent had never had children.

Between three-quarters and four-fifths of the old people in the three countries possessed surviving children. Among the British elderly were found the highest proportion of childless persons, the highest proportion of persons who had only one or two children, and the smallest proportion of persons with large families. This is perhaps one of the most surprising features of the results and reflects the fact that the married population which brought about the decline in family size in the first three decades of this century are now mostly of pensionable age.[7] Large families were

Table VI–2: PERCENTAGE OF MEN AND WOMEN WITH AND WITHOUT SURVIVING CHILDREN (*Percentage Distribution*)

Surviving Children and Marital Status of Respondent	DENMARK			BRITAIN			UNITED STATES		
	Men	Women	All	Men	Women	All	Men	Women	All
None									
Single	4	10	8	5	14	10	3	6	5
Married or widowed	12	9	10	15	12	13	14	12	13
At least one	84	81	82	80	74	76	83	82	82
Total	100	100	100	100	100	100	100	100	100
N=	1,144	1,301	2,445	1,004	1,496	2,500	1,081	1,361	2,442

found most frequently in the United States, though it should be emphasized that in all three countries over two-fifths (and in Britain over a half) of those with children had only one or two. Slightly more of the women than of the men had six or more children. This was principally because the women were older and therefore belonged to cohorts who had had larger families. But with this exception, the distribution of different numbers of children among men and women was practically the same. The mean number of surviving children of old people in each of the countries was about three.

Families consisting of children of the same sex are commoner than is generally realized. Nearly 10 per cent of old people in all three countries had two or more sons but no daughters. In Britain 10 per cent had two or more daughters but no sons; it would seem reasonable to deduce that this percentage is approximately 10 in the United States and in Denmark as well. Altogether there appear to be nearly as many families consisting of two or more children of the same sex as there are families consisting of an only child, as Table VI–4 shows. It is hypothesized that the living

Table VI–3: PERCENTAGE OF PERSONS WITH SURVIVING CHILDREN, BY NUMBER OF CHILDREN (*Percentage Distribution*)

Number of Surviving Children	DENMARK		BRITAIN		UNITED STATES	
1	24		25		20	
2	25		26		23	
3	18		18			
4	12	37	9	35		38
5	7		8			
6	6		6			
7	2		3			
8	2	14	2	13		19
9 or more	4		2			
Total	100		100		100	
N=	2,010		1,911		2,011	

arrangements, social relationships, and social security of old people may be dependent not only on the number of their children but also on whether their children are all sons, all daughters, or include both sons and daughters.

Although most old people have children who are married or widowed, a few have children all of whom are too young to be married or who have remained single. Table VI–5 shows that in the 1962 survey from 3 to 6 per cent of persons with children in the three countries did not have any child who was married or widowed. The numbers having a married or widowed daughter ranged from 71 to 79 per cent; and the numbers having a married or widowed son ranged from 70 to 74 per cent. In the United States and Britain relatively more had married or widowed daughters than married or widowed sons.[8] In Denmark, on the other hand, the propor-

Table VI–4: PERCENTAGE OF MEN AND WOMEN BY SEX OF THEIR CHILDREN (*Percentage Distribution*)

Type of Family	DENMARK			BRITAIN			UNITED STATES		
	Men	Women	All	Men	Women	All	Men	Women	All
One son only	12	12	12	12	11	12	8	8	8
One daughter only	11	12	11	14	13	14	12	12	12
Two or more sons	10	10	10	9	10	9	8	10	9
Two or more daughters	67	66	67	12	9	10	71	70	70
Children of both sexes				53	56	55			
Total	100	100	100	100	100	100	100	100	100
N=	959	1,043	2,002	807	1,104	1,911	900	1,111	2,011

Table VI-5: PERCENTAGE OF PERSONS HAVING CHILDREN, WHOSE
CHILDREN WERE MARRIED OR WIDOWED

Persons with Children	DENMARK	BRITAIN	UNITED STATES
With a married or widowed daughter (%)	71	72	79
With a married or widowed son (%)	72	70	74
With a married or widowed daughter or son (%)	94	95	97
Number with children	2,002	1,911	2,012

tions were nearly equal. Taken with Table VI–4 it appears that the
elderly population of the United States and Britain differ from that of
Denmark in having a slight excess of daughters over sons. This fact is of
some importance in explaining slight differences in family relationships,
as will be seen later.

The vast majority of those who have a married child also have grandchildren. Altogether nine in ten old people with surviving children have
grandchildren as well: 93 per cent in the United States and in Denmark
and 89 per cent in Britain. The figures for men and for women with children are very similar. A more surprising finding for all three countries is
the substantial proportion who also have great-grandchildren. More
women than men in all three countries have great-grandchildren.

Some old people who lack a spouse and children have brothers and
sisters on whom they can depend. In general nearly four-fifths of the old
people in the surveys in all three countries had surviving siblings. As

Table VI-6: PERCENTAGE OF PERSONS WITH CHILDREN WHO ALSO HAVE
GRANDCHILDREN AND GREAT-GRANDCHILDREN (*Percentage Distribution*)

Persons with Children	DENMARK			BRITAIN			UNITED STATES		
	Men	Women	All	Men	Women	All	Men	Women	All
With grandchildren	92	93	92	89	90	89	93	94	93
With no grandchildren	8	7	8	11	10	11	7	6	7
Total	100	100	100	100	100	100	100	100	100
N=	951	1,029	1,980	805	1,103	1,908	897	1,100	2,007
With great-grandchildren	19	27	23	18	26	23	34	45	40
With no great-grand- children	81	73	77	82	75	77	66	55	60
Total	100	100	100	100	100	100	100	100	100
N=	951	1,029	1,980	801	1,095	1,896	882	1,094	1,976

Table VI-7 shows, rather more than half of them in Denmark and Britain had just one, two, or three siblings. The range was wide, however. Between 1 and 2 per cent of the elderly in Denmark and Britain had nine or more surviving siblings. As many as 18 per cent and 13 per cent respectively had five or more. On the other hand the small but important minorities lacking both children and siblings should be noted. They range from 3 per cent in Denmark to about 5 per cent in Britain and in the United States.

Table VI-7: PERCENTAGE OF PERSONS WITH DIFFERENT NUMBERS OF SURVIVING SIBLINGS (*Percentage Distribution*)

Surviving Siblings and Marital Status of Respondent	DENMARK			BRITAIN			UNITED STATES		
	Men	Women	All	Men	Women	All	Men	Women	All
None									
Unmarried persons, no children	1	3	2	2	5	4	2	5	3
Married persons, no children	2	1	1	2	1	1	2	1	2
Unmarried or married persons, with children	17	17	17	18	17	18	14	18	16
All with no siblings	20	21	21	22	23	23	18	24	21
All with siblings									
1	19	21	20	21	23	22			
2	17	19	18	17	19	18			
3	13	13	13	16	14	15	82	76	79
4	12	9	11	11	9	9			
5 or more	19	17	18	13	13	13			
Total	100	100	100	100	100	100	100	100	100
N=	1,135	1,292	2,427	996	1,489	2,485	1,076	1,358	2,434

It is of course possible to analyze the possession of siblings in various ways. The scope and character of reciprocal help and social relations between two siblings may be limited because they are widely different in age or because they are of the same sex. In Britain, for example, 16 per cent of the men with siblings had sisters only. Only 39 per cent of the entire sample had siblings of both sexes. Again persons with few or no children may have several siblings or a range of other relatives, such as siblings' children. In Britain, for example, 19 per cent of the entire sample had only one child but this figure is made up of 4 per cent with no siblings, 4 per cent with 1 sibling, 3 per cent with 2, and 8 per cent with 3 or more siblings. In the entire sample 5 per cent had neither siblings nor children; but, at the other extreme, 5 per cent had 5 or more siblings *and* 5 or more children. It is evident that a substantial proportion of old persons having only one child *may* have alternative or supplementary sources of social support from siblings or from siblings' children. On the other hand, a substantial proportion of old people have no possibility of such support. Some of those lacking siblings in old age will never have had them.

The wider ramifications of family structure could not be explored in the cross-national survey but the reader should remember that there are other categories of relatives with whom the old person may be in touch. Those without children and siblings may have brothers-in-law; or they may have cousins, from either their mother's or father's side of the family. In other words, for many people a very large network of kin can be traced. However, our knowledge of the marital status of old people, the number of children they possess of each sex, and whether or not they possess grand-children, great-grandchildren, and siblings, does allow us to characterize the structure of their families and, approximately, the proportions who are members of structures of one generation or from two to four generations.

Table VI-8: PERCENTAGE OF OLD PERSONS BELONGING TO AN IMMEDIATE FAMILY STRUCTURE OF ONE, TWO, THREE, OR FOUR GENERATIONS (*Percentage Distribution*)

Number of Generations in the Family	Possession of Near Relatives	Denmark	Britain	United States
One[a]	Childless, unmarried, no siblings	2	4	3
	Childless, unmarried, with siblings	9	12	8
	Childless, married, no siblings	1	1	2
	Childless, married, with siblings	5	6	5
	Total	18	24	18
Two	One son only, no grandchildren	3	2	2
	One daughter only, no grandchildren	2	4	2
	More than one child, no grandchildren	2	3	2
	Total	7	9	6
Three	One son only, and grandchildren	6	6	4
	One daughter only, and grandchildren	7	6	6
	More than one child, and grand-children	44	39	35
	Total	56	51	44
Four	One child only, grandchildren, and great-grandchildren	2	2	3
	More than one child, grandchildren, and great-grandchildren	17	16	29
	Total	19	17	32
	Total	100	100	100
	N=	2,435	2,485	2,436

[a] Childless persons having grandchildren or great-grandchildren (numbering 16 in Britain and 11 in Denmark) have been classified with those of "one generation." The number for the United States is unknown, since those who were asked about grandchildren and great-grandchildren were persons with children only.

Table VI–8 presents a summary of some of the previous information. The great majority of old people belong to families of three or four generations.[9] More than half in all three countries have more than one child and also grandchildren (55 per cent in Britain, 61 per cent in Denmark, and 64 per cent in the United States). They could be said to have good potential family resources for help in old age. Another fifth have resources in depth over two, three, or four generations, but either they have only one child or, if they have two or more children, they have no grandchildren (23 per cent in Britain, 23 per cent in Denmark, and 19 per cent in the United States). The remaining persons have no direct descendants alive (23 per cent in Britain, 17 per cent in Denmark, and 18 per cent in the United States). Only about a third of them are married, and some who are single or widowed have no surviving siblings. The last-named are a small but very important minority because they are potentially the most vulnerable to the crises of old age. Britain apparently has the largest proportion who seem to be potentially insecure, from the viewpoint of being old and without family. It should also be remembered that not all those who have children are necessarily more secure. In particular, those having one son only may not be much better off than many childless people. Because of his occupational commitments the son may be unable to play a supportive role and his wife may have commitments to parents of her own. If to those who are childless we add those having a family of two or three generations but only one son, the resulting figure is 32 per cent of old people in Britain, 27 per cent in Denmark, and 23 per cent in the United States.

The Span Between the Generations

The ages at which individuals marry and the ages at which they become parents will determine the general span in years between different generations in society. In demographic literature there is surprisingly little information about age differences between parents and their eldest, youngest, and other children. There is none, or virtually none, about the difference in age between grandparents and their grandchildren.

Average ages at first marriage have diminished and for women in the United States have been relatively low throughout this country, as Table VI–9 shows. In England and Wales men have been on average around two years, in Denmark about three years, and in the United States around three or four years, older than their wives, though in the United States the difference is diminishing. The variation in age at marriage and in age difference between husbands and wives is very large.[10]

The age of parenthood has also been diminishing. In the United States the median age of women at the birth of their first child was 23 years for those born between 1920 and 1930, but 21.5 for those born between 1930 and 1939. Because also of the decreasing number of large families the median age of women at the birth of their last child has fallen from 33 for those born between 1880 and 1890 to 30 or 31 for those born between 1920 and 1930.[11] Table VI–10 shows some of the changes taking place

Table VI–9: AVERAGE AGE AT FIRST MARRIAGE FOR SELECTED YEARS[a]

Year	DENMARK		ENGLAND AND WALES		UNITED STATES	
	Men	Women	Men	Women	Men	Women
1900	29.1	26.1	26.9	25.4	25.9	21.9
1930	27.6	24.9	27.4	25.5	24.3	21.3
1960	25.9	22.9	25.9	23.5	22.8	20.3

[a] Figures for England and Wales are for the years 1901–05, 1931–35, and 1955–60 respectively. Danish figures refer to the years 1901–05, 1931–35, and 1960. The Danish material for 1900 refers to the average age of *all* persons marrying, including those marrying for other than the first time. The United States figures are medians.

between the 1880's and the 1930's in the life cycle of women. Earlier marriage, earlier childbirth, and fewer large families inevitably contribute towards a narrowing of the average span in years between successive generations.

Information about age differences between old people and their surviving children and grandchildren was collected and analyzed in the British part of the cross-national survey. The oldest surviving child is not necessarily the first-born child of an old person. As already stated, 3 per cent of the sample had once had children but at the time of the survey had none surviving. Others with surviving children had lost at least one child, sometimes the first-born, during their lifetime. A woman of 65 years of age or over in the British survey was on average 26.4 years, and a man 29.0 years, older than the eldest or only child. But there was considerable variation. Some persons had stepchildren who were almost as old as themselves. Two per cent of men and 7 per cent of women were less than

Table VI–10: MEDIAN AGE OF WOMEN AT SELECTED STAGES OF THE LIFE CYCLE (UNITED STATES)

Stage of Family	Born 1880–89	Born 1930–39[a]
First marriage	21.6	19.9
Birth of first child	22.9	21.5
Birth of last child	32.9	30.0 to 31.0[b]
First marriage of last child	56.2	51.5 to 52.5
Death of one spouse	57.0	64.4

Source: Paul C. Glick and R. Parke, "New Approaches in Studying the Life Cycle of the Family," *Demography*, II (1965).

[a] Some figures are estimated on the basis of incomplete data.

[b] For mothers born 1920 to 1929.

20 years older than the eldest child; while 16 per cent and 8 per cent respectively were more than 35 years older. Such a variation does of course hold implications for the relationships between old people and their children. It is even more striking if youngest children are considered. Women were on average 35.3 years older, and men 37.9 years, than the youngest child. But while some were less than 20 or 25 years older, 28 per cent were from 40 to 49 years older, and a further two per cent 50 or more years older. Thus, the variation in age difference between parent and child, which is already quite wide for the eldest children in the family, becomes even wider for the youngest children. It is wider still between grandparent and grandchild, ranging from just over 30 to 80 years and more. Table VI-11 indicates the age at which elderly men and women in Britain reached certain stages in the life cycle. When compared with Table VI-10 the data suggest that elderly women in the United States passed through certain stages of the life cycle sooner than their peers in Britain.

Table VI-11: MEAN AGE OF MEN AND WOMEN AT SELECTED STAGES OF THE LIFE CYCLE (BRITAIN)

Stage of Family	Born 1897 or Earlier and Still Surviving in 1962	
	Men	Women
First marriage	approx. 27	approx. 25
Birth of first child	29	26
Birth of last child	38	35
Birth of first grandchild	57	54
Birth of first great-grandchild	approx. 75	approx. 72
Expected death for those aged 65	[77]	[80]

Grandmothers in the sample (who of course do not represent a sample of *all* grandmothers) were on average about 54 years older, and grandfathers about 57 years older, than their first grandchildren. But the range was large, some persons in the sample being less than 45 years older and others more than 65 years older than their grandchildren. Finally, there are the great-grandparents of advanced age. Women with great-grandchildren were on average aged about 72 when they became great-grandmothers, and men were aged about 75. For these individuals it is noticeable that the average span in years between the generation of grandparents and the generation of great-grandparents has diminished. This is because only those who marry and have children earlier than average, and whose children themselves have children earlier than average, are likely to have great-grandchildren.

Despite the scope that clearly exists for structural variation in family-building, substantial numbers of old people had proceeded through similar stages at roughly comparable ages. Over a third of the men with grandchildren had had their first child between the ages of 25 and 34 *and* their first grandchild between the ages of 50 and 59. Over a third of the women had had their first child between the ages of 20 and 24 *and* their first grandchild between the ages of 45 and 54. Others were fairly close to this programming of the life cycle. Nevertheless the variation was wide. There were such instances as the woman who had had her first child before she was 20 but did not become a grandmother until she was over 65 years old; and the man who did not become a father until the age of 50 but yet became a grandfather before he was 70. It is a recurring theme of this chapter that structural variations like these, and their systematic revelation, may be of considerable importance to the understanding of the quality and character of family relations.

Aging and Family Structure

The structure of the families of old people in the three countries has been described in broad outline. Kinship structure changes over time but the individual's place in it also changes as he gets older. New members are recruited by birth or marriage; older members are discharged by death. An individual's roles and his network of relationships change with age. Some of the changes that take place after the age of 65 will now be described.

We will first consider the changes in the generation to which the old person belongs. These are primarily losses experienced with advancing age. Table VI–12 shows that with increasing age the proportion of women with a husband alive falls very steeply, and the proportion of men with a wife alive falls less steeply, in all three countries. Only between a tenth and a fifth of women, although a larger fraction of men (from nearly a half to three-fifths), remain married among those aged 80 and over. The proportions who are widowed increases correspondingly. Significantly more of the women in Denmark in each age-group are married than of women in the other two countries. This might be attributed to the more favorable ratio of male to female mortality in Denmark than in the other countries.[12]

The proportion having siblings alive also falls steeply in all three countries—from around 85 per cent of those aged 65 to 69 to around 70 per cent of those aged 75 and over. (See Table VI–13.) Similarly, older persons who have siblings alive tend to have fewer of them. In Denmark, for example, 36 per cent of persons aged 65 to 69 but only 17 per cent of persons aged 75 and over, had four or more siblings. Variations in birth-order and age should be remembered, however; for example, two old people aged 70 might both have had ten siblings but because one was the eldest and one the youngest, one of the two might have no surviving siblings and the other ten.

With time the elderly lose husbands or wives and siblings. They are also likely to lose other contemporaries—such as brothers-in-law, sisters-in-law, and first and second cousins. To many old people such relatives may not be functionally important but to some they are.

Table VI–12: PERCENTAGE OF PERSONS IN EACH AGE GROUP WHO ARE
MARRIED, WIDOWED, AND SINGLE

Age	DENMARK		BRITAIN		UNITED STATES	
	Men	Women	Men	Women	Men	Women
Married (%)						
65–66	88	60	82	54	81	54
67–69	80	51	75	46	87	46
70–74	69	43	71	31	78	40
75–79	61	30	58	27	71	29
80+	45	19	60	18	56	10
All ages	70	42	70	34	76	37
Widowed, Divorced, Separated (%)						
65–66	8	31	14	33	15	40
67–69	15	39	20	42	12	47
70–74	25	45	24	53	18	54
75–79	33	60	36	56	26	67
80+	52	70	36	68	42	81
All ages	26	48	25	52	21	56
Single Persons (%)						
65–66	4	9	4	12	4	5
67–69	4	10	4	12	1	6
70–74	4	11	4	15	4	6
75–79	6	9	6	17	3	4
80+	3	10	4	13	2	9
All ages	4	10	5	14	3	6
Number of Cases						
65–66	183	219	164	212	176	205
67–69	262	269	226	286	230	303
70–74	318	396	287	438	347	423
75–79	223	250	202	293	182	226
80+	156	166	125	267	146	191
All ages	1,142	1,300	1,004	1,496	1,081	1,348

There is no marked or consistent trend with age among older people possessing children. For Britain the proportion of married and widowed women with children falls from 89 per cent of those aged 65–66 to 82 per cent of those aged 80 and over. For the United States the proportion of married and widowed women with children, after varying slightly between 85 and 90 per cent in the 60's and 70's, also falls among those aged 80 and over, to 84 per cent. It is likely that in the recent past the more favorable expectation of life of the childless than of women who have borne children helps to explain this slight trend. But in Denmark the percentage of married and widowed women with children fluctuates only marginally around 90 per cent for each age-group.

When account is taken of the total number of children, however, there are pronounced differences with increasing age, at least in the two

Table VI–13: PERCENTAGE OF PERSONS OF DIFFERENT AGE WITH
VARYING NUMBERS OF SIBLINGS (*Percentage Distribution*)

Number of Siblings	DENMARK			BRITAIN			UNITED STATES		
	65–69	70–74	75+	65–69	70–74	75+	65–69	70–74	75+
None	13	16	33	15	20	33	14	22	29
1	15	23	23	18	23	25			
2	21	16	16	20	17	17			
3	14	13	11	16	15	13	86	78	71
4	13	11	8	13	11	5			
5 or more	23	21	9	18	15	7			
Total	100	100	100	100	100	100	100	100	100
N=	923	710	791	883	722	880	910	769	742

European countries. As Table VI–14 shows, more of the people in Denmark and Britain aged 65 to 69 than of the people aged 80 and over have only one or two children and fewer of them have six or more children. This reflects the rapid decrease that took place among those marrying in the latter part of the nineteenth and early part of this century in the numbers of large families produced. Similar trends were not found among the United States sample, although future surveys are likely to find increases in the proportions of the population aged 65 to 69 who have only one or two children and corresponding decreases in the proportions having several children.

Differences found at present between old people in their 60's and those in their 80's in the number of children they have are therefore attributable chiefly to generation differences in the numbers of children borne rather than aging as such. If the distribution by family size were constant from one generation to the next we could predict a slight decrease between the age of 65 and the most advanced ages in the proportions of men and women having children. Some children in small families are bound to die before both their parents. Thus in Britain approximately 3 per cent of those who were married or widowed had once had children but now had none surviving. There were a few persons in the sample (less than one per cent) who had no surviving children and yet possessed grandchildren.

In completing this account of aging and family structure it must be emphasized that there are replacements in the family structure for the losses sustained by old people. Representatives of new generations are born as contemporaries die. Interestingly enough, the proportion of old people in their 80's who had grandchildren was not markedly higher than the proportion of people in their 60's. Indeed, in Britain and the United States there was not a distinct or regular increase from age-group to age-group in the proportion having grandchildren. Ages at marriage and at childbirth have been such in these two countries that nearly all who become grandparents reach this stage in their early 60's.[13] Much the same appears

Table VI–14: PERCENTAGE OF PERSONS OF DIFFERENT AGE WITH
VARYING NUMBERS OF CHILDREN (*Percentage Distribution*)

Sex of Respondent and Number of Surviving Children	DENMARK				BRITAIN				UNITED STATES			
	65–9	70–4	75–9	80+	65–9	70–4	75–9	80+	65–9	70–4	75–9	80+
All persons												
1	28	23	21	18	26	25	26	22	21	20	18	22
2	26	25	24	23	28	28	21	26	24	21	22	25
3–5	35	39	38	42	36	34	34	37	37	41	38	36
6 or more	12	13	17	17	10	13	19	15	18	19	22	17
Total	100	100	100	100	100	100	100	100	100	100	100	100
N=	755	587	397	271	697	554	367	293	758	630	344	273
Men												
1	28	19	24	16	26	29	21	23	20	22	18	22
2	27	25	24	21	28	27	22	28	26	21	22	24
3–5	35	43	37	41	35	30	41	33	38	42	37	35
6 or more	10	12	15	22	11	13	15	16	17	15	23	19
Total	100	100	100	100	100	100	100	100	100	100	100	100
N=	359	275	190	139	315	234	155	103	337	281	155	127
Women												
1	27	27	19	20	26	21	30	22	21	18	17	23
2	24	24	24	25	29	28	21	25	23	21	22	25
3–5	35	35	38	43	37	38	28	38	36	40	39	36
6 or more	13	14	19	12	8	13	21	15	19	21	22	16
Total	100	100	100	100	100	100	100	100	100	100	100	100
N=	396	312	207	132	382	320	212	190	421	349	189	146

to be true of women in Denmark, although in that country the proportion of men who are grandfathers is lower among those in their 60's than among those in their 70's and 80's. Nevertheless, while there may be little further change after the age of 65 in the proportion of each age-group having at least one grandchild, the total number of grandchildren old people have will probably increase between the age of 65 and the late 80's. We did not collect information about these numbers.

In all three countries the proportion of old people having great-grandchildren increased steeply with advancing age. As Table VI–15 shows, by the age of 80 and over, two-fifths of the men and half the women in Britain, nearly half the men and two-thirds of the women in Denmark, and over half the men and two-thirds of the women in the United States, had great-grandchildren.

Thus, as old people advance in age from their 60's to their 70's and 80's the growing number of their grandchildren and the birth of one or more great-grandchildren tend to balance, at least in numbers, the loss of spouse and siblings. Figure VI–5 shows some of the main changes with increasing age. These changes are not experienced equally by all old people, however. Some of those lacking children lose their spouses and siblings and, if there

Table VI-15: PERCENTAGE OF MEN AND WOMEN OF DIFFERENT AGE, HAVING CHILDREN, GRANDCHILDREN, AND GREAT-GRANDCHILDREN

Country and Sex		With Grandchildren (%)					With Great-grandchildren (%)				
		65–66	67–69	70–74	75–79	80+	65–66	67–69	70–74	75–79	80+
Denmark	Men	87	87	93	91	96	5	8	15	29	46
	Women	89	93	92	93	95	12	15	23	41	64
	N=	327	425	584	397	271	327	425	584	397	271
Britain	Men	88	84	90	97	92	4	9	16	30	43
	Women	90	87	92	93	92	5	11	23	38	52
	N=	302	393	552	362	292	298	389	549	362	292
United States	Men	92	94	91	95	92	15	27	34	40	57
	Women	95	91	95	97	90	32	29	45	59	68
	N=	308	449	628	343	273	301	437	624	336	273

are no nephews and nieces or more distant relatives who act as substitutes, such persons become even more isolated. By contrast, some old people with several children find that the number of grandchildren and great-grand-children multiplies. One elderly widow in Britain maintained a stock of two dozen birthday cards for grandchildren in a kitchen drawer because she found she needed one, on average, every week or fortnight. Since the principal kinship ties in Western society seem to be between descendant and ascendant rather than among collateral or affinal kin, the main change experienced with increasing age is for old people to find them-selves nearer one of two extremes—experiencing the seclusion of the spinster or widow who lacks children *and* surviving brothers and sisters, or pushed towards the pinnacle of a pyramidal family structure of four generations which may include as many as four or five children, their husbands or wives, and twenty or thirty grandchildren and great-grandchildren.

Effects of Family Structure on Family Organization

THE HOUSEHOLD

Kinship structure does not by itself determine individual household organization and social relationships, but it will tend to limit the number of alternative possibilities there are for organization and action, and, in the widest sense, will influence social norms. We will discuss household composition, the proximity of kin, and frequency of contacts with children in turn. A fuller account of living arrangements and family relationships will be given in later chapters. Here the emphasis is on showing some of the ways in which structure may correlate with organization.

Figure VI–5: CHANGES WITH INCREASING AGE IN THE PERCENTAGES OF OLD
PEOPLE WITH CERTAIN KINDS OF RELATIVES

1. Percentage of all old people with
   no siblings

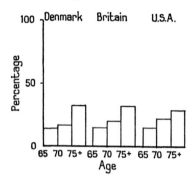

2. Percentage of those with four
   or more siblings

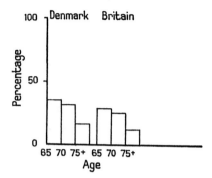

3. Percentage of men with wife alive

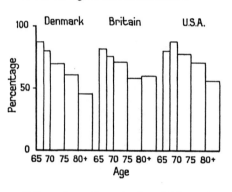

4. Percentage of women with husband alive

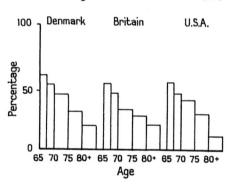

5. Percentage of men having children, who
   have great-grandchildren

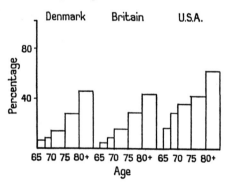

6. Percentage of women having children,
   who have great-grandchildren

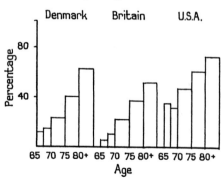

Some of the differences in the living arrangements of old people in Denmark, Britain, and the United States can be explained by differences in family structure. More of the elderly in Britain, for example, are women, widowed or single, and persons with only one or two children. These and other factors help to explain differences in the patterns of living arrangements of the three elderly populations. We will say more about this later. But there are certain consistent patterns according to family structure in each of the three elderly populations, and some of these will now be described.

First, whether old people are married or not affects the composition of the rest of the household. More widowed than married old persons in all three countries were found to be living with married children. This is not explained either by the greater age or incapacity of these old persons, though incapacity seems sometimes to be a contributory factor. Twenty-three per cent of the widowed in Britain, 16 per cent in the United States, and 8 per cent in Denmark, compared with 5 per cent, 2 per cent, and 1 per cent respectively, of the married, lived with married children, as Table VI–16 shows.

Second, whether or not an old person is single or widowed affects the composition of the household. A much smaller percentage of widowed than of single old persons in all three countries were found to live with siblings —1 per cent in Denmark, 4 per cent in Britain, and 4 per cent in the United States, compared with 22 per cent, 38 per cent, and 47 per cent respectively. This difference is not explained by the numbers of widowed

Table VI–16: LIVING ARRANGEMENTS OF MARRIED AND OF WIDOWED, DIVORCED, AND SEPARATED PERSONS (*Percentage Distribution*)

Household Composition[a]	DENMARK		BRITAIN		UNITED STATES	
	Married	Widowed and Divorced	Married	Widowed and Divorced	Married	Widowed and Divorced
Living alone	—	62	—	43	—	49
Living with spouse only	82	—	68	—	79	—
Living with married daughter (and others)	0	4	4	17	1	12
Living with married son (and others)	1	4	1	6	1	4
Living with unmarried children (and others)	13	16	22	23	12	20
Living with others	4	14	6	11	7	15
Total	100	100	100	100	100	100
N=	1,338	913	1,210	1,029	1,335	991

[a] This is a priority code, i.e., households with married children may also include unmarried children, etc.

persons who lived with children because, as Table VI–17 shows, relatively *more* widowed than single persons lived alone in Denmark and in the United States, and the same proportion of both widowed and single persons lived alone in Britain. If we take account, on the one hand, simply of widowed persons who in fact had children and, on the other hand, of single persons who in fact had siblings, it can be said a widowed person was less likely, in all three countries, to live with a child than a single person was to live with a sibling. This is perhaps an unexpected finding but it may suggest that in the absence of children and grandchildren people often maintain extremely close relationships with one or more of

Table VI–17:   LIVING ARRANGEMENTS OF WIDOWED AND OF SINGLE PERSONS (*Percentage Distribution*)

Household Composition[a]	DENMARK		BRITAIN		UNITED STATES	
	Widowed and Divorced	Single	Widowed and Divorced	Single	Widowed and Divorced	Single
Living alone	62	55	43	43	49	39
Living with married and/ or unmarried children (and others)	24	4	46	2	36	0
Living with siblings (and others)	1	22	4	38	4	47
Living with others	12	19	7	17	11	15
Total	100	100	100	100	100	100
N=	913	182	1,029	260	991	116

[a] See footnote *a*, Table VI–16.

their siblings. Such close relationships are not maintained by those who have children. When the children marry and leave home and husbands or wives die, these old people more often continue living alone than attempt to renew close relationships with siblings. Such close relationships are not even maintained by people who marry but fail to have children, or lose their children. As many as 68 per cent of widowed persons in Denmark and Britain who were childless, and 61 per cent in the United States, lived alone—compared with 58 per cent, 44 per cent, and 39 per cent respectively, of the single. Fewer lived with siblings. For reasons such as the need to acknowledge the integrity and privacy of marriage and to maintain distance between the adult generations, large numbers of those with children also chose not to live with their children.

Third, the household composition of the elderly is further affected by the number and the sex of old people's children. Table VI–18 presents a rather elaborate picture of the relationship between family structure and household composition. It is intended to illustrate the influence of structural variation. We have already commented on the large proportion of single persons who lived with siblings and the large proportion of childless widowed persons who lived alone.

Few married couples in any country lived with married children, and in Denmark only tiny minorities of the widowed did so. Moreover, in that country the few who did live with married children chose to live with sons and daughters in roughly equal proportions. In this respect Denmark differed from the other two countries. In Britain and the United States roughly three times as many old persons lived with married daughters as with married sons. It would seem that in these two countries greater emphasis is placed on the parent-daughter, and particularly the mother-daughter, relationships. In all three countries slightly more old persons with sons than with sons and daughters or daughters only were found to be living with siblings. Widowed persons with sons only were also more likely to be found living alone. In the United States, for example, 61 per cent of widowed persons with one son only, compared with 40 per cent of those with one daughter only, lived alone. Again this suggests the emphasis that is placed on the parent-daughter relationship and the tendency for some people to prefer sharing a household with some relative other than a son or, perhaps more relevantly, a daughter-in-law.

A fascinating fact is that in Denmark and the United States more of the widowed than of the married lived with *unmarried* children. This was true for old people with every type of family. In Britain it was true of those with an only son and an only daughter, but not of those with more than one child. In Denmark 15 per cent of the widowed persons with an only daughter were, in fact, living with an *unmarried* daughter, compared with only 2 per cent of married persons. For Britain the figures are 25 per cent and 14 per cent respectively; and for the United States, 22 per cent and 6 per cent. It is not easy to account for this difference. When a detailed comparison was made between the widowed and married in the British sample who had only one surviving child, it was found that the widowed old people were older, their sons or daughters tended to be older than the children of the married persons, and those who lived with an unmarried child were likely to have been widowed when the child was young more often than those who did not live with an unmarried child. Unfortunately, we were not able to check whether more of the two-person households consisting of a widowed old person and an unmarried child were of opposite than of like sex. But in general the evidence suggests that at least one of the children of a widow or widower .may postpone marriage, sometimes indefinitely, if the other parent dies at a time when the child is adolescent or in his or her 20's. This appears to be one of the ways by which a family adjusts to the loss of one of its members and compensates the individual who is most affected.[14]

Another form of compensation is indicated by the greater degree to which the single and widowed without children are found to be living with other relatives or with non-relatives. There are hints of the same thing in the figures for those with an only son or daughter, compared with the figures for those with two or more children.

Table VI–18a: HOUSEHOLD COMPOSITION OF SINGLE, WIDOWED, AND DIVORCED PERSONS WITH DIFFERENT NUMBERS OF SONS AND DAUGHTERS (Percentage Distribution)

Household Composition	No Living Children — Single	No Living Children — Widowed	One Son Only	One Daughter Only	Two or More Sons Only	Two or More Daughters Only	Son(s) and Daughter(s)	All Unmarried Persons
Denmark								
Living alone	58	68	64	59	67		60	61
Married daughter	—	—	—	8	—		5	3
Married son	—	—	12	—	5		3	3
Unmarried child	—	—	12	15	15		21	14
Siblings	23	5	1	1	2		1	5
Grandchildren	—	—	—	3	2		1	1
Other relatives	4	6	1	1	1		1	2
Non-relatives	15	20	10	13	8		8	11
Total	100	100	100	100	100		100	100
N=	167	111	91	95	89		553	1,107
Britain								
Living alone	44	68	55	35	54	42	33	43
Married daughter	—	—	—	27	—	25	25	14
Married son	—	—	14	—	18	—	17	5
Unmarried child	—	—	14	25	18	28	31	18
Siblings	39	14	8	4	4	1	1	11
Grandchildren	—	1	2	2	—	1	—	1
Other relatives	6	8	2	2	—	1	1	3
Non-relatives	11	10	5	4	6	—	3	6
Total	100	100	100	100	100	100	100	100
N=	254	146	104	102	90	73	520	1,289
United States								
Living alone	39	60	61	40	51		45	48
Married daughter	—	—	—	24	—		16	11
Married son	—	—	8	—	12		3	3
Unmarried child	—	—	18	22	23		26	18
Siblings	46	14	5	3	3		2	9
Grandchildren	—	2	—	5	3		2	2
Other relatives	7	11	3	2	—		1	3
Non-relatives	8	12	5	5	9		4	6
Total	100	100	100	100	100		100	100
N=	116	148	74	116	78		574	1,107

Table VI–18b: HOUSEHOLD COMPOSITION OF MARRIED PERSONS WITH DIFFERENT NUMBERS OF SONS AND DAUGHTERS
(Percentage Distribution)

Household Composition[a]	NUMBER AND SEX OF CHILDREN						All Married Persons
	No Living Children	One Son Only	One Daughter Only	Two or More Sons Only	Two or More Daughters Only	Son(s) and Daughter(s)	
Denmark							
Living with spouse only	97	90	92	78		78	82
Married daughter	—	—	—	—		1	*
Married son	—	4	—	6		*	1
Unmarried child	—	2	2	13		18	13
Siblings	—	1	2	—		1	*
Grandchildren	1	—	—	—		*	1
Other relatives	—	—	2	—		*	*
Non-relatives	3	2	3	4		2	2
Total	100	100	100	100		100	100
N=	155	138	135	107		784	1,336
Britain							
Living with spouse only	89	74	77	70	65	56	68
Married daughter	—	—	4	—	5	—	4
Married son	—	3	—	—	—	7	1
Unmarried child	5	13	14	30	26	32	22
Siblings	—	5	3	—	1	—	2
Grandchildren	3	2	—	—	2	—	1
Other relatives	3	2	1	—	—	1	1
Non-relatives	3	2	1	—	2	1	1
Total	100	100	100	100	100	100	100
N=	189	117	160	91	125	529	1,211
United States							
Living with spouse only	87	80	85	78		77	79
Married daughter	—	—	1	—		1	1
Married son	—	1	—	—		1	1
Unmarried child	5	12	6	13		17	13
Siblings	—	2	5	3		1	2
Grandchildren	3	—	2	2		2	2
Other relatives	—	2	2	3		—	1
Non-relatives	4	2	2	2		1	1
Total	100	100	100	100		100	100
N=	166	93	124	110		842	1,335

* Less than one per cent.   [a] See footnote a, Table VI–16.

Two supplementary conclusions can be drawn about household composition from other data. Old people in Denmark and the United States who were separated or divorced were less likely than the widowed to be found living with one of their children. In the United States, for example, 45 per cent of the widowed with children lived with one of them, compared with 22 per cent of the divorced. Although numbers were small, the difference between the divorced or separated and the widowed appears to exist for men and women separately, and for men and women of each type of family structure. (More of the separated than of the widowed also lived at a considerable distance from their children.) It is likely that once parents are divorced or separated, children tend to maintain close relations with one but not both of them.

Table VI–19: PERCENTAGE OF WIDOWED WOMEN WITH AN ONLY CHILD WHO LIVE WITH THAT CHILD

Sex of Only Child	Widowed Women*	
	Per cent	Total Number
Son		
Denmark	25	67
Britain	25	80
United States	29	59
Daughter		
Denmark	20	71
Britain	55	78
United States	53	83

* There were fewer than 50 men in all three samples with an only son or an only daughter. Separated and divorced women are included with the widows.

Another conclusion is that in Britain and the United States but not in Denmark certain pairings of old people and their children are much more likely than others; for example, among those with an only child, widows are much less likely to live with a son than with a daughter (Table VI–19).

PROXIMITY OF DIFFERENT HOUSEHOLDS

Family structure helps to explain the geographical distribution of the family as well as the composition of the household. In all three countries more married than widowed persons lived over thirty minutes journey from their nearest child. This finding holds for nearly all family types in every country, as Table VI–20 shows. Again, a rather elaborate table is given to bring out the differences between those with different types of family as well as the differences between the married and the widowed. In the United States, 44 per cent of married persons with an only daughter,

Table VI–20a: PERCENTAGE OF WIDOWED, SEPARATED, AND DIVORCED PERSONS WITH DIFFERENT NUMBERS OF SONS AND DAUGHTERS, ACCORDING TO DISTANCE FROM NEAREST CHILD (*Percentage Distribution*)

Proximity of Nearest Child	NUMBER AND SEX OF CHILDREN					
	One Son Only	One Daughter Only	Two Sons or More	Two or More Daughters	Son(s) and Daughter(s)	All Widowed, Separated, and Divorced Persons
Denmark						
Same household	20	22	17	29		26
Within 10 minutes	22	22	27	35		31
11–30 minutes	20	17	28	20		12
31–60 minutes	14	17	17	10		21
More than an hour, less than a day	15	21	10	5		8
A day or more	9	1	1	1		2
Total	100	100	100	100		100
N=	86	88	88	545		807
Britain						
Same household	29	53	36	51	63	54
Within 10 minutes	24	12	24	19	19	20
11–30 minutes	19	9	14	16	10	12
31–60 minutes	10	10	11	5	4	6
More than an hour, less than a day	14	13	13	5	3	7
A day or more	4	4	1	3	1	2
Total	100	100	100	100	100	100
N=	104	102	99	73	520	889
United States						
Same household	26	46	35	46		43
Within 10 minutes	20	9	26	30		26
11–30 minutes	19	12	18	13		14
31–60 minutes	14	4	9	4		5
More than an hour, less than a day	12	16	9	6		8
A day or more	9	13	4	1		4
Total	100	100	100	100		100
N=	74	115	78	573		840

for example, and 51 per cent with an only son, lived more than thirty minutes journey away from that child, compared with 33 per cent and 35 per cent respectively of unmarried persons. It is also important to note that while proportionately more widowed than married persons lived with one of their children, proportionately *fewer* lived within ten minutes journey. In all countries it was more likely for widowed old people to be found living with one of their children than near them. In Denmark and in

Table VI–20b: PERCENTAGE OF MARRIED PERSONS WITH DIFFERENT NUMBERS OF SONS AND DAUGHTERS, ACCORDING TO DISTANCE FROM NEAREST CHILD (*Percentage Distribution*)

Proximity of Nearest Child	One Son Only	One Daughter Only	Two Sons or More	Two or More Daughters	Son(s) and Daughter(s)	All Married Persons
			NUMBER AND SEX OF CHILDREN			
Denmark						
Same household	15	2	18	18		16
Within 10 minutes	21	29	28	36		33
11–30 minutes	18	25	23	26		25
31–60 minutes	14	15	14	11		12
More than an hour, less than a day	28	27	15	8		13
A day or more	4	2	2	1		1
Total	100	100	100	100		100
N=	155	128	108	790		1,189
Britain						
Same household	17	19	30	29	40	32
Within 10 minutes	20	26	35	27	27	27
11–30 minutes	25	15	20	15	20	19
31–60 minutes	12	10	5	19	6	9
More than an hour, less than a day	19	26	9	10	6	11
A day or more	8	5	1	1	1	2
Total	100	100	100	100	100	100
N=	117	160	91	124	529	1,021
United States						
Same household	13	6	13	19		17
Within 10 minutes	21	30	39	42		39
11–30 minutes	15	20	15	17		17
31–60 minutes	12	6	15	8		9
More than an hour, less than a day	22	23	15	11		13
A day or more	17	15	4	4		6
Total	100	100	100	100		100
N=	92	124	109	842		1,167

the United States, it was more likely for married persons to be found living near their children than with them. In Britain, however, married persons tended to be younger, and widowed persons older, than in the other two countries, and married persons with several children more often had at least one single child still living at home. The social norm that elderly married couples should maintain households independent of their married children was not so often fulfilled in Britain as in the other two countries.

In Britain and the United States but not in Denmark widowed persons were more likely to be found living with a daughter than with a son. They were also less likely to be found living more than thirty minutes journey away from any of their children.

When the data are consolidated to find whether there are any general differences between sons and daughters in their nearness to old people, it can be concluded, first, that in Denmark there are very small differences in the distribution of children according to sex; and, secondly, that in Britain and the United States, although a markedly higher proportion of nearest daughters than of nearest sons are to be found living in the household, the difference is largely cancelled out by the higher proportion of nearest sons than of nearest daughters who are found to be living within ten minutes or thirty minutes journey of the old people. A special analysis of the British data gave further confirmation that although married daughters more often live *with* old people than do married sons they are not in general more likely to live *near* old people. On a broad national basis, then, there is no evidence of marked matrilocal family organization.[15]

A final conclusion to be drawn from the data on proximity may seem obvious but is crucial. In all three countries the chances of living further than thirty minutes journey from the nearest child are greater the smaller is the number of children. Table VI–21 shows that from about two-fifths to a half of those who have either an only son or an only daughter live at this

Table VI–21: DISTANCE OF PERSONS WITH DIFFERENT NUMBERS OF SONS AND DAUGHTERS FROM THEIR NEAREST MARRIED OR WIDOWED CHILD (*Percentage Distribution*)

Proximity of Nearest Child	One Son	One Daughter	Two or More Sons	More than One Child—at Least One Daughter
Denmark				
Same household	8	5	6	5
Within 30 minutes	46	52	60	69
More than 30 minutes	46	43	34	26
Total	100	100	100	100
N=	192	193	192	1,313
Britain				
Same household	11	20	12	23
Within 30 minutes	50	40	62	57
More than 30 minutes	38	41	25	20
Total	100	100	100	100
N=	192	215	178	1,038
United States				
Same household	8	21	10	16
Within 30 minutes	43	39	57	61
More than 30 minutes	49	40	33	23
Total	100	100	100	100
N=	141	221	185	1,395

distance from their nearest married child, whereas about a fifth to a quarter of those who have more than one child, including at least one daughter, live at this distance.

Effects of Family Structure on Family Relationships

The over-all frequency of contact between old people and their children, as judged primarily by the shortest period since they had seen one of their children, is remarkably similar for the three elderly populations of Denmark, Britain, and the United States.[16] But, as we shall find, differences attributable to structural factors tended to cancel each other out. We can start by showing how similar are the over-all patterns of contact for the three countries. Between 62 and 69 per cent of old people in the samples in Denmark, Britain, and the United States lived with one of their children or had seen one the same day or the previous day. However, as shown earlier, the three populations varied structurally: more old people in Britain than in the United States and Denmark had single children; fewer were married; slightly more had only one or two children. We will consider such differences in turn. First, the over-all difference between old people in Britain and old people in the United States according to their most recent contact with their children becomes negligible once single children are left out of account. Between 58 and 59 per cent of old people in both countries with a married child had seen one the same or the previous day. The percentage not seeing a married child in the previous year was 3 per cent in both countries.

Second, in almost all types of families in the three countries, more widowed than married persons had seen a child the same day or the

Table VI-22: PERCENTAGE OF PERSONS WITH CHILDREN, ACCORDING TO THE SHORTEST PERIOD SINCE THEY HAD LAST SEEN A CHILD (*Percentage Distribution*)

Shortest Period Since Last Saw Child	DENMARK		BRITAIN		UNITED STATES	
	Any Child, Single or Married	Married Child	Any Child, Single or Married	Married Child	Any Child, Single or Married	Married Child
Today or yesterday[a]	62.3	50.9	69.4	58.5	65.4	58.9
2–7 days	21.9	28.8	17.2	23.2	18.6	22.1
8–30 days	9.8	12.6	7.3	9.4	6.7	8.0
31 days–1 year	4.7	6.4	4.2	6.0	6.9	8.1
Not in last year	1.3	1.3	1.8	2.9	2.4	2.9
Total	100	100	100	100	100	100
N=	1,999	1,828	1,906	1,806	2,002	1,934

[a] Including those in same household.

Table VI–23: WIDOWED AND MARRIED PERSONS HAVING DIFFERENT TYPES OF FAMILY, ACCORDING TO THE SHORTEST PERIOD SINCE THEY HAD LAST SEEN A MARRIED OR WIDOWED CHILD (*Percentage Distribution*)

Shortest Period Since Last Saw Child	Widowed, Separated, and Divorced			Married		
	Denmark	Britain	United States	Denmark	Britain	United States
Persons with One Son Only						
Today or yesterday[a]	43	53	45	38	27	32
2–7 days	27	27	21	33	31	17
8–30 days	13	10	13	16	23	25
31 days–1 year	9	6	14	13	9	21
Not in last year	8	3	8	0	10	5
Total	100	100	100	100	100	100
N=	78	88	63	112	103	77
Persons with One Daughter Only						
Today or yesterday[a]	51	66	56	45	41	44
2–7 days	23	8	16	25	27	27
8–30 days	11	9	11	25	15	3
31 days–1 year	12	12	10	3	13	17
Not in the last year	4	5	8	3	4	9
Total	100	100	100	100	100	100
N=	75	80	104	114	135	118
Persons with Two or More Sons Only						
Today or yesterday[a]	47	51	48	43	51	42
2–7 days	31	27	30	33	33	37
8–30 days	8	9	9	14	9	6
31 days–1 year	10	11	8	8	6	12
Not in the last year	3	1	5	2	1	3
Total	100	100	100	100	100	100
N=	87	88	77	104	87	108
Persons with at Least One Daughter, More than One Child						
Today or yesterday[a]	57	72	71	51	57	60
2–7 days	27	17	17	30	26	23
8–30 days	10	6	6	13	9	8
31 days–1 year	5	3	4	6	5	7
Not in the last year	1	2	2	0	2	1
Total	100	100	100	100	100	100
N=	540	580	564	773	645	823

[a] Including those sharing a household.

previous day (Table VI–23). This difference between married and widowed persons, however, is chiefly attributable to the fact that relatively more widowed persons are living with a married child. Indeed, once we consider, at the other extreme, the numbers of old people who have not seen a married child within the last thirty days, including some who have not seen one within the previous year, it emerges that proportionately more widowed than married persons in some types of family are at a disadvantage.

Third, there was a distinct trend in all three countries for fewer old people with the smallest families to have seen a child the same or the previous day and for more of them not to have seen a child within the previous month. And more of those with daughters than with sons had seen one the same or the previous day. Table VI–23 shows these important findings, and the pattern is clear and consistent (with the sole exception that a relatively higher proportion in Britain of widowed persons whose only child was a daughter rather than a son had not seen that child within the previous month).

One feature of these findings is that there is a marked difference between sons and daughters in patterns of contact. The difference is more marked than in the case of proximity. Even when living at comparable distances a daughter is more likely than a son to have been seen within a recent period. This is much as might be expected and could be shown with a variety of evidence from other studies in Western countries. What is surprising is that the difference is not more marked than it is, and that so many old people are in such frequent contact with sons. Again, however, the emphasis on the relationship with daughters that is found in Britain and the United States is virtually imperceptible in Denmark. Thirty-one per cent of old people in that country with at least one married daughter in their families had not seen a married daughter within the previous week, compared with 34 per cent who had not seen a married son in the same period.

Table VI–24 brings out very clearly the relative lack of a variable pattern of contact in Denmark, although it reveals a fascinating one for the other two countries. When persons are widowed in old age there are four possible relationships they can have with married children: widow/married daughter, widow/married son, widower/married daughter, and widower/married son. In both the United States and Britain there was, as these four relationships were traced in turn, a marked fall in the proportions having contact with a child within the previous week. No doubt further research will show other subtleties in the relationships (depending, for instance, on whether the children involved are married or widowed, and have, or do not have, children). But Table VI–24 certainly suggests there is an important sexual pattern in intergenerational relationships within the family, at least in the United States and Britain, and that particular importance is placed on the relationship between widowed mother and married daughter.

But patterns of contact are affected (or perhaps determined) not only by whether or not the children are sons or daughters, but by the size of the family and the exact ratio between the sexes. Independent of proximity, patterns of contact are more frequent in some types of family. Thus, taking only those persons living within ten minutes journey of their children, we found that more of those with only one son than with two or more sons had seen a son recently.

Table VI—24: WIDOWS AND WIDOWERS, ACCORDING TO THE SHORTEST PERIOD SINCE THEY HAD LAST SEEN A MARRIED DAUGHTER OR MARRIED SON (*Percentage Distribution*)

Shortest Period Since Last Saw Child	Married Daughter		Married Son	
	Widows[a]	Widowers[a]	Widows[a]	Widowers[a]
Denmark				
Today or yesterday[b]	41	41	42	39
2–7 days	30	24	26	30
8–30 days	17	17	19	12
More than 30 days	12	18	14	20
Total	100	100	100	100
N=	389	186	403	189
Britain				
Today or yesterday[b]	62	58	41	41
2–7 days	19	18	29	25
8–30 days	9	8	15	13
More than 30 days	10	16	16	22
Total	100	100	100	100
N=	477	154	507	155
United States				
Today or yesterday[b]	59	49	45	33
2–7 days	21	25	27	23
8–30 days	10	6	10	14
More than 30 days	10	20	18	30
Total	100	100	100	100
N=	497	149	469	122

[a] Widows and widowers include divorced and married but separated persons.

[b] Including those sharing a household.

Although we would hope that further research with larger samples will identify a larger range of structural types of family and will show in more detail the differences in organization and behavior among such types, the present analysis has at least demonstrated the importance of structural variation. It has shown that (i) the composition of households, (ii) the geographical distribution of related households, and (iii) the patterns of contacts among relatives are affected by the structure of the extended family.

More important, it has tended to overshadow "cultural" variation in offering an explanation of the data. The differences between certain types of family tend to be greater than the differences between the countries. Suppose we compare the patterns of contact between old people and their children for each family type, country by country. It can be said that in general more old people in Britain than in the United States and Denmark have seen a child within the previous day and fewer have not seen one within the previous month. But although there is such a trend it should not be exaggerated. Some of the figures in Table VI–23, for example, do not follow the trend and others represent such small differences, particularly between Britain and the United States, that they are not statistically significant. Moreover, it should also be remembered that the ratio of widows to widowers is higher in Britain than in the United States and this accounts for part of the differences between the countries.

Much is explained by this analysis of structural variation. More of the elderly in Britain than in the United States have only one or two children, have a son or sons only, or are widowed. Other things being equal, this would lead us to conclude that fewer of them would have had recent contact with a child. However, widowed persons are more likely than married persons to live with a married child, proportionately more old people with every type of family live with or near their children in Britain than in the United States, rates of contact for similar categories of family are slightly higher in Britain, and, finally, more old people in Britain than in the other countries have a single child. This is why the over-all frequency of contact between the generation of old people and their children is about the same in the two countries.

Compensation and Substitution

Two features of social structure have been illustrated several times in the foregoing analysis. They help to explain not only how the structure is kept in equilibrium but how individuals are bound into society and given its protection. They may be called the principles of *compensation* and *replacement*. An individual's relationships adjust to variations in family structure. One of the functions of kinship associations is to provide replacements for intimate kin lost by death or migration. A second function is to compensate for the absence of children, grandchildren, or siblings by providing substitutes or preserving into old age some of the ties of childhood and adolescence. In a sense the extended family of three and four generations is a self-balancing or self-correcting system to which the principles of replacement and compensation are fundamental.

Thus old people who have never married tend to maintain much closer relationships with their brothers and sisters than those who marry and have children. Persons without children tend to resume closer associations with siblings upon the death of a spouse, but, interestingly, not as close as single persons. Widowed persons tend to have closer contacts than married persons with their married children. And although more of those with several children than with one or two children are likely to have frequent contact with at least one of their children, parent-child relationships tend to be closer (as measured by living arrangements and frequency of contact) in the small family.

A particularly interesting question raised by the data is whether children who lose their fathers postpone marriage. In all industrial countries a considerable proportion of women are widowed by the mid-50's. By the mid-60's between 3 and 4 in 10 are widowed (see Table VI–10). This means that for a large number of children the father dies during their adolescence or early adult life. The last child in the family to remain single may feel under a special obligation to take over the roles of breadwinner and of household companion in relation to the widowed mother and may, as a consequence, postpone marriage or even remain single.[17] Without suppositions of this kind it is difficult to account for the figures in Table VI–25. They show, for all three countries, a larger percentage of widowed than of married persons at different ages living with a

Table VI–25: PERCENTAGE OF MARRIED AND OF WIDOWED WOMEN, OF DIFFERENT AGE, WHO LIVE WITH AN UNMARRIED CHILD

Age	DENMARK		BRITAIN		UNITED STATES	
	Married	Widowed, Separated, and Divorced	Married	Widowed, Separated, and Divorced	Married	Widowed, Separated, and Divorced
65–66	15	21	27	34	11	22
67–69	10	17	19	21	13	24
70–74	9	12	22	26	9	23
75–79	5	24	14	20	11	13
80+	a	15	a	21	a	26
All ages	10	17	21	24	10	22
N=						
65–66	130	68	115	71	111	83
67–69	134	105	131	121	141	144
70–74	171	180	138	233	170	229
75–79	76	151	78	165	65	151
80+	32	117	48	183	19	154
All ages	543	621	510	773	510b	767b

a Percentages not computed on a base of less than 50.

b Six widowed, divorced, and separated women, and 4 married women of unknown age, are included in the totals.

single child. It may be hypothesized that the difference can be explained by more of the single children of married people moving out in order to live away from home. But in fact this does not account for more than a tiny fraction of the difference. Further research to explore the reasons for postponement of marriage would seem to be called for.[18]

Sometimes a child will marry and yet maintain a particularly close relationship with a parent widowed in the period before marriage. The following is an example from Denmark.

> Mr. Meduk is a man of 82 who lost his wife 18 years previously. At that stage he lived with his youngest daughter, who was single. When she married he went to live with her. He is still active, can go outdoors on his own, and helps

with shopping and light housework. He has an older daughter and a son, who live about an hour's journey distant, but he has not seen them in the past twelve months. He never sees other relatives. He never feels lonely and does not want to move, because, as he says, he enjoys living with his daughter.

There is also the increasingly common instance of the man or woman who is not widowed until a fairly advanced age and who goes to join a married child largely because he or she is too infirm to continue living alone. This is a form of familial "compensation" for social loss, reinforced by acknowledged physical need. Even allowing for those living in institutions, more old people with children in Denmark, Britain, and the United States who were incapacitated lived with or near their families and saw them frequently.

The present data supply only a preliminary indication of the operation of the principles of compensation and substitution as they affect individuals and individual relationships in the social structure.[19] More detailed information could be collected. For example, old people possessing sons and not daughters appear to have closer and more affectionate relationships than others with daughters-in-law. And if the daughters-in-law in question do not themselves have surviving parents, the relationships appear to be further reinforced. Plainly, the ramifications of this type of analysis are considerable.

Effects of Changes in Population Structure

During the last hundred years the trends in population structure in Denmark, Britain, and the United States have taken a broadly similar direction. It is true that some changes have been smaller or more gradual. Thus, the proportion of persons aged 65 and over has increased much less sharply in Denmark than in Britain, with the United States intermediate. Or, again, family size and age at marriage have decreased less in the past 50 years in the United States than in Denmark and Britain.[20] But in all three countries there have been trends towards more marriage, earlier marriage, earlier childbirth, fewer large families, and longer expectation of life, particularly at younger ages.[21]

These changes have altered the structure of the kinship network and the extended family in the following ways. They have reduced the average span in years between the generations, and allowed the emergence of four generations of surviving relatives, as described above. They have contributed to the strengthening of relationships with ascendant and descendant kin, and of affinal kin, as compared with collateral kin. In a sense, there is greater stability at the center. More people marry. More marry young. More survive as married couples until an advanced age. Consequently the number of middle-aged and elderly spinsters acting as universal aunts has diminished; there are fewer "denuded" immediate families and fewer extended families of certain types—such as widowed women linking with collateral married or unmarried kin for the purpose of rearing children and overcoming hardship. The broken marriage and the broken "home" are no longer dominant constituents of the extended family. A model type

Figure VI-6A: CHANGES IN POPULATION AND KINSHIP STRUCTURE, ENGLAND AND WALES, 1861–1961

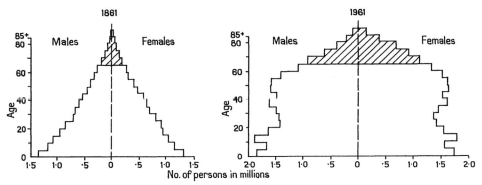

England and Wales – Actual Population Pyramids 1861 and 1961

of extended family is beginning to replace a wide variety of families and households, ranging from lone individuals at one extreme to kinship "tribes" at the other. Figures VI-6 A and B illustrate the changes taking place in kinship structure which correspond to the changes taking place in population structure.

What are the implications of these changes? Old people can be divided into two broad categories—those belonging to the third (or grandparental) and those belonging to the fourth (or great-grandparental) generation. Those belonging to the third generation more often have a surviving husband or wife than did persons of their age at the turn of the century. Fewer have single children remaining at home and grandchildren who are in their infancy. Since these old people represent the "younger" section of the elderly, fewer of their children will have to look after them in infirmity, or illness, and they will have more energy to spare for their grandchildren. In various ways it is likely that the rapid relative increase in importance of

Figure VI-6B

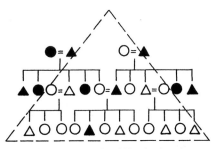

1. Characteristic example of kinship structure around 1900

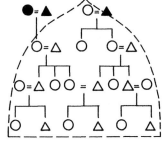

2. Characteristic example of kinship structure – second half of twentieth century

the third generation, with its younger age-span, will result in much greater emphasis being placed in the future than formerly on the reciprocal relations between the second and third generations. This will alter, and complicate, the whole pattern of kinship activity. Moreover, a fourth generation of relatively frail people is also being established.

The nature of the problems of old age is therefore changing. A common instance in the past has been the middle-aged woman faced with the problem of caring for an infirm mother as well as her young children. A common instance of the future will be the woman of 60 faced with the problem of caring for an infirm mother in her 80's. Her children will be adult but it is her grandchildren who will compete with the mother for her attentions. Similarly, there may be a shift of emphasis from the problem of which of the children looks after a widowed parent to the problem of how a middle-aged man and wife can reconcile dependent relationships with *both* sets of parents.

Changes in population structure have far wider and deeper effects than we have been able to indicate here. Insufficient attention has been paid to them in discussing relationships between parents and their children, between husbands and wives, between generations, and generally among households and families.

Theories of Change in Family Life

The full analysis of structural change in the extended family and the kinship network as well as in the population has major implications for our understanding of changes over time in the family. Theorists have alleged the disintegrating effects upon the extended family of industrialization and urbanization, and much has been written about the isolation of the immediate or nuclear family in contemporary society. We are not here concerned with modern exaggeration of the residential and economic unity that the extended family had in the past. But we are concerned with the assumptions that have been made about the end-results of change. These assumptions might be listed as follows: (a) that since a minority of households comprise relatives of three generations, the extended family has "disintegrated" and has lost its functions; (b) that children gain enormously from their parents during the period of socialization but not thereafter, and tend to move away, both physically and emotionally, to begin the cycle all over again, this time as parents; (c) that the middle-aged and elderly have dissimilar interests from those of their children's generation and are likely to have associations with peers rather than with *either* younger unrelated persons *or* younger relatives; (d) that the extended family is inimical to the demands of an industrial society for occupational and social mobility; and (e) that older individuals and younger related immediate families tend to live independently even if traditions of friendly visiting and reunions are maintained.

Without commenting on all these assumptions it can be argued that the data collected in the cross-national survey, and the analyses subsequently made, show, first of all, why much more attention must be devoted to precise definition of different types of family, and to family relationships and functions. Second, they show that relatives not belonging to the household structure do nonetheless carry out important, even everyday, functions for individuals who may be living alone or with other people (as described, for example, in Chapter 5). Third, they show that the structure of the kinship network has been changing more radically than has been supposed. And, fourth, they show that this has had its inevitable repercussions on both family and social organization.

As a consequence the structural determinants of changes may have been underestimated and the economic and educational determinants overestimated. Changes in family organization and relationships may have been affected less by changes in industrial and economic organization, occupational recuitment, and educational selection and organization and more by changes in population structure. Specific changes in birth and mortality rates, size of family, marriage rates, and age of marriage may have had a more pervasive effect than we have realized hitherto. If this conclusion is correct, then theories of the process of urbanization and of the social effects of industrialization may need to be revised.

Summary

The main theme of this chapter is that family structure is a crucial analytic variable in understanding social organization and relationships and therefore individual processes of aging.

First, the structural characteristics of the families of old people in the three countries can be described. Nearly half the elderly population in Denmark and the United States, and just over half in Britain, are single or widowed. Nearly a fifth in the former countries, and nearly a quarter in the latter country, have no surviving children. Rather more old people in the United States than in Denmark or Britain have six or more children but in each of the countries from two-fifths to a half of those with children have only one or two. One of the interesting features of family structure is the large proportion who have children of one sex only. Apart from the fifth to a quarter of the elderly who have one son only or one daughter only, around another fifth have two or more sons or two or more daughters only. The vast majority of those with children have grandchildren, and more than a fifth in Denmark and Britain and more than two-fifths in the United States have great-grandchildren. The fact that the four-generation family is already a common phenomenon in industrialized societies is one of the more surprising results to emerge from the cross-national survey.

Nearly four-fifths of the elderly population have surviving brothers or sisters; a large minority have five or more. Some people can depend on their siblings for companionship and help if they have no children, so it is useful to consolidate the information about children, grandchildren, and siblings. It emerges that from a half to three-fifths of the elderly in the three countries belong to an immediate family structure of three or four generations and also have more than one surviving child. They might be said to have good potential family resources for help in old age. Another fifth have resources in depth over two, three, or four generations, but either they have only one child or, if they have two or more children, they have no grandchildren. The remaining persons, amounting to rather less than a fifth in Denmark and the United States, but nearly a quarter in Britain, have no direct descendants alive. A minority of from 2 to 4 per cent are childless, are single or widowed, *and* have no siblings. (At the other extreme there is a similar minority with five or more children *and* five or more siblings.)

One important feature of structure is the difference in years between the generations. In all three countries the trends towards earlier marriage, earlier childbirth, and fewer large families inevitably contribute towards a narrowing of the average span in years between successive generations. In Britain the difference in age between old people and their eldest children was 26.4 years for women and 29.0 for men, and between old people and their first grandchildren about 54 years for women and 57 for men. But the range is extremely wide, with some old people having young dependent children and others having middle-aged grandchildren.

As age increases the structure of the family changes—at least from the viewpoint of the individual. Old people experience the loss of family members. For example, at the age of 65 to 66 over half the women in all three countries have a husband alive, whereas over the age of 80 from only a tenth to a fifth of the women have a husband alive. Again, in the late 60's six in seven women have a sibling alive, but after the age of 75 only two in three old people have siblings alive. But just as old family members are discharged by death, new ones are recruited by birth. For example, by the age of 80 and over, nearly half the old people with children in Britain, over half in Denmark, and over two-thirds in the United States have great-grandchildren. With increasing age old people tend to find themselves nearer one of two extremes—experiencing the seclusion of the spinster or widow without children and surviving brothers and sisters, or pushed towards the pinnacle of a pyramidal family structure of four generations.

Second, having outlined the structural characteristics of the families of old people in the three countries, some of the consequences for family organization and interaction can be described. The composition of the rest of the household is affected by whether or not old people have a spouse or are single or widowed, and is further affected by the number and sex of old peoples' children. Compared with widowed old persons, for example, married persons more often maintain households independent of their married children and less often share them with other relatives. Single persons are more likely than widowed persons—even than widowed persons who lack children—to share households with siblings. A widowed person is in fact less likely in all three countries to live with a child than a single person is to live with a sibling. Widowed persons with sons only are more likely to be living alone than widowed persons with daughters only. Divorced persons are less likely to live with their children than widowed persons.

Findings such as these imply various conclusions about family organization. They suggest a structural explanation for existing patterns of household composition, given certain social norms. The integrity of marriage is respected, partly by recognizing the right of a married couple to live in an independent household. Social distance between the adult generations in the family is also observed. Preferment is given in family organization and management to relations with daughters over relations with sons. Preferment is given to relations with children over relations with siblings, but if people do not marry, or if they marry and do not have children, then relations with siblings can be maintained throughout life—especially with other childless or single siblings. Once weakened, family relationships are difficult to renew or repair; they need to be regularly reinforced—like conditioned reflexes.

Family structure also affects the geographical distribution of family members. Fewer widowed than married old persons live at considerable distances from their children. Again, it is more common for widowed persons to be living with a child than near him but it is more common for married persons to be living near a child than with him. The chances of living further than thirty minutes journey from the nearest child are greater the smaller is the number of children, though children in the small families tend to compensate: proportionately *more* of them live with or near their parents. Although married daughters more often live with old people than married sons, they are not in general more likely to live near old people. On a broad cross-national basis, then, there is no evidence of marked matrilocal family organization.

One important finding about family organization is the working of a principle of compensation or substitution. More widowed than married old people of comparable age live with unmarried children. It is hypothesized that children sometimes postpone marriage if a father or mother, particularly a father, dies during their adolescence or early adulthood. There are other examples of such compensation. A child in a small family tends to "make good" the inadequacy of numbers; in other words, he tends to live closer and see more of his elderly parents than a comparable "average" child in a large family. Again, a person without children will often share a household with a sibling, or see more of his siblings than a person with both children and siblings.

Finally, family structure affects individual relationships. The shortest period since an old person saw a child was taken as one simple measure which would reveal this. In the 1962 cross-national survey more of the widowed than the married, more of those with several children than one child only, and more of those with daughters than with sons only, had seen a child the same or the previous day. Broadly speaking, fewer in these categories had not seen a child within the previous month. Even when living at comparable distances daughters tended to have been seen more recently than sons. Nevertheless, in all three countries contacts between old persons and their sons were frequent.

Two interesting conclusions emerged about the elderly in individual countries. First, slightly more of the elderly in most types of family in Britain, defined according to sex and number of children, had frequent contacts with their children. Second, relationships in Denmark between old people and their children tended to be more loose-knit than in the other two countries (for example, fewer shared a household) and were also bilateral (for example, relations with sons were nearly as frequent as those with daughters). In Britain and the United States there was greater emphasis on the mother-daughter relationship. Three times as many widowed persons lived with married daughters as with married sons, and in tracing the four possible relationships of widow/married daughter, widower/married daughter, widow/married son, and widower/married son, the proportion seeing a child on the same or the previous day tended to decrease and the proportion not seeing a child in the last month tended to increase.

Both these conclusions, however, tended to be overshadowed by the broad similarity in pattern of family contacts. Since more of the elderly in Britain than in the United States had only one or two children and had sons only, the over-all difference between the elderly populations in patterns of contacts with children were relatively small. Over three-fifths in each of the three countries had seen a child the same or the previous day and another fifth within the previous week. The surprising conclusion for many readers will be that despite structural variations the over-all patterns are so similar.

NOTES

1 See Clark Tibbitts, "Origin, Scope and Fields of Gerontology," in Clark Tibbitts, ed., *Handbook of Social Gerontology* (Chicago: University of Chicago Press, 1960), pp. 3–26.

2 Talcott Parsons has referred repeatedly to the structural isolation of the conjugal family. "The most important distinctive feature of our family structure is the isolation of the individual conjugal family. It is impossible to say that with us it is natural for any other group than husband and wife and their dependent children to maintain a common household." Talcott Parsons, "Age and Sex in the Social Structure of the United States," in *Essays in Sociological Theory* (New York: The Free Press of Glencoe, 1964; rev. paperback ed.), p. 102.

3 It is undoubtedly true that there are large selections of kin that can be considered as "groups," since they serve particular if less continuous functions. Examples are the "family" that is invited to a funeral or wedding, and the "family" sharing a particular surname.

4 Between 1900 and 1960 the per cent of men aged 65 and over who were widowed decreased from 26.4 to 22.6, and of women from 59.3 to 55.3. U.S. Bureau of the Census, *Twelfth Census of the United States, 1900, Population*, Vol. II, Part II (Washington, D.C.: U.S. GPO, 1902), Table 49. In England and Wales the percentages also decreased, of widowers from 35 in 1901 to 22 in 1961. General Register Office, *Census, 1961*, England and Wales, Age, Marital Condition and General Tables (London: HMSO, 1965), Table 13.

5 For all three countries the single appear to have been underrepresented. For Denmark and the United States the married have been overrepresented.

6 See General Register Office, *Census, 1961*, England and Wales, Age, Marital Condition and General Tables, *op. cit.*

7 In Britain family size decreased appreciably during the latter part of the nineteenth century and the early part of this century. Among couples married in 1900–1909 the average number of children born was two less than among couples married in the

1850's and 1860's. Couples married in 1925–29 had one child fewer on average than couples married in 1900–1909. Couples marrying in 1925–29 had an average of just over two children compared with the five or six children of couples marrying sixty or seventy years earlier. With allowances for the death of some of their children a similar drastic change has been taking place in the family circumstances of the aged population. By 1962 the distribution of families of different sizes among the aged had come to resemble closely the distribution of families of different size resulting from marriages taking place in the 1920's. Among persons who married around 1860 only 9 per cent produced no children, whereas 53 per cent had six or more children. Among persons who married in the 1920's 17 per cent produced no children and 7 per cent had six or more children. These percentages from 1920's marriages corresponded broadly with the number of married and widowed old people in the 1962 sample having no surviving children and having six or more (15 per cent and 11 per cent respectively). *Report of the Royal Commission on Population* (London: HMSO, 1948).

8 For Britain the difference is not statistically significant; however, a second national survey carried out among the elderly late in 1962 also showed that rather more persons had a married or widowed daughter than a married or widowed son.

9 The proportions are, if anything, slight underestimates. Some people who were interviewed had a parent alive. There were also some who had great-great-grandchildren and who had living representatives of all five generations.

10 For example, a survey of first marriages taking place between 1947 and 1954 in the United States, showed that in 6 per cent the husband was 10 or more years older than his wife and a further 23 per cent was from 5 to 9 years older, but in 6 per cent he was 3 or more years younger than his wife. Paul C. Glick, *American Families* (New York: John Wiley and Sons, Inc., 1957), p. 125. The census for 1951 in England and Wales revealed that 3 per cent of husbands of all wives aged 50 or under were 13 or more years older, and a further 8 per cent from 8 to 12 years older, than their wives, but that 6 per cent were 3 or more years younger. Although the majority of wives had married in their 20's, 6 per cent had married in their late 30's and another 2 per cent in their 40's or later. General Register Office, *Census, 1951*, England and Wales, Fertility (London: HMSO, 1954), Tables 2, 13, p. xxxii.

11 Paul C. Glick and R. Parke, "New Approaches in Studying the Life Cycle of the Family," *Demography*, II (1965); also Paul C. Glick, "The Life Cycle of the Family," *Marriage and Family Living*, XVII, No. 1 (Feb., 1955).

12 Expressed as a percentage of the male expectation of life at age 65 the female expectation of life at that age is 109 in Denmark, but 123 in the United States and 127 in England and Wales. *U.N. Demographic Yearbook* (New York: United Nations, 1963), Table 26, p. 668.

13 In the British survey, for example, it was found that only about 10 per cent of those aged 70 and over with grandchildren had become grandparents after the age of 65.

14 For a discussion of similar findings in one area of London, see Peter Townsend, *The Family Life of Old People* (London: Routledge & Kegan Paul, 1957), pp. 81–82.

15 Of those with both married sons and married daughters, 44 per cent lived nearer the married daughter and only 30 per cent nearer the married son (with the remaining 27 per cent at about equal distances). However, when those with children living in the same household were excluded, the percentages were both 32 (with a further 35 per cent having a son and a daughter at equivalent distances). An aggregate analysis of the proximity of old people to *all* their sons and daughters shows that while rather more daughters than sons share a household, rather fewer live within ten minutes journey.

16 Old people were asked when they had last seen each of their children, beginning with the eldest. In Britain they were also asked how often they usually saw each child.

17 The single children of old people tend to fall into two categories: (i) younger persons who were born relatively late and who are only now of the usual marriageable age, or approaching that age (such as the youngest child of a large family, or the only child born relatively late in an otherwise childless marriage); and (ii) older persons who have remained unmarried—sometimes as a direct consequence of structural change and developments in the family. Thus, it is suggested that only children may sometimes postpone marriage indefinitely, especially if they experience the loss of their

fathers during adolescence and feel, or are encouraged to feel, the need to provide companionship and support to their widowed mothers. A direct check of this supposition is not easy to devise. The cross-national survey simply found that in all three countries relatively more of the only children were single, despite their older age.

18 In Britain, for example, it was very uncommon for single children to be found living apart from either their widowed or their married parents. A brief discussion of some of the issues is given by Peter Townsend, *The Family Life of Old People, op. cit.*, pp. 81–82.

19 There are some interesting examples in the recent literature. For example, "Living with the husband's parents did seem to work in several cases when the wife's own mother was dead. 'She's been a second mother to me. I don't know what I'd have done without her,' was a typical comment. Clearly the need for someone to fill the gap in these women's own family relationships made by the death of their own mothers made trivial any smaller differences between them and their mothers-in-law, which had their own mothers been alive, would probably have been crucial. One useful function that relations acquired at marriage can perform is clearly to fill the blank spaces in the ranks of one's own family." Colin Rosser and Christopher Harris, *The Family and Social Change* (London: Routledge & Kegan Paul, 1965), p. 260.

20 Thus in the United States the median age at marriage of women born between 1880 and 1890 was 21.6, compared with 19.9 for those born between 1930 and 1940. Again, the average number of children per woman ever married by the end of the child-bearing period fell from 3.4 for those born between 1880 and 1890 to 2.5 for those born between 1910 and 1920, but it rose again to 3.1 for those born between 1920 and 1930. P. C. Glick and R. Parke, *op. cit.*

21 In the United States, the main differences between the youngest women and those 40 or 60 years their seniors, who were young at the beginning of the century, are as follows: "The youngest women marry one or two years younger; their age at the marriage of their last child is four to five years younger, and their length of married life is about nine years longer." P. C. Glick and R. Parke, *op. cit.*

7 : *The Household and Family Relations of Old People*

The social context within which individual aging takes place may be described as a social network of contacts encompassing several generations of kinsfolk, friends, and acquaintances. This social network consists of the household, the immediate and the extended family of the older person, as well as any other individual or group with which the older person maintains contact. This network can be smaller as well as larger than the family structure described in the previous chapter. For the extremely isolated individual the social network has shrunk. Normally, however, the social network will consist of members of the household of which the older person is part—some or all of his adult children, grandchildren, and friends, acquaintances, and individuals such as neighbors, shopkeepers, the postman, or the district nurse.

This chapter will analyze only two parts of this social network: that part which is determined by the organization of the household in which the older person lives, and that part which is established through contact with children, grandchildren, siblings, and other relatives. The general theme of this chapter is the extent to which older people are part of an extended family.

We will comment briefly on the shortcomings of existing theoretical assumptions about the family relationships of older people, and then go on to discuss the approach and some of the definitions used in this cross-national survey. We will successively deal with three different topics: first, the organization of the extended family as it is revealed by household structure and the proximity of children; second, the structural integration of the extended family as demonstrated through the frequency of the old person's contact with children, siblings, and other relatives and by reciprocal help patterns; and third, the influence of age, sex, and physical capacity on the family relations of older people. Later in this chapter we will summarize and discuss some of our main findings and compare the similarities and differences between the family relations of older people in the three countries involved in this cross-national study.

Family Relations in Later Life, Myth or Theory?

As has been pointed out earlier, family sociologists have hitherto shown a reluctance to deal with family relationships in the last stages of the life cycle. Until recently the preoccupations of sociologists have been with the establishment, structure, and functioning of the nuclear family. The last stages in the development of this family have been systematically disregarded.[1] Instead of a body of theoretical work on the development of family relations in later life we have been offered only pessimistic predictions of a dissolution of family relations in industrial societies.

Sociological literature on the development of the family in industrial societies has succeeded in creating the impression that industrialization and urbanization result in a type of family which is "atomistic," "particularistic," "loose-knit," and "unstable," or even "dissolved." In the 1930's, Sorokin, for example, predicted the future development of the family as follows:

> The family as a sacred union of husband and wife, of parents and children, will continue to disintegrate. Divorces and separations will increase until any profound difference between socially sanctioned marriages and illicit sex-relationship disappears. Children will be separated earlier and earlier from parents. ... The main sociocultural functions of the family will further decrease, until the family becomes a mere incidental cohabitation of male and female, while the home will become a mere overnight parking place mainly for sex relationships.[2]

Other "pessimistic" assumptions about relations between generations prevalent in the 1930's and early 1940's are to be found in statements stressing the tendency towards the development of an integrated, but isolated, nuclear family. Parsons' articles on "Age and Sex in the Social Structure of the United States" and "The Kinship System of the Contemporary United States," published in 1942 and 1943 respectively (and reprinted unamended until very recently), include some "classical" statements which stress structural isolation of the nuclear family and disintegration of the extended kin network. For example:

> It is impossible to say that with us it is "natural," for any other group than husband and wife and their dependent children to maintain a common household. Hence, when children of a couple have become independent through marriage and occupational status the parental couple is left out without attachment to any continuous kinship group. It is, of course, common for other relatives to share a household with the conjugal family but this scarcely ever occurs without some important elements of strain.[3]

Elsewhere Parsons says:

The obverse of the emancipation, upon marriage and occupational independence, of children from their families of orientation is the depletion of that family until the older couple is finally left alone. This situation is in strong contrast to kinship systems in which membership in a kinship unit is continuous throughout the life cycle.[4]

As late as 1950 Homans was able to write: "Our own society has a single kinship unit, the nuclear family . . ."; and, further: "The nuclear family first left the household and then even the neighborhood of other kinsmen."[5]

In general, theories about family development seem either to have stressed a trend towards family dissolution or a trend towards the predominance of an isolated nuclear type of family. Both approaches imply an idealization of the traditional extended family, consisting of three or more generations and often of two nuclear families, living and working in the same household. It is obvious that there is a substantial time-lag between theoretical assumptions concerning the isolation of the nuclear family and the weakening of relations between generations, and the development of empirical evidence about existing family systems in highly industrialized societies. During recent years evidence on the existence of close relations between generations as well as kinsfolk has accumulated in both the United States and Great Britain.[6] As Sussman and Burchinal put it:

> . . . there appears to be an academic "cultural lag" between antiquated nuclear family theory and empirical reality. The theory stresses the social isolation and social mobility of the nuclear family, whereas current findings from empirical studies reveal an extended kin family system functioning within a network of relationships and mutual assistance patterns along bilateral kinship lines, and encompassing several generations.[7]

Predictions about the dissolution of the family may be said to conceal a false premise. Traditional family sociologists have apparently failed to recognize that the modern family, as in former times, continues to adapt itself to a rapidly changing society. Much of the reasoning about the development of relations between generations has been governed by conditions of "*ceteris paribus*." As an example of the flexibility of the family, let us consider the effect of migration on the relationship between generations. In a society which lacks means of communication, migration must lead towards a disintegration of family ties. In contemporary industrial society, however, physical distance between generations is only a minor problem. The aged may have their children living at a considerable distance from the parental home, but communication is possible by telephone, correspondence, or mutual visiting. Modern means of transportation and communication have diminished the importance of physical distance. The removal of adult children to households separate from that of their parents does not necessarily imply the termination of parental functions in relation to the children and vice versa. Parents in their 40's, 50's, and 60's lose as well as gain functions within the structure of their families. They lose the obligation to care for their children and the responsibilities implicit in this function; they gain the role and the responsibilities of the grandparent.

Further, sociologists have often overemphasized the predominance as well as the stability and integration of the large household in pre-industrial societies. It seems quite certain that this functionally inter-dependent and economically self-supporting household has existed in the past and still does occur in certain middle European agricultural areas. Recent historical research, however, has revealed that only relatively few such households existed in pre-industrial England and in certain regions in France. Individuals who survived to old age were surprisingly often left to live and die alone.[8]

It seems obvious that the integration of the pre-industrial household to a large extent was due to external factors rather than internal factors. Strong social control maintained by the community has given these house-holds a reputation of stability and integration.

Again we are faced with the tendency to idealize the past. The large household, consisting of several generations living and working together, may have been a stable unit, if by stable is meant "remaining together," but the apparent stability of this autocratic type of family may have con-cealed more tensions than harmony. Nevertheless, many of the traditional family sociologists have been of the opinion that "living apart from each other" in separate households, which is the established pattern for different generations in most industrial societies today, militates against inter-generational contacts. The common belief has been that the family necessarily disintegrates when the household becomes smaller. But as Rosenmayr and Köckeis point out, "joint living is not the most important factor in the relations between old people and their grown up children ... without it, there can be many practical demonstrations of mutual goodwill."[9] No positive correlations need be expected between joint living and family adjustment. On the contrary, it seems that family adjustment can be demonstrated through the establishment of extended family systems whose members see one another regularly and who expect a certain amount of mutual help each from the other.

The traditional assumptions about the changes in the family and the disintegration of relations between the generations in modern societies have never been supported by empirical evidence. On the contrary, a number of studies have demonstrated that the generations, although preferring to live apart, maintain contact and exchange mutual services. What is found between the generations is "intimacy" at a distance rather than isolation.

It is not logical to expect a single "ideal type" of family in highly differentiated industrialized societies. What can be expected is "family diversity" rather than "family uniformity." Industrial societies create every possible form of family life, varying from the highly integrated extended family in which the older person has a secure and respected role, to the highly dispersed network on whose periphery the older person has an isolated position. Evidence of this diversity has already been provided in some contemporary research on relations between generations. The present survey, however, is the first of its kind to compile data on the family relations of older people in three countries, of which one, Denmark, is quite unexplored in this respect. If our hypothesis about family diversity in industrial societies holds true, we may, in this cross-national context, expect more variation in the relations between generations *within* each country, than *between* the three countries involved.

Some General Problems of Approach

Every method of data collection has its advantages and disadvantages. Research in the field of family relations of older people which tries to obtain information about the extent to which older people belong to an extended family, the frequency of contact of older people with family members, as well as the functions of the extended family, must employ painstaking and therefore time-consuming questionnaires. Since it was decided at an early stage that the present study would cover a variety of topics all related to the social well-being and living conditions of the aged in the three countries, the possibility for an elaborately detailed analysis of family relations has been somewhat restricted. Bearing in mind the over-all character of the questionnaire as well as its length, it has been necessary to limit ourselves to gathering detailed information about the overt relations between older people and their children, and somewhat less detailed information about the relations of older people with siblings and other relatives.

The data about the family relations of older people, in the present survey, cover the following topics:

1. The number of living children; number of sons and daughters.
2. For each child: sex, marital status, proximity to the home of the older person, time of last contact.
3. Help given to and received from children.
4. Help from children (among others) in a number of specific situations, such as household activities, shopping during illness, et cetera.
5. Number of living siblings.
6. Last contact with siblings.
7. Help from siblings and other relatives, both in general and in specific situations.

The cross-national survey enables us to reach some rough estimates of the degree of contact between older persons and their children and other relatives. It provides us with useful but limited information about the role of the family in later life, that is, the functions of the family vis-à-vis its aging members. It does not enable us to evaluate the attitudes that lie behind the pattern of contacts as we observe it. Nor does it evaluate the quality of family relationships, or the relative importance of family contacts in relation to the total network of contacts that may be maintained by older persons.

All research projects leave unanswered a number of questions. At the same time, research raises new questions. Cross-national and other comparative investigations are in a special position in this respect. Comparisons between countries may reveal unexpected similarities as well as differences which demand interpretation. Often, however, it is not possible to supply an adequate interpretation of such findings, since the research design may not include those variables that are needed for more detailed analysis of unexpected cross-national similarities and differences. For example, we find that old people in Denmark, more than in Britain and the United States, tend to live apart from children. On the other hand, we find that the proportions of older persons who have had contact with at least one child within the last week are very much the same in each of the countries. We also find that older persons in Denmark seem to get less help from children and give less help to children than older people in Britain and in the United States. These differences are so marked that they cannot be due to possible differences in the approach used by the interviewers or to the older person's interpretation of the questions. In this, and in other cases, we are confronted with results which raise new questions that we are unable to answer. These questions, however, can provide a fruitful basis for future cross-national as well as national research. Meanwhile, in the absence of complete data some tentative explanations of cross-national similarities and differences must be sought in the cultural and institutional background of each of the three countries.

Concepts and Definitions

The main theme of this chapter is the extent to which the aged can be said to belong to an extended family. The concept "extended family," as we use it in the present research, covers a social system that consists of parents, adult children, siblings, and other relatives, who do not necessarily live in the same household, but who nevertheless contrive to see each other frequently. The extended family need not be one integrated group, but can equally well consist of a more loosely knit web of individual or groups of relatives who frequently interact with the older person.[10] The crucial point is that when we use the concept "extended family," we refer to the categories of children, siblings, and relatives (individuals as well as whole families), who tend to have frequent contacts with the older person. Since "frequent contact" is an ambiguous term, the measure "contact within the past week" can be and was used.

The private household—as the concept is defined internationally and employed in this chapter—consists of persons who sleep under the same roof and eat around the same table. In practice, difficulties can arise in applying this definition. It may cut through existing social systems or it may unite separate systems. A widow who lives alone in a flat but who spends most of her time with the family of one of her children, who live around the corner, is classified as "living alone." Further, in some instances where the older person lives under the same roof with relatives or nonrelatives it can be extremely difficult to say who is in the household and who is not.[11] By and large, errors introduced by the limitations of the "household" concept will cancel each other. Nevertheless it is important to realize that household categories like "older person living alone," "older person living with relative," "older person living with non-relative" in practice may not be as exclusive as the definition implies. The social structure of which the older person who lives alone is a part may range from almost total isolation from others to being more or less part of another household. On the other hand, the older person who lives with relatives or non-relatives may not necessarily be involved in their daily lives.

The proximity of children and relatives plays an important role in the organization of the extended family. Physical nearness is one of the most important conditions through which the extended family is able to operate. Those closest to the older person are the other members of the household of which he is part. Nearly as close are those members of the extended family who have a household of their own, but who may actually live in the same physical structure. In the present survey we found that it is sometimes not a simple matter to decide whether or not two families (or households) occupy separate dwellings. If a semi-detached house consists of two apartments, the two families can be said to live in the same house but to occupy separate dwellings. We therefore treated all children who lived outside the dwelling occupied by the older person's household as neighbors even though they may in fact be occupants of the same physical structure.

The proximity of children is measured by "transport distance." By transport distance we mean the time usually taken by the older person or the child to cover the distance between the two houses when employing the "usual" means of transport (that is, whether on foot, by public transportation, car, train, air, et cetera).

Contacts between older people and their children and other relatives were determined by asking the older person when he had last seen each child, a sibling, and a relative. By asking about "the last contact" we obtain a crude indirect measure of frequency of family contacts. We did not ask old people how often they usually saw members of the family. Such questions about "usual" frequencies too easily result in an over-estimation of the actual amount of maintained contact. Questions about "the last contact" give a much better estimate of the proportion of older people at either extreme of the scale, that is, the proportion of those who have little or no contact, and of those who have a great deal of contact. As mentioned earlier, information was obtained about contact with each individual child. Since we have no information about the length, content, and importance of individual contacts, each contact has been weighted equally and summarized into a single code: "When did the older person last see one of his children?" Similar summary codes have been constructed for the last contact with daughters, sons, and single and married children.

Proximity to Children: Some Structural Aspects of the Extended Family

In this section we consider three aspects of what might be termed the geographical organization of the extended family as it affects the old person. First, we investigate the core of the extended family, the household, which includes the older person. The word "core" is perhaps misleading, in that it implies that the older person is the central figure of the extended family. Within the over-all structure of the extended family, and from the point of view of its individual members, this need not be the case. For the purposes of this discussion, however, let us consider the aged person's immediate household as the center of his family relations.

Second, we consider the housing situation of the older person. Two factors interest us: the size of the dwelling in which the older person lives, and the length of his stay both in this dwelling and in the neighborhood. The size of available housing is an important condition for the establishment of large households. Small housing may in fact prevent such establishments and so influence the geographical organization of the extended family. Length of residence may be considered as an indicator of integration within a given social structure, of which the extended family perhaps forms a part. The longer an older person has lived in a certain house and/or area, the stronger the likelihood that he is part of a social network which makes living in the area valuable to him in and of itself.

Finally, we will examine the geographical distance between the older person and those of his children who live outside his household. We will gauge the extent to which older persons who no longer live with children live close to one among them.

THE STRUCTURE OF THE HOUSEHOLD

The majority of elderly persons in the three countries are part of a family structure consisting of at least three generations (see Chapter 6). In all three countries it is unusual for three successive generations to share a common household. In Denmark approximately 5 per cent, in the United States 8 per cent, and in Britain 13 per cent of the respective samples live in such households.[12] The three-generation household represents a structure which is rare in almost all industrial societies. In Europe this type of household is found mostly in the less prosperous agricultural areas, a last remnant of the self-supporting farm family, consisting of two, three, or four generations living and working together.[13] The three-generation household can also be found in urban areas of Europe, often established as a temporary arrangement to solve an acute housing or other social problem of one of its members. Three-generation households are seldom maintained continuously throughout adult life. Either they are temporary, or they are re-established as permanent arrangements when other relationships are severed.[14]

About a quarter of the aged population in Denmark (28 per cent), in Britain (22 per cent) and in the United States (22 per cent) live alone.

One-third of the elderly population in Britain and slightly less than half in Denmark and in the United States live as married couples, in a household of their own, without other members. The remainder of the elderly, 27 per cent in Denmark, 45 per cent in Britain, and 35 per cent in the United States live in households which have a more differentiated structure. Most of these households include an adult child, especially an unmarried or a previously married child.

For the generations of older people represented in the three national samples, the last child normally would have left the parental home as the parents approached their late 50's. Nevertheless, approximately 14 per cent of all married elderly couples in Denmark and in the United States, and 23 per cent of those in Britain, live with an unmarried child. Among those who are widowed and divorced, 15 per cent in Denmark, 18 per cent in Britain, and 20 per cent in the United States live with an unmarried child.

There are several reasons for the establishment and/or maintenance of households consisting of aged parents and unmarried adult children. Some illustrations may perhaps clarify the different characteristics of such households.

Mr. and Mrs. S. live in a bungalow in an older residential area of Copenhagen. They have four children, the two eldest and the youngest of whom are married. The third child, a daughter aged 42, has never been married. She cares for her parents, and performs nearly all household tasks.

Mrs. J. is a widow whose husband died five years ago. She lives in a provincial town and runs a shop. Aged 78, she lives together with a son who is 60. Mrs. J. says that she will retire as soon as her son gets a pension. Her son will not continue the small family business. He is not very bright, she says, but he has always been willing to help her.

Mrs. L. has been divorced for twenty years. She is 66 and has just retired from a job as a secretary in a large industrial firm. She lives together with her eldest daughter, aged 42, whose husband died two years ago. Her daughter has three children, one of whom lives in the same household.

These three examples each represent quite different types of households, although each of them consists of older people and their unmarried, or previously married, child. The first case represents the classical instance of the daughter who fails to marry and remains with her parents. In this case it is the younger person who gradually acquires responsibility for the older. In the second case, we find the reverse. Here an energetic and healthy 78-year-old mother is still in command of the household and taking care of a son who has never done very well. The third case represents a re-establishment of a household consisting of an aging parent and an adult child, perhaps for convenience, or perhaps because the daughter had difficulty in finding a place to live, or perhaps because of strong emotional ties between mother and daughter.

What are the general characteristics of those elderly people who live with unmarried children? Our results show that the picture is much more differentiated than might have been expected. First of all, we find that in

Table VII–1: PERCENTAGE OF UNMARRIED AND MARRIED PERSONS, BY HOUSEHOLD COMPOSITION[a] (*Percentage Distribution*)

Household Composition	DENMARK Unmarried			DENMARK Married			BRITAIN Unmarried			BRITAIN Married			UNITED STATES Unmarried			UNITED STATES Married		
	Men	Women	All	Men	Women	All	Men	Women	All	Men	Women	All	Men	Women	All	Men	Women	All
Living alone	58	63	61	—	—	—	37	45	43	—	—	—	52	46	48	—	—	—
Living with spouse only	—	—	—	80	84	82	—	—	—	67	68	68	—	—	—	77	82	79
Living with married child (and others)[b]	9	5	7	2	1	1	23	17	19	5	1	5	12	15	14	2	2	2
Living with unmarried child (and others)	11	16	15	15	13	14	18	20	18	24	24	23	17	22	20	16	13	15
Living with siblings or other relatives	6	7	7	1	—	—	14	13	13	3	5	3	11	12	12	3	2	3
Living with others	16	9	10	2	2	3	8	5	6	1	2	1	8	5	6	2	1	1
Total	100	100	100	100	100	100	100	100	100	100	100	100	100	100	100	100	100	100
N=	349	758	1,107	796	543	1,339	303	986	1,289	701	510	1,211	256	851	1,107	825	510	1,335

[a] Detailed information on non-response is not given in this or subsequent tables if 98 per cent or more of all eligible respondents have answered the question.

[b] This is a priority code, i.e., households with married children may also include unmarried children, etc.

both Denmark and the United States relatively more widowed and divorced persons than married persons tend to live with unmarried children. In these two countries, we also find pronounced sex differences in the proportions of people who live with unmarried children. Table VII-1 shows clearly that in Denmark as well as the United States significantly more unmarried women than men live in a household with an unmarried child. The reverse is true for the married, among whom we find slightly more men than women living in a household with unmarried children. As has been shown in Chapter 6, in all three countries older people who live with unmarried children tend to have large families. Finally, as will be demonstrated, our data reveal some unexpected class differences in the proportions of older people who live together with unmarried children. In Denmark such households exist nearly twice as frequently among farmers as among white and blue collar workers. In both Britain and the United States we find slightly more persons of blue collar background than of white collar background living with unmarried children. (For a more detailed discussion of class differences, see Chapter 8 in this volume.)

A household consisting of an aged parent and the family of one of his married children differs greatly in structure as well as origin, from households consisting of aged parents and unmarried adult children. The fact that most of these former households consist of a widowed parent and a married child clearly shows that this arrangement often arises from the need of a surviving parent for care. This is by no means the only reason for the establishment and maintenance of such households, however. Again we must consider a variety of conditions that can lead to a joint household consisting of an aging parent and an adult married child. Examples from the Danish study provide some illustrations.

Mr. and Mrs. P. live in a provincial town. Mr. P. is a self-employed carpenter living in a six-room detached house. Mr. P. is still actively employed. Both Mr. and Mrs. P. are in good health. They have three children—all of them are married. The eldest and the youngest live in the neighborhood. The second child, a daughter, lives with her husband and 9-month-old child, together with her parents. It is a temporary arrangement, which will end as soon as Mr. P. has finished the house which he is building for his daughter and her family.

Mrs. R. is a 67-year-old widow in good health. She lives in a suburb in the Copenhagen area in a house with seven rooms. Her youngest daughter, the daughter's husband, and their three children aged 2, 4, and 7 live with her. Mrs. R. takes care of the grandchildren and is involved in the greater part of the everyday household work, as both her son-in-law and her daughter are working. Mrs. R. says that time never passes slowly and she never feels lonely.

Mrs. Z. is a 77-year-old widow, living on a farm, which is now run by her second eldest son. Her son is married and has five children aged from 9 to 19. Mrs. Z. has difficulty in getting about, she is hard of hearing, and does not help her daughter-in-law in household activities. She says she sometimes feels lonely.

The three households described above each have their own origin and *raison d'être*. They also serve to illustrate that the household consisting of older people and the family of a married child differs in structure and

character at different stages of the life-cycle. The case of Mrs. Z. is a
typical example of a household that includes an elderly widow in need of
care. It also illustrates the instance of the family that has run a farm for
several generations, with one of the sons taking over operation of the farm
while the parents continue to share the farm homestead. The case of
Mrs. R. is quite different. Since the relations between Mrs. R. and her
daughter are good, her married daughter and the latter's family have taken
over part of a large house. In contrast to the case of Mrs. R., the situation
of Mr. and Mrs. P. is more temporary. Mr. and Mrs. P. have space
enough to solve the immediate housing problem of their daughter, but
it seems to have been agreed from the beginning that the daughter should
have a separate dwelling.

It is obvious that the sex and marital status of the older person and the
sex of the married child are decisive factors for the establishment of
households consisting of older parents and married children. Far more
widowed than married older people live together with married children.
In Britain we find only 5 per cent of the married against 19 per cent of the
widowed living with married children, in the United States 2 per cent
against 14 per cent, and in Denmark one per cent against 7 per cent.

In the United States and Britain, but not in Denmark, it is more common for widowed persons to live with the family of a married daughter
than with a married son. In all three countries we find about equal

Table VII–2: PERCENTAGE OF UNMARRIED MEN AND WOMEN IN THE
HOUSEHOLD OF A MARRIED SON OR DAUGHTER

Household Type	DENMARK		BRITAIN		UNITED STATES	
	Men	Women	Men	Women	Men	Women
Living with						
Married daughter	4	3	15	13	10	12
Married son	5	2	8	4	3	3
N=	349	758	303	986	256	842

proportions of widowed men and women living with married daughters.
And, in Britain and Denmark, but not in the United States, we find twice
as many widowed men as widowed women living in the same household
with a married son.

Most of the elderly people who live with siblings or other relatives are
to be found among the widowed, divorced, and single. It is obvious that
the possession or lack of children is a decisive factor in these living
arrangements. In old age, as has been demonstrated, the absence of
children seems to be compensated for by more active relations with
siblings and other kin. (For a more elaborate discussion of the influence of
children on family structure, see Chapter 6.) People who never marry will
often maintain active relations with at least one member of their family of

orientation. Such a relationship may endure until the later stages of the life-cycle. We may say that widowed and divorced elderly people, when they do not live alone, live with children, and that single elderly people live with siblings or relatives.

In Denmark and Britain but not in the United States, it seems that childlessness is less isolating for men than for women. In both countries we find relatively fewer childless unmarried men than women living alone, and more living with siblings and non-relatives.

Table VII-3: PERCENTAGE OF CHILDLESS, UNMARRIED MEN AND WOMEN, BY TYPE OF HOUSEHOLD (*Percentage Distribution*)

Household Type	DENMARK		BRITAIN		UNITED STATES	
	Men	Women	Men	Women	Men	Women
Living alone	54	66	42	56	53	50
With siblings	19	14	33	29	19	32
With other relatives	3	6	8	6	12	10
With non-relatives	24	14	17	9	16	8
Total	100	100	100	100	100	100
N=	83	194	88	312	73	191

Living with relatives, other than siblings, is most common in the United States and least common in Denmark. Differences between the sexes in this respect are small and inconsistent. Attention should finally be given to the fact that the relatively small proportion of childless people living with siblings or other relatives in Denmark is counterbalanced by a very large proportion of childless people who live with non-relatives. In part, this is explained by the Danish tradition, particularly strong in rural areas, of widowers acquiring a housekeeper after bereavement.

THE SIZE OF DWELLING OCCUPIED BY DIFFERENT TYPES OF HOUSEHOLDS[15]

The establishment of households that include elderly people and adult children, whether such an arrangement is a permanent or a temporary one, is dependent on the availability of adequate housing. Denmark, in common with all other Scandinavian countries, has a tradition of small housing. About 60 per cent of all dwellings have less than four rooms compared with 23 per cent in Britain. In Britain almost half of both the unmarried as well as the married elderly live in dwellings that contain five or more rooms. In Denmark less than one of five unmarried elderly people, and only one in four married persons, occupy dwellings of that size.

Table VII–4: PERCENTAGE OF MARRIED AND UNMARRIED PERSONS, BY SIZE OF DWELLING, IN DENMARK AND BRITAIN (*Percentage Distribution*)

Number of Rooms	DENMARK			BRITAIN		
	Married	Unmarried	All	Married	Unmarried	All
1–3	51	62	56	28	30	29
4	24	19	22	24	22	23
5 or more	25	19	22	48	48	48
Total	100	100	100	100	100	100
N=	1,323	1,079a	2,402	1,209	1,284	2,493

a 97.4 per cent of eligible respondents answered this question.

Some of the difference between the proportion of elderly people who live with children in Denmark and England can be explained by the considerable difference in the average size of family dwellings in the two countries. The correlation between size of dwelling and the occurrence of large multi-generational households which include elderly people explains only a part of the difference between the living arrangements of elderly people in Britain and Denmark. The United States is also a country with

Table VII–5: LIVING ARRANGEMENTS OF MARRIED AND UNMARRIED PERSONS, AGED 65 AND MORE, BY SIZE OF DWELLING, IN DENMARK AND BRITAIN (*Percentage Distribution*)

Marital Status and Living Arrangements	DENMARK				BRITAIN			
	No. of Rooms			Total	No. of Rooms			Total
	1–3	4	5		1–3	4	5	
Married								
Living with spouse only	91	79	66	82	82	69	59	68
With married child	—	—	5	1	1	2	8	4
With unmarried child	8	16	23	14	13	23	27	22
With others	1	5	6	3	4	6	6	6
Total	100	100	100	100	100	100	100	100
N=	672	322	329	1,323	337	295	577	1,209
Unmarried								
Living alone	77	37	36	62	69	49	25	43
With married child	2	7	18	6	5	16	28	19
With unmarried child	11	25	19	15	15	21	20	19
With others	10	31	27	17	11	14	27	19
Total	100	100	100	100	100	100	100	100
N=	667	206	206	1,079a	379	287	618	1,284

a 97.4 per cent of eligible respondents answered this question.

typically large housing facilities. In spite of this, the proportion of elderly people who live together with children is lower there than in Britain.

One must bear in mind that in Denmark, contrary to Britain, large dwellings first of all are found in the rural parts of the country. Furthermore, living together with children is much more common in the rural areas of Denmark than in the urban. As Ethel Shanas points out in the next chapter, sharing a home with children is most common among widowed working class men and women in Britain, working class widows in the United States, and widowed farmers and farm wives in Denmark (see Chapter 8). In that country, about 40 per cent of all elderly people who live with children were found among farmers.

As a consequence of the traditional policy of small housing in urban areas, many elderly people in Denmark have little opportunity to live together with adult children. Once children have left the family, the parents continue to live on their own. Recent trends in housing policy for the aged as well as in development of welfare services in Denmark show that everything possible is done to keep old people independent within their own dwelling.

LENGTH OF RESIDENCE IN DWELLING AND NEIGHBORHOOD

The longer people have lived in a certain dwelling or area, the more they develop a feeling of belonging to both place and area. The length of residence in a certain dwelling and neighborhood may to some extent be considered as an indicator of integration. The longer the older person has lived in a certain area, the more likely it is that he or she has developed a network of contacts in this particular area and feels at home in it.

Older people in Denmark and Britain seem to be somewhat less mobile than their counterparts in the United States. In Denmark as well as in Britain approximately 75 per cent of all people aged 65 and more have lived for 20 or more years in the same neighborhood. Data from a 1957 survey of the elderly in the United States indicate that only about 50 per cent of the elderly have lived in the same neighborhood 25 years or more.[16] In Denmark only about 15 per cent and in Britain about 20 per cent of the aged changed their dwelling within the last 5 years. Recent census data from the United States reveal that 36 per cent of persons aged 65 and more moved to a different residence in the period 1955-60.[17]

The mobility patterns of the aged in different household types are not the same in Britain and Denmark. In general, the Danes are less mobile than the British. In Britain those who are most likely to have moved recently are single people who live with married children. Those who are least mobile are single persons either living alone or with others, and married couples either living alone or sharing a household with others. In Denmark single people who live alone and married couples who have their own household tend to be slightly more mobile than single and married people who share a household with others. The differences in the mobility patterns between the two countries can be partly explained by the differences in population structure.

Table VII–6: LENGTH OF RESIDENCE IN DWELLING OF OLD PERSONS,
BY HOUSEHOLD TYPE, DENMARK AND BRITAIN (*Percentage Distribution*)

Length of Residence	Married Persons		Unmarried Persons			All Persons
	Living with Spouse Only	Living with Others[a]	Living Alone	Living with Married Children	Living with Others	
Britain						
Less than 6 years	20	16	20	37	21	21
6–10 years	14	9	10	17	11	12
11–20 years	14	14	13	10	15	14
21 or more years	52	61	57	36	53	53
Total	100	100	100	100	100	100
N=	812	388	553	241	490	2,484
Denmark						
Less than 6 years	15	8	16	—	13	14
6–9 years	14	11	17	—	10	14
10–19 years	21	16	21	—	18	20
20 or more years	50	66	46	—	59	53
Total	100	100	100		100	100
N=	1,087	235	662		376	2,360[b]

[a] Living with others includes married children.
[b] 96.3 per cent of all eligible respondents answered this question.

As mentioned previously, that part of the elderly population in Denmark which shares a household with others, mostly children, is largely rural. Extended households in rural areas are more permanent in character than equivalent households in urban areas. Therefore, it may be expected that elderly people in extended households in Denmark, that is, those living with children, belong to the least mobile category among the aged in Denmark, while they are among the most mobile category in Britain. Thus it is probable that a large proportion of the relatively few extended households in Denmark represent permanent structures, while a large proportion of such households in Britain may be predominantly re-established households. The latter type of household is more typically urban, and the former more rural, in structure and character.

THE PROXIMITY OF CHILDREN

In all three countries the majority of old people tend to live apart from their children in their own households. This is most pronounced in Denmark where only 20 per cent of men and women were found living together with children, and least pronounced in Britain where 39 per cent of all aged men and 44 per cent of all aged women share a household with an adult child. The living arrangements of the aged in the United States are more similar to those in Denmark, with 23 per cent of older men and 32 per cent of older women living together with married or unmarried children.

Table VII-7: PROXIMITY OF THE NEAREST CHILD TO PERSONS AGED
65 AND OVER (*Percentage Distribution*)

Proximity of Nearest Child	DENMARK			BRITAIN			UNITED STATES		
	Men	Women	All	Men	Woman	All	Men	Women	All
Same household	20	20	20	39	44	42	23	32	28
10 minutes journey or less	32	32	32	23	24	24	33	33	33
11–30 minutes journey	22	24	23	17	15	16	16	15	16
More than 30 minutes journey	26	24	25	21	17	18	28	20	23
Total	100	100	100	100	100	100	100	100	100
N=	961	1,047	2,008	807	1,104	1,911	897	1,110	2,007

From the point of view of both the aged and their children, "living apart from each other" seems to be the preferred type of organization of the family network.[18] It also seems evident that living apart is preferred within certain geographical limits—that is, parents and children prefer to be not too far from one another. Our data from the three countries show clearly that the majority of the aged have at least one child within easy access. Indeed, the similarities between the three countries in this respect are striking. In Denmark 75 per cent of the aged with living children have at least one of their children within thirty minutes distance. The equivalent proportion in Britain is 82 per cent and in the United States 77 per cent.

The sex of the older person does not seem to affect the geographical organization of the extended household in either Denmark or in Britain. In neither of these countries are there significant differences in the proportions of older men and women living close to or far from the nearest child. In the United States, however, 56 per cent of the older men compared to 65 per cent of the older women live ten minutes distance from a child or share the household with one; conversely, we find that relatively more men than women live more than thirty minutes distance from their nearest child.

It is clear that variations in the proportion of older persons who live together with children influence the relative number of older persons who live near to their children in the three countries. As Table VII-7 shows, the fact that Britain has the highest proportion of older persons who live within thirty minutes journey from at least one child is due largely to the high proportion of old people who share a household with children. Table VII-7 also indicates that high proportions of people living apart from their children (especially in Denmark) are offset by similarly high proportions of people having a child within less than ten minutes journey.

It seems odd that a small country like Denmark has as high a proportion as the United States of unmarried elderly people living at a relatively long distance from their nearest child. It might be expected that the rural and small-town character of large parts of Denmark would stimulate cohesion of extended family relations and narrow the geographical boundaries of the extended family network; yet this does not seem to be the case. The above findings lead us to a more general question: What is the influence exerted by urbanization on the geographical organization of the extended family? The familiar assumption that urbanization has led towards spatial separation of generations cannot be verified by our Danish data. On the contrary, we find a striking similarity between the proportions of older people in urban and in rural areas whose nearest child lives at a relatively short distance. In Denmark approximately 75 per cent of the elderly population in urban as well as in rural areas live within thirty minutes transport distance from their nearest child.

Let us now turn to another question. What are the effects of marital status of the old person on the proximity of children? Do widowed people, compared to married people, live closer to their children? Do widows, compared to widowers, live nearer to their children? We have already demonstrated that more widowed than married older persons tend to live together with at least one of their children. Apart from this, however, one is inclined to ask whether or not changes in marital status affect the geographical organization of the extended family.

When we concentrate on the category of older people who do not share a household with one of their children, we find little or no evidence that widowed persons compared to married persons live nearer to one of their children. In fact, there is a striking similarity between the three countries in the proportions of old people who do not live with a child but whose nearest child lives at either a short or long distance.

There is no consistent evidence that widows, compared to widowers, tend to live nearer to their children. In Denmark slightly more widowed men than women live within ten minutes distance from a child or share a

Table VII–8: PROXIMITY OF THE NEAREST CHILD OF MARRIED AND UNMARRIED PERSONS AGED 65 AND OVER, WHO DO *NOT* SHARE A HOUSEHOLD WITH A CHILD *(Percentage Distribution)*

Proximity of Nearest Child of Those Persons Not Living with Children	DENMARK		BRITAIN		UNITED STATES	
	Married	Unmarried	Married	Unmarried	Married	Unmarried
Within 10 minutes journey	39	43	39	42	46	45
11–30 minutes journey	30	27	28	26	20	25
More than 30 minutes journey	31	30	33	32	34	30
Total	100	100	100	100	100	100
N=	994	609	698	412	971	480
Proportion of total sample living with a child	16	26	32	54	17	43

household with one. In Britain we find the reverse to be true, but the difference is not significant. Only in the United States are there a remarkably large proportion of widows compared with widowers (71 per cent compared to 58 per cent) living within short distances of children.

The general conclusion to be drawn from our data on the proximity of children to older people is that in each of the three countries most elderly people tend to live in the vicinity of at least one of their children. In all three countries widowed persons are more likely than married persons to be found sharing a household with a child. In Denmark and the United States, married persons are more likely not to share the same household with a child, but to live near them. There are indications, in these two countries, of a tendency to compensate—that is, people who do not share a household with a child tend to live near at least one of their children. Such compensation is particularly noticeable in Denmark, the country with the lowest proportion of older persons living together with children.

Integration within the Extended Family

The most frequently occurring types of households are those of older persons who live either with a spouse only or who live alone. In the three countries in this survey it is obvious that older persons prefer to live apart from but still near to their children. Does close proximity to children, however, in general also imply frequent contacts with children?

The following paragraphs are concerned with relations between older people and their families and comprise descriptions, first, of contacts with children, siblings, and relatives; and second, patterns of mutual help and assistance. A complete picture of the quality of family relations of older people is beyond our scope. We cannot attempt an over-all evaluation of the relative importance of different kinds of relations within the extended family, nor can we estimate the emotional content of these relationships. We do not know if the extended family functions satisfactorily from the aged individual's point of view. Nevertheless, each item of information that we have collected, as well as the over-all emerging pattern of family interaction, gives valuable indications of the degree of integration between the older person and his immediate as well as his extended family.

CONTACT WITH CHILDREN

In all three countries most older parents maintain regular contact with at least one of their children. The proportion of elderly people who had seen at least one child during the twenty-four hours prior to interview was 62 per cent in Denmark, 69 per cent in Britain, and 65 per cent in the United States. The similarities between the three countries are striking, especially when we take into account the differences in the proximity of children to older people.

Slightly more women than men reported recent contact with a child. Relatively more widowed than married persons, and more widows than widowers, reported some contact with at least one child during the

Table VII–9: WHEN PEOPLE AGED 65 AND OVER LAST SAW ONE OF THEIR CHILDREN (*Percentage Distribution*)

Last Time Child Seen	DENMARK			BRITAIN			UNITED STATES		
	Men	Women	All	Men	Women	All	Men	Women	All
Today or yesterday[a]	61	64	62	66	72	69	62	68	65
2–7 days ago	21	22	22	17	17	17	20	17	18
8–30 days ago	11	9	10	9	6	8	7	7	7
More than 30 days ago	7	5	6	8	5	6	11	8	10
Total	100	100	100	100	100	100	100	100	100
N=	957	1,035	1,992	807	1,104	1,911	896	1,106	2,002

[a] Includes those who live in the same household with a child.

previous week. These differences, however, are not very marked. Certainly they are by no means large enough to demonstrate that ties between mothers and adult children in later life are stronger than ties between fathers and children.

As we have shown earlier in this chapter, about twice as many elderly in Britain as in Denmark and the United States live together with at least one of their children. To what extent is living apart from children compensated for by more frequent contacts with children? Is it possible to observe a kind of compensation in those countries where relatively many old people do not share a household with one of their children?

In each of the three countries, approximately 50 per cent of those who have children, but who live apart from them, had some contact with a child within the last twenty-four hours before the interview. This proportion is largest in Denmark and lowest in Britain. In other words, our data presented in Table VII–10 seem to indicate that the absence of children from the household of the older person—which is especially typical among the aged in Denmark—is to some extent counterbalanced by more frequent contacts with children.

Table VII–10 shows further that there is very little difference between the proportions of married couples and unmarried people living alone, who had recent contact with a child. When, however, we compare these two categories with the third—those old persons who have children, but who share a household with relatives or non-relatives—differences in contact become more pronounced. In the last-named group only 32 per cent in Denmark, 36 per cent in Britain, and 44 per cent in the United States had seen one of their children during the last twenty-four hours. For old people who have children but who have no child in the household, living together with relatives or non-relatives seems to compensate for less frequent contacts with their children.

Table VII-10: WHEN MARRIED AND UNMARRIED PERSONS NOT LIVING WITH A CHILD LAST SAW ONE OF THEIR CHILDREN

(Percentage Distribution)

| Last Time Child Seen | Married and Living with Spouse Only[a] | | | Unmarried | | | | | | | All Who Live Apart from Children[b] | | |
| | | | | Living Alone | | | Living with Others, Except Children | | | | | |
	Denmark	Britain	United States	Denmark	Britain	United States	Denmark	Britain	United States	Denmark	Britain	United States
Today or yesterday	53	47	53	58	53	53	32	36	44	53	47	52
2–7 days ago	27	30	26	27	27	26	29	23	23	27	30	26
8–30 days ago	14	13	9	8	9	10	16	18	13	12	13	9
31 days to 1 year	5	7	9	5	7	8	16	15	14	6	7	10
More than 1 year ago	1	1	3	2	4	3	7	8	6	2	3	3
Total	100	100	100	100	100	100	100	100	100	100	100	100
N=	940	652	900	501	344	390	98	66	90	1,583	1,111	1,446

[a] Married people with children who do not share a household with a child but who do share a household with a relative or non-relative are excluded from these tabulations since these groups are too small. Denmark: N=44; United States: N=66; Britain: N=49.

[b] Includes the category mentioned in footnote a.

CONTACTS WITH SIBLINGS AND OTHER RELATIVES

Between 75 per cent and 80 per cent of all aged persons in the three countries have living children and about the same proportion have living siblings. It has been demonstrated earlier that the proportion of old persons with living children is relatively constant for all age groups. The proportion of old persons who have living siblings, however, decreases with advancing age. About two-thirds of the elderly in each of the three countries have both children and living brothers or sisters. The proportion of old people who have neither living children nor siblings is about one per cent in the United States and in Denmark and about 3 per cent in Britain.

Contacts with siblings are less frequent than contacts with children. In each of the three countries a little more than one-third of those old people who reported that they had living siblings had seen one of their siblings during the previous week. More than half of the aged in Denmark, about

Table VII–11: PERCENTAGE OF OLDER MEN AND WOMEN WHO REPORTED CONTACT WITH AT LEAST ONE OF THEIR SIBLINGS

Contact with Sibling	DENMARK		BRITAIN		UNITED STATES	
	Men	Women	Men	Women	Men	Women
During the previous week	32	37	28	41	34	43
During the previous month	55	60	45	56	39	44
N=	901	1,020	781	1,151	888	1,042

half of those in Britain, and less than half in the United States, reported some contact with siblings during the previous month. In Denmark, contacts with other relatives occur less frequently than contacts with siblings but in Britain relatively more older persons, especially men, had contacts with relatives other than siblings during the previous week. In the United States these differences in contacts between siblings and other relatives are insignificant.

In all three countries more women than men reported recent contacts with siblings or other relatives. The differences between the proportion of women and men who had seen a sibling during the previous week are particularly marked in Britain and in the United States. Those to whom contact with siblings is most significant are spinsters and bachelors. In the three countries approximately two-thirds of those who never married, compared with one-third of the married, widowed, and divorced, had some contact with a sibling during the previous week. We have shown earlier that the proportion of single older persons living with siblings is nearly equal to the proportion of married or widowed old people living with an adult child. Childlessness among the aged is not entirely compensated for by contacts with siblings, but it is evident that for childless single persons siblings represent an important link with the extended family.

Not all elderly persons have children. In an over-all evaluation of the contacts of the elderly person with his family, it is necessary to consider the role of siblings and relatives. Even where an elderly person has children, it may be that his relationship with a sibling or other relative is closer than with a child. It is also possible that an older person, despite having children, relatives, and siblings, has no family contacts at all.

We have already shown that in all three countries approximately two of every three elderly people who have children had contact with at least one of them during the twenty-four hours prior to the interview, and that about three of every four had some contact with a child during the previous

Table VII–12: PERCENTAGE OF OLDER MEN AND WOMEN, BY MARITAL STATUS, WHO HAD SEEN A SIBLING DURING THE PREVIOUS WEEK

Marital Status	DENMARK		BRITAIN		UNITED STATES	
	Men	Women	Men	Women	Men	Women
Married	31	30	23	38	34	38
Widowed, divorced, separated	32	38	35	35	33	41
Single	45	64	64	68	a	81
N=	901	1,020	781	1,151	888	1,042

a Per cents not computed on base less than 50.

week. Let us now look briefly at the family contacts of those categories of elderly people who did not have recent contacts with children or who do not have living children. (A detailed discussion of the role of the extended family and of child substitutes appears in Chapter 6.)

Approximately 70 per cent of all respondents in the three national samples reported contact with a child during the week prior to the interview. The proportion of elderly people who reported contacts with children and/or siblings and other relatives during the previous week varies from 81 per cent in Denmark to 83 per cent in Britain and 86 per cent in the United States. Among elderly people who have children but who saw none of them during the last week, we find that about 28 per cent of those in Denmark, 38 per cent in Britain, and 45 per cent in the United States saw a sibling or other relative during that period. In every country, persons who have no children reported more frequent contact with siblings or relatives than did those persons who have children but who had not seen a child during the preceding week.

Finally, we can raise the question of the extent to which variations in

Table VII–13: FAMILY CONTACTS OF OLD PEOPLE WHO DID NOT SEE A
CHILD DURING THE PREVIOUS WEEK AND OF OLD PEOPLE WHO HAVE
NO CHILDREN (*Percentage Distribution*)

Family Contacts	DENMARK			BRITAIN			UNITED STATES		
	Men	Women	All	Men	Women	All	Men	Women	All
Persons who did not see a child in past week:									
Saw a sibling or other relative during last week	22	35	28	34	42	38	37	54	45
Did not see a sibling or other relative during last week	76	64	70	48	38	43	61	45	54
Have no siblings or relatives	2	1	2	18	20	19	2	1	1
Total	100	100	100	100	100	100	100	100	100
N=	220	198	418	135	126	261	171	165	336
Persons who have no living children:									
Saw a sibling or other relative last week	40	54	48	53	63	60	55	66	62
Did not see a sibling or relative during last last week	55	42	48	36	22	27	43	30	35
Have no siblings or relatives	5	4	4	11	15	13	2	4	3
Total	100	100	100	100	100	100	100	100	100
N=	155	222	377	197	392	589	180	250	430

the structure of the household tend to influence the over-all pattern of
contacts between older persons and their children or siblings and other
relatives. Table VII–14 gives the pattern of family contacts of all older
persons in the three countries with the exception of those who share a
household with their children.

The likelihood of persons who do not live with children seeing neither
children nor siblings within a recent period is greatest in Denmark and
smallest in Britain. Living apart from children, a common pattern for the
elderly population in Denmark, is not entirely compensated for by more
frequent contacts with children, siblings, or relatives.

STAYING WITH CHILDREN AND HAVING CHILDREN TO STAY

In addition to visiting, people may also go to stay with their children or
have their children to stay with them. The reasons why old people stay
with children are many. For example, children may live at a considerable
distance so that an overnight or week-end visit is necessary if any visiting
at all is to take place. This is the case with Mrs. S. and Mr. and Mrs. J.

Table VII–14: FAMILY CONTACTS OF OLDER MEN AND WOMEN, EXCLUDING THOSE WHO SHARE A HOME WITH CHILDREN (*Percentage Distribution*)

Family Contacts	DENMARK			BRITAIN			UNITED STATES		
	Men	Women	All	Men	Women	All	Men	Women	All
Saw child during the previous week	63	63	63	63	63	63	63	63	63
No contact with child, but saw a sibling or other relative during last week	5	5	5	7	5	6	7	9	8
Have no children, but saw sibling or other relative during last week	6	10	9	15	25	21	12	17	14
No family contacts during last week	24	21	22	19	13	15	21	14	18
Have neither children, siblings, nor relatives	2	1	2	7	8	8	—	1	1
Total	100	100	100	100	100	100	100	100	100
N=	935	1,086	2,021	692	1,006	1,698	878	1,008	1,886

Mrs. S. is a widow, whose husband died three years ago. Her daughter lives eight hours journey by train and her only son lives at an even greater distance. Since her husband died Mrs. S. has gone to stay with either her daughter of her son at least two or three times a year, for a period of two or three weeks each time. She sometimes also comes when one of the children needs help in the household. Before Mrs. S.'s husband died, both parents frequently stayed with one of the children, especially during the holidays.

Mr. and Mrs. J. have three married children, two of whom live in another town, at a distance of about three hours driving. Mr. and Mrs. J. live in an attractive area, and every year either the children or the grandchildren, or both, come and stay with them for some time. The J.'s have also taken care of grandchildren when the children's parents were on a holiday.

These two examples are typical of many elderly persons who are still in good health and who maintain contact with children living at a distance by staying with the children or having them to stay. Distance, however, is not the only reason for this form of contact with children.

Mrs. N. is a widow, 86 years of age, who lives with her unmarried daughter. She is still very active, but not quite as strong as she used to be. It is a great help for her to have her daughter living with her in the same flat. For the daughter, who is an office worker, living with her mother sometimes becomes a strain. During holidays, at least twice a year, she travels abroad. Mrs. N. does not like to be alone and one of her other children arranges to stay with her at night.

Overnight stays are far more common in the United States than in either of the other two countries. Nearly half of the American respondents report that they had children to stay and/or that they themselves had stayed overnight with one of their children during the previous twelve months. In Britain only between a quarter and one third of the older population, and in Denmark only one of every five older persons, report this kind of contact with their children.

In all three countries the proportion of old people who go to stay with children is highest among the widowed or divorced who live alone, and lowest among the married. We also find that relatively more married than widowed older persons reported that children came to stay with them. The patterns of overnight stays reveal a tendency for the elderly couple to remain the core of family life, but for that family life to become more

Table VII–15: PROPORTION OF OLDER MEN AND WOMEN WHO STAYED WITH CHILDREN OVERNIGHT OR HAD CHILDREN VISITING WITH THEM, BY MARITAL STATUS AND LIVING ARRANGEMENTS

Marital Status and Overnight Stays	DENMARK			BRITAIN			UNITED STATES		
	Men	Women	All	Men	Women	All	Men	Women	All
Stayed overnight with children									
All married persons	16	17	17	27	28	27	38	43	40
All widowed and divorced persons	21	28	25	28	34	32	37	52	48
Widowed and divorced, who live alone	24	33	30	39	46	44	42	66	60
All persons with children	17	22	20	27	32	30	37	47	42
Children stayed overnight									
All married persons	24	22	23	31	30	31	52	52	52
All widowed and divorced persons	16	17	17	17	23	21	32	43	40
Widowed and divorced, who live alone	15	18	17	24	24	24	33	54	49
All persons with children	21	19	20	27	26	26	48	46	47
N=	963	1,042	2,005	799	1,097	1,896	882	1,084	1,966

dispersed on the death of one of the parents. Married elderly couples apparently attract children; and children, in turn, attract their widowed and divorced parents. This may be further illustrated by the way elderly people spend Christmas. As long as both parents are alive, many families maintain the tradition of spending Christmas in the home of the elderly parents. When one of the parents dies, one of the children invites the surviving parent to spend Christmas in his or her home.

When the United States is compared with Britain and Denmark, the differences in the proportion of elderly people who stayed with their children, or had children to stay overnight, require an explanation. First of all, it must be remembered that elderly people in the United States have more living children than the elderly in either of the two other countries. These differences in family structure might perhaps explain part of the varying patterns of parent-child visiting. Second, it is necessary to take physical distance into consideration. It may well be that the children of the aged in the United States are more scattered, geographically speaking, than in Britain and Denmark, and that a relatively larger proportion of the elderly in the United States than in the other two countries have at least one child living at a great distance.

When Britain and the United States are compared, the fact that relatively fewer older people in Britain tend to stay with children or have children to stay with them can to some extent be explained by the large proportion of older people in Britain who share a home with a child. Living with a child makes traveling to other children and having them to stay less necessary. In Denmark, however, as in the United States, relatively few elderly live with children. In both countries, too, relatively few elderly people have their nearest child at more than one hour's traveling distance. Denmark is physically a small country, but, apart from the matter of distance, it is likely that the housing situation in Denmark makes it impossible for the aged and their children to have each other to stay overnight. Relatively few Danish families have a spare room, or housing large enough to accommodate an overnight visitor easily.

PATTERNS OF MUTUAL HELP AND ASSISTANCE

Given that the generations, in all three countries, tend to live apart from each other, are they nonetheless involved in one another's daily lives? A number of studies during the last fifteen years in both the United States and Britain indicate that patterns of kin assistance are typical in old age. Adult children help their parents, and parents help their adult children. Patterns of help take many forms and include the exchange of services, gifts, advice, help in emergencies, transport, and, to some extent, financial aid. Sussman and Burchinal in a summary of American research indicate that help flows two ways between parents and children and to a lesser extent between the elderly and their siblings.[19]

Mutual help patterns are an important indicator of the content of the relations between generations. They are more than evidence of mutual expectations. They constitute sources of information on what takes place in the relations between parents and children in later life. We can distinguish two different forms of help. First, there are the numerous small services people tend to perform for each other. Parents and children rarely consider visiting or staying with each other as "help." During such time spent together, help is informally offered and accepted. When an aged widow asks her son to carry some parcels downstairs it is doubtful if either will consider the action as "help." The small services which people perform for each other simply because they spend some time together differ in character from the second form of help. This form of help is deliberately organized. As an example, an aged mother may take charge of a child's household in an emergency or a daughter may arrive twice a week to do the heavy housework and the shopping for her mother.

These latter types of help are often seen as "real" help, compared with those usual services which entail little effort. In general, this means that older people who have frequent contacts with their children or with other people both give and receive more help of the first kind than older people with relatively few contacts.

By asking older persons, in the cross-national survey, "Do you help your children?" "Who helps you?" and similar questions, the more organized forms of help between parents and children will tend to be stressed, even though interviewers asked about "help with even small things."

The help that elderly parents give to children or grandchildren takes a variety of forms. For those persons who have children still in their late teens or early 20's, either in the same household or living apart from them,

Table VII–16: PROPORTION OF OLDER MEN AND WOMEN WHO HELPED CHILDREN WHO REPORT SPECIFIC KINDS OF HELP

Kinds of Help	DENMARK		BRITAIN		UNITED STATES	
	Men	Women	Men	Women	Men	Women
Help with grandchildren	15	32	13	17	21	31
Gifts	31	38	16	5	38	28
Emergency help	1	5	2	3	4	4
Home repairs	26	5	28	4	32	4
Housekeeping	4	34	17	42	7	52
Other	26	8	9	7	3	1
N=	225	329	336	501	350	520

help can range from cooking, doing the laundry, and sending gift parcels, to economic support. In these instances the "help" given is virtually an extension of normal parental functions in relation to children. In other instances, help may involve financial assistance to newly or recently married children, gifts of clothing, furniture, food, et cetera, help in the daily maintenance of the child's household, baby-sitting, and being available for advice and for emergencies.

The forms of help given by parents to their children vary with the sex of the parent. Home repairs are a typically masculine job, while help with housekeeping is a typically feminine job as indeed is baby-sitting (although baby-sitting was also cited by relatively many elderly grandfathers). The differences in forms of help between the three countries are not very pronounced, except that a relatively smaller proportion of the British mentioned "gifts" as a form of help.

There is a wide variation in the proportions of elderly people in the three countries who reported that they were able to help their children. In the United States more than half of all respondents with children reported that they helped their children; in Britain the proportion helping children is somewhat less than half; and in Denmark it applies to only a quarter of the sample. Again, we must remember that if they live with each other, both the elderly people and their children are in a better position to give help as well as to receive it.

It is therefore somewhat unexpected that the proportion of older people who help their children is greater in the United States than in Britain, for in the latter country substantially more of the aged population live with children. In evaluating these differences, however, one must recall that

Table VII–17: PROPORTION OF OLDER MEN AND WOMEN GIVING HELP TO AND RECEIVING HELP FROM CHILDREN AND GRANDCHILDREN

Help Patterns	DENMARK			BRITAIN			UNITED STATES		
	Men	Women	All	Men	Women	All	Men	Women	All
Gave help to children	24	32	28	40	48	44	59	60	60
Gave help to grandchildren	9	18	13	32	33	33	50	49	50
Received help from children and relatives[c]	17	21	19	53	63	59	61	75	69
Regular money help	1	3	2	2	5	4	1	7	4
Occasional money gifts	4	8	6	14	25	20	25	43	35
N=[a]	956	1,039	1,995	803	1,100	1,903	901	1,111	12,012
N=[b]	864	940	1,804	716	996	1,712	826	1,025	1,851

[a] Help to children.

[b] Help to grandchildren: 96.9 per cent of the eligible men respondents and 94.7 per cent of the eligible women respondents in Denmark answered this question. In Britain and in the United States more than 98 per cent of all eligible respondents answered this question.

[c] The proportions of persons who said they received help from children cannot be compared with the proportions who received help from children in the performance of certain activities and household duties, as reported in Chapter 4. In the tables in Chapter 4 a priority code for "helpers" was used and help from spouse had priority over help from children.

the question "Are you able to help your children?" is apt to bring about that kind of response that is related to the more organized forms of help. This is perhaps one of the reasons why, although relatively more elderly people in Britain than in the United States live with children, fewer among the British than among the American respondents reported that they helped their children.

The proportion of elderly people reporting help to grandchildren shows a similar pattern. Nearly half of the respondents in the United States compared with one of three in Britain and one of eight in Denmark said that they helped their grandchildren. Women report more help to children than do men in both Denmark and Britain, but not in the United States where both men and women are equally likely to report help to children. Help to grandchildren is reported by twice as many women as men in Denmark, but in both the United States and Britain roughly equal proportions of men and women report that they help their grandchildren.

The reports that old people give on help they receive from children and relatives show a pattern similar to their reports of help to children. There is a striking difference between Denmark on the one hand, and Britain and the United States on the other, in the proportions of elderly people who say that they are helped by children or relatives with different things. In Denmark less than 20 per cent of the elderly say that they receive help from children, in the United States, nearly 70 per cent. The answers to the question about help received from children and other relatives probably are indicative of only a minimum of the help actually received by the elderly. The response to this question is based on what the older person considered as help and not on some assessment of all those activities that in fact were performed in order to help him. Since this interpretation was used for all three countries, however, it does not explain the marked differences between Denmark and the other two countries in the proportion of aged parents who reported help from children.

The aged appear to be generally independent of regular monetary help from children. In the United States and Britain about 4 per cent, and in Denmark only 2 per cent, of old people reported receiving regular money allowances from children. In all three countries pension schemes seem to have provided a minimum level of existence, which guarantees old people some economic independence from their children.[20] Occasional money gifts in the form of gifts for special occasions, paying for travel, and similar kinds of support are more usual than regular monetary support. Acrans Denmark has the lowest proportion of old persons (about 6 per cent) reporting occasional money gifts from their children. In Britain about 20 per cent and in the United States as many as 35 per cent of the elderly with children said that their children had made them a gift of money during the past twelve months. For all three countries, women are more likely than men to receive some economic support from their children, whether regular or occasional.

The Effect of Age on the Household Composition and the Family Relations of Older People

With advancing age the older person experiences a variety of changes. First of all, there are changes in state of health and especially in physical capacity. Secondly, there are the changes in family life primarily due to losses within the immediate household and in the extended family. At the same time the older person is experiencing the general technological and cultural changes which occur in the society in which he lives. The impact of each type of change on the social situation of aging individual, can hardly be isolated. In some instances they reinforce each other, while in other instances the effect of one kind of change is more or less compensated for by other changes, which take place about the same time.

From a sociological and psychological point of view, two processes are particularly conspicuous in the changing family relations of older people in highly developed societies: first, their increased dependency on help and assistance from other people; and, second, their increased isolation. We will concentrate primarily on the evidence that can be found about the changes in the household composition and the family relations of older people in relation to these processes. In other words, do our data indicate that relatively elderly people are less integrated within their families as they grow older?

VARIATIONS, BY AGE, IN HOUSEHOLD COMPOSITION

The changes in the social structure of which the aging individual is a part affect the composition of the household as well as the general arrangement of contacts with the extended family. Let us first consider the structure of the households of unmarried and married old people in different age groups. We will begin with an analysis of the structure of the household of unmarried persons.

With increasing age there is a decrease in the proportion of unmarried persons who live alone and an increase among those who live with married or unmarried children. These age changes are more marked for men than for women, and are especially obvious in Denmark. In that country the proportion of single men who live alone falls from 69 per cent for the age group 65 to 69, to 46 per cent for those aged 80 and over. The proportion of single women who live alone also decreases with increasing age, but the pattern is less consistent than that for men.[21]

The proportion of single elderly people who live with married children rises with increasing age. Among single men in Denmark, almost none in the age group 65 to 69 live with married children, but in the age group 80 years and over nearly one of four men live with such children. A similar pattern of household formation is found in the United States. In Britain the proportion of elderly single men living with married children is constant for all those over the age of 70. For single women in that country, however, there is an increase with age in the proportion who live with married chidren. Table VII–18 clearly indicates that a household composed of unmarried elderly persons and their children is far more common for those in their 70's and 80's than for those in their 60's.

Among married couples, the majority of surviving couples in all three countries maintain themselves in an independent household even throughout the last stages of their life-cycle. The proportion of married couples living together with unmarried children decreases with increasing age —especially in Denmark and the United States. The decline with age in the proportion of married persons living with unmarried children is comparable to the increase with age in the proportion of single elderly people living with unmarried children. Very few elderly married couples

Table VII-18: PROPORTION OF UNMARRIED MEN AND WOMEN, BY AGE GROUP AND LIVING ARRANGEMENTS
(Percentage Distribution)

Living Arrangements[a]	MEN				WOMEN				TOTAL		
	65–69	70–74	75–79	80+	65–69	70–74	75–79	80+	Men	Women	All Persons
Living alone											
Denmark	69	67	49	46	65	67	63	58	58	63	61
Britain	34	38	44	24	47	42	52	40	37	45	43
United States	56	53	47	52	46	47	50	42	52	46	48
Living with married children											
Denmark	—	4	9	22	4	4	5	10	9	5	6
Britain	15	28	25	26	10	18	18	26	23	17	19
United States	6	13	11	19	12	13	21	16	12	15	14
Living with unmarried children											
Denmark	6	6	14	19	16	11	23	17	11	16	15
Britain	21	16	10	32	21	21	17	17	18	20	19
United States	16	12	21	20	22	23	13	25	17	22	20
Living with others											
Denmark	25	23	28	13	18	18	9	15	22	16	18
Britain	30	18	21	18	22	19	13	17	22	18	19
United States	22	22	21	9	20	17	16	17	19	17	18
N=											
Denmark	76	98	89	86	224	225	175	134	349	758	1,107
Britain	86	83	84	50	252	300	215	219	303	986	1,289
United States[b]	63	76	53	64	256	253	161	172	256	842	1,098

[a] This is a priority code.

[b] Nine women of unknown age are excluded from this distribution.

Table VII-19: PROPORTION OF MARRIED MEN AND WOMEN, BY AGE GROUP AND LIVING ARRANGEMENTS (*Percentage Distribution*)

Living Arrangements[a]	MEN				WOMEN				TOTAL		All Persons
	65–69	70–74	75–79	80+	65–69	70–74	75–79	80+	Men	Women	
Living with spouse only											
Denmark	78	81	82	83	81	85	91	b	80	83	82
Britain	67	69	67	68	67	64	76	b	67	68	68
United States	73	80	82	82	81	82	83	b	77	82	79
Living with spouse and married children											
Denmark	1	2	0	4	2	1	0	b	2	1	1
Britain	3	6	7	5	4	6	8	b	5	1	5
United States	2	1	3	2	1	4	0	b	2	1	2
Living with spouse and unmarried children											
Denmark	18	14	13	10	14	9	5	b	15	13	14
Britain	27	21	22	22	23	25	15	b	24	24	23
United States	21	14	12	11	15	10	14	b	16	13	15
Living with others											
Denmark	3	3	5	3	3	5	4	b	3	3	3
Britain	3	4	4	5	6	5	1	b	4	7	4
United States	4	5	3	5	3	4	3	b	5	4	4
N=											
Denmark	370	220	136	70	264	171	76	[32]	796	543	1,339
Britain	304	204	118	75	246	138	78	[48]	701	510	1,211
United States	343	271	129	82	252	170	65	[19]	825	506	1,331

a This is a priority code.

b Percentages are not computed where base is less than 50.

live together with married children, siblings, or other relatives or non-relatives.

In general the variations in the composition of the household of elderly people of differing ages suggest three conclusions. First, the main changes in the living arrangements of elderly people are related to widowhood. As long as husband and wife are both alive they tend to live in their own household. Second, changes in household composition by age are more pronounced for unmarried men than for unmarried women. This can perhaps be explained by the fact that the loss of a spouse often creates more practical problems for men than for women. Third, living with children is most common among the oldest age groups in the elderly population of Denmark and the United States, and frequent among all age groups in Britain. The absence of pronounced age variations in the living arrangements of older people in the last-named country suggest that in Britain "sharing a household with adult children" is less a function of "aging" and to a greater extent a reflection of a particular family culture.

VARIATIONS, BY AGE, IN THE PROXIMITY OF CHILDREN

The fact that more people in their 80's than in their late 60's live with adult children suggests that, with increasing age, relatively more elderly people may be found living close to their children. In other words, with increasing age either the older person is likely to move into the household of a child, or the child to join an elderly enfeebled parent. But, to what extent do older people or their children move into closer proximity to one another without necessarily moving into the same household? This has been suggested as an explanation of the geographic mobility of the elderly in the United States, for example.

Our findings for the three countries, however, do not indicate any large-scale movement by old people into the vicinity of their children. What apparently happens with increased age is a movement into a joint household rather than a move so that the old person can live close to a child.

VARIATIONS, BY AGE, IN CONTACTS WITH CHILDREN, SIBLINGS, AND RELATIVES

To what extent is the contact between the aged and their children and relatives influenced by the age of the old person? Changes in the composition of the household and losses within the extended family affect the over-all pattern of the contact of old people with children and relatives, of course. But if a gradual contraction of the net of contacts maintained by older persons were in fact a general phenomenon of advancing age, we could expect a decrease with age in the proportions of older persons who report recent contacts with their children, siblings, and relatives. This does not seem to be the case, however. As shown by Table VII-21, in all three countries the proportion of older persons having contact with at least one

Table VII–20: PERCENTAGE OF PERSONS, BY AGE GROUP, WHO LIVE
WITH A CHILD OR WITHIN 10 MINUTES DISTANCE FROM A CHILD

Age	DENMARK		BRITAIN		UNITED STATES	
	Men	Women	Men	Women	Men	Women
Live with children						
65–69	19	20	38	37	26	27
70–74	16	15	38	47	18	31
75–79	24	20	37	43	22	32
80 and over	26	30	46	55	25	47
Total	20	20	39	44	23	32
Live apart from children, but within 10 minutes						
65–69	33	36	37	40	42	44
70–74	43	40	34	47	42	49
75–79	45	49	43	43	44	58
80 and over	44	44	38	44	47	51
Total[a]	40	40	37	43	43	49

[a] Percentages are based on all in particular age group who had children but who lived apart from a child.

child during the 24 hours before the interview either remains constant or else increases slightly with advancing age. For women in all three countries there is in fact a marked increase with age in the number of those who saw a child during the previous day.

The over-all pattern of stability is only slightly modified if account is taken of the marital status and composition of the household of the old person. In both Britain and the United States, the proportion of married men and women in their 70's and 80's who have seen a child within the last 24 hours is slightly smaller than the proportion of married men and women in their late 60's who have seen a child. In Denmark the differences between the age groups are not significant. Conversely, in all three countries a higher proportion of widowed women aged 70 years or more than of women in their late 60's had seen a child during the last 24 hours. There are no marked age differences in the proportions of widowed men who had seen a child within that time period.

We have shown, earlier in this chapter, that not living together with children in old age is compensated for by more frequent visiting among parents and children. With increasing age the proportion of men as well as women in Denmark who do not live with a child but who saw a child within the last 24 hours rises sharply. The same is true for women in the United States, but not for men. No such pattern of additional contacts with children with increasing age appears in Britain. If daily contacts with children are to be maintained with increasing age in that country, such contacts are achieved by sharing a joint household.

Earlier in this chapter we pointed out that the proportion of older

Table VII–21:   WHEN PEOPLE IN DIFFERENT AGE GROUPS LAST SAW ONE
OF THEIR CHILDREN (*Percentage Distribution*)

Last Time Child Seen	MEN				WOMEN			
	65–69	70–74	75–79	80+	65–69	70–74	75–79	80+
Today or yesterday[a]								
Denmark	59	58	63	71	59	64	66	73
Britain	68	65	68	63	70	72	70	76
United States	65	59	60	62	64	66	73	80
2–7 days ago								
Denmark	20	26	22	15	26	19	21	18
Britain	16	18	19	16	19	18	16	14
United States	19	20	25	18	19	20	16	7
8–30 days ago								
Denmark	13	9	10	9	9	10	9	7
Britain	8	10	8	13	5	6	8	7
United States	5	9	6	10	8	6	3	6
More than 30 days ago								
Denmark	8	7	5	5	6	7	4	2
Britain	8	7	5	8	6	4	6	3
United States	11	12	9	10	9	8	8	7
N=								
Denmark	358	274	186	139	392	309	204	130
Britain	315	234	155	103	382	320	212	190
United States	336	280	154	126	419	348	188	145

[a] Includes those who live in the same household with a child.

persons who have living children remain stable for all age groups, while
there is a decrease with age in the proportion of aged persons who have
living siblings. Correspondingly, we find that with advancing age there is
a decrease in the proportion of men as well as women who had some
contact with siblings during the previous week. Such a decline in recent

Table VII–22:   PERCENTAGE OF PERSONS, BY AGE GROUP, WHO LIVE
APART FROM CHILDREN BUT WHO SAW AT LEAST ONE CHILD WITHIN
THE PAST 24 HOURS

Age Group[a]	DENMARK		BRITAIN		UNITED STATES	
	Men	Women	Men	Women	Men	Women
65–69 years	48	49	48	51	52	51
70–74 years	50	57	43	47	49	50
75–79 years	54	55	47	48	48	60
80 and over	57	64	29	47	49	62

[a] For total number of cases in each age group see Tables VII–18 and VII–19.

Table VII–23: PERCENTAGE OF PERSONS, BY AGE GROUP, WHO REPORTED
CONTACT WITH AT LEAST ONE OF THEIR SIBLINGS OR RELATIVES DURING
PAST WEEK[a]

Age of Elderly Person and Type of Contact	DENMARK		BRITAIN		UNITED STATES	
	Men	Women	Men	Women	Men	Women
Sibling						
65–69	34	41	30	49	39	47
70–74	36	34	29	40	33	42
75 and over	25	35	22	26	27	39
Other relatives						
65–69	23	27	41	44	31	35
70–74	22	26	38	40	33	36
75 and over	21	23	29	42	33	38

[a] For number of cases see Table VI–13.

contact is not observed in the interaction of older persons and their other relatives. Apparently this type of interaction remains reasonably stable throughout the age span.

VARIATIONS, BY AGE, IN PATTERNS OF MUTUAL HELP AND
ASSISTANCE

The ability to help children is to some extent related to the age of the parents. As Table VII–24 indicates, in both Britain and the United States, the proportion of older persons who reported that they helped their children is highest for those in their late 60's, slightly lower for those in their 70's, and lowest of all for the oldest age groups.

The decrease with age in the proportion who report giving help is not very great. In the United States, for example, about two-thirds of those in their late 60's against half those in their 70's gave help to children. This absence of a sharp decrease with age in those reporting help to children lends support to the hypothesis that the aged parent participates in family activity irrespective of his years.

Similarly, the amount of help received from children is clearly related to the age of the parents. The older the parent is, the more likely it is that he receives help from a child. The nature of such help varies but it is of some interest that the proportion of older persons who receive occasional economic support from children increases with advances in age in every country.

In general, our observations concerning the effect of advances in age on contacts between the aged and their children and relatives, point up that regular family contact is constant for old people in all age groups. This is clearly demonstrated by the stable and sometimes increased proportions of old persons in each successive age group reporting recent contacts with

Table VII–24: PROPORTION, BY AGE GROUP, OF OLDER MEN AND WOMEN
GIVING HELP TO AND RECEIVING HELP FROM CHILDREN

Age and Help Patterns[a]	DENMARK		BRITAIN		UNITED STATES	
	Men	Women	Men	Women	Men	Women
Gave help to children						
65–69	21	27	56	60	66	66
70–74	28	29	42	50	62	57
75 and over	24	27	34	37	47	55
Received help from children						
65–69	12	18	55	60	60	72
70–74	19	16	50	60	57	72
75 and over	23	32	54	75	66	79
Received regular money help						
65–69	1	3	3	5	1	5
70–74	1	3	3	8	1	8
75 and over	2	4	2	4	2	7
Received occasional money gifts						
65–69	3	6	12	23	21	39
70–74	3	8	17	25	23	43
75 and over	4	10	14	28	31	48

[a] For number of cases see Table VI–14.

children, and also by the increase in the amount of help that flows from children to aged parents. It is only when losses occur within the older persons' generation, as in the loss of siblings, that we find a contraction with age in the amount of contacts reported by old people.

Health and Incapacity, the Organization of the Household, and Contact Between the Aged and Their Children

Does increased incapacity and the resulting inability of the old person to care for himself in various ways influence household organization in old age and the over-all pattern of contact between the aged person and his children and relatives? It may be expected that a reduction in the capacity for self-care of the old person increases his dependency on family members either within or outside the household. It may also be expected that the old person's flow of contacts with the outside world changes with each decrease in health. The more the older person becomes dependent on others, the more likely it is that the flow of contacts will be initiated not by him but by other members of the extended family. Restricted mobility limits the older person's radius of action. Travel and the use of public transport become more difficult for him. Problems in orientation and fear of heavy traffic restrict his mobility. The greater these difficulties become, the more likely it is that the role of the old person changes from that of a visitor to that of one dependent on the visits of others.

When these circumstances are taken into consideration, it is somewhat surprising that the proportion of older persons who had recent contacts with children remains roughly the same for all age groups. Particularly for those who are unmarried and live alone, limitations on mobility may change the whole pattern of contacts with others. The following examples come from Denmark:

> Mrs. H. is a widow, whose husband died many years ago. Although she is childless, Mrs. H. has had very close contacts with her brother's two daughters. They used to visit her and she them, once or twice a week. At the age of 68, however, Mrs. H. became nearly blind—and after that, although they lived within only fifteen minutes distance, it was impossible for her to walk to these two families on her own. Sometimes someone came to fetch her—but the contact, although maintained, changed from regular visits each week (when she spent the whole day with the two families, who regarded her as a grandmother)—to more irregular visits which her brother's children and grandchildren paid her when they could find the time.

A change in the health situation of an old person may influence the pattern of contacts maintained with children and relatives by a married couple.

> Mr. A. is a retired salesman. After retirement he and his wife settled in the country. Mr. and Mrs. A. have three children and eight grandchildren—and enough room to have at least one of the children's family stay with them during week ends or holidays. At the age of 72 Mrs. A. had a heart attack, and although she survived she never recovered completely. Mr. A. was able to take care of her but the A.'s had to stop traveling. It also became more difficult to have their children and especially their grandchildren stay with them. Mr. and Mrs. A. continued to see their children regularly—but the content of this contact and its character changed markedly.

In all three countries incapacity (as measured by our index) seems to have a greater impact on the household arrangements of single and widowed persons rather than on the arrangements of married persons. As Table VII–25 shows, among the older unmarried aged (those over 70) twice as many people who live with children as those who live alone have high incapacity scores. (For a discussion of the Index of Incapacity, see Chapter 1; for a consideration of incapacity and living arrangements, see Chapters 4 and 5.) The problems associated with a decrease of physical capacity are most pronounced for elderly people who live alone. In all three countries, one-fourth of all persons with high incapacity scores live alone. These persons constitute one per cent of the elderly male population of each of the three countries, and 3 per cent of elderly women in the United States, 4 per cent in Britain, and 5 per cent in Denmark. By and large our data support the hypothesis that the weaker the older person becomes, the greater is the tendency to live with children or relatives. The evidence, as has been shown earlier, is most marked for persons who are unmarried. It must be remembered, however, that the fact that an old person of limited capacity lives with a child does not necessarily indicate that health was the decisive factor in the establishment of a joint

Table VII–25: LIVING ARRANGEMENTS OF UNMARRIED PERSONS AGED 70 AND OVER, BY INCAPACITY SCORES[a] (*Percentage Distribution*)

Incapacity Score and Living Arrangements	DENMARK	BRITAIN	UNITED STATES
Living alone			
0–2	77	74	83
3–4	11	12	8
5+	12	14	9
Total	100	100	100
N=	479	401	369
Living with children or grand-children			
0–2	59	64	70
3–4	20	13	13
5+	21	23	17
Total	100	100	100
N=	179	364	279
Living with relatives or others			
0–2	69	61	84
3–4	15	19	9
5+	16	20	7
Total	100	100	100
N=	133	121	128

[a] Excludes those persons "too ill to be interviewed" for whom proxy interviews were secured.

household. The joint household may have preceded the parent's incapacity.

The extent to which a decrease in physical capacity affects the contacts between older people and their families is difficult to determine without controlling the age factor—as has been done in Table VII–27. The evidence does not reveal a consistent pattern. In Britain and the United States we find some support for the hypothesis that the proportion of elderly people, within different age groups, who had recent contacts with children is highest for those who have high incapacity scores and lowest for those with zero scores. Correspondingly, we find a decrease in the proportion of elderly people with high incapacity scores who had contact with neither children nor other relatives during the week prior to the interview. In Denmark, however, contact with children seems to be more a function of age than of physical capacity. The proportions of older people in different age groups who reported recent contacts with children are remarkably similar for those with respectively low and high scores on the incapacity index.

Our data do not enable us to distinguish between those who visited, and those who were visited by, children and relatives. The remarkable stability of the interaction between old people and their children and relatives for different age cohorts and different degrees of incapacity implies a structural

Table VII-26: LIVING ARRANGEMENTS OF PERSONS AGE 65 AND OVER
WITH INCAPACITY SCORES OF 5 OR MORE[a] (*Percentage Distribution*)

Marital Status and Living Arrangements[b]	DENMARK			BRITAIN			UNITED STATES		
	Men	Women	All	Men	Women	All	Men	Women	All
Unmarried									
Living alone	8	36	25	16	28	25	11	31	25
Living with married child	8	8	5	11	20	18	4	19	15
Living with unmarried child	3	15	11	7	17	15	2	18	13
Living with relatives or others	9	9	9	7	10	10	8	7	7
Married									
Living with spouse only	65	26	41	34	17	21	56	19	29
Living with spouse and married child	—	1	—	4	2	2	2	—	1
Living with spouse and unmarried child	12	4	8	16	5	8	17	5	9
Living with others	2	1	1	5	1	1	—	1	1
Total	100	100	100	100	100	100	100	100	100
N=	101	156	257	56	221	277	52	131	183

[a] Excludes persons "too ill to be interviewed" for whom proxy interviews were secured.

[b] This is a priority code.

change in the pattern of contact maintained by older persons and their families. Increasing disability prevents the older person from visiting others; consequently more visits must be initiated by children and other members of the extended family. A decline in physical capacity need not decrease the number of contacts between parents and children, but it does change the direction of these contacts. The old person becomes increasingly dependent on children and relatives.

The Diversity of the Family Relations of Older People

Within the aged populations of Denmark, Britain, and the United States, a wide variety of family relations have been observed and reported. There are some older people who live near to children and who maintain frequent contacts with them, others who are involved in helping their children, and others who receive help. In brief, it seems obvious that in dealing with the family relations of old people a distinction must be drawn between several major categories of such persons, as well as among several minor groups. The former are represented by those married and widowed older persons who maintain frequent contacts with children and who are able to get around on their own. An example of one of the minor categories is the small group of dependent, widowed, and disabled persons who live alone and have infrequent contacts with their families.

Table VII–27: FAMILY CONTACTS OF OLDER PEOPLE, BY AGE AND INCAPACITY

Type of Contact and Age	Per cent with Given Type of Contact											
	DENMARK				BRITAIN				UNITED STATES			
	Incapacity Score				Incapacity Score				Incapacity Score			
	0	1–2	3–4	5+	0	1–2	3–4	5+	0	1–2	3–4	5+
Saw child last 24 hours												
65–69	46	47	54	51	53	52	62	[66]a	52	58	59	52
70–74	49	47	62	50	49	54	61	59	50	54	55	61
75–79	55	50	48	61	49	57	46	53	49	58	74	
80 and over	63	59	59	58	48	53	53	60	47	63	69	
All persons	50	49	56	55	51	53	55	58	50	56	62	64
Saw child within week												
65–69	66	65	70	73	67	67	73	[73]a	67	72	72	73
70–74	67	66	78	64	65	65	75	69	64	76	77	59
75–79	69	73	70	79	63	66	59	69	68	75	78	
80 and over	76	74	72	74	61	63	63	70	56	71	71	
All persons	68	68	72	72	—	65	68	70	66	72	74	69
No family contacts during last week												
65–69	19	22	14	18	16	15	11	[17]a	14	16	11	19
70–74	22	23	17	19	16	15	10	9	16	13	8	11
75–79	21	18	16	18	20	16	20	13	15	16	12	
80 and over	17	17	18	7	17	20	17	13	21	13	14	
All persons	20	21	18	16	17	16	14	12	15	14	11	14
N=	1,275	633	207	287	1,346	577	244	277	1,526	540	183	183

a Per cent for ages in brackets based on N of less than 50.

We are able to distinguish between five major types of households in all three countries:

1. Households consisting of an elderly person living alone, who has never been married. These households include about 4 to 8 per cent of all people aged 65 and over.
2. Households consisting of a widowed (sometimes a divorced or separated) parent, living alone. About 22–28 per cent of those aged 65 and over.
3. Households consisting of a married couple only. About 35–45 per cent of those aged 65 and over.
4. Households consisting of a married couple and married or single children. About 7–14 per cent of those aged 65 and over.
5. Households consisting of a widowed (or divorced or separated) parent and married or unmarried children. About 9–20 per cent of those aged 65 and over.

These five types of household represent the most frequent living arrangements of older people in the three countries and our discussion therefore can be limited to a consideration of these types only. Let us first consider those households that include both aged parents and adult children, and those households in which old people either live apart from children or have no living children. The household that includes both an aged parent and an adult child exhibits a variety of different structures, dictated by such diverse factors as the different emotional ties between generations, the role of the older person within the household, and the aims pursued by members of the household, through its establishment and maintenance. By isolating two dimensions—the gradual change by which old people surrender independence and become dependent on help and support from their families, and the planned duration of the existing household structure—and combining these two variables, we can distinguish four different types of household, each consisting of two or more generations.

Figure VII-1: FOUR TYPES OF HOUSEHOLD ARRANGEMENTS OF ELDERLY PARENTS AND ADULT CHILDREN

Aged Person's Need for Care	Planned Duration of Household Structure	
	Temporary	Permanent
Independence	I Parents living with children who are awaiting a new dwelling	II The classical extended family of two or more generations living and working together
Dependence	III Widowed or disabled parent was moved into the household of a married child while awaiting institutionalization	IV Widowed or divorced parent sharing a household with a child who will take care of her/him, if incapacity increases

Data from the three countries and from other research indicate that arrangement II, independence-permanent, is unusual in Western societies and occurs mainly in rural areas. Since relatively few older persons in all three countries live in institutions, our data support the hypothesis that households represented by types I and IV, independence-temporary, and dependence-permanent, are the ones that occur most frequently. The last type, dependence-permanent, is found mostly among the oldest and those most frail in the elderly population.

Let us now consider those households in which the elderly live apart from children. Living apart from children but in the close vicinity of at least one child seems to be the preferred arrangement between generations in all three countries. A relatively large proportion of older persons who do not live with children live within ten minutes distance of at least one child. Thus living apart from children is often compensated for by having a child who lives in the neighborhood.

Contacts with children occur about twice as frequently as contacts with siblings or other relatives. People who have never been married, however, substitute frequent contacts with siblings for the contacts that older parents have with their adult children.

It has often been maintained that women are closer to the center of family relations than men, and that they constitute the emotional center of the nuclear family and the pivot of relationships within the extended family. The present cross-national study has not dealt with the affectional integration of elderly people in the family and therefore neither supports nor refutes this hypothesis. From a structural point of view, however, our data indicate that in all three countries about equal proportions of both elderly men and elderly women seem to be integrated within a modified extended family system. In general, there are only small differences in the living arrangements of older men and women and in the proportions of men and women who enjoyed recent contacts with children or other relatives.

There are some exceptions to this categoric statement. We do find that with the exception of Denmark, more older persons live with married daughters than with married sons. Further, when marital status is taken into account, differences between the sexes become more pronounced: relatively more single men than single women live with married children and more women than men live with unmarried children. In all three countries relatively more single women than men reported some recent contacts with children, siblings, or other relatives. No significant differences in such contacts were observed between married men and women. More women than men tend to stay with children or have children to stay. Again, these differences are most pronounced between single men and single women and least pronounced between married. More women than men report that they helped their children, received help from children, or received regular or occasional economic support from them. Again, however, we must stress that the observed differences between men and women, though consistent, are by no means striking.

Family relationships of the elderly change with age, and such variations occur in strikingly similar patterns in all three countries. With increasing age we find that in all three countries:

1. More old people live with children, both married and unmarried.
2. More old people live close to children.
3. More old people report recent contacts with children.
4. More old people report help from their children.
5. Fewer old people report that they are able to help their children.

While there is a high degree of stability with age in the contacts between older people and their families, there is a change in the pattern of flow of contacts. With advancing age and disability, an increasing amount of contact between parents and children is initiated by children or other relatives, and fewer contacts are initiated by the older person himself. The change from independence towards dependence on the part of the older person includes a change in role, from being a visitor to becoming one who is visited.

The role of the older person in his modified extended family is dependent partly on his degree of integration or family involvement, partly on his degree of dependence on contact and support from other people. Again, we can make a distinction between four types of situations that have been observed in the family relations of older people. At the one extreme, we have the isolated nuclear family and the dependent but isolated aged individual who lives alone or has become resident in a home for the aged.

Figure VII–2: FOUR EXAMPLES OF THE DEVELOPMENT OF FAMILY RELATIONS IN LATER LIFE

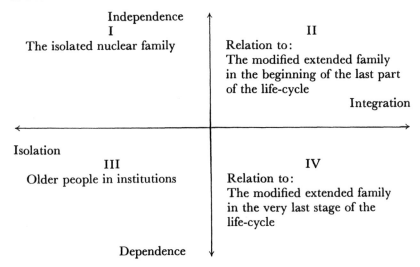

At the other extreme we find the integrated modified extended family, in which integration is demonstrated by a relatively large degree of mutual contacts, help, and support. The stability with age in the family relationships of older people, as well as the relatively large proportion of older persons who maintain contacts with children, siblings, and relatives, suggests that for a large proportion of the aged in all three countries, "aging" implies a gradual change from a state of independence to a state of dependence within an integrated social structure represented by the extended family. Aging does not necessarily lead towards isolation.

The majority of the aged in all three countries have children, live in the vicinity of at least one of these children, and maintain regular contacts with their families. The normal pattern of family relations in later life is one of continuing integration rather than growing isolation. There are isolated people in all three countries, of course. These persons represent a small minority of all old people. Nor do all isolated people represent a "problem group." Some of them are able to care for themselves without the kind of help received by their more integrated counterparts. A small minority of older people, however, are in poor health and isolated from their families. The majority of these are women.

Variations Between Denmark, Britain, and the United States

Our observations in the three countries lend support to the general hypothesis that in industrial societies family relations in later life have developed towards a modified extended family system rather than towards isolation and the breaking of family ties. The over-all pattern revealed in the relations between older people and their families shows clearly that most elderly people in each of the three countries are likely to maintain fairly frequent contacts with children as well as relatives. Comparisons between the three countries, however, reveal certain variations in the structure and function of the extended family. Table VII–28 summarizes some of our main findings.

Table VII–28: MAIN SIMILARITIES AND DIFFERENCES IN FAMILY RELATIONS OF OLDER PEOPLE IN DENMARK, BRITAIN, AND THE UNITED STATES

Characteristics	Per Cent with Each Characteristic		
	Denmark	Britain	United States
Proximity of children:			
Children in the same household	20	42	28
Nearest child more than one hour distant	12	11	16
Contact with children:			
Saw at least one child today or yesterday	62	69	65
Stayed overnight with child(ren) within last 12 months	20	30	43
Had children staying overnight within last 12 months	20	26	46
Help to children:			
Gave help to children	28	44	60
Gave help to grandchildren[a]	13	33	50
Help from children:			
Received a regular money allowance	2	4	4
Received occasional money gifts within last months	6	20	35
N=	2,012	1,911	2,012

[a] Only for those who have grandchildren. Denmark: N= 1,845; Britain: N= 1,719; United States: N=1,873.

In Denmark we find that relatively few elderly persons live with children and few older persons are helped by children. About the same proportion of older persons in Denmark as in Britain and the United States saw at least one child in the twenty-four hours before the interview.

said: ". . . Of course we visit our children regularly. They often
to come."

raditional family system that stresses functional independence
:n generations can also be traced in the Danish social and fiscal
:ion. Denmark early established both a tradition of public care for
:d and a general pension system. The latter system was a product
:eral recognition, on the part of prosperous middle classes and the
ing elite, of an inevitable need, rather than a result of class struggle.
:rmore, as far back as the first codifications of 1708 and 1799 on help
poor, sick, and the aged, Danish social security Acts have never
that public relief of the aged and other groups can be granted only
:stablishment of an applicant's inability to obtain support from
:n or other relatives.[24] Even before the earliest social security acts,
ots to provide for the destitute placed the burden of support on the
unity and disregarded family obligations. Parents are responsible
: support of their children; husbands and wives equally are respon-
or their children's welfare and the functioning of the nuclear
; but children have no responsibility towards their parents.
ves' Responsibility Acts never existed in Denmark in spite of the
at such legislation has remained in the constitutions of many other
rn societies, although with less rigorous application than formerly.
: Danish system of taxation stresses independence between genera-
Economic support of family members is not a deductible item in the
l tax returns. Tax concessions are therefore unavailable to parents
ucational or other purposes concerned with children's economic
rt. Adult children may not deduct occasional money gifts to their
ts from their annual income declaration, but some exceptions are
in cases where the taxpayer furnishes proof of a commitment to
r economic support of parents or others.

ally, the Danish tradition of cooperative movements and voluntary
ations as well as the apprenticeship system must be emphasized. The
r led to the establishment, as early as the latter part of the nineteenth
y, of health insurance societies in nearly all parts of the country,
as well as urban. As a result of the latter, the Danish middle class
lways been less dependent on help from their children than have
rs and craftsmen in other European countries outside Scandinavia.
radition has grown for children to leave home at an early age in
to work for others rather than remain on their parents' farm or in
mily business.

gether, there would seem to be a certain correspondence between
pe of relations that develop between generations and the institutional
round to these relations. The more loosely knit system of relations
holds between generations in Denmark, especially in comparison
3ritain, far from being the product of early developments in welfare
, in all likelihood fostered the ideal circumstances for the early
ence of a social security system.

: structural similarities between Denmark, Britain, and the United
in the development of contacts of the elderly with their children,
ing arrangements of the elderly, and family patterns of mutual help

Contacts with relatives and siblings reveal the
and the United States, although fewer elderly
in Denmark than in the other two countries. I
than in Britain or the United States either to s
them to stay overnight.

In the United States we also find relatively
with children (but a larger proportion than in
all old people saw at least one child in the tw
interview, and almost the same proportion rece
is very common to have children to stay or to st

In Britain a large proportion of the elderly
half the elderly possessing children receive hel₁
mately the same proportion give help to childı
or having them to stay is more common than in I
than in the United States.

The main difference between the family rel₂
Denmark on one hand, and Britain and the Un
that although older people in Denmark, just as
Britain, report frequent contacts with childre
involvement in the daily lives of their children ar
In other words, the relatively small amount of
generations in Denmark seems to indicate less ₁

Why is Denmark different from Britain and
respect? Is this a recent development or is it
culture dissimilar to the culture in the other t
provide an adequate answer to these question
characteristics of the Danish institutional struct
all suggest that in Denmark the generations li
each other than in either Britain or the United
system seems to be more "particularistic" thar
two countries. In fact Frédéric Le Play and h
make this observation in the latter half of the
they pointed out that Scandinavia gave birth t
family.[22] This family

> . . . enables its young people to manage their own
> dently and to establish themselves in a definite fi
> great deal of individual initiative. Thanks to it, t
> highly appreciated. The individual is the organiz
> groupings in this type of society.[23]

It is the author's opinion, based on researcl
countries, that family relations in Denmark
formality than in either the Netherlands or E
"family evening," for example, is quite unknov
Sundays at the home of an aged parent are uncoı
This does not mean to imply that elderly peopl
their children, but rather that contacts are m₁
invitation than on spontaneous arrival. As one ʳ

and assistance all underline the importance of family dynamics. Differences in the level and content of relations between older people and their families, however, point in the direction of cultural variations. The survey findings emphasize the need for the development of family theory that can explain diversity as well as similarity in family relations.

NOTES

1 See Belle Boone Beard, "Are the Aged Ex-Family?" *Social Forces*, XXVII (1949), 274–279. In 1949, Beard listed a score of standard works on the family which omitted discussion of the family life of old people.

2 Pitirim A. Sorokin, *Social and Cultural Dynamics* (New York: American Book Company, 1937), IV, 776.

3 Talcott Parsons, "Age and Sex in the Social Structure of the United States, 1942," *Essays in Sociological Theory* (New York: The Free Press of Glencoe, 1964; rev. paperback ed.), pp. 102–103.

4 Talcott Parsons, "The Kinship System of the Contemporary United States, 1943," in Parsons, *op. cit.*, pp. 194–195.

5 George C. Homans, *The Human Group* (New York: Harcourt, Brace, 1950), pp. 263, 279.

6 See Marvin B. Sussman, "Relationships of Adult Children with their Parents in the United States," in Ethel Shanas and Gordon F. Streib, eds., *Social Structure and the Family: Generational Relations* (New York: Prentice-Hall, Inc., 1965), pp. 62–92; Marvin B. Sussman and Lee Burchinal, "Reappraising Kin Networks in Urban Society," Paper prepared for the Meeting of the American Sociological Association, Washington, D.C., 1962; Peter Townsend, in a new concluding chapter in *The Family Life of Old People* (Harmondsworth, Middlesex: Penguin Books, Ltd., 1962); Ethel Shanas, *The Health of Older People: A Social Survey* (Cambridge, Mass.: Harvard University Press, 1962).

7 M. B. Sussman and L. Burchinal, *op. cit.*, 1962.

8 Peter Laslett, *The World We Have Lost* (London: Methuen, 1965).

9 Leopold Rosenmayr and Eva Köckeis, "Propositions for a Sociological Theory of Aging and the Family," in *International Social Science Journal*, XV, No. 3 (1963), 416.

10 The use made of the concept of "extended family" in this volume does not entirely correspond with the utilization of this concept in other literature. A number of authors are apt to use the concept in describing a household that consists of three or more generations and at least two nuclear families, who live in the same dwelling. See, for example, Eugene A. Friedmann, "The Impact of Aging on the Social Structure," in Clark Tibbitts, ed., *Handbook of Social Gerontology* (Chicago: University of Chicago Press, 1960); and Richard T. La Piere, *Social Change* (New York: McGraw-Hill Book Company, Inc., 1965), p. 337. Others stress that the extended family consists of two or more nuclear families, not necessarily living under the same roof. See George Murdock, *Social Structure* (New York: The Macmillan Company, 1949), pp. 1–2; Michael Young and Peter Willmott, *Family and Kinship in East London* (Harmondsworth, Middlesex: Penguin Books, Ltd., 1962), p. 48. These definitions deviate from our utilization of the concept, partly because they lay emphasis on "working and living together in the same household" and/or because they stress that the extended family consists of "two or more nuclear families."

11 See also P. Townsend, *op. cit.*, p. 35.

12 Jan Stehouwer, "Relations between Generations and the Three-Generation Household in Denmark," in E. Shanas and G. F. Streib, eds., *op. cit.*, p. 152.

13 *Ibid.*, pp. 148–151.

14 L. Rosenmayr and E. Köckeis, "A Method to Assess Living Arrangements and Housing Problems of the Aged," paper prepared for the International Social Science Research Seminar in Gerontology, Markaryd, Sweden, 1963.

15 Because detailed information on housing the elderly in the United States was available elsewhere, housing material was collected only in Denmark and Great Britain. Parts of the notes and tables about the housing situation of the aged have been prepared by Mrs. Sylvia Tunstall, University of Essex.

16 Unpublished data from the study reported in Ethel Shanas, *op. cit.*

17 Anthony Lenzer, "Mobility Patterns among the Aged, 1955–1960," *The Gerontologist*, V, No. 1 (1965), 12.

18 This has been indicated by numerous local as well as a few national sample surveys. See, for example: Peter Townsend, *op. cit.*, p. 37; Ethel Shanas, *op. cit.*, pp. 94 ff.; Rosenmayr and Köckeis, "A Method to Assess Living Arrangements . . . ," *op. cit.*

19 M. L. Sussman and L. Burchinal, *op. cit.*, 1962.

20 Living together with children is often a financial necessity for the old persons. Such an arrangement is not usually considered a "help."

21 In interpreting these findings it must be remembered that in part the decrease in the relative number of older people living alone reflects the fact that the proportion of unmarried people who move into institutions increases with age.

22 Frédéric Le Play, *Les Ouvriers Européens* (Paris: 1855). See also H. De Tourville, *The Growth of Modern Nations, A History of the Particularist Form of Society* (English trans., in 1907), pp. 74 ff.

23 R. Pinot, "La Classification des Éspeces de la Famille," p. 64; cited in P. A. Sorokin, *Contemporary Sociological Theories* (New York: Harper & Row, 1964; Torchbook ed.), p. 87.

24 Forordning af 24. september 1708: Om forhold med Betlere, fattig Børn, retti Almisse-Lemmer og Løsgiaenger i Kiøbenhavn, sa og om Almisse til deres Underhold- (Kiøbenhavn: Skous Forordninger, 1795); Kgl. approberet og Plan for Fattig. vaesenets Indretring og Bestyrelse i Staden Kiøbenhavn og dens forstaeder, af 1, juli 1799 (Sch. 1800).

8 : *The Family and Social Class*

Students of the family usually concentrate their attention on the conjugal nuclear family, the family of husband and wife and their children. Studies of dating and courtship, early marriage, and patterns of child-rearing are routinely reported in the literature. While some few scholars have considered family life in the so-called "empty nest period," the time when children are grown and have left the parental home, these analyses almost invariably assume that association between parents and adult children is negligible during this period.

Old people and their place in the family, as has been pointed out earlier, are often ignored in family research. If the old are mentioned at all they are discussed as though they were outsiders to the total family configuration, who served only to create problems for the middle generation and the young.[1] This tacit assumption that old people have essentially a negative role in the family results from the belief that the conjugal nuclear family is the ideal family type within industrial societies. It has been postulated that such a family, in terms of its social and physical mobility, is most likely to survive successfully and to maintain itself in an urban environment.

Contemporary students of the family would argue that the modified extended family, rather than the nuclear conjugal family, has emerged as the ideal type in present-day Western society.[2] In this modified extended family old people, as parents or grandparents or as relatives by blood or marriage, interact with children, grandchildren, and with other kin. The role of the elderly within the kin network, may be a positive one. The old are often the givers as well as the receivers of help. Adult children may come to aged parents for advice and counsel. The elderly may be accepted by their kin rather than avoided by them. And, further, old people are often the stable polar element around which the kin network is organized.[3]

Detailed comparative studies of old people and their families suggest that the family life of old people differs within each social class. British studies in particular stress that for old people in working class families the kinship system and the kin network develop primarily through relationships between mothers and daughters. It is "Mum" and her daughters who serve as a focal point for the extended family. For old people in middle class families, however, the kinship system seems to develop less through the mother-daughter relationship and to be more dependent on the nature of the relationship between the husband and wife. Nevertheless, despite the possibly different organization of the kin network and its effect on details of family life, " . . . the family is as much of a support to its aged members in the suburb as in the East End."[4]

In the present chapter we shall concentrate on only one aspect of the family life of old people, namely, how the interaction of an old person with his family is affected by his class position. We shall first consider how the structure of the family in old age differs within each social class; then, the interaction of old people in each class with their children and relatives; and finally, the patterns of family help within social classes. As each topic is analyzed, whenever pertinent we shall compare the findings for old men and old women. In summary, we shall make some over-all comparisons of old people in the family in different social classes in Denmark, Britain, and the United States.

While many criteria of social class are possible (for example, economic status, education, social position, occupation, or some combination of these), to facilitate comparisons between the three countries we have used occupation as an index of class.[5] Occupation is necessarily a rough indicator of class position, but it was the index most readily available to us for the three-country analysis. Men and single women are classified by their own jobs, married women and widows by the occupation of their husbands.[6] We have grouped old people into four broad categories: white collar, blue collar, service workers, and agricultural workers. Our white collar workers are comparable to the usual "middle class" category; our blue collar and service workers are both "working class." In the analysis of marital status and social class, the findings for persons of blue collar and service backgrounds are analyzed separately; elsewhere, these two groups are combined into the single category of "working class." The most ambiguous of our class divisions is that of agricultural worker. Because of the wide range of agricultural establishments in the three countries, this category includes agricultural laborers, sharecroppers, and farmer-owners who may range from smallholders to large ranch owners.[7] The chief virtue of grouping all these persons together in our analysis is that the agricultural worker category serves to differentiate those old people of essentially rural backgrounds from old people in cities and towns.

Social Class and Family Structure

Widespread popular reports of the alienation of old people from their families usually ignore the fact that an old person must have living relatives—children, brothers and sisters, other kin—before he can be part of a kin network or a family configuration. To put it bluntly, one cannot be alienated from one's family if one has no family. The family life of old people therefore must obviously differ by whether the old person is married, widowed, or single, by whether he has surviving children, and by whether he has relatives, particularly brothers and sisters, who are still alive. (See in this connection the discussion of the structure of the family in Chapter 6.)

The class position of an old person in Denmark, Britain, and the United States influences both his chances of being married and the size and structure of his immediate family. Class position, however, seems to be unrelated to the possession of living brothers and sisters.

MARITAL STATUS

In each country and in each social class, old men are more likely than old women to be married. This is partly a result of men marrying women younger than they are, partly due to widowed men being more likely than widowed women to remarry, and partly due to the greater longevity of women compared to men. In all three countries, however, an old man's chances of being married are affected by his social class.

In both Britain and the United States middle class men with white collar backgrounds are more likely than other men to be married. From our data we cannot determine whether this difference between middle class men and other men (a) is the result of differential longevity—that is, of men in the white collar occupations being more likely than other men to survive into old age—or (b) whether it is the result of these men marrying women considerably younger than they are, or (c) whether it results from a greater incidence of remarriage among these old men. All three of these causal factors may be operating to create the differences in the two countries between the proportions of middle class men and of other men who are married. In Denmark, unlike Britain and the United States, an equally high proportion of old men of both white collar and working class backgrounds are married. Significant differences in marital status appear only when men in these two classes, both largely urban, are compared with men of agricultural background.[8] It may be that in Denmark, more than either in Britain or in the United States, urban and rural styles of living are more important than social class in influencing the family structure of the elderly. We will look for further evidence to support this hypothesis as we analyze the family life of old people in relation to their social class.

In all three countries, while most older men are married, most older women are unmarried—that is, they are either widowed or they have never married. In both Britain and the United States, a higher proportion of widows are found among women of blue collar background than among women of white collar background. Again, Denmark differs from the other two countries. Here women of white collar background are somewhat more likely than women of blue collar background to be widowed.

In both Britain and Denmark a substantial proportion of old women have never married. The proportion of older women who are unmarried is

Table VIII-1: PROPORTION OF PERSONS AGED 65 AND OVER IN EACH MARITAL STATUS, BY SOCIAL CLASS

Marital Status	White Collar			Blue Collar			Service Workers			Working Class—Blue Collar and Service Workers			Agricultural Workers		
	Men	Women	All	Men	Women	All	Men	Women	All	Men	Women	All	Men	Women	All
Married															
Denmark	72	41	55	73	52	63	[a]	10	18	72	40	55	64	52	59
Britain	77	33	50	68	38	50	[a]	21	35	68	36	49	67	[a]	62
United States	83	41	59	75	37	57	70	46	56	74	40	56	73	35	50
Widowed, separated, divorced															
Denmark	24	49	38	24	42	33	[a]	66	62	25	49	38	28	47	37
Britain	20	49	37	27	59	45	[a]	27	29	27	56	44	23	[a]	32
United States	14	54	37	22	62	41	27	50	41	23	58	41	24	65	49
Single															
Denmark	4	10	7	3	6	4	[a]	23	20	3	11	7	7	1	4
Britain	3	18	12	5	4	4	[a]	52	36	5	8	7	10	[a]	6
United States	3	5	4	3	1	2	3	4	3	3	2	2	3	—	1
Total															
Denmark	100	100	100	100	100	100	[a]	100	100	100	100	100	100	100	100
Britain	100	100	100	100	100	100	[a]	100	100	100	100	100	100	[a]	100
United States	100	100	100	100	100	100	100	100	100	100	100	100	100	100	100
Number of cases[b]															
Denmark	386	473	859	414	373	787	28	155	183	442	528	970	310	270	580
Britain	257	408	665	622	861	1,483	47	94	141	669	955	1,624	61	42	103
United States	300	392	692	454	413	867	117	175	292	571	588	1,159	202	295	497

[a] Per cents are not computed when base is less than 50.

[b] The percentage of eligible respondents who answered this question are: Denmark, total 98.5, men 99.4, women 97.7; Britain, total 95.7, men 98.3, women 93.9; United States, total 96.2, men 99.3, women 99.3. Non-response for social class in both Britain and the United States is concentrated among single women.

twice as great in Britain and one and one-half times as great in Denmark as in the United States. In both Denmark and Britain, elderly spinsters are concentrated in two social class groups. They are either white collar workers—teachers, clerks, office employees—or women in service occupations—maids, housekeepers, and companions. About one-third of the single women in the American sample did not report their occupations and thus could not be assigned to social class categories. There is reason to believe, however, that if full reports of occupations had been received from these American spinsters, they too would cluster in the predominately female occupations, in either white collar or service categories.

What conclusions can be drawn from the data on marital status and social class in the three countries? In Britain and the United States, older couples—that is, couples where the man is 65 years or older—are most likely to be found among the middle class. It is these white collar, middle class couples who occupy the retirement communities of the United States and Britain, and it is among these couples that one is likely to find a companionate, sharing, close relationship between husband and wife.[9] In both these countries the elderly widow is more likely to be found among the blue collar than among the white collar group. This disparity in the proportion of blue collar and white collar widows is particularly marked in Britain. In Denmark, in contrast to the other two countries, elderly couples are equally common among both the white collar and blue collar groups, while elderly widows are more often found among women of white collar than of blue collar background.

FAMILY SIZE

Let us now consider what effect the social class of the old person may have on the size and structure of his family. Family size, or more specifically the number of surviving children available to the old person, is especially important in old age. Aging parents turn to their children for help in meeting daily responsibilities; mature children, for their part, turn to their parents for various forms of help and support. As other sources of gratification lessen and disappear, children and particularly grandchildren become an increasingly important source of psychic satisfaction to the old person. Since old people more and more depend on their children, the number of children readily available to the old person is especially important in understanding the family life of the elderly. A single daughter who takes the responsibility of shopping, doing the housework, and meeting the psychological demands of an aged mother, may soon find her situation intolerable in view of her other responsibilities. Several daughters of an aged mother may not only free one another for their usual activities, but also share the psychological demands of their mother.

What is the relationship of the social class of the old person to his number of living children? In each country—Denmark, Britain, and the United States—old people with white collar backgrounds have the smallest number of children, those with blue collar backgrounds a substantially larger number of children, and agricultural workers the largest families of all. The average number of children for every old person in Denmark is 2.8; in Britain, 2.5; and in the United States, 3.1. In each country, old people of working class and agricultural backgrounds have more children than the national average; old people of white collar background, fewer children than the average.

In each country between one-fifth and one-fourth of all old people have no surviving children. The absolute percentages of old people without children are: Denmark, 18 per cent; Britain, 24 per cent; and the United States, 18 per cent. Childlessness among older women in particular is

Table VIII–2: PROPORTION OF ALL PERSONS AGED 65 AND OVER WITH EACH NUMBER OF LIVING CHILDREN, BY SOCIAL CLASS

Number of Living Children	White Collar			Working Class—Blue Collar and Service Workers			Agricultural Workers		
	Men	Women	All	Men	Women	All	Men	Women	All
None									
Denmark	15	22	19	15	19	17	18	10	14
Britain	23	35	30	18	19	19	21	a	18
United States	16	21	19	18	13	16	14	9	11
1–2									
Denmark	47	44	45	39	39	39	34	36	34
Britain	51	39	44	40	39	39	31	a	31
United States	47	43	45	33	35	34	30	29	29
3–5									
Denmark	31	28	29	32	29	31	35	34	35
Britain	22	21	21	30	30	30	25	a	29
United States	29	28	28	35	34	34	30	34	32
6 or more									
Denmark	7	6	7	14	13	13	13	20	16
Britain	4	5	4	12	12	12	23	a	22
United States	8	8	8	14	18	16	26	27	27
Total									
Denmark	100	100	100	100	100	100	100	100	100
Britain	100	100	100	100	100	100	100	a	100
United States	100	100	100	100	100	100	100	100	100
Average number of children									
Denmark	2.5	2.3	2.4	3.0	2.8	2.9	2.9	3.5	3.2
Britain	1.9	1.8	1.9	2.8	2.7	2.7	3.3	a	3.4
United States	2.5	2.4	2.5	3.0	3.3	3.2	3.7	4.0	3.9
Number of cases[b]									
Denmark	389	473	862	443	529	972	310	270	580
Britain	257	408	665	669	955	1,624	61	42	103
United States	300	392	692	571	588	1,159	202	295	497

[a] Per cents are not computed when base is less than 50.

[b] The percentages of eligible respondents who answered this question are: Denmark, total 98.7, men 99.7, women 97.8; Britain, total 95.7, men 98.3, women 93.9; United States, total 96.2, men 99.3, women 93.7.

related to their class position. In all three countries, women of white collar background are more likely than women of working class background to be childless. Among older men the relation of childlessness and class position is less clear-cut. In Denmark and in the United States, men of all social classes are equally likely to be childless; in Britain, it is white collar men who are likely to be childless. In general, while family size among the aged seems to be clearly related to class position, no straightforward case can be made from our findings that class position affects the probability of both older men and older women being childless.

Those studies of old people that investigate the importance of children in the maintenance of family life in old age have concentrated on the key role of the daughter. The dependence of working class old people on a daughter is one of the major themes of the Townsend study of old people in East London.[10] An American study suggests that, irrespective of social class, old people ask their daughters to help them more often than they ask their sons. A national sample of old people in the United States were asked to whom (other than husband or wife) they would turn in a health crisis. In nine cases of every ten, those old people who had children said a child would help them. Men and women both were twice as likely to say that they would turn to a daughter rather than to a son.[11]

If daughters are more important than sons in providing assistance to the elderly, then it is of some importance to know whether daughters are equally available to all sections of the elderly population. In other words, does the social class of the old person affect whether or not he has a surviving daughter? Both men and women of white collar background are less likely than persons of either blue collar or agricultural background to have surviving daughters. In each country, older men and women of white collar backgrounds are the most likely of all persons to have only a single surviving child, either a son or a daughter. The data on the family structure of old people suggest that the middle classes in Denmark, Britain, and the United States were limiting the size of their families even a half century ago. Since it may be assumed that the children of middle class people were less likely than the children of blue collar or agricultural workers to have died in infancy or in early childhood, we can only conclude that (particularly if the first child in a middle class family was a son) no further children were wanted.

The limitation of the size of their families among old people of white collar background results in a pattern of child-parent help in old age that differs from that of blue collar workers. Among old people of blue collar background the flow of help is mainly from daughter to parent, while among old people of white collar background help flows from son or daughter to parent, or, if there are no children, it is non-existent. The mutual dependence of the elderly middle class husband and wife remarked upon by other investigators may be a result of the family structure of the middle class. Since these old persons are likely to have only a single child or no children, they are forced by circumstances to turn to each other.

While social class affects the size of an old person's immediate family, class position is not related to the old person's chances of having living

Table VIII–3: PROPORTION OF PERSONS AGED 65 AND OVER IN EACH
TYPE OF FAMILY STRUCTURE, BY SOCIAL CLASS

Family Structure	White Collar			Working Class—Blue Collar and Service Workers			Agricultural Workers		
	Men	Women	All	Men	Women	All	Men	Women	All
No children									
Denmark	15	22	19	14	19	17	18	10	15
Britain	23	35	30	18	19	19	21	a	18
United States	16	21	19	18	13	16	14	9	11
One son only									
Denmark	13	11	12	10	9	9	7	10	9
Britain	13	11	12	8	8	8	8	a	7
United States	12	8	10	5	7	6	7	5	6
One daughter only									
Denmark	9	13	12	10	8	9	7	7	7
Britain	14	9	11	11	11	11	6	a	8
United States	11	11	11	10	10	10	7	8	8
Several children, at least one daughter									
Denmark	53	45	48	59	56	57	59	67	62
Britain	45	39	41	55	54	54	59	a	65
United States	54	49	51	61	62	61	64	69	67
Two or more sons, no daughters									
Denmark	9	9	9	7	8	7	9	6	7
Britain	5	6	6	8	8	8	5	a	3
United States	7	11	9	6	8	7	8	9	8
Total									
Denmark	100	100	100	100	100	100	100	100	100
Britain	100	100	100	100	100	100	100	a	100
United States	100	100	100	100	100	100	100	100	100
Number of cases[b]									
Denmark	388	472	860	442	529	971	310	270	580
Britain	257	409	666	669	954	1,623	61	42	103
United States	300	392	692	571	588	1,159	201	295	496

[a] Per cents are not computed when base is less than 50.

[b] Includes persons with no surviving children, childless married persons, and single persons. See footnote *b*, Table VIII–2.

brothers and sisters. Birth control was not prevalent seventy-five years ago, and mortality in this generation has undoubtedly blurred any differences there may have been in family size between the classes. In each country, irrespective of social class, roughly four of every five older men and women have living brothers or sisters. Brothers and sisters, like children, are a source of social support for older people. As has been shown earlier, in many instances these brothers and sisters play a major part in the kin network of the elderly.

What have we learned up to now about the family and social class in old age? Over-all, we have concentrated on the effect of social class on family structure. We have demonstrated that the social class of the old person affects whether or not he is married, his number of surviving children, and the structure of his immediate surviving family. Although, in every class, men are more likely than women to be married, in Britain and the United States men of white collar background are most likely of all men to be married. In all three countries, old people with white collar backgrounds have the fewest surviving children. Again, in each country, old people with white collar backgrounds are the most likely of all old persons to have only a single surviving child—and the least likely of all old people to have a surviving daughter.

Family Interaction and Social Class

SOCIAL CLASS AND LIVING ARRANGEMENTS

The interaction of the old person with his family is dependent upon his living arrangements as well as upon the structure of his immediate family. It is certainly easier for the old person to see his children and relatives and to share their activities if he lives in the same house with them or only a short distance away. Then, too, some children may play a more important role in the family configuration than others. Eldest children may be more closely involved with parents than younger children, married daughters may be on more intimate terms with aged parents than married sons.

Let us first illustrate the importance of family interaction within the life of the old person by describing two different men.

Victor Morrison is a retired man of 72. He lives with his wife and two young unmarried daughters on the West Coast of the United States. Mr. Morrison used to have a small restaurant, but he sold it recently because he felt that the work was too hard for him. Mr. Morrison is "middle class" on our occupational scale.

The Morrisons have two sons and four daughters. Four of these children are married and live within ten minutes of their parents. The two youngest girls live at home. Mr. Morrison saw all of his children but one within the last twenty-four hours. The remaining child, a daughter, he saw within the last week. Although he has three sisters, he did not see any of them within the past month.

Mr. Morrison has 23 grandchildren. He sees them often—some every day. He says: "I pick them up at school when it rains; I work in the garden with them; we do lots of things together."

John Vaughn, like Victor Morrison, is also 72 years old and lives on the West Coast of the United States. Mr. Vaughn is a farmer and is classified as an agricultural worker on our occupational scale. He works 77 hours a week.

Mr. and Mrs. Vaughn live alone. They have two children, a daughter and a son, both married and both living over a day's journey from them. They have seen their daughter during the past year—she came, with her children, to visit the family farm—but they have not seen their son. Mr. Vaughn has one brother whom he sees often. He saw him last within the past week.

Mr. Vaughn says of his children: "They send us presents on all holidays. They're really good kids."

Mr. Morrison and Mr. Vaughn both seem to be well-adjusted old men. Yet, it may be suggested that if Mr. Vaughn were to stop working, unlike Mr. Morrison, he would find it difficult to fill his time. Life would be empty for Mr. Vaughn. He would have no children close by to visit, no grandchildren to help and to supervise.

The brief accounts of Mr. Morrison and Mr. Vaughn give us some feeling of what family life may be like in old age. Not all people have the same living arrangements nor the same chances to be with their family members.

Let us now consider how social class affects the life of the old person. Does the old person's social class affect whether he lives with or apart from his children or relatives? Does it affect how far he is from his nearest child? What of class and his interaction with specific children: does his eldest child live near or far? Does social class affect the proximity of the old person to a married daughter or son?

Distance from children, however, is only a crude indication of family visiting patterns. How often do parents and children actually see one another? Do parents see married daughters more often than married sons? How often do old people see their brothers and sisters and other relatives? What is the effect of social class on visiting patterns?

In all three countries—Denmark, Britain, and the United States— most old people who are married live apart from their children and relatives. And in Western cultures this is what old people want—to live independently in their own homes as long as possible.[12] In both Britain and the United States, however, social class clearly affects the living arrangements of old couples. Elderly couples with a white collar background are far more likely than those with either working class or agricultural backgrounds to live apart from children and relatives. A possible explanation of these class differences in living arrangements is the difference in the size of families of the white collar and other classes. Old people with working class or agricultural backgrounds have larger families than old people of white collar background and thus even after 65 are more likely to have a young unmarried adult child still in the home. On the other hand, the economic explanation for the differences in the living arrangements of old couples of various classes must not be ruled out. Living together in a joint household is often the way in which adult children and other relatives assist in the support of aged persons.[13] The fact that more white collar couples than other couples live alone may simply reflect their more comfortable economic status.

In Denmark, in contrast to Britain and the United States, the differences in the proportion of older couples with white collar and blue collar backgrounds who live apart from children and relatives are negligible. Differences in living arrangements among old couples in Denmark are less between the middle class and the working class than between these two groups and agricultural workers. Old couples with agricultural back-

Table VIII-4: PROPORTION OF MARRIED PERSONS AGED 65 AND OVER, BY SOCIAL CLASS AND TYPE OF LIVING ARRANGEMENTS

Living Arrangements	White Collar			Working Class—Blue Collar and Service Workers			Agricultural Workers		
	Men	Women	All	Men	Women	All	Men	Women	All
Living with spouse only									
Denmark	82	87	84	83	85	84	72	81	75
Britain	74	72	73	66	68	67	a	a	48
United States	82	85	83	78	82	79	68	77	72
Living with spouse and children									
Denmark	14	7	11	14	11	13	25	16	21
Britain	20	19	20	29	27	28	a	a	45
United States	11	9	10	18	13	16	22	14	18
Living with spouse, relatives, and/or others									
Denmark	4	5	5	3	3	3	3	3	3
Britain	6	9	7	5	5	5	a	a	6
United States	7	6	7	5	5	5	11	9	10
Total									
Denmark	100	100	100	100	100	100	100	100	100
Britain	100	100	100	100	100	100	a	a	100
United States	100	100	100	100	100	100	100	100	100
Number of cases[b]									
Denmark	270	190	468	317	211	528	198	141	339
Britain	198	135	333	453	345	798	41	23	64
United States	250	161	411	421	234	655	148	102	250

[a] Per cents are not computed when base is less than 50.

[b] See footnote b, Table VIII-2.

grounds are one and one-half times as likely as elderly couples of white collar or working class backgrounds to share a home with one of their children or their relatives.

In both Britain and the United States the social class of unmarried old people affects their living arrangements. Substantial numbers of un-unmarried old people have no children (29 per cent in Denmark and in Britain and 24 per cent in the United States) and therefore cannot be expected to live with children. (As has been pointed out earlier, however, relatives tend to replace children for many childless old people.) In both Britain and the United States substantially higher proportions of unmarried working class aged than of unmarried white collar aged live with children and relatives. Again, as with elderly couples, in Denmark there is no marked difference in the proportion of white collar and of blue collar unmarried old people living *with* children and relatives. On the other hand, unmarried persons of agricultural backgrounds are almost

Table VIII–5: PROPORTION OF UNMARRIED PERSONS AGED 65 AND OVER, BY SOCIAL CLASS AND TYPE OF LIVING ARRANGEMENTS

Living Arrangements	White Collar			Working Class— Blue Collar and Service Workers			Agricultural Workers		
	Men	Women	All	Men	Women	All	Men	Women	All
Living alone									
Denmark	62	62	62	67	71	70	42	49	46
Britain	41	42	42	35	47	44	a	a	a
United States	54	51	52	47	36	39	64	55	57
Living with children									
Denmark	15	18	17	18	15	16	29	41	35
Britain	30	33	32	46	41	42	a	a	a
United States	24	27	26	31	46	41	20	34	31
Living with relatives									
Denmark	5	9	8	6	6	6	9	6	8
Britain	15	19	18	13	9	10	a	a	a
United States	18	15	15	13	11	12	11	9	10
Living with others									
Denmark	18	11	13	9	8	8	20	4	11
Britain	14	6	7	6	3	4	a	a	a
United States	4	7	7	10	7	8	5	2	2
Total									
Denmark	100	100	100	100	100	100	100	100	100
Britain	100	100	100	100	100	100	a	a	a
United States	100	100	100	100	100	100	100	100	100
Number of cases[b]									
Denmark	111	283	394	126	318	444	111	129	240
Britain	59	273	332	216	610	826	20	19	39
United States	50	231	281	150	354	504	55	193	248

[a] Per cents are not computed when base is less than 50.

[b] The percentages of eligible respondents who answered this question are: Denmark, total 97.7, men 100, women 96.7; Britain, total 92.9, men 97.3, women 91.5; United States, total 93.3, men 99.6, women 91.4.

twice as likely to live with children or relatives as persons of white collar or blue collar backgrounds.

The findings indicate that in Britain and the United States, the social class of an old person affects whether or not he lives with his children and relatives. In both these countries, persons with white collar backgrounds, whether married or unmarried, are the least likely of all persons to live with children and relatives. The sharing of a home with children is most common among widowed working class men and women in Britain and among widowed working class women in the United States.

The living arrangements of old people in Denmark differ from those of old people in the other two countries. In Denmark both white collar and blue collar workers live apart from children and other relatives. Sharing a home with children and relatives is apparently a rural rather than a working class phenomenon in Denmark. Our findings indicate that widowed farm wives are the most likely of all aged persons to share a home with children or relatives. As Jan Stehouwer has indicated elsewhere, irrespective of whether old people in Denmark are of white collar or blue collar background, in both the provincial towns and in the urbanized Copenhagen area they live apart from their children and relatives.[14]

SOCIAL CLASS AND PROXIMITY OF SPECIFIC CHILDREN

We now turn from describing the specific household arrangements of the elderly, to consideration of the distance that older people live from their children. More specifically, is this distance affected by the social class of the old person?

In each country, and for every social class, old people who live apart from children tend to have at least one child in the immediate vicinity. Half of all old people, irrespective of class, either share a household with a child or live within ten minutes distance from a child. Further, in all three countries, despite their differences in size, it is unusual for an old person to have his nearest child one hour or more distant from him. The proportion of old people who are this far from their nearest child ranges from 11 and 12 per cent in Britain and in Denmark to 16 per cent in the United States. There are some class differences, however, among those old people who live this far from their nearest child. In both Britain and the United States persons of white collar backgrounds are the most likely of all old persons to report that they live an hour or more from their nearest child. In Denmark, persons of both white collar and blue collar backgrounds are equally likely to report that they live this far from their nearest child. The class differences in Denmark are between white collar and blue collar workers and their wives on the one hand, and those of agricultural background on the other.

In view of the differences in physical size and in the style of housing in Denmark, Britain, and the United States, these findings on the proximity of older parents and their children for each of the social classes are striking. The evidence is diametrically opposite to the common belief that aged parents within any social class are physically separated from their children. The immediate household of the old person differs by whether he is of white or blue collar background in Britain and the United States, and by whether he is of these or of an agricultural background in Denmark. However, in most instances, if an old person has children and there is no child in his immediate household, then there is a child living within ten minutes distance from him. The responsibility or attachment of adult children to aged parents appears to override class and possibly urban-rural differences in style of life.

Studies of the family life of old people have investigated the relationship of aged parents with separate children in the family. In his study of East London, Townsend suggests that married daughters are more likely to live in close proximity to their aged parents than are married sons.[15] It has also been suggested that eldest children may be the most likely of all

Table VIII–6: PROPORTION OF PERSONS AGED 65 AND OVER, BY SOCIAL CLASS AND PROXIMITY OF NEAREST CHILD (*Percentage Distribution*)

Proximity of Nearest Child	White Collar			Working Class— Blue Collar and Service Workers			Agricultural Workers		
	Men	Women	All	Men	Women	All	Men	Women	All
Same household									
Denmark	16	17	17	17	16	16	31	31	31
Britain	27	43	36	42	45	44	a	a	49
United States	16	25	21	26	37	32	25	30	28
10 minutes or less									
Denmark	30	30	30	32	36	34	34	29	31
Britain	22	20	21	23	25	24	a	a	21
United States	31	33	32	34	31	33	34	37	36
11–30 minutes									
Denmark	22	23	23	26	26	26	18	21	19
Britain	18	14	16	16	15	16	a	a	14
United States	17	14	15	17	16	16	15	14	15
31–60 minutes									
Denmark	16	15	16	11	11	11	8	11	10
Britain	13	9	10	8	7	7	a	a	5
United States	11	9	9	7	4	5	13	6	8
One hour or more									
Denmark	16	14	15	14	11	13	9	8	8
Britain	20	14	17	11	8	9	a	a	11
United States	25	19	22	16	12	14	14	13	13
Total									
Denmark	100	100	100	100	100	100	100	100	100
Britain	100	100	100	100	100	100	a	a	100
United States	100	100	100	100	100	100	100	100	100
Number of cases[b]									
Denmark	330	368	698	376	430	806	252	243	495
Britain	198	266	464	547	773	1,320	48	37	85
United States	253	307	560	465	510	975	174	267	441

[a] Per cents are not computed when base is less than 50.

[b] See footnote *b*, Table II–2.

children to assume responsibilities for aged parents. We would like to know something more about these two hypotheses. Are the relationships of old people and specific children affected by differences in social class among the aged? Does their social class affect the proximity of aged parents and their eldest child? Are there class differences that affect the proximity of parents and their married children, both sons and daughters?

In all three countries, irrespective of social class, roughly one-third of all old people are either in the same household as their eldest child or no more than ten minutes distance from him. There are class differences within each country, however, in the sharing of a household by old people and their eldest child. In the United States, white collar, working class,

Table VIII-7: PERSONS AGED 65 AND OVER, BY SOCIAL CLASS AND
PROXIMITY OF ELDEST CHILD (*Percentage Distribution*)

Proximity of Eldest Child	White Collar			Working Class—Blue Collar and Service Workers			Agricultural Workers		
	Men	Women	All	Men	Women	All	Men	Women	All
Same household									
Denmark	8	8	8	6	6	6	14	11	13
Britain	15	20	18	17	17	17	a	a	10
United States	6	13	10	6	16	12	5	11	9
10 minutes or less									
Denmark	19	19	19	20	23	22	19	20	19
Britain	18	18	18	19	22	20	a	a	27
United States	21	20	20	24	24	24	23	24	24
11–30 minutes									
Denmark	20	23	22	24	26	25	19	23	21
Britain	16	21	19	23	23	23	a	a	15
United States	17	14	15	17	16	17	15	15	15
31–60 minutes									
Denmark	18	18	18	20	18	19	16	21	18
Britain	14	11	12	13	11	12	a	a	19
United States	13	10	11	13	9	10	13	12	12
One hour or more									
Denmark	34	31	33	30	27	28	32	25	29
Britain	37	30	33	28	28	28	a	a	29
United States	44	43	43	40	35	37	44	38	40
Total									
Denmark	100	100	100	100	100	100	100	100	100
Britain	100	100	100	100	100	100	a	a	100
United States	100	100	100	100	100	100	100	100	100
Number of cases[b]									
Denmark	330	367	697	376	430	806	252	243	495
Britain	196	262	458	544	769	1,313	42	37	79
United States	253	307	560	462	508	970	174	267	441

[a] Per cents are not computed when base is less than 50.

[b] The percentages of eligible respondents who answered this question are: Denmark, total 99.4, men 99.5, women 99.3; Britain, total 96.8, men 96.9, women 96.7; United States, total 98.0, men 98.7, women 97.4.

and agricultural workers are all equally likely to share a home with their eldest child. In Britain, both white collar and working class old people are almost twice as likely as those of agricultural backgrounds to live with an eldest child. In Denmark, the sharing of households by old people and their eldest child is diametrically opposite to the situation in Britain. The eldest child of those of agricultural background is almost twice as likely as the eldest child of white collar or blue collar parents to live with an aged parent. The only consistent class differences in all three countries in the proximity of old people to their eldest children is that old people of white collar background, both men and women, are slightly more likely than other old people to have their eldest child living an hour or more distant from them.

The relationships between the social class of an old person and his proximity to his eldest child seem very slight. About the same proportion of old people in each social class live either with an eldest child or within ten minutes distance of him. We may still ask, however, whether there are class differences that affect the proximity of aged parents and married children.

In both Britain and the United States the class position of the old person affects how close he lives to his nearest married child. Old people

Table VIII–8: PROPORTION OF PERSONS AGED 65 AND OVER, BY SOCIAL CLASS AND DISTANCE (WITHIN 10 MINUTES OR LESS, OR OVER AN HOUR OR MORE) FROM THEIR NEAREST MARRIED OR WIDOWED SON OR DAUGHTER

Proximity of Nearest Married or Widowed Child	MEN			WOMEN			ALL		
	Son	Daughter	Any Child	Son	Daughter	Any Child	Son	Daughter	Any Child
White Collar									
Same household									
Denmark	2	3	4	3	5	5	2	4	4
Britain	8	7	10	10	23	23	10	16	17
United States	3	5	6	6	15	16	4	11	11
10 minutes or less									
Denmark	26	28	34	29	24	33	28	26	33
Britain	26	19	26	28	20	29	27	19	28
United States	31	24	34	29	29	35	30	26	35
One hour or more									
Denmark	27	21	19	26	22	15	27	22	17
Britain	33	38	28	26	24	19	29	31	23
United States	35	40	29	34	33	22	35	36	25
Working Class—Blue Collar and Service Workers									
Same household									
Denmark	3	2	3	2	3	4	2	3	4
Britain	6	19	19	9	23	24	8	21	22
United States	3	11	12	8	21	24	6	16	18
10 minutes or less									
Denmark	24	25	33	32	26	37	28	26	35
Britain	33	30	35	33	31	37	33	31	36
United States	36	28	40	38	29	38	37	28	39
One hour or more									
Denmark	23	22	16	21	23	13	22	22	14
Britain	20	19	13	20	18	12	20	18	12
United States	31	28	20	25	21	15	28	24	17

Proximity of Nearest Married or Widowed Child	MEN			WOMEN			ALL		
	Son	Daughter	Any Child	Son	Daughter	Any Child	Son	Daughter	Any Child
Agricultural Workers									
Same household									
Denmark	7	5	9	7	3	8	7	4	8
Britain	a	a	a	a	a	a	6	17	19
United States	4	4	7	9	15	19	7	11	14
10 minutes or less									
Denmark	30	21	36	25	25	33	28	23	35
Britain	a	a	a	a	a	a	36	18	33
United States	34	31	44	39	31	44	37	31	44
One hour or more									
Denmark	22	22	12	20	18	11	21	20	11
Britain	a	a	a	a	a	a	24	15	15
United States	25	28	18	23	25	15	24	26	16
White Collar									
Number of cases[b]									
Denmark	231	218	304	255	245	345	486	463	649
Britain	122	138	189	183	172	252	305	310	441
United States	173	186	240	211	220	294	384	406	534
Working Class—Blue Collar and Service Workers									
Number of cases[b]									
Denmark	265	273	357	312	312	409	577	585	766
Britain	376	401	517	569	565	734	945	966	1,251
United States	355	384	457	379	404	490	734	788	947
Agricultural Workers									
Number of cases[b]									
Denmark	180	183	234	188	186	235	368	369	469
Britain	38	39	47	25	33	35	63	72	82
United States	134	138	168	210	221	263	344	359	431

[a] Per cents are not computed when base is less than 50.

[b] See footnote *b*, Table II–2.

of working class background or agricultural backgrounds in these two countries are more likely to live either with or near a married child than old people of white collar backgrounds. The sharing of households by working class people and their married children is especially marked in Britain. Once again, Denmark differs from either Britain or the United States. In general, old people in Denmark, irrespective of social class, are unlikely to share a household with a married child or to live within ten minutes of a child. Roughly four of every ten aged persons in Denmark, irrespective of social class, are physically this close to their nearest married child—with some indication that such physical proximity is most common for old people of agricultural background. In all three countries old persons of white collar background are more likely than other old persons to report that their nearest married child is an hour or more distant from them.

The findings on their nearest married child's proximity to parents of white collar background tend to corroborate the reports of the proximity of eldest children to their parents. In all three countries the adult children of white collar parents are more mobile physically than adult children of other backgrounds. Such mobility shows itself in parents and children living in separate households in all three countries and—even more important—in parents and eldest children or married children living at greater distances from one another.

The findings presented thus far, however, still leave certain key questions unanswered. These questions relate to the behavior of daughters, as opposed to the behavior of sons, and to the relationship of mothers and their grown children as opposed to the relationship of fathers. Do the married sons and the married daughters live at equidistance from their elderly parents? Specifically, do married daughters of working class families continue to live in close proximity to aged parents, while the married sons of such families, like the married sons of white collar parents, move away? Are old women more likely than old men to live near married daughters? Among old people of agricultural background, are married sons, the inheritors of the family property, more likely than married daughters to live close to their parents?

In both Britain and in the United States, men and women of white collar origins are less likely than men and women of blue collar origins to live with or close to a married son or a married daughter. In other words, in these two countries, irrespective of the sex of the child, the married children of middle class parents are more physically mobile than the married children of blue collar parents. In Denmark these differences in the mobility of the married children of white and blue collar workers are virtually non-existent. In both Britain and the United States, old people of working class backgrounds are more likely to live near a married daughter than a married son. Again, these differences between sons and daughters of working class families are not reported in Denmark. Indeed, in that country women of working class backgrounds are more likely to live with or near a married son than a married daughter.

In general, for both Britain and the United States the findings indicate that old women are more likely than old men to live near a married daughter. Old women in Britain, in every social class, and old women in the United States of white collar and agricultural backgrounds, are more likely than old men of the same respective classes to live near a married daughter. In Denmark, on the contrary, old men and old women in each occupational class are equally likely to live near a married daughter.

In Denmark and the United States we are able to test whether the married sons of old people of agricultural origins are more likely than their daughters to live near these parents. Again, the findings are not consistent for both men and women in the two countries. In Denmark the married sons of both old men and old women of agricultural background are more likely than married daughters to live close to their parents. In the United States, only the married sons of old men of agricultural background are more likely than married daughters to live near their parents. Old women of agricultural background are physically closer to married daughters than to married sons.

The findings on the proximity of old people of various social classes and their children indicate the operation of two separate kinds of family logistics. In general, irrespective of class, about half of all old people either live with a child or within ten minutes distance of a child. About a third of all old people, again irrespective of social class, live with or in close proximity to their eldest child. Whether an old person lives close to a married child, however, is affected by his social class. In both Britain and the United States old people of white collar backgrounds are the least likely of all old people to live in the immediate vicinity of a married child. The data suggest both greater physical mobility on the part of the married children of white collar parents in Britain and the United States (a finding already reported for all children of white collar parents) and, simultaneously, greater sharing of households among working class old people and their married children. In Denmark, irrespective of class, sharing a household with a married child or living close to a married child is less common than in either Britain or the United States. Among old people in Denmark men with farm backgrounds are somewhat more likely than other old people to live close to a married child (in this instance married sons), reflecting a cultural pattern in which the son is likely to inherit the family farm or to work on the farm along with his father.

SOCIAL CLASS AND FREQUENCY OF CONTACT WITH CHILDREN

The physical distance between parents and children is only a clue to the amount of interaction that occurs between them. Living within ten minutes distance of an adult child, while it increases the probability that the old parent and the child will see one another, does not guarantee that such interaction will take place. A better index of interaction is how recently old people saw their children. Are there class differences in how recently aged parents saw a child—or are old people of the various social classes equally likely to have seen a child within a given period? What of married children? Are there class differences in how recently old people saw a married child?

In all three countries at least six of every ten old people saw one child within the 24 hours preceding the interview—either that same day or a day earlier. In every country old people of agricultural backgrounds, farmers or the wives of farmers, are the most likely of all old people to have seen one of their children within the last 24 hours and the least

Table VIII–9: PERSONS AGED 65 AND OVER, BY SOCIAL CLASS AND
SHORTEST PERIOD SINCE ANY CHILD SEEN (*Percentage Distribution*)

Shortest Period Since Any Child Seen	White Collar			Working Class— Blue Collar and Service Workers			Agricultural Workers		
	Men	Women	All	Men	Women	All	Men	Women	All
Same household									
Denmark	16	17	17	16	16	16	31	31	31
Britain	27	43	36	42	45	44	a	a	49
United States	16	25	21	26	37	32	25	30	28
Today or yesterday									
Denmark	40	46	43	42	45	43	41	39	40
Britain	29	23	26	27	28	27	a	a	29
United States	40	40	40	36	31	33	44	42	43
Within past 2–7 days									
Denmark	24	21	23	23	25	24	17	19	18
Britain	21	20	20	17	16	17	a	a	9
United States	21	18	20	21	18	20	16	15	15
Within past 8–30 days									
Denmark	12	11	12	11	8	10	8	7	7
Britain	12	8	10	8	6	7	a	a	6
United States	11	7	9	5	7	6	7	5	6
More than one month ago									
Denmark	7	5	6	8	6	7	3	4	4
Britain	11	6	8	6	5	5	a	a	6
United States	12	10	10	12	7	9	9	8	8
Total									
Denmark	100	100	100	100	100	100	100	100	100
Britain	100	100	100	100	100	100	a	a	100
United States	100	100	100	100	100	100	100	100	100
Number of cases[b]									
Denmark	330	367	697	376	428	804	248	242	490
Britain	198	266	464	545	769	1,314	48	37	85
United States	253	305	558	465	509	974	173	266	439

[a] Per cents are not computed when base is less than 50.

[b] The percentages of eligible respondents who answered this question are: Denmark, total 99.0, men 99.1, women 99.0; Britain, total 97.5, men 98.0, women 97.1; United States, total 98.0, men 98.9, women 97.2.

likely of all old people to say that as long as a week has elapsed without their seeing a child. That many of these old people are actually sharing a common job with their children is undoubtedly reflected in such reports of family interaction. In both Britain and the United States, old people of white collar background, both men and women, are the least likely of any old people to say that they saw a child within the past 24 hours, the most likely to say that they have not seen any child for a week or more.

The pattern of interaction of old people with their married children is similar to their interaction with any child. Once again, in every country, old people with agricultural backgrounds are the most likely of all old people to have seen a married child in the last 24 hours. Again, in both Britain and the United States, but not in Denmark, both men and women of white collar background are the least likely of all people to have seen a married child within that time period.

It had been expected that there would be a difference in the relative frequency with which old people saw their married sons and their married daughters. It was thought that old men of agricultural background would be more likely to see their married sons than their married daughters in the last 24 hours, but that other old persons would be more likely to have recently seen a daughter than a son. It was believed that visiting patterns between the old and their children would be affected by the small tasks which daughters perform for old parents, the help with housekeeping, shopping, and errands. The findings for both Britain and the United States are in keeping with this general hypothesis. In the United States old men of agricultural background are more likely to have recently seen a married son than a married daughter. With this exception, old people in each social class in both Britain and the United States are more likely to have seen a married daughter than a married son within the past 24 hours. In Denmark, however, in contrast to Britain and the United States, there are no marked class differences affecting how recently old people saw a married son or a married daughter. In that country both men and women of agricultural background are slightly more likely to have recently seen a married son than a married daughter, but men and women of white collar and blue collar backgrounds are equally likely to have seen either a married son or a daughter in the last 24 hours.

The findings from the survey on how recently old people saw their children show that, regardless of class, a majority of old people saw at least one of their children during the past 24 hours and that an additional group of old people saw at least one of their children during the past week. Only a minority of old people, about one in every six persons in the three countries, failed to see one of their children within the past week. In Britain and in the United States old persons of white collar background are less likely than those of blue collar or agricultural backgrounds to have recently seen a child and are thus overrepresented in this minority. This effect of social class on family life of the elderly seems quite clear for these two countries. In Denmark, however, both white collar and blue collar workers are overrepresented among those who have not seen a child. It is agricultural workers and their wives who are most likely to live with children and to see their children.

VISITING WITH CHILDREN

To some extent, old people and their children compensate for their physical separation and for not seeing one another by extended visiting. Parents come to stay overnight with a child living at a distance; children come to stay with parents. Such overnight visiting is much more common in the United States than in either of the two European countries.

Undoubtedly this visiting pattern results in part from the differences in physical size in the three countries and the greater distances which parents and children in the United States need travel in order to see one another. In both Britain and the United States, however, old persons of white collar origins, both men and women, were the most likely of all old people to visit overnight with a child during the past year. Just as these persons were the most likely of all old people to report that their children lived at a distance, so they were the most likely of all old people to say that they stayed overnight with a child. In Denmark, the patterns of visiting overnight with children are less clear-cut for the different social classes.

Table VIII–10: PROPORTION OF PERSONS AGED 65 AND OVER, BY SOCIAL CLASS, WHO SAW A MARRIED OR WIDOWED SON OR DAUGHTER WITHIN THE WEEK

Married or Widowed Child Seen within Week	MEN			WOMEN			ALL		
	Son	Daughter	Any Child	Son	Daughter	Any Child	Son	Daughter	Any Child
White Collar									
Same household									
Denmark	2	3	4	3	4	5	2	3	4
Britain	8	7	10	10	23	23	9	16	18
United States	3	5	6	6	16	16	5	11	11
Today or yesterday									
Denmark	35	36	43	37	41	49	36	38	46
Britain	26	33	35	27	28	32	27	30	34
United States	37	31	44	32	37	43	34	34	44
Within past 2–7 days									
Denmark	31	28	28	28	28	26	30	28	27
Britain	27	21	24	32	25	27	30	23	25
United States	21	26	24	28	21	22	25	23	23
Working Class—Blue Collar and Service Workers									
Same household									
Denmark	2	2	3	2	3	4	2	3	4
Britain	6	19	19	9	23	24	8	21	22
United States	3	11	12	8	21	24	6	16	18
Today or yesterday									
Denmark	33	34	43	39	35	47	36	34	45
Britain	30	33	37	30	36	39	30	34	39
United States	31	34	43	32	32	38	31	33	40
Within past 2–7 days									
Denmark	30	32	31	30	32	30	30	32	31
Britain	30	26	24	31	22	22	31	24	23
United States	29	26	25	30	25	22	30	25	24

Table VIII–10—continued

Married or Widowed Child Seen within Week	MEN			WOMEN			ALL		
	Son	Daughter	Any Child	Son	Daughter	Any Child	Son	Daughter	Any Child
Agricultural Workers									
Same household									
Denmark	7	5	9	7	3	8	7	4	8
Britain	a	a	a	a	a	a	6	17	20
United States	4	4	7	9	15	19	7	11	15
Today or yesterday									
Denmark	37	35	47	32	35	44	34	35	45
Britain	a	a	a	a	a	a	33	36	44
United States	46	40	55	41	35	49	43	37	51
Within past 2–7 days									
Denmark	26	28	25	28	36	31	27	32	28
Britain	a	a	a	a	a	a	23	14	17
United States	20	30	20	24	22	17	23	25	18
White Collar									
Number of cases[b]									
Denmark	231	215	304	254	245	345	485	460	649
Britain	122	137	189	183	171	251	305	308	440
United States	172	185	240	208	218	292	380	403	532
Working Class—Blue Collar and Service Workers									
Number of cases[b]									
Denmark	263	273	357	311	309	407	574	582	764
Britain	374	401	514	564	563	730	938	964	1,244
United States	354	382	455	378	401	489	732	783	944
Agricultural Workers									
Number of cases[b]									
Denmark	176	180	231	186	185	234	362	365	465
Britain	36	39	47	25	33	35	61	72	82
United States	133	134	166	208	219	262	341	353	428

[a] Per cents are not computed when base is less than 50.

[b] The percentages of eligible respondents who answered these questions are: married or widowed sons—Denmark, total 99.0, men 99.0, women 99.1; Britain, total 98.0, men 98.5, women 97.6; United States, total 98.5, men 99.4, women 97.8; married or widowed daughters—Denmark, total 98.7, men 98.5, women 98.9; Britain, total 97.7, men 98.1, women 97.3; United States, total 98.5, men 99.1, women 97.9; any married or widowed child—Denmark, total 99.3, men 99.3, women 99.2; Britain, total 97. 8 men 98.3, women 97.4; United States, total 98.4, men 99.3, women 97.7.

Table VIII–11: PROPORTION OF PERSONS AGED 65 AND OVER, BY SOCIAL CLASS, WHO EITHER VISITED AN ADULT CHILD OVERNIGHT OR HAD AN ADULT CHILD VISITING OVERNIGHT

Visiting with Children and Social Class	DENMARK			BRITAIN			UNITED STATES		
	Men	Women	All	Men	Women	All	Men	Women	All
Visiting with adult child									
White collar	20	24	22	36	36	36	44	56	50
Working class—blue collar and service workers	15	24	19	27	34	31	37	50	44
Agricultural workers	19	20	19	a	a	24	40	52	47
Adult child visiting over- night									
White collar	21	20	20	38	33	35	53	53	53
Working class—blue collar and service workers	20	17	19	26	27	26	44	43	44
Agricultural workers	26	22	24	a	a	28	60	58	59
Number of cases[b]									
White collar	320	352	672	182	236	418	244	282	526
Working class—blue collar and service workers	371	421	792	502	704	1,206	444	462	906
Agricultural workers	245	237	482	46	36	82	160	243	403

[a] Per cents are not computed when base is less than 50.

[b] The percentages of eligible respondents who answered this question are: Denmark, total 99.1, men 99.5, women 98.8; Britain, total 96.7, men 97.1, women 96.4; United States, total 96.1, men 97.2, women 95.1.

Whether children come to stay overnight with aged parents is a function not only of how far children live from their parents but also whether their parents have room to put them up for an extended visit. In both Britain and the United States old people of blue collar background are the least likely to report that children visited overnight with them; old people of white collar background are the most likely to report such visits. In Denmark there are no marked differences between white collar and blue collar persons in their reports of children visiting overnight.

CONTACT WITH BROTHERS AND SISTERS

Brothers and sisters also play an important role in the social life of old people. In each country, about one-third of all old persons who had brothers and sisters saw at least one of them during the week before the interview. Social class is not the chief determinant of whether an old person sees his brothers and sisters. The significant factor in the mainten- ance of relationships with brothers and sisters is whether the old person has ever been married. It is single men and women of every social class who are most likely to have frequent contact with their brothers and sisters.

CLASS DIFFERENCES IN PATTERNS OF FAMILY CONTACT

To this stage we have discussed the effect of social class on various kinds of family interaction: whether an old person lives with or apart from his children, how recently an old person saw his children, whether he and his children visit overnight with one another, and whether he visits with his brothers and sisters.

The pattern of family contacts of old men and women in the various social classes in Denmark, Britain, and the United States in the week before their interview is given in summary form in Table VIII–12. In this analysis old people are divided into those who have children and those who have no children. For those who have children but who have not seen them during the past week and for those old people without children, there is a further analysis of whether they have seen brothers, sisters, or other relatives during the week.

Is there a class difference in these patterns of family contact? Are middle class old people less likely than working class people to see their families and their relatives as often as every week? Further, is there a

Table VIII–12: PERSONS AGED 65 AND OVER, BY SOCIAL CLASS AND BY FREQUENCY OF CONTACTS WITH CHILDREN AND FAMILY (*Percentage Distribution*)

Family Structure and Frequency of Contact	DENMARK			BRITAIN			UNITED STATES		
	Men	Women	All	Men	Women	All	Men	Women	All
White Collar									
Have children	86	80	82	77	65	70	84	79	81
Saw child in past week	71	68	69	59	56	57	65	65	65
Today or yesterday	50	51	50	43	43	43	65	65	65
In past 2–7 days	21	17	19	16	13	14	18	14	16
Child not seen in past week	14	12	13	18	9	13	20	14	16
Live with or saw sibling	5	5	5	6	3	4	7	6	6
Saw no relative	9	7	8	9	4	6	13	8	10
Have no relatives	*	*	*	3	2	3	—	—	—
Have no children	14	20	17	23	35	30	16	21	19
Live with or saw sibling or relative	5	11	8	9	22	17	10	12	12
Saw no relative	8	8	8	11	9	9	5	8	6
Have no relatives	1	1	1	3	4	4	*	1	1
Total	100	100	100	100	100	100	100	100	100
N=a	372	455	827	257	408	665	300	392	692

Table VIII–12—continued

Family Structure and Frequency of Contact	DENMARK			BRITAIN			UNITED STATES		
	Men	Women	All	Men	Women	All	Men	Women	All
Working Class—Blue Collar and Service Workers									
Have children	87	83	85	82	81	81	82	87	84
Saw child in past week	71	72	71	70	72	71	68	75	71
Today or yesterday	51	51	51	56	59	58	50	59	55
In past 2–7 days	20	21	20	14	13	13	18	16	17
Child not seen in past week	16	11	13	12	9	10	14	12	13
Live with or saw sibling	6	4	5	4	4	4	5	7	6
Saw no relative	9	7	8	6	3	4	8	5	6
Have no relatives	1	*	*	2	2	2	1	*	*
Have no children	13	17	15	18	19	19	18	13	16
Live with or saw sibling or relative	5	10	7	11	12	12	9	9	9
Saw no relative	8	7	8	6	4	5	9	4	6
Have no relatives	*	*	*	1	3	2	*	*	*
Total	100	100	100	100	100	100	100	100	100
N=ª	426	511	937	669	955	1,624	571	588	1,159
Agricultural Workers									
Have children	84	92	88	79	b	85	86	91	89
Saw child in past week	75	82	78	67	b	73	72	79	76
Today or yesterday	61	65	63	61	b	65	59	65	63
In past 2–7 days	14	17	15	6	b	8	13	14	13
Child not seen in past week	9	10	10	12	b	12	14	12	13
Live with or saw sibling	2	3	3	5	b	6	5	7	6
Saw no relative	7	7	7	6	b	6	9	5	7
Have no relatives	*	—	*	—	b	—	—	—	—
Have no children	16	8	12	21	b	16	14	10	11
Live with or saw sibling or relative	8	2	5	8	b	7	9	7	8
Saw no relative	7	6	6	6	b	4	4	3	3
Have no relatives	1	—	1	6	b	5	—	—	—
Total	100	100	100	100	b	100	100	100	100
N=ª	294	263	557	61	42	103	203	295	498

ª The percentages of eligible respondents who answered this question are: Denmark, total 95.0, men 95.5, women 94.5; Britain, total 96.9, men 98.6, women 93.8; United States, total 96.1, men 98.4, women 93.4.

b Per cents are not computed when base is less than 50.

* Less than one per cent.

difference between men and women in their pattern of family contacts that may prove to be more important than class differences if such differences exist?

A very small proportion of old people, about one in a hundred in Denmark and in the United States and three in a hundred in Britain, have neither children, nor brothers and sisters, nor other relatives. These persons, who are truly without family, are scarce in every social class in Denmark and the United States and are most likely to be found among those of white collar background in Britain. In all three countries a substantial group of all old people—17 per cent in Denmark, 16 per cent in Britain, and 14 per cent in the United States—saw neither children nor relatives during the week preceding their interview. For this period, at least, these old people saw no member of their immediate families other than their husband or wife, if they were married.

Class differences among these old people with limited family contacts are most obvious in Britain. Old people with white collar background, both men and women, are substantially more likely than other old people to have seen neither children nor relatives during the past week. In the United States, middle class women are more likely than other women to have seen neither children nor relatives, but middle class and working class men are equally likely not to have seen these family members. Among American men, workers in agriculture apparently have the greatest amount of contact with their children and their other relatives. The pattern of family contacts of old people in Denmark is different from that in the other two countries. There are no significant differences in that country in the family contacts of persons of white collar and blue collar background. While there is some indication that men and women of agricultural background are more likely than other persons to have seen their family members, the differences between the groups are very small.

In every country, women were more likely than men to have seen their children and relatives during the past week. There are several reasons for this: old women are more likely to be widowed and to live with children; they are also more likely than men to share a home with their relatives, particularly their brothers and sisters. In the three countries there is no consistent class pattern in the degree of difference between men and women in their contacts with their families. In Britain, white collar women are noticeably more likely than men to have seen children or relatives during the past week; in the United States and Denmark it is among the blue collar group that women are much more likely than men to have seen their children or relatives.

The summary of the pattern of family interaction in Table VIII-12 reinforces the previous findings reported in this chapter. Just as the social class of the old person affects his family structure in old age, so social class affects his interaction with his family. Frequent contact with children and relatives is most common among the working class in Britain and among those of agricultural background in the United States and, to some extent, in Denmark. If old people lack contact with their children and relatives, such lack is not likely to be reported by persons of white collar background in both Britain and the United States. In Denmark, however, the findings show similar patterns of family contact among both white collar and blue collar persons.

The patterns of family contact for old people of various social classes show that most old people, irrespective of class, are not isolated from their families. If the nuclear isolated family exists at all in old age, however, it is likely to be a middle class, white collar family in Britain and in the United States and perhaps a city or town family in Denmark. Certainly it is not the *typical* family for old people, irrespective of class, in any country.

Family Help Patterns and Social Class

Old people and their families share housing, see one another regularly, and visit overnight. The children and relatives of old people come to their assistance in times of emergency, give them gifts on birthdays and holidays, help them with housekeeping and home repairs, take them on outings, and often provide them with transportation. Old people for their part come to the assistance of their children in times of emergency, give them gifts on birthdays and holidays, help them with housekeeping and home repairs, help take care of their grandchildren, and entertain children and grandchildren as visitors and week-end guests. The reciprocal help patterns among old people and their children are fully discussed elsewhere. At this time, however, we shall concern ourselves with the effect of social class on family help patterns. Does social class make a difference in the proportion of old people who report that they receive help from their children or relatives or who help their children in any way?

Roughly half of all old persons in both Britain and the United States said that they received help from their children during the past month. In Denmark less than one-fifth of all old people received help from their children. Women in every social class in Britain and the United States are more likely than men to receive help from children or relatives. There are no major differences between white collar and blue collar women in the proportion who receive help from children, but there are class differences in the proportions of men who receive such help. In both Britain and the United States, middle class men are the least likely of all men to report that they had help from children.

About 5 of every 10 old people in Britain, and 6 of every 10 in the United States, reported that they gave help to their children during the past month. In Denmark only 3 of every 10 old people gave help to their children. Three of every 10 persons in Britain, and 5 of every 10 in the United States, specifically said that they helped their grandchildren. Undoubtedly some help to grandchildren is included among the help old people said they gave their children. It is therefore the report of help to children which is most useful here.

In all three countries persons of white collar background, both men and women, were more likely than those of blue collar background, to say that they helped their children. Indeed white collar old people were more likely to report that they gave help to children during the past month than that they received help. Working class men in the United States and agricultural workers in Denmark were also noticeably more likely to say that they had given help rather than that they had received it.

Table VIII–13: PROPORTION OF PERSONS AGED 65 AND OVER, BY SOCIAL CLASS, WHO GAVE HELP TO CHILDREN AND GRANDCHILDREN OR WHO RECEIVED HELP FROM CHILDREN DURING PAST MONTH[a]

Help Patterns and Social Class	DENMARK			BRITAIN			UNITED STATES		
	Men	Women	All	Men	Women	All	Men	Women	All
Gave help to child									
White collar	25	33	29	55	56	56	66	70	68
Working class	17	28	23	42	47	45	57	58	57
Agricultural workers	29	37	33	b	b	40	58	57	58
Gave help to grandchild									
White collar	c	c	c	39	38	39	58	58	58
Working class	c	c	c	29	32	31	49	48	48
Agricultural workers	c	c	c	b	b	27	40	43	42
Received help from child									
White collar	c	c	18	40	55	49	37	59	49
Working class	c	c	17	45	55	51	45	59	52
Agricultural workers	c	c	25	b	b	46	55	67	62
Number of cases[d]									
Gave help to child									
White collar	323	365	688	197	266	463	253	308	561
Working class	374	425	799	544	769	1,313	468	510	978
Agricultural workers	247	242	489	48	37	85	175	267	442
Gave help to grandchild									
White collar	c	c	c	166	229	395	221	269	490
Working class	c	c	c	491	706	1,197	431	471	902
Agricultural workers	c	c	c	46	35	81	158	255	413
Received help from child									
White collar	c	c	681	190	258	448	253	308	561
Working class	c	c	803	540	756	1,296	468	510	978
Agricultural workers	c	c	493	47	37	84	175	267	442

[a] Danish data are based on help given or received at any time, not only during past month. Twenty per cent in Britain and 28 per cent in the United States who gave help to children, gave no help in the past month.

[b] Per cents are not computed when base is less than 50.

[c] Data not available.

[d] The percentages of eligible respondents who answered the questions on social class and on (1) help to children, are: Denmark, total 97.9, men 97.8, women 97.9; Britain, total 97.2, men 97.4, women 97.1; United States, total 98.5, men 99.4, women 97.7; on (2) help to grandchildren, are: Britain, total 97.3, men 97.6, women 97.1; United States, total 96.4, men 97.2, women 95.7; on (3) help from children, are: Denmark, total 97.9; Britain, total 95.7, men 96.3, women 95.2; United States, total 98.5, men 99.4, women 97.7.

In general, the findings on the help patterns of old people and their adult children show an amazing amount of assistance between the two groups. The pattern of help is clearly class-determined only in Britain, where white collar parents give help and working class parents receive help. One other clear finding emerges from the analysis: in Denmark, compared to the United States and Britain, old people report both giving less help to children and receiving less help from them.

Social Class and Family Life in Old Age

Our analysis of social class and family life in old age has been highlighted by a consistent theme. This may be summarized as follows.

In Britain and in the United States the family life of old people differs by whether they are of white collar or blue collar backgrounds. These class differences show themselves in the area of family structure and in the proximity of parents and children. Class differences, however, are not as great as many students of the family would have had us believe.

In Denmark old people of white collar and those of blue collar backgrounds show no marked differences in family life. The major differences in Denmark are between agricultural workers and their wives on the one hand—and other old people, regardless of their class, on the other.

Middle class, white collar persons in both Britain and the United States are more likely than working class persons to have only a few children and to live at a greater distance from their children. The married children of middle class families, both sons and daughters, tend to live apart from their parents, not only in separate households, but also at a greater distance from them. In some degree this physical separation of parents and children is compensated for by more overnight visiting on the part of white collar families. The average old person of white collar background maintains strong relationships with his children. He is more likely than his blue collar counterpart, however, to see his children infrequently or not at all. In the case of white collar parents, the patterns of help in old age flow from parents to children; in the case of blue collar parents, they flow from children to parents.

In Denmark, different styles of family life in old age are reported by white collar and blue collar persons on the one side, and agricultural workers on the other. Middle class and working class appear to merge into a common classless pattern.

The analysis of the family and social class in old age points up social class as a major source of the heterogeneity of the elderly. White collar, blue collar, and agricultural workers differ in life styles in the middle years. These same differences, reinforced by time, continue into old age.

NOTES

1 An excellent discussion of this problem-centered view of the elderly in the family appears in Alvin L. Schorr, *Filial Responsibility in the Modern American Family* (Washington, D.C.: U.S. GPO, 1960), pp. 12–13.
2 See Eugene Litwak, "Extended Kin Relations in an Industrial Democratic Society," in Ethel Shanas and Gordon F. Streib, eds., *Social Structure and the Family: Generational Relations* (Englewood Cliffs, N.J.: Prentice-Hall, Inc., 1965).
3 For studies that illustrate the role of the elderly see Peter Townsend, *The Family Life of Old People* (New York: The Free Press of Glencoe, 1957); and Robert J. Havighurst and Ruth Albrecht, *Older People* (New York: Longmans, Green, Inc., 1953).
4 Peter Willmott and Michael Young, *Family and Class in a London Suburb* (London: Routledge and Kegan Paul, 1960), p. 58. See also Michael Young and Peter Willmott, *Family and Kinship in East London* (London: Routledge and Kegan Paul, 1957).
5 The Index of Social Economic Status developed by W. Lloyd Warner, Marchia Meeker, and Kenneth Eells, in their *Social Class in America* (Chicago: Science Research Associates, Inc., 1949) has been widely used as an index of class. Bernard Barber argues that the family kin network determines family status. "Family Status, Local Community Status, and Social Stratification: Three Types of Ranking," *Pacific Sociological Review*, IV (Spring, 1961), 3–10. See also D. V. Glass, ed., *Social Mobility in Britain* (New York: The Free Press of Glencoe, 1954); and Edward Gross, "The Occupational Variable as a Research Category," *American Sociological Review*, XXIV (October, 1959), 640–649.
6 We are aware that many women have been widowed for long periods and that there have been changes in their scale of living since widowhood. Nevertheless, it is doubtful that the values associated with the class position of a couple would change radically in the woman's widowhood.
7 The class categories are based on occupational groupings of the United States Bureau of the Census. In each country all persons were classified using the *Alphabetical Index of Occupations and Industries* of that Bureau. U.S. Bureau of the Census, *1960 Census of Population, Alphabetical Index of Occupations and Industries* (Washington, D.C.: U.S. GPO, 1960; rev. ed.). The occupations in each category are: *white collar:* professionals, technical workers, managers, officials and proprietors (except farm), clerical and sale workers; *blue collar:* craftsmen, foremen, operatives and laborers (except farm); *service workers:* private household workers and other service workers; *agricultural workers:* farm owners, managers, laborers, and foremen.
8 Not all white collar and blue collar older men in Denmark are urban. Jan Stehouwer states that about 30 per cent of the white collar aged in Denmark and about 22 per cent of the blue collar aged live in rural areas.
9 For a British study of elderly men and their wives, see Willmott and Young, *op. cit.*, p. 76. For an American study, see Alan C. Kerckhoff, "Nuclear and Extended Family Relationships: A Normative and Behavioral Analysis," in *Social Structure and the Family: Generational Relations, op. cit.*
10 Townsend, *op. cit.*
11 Ethel Shanas, *The Health of Older People: A Social Survey* (Cambridge, Mass.: Harvard University Press, 1962), p. 113.
12 *Ibid.*, pp. 94–116.
13 See Schorr, *op. cit.*, pp. 19–21.
14 Jan Stehouwer, "Urban-Rural Differences in the Contact between the Aged and Their Children in Denmark" (unpublished paper prepared for the International Social Science Seminar in Gerontology, Markaryd, Sweden, 1963).
15 See Townsend, *op. cit.*

9 : *Isolation, Desolation, and Loneliness*

Isolation and loneliness are thought to be common problems in old age. By comparison with the young and the middle-aged, the old are known to be liable to a loss of attachments and activities. But their vulnerability may be exaggerated. The change in their social and emotional experiences may not be as dramatic or as widespread as many people in Western societies fear, and is therefore worth investigating carefully.

Considerable emphasis has been placed in previous chapters on the large numbers of old people who remain active and who continue to see their relatives frequently, particularly their children and grandchildren. Decrepitude and solitude are not in fact predominant features in old age, even in advanced industrial societies. So much is clear. But how many old people do in fact lead solitary lives? And why do they do so? This chapter offers a provisional account of isolation and loneliness among old people in the three countries. It starts by discussing "isolation" and related concepts and goes on to describe how many old people are isolated, at least in relation to their contemporaries, and to ask whether loneliness is explained by such isolation or whether it has a more complicated etiology. Although no information has been collected from persons at successive dates as they grow older, the whole frame of argument and explanation has to be couched in terms of interaction between the individual and society during the last stage of the life-cycle. Otherwise it is impossible to understand what are the social and psychological processes at work. We hope that the concepts and the kind of data described in this chapter will be further explored and elaborated by others.

The Concept of Isolation

By "social isolation" some people mean the universal and necessary lack of communion between man and his fellows: the isolate is an individual who cannot properly communicate his feelings and experiences—even when he is totally and continuously immersed in social activities. As Halmos vividly describes it, "He is shut up amidst the fellow-members of his community into a cubicle where he is engaged in a lifelong conversation with himself."[1] The title of Riesman's book *The Lonely Crowd* conveys this meaning precisely.[2] Others use the term "isolation" to describe the lack of integration of a particular group, such as an ethnic minority, into society, *even when individual members of the group enjoy a great deal of interaction*. They can nonetheless be said to be "socially isolated." Sometimes "isolation" is taken to refer to members of a group (such as those in certain work-groups or suburban neighborhood-groups) who have virtually no social relationships with other members of the group, *even when they enjoy other kinds of social interaction*. There are other uses of the term. Thus, individuals may have few relationships and activities—by comparison with other persons in society, or with their predecessors, their age contemporaries, or even themselves at an earlier stage in life.

These different possibilities are rarely allowed and distinguished in the social sciences, and some have received a lot more attention than others. As a result of the interest in theories of social evolution and the social consequences of industrialization, there is a large amount in the literature about "desocialized" modern society and the impersonality and solitude of urban life. With the coming of the Industrial Revolution, it is supposed:

> We see the emergence of a mass society in which the individual is thoroughly weaned from his community and begins to live either in solitude or in mobs and audiences. . . . Certainly, ours is a desocialized society in which social isolation is widespread.[3]

But whatever the accuracy of such inferences about the direction of social change, few serious attempts have been made to specify and measure the various kinds of isolation that are experienced. This applies particularly to the diversity of individual experience. Just as economists have been concerned primarily with aggregates of income in different sectors of the economy rather than with its distribution among individuals and families, so sociologists have been concerned with general levels of social participation and interaction rather than with their distribution among individuals.

In considering social isolation in old age we can usefully start by distinguishing between objective and subjective states. Questions about the extent to which the individual interacts with society can be answered objectively, at least in principle. His behavior can be observed and plotted. How he feels is another matter. Although we can often make accurate inferences from behavior to feeling, we are sometimes wrong. There are all kinds of objective cues to subjective states of happiness, depression, and loneliness, for example, but at times the pattern of cues is inconsistent and at others the cues are flatly contradicted by the assertions to the contrary of the individuals concerned. Someone who has a full social life, a happy family, and a brilliantly successful career may claim he is perpetually unhappy or lonely. Equally, someone living in poverty who leads the life of a vagabond and has no contact with friends or relatives may claim he is happy and never feels lonely. It is the sociologist's task to explore the contiguity of objective and subjective states to find recurring patterns.

Old people may be isolated from society in the following senses:

1. By comparison with their contemporaries; this might be termed *peer-contrasted isolation*:
2. By comparison with younger people; this might be termed *generation-contrasted isolation*:
3. By comparison with the social relationships and activities enjoyed by the same people at an earlier stage of the life-cycle, in youth or middle age; this might be termed age-related isolation or *desolation*:
4. By comparison with the preceding generation of old people; this might be termed *preceding cohort isolation*.

In this report, we will be concerned primarily with the first of these four types of isolation. It should be remembered also that social isolation can be partial in each of the senses listed. An old person may be isolated from his peers but fully integrated into his family; he may belong to fewer associations than does the average member of the younger generation but may spend more time with different members of his family, with neighbors and with fellow-members of the principal club or association to which he belongs; and finally, he may lose a wife and the associations of work but not children and friends. Again, isolation can be lifelong, intermittent, initial, or terminal in relation to the individual life-cycle.

The Difficulty of Providing an Operational Definition

If we seek to compare the degree of isolation among old people there are difficulties in measuring the intensity, range, and kind of social participation. First, intensity: An old man may visit a pub for two minutes or two hours. If he stays for two hours he may do one of three things—drink alone, drink and converse with a single companion, or drink and converse with a variety of other people. One woman may live with a son; another may be visited by a son for two hours every evening; and a third may be visited fleetingly by a son every day on his way to work. How far is it possible to discriminate between these situations in any "measure" of the extent of social participation?

Second, range: One man may belong to a club and visit it five times a week; another may belong to five different clubs and visit each of them once a week. Should their levels of social participation be treated as broadly the same?

Third, kind: One man living alone may visit a married daughter and spend holidays with her and her family; he may also meet one or two of his former workmates every day at a habitual meeting-place. Another man living alone may have no contact with relatives or former workmates, but he may belong to a football spectators' club and an old people's club, attend various functions arranged by welfare agencies, and spend holidays in a special hotel for the elderly. If the number, intensity, range, and duration of social contacts of these men are broadly the same, should their level of social participation also be treated as the same, even if the second man lacks some of the main types of social interaction enjoyed by the elderly?

There have been a number of attempts to develop a general scale of social participation. Most are unsatisfactory, however, because investigators have tried to find a short cut through the laborious task of collecting information about the huge range of human social activities. One general scale is unsatisfactory because it simply counts the number of individual affiliations to associations and tends to ignore individual membership in primary groups.[4] Another investigation has used a simple index of isolation for the old. Account was taken of (*a*) seeing children at least once a month, (*b*) seeing relatives at least once a month, (*c*) having very close friends living, (*d*) having personal friends, and (*e*) having made new friends.[5] The trouble is that this is inconsistent and crude. The scale switches from a certain frequency of associations to the mere existence of certain associations; moreover, the chosen frequency can accommodate widely different experiences. Thus, a man in full-time employment and leading a rich life with his family could be classified as socially isolated because he does not satisfy three of the five criteria of the scale; whereas a retired man living alone who sees a daughter and a brother only once a month and friends only once or twice in the year may yet count as fully integrated. A more elaborate index has been developed in a series of British studies.[6] As much information as possible is collected about every kind of social activity for the purpose of estimating the average number of social "contacts" per week.[7] This method takes no account of intensity and kind of contact but seems reliable enough to distinguish those who are relatively isolated in the elderly population. The broad approach and variations in method are discussed carefully by Tunstall.[8]

MEASURES USED IN THE CROSS-NATIONAL SURVEY

It was not possible to develop a precise index of isolation in the cross-national survey. To do so would have meant including a large number of questions on social activities—probably at the expense of obtaining data on incapacity, retirement, and income. Instead, we sought to develop four simple categorizations: (i) persons living alone; (ii) among those living alone, persons who had had no human contact on the day previous to interview (specially identifying also, within this group, persons who had not been visited in the week previous to interview); (iii) persons who declared themselves to be often alone; and (iv) persons who had no surviving spouse, children, siblings, or other relatives, or who, if they had one or more relatives in these categories, had not seen any within the previous seven days.

The second and fourth of these categorizations depended on summarizing the answers to a series of questions. Thus, those living alone were asked whether they had been involved in a range of activities the previous day, including whether they had been visited, whether they had met or visited friends, and whether they had had a telephone conversation. Those having had no human contact the previous day were then further divided according to whether or not they had had visitors in the previous week.[9]

The Over-all Degree of Isolation

Table IX–1 shows in summary form the numbers in the three countries who were isolated according to these various criteria. The similarities between the three populations are again more notable than the differences. Broadly speaking, only a very small minority were found to be living in extreme isolation, in the sense that a week or even a day could pass without human contact. Between 2 per cent and 3 per cent of the elderly in the three countries lived alone, had had no visitors in the previous week, *and* had had no human contact on the day previous to interview. The proportion lacking relatives or having no recent contact with them was not much larger, which suggests that in old age the family plays a primary role in maintaining some degree of integration with society. The number with no relatives ranged from one per cent to 3 per cent, and the number having no contact with any relative in the past week from 13 per cent to 18 per cent.

Although these and other data suggest that in each of the three countries fewer than 5 per cent of the elderly live in extreme isolation, nevertheless a much larger minority live in a state of semi-isolation, or else feel themselves to be often alone. Rather fewer than a quarter of the elderly in Britain and the United States and rather more than a quarter in Denmark actually live alone, and the numbers who say they are often alone are similar. This is a considerable proportion whose circumstances need to be studied carefully.

The Characteristics of Isolated Persons

More women than men tend to be isolated, except in contacts with relatives, as Table IX–1 shows. In all three countries the proportion of women who say they are often alone or who live alone is more than double or nearly double that of men. Whether more women than men are living in extreme isolation is much less certain, and there was no possibility in the cross-national survey of asking the complex range of questions necessary to establish a reliable answer. But it should be noted that slightly more women than men in both Britain and Denmark had had no human contacts on the day before the interviews.

What accounts for the broad difference in isolation between men and women? In the first place, those living alone are either single, widowed, divorced, or separated. Relatively more of the widowed, divorced, and separated than of the single in Denmark and the United States live alone (62 per cent and 49 per cent, compared with 55 per cent and 39 per cent, respectively). In Britain the proportions are the same (43 per cent). Secondly, in all three countries the chances of living alone once widowed are highest for those without children and lowest for those with several children—persons with one or two children being intermediate. Finally, they are higher still for those who not only lack children but also lack siblings. These data imply, in short, that there is likely to be a strong correlation between the number of persons involved in an individual's immediate family network and the chances of living alone in old age.

Table IX–1: PERCENTAGE OF MEN AND WOMEN LIVING IN ISOLATION[a]

Category of Isolation	DENMARK			BRITAIN			UNITED STATES		
	Men	Women	All	Men	Women	All	Men	Women	All
Living alone									
All living alone	18	37	28	11	30	22	12	29	22
No visits in previous week and no human contact yesterday	2	3	3	1	3	2	1	1	1
No human contact yesterday	0	1	1	0	1	1	1	1	1
Human contact yesterday	16	33	24	10	26	19	11	27	20
Not living alone	82	63	72	89	70	78	88	71	78
Total	100	100	100	100	100	100	100	100	100
N=	1,144	1,301	2,445	1,004	1,496	2,500	1,081	1,361	2,442
Often alone									
Often alone	17	32	25	16	35	27	18	33	26
Not often alone	83	68	75	84	65	73	82	67	74
Total	100	100	100	100	100	100	100	100	100
N=	1,139	1,298	2,437	1,002	1,487	2,489	1,073	1,354	2,427
No family or isolated from family									
No relatives at all	1	1	1	2	4	3	0	1	1
Relatives, none seen in last week	20	17	18	16	11	13	17	10	13
Relatives, one or more seen in last week	79	82	81	82	85	84	83	89	86
Total	100	100	100	100	100	100	100	100	100
N=	1,139	1,296	2,435	1,004	1,496	2,500	1,081	1,361	2,442

[a] Detailed information on non-response is not given in this or subsequent tables if 98 per cent or more of all eligible respondents have answered the question.

Now, the main difference between men and women in their structured integration with the family is that a much higher proportion of the women are widowed, and slightly more of them are older and therefore are more likely to have no siblings or only one. This chiefly explains the slight tendency, at least in Britain and the United States, for more women than men to be isolated from all family contact. Next, the fact that so many more women than men are widowed also largely explains the big difference between the sexes in the numbers living alone and saying they are often alone. If the same proportions of widowed persons were found among both men and women, the numbers of each sex found to be living alone would not be strikingly different.

Three further factors must be mentioned. First, more women than men tend to be infirm, and this sets them at a disadvantage in making visits and otherwise maintaining outgoing social communications. Second, the roles women have played in life, by and large, make it easier for them than for men to be self-sufficient in the eventuality of the death of a spouse. Their social roles have been, and can remain, predominantly home-centered. They have been accustomed to perform the range of activities that are necessary to maintain an independent household, whereas men have been accustomed not only to perform more dependent roles in the household, but also to perform narrowly specialized rather than flexible roles outside. Third, social values support the independent maintenance of a household by the different generations. Therefore, except when newly married children are having difficulty in finding a home, when a parent is bereaved in extreme old age, or when an already widowed parent becomes very infirm, the oldest and the second oldest generations are reluctant to initiate arrangements to share households. In Britain, for example, 90 per cent of those living alone said they preferred to continue living alone. There is evidence from the United States that neither generation was more eager than the other to live in a joint household.[10]

Old people who are, when compared with their contemporaries, isolated, are generally found to be persons who are (i) older than average, (ii) single or widowed, (iii) lacking children and other relatives living nearby, (iv) retired from work and infirm. It is usually the combination of three or more of these factors rather than any one factor that produces isolation.

LIVING ALONE

"Living alone" is the first of our types of isolation, but the term must not be misinterpreted. We are speaking of persons who share a room, a flat, or a house with no one else and who, by implication rather than by accredited fact, normally eat alone in such an "independent" dwelling. It will be as well to remember that the designations of single-person and multi-person households in national censuses and surveys do not correspond neatly with possible designations of people into those who are isolated and those who are integrated, nor even those who are alone and those who have company. There are old people who spend their days at work or with their friends and families and who only sleep at their "permanent" addresses. Equally, there are old people sharing a house with a younger family who spend all but a few minutes each day alone in their rooms. There are also elderly married couples who lead extraordinarily secluded lives. But so long as these exceptions are borne in mind, it remains true that those occupying a household alone tend to be limited in their "bridge" contacts with society and that they include among their numbers most of the persons who are severely isolated.

Table IX–2: PERCENTAGE OF PERSONS LIVING ALONE WHO HAVE A
CHILD LIVING WITHIN TEN MINUTES JOURNEY (*Percentage Distribution*)

Proximity of nearest Child	DENMARK			BRITAIN			UNITED STATES		
	Men	Women	All	Men	Women	All	Men	Women	All
Within 10 minutes journey	51	43	45	38	48	46	36	50	47
11–60 minutes journey	38	47	44	40	36	37	40	31	33
More than 60 minutes journey	11	10	10	22	16	17	24	19	20
Total	100	100	100	100	100	100	100	100	100
N=	154	350	504	73	271	344	92	298	390

Table IX–2 shows that nearly half of those with children who lived
alone were in fact within ten minutes journey of at least one of their
children. More than half had seen one or more of their children within the
previous day.

Of all the old people living alone in the United States, for example,
53 per cent of those with children had seen one or more of their children
within the previous day and 76 per cent had stayed overnight with their
children or had their children to stay with them on one or more occasions
during the previous year.

Table IX–3: PERCENTAGE OF PERSONS LIVING ALONE WHO SEE
RELATIVES FREQUENTLY (*Percentage Distribution*)

Frequency of Contact	DENMARK			BRITAIN			UNITED STATES		
	Men	Women	All	Men	Women	All	Men	Women	All
Seen child yesterday/to-day	44	45	45	34	33	33	29	43	39
Seen child within previous week	23	20	21	16	17	17	18	19	19
Seen other relatives within previous week[a]	10	18	15	25	26	26			
Seen no relatives within week	24	16	18	19	16	16	53	38	42
Has no relatives	0	1	1	6	9	8			
Total	100	100	100	100	100	100	100	100	100
N[b]=	189	451	640	110	444	554	133	391	524

[a] Includes persons without children who had seen other relatives yesterday or today.

[b] The percentages of eligible respondents giving information are: Denmark, men 96.9
women 95.4; Britain and the United States, more than 98. The data for the United
States give contacts with children only.

Many of those not having children but having other relatives were in close touch with them. Substantial minorities were isolated, however. Nineteen per cent of those living alone in Denmark, and 24 per cent in Britain either had no relatives or had not seen any of them for at least a week (Table IX-3).

ACTIVITIES OF THOSE LIVING ALONE

How did those living alone pass their time? We asked these people which of a list of activities they had engaged in during the previous day. In general the numbers having various activities proved to be larger than is often assumed of old people. The average individual named 3 activities among the 7 listed—rather more than 3 in the United States, almost exactly 3 in Denmark, and slightly less than 3 in Britain. Table IX-4 shows the proportions reporting different activities.

Table IX-4: PERCENTAGE OF PERSONS LIVING ALONE, ACCORDING TO THEIR ACTIVITIES THE PREVIOUS DAY

Activity	DENMARK			BRITAIN			UNITED STATES		
	Men	Women	All	Men	Women	All	Men	Women	All
Listening to radio	79	78	78	61	65	63	59	55	56
Going for walk	56	48	50	52	38	41	67	44	50
Doing shopping	41	52	49	44	39	40	44	30	33
Having visitors	31	41	38	37	43	42	34	52	48
Watching television	28	32	31	38	37	37	44	56	53
Visiting friends	27	29	29	24	27	27	29	42	39
Meeting friends somewhere	33	19	23	27	26	26	54	38	42
None of these things	5	2	3	0	2	2	a	a	a
Mean number of activities	3.0	3.0	3.0	2.8	2.8	2.8	3.3	3.4	3.4
N=b	193	472	665	109	432	541	133	391	554

a Not known.

b The percentage of eligible respondents giving information was more than 98 in Denmark for all activities; it was 99.1 in Britain for men and 97.3 for women for all activities; and it varied between 98.5 and 94.0 for men and between 98.5 and 95.4 for women in the United States.

In all three countries radio-listening was found to be the most common activity, the percentage of persons involved in Denmark being higher than in Britain and higher still than in the United States. Predictably, this order is reversed for the proportions watching television. In Denmark and Britain the percentage watching television is almost exactly the same as the percentage having sets (being 28 and 38 respectively).

More of those living alone in the United States than in the European countries have visitors, more visit friends, and more meet friends somewhere, but fewer do shopping. In general men are not strikingly more mobile than women. It is simply that their activities are not so often home-centered. More women than men have visitors but more of them also visit friends. On the other hand, more men than women go for a walk and meet friends outside the home. Interestingly, more of the men than of the women living alone in Britain and the United States do some shopping in the day.

OFTEN ALONE IN THE DAY

The great majority, but not all, of those living alone say they are often alone. But a minority of persons living with others, and in fact a substantial minority of persons living with their children, also say they are often alone. Table IX–5 shows how far subjective assessment corresponds with structural designation. Two particularly interesting conclusions can be drawn from the table. First, in each country fewer persons who live with a spouse than persons who live with children or with others say they are often alone. The figures plainly testify to the companionship that marriage is felt to provide in old age. Secondly, except for those living physically alone, more women than men in different types of households tend to say they are often alone. Husbands and married children may be at work in the day and these women may spend a lot of time alone at home. And although some men may sacrifice work and other outside activities to care for their wives when the latter become infirm before they do, most may find it difficult to do so.

Table IX–5: PERCENTAGE OF PERSONS, BY TYPE OF HOUSEHOLD, WHO SAY THEY ARE OFTEN ALONE[a]

Sex and Country	Living Alone	Married Couple Alone	Living with Children		Living with Others	
			Unmarried	Married	Unmarried	Married
Denmark						
Men	78	3	12	3	16	b
Women	68	6	15	5	37	b
Britain						
Men	73	6	19	5	15	b
Women	72	15	27	14	17	b
United States						
Men	88	6	31	3	17	5
Women	74	10	28	7	19	b

[a] The percentage of eligible respondents giving information was more than 98 in all three countries.

[b] Percentages are not computed on a base of fewer than 50.

People who have some personal incapacity are more likely than those who do not to say they are often alone, but the correlation is not marked, as Table IX–6 shows. Slightly more of those who have some incapacity than of those who do not are found to be living with others, but when household arrangements are standardized the correlation between feelings of aloneness and incapacity is not striking. The crucial determinants of old people's feelings of aloneness seem to be: sleeping in a structurally separate dwelling alone; the loss of the physical proximity of a spouse; and several hours spent alone in the day—in that order.

Table IX–6: PERCENTAGE OF PERSONS WITH VARYING DEGREES OF PERSONAL INCAPACITY WHO SAY THEY ARE OFTEN ALONE

Incapacity Score	DENMARK		BRITAIN		UNITED STATES	
	Men	Women	Men	Women	Men	Women
Per cent						
0	18	28	12	32	16	29
1–2	19	37	23	38	25	41
3–4	16	32	18	40	19	33
5+	11	36	25	37	18	38
N=						
0	653	618	637	705	735	784
1–2	289	343	218	359	220	318
3–4	83	167	72	171	67	114
5+	100	156	56	220	50	129

Family Activities in Relation to Other Social Activities

In previous chapters particular attention has been paid to family relationships in the social integration of old people. Have we exaggerated the importance of these relationships? Are social activities—such as visits to clubs or churches, or relationships with neighbors and friends—as important, or even more important, than family relationships? To answer these questions satisfactorily requires much more information than we could collect. Moreover, there are difficulties in securing comparable information cross-nationally when voluntary associations vary so widely in name, function, and membership. But enough information was obtained to indicate a first approximate outline of an answer.

Those living alone were asked who had visited them the previous day. Relatives, rather than neighbors or friends, tended to predominate among the replies. (See Table IX–7.) In the United States neighbors and friends were almost as well represented among the visitors as relatives. In Britain, on the other hand, the proportions receiving visits from neighbors or more particularly friends were much smaller. The figures provide a fairly strong indication of the major role played by the family, because those living alone include many persons who in old age have lost contact with the family or have no close relatives alive.

But are people who are not integrated into an extended family socially active in other ways, and vice versa? Are friendships or membership in a club or a church a substitute for the family in old age? These are extremely important questions which deserve far more attention than they have yet attracted. In the British part of the cross-national survey it was found that 7 per cent of the men and 13 per cent of the women were members of an old people's club, 23 per cent and 15 per cent respectively of other types of clubs, and 32 per cent and 46 per cent respectively of a church or chapel.[11] A large number reported participation during the last week or

Table IX-7: PERCENTAGE OF PERSONS LIVING ALONE WHO WERE VISITED BY A NEIGHBOR, FRIEND, OR RELATIVES THE PREVIOUS DAY

Visitor Previous Day	DENMARK	BRITAIN	UNITED STATES
	All Persons	All Persons	All Persons
Neighbor	50	33	59
Friend	37	26	46
Relative(s)	61	57	60
N[a]=	220	223	219

[a] The percentages of eligible respondents giving information are: 86.9 for Denmark, 98.7 for Britain, and between 87.4 and 89.0 for the United States. Some of those who had a visitor were visited by persons other than a neighbor, friend, or relative.

the last month. Yet these persons did not differ strikingly from non-members in the degree to which they were integrated into an extended family. Some individuals certainly seemed to find compensation in club and church activities for their lack of close relatives, but others seemed to have added club and church activities as well as friendships to a family life that was itself rich already. Three-quarters of those who had no relatives or who saw them infrequently did not belong to any club at all. The categories in Table IX-8 may be broad but there is no sign of an inverse correlation between familial and extra-familial participation. A number of previous studies in the United States and Europe have pointed to the same conclusion.[12]

Loneliness in Old Age

So far the circumstances of isolated persons, but not their reactions to those circumstances, have been described. Loneliness may be defined as an unwelcome feeling of lack or loss of companionship. The degree of loneliness felt by an old person is not easy to determine, but most people under-

Table IX–8: PERCENTAGE OF PERSONS WHO HAVE NO FAMILY OR WHO
ARE ISOLATED FROM THEIR FAMILY, BY MEMBERSHIP IN CLUBS AND
CHURCH (BRITAIN)

Family Relationship	Type of Membership					
	MEN			WOMEN		
	Old People's Club	Other Clubs	None	Old People's Club	Other Clubs	None
No relatives	1	4	2	3	3	4
Relatives, none seen	13	17	16	10	12	11
Relatives, one or more seen in last week	85	79	82	87	85	85
Total	100	100	100	100	100	100
N=	68	230	706	192	228	1,073
	Church Member	Non-Church Member		Church Member	Non-Church Member	
No relatives	2	3		2	4	
Relatives, none seen	17	17		11	11	
Relatives, one or more seen in last week	81	81		85	85	
Total	100	100		100	100	
N=	314	688		720	772	

stand the question "Are you lonely?" readily enough and, judging by their manner, have plainly reflected upon it many times. When relatives are present during an interview there is a danger of getting an answer that is different from the one that would be given by the old person alone. There are old people who tell their children they are lonely to encourage them to call as often as possible. Yet these same persons recognize that they do not feel lonely in a profound sense of that term. Accordingly, interviewers were urged to check answers given in such conditions whenever possible. It should be emphasized, however, that although the answers are generally regarded as reliable, they were given at a particular time and should not be regarded as representing uniformly permanent individual attitudes.

Relatively few old people feel lonely often. Table IX–9 shows how wide of the mark has been much of the pessimistic and misleading speculation about the loneliness of the elderly in industrialized countries. Here there is evidence of the subjective attitudes of the majority of the aged, adding to the evidence in this report of their objective integration. But extreme loneliness is not a rare phenomenon and occasional loneliness is quite a common one. In general a substantial minority of the elderly say they experience some degree of loneliness, though the prevalence for this is rather greater in Britain and the United States than in Denmark. Adjustment to the lack or loss of companionship in old age may be easier for more people in Denmark, perhaps because social networks in that country are found to be slightly more loose-knit, with less emphasis placed on the norms and sponsoring activities of sub-groups, and on class differentiation, and with more emphasis being placed on individually reliant behavior. The evidence reported in Chapter 7 of fewer elderly persons receiving help from children may imply that fewer *expect* help. Denmark compared with Britain and the United States is a more homogeneous society and people neither need to identify quite so strongly with social sub-classes and groups nor do they miss these sub-classes and groups quite so keenly when they are detached from them. As elsewhere in this report, however, the contrast between Denmark, on the one hand, and Britain and the United States, on the other, is not sharp enough to justify a recognition of a difference of kind rather than of emphasis in explaining the type of society to which older people are expected to adjust.

Table IX-9: PERCENTAGE OF MEN AND WOMEN WHO SAY THEY FEEL LONELY (*Percentage Distribution*)

"*Lonely*"	DENMARK			BRITAIN			UNITED STATES		
	Men	Women	All	Men	Women	All	Men	Women	All
Often	3	5	4	5	8	7	8	9	9
Sometimes	9	16	13	15	26	21	16	25	21
Rarely or never	88	79	83	81	66	72	76	66	70
Total	100	100	100	100	100	100	100	100	100
N=	1,138	1,298	2,436	998	1,485	2,483	1,064	1,348	2,417

LONELINESS AND ISOLATION

Who are the people who feel lonely? Above we found that the widowed and the single rather than the married tend to be the most isolated and, indeed, we find that more of them experience loneliness, as Table IX-10 shows. Earlier we also found that more women than men live alone or are often alone and, again, we now find that more women than men of the same marital status, with the exception of widowed persons in the United States, "often" and "sometimes" experience loneliness. But the difference between men and women is not very striking and is largely explained by differences in marital status and living arrangements. First, significantly more widowed than single persons say they are lonely and this remains true even when only those single and widowed persons who live alone are considered. The fact that about half the widowed persons who live alone have daily contacts with their children should also be remembered.

Second, a significantly larger proportion of those who have been

Table IX–10: PERCENTAGE OF MEN AND WOMEN OF DIFFERENT MARITAL STATUS WHO SAY THEY FEEL LONELY

"*Lonely*"	DENMARK			BRITAIN			UNITED STATES		
	Men	Women	All	Men	Women	All	Men	Women	All
Married									
Often	1	2	1	3	4	3	3	5	4
Sometimes	6	12	8	11	18	14	13	20	16
Rarely or never	93	86	91	86	78	83	84	76	81
Total	100	100	100	100	100	100	100	100	100
N=	797	544	1,341	699	505	1,204	809	505	1,314
Widowed/divorced/ separated									
Often	9	8	8	9	12	11	23	13	16
Sometimes	18	21	20	24	31	29	28	30	30
Rarely or never	73	72	72	67	57	59	48	57	55
Total	100	100	100	100	100	100	100	100	100
N=	290	621	911	252	769	1,021	223	759	982
Single									
Often	a	4	4	a	4	5	a	4	9
Sometimes	a	14	13	a	24	23	a	12	12
Rarely or never	a	83	82	a	72	72	a	84	78
Total	100	100	100	100	100	100	100	100	100
N=	49	132	181	46	211	257	32	84	116

a Percentages not computed on a base of less than 50.

widowed recently, as compared with those widowed several or many years ago, feel lonely. Many of the former are living alone.

> Mrs. Dreall is a widow aged 80 living alone in a bungalow in a Yorkshire dale. Her husband, who was a platelayer, working for British Railways, died four months ago. A son lives nearby, and she sees him and his family every day. Her only other child, also a son, lives more than an hour's journey away and last saw her a month ago. She sees little of other relatives and does not belong to a club or attend church. On the day before the interview she went for a walk, listened to the radio, and was visited by her son's family. She says that although she prefers to live alone, she is often lonely and that time often passes slowly. She also says that she is often alone.

In Britain 55 per cent of women widowed within the last five years, and in Denmark 35 per cent widowed within the last six years, were often or sometimes lonely, compared with 38 per cent and 23 per cent respectively of women widowed 20 years or more. Although the numbers do not allow refined analysis, this finding remains true irrespective of certain kinds of social circumstances—for example, whether living alone or with others, and whether having seen children recently or not. In Britain rather more of those who had been widowed recently, rather than several or many years ago, lived with children or other people—and yet more of them said that they felt lonely.

Table IX–11: PERCENTAGE OF WIDOWS, ACCORDING TO DURATION OF WIDOWHOOD, WHO SAY THEY FEEL LONELY (*Percentage Distribution*)

"*Lonely*"	0–4 Years[a]	5–9 Years[a]	10–19 Years	20 Years or More	All
Britain					
Often	18	13	8	12	13
Sometimes	37	30	32	26	30
Rarely or never	45	57	59	62	57
Total	100	100	100	100	100
N[b]=	137	154	221	228	740
Denmark					
Often	13	6	5	6	8
Sometimes	22	25	23	18	22
Rarely or never	65	69	71	77	71
Total	100	100	100	100	100
N[b]=	155	93	175	142	565

[a] Denmark: 0–5 years and 6–9 years.

[b] More than 98 per cent of eligible respondents in Britain and 96.9 per cent in Denmark gave information.

Third, many isolated people do not feel lonely and some "integrated" people do feel lonely. Isolation and loneliness are not coincident. This is perhaps one of the most important findings of the cross-national survey. The following are examples of isolation.

Mr. Budingen, aged 75, lives alone in an English town in the Midlands. He used to be a mole-catcher. He is married but has been separated from his wife since the First World War and has not seen his two children since she took them away with her. None of his siblings is alive, and he does not belong to clubs and societies and does not attend church. He had not had any visitors in the past seven days and claimed to have had no conversations with anyone. He says he is often alone but never lonely. He does not find that time passes slowly. He watches television, and the garden is a credit to him (though the house is very untidy and bedecked with cobwebs). "I'm as happy as can be." He now walks a little unsteadily and has difficulty in climbing stairs. In the spring and summer he visits friends in a neighboring village every week or so and helps them with their gardening.

Miss Deepling is 70 years of age and lives alone in a terraced cottage on the outskirts of a small country town in the south of England. She used to serve in a shop but has not had a paid job for ten years. She has no living brothers or sisters—"I'm the last one of my family"—and her closest relative, a niece, lives a hundred miles away. She says she is often alone but that time never passes slowly and she is never lonely. "I like being alone. I think there's nothing like it. My clocks go so fast. All my visitors say so." She has brief visits from a friend on most days, and her vicar calls once a month. Once a week she pays privately for domestic help.

By contrast, there are people who do not live alone and who lead quite active social lives but who nonetheless say that they are lonely. The following woman is an example.

Mrs. Iselforth is a widow, 82 years of age, living with her single daughter of 50. She has not worked for more than 25 years but despite some infirmity (she suffers from arthritis and is limited in walking and climbing stairs) leads an active life, belonging to two women's guilds and the local Methodist sisterhood. She attends meetings or goes shopping most afternoons of the week, occasionally visits cinemas and theaters, and sees two or three of her brothers and sisters every week and other relatives less often. She also has friends living locally. Her husband died a few years previously. She is conscious that her sight has been getting worse lately but still prepares all the meals for the household and does most of the housework. Her daughter is plainly solicitous. "She buys me presents, treats me to the pictures and theaters, and takes me out for bus rides and on holidays." But her daughter is at work in the week and, despite her activity in the home and outside, Mrs. Iselforth says she is frequently alone, that time often passes slowly, and that she is often lonely.

From half to four-fifths of single and widowed men and women surveyed in the three countries said they were never or rarely lonely. From half to two-thirds of the men and women living alone said the same (Table IX–12). Of all those who said they were often lonely only just over half in Britain and Denmark and rather less than half in the United States were actually living alone. Around one-fifth lived with a spouse only, but just under another third were actually living with children or others.

Although our measures of social interaction and integration are neither as full nor as specific as we should prefer them to be, the evidence presented

Table IX–12: PERCENTAGE OF UNMARRIED MEN AND WOMEN IN DIFFERENT TYPES OF HOUSEHOLD WHO SAY THEY FEEL LONELY (*Percentage Distribution*)

"Lonely"	DENMARK			BRITAIN			UNITED STATES		
	Living Alone	Living with Children	Living with Others	Living Alone	Living with Children	Living with Others	Living Alone	Living with Children	Living with Others
Men									
Often	10	9	6	18	4	4	32	17	9
Sometimes	21	12	9	35	16	18	27	29	21
Rarely or never	69	79	85	48	80	77	41	54	70
Total	100	100	100	100	100	100	100	100	100
N=	196	68	80	107	120	71	133	69	53
Women									
Often	7	9	3	16	6	5	15	11	6
Sometimes	23	13	15	39	24	18	30	30	20
Rarely or never	70	78	82	45	70	76	55	59	74
Total	100	100	100	100	100	100	100	100	100
N=	477	150	131	442	356	182	391	286	166

here demonstrates that loneliness is not conditioned exclusively by physical or social segregation—or rather, to use the terminology tentatively suggested earlier, it is not conditioned by *peer-contrasted* isolation. In particular, people who, by comparison with their peers, are lifelong isolates are not usually lonely. As Marjorie Fiske Lowenthal has affirmed, many people who are extremely isolated are not lonely. She found one major group of the extremely isolated to be self-sufficient and self-possessed. They were alienated from society: "male, single, and rather likely to be foreign born, with a history of considerable occupational and geographic mobility; more often than not, they wind up as alcoholics and live on Skid Row or its environs. . . . Interviewers often found them courtly, charming and satisfied with their way of life."[13] The other major group of extreme isolates consisted of nearly as many women as men. Many had achieved a high occupational level, had married but had usually been separated or widowed. Few had had children, or if they had them they were estranged from the children. "Problems having to do with personal losses in childhood or early adulthood figure frequently in their life stories—the death of a parent, usually the mother, or a sibling, for example. . . . They give the impression of having tried but failed and the bulk of their adult lives is characterized by marginal if not precarious social adjustment. We have called them the *defeated*."[14]

Loneliness is not, therefore, a necessary reaction of those who are extremely isolated. Some students have gone on to point to a multiplicity of causes. Shortly after World War II Sheldon showed that among old people in the town of Wolverhampton the lonely tended to be widowed and single people, living alone, in their 80's rather than in their 60's, and relatively infirm. (The cross-national study has in these respects confirmed his study and other local studies.) But Sheldon also found that not all the people in these conditions were lonely, and he concluded:

> Loneliness cannot be regarded as the simple direct result of social circumstances, but is rather an individual response to an external situation to which other old people may react quite differently.[15]

There seemed to be no single "cause" of severe loneliness.

But once the question is studied in the context of the life-cycle rather than in the context of scattered social conditions and affiliations, it is possible to see a more consistent and comprehensive explanation.

DESOLATION AND LONELINESS

A persuasive hypothesis is that loneliness is attributable to age-related isolation or *social desolation*. A person who has lost a social intimate (usually someone he or she loves, such as a husband, or wife, a relative, or a close friend) is isolated relative to a previous situation. For younger persons time "heals" in the sense that there is a chance they will remarry or else replace the close relative or friend who has been lost, with another relative in the extended family or with a new friend. For older persons this process of healing also occurs, as Table IX–11 suggests, but it is normally less rapid and substitutes tend to fall short of former intimates in the roles they play in the lives and affections of old people.

The crucial social losses sustained by old people seem to be the following: spouse, child, sibling, grandchild, friends, and acquaintances at work or in the locality. If they are deprived of the company of a close relative, usually a husband or a wife or a child (through death, illness, or migration), they will complain of loneliness. If they have no family or if relationships with the family are relatively weak, then they will tend to be lonely if they are deprived of the company of friends and acquaintances. In the cross-national survey two particularly noteworthy examples of the importance of "loss" or deprivation in understanding loneliness were, first, that fewer persons who had never been married than persons who had been married but were now widowed felt lonely; second, that whereas childless but married old people were no more likely to be lonely than married people who had seen a child very recently, this was quite different with the widowed. Many more of them were lonely if they had no children.

Loneliness is related much more to "loss" than to enduring "isolation." There is evidence not only that the recently widowed are much more likely to be extremely lonely than those widowed for many years, but also that persons whose children die or who have become separated from their children, and persons who have been detached in other ways from their social circle (such as people who are moved into a house or flat in a new district), feel lonely.[16]

Social loss is inextricably bound up with physical decrescence. More old people in the three countries who are personally incapacitated than who are not, are lonely, as Table IX–13 shows. Even when account is taken of the fact that more of those who are widowed are incapacitated, the correlation between loneliness and increasing personal incapacity is independent of marital status. Earlier we found that there was only a slight and rather irregular correlation between the state of being often alone and increasing incapacity (Table IX–6). Moreover, slightly fewer of those with severe incapacity were found to be living alone. The trend shown in Table IX–13 is therefore important. Even when living in a household with others, some old people become depressed and lonely through the social losses forced upon them by their infirmity and through the knowledge that their infirmity will obstruct social initiative. Interestingly, it is clear from some older people's comments that the latter is often as catastrophic as the former. The loss of the possibility of enjoying certain forms of social participation can reinforce loneliness as much as the actual loss of those forms of participation.

Just as there is a correlation between increasing incapacity and loneliness, so there is a similar correlation between self-evaluations of poor health and loneliness. More old people rating their own health as fair or poor than those rating their health as good also said they were lonely, irrespective of whether they lived alone or not. (See Tables III–5 and III–7 above.)

Table IX–13: PERCENTAGE OF MEN AND WOMEN WITH DIFFERENT
DEGREES OF INCAPACITY WHO SAY THEY FEEL LONELY (*Percentage
Distribution*)

"*Lonely*"	DENMARK			BRITAIN			UNITED STATES		
	0	1–4	5+	0	1–4	5+	0	1–4	5+
Men									
Often	1	5	7	3	6	16	6	9	ᵃ
Sometimes	6	11	19	10	23	25	13	24	ᵃ
Rarely or never	93	84	74	87	71	59	80	68	ᵃ
Total	100	100	100	100	100	100	100	100	100
N=	652	372	88	636	288	73	729	286	48
Women									
Often	3	5	13	5	8	18	4	11	30
Sometimes	13	18	23	20	31	32	30	33	29
Rarely or never	84	77	65	76	61	50	76	56	41
Total	100	100	100	100	100	100	100	100	100
N=	619	509	150	704	529	252	777	432	130

ᵃ Percentages are not computed on a base of less than 50.

Mitigation of Loneliness

Some old people who live with their children and grandchildren are often
lonely. They are usually persons who have recently lost a husband or wife
or have sustained the loss of some other person who had been very closely
related to them in their social existence. The practical conclusion to be
drawn from this fact may seem to be that it is difficult through social
policy to relieve grief or distress. But how far can company mitigate acute
feelings of loneliness? Although it is not easy to distinguish cause and
effect, nevertheless the data suggest that the feelings of some of those who
have experienced severe social loss are relieved by other contacts and
relationships. For example, Table IX–14 indicates—much more strongly
in Britain than in Denmark and the United States—that persons who are
widowed and have seen their children within the last day are slightly less
likely to experience loneliness than others. It is difficult, because of the
numbers involved, to separate the data into finer categories. The period
of widowhood was established for persons in Denmark and Britain. It
seemed that the recently widowed were much less likely to feel lonely if
they reported seeing their children the same or the previous day than if
they reported seeing them a week or more before. For example, among
women widowed within the previous five years in Britain, 52 per cent of
those who had seen their children the same day or the previous day, but
only 37 per cent of those who had not seen their children the same or the
previous day, said they were never lonely.[17]

When we turn to consider only those widowed persons living alone, the
evidence is mixed. For Britain, and to a lesser extent for the United States,
a significantly smaller proportion of those seeing a child very recently,

Table IX-14: PERCENTAGE OF WIDOWED PERSONS WITH DIFFERENT
KINDS OF CONTACT WITH CHILDREN WHO SAY THEY FEEL LONELY

"*Lonely*"	WIDOWED		
	With Child		With No Child
	Seen Yesterday or Today	Not Seen Yesterday or Today	
Denmark			
Often	8	6	10
Sometimes	20	27	24
Never	72	67	66
Total	100	100	100
N=	497	261	83
Britain			
Often	7	18	19
Sometimes	28	34	30
Never	65	48	51
Total	100	100	100
N=	677	198	142
United States			
Often	13	19	19
Sometimes	29	30	27
Never	58	51	54
Total	100	100	100
N=	562	199	124

rather than some time ago, said they were often lonely, but for Denmark the proportion was not significantly different (Table IX–15). Generally, the result for the three samples points in a consistent direction, however, and we should remember that division of widowed persons living alone into the three broad categories of Table IX–15 takes no account of all kinds of compensatory social relationships and activities. Some of those not seeing children every day see other relatives or friends every day. Some of those seeing children every day see them only fleetingly and, because of infirmity, spend much of their time alone at home. Information in greater depth and for larger numbers of people is required before realistic social continua can be devised and the theory properly elaborated.

Isolation, Loneliness, and Suicide

We have seen that desolation, in particular the loss of someone who is loved, explains the loneliness of old people more appropriately than peer-contrasted social isolation (though we have also seen that substitute or compensating social involvement can be an important mitigating factor). Severe social loss may explain more than loneliness, however. Health and state of mind may be seriously affected.

Table IX-15: PERCENTAGE OF WIDOWED PERSONS LIVING ALONE, BY
FREQUENCY OF CONTACT WITH CHILDREN, WHO SAY THEY FEEL LONELY
(*Percentage Distribution*)

"*Lonely*"	DENMARK			BRITAIN			UNITED STATES		
	Child Seen Yester-day or Today	Child Seen in Last 7 Days	No Child Seen /No Child	Child Seen Yester-day or Today	Child Seen in Last 7 Days	No Child Seen /No Child	Child Seen Yester-day or Today	Child Seen in Last 7 Days	No Child Seen /No Child
Often	7	10	8	11	21	24	15	21	25
Sometimes	26	23	24	43	35	35	32	28	28
Rarely or never	67	67	68	46	44	41	53	52	47
Total	100	100	100	100	100	100	100	100	100
N=	268	127	119	178	86	159	194	87	96

The study of mortality and morbidity rates of older people in relation
to social state or social loss is complex and is still in its infancy.[18] Rather
more (but still not very much) attention has been paid to suicide rates.
As long ago as 1897 Durkheim pointed out that the rates increase more
sharply among single and widowed persons in old age than they do among
married persons.[19] He argued in general that suicide varied inversely with
degree of integration into domestic society, and he showed that this applied
both to those who had never been integrated (for example, the unmarried)
as well as to those who had been integrated but whose domestic circle had
been broken (for example, the widowed, with and without children). But
he did not attempt to discuss his three types of suicide—egoistic, altruistic,
and anomic—in relation to aging. Halbwachs drew a distinction between
isolation and "the feeling of being suddenly alone." (This corresponds
closely with the emphasis on "desolation" in this chapter.) Halbwachs
contended that the latter precipitated suicide.[20]

A study of the suicide rates in the three countries shows that the rates
are greater for men than for women in each country at all ages; whereas
suicide rates continue broadly to rise for men in late life, for women they
level off or fall after middle age; suicide rates in old age are highest in
Denmark, though the rates for men in both other countries are not much
lower; and the rates for older women in the United States are notably low.

In both the United States and England and Wales the rates display the
same characteristics, for men rising to a peak in the late 70's or early 80's
(between 50 and 60 per 100,000) and then falling slightly, but for women
falling markedly between the 60's and the late 80's (from between 10 and
20 per 100,000 to less than 5 per 100,000). The Danish rates are more
variable.

Suicide rates are not easy to relate to changes in occupational role.
Upon retirement men often have to change virtually their whole style of

living. They lose the associations of work, the status of breadwinner, and to a considerable extent even the income to finance substitute activities and interests. Unless their wives become infirm they are not always encouraged to adopt substitute occupational roles in the household. The functionless retired man, with time to stand at a street corner, is found in all industrial societies. Yet if the stress of retirement is closely associated with suicide one would expect the rates in the mid- and late 60's to be much higher, in relation to the rates at older ages, than they are. Proportionately far more men of each specific age retire in the 60's than in later years.[21]

There are no well-founded theories of suicide in relation to aging, but some of the factors discussed in this chapter are likely to be important in the development of such theories. These factors are: loss of spouse (especially by men), loss of child or other emotionally close relative, loss of paid employment (especially by men), and loss of physical and mental agility. Two or more of these factors rather than only one of them, plus some ancillary factors, are likely to affect the propensity to suicide in old age.

Aging and Disengagement

In interpreting the data on isolation and loneliness we have been driven repeatedly to take account of changes that occur during the latter stages of the life-cycle. The emphasis given to desolation rather than to isolation has provided the emerging theme of our analysis. For simplicity of presentation we have so far avoided detailed comparison between persons of different age. At the more advanced ages are people more isolated? Do they become more lonely? Do they withdraw from social participation? These are questions we will now take up.

It is evident from this report that as people get older more are found to be infirm, fewer are employed, and, in general, fewer have a large number and range of activities. This would be expected. Some theorists have read more into the decline of activity, however, than just infirmity. René König and others have used the concept of "desocialization" (in contrast to that of "socialization") to describe the social and psychological changes of old age. Cumming and Henry have developed the concept of "disengagement."[22] They suggest that, independent of physical decrescence and falling standards of living,

> normal aging is a mutual withdrawal or "disengagement" between the aging person and others in the social system to which he belongs—a withdrawal initiated by the individual himself, or by others in the system.[23]

The individual "prepares" for death and tends to disengage. He becomes preoccupied with himself and is less concerned with others around him. Society withdraws its integrating pressures. Roles are given up, social relationships are restricted in number and scope, and there is less commitment to social norms and values. Disengagement and preparation for death suggest an "ultimate biological basis for a reduction of interest or involvement in the environment."[24]

The theory is persuasive, because the departure of children upon marriage from the household, retirement, and bereavement are characteristic experiences in the latter stages of the individual life-cycle. But what evidence is there of (i) increasing isolation in old age, and of (ii) decreasing emotional investment in individuals and groups with whom the elderly have relationships? Table IX–16 provides a summary of changes with age in the proportions of old people in the three countries experiencing different forms of isolation, loneliness, and boredom. At first sight there appears to be a marked increase in the proportions experiencing isolation. In all three countries substantially more persons in their 80's and over, than in their 60's, say they are often alone. But in terms of recent contacts with relatives there is either no conclusive trend or, in the case of Denmark, contrary evidence. And the most critical measure of all, of the numbers living alone *and* having no contact the previous day with any human being, produces no sudden, but only a slight, increase with age. Moreover, it should be noted that on none of our measures are more than two-fifths of those in their 80's isolated. Further, in terms of living alone, being often alone, and having no recent contacts with relatives, from nearly a fifth to a quarter of old people in their 60's *are* isolated. If the disengagement hypothesis holds then it would seem that either a substantial number of people prepare for death at a rather early stage of life, or that many do not prepare for it even at a very advanced age.

When different groups of the elderly are studied, the pattern of change becomes more complex. A good part, but not all, of the increase in isolation with age is explained by the rapid increase in the proportion of old people who are widowed and in the increasing excess of women over men. With age there is, in fact, as Jan Stehouwer has shown in Chapter 7, a *decrease* in the proportion of single and widowed men and women who are living alone; an increase in the proportions both living with children and, when not living with them, living within ten minutes journey; and an *increase* in the proportion of women, and in Denmark in the proportion of men as well, who have seen one of their children the same or the previous day, and a corresponding decrease in the proportions not seeing one of the children during the previous month (with the exception of men in Britain and the United States, for whom there is no marked trend either way). When persons become more isolated by virtue of losing a spouse it is evident that some among them, particularly if they are also infirm, are drawn into living with or near their children. Certainly this may not be adequate compensation or replacement, but it is an example of society offering repair rather than "withdrawing."

Among persons living alone slightly more of those in their 80's and 90's than in their 60's said they were often alone (76 per cent compared with 69 per cent in Denmark, and 80 per cent compared with 63 per cent in Britain). In all three countries the proportion of persons living alone who said they visited friends the previous day diminished, according to their age, but in Britain and Denmark the proportion having visitors increased significantly, and in the United States it fell only marginally. In general, there was only a small decrease in the proportions of people engaging in

Table IX–16: PERCENTAGE OF PERSONS OF DIFFERENT AGE WHO HAVE
PARTICULAR CHARACTERISTICS AND REACTIONS

Characteristics	Country	65–69	70–74	75–79	80+
Living alone	Denmark	20	30	32	36
	Britain	17	22	30	25
	United States	17	21	26	31
Living alone and no human contact	Denmark	1	3	5	6
yesterday	Britain	2	2	4	5
	United States	2	1	3	3
Often alone	Denmark	20	27	27	33
	Britain	24	24	33	33
	United States	24	25	27	38
No relatives or none seen in last	Denmark	20	19	15	12
week	Britain	—	—	—	—
	United States	25	26	22	28
Reactions					
Time often passes slowly	Denmark	2	4	5	8
	Britain	7	9	8	12
	United States	10	11	18	19
Often or sometimes lonely	Denmark	13	17	19	25
	Britain	24	26	27	41
	United States	25	29	35	38
Often or sometimes lonely (widows	Denmark	22	27	26	33
and single women only)	Britain	38	38	38	47
	United States	37	40	43	43
N=[a]	Denmark	934	714	476	322
	Britain	888	725	495	392
	United States	914	770	408	337

[a] The totals given are maxima. For certain items the totals were up to 8 fewer. The percentages of eligible respondents giving information were in all instances more than 98.

various activities. In the United States, in particular, activities tended to be maintained, as Table IX–17 shows.

Much of the fall in activities is clearly attributable to the infirmity of larger numbers at the advanced than at the less advanced ages. Table IX–18 repeats part of the analysis given in Table IX–16, but only for those having no personal incapacity—that is, those scoring 0 in the incapacity index. The number saying they were often alone increased from around 20 per cent, for those in their late 60's, to around 30 per cent for those in their 80's and 90's. The number living alone, in Denmark and the United States, increased more sharply, but the figures conceal a shift in

Table IX–17: PERCENTAGE OF PERSONS OF DIFFERENT AGE LIVING ALONE WHO HAD PARTICULAR ACTIVITIES ON THE PREVIOUS DAY

Activity	DENMARK				BRITAIN				UNITED STATES			
	65–9	70–4	75–9	80+	65–9	70–4	75–9	80+	65–9	70–4	75–9	80+
Listening to radio	83	76	79	69	62	67	65	69	58	57	49	59
Going for walk	49	53	52	42	49	43	37	33	45	53	47	55
Doing shopping	56	50	49	34	40	47	37	34	32	34	34	35
Having visitors	31	36	40	50	42	34	41	53	49	53	40	46
Watching TV	35	35	27	21	45	41	34	23	60	56	48	46
Visiting friends	33	29	25	25	32	32	22	17	47	42	38	28
Meeting friends	26	22	30	12	32	29	23	19	48	39	36	43
None of these	2	2	3	8	2	1	2	4	b	b	b	b
Mean number of activities	3.1	3.0	3.0	2.5	3.2	2.9	2.6	2.4	3.4	3.3	2.9	3.1
N=a	190	210	153	117	146	155	142	98	c	c	c	c

The percentage of eligible respondents giving information was more than 98 in Denmark for all activities; it was 98.1 in Britain for men and 97.3 for women for all activities; and it varied between 98.5 and 94.0 for men and between 98.5 and 95.4 for women in the United States.

b Not known.

c The number of persons replying varied for the different activities between 143 and 149 for persons aged 65–69, between 151 and 157 for persons aged 70–74, between 102 and 104 for persons aged 75–79, and between 78 and 103 for persons aged 80 and over.

the proportions of different marital status. When widowed and single persons alone are considered the number tends, if anything, to fall, as the table shows. Unfortunately the samples were too small to allow us to control more than a few variables, but these preliminary data offer little evidence of "withdrawal."[25]

This is, of course, only a provisional analysis of what is an important subject for research. The data on isolation collected in the cross-national survey were not comprehensive. Moreover, the survey was carried out at a particular point in time and any conclusions that may be drawn about the aging process have to be based on comparisons between age cohorts, people in their 60's and people in their 80's.

While not a great deal can be said about changes in the level of social interaction, even less can be said about changes in attitudes and values and in the quality of relationships. Table IX–16 shows that the proportions saying that time often passed slowly for them increased with age, though not very much. Table IX–18 shows that most of even this trend is explained by more people being incapacitated at the advanced ages and, when the drastic changes between the 60's and the 80's in employment levels are

Table IX–18: PERCENTAGE OF NON-INCAPACITATED PERSONS OF
DIFFERENT AGE WHO HAVE PARTICULAR CHARACTERISTICS AND REACTIONS

Characteristics	*Country*	65–69	70–74	75–79	80+
Living alone	Denmark	18	31	35	40
	Britain	15	21	31	21
	United States	16	20	21	36
Living alone: widowed and single persons only	Denmark	62	57	65	55
	Britain	42	42	55	39
	United States	72	53	47	52
Often alone	Denmark	19	25	24	32
	Britain	21	20	29	29
	United States	20	22		27
Reactions Time often passes slowly	Denmark	2	2	2	2
	Britain	5	4	4	5
	United States	5	5	9	13
Often or sometimes lonely	Denmark	10	13	13	10
	Britain	18	21	21	24
	United States	20	24	25	26
$N^{=a}$	Denmark	569	388	218	100
	Britain	620	318	228	101
	United States	628	499	233	150

[a] The totals given are maxima. For certain items the totals were up to 11 fewer. The percentage of eligible respondents giving information was in all instances more than 98.

borne in mind, it is perhaps surprising that more did not complain of extreme boredom.

There was a marked increase in the over-all proportions saying they were lonely, but this was partly attributable to the relative increase in the number of widowed persons at the advanced ages. Table IX–16 shows that the "age-gradient" for loneliness is not very marked, for example, for widowed and single women. Table IX–18 again suggests that when the rising prevalence of incapacity is taken into account, the changes with age in the proportions expressing deprivation and loss are minimal.

The main argument being developed in this chapter is that desolation, and particularly the bereavement from a spouse, is a common and particularly important experience in old age, but that the individual old person, his family, and even society in general seek mitigation or substitution, with some success, for both emotional and social loss. It is not sufficiently recognized that the evidence for "withdrawal" or "disengagement" is primarily based on the facts of bereavement (when it is not based on growing infirmity). Yet bereavement can in no meaningful sense be said to be "initiated" by the individual old person or by society. The experience is undoubtedly more common in later life.

Both the bereaved person and society have difficulty in finding replacements. But the evidence so far suggests that the same kind of responses are made by the old and for the old as at any other stage of life. The adjustments that are made in an old person's social structure as a consequence are neither gradual nor terminal. They are major reconstructions. The kind of theory we need is one that suggests not the image of erosion but, rather, that of sudden, if partial, disintegration and patched-up reconstruction.

Summary

In this chapter we have pursued the twin themes of *isolation* and *desolation*. We began by distinguishing different types of isolation and showing how difficult it is to get a rational measure of social interaction. One important meaning of social *isolation* is to have little contact or relationship, by comparison with persons of the same age, with family, local community, and society. In all three countries only a very small minority (4 per cent or fewer) of old people were found to be living in extreme isolation in the sense that a week or even a day could pass without human contact. Few people were without meaningful everyday relationships and social activities. A larger proportion (a quarter in each country) said they were often alone. Relatively more women than men said they were often alone, and this tended to correspond with the larger proportion of women who were found to be widowed and living alone.

Those who were isolated were generally persons who were living alone, older than average, single or widowed, lacking children and other relatives living nearby, retired, and infirm. Three or more of these factors acting together were more likely to produce social isolation than was any single factor.

Desolation, a special form of isolation related to a previous individual situation, is typified by the loss (by death, hospitalization, or migration) of a social intimate, usually someone who is loved, such as a spouse or another close relative. The proportion of old people who have experienced the recent loss of a spouse, close relative, or friend is high—and seems to be higher still at the advanced ages. Desolation and peer-contrasted isolation overlap but do not coincide.

The data tended to support the hypothesis that desolation rather than peer-contrasted isolation is the causal antecedent of loneliness (defined as the unwelcome feeling of lack or loss of companionship) and may also be more important than isolation in explaining the propensity to suicide in old age. But we also found that the feelings of some of those who have experienced severe social loss are relieved by remaining or substitute contacts and relationships, particularly with members of their families. Companionship may thus prevent or mitigate loneliness, although lack of companionship does not appear to be a strong causal antecedent of loneliness.

Finally, we considered whether people disengage from society in advanced old age. We found that in all three countries substantially more persons in their 80's than in their late 60's are living alone and say they are often alone. But the trend towards isolation with age is not steep, and on none of our measures are more than two-fifths of those in their 80's "isolated" or alone. The small minority of extreme isolates increases marginally in Britain and the United States, and rather more sharply in Denmark, but still only to 6 per cent. Moreover, there is some evidence that when people become widowed or infirm they move to join their children.

The great majority of those living alone have a number of daily social activities and relationships and, although there is some falling off with increasing age, the fall is not marked and much of it is attributable to the higher prevalence of infirmity. While the data do not allow more sophisticated handling they do not suggest that, independent of growing infirmity, social disengagement is a widespread phenomenon. Bereavement is perhaps the most important isolating experience in old age and yet even this, as at other ages, draws a chain of "reintegrating" responses from family and community. Once he overcomes his initial grief, the old person himself often finds that compensating relationships provided by his family and friends may gradually mitigate his sense of loneliness.

NOTES

1 Paul Halmos, *Solitude and Privacy: A Study of Social Isolation: Its Causes and Therapy* (London: Routledge and Kegan Paul, 1952), p. xv.
2 David Riesman, *The Lonely Crowd* (New Haven, Conn.: Yale University Press, 1950).
3 P. Halmos, *op. cit.*, pp. 44, 89.
4 F. Stuart Chapin, *Experimental Designs in Sociological Research* (New York: Harper Brothers, 1947), and F. Stuart Chapin, *Social Participation Scale* (Minneapolis: University of Minnesota Press, 1952).
5 Bernard Kutner, David Fanshel, Alice M. Togo, and Thomas S. Langner, *Five Hundred over Sixty* (New York: Russell Sage Foundation, 1956).
6 Peter Townsend, *The Family Life of Old People* (London: Routledge and Kegan Paul, 1957), pp. 166–172; Peter Willmott and Michael Young, *Family and Class in a London Suburb* (London: Routledge and Kegan Paul, 1960); and Jeremy Tunstall, *Old and Alone: A Sociological Study of Old People* (London: Routledge and Kegan Paul, 1965).
7 "By 'contact' is meant a meeting with another person, usually prearranged or customary at home or outside, which involves more than a casual exchange of greetings between, say, two neighbors in the street." P. Townsend, *ibid.*, p. 167.
8 J. Tunstall, *op. cit.*, Chapter 3; see also Appendix 3.
9 In the interview people living alone were asked about their activities the previous day and the following were prompted: watch TV, listen to radio, go for a walk, do shopping, meet friends somewhere, visit friends or relatives, have any visitors. If they had no visitor they were asked a further question "Did anyone call on you?" and again there was a check, by prompting, whether a neighbor, friend, or relative had called. Finally, all those living alone were asked whether they had had a talk with anyone the day before, either personally or on the phone and whether, apart from the day before, they had had any other visitors in the last seven days.
10 "Both older people and their responsible relatives were in agreement that older people should live in their own homes if possible." Ethel Shanas, *The Health of Older People* (Cambridge, Mass.: Harvard University Press, 1962), p. 118. Beyer and Woods found that when elderly persons were asked "What arrangements do you think are

best for people over 65 who are able to take care of themselves?" only 17 per cent said that they should live with their families; 31 per cent thought that they should live by themselves "away" from relatives, and as many as 52 per cent "near" their relatives. Glenn H. Beyer and Margaret E. Woods, *Living and Activity Patterns of the Aged* (Ithaca, N.Y.: Center for Housing and Environmental Studies, Cornell University, 1963).

11 Membership was defined in the sense of attending at least occasionally.

12 For example, see Arnold M. Rose, "Group Consciousness Among the Aged," in Arnold M. Rose and Warren A. Peterson, eds., *Older People and Their Social World* (Philadelphia: F. A. Davis Company, 1965).

13 Marjorie Fiske Lowenthal, "Social Isolation and Mental Illness in Old Age," in P. From Hansen, ed., *Age with a Future*, Proceedings of the Sixth International Congress of Gerontology, Copenhagen, 1963 (Copenhagen: Munksgaard, 1964), p. 467.

14 *Ibid.*

15 Joseph H. Sheldon, *The Social Medicine of Old Age*, Report of an Inquiry in Wolverhampton (London: Oxford University Press, 1948), p. 130.

16 P. Townsend, *op. cit.*, pp. 173–178; J. Tunstall, *op. cit.*, Chapter 4.

17 This statement is made possible by the amalgamation of data collected during the cross-national survey with data collected in a second, almost identical, survey carried out later in 1962 in Britain. The total numbers of widows with children in the two categories were 140 and 51 respectively.

18 A number of experimental studies have been and are being carried out. Marjorie Fiske Lowenthal found that lifelong extreme isolation was "not necessarily conducive to mental illness in old age—but that there was some evidence of a higher prevalence among the marginally isolated and those who had become isolated late in life. However, since there was some evidence also that physical illness or disability had preceded both their social isolation and their psychiatric problems, further research was required before definite conclusions could be drawn." M. F. Lowenthal, "Social Isolation and Mental Illness in Old Age," in P. From Hansen, ed., *op. cit.*, p. 467. Unexpectedly high rates of mortality among men widowed less than six months are discussed by Michael Young, Bernard Benjamin, and Chris Wallis, "The Mortality of Widowers," *The Lancet*, August 31, 1963.

19 Emile Durkheim, *Suicide: A Study in Sociology* (London: Routledge and Kegan Paul, 1952; English ed.), pp. 175–179.

20 Maurice Halbwachs, *Les Causes du Suicide* (Paris: Libraire Felix Alcan, 1930), p. 420.

21 It is sometimes argued that the evidence of the war years confirms the relationship between the employment rate and the suicide rate among elderly men. Sainsbury, for example, pointed out that "during the war . . . when elderly men were able to obtain useful employment, the suicide rate among them fell more than that of younger men." But other social changes induced by war (such as local cohesion brought about by organization against air raids) may be as important as better employment opportunities in reducing suicide rates. Peter Sainsbury, *Suicide in London*, Maudsley Monographs No. 1 (London: Chapman and Hall, 1955), p. 81.

22 Elaine Cumming and William E. Henry, *Growing Old: The Process of Disengagement* (New York: Basic Books, Inc., 1961). Among papers of interest are, William E. Henry, "The Theory of Intrinsic Disengagement," and Robert S. Havighurst, Bernice L. Neugarten, and Sheldon S. Tobin, "Disengagement, Personality and Life Satisfaction in the Later Years," in P. From Hansen, ed., *op. cit.*, pp. 415–425.

23 Elaine Cumming, "Further Thoughts on the Theory of Disengagement," *International Social Science Journal*, XV (1963), No. 3, 377.

24 *Ibid.*, p. 379.

25 Comparisons between the numbers of those in their late 60's and those in their late 70's and over who engage in different activities showed surprisingly little difference once those with any incapacity were ruled out. For example, in Britain 34 per cent of the former, compared with 32 per cent of the latter, had visited friends on the previous day; 44 per cent compared with 43 per cent had gone shopping; 56 per cent compared with 46 per cent had gone for a walk; 33 per cent compared with 23 per cent had met friends outside the home; and 40 per cent, compared with 38 per cent, had had visitors at home.

10 : *Work and Retirement*[1]

Various studies have suggested that the pattern of retirement is strongly influenced by the person's occupation. Such patterns vary considerably from one trade to another. Farm work, for example, is often continued until late in life. Certain kinds of manual work, on the contrary, are so strenuous that they are usually discontinued by the person at a relatively early age, say somewhere around 65 years.

Patterns of retirement also vary between the self-employed and those who are working for hire. The self-employed person has a choice of retiring gradually either by reducing the number of hours (and days) he actually works or by employing more assistance, or of continuing to work past the usual retirement age. Unlike most self-employed persons, many employees have to retire completely on reaching a fixed age limit, and many have no choice between working full-time and not working at all.

Retirement is also heavily influenced by both the absolute and relative level of pensions available to the worker, and by the age limits for obtaining such pensions. Among a series of other factors influencing retirement patterns, we should also mention the level and character of unemployment. If general unemployment is rather high, and to some extent caused by ongoing technological changes, the problems of retirement may turn out to be particularly pertinent to younger men, say men in their 50's who want to remain in the labor force. Furthermore, if general unemployment is high, it may be difficult to distinguish between wage-earners who are long-standing unemployed and wage-earners who have definitely left the labor force.

Taking into account all the factors influencing how and when people retire from work, it is obvious that there must be differences between retirement patterns in Denmark, Britain, and the United States. The problem put before us is to distinguish between those differences arising from differences in the occupational structure and pension schemes of our three countries, and those differences due to different kinds of behavior in the three countries. Or to put it another way: Are there, when structural differences in occupational conditions and pension schemes are accounted for, any differences left between the retirement and working habits in the three countries? If so, such remaining differences may be explained by differences in the social value systems, the cultural patterns, the national character and tradition of the three countries—and this would open up new fields of research in order to trace the nature and causes of such differences. If not—if it is possible to explain all or most differences in retirement habits by differences in the structure of the three societies— then the result may be taken as an indication that a man's belonging to a certain occupation, a certain social class, his being entitled to certain pension schemes, is more decisive for his behavior in retiring than is his belonging to a certain nation. If the latter should be the case, the research results may be useful as a means of predicting future patterns of retirement in each country. For example, once we know something about how retirement in the United States is influenced by an occupational structure still unknown in Denmark, we have a chance of forecasting the way in which changes towards a similar occupational structure will influence retirement, when such changes eventually reach the shores of Denmark.

Definitions and Main Results

The findings of analyses on work and retirement are in some measure dependent upon the definitions used. In this study a person is considered a member of the labor force if he or she has been at work within the last week, irrespective of the number of hours worked, or if he or she has been temporarily absent from work owing to illness, unemployment, holidays, and so forth. Following this definition, our cross-national analyses show a marked difference between the labor force status of old people in Great Britain on the one side, and Denmark on the other, with the United States in between. In Great Britain only 28 per cent of all men aged 65 years and more are in the labor force, in Denmark 38 per cent of these men are in the labor force, and in the United States, 32 per cent.

The corresponding labor force participation rates among women, 65 years of age and more, are 8 per cent in Great Britain, 13 per cent in the United States, and 8 per cent in Denmark. In spite of the fact that an increasing number of women have entered the labor force in recent years, the problems of work and retirement are still most relevant to men. Consequently the analyses in this chapter are concentrated on men.

Comparisons between our samples and the official labor market statistics expose the same main tendencies in the differences between the working status among old men in the three countries. The number of men temporarily absent from work and unemployed is very small. But it must be borne in mind that the distinction between long-standing unemployment and retirement is difficult to make.

The starting point for the analysis is thus that 32, 28, and 38 per cent respectively of American, British, and Danish men of 65 years and more in our sample are still in the labor force. In order to indicate more precisely the factors causing these country-by-country differences, we will examine the labor force participation rates (a) for smaller age groups within those

Table X–1: DISTRIBUTION OF THE MALE SAMPLES, BY WORK STATUS

Work Status	DENMARK		BRITAIN		UNITED STATES	
	Number	Per Cent	Number	Per Cent	Number	Per Cent
At work last week	418	37	252	25	290	27
Temporarily absent	19	1	24	2	42	4
Unemployed	2	—	1	1	12	1
Total in the labor force	439	38	277	28	344	32
All men	1,145	100	1,004	100	1,081	100

65 years and more, (b) for different occupational groups, and (c) for age groups within occupational groups, and (d) within groups of differing marital status. After that, we will examine the contributions of the aged to the work force in terms of their hours of work; and finally, we will compare the reasons for retirement in the three countries.

Labor Force Participation by Age Groups

In all three countries the older work force is heavily weighted with men under 70 years of age. But, on the whole, the Danish older work force is somewhat younger than the British and the American. Sixty-three per cent of Danish men over 65 years still at work are under 70 years of age as opposed to 59 per cent in Great Britain and 54 per cent in the United States. The retired group in all countries is heavily weighted with men over 70 years of age, with retired men in Denmark being generally an older group than retired men in Great Britain and the United States. Among retired men over 65 years of age in Denmark, 76 per cent are over 70 years old—as opposed to 69 per cent of the British and 70 per cent of the American retired men.

It is true that the age distribution of men within the samples varies somewhat from country to country. The United States, in particular, has a greater accumulation of men in the group 70–74 than the other countries and correspondingly fewer men in the age brackets 67–69 and 75–79. But these small differences in the age distribution of men in the three countries cannot explain the differences in the age of the retired and of the work force. An examination of the percentage of each age group in the labor force shows that the heavy employment of older men in Denmark compared with both Britain and the United States is consistent for all age groups up to 75. The higher Danish employment rate among older men is clearly shown in Table X–5. Here the Danish employment rate for each age group has been computed using the comparable employment rates in both Britain and the United States as a base. The computations highlight two main tendencies:

Table X–2: AGE DISTRIBUTION OF MEN AGED 65 AND OVER IN THE LABOR FORCE AND IN RETIREMENT[a] (*Percentage Distribution*)

Age Group	In Labor Force			Retired		
	Denmark	Britain	United States	Denmark	Britain	United States
65–66	32	29	26	6	12	12
67–69	31	30	28	18	19	18
70–74	23	25	30	31	30	33
75 and over	15	16	16	45	39	37
Total	100	100	100	100	100	100
N=	439	277	344	706	727	737

[a] The total number of men in each age group for each country is:
Denmark—65–66, 184; 67–69, 262; 70–74, 318; 75 and over, 381; all men, 1,145.
Britain—65–66, 164; 67–69, 226; 70–74, 287; 75 and over, 327; all men, 1,004.
United States—65–66, 176; 67–69, 230; 70–74, 347; 75 and over, 328; all men, 1,081.

One hundred per cent of the eligible respondents answered this question in all three countries. In subsequent tables, where 98 per cent or more of eligible respondents have answered the question, data on non-response will be omitted.

Table X–3: AGE DISTRIBUTION OF MEN WITHIN THE TOTAL POPULATION AND WITHIN THE THREE SAMPLES (*Percentage Distribution*)

Age Group	Total Population			Sample Distribution		
	Denmark[a]	Britain[b]	United States[c]	Denmark	Britain	United States
65–66	17	}41	38	16	16	16
67–69	21			23	23	21
70–74	28	30	29	28	29	32
75–79	19	15	}33	20	20	17
80 and over	15	14		13	12	14
Total	100	100	100	100	100	100

[a] As of January, 1962. *Statistisk Arbog* (Copenhagen: Det statistiske departement, May 1963).

[b] As of June, 1962. Central Statistical Office, *Annual Abstract of Statistics* (London: HMSO, 1965).

[c] As of April, 1960. United States Bureau of the Census, *Statistical Abstract of the United States* (Washington, D.C.: U.S. GPO, 1962).

1. The Danish higher rate of employment is mostly found in the age bracket 65–69. In other words, the United States and the Danish labor force percentages come rather close to each other from the age of 70 upwards.
2. The generally lower rate of employment in Great Britain compared to Denmark is more distinct after the age of 67. That is to say, the British and the American labor force percentages are rather on a par in the age group 65–66 years.

Table X-4: PROPORTION OF MEN IN EACH AGE GROUP IN LABOR FORCE

Age Group	DENMARK	BRITAIN	UNITED STATES
65–66	76	49	51
67–69	52	37	42
70–74	31	24	29
75–79	18	15	19
80 and over	15	10	15
All men	38	28	32
N=	1,145	1,004	1,081

Table X-5: DANISH RATE OF EMPLOYMENT AS A PROPORTION OF BRITISH AND AMERICAN EMPLOYMENT IN EACH GROUP

Age Group	Danish Rate of Employment	
	With the British Rate as 100	With the United States Rate as 100
65–66	155	149
67–69	140	124
70–74	129	107
75–79	120	95
80 and over	150	100

The exceedingly higher rate of employment in Denmark till the age of 67, the somewhat lesser rate in the interval 67–69 years, and (compared to the American findings) the still decreasing higher rate of employment after the age of 70, are presumably largely the results of the different pension age in the three countries. The age limit at which men are entitled to full public old age pensions is 65 in the United States and Great Britain; in Denmark, however, it is 67. For most civil servants and persons entitled to private pensions the retirement age is normally age 65 in the United States, ages 60–65 in Britain, but ages 67–70 in Denmark. Danish wage-earners, like American and British, remain in the labor force until the normal pension age which, as has been noted, is 67 in Denmark as opposed to 65 or less in the United States and Great Britain respectively.

Because the prevalent age limit for public pensions in the United States and in Britain lies at the lowest age limit of the sample, and in Denmark, above it, the value of the sample is limited in an illustration of retirement patterns. In both the United States and Great Britain there is, beginning at the age of 65, roughly the same decrease in the percentage of employed men from one age group to another, while in Denmark the decrease in the proportion of employed men appears enormous—24 percentage points at age 67, the age at which men are entitled to public pensions, and 21 percentage points at age 70, the prevailing pension age for civil servants.

Table X-6: NUMERICAL DECREASE IN PERCENTAGE OF MEN IN THE LABOR FORCE FROM ONE AGE GROUP TO THE NEXT[a]

Age	DENMARK	BRITAIN	UNITED STATES
At age 67	24	12	9
At age 70	21	13	13
At age 75	13	9	10
At age 80	3	5	4

[a] Calculated on the basis of the proportion of men in the labor force at ages 65–66.

The effect of the age of entitlement for public pensions on a man's leaving the labor force is probably most noticeable among manual workers. Self-employed persons in the middle and higher income brackets very often have a chance of diminishing the pressures of work; thus, they can continue in the labor force. The same may hold true for certain non-manual wage-earners, who will often remain in the labor force until they reach the age limit for compulsory retirement in their occupation. In Denmark and the United States this age limit is sometimes higher than the age at which a person is entitled to a public pension. It is expected that self-employed persons and certain special groups of non-manual wage-earners will form the main part of those still employed at ages greater than the age limits for public pensions.

Labor force participation rates are nearly the same, 51, 49, and 52 in the United States, Britain, and Denmark respectively, in the age group just after normal pension age. Thus, in all three countries about half of all men do not retire as soon as they reach the age entitling them to full old-age benefits—irrespective of the fact that this age limit is two years higher in Denmark than in the other two countries. As the health of old Danish men does not seem substantially better than that of British and American men, there is evidence for the view that pension age has a strong influence on forming retirement norms. Certainly, this seems to be the case in the age group between 65 and 70 years of age. (The reader is referred to Chapter 2 for a discussion of the level of capacity of men in the three countries.)

The general lower rate of employment of older men in Great Britain compared to Denmark and the United States is demonstrated in Table X–7. This table shows the percentage of men in the labor force as a percentage of the comparable labor force rates in the United States and

Table X–7: BRITAIN'S EMPLOYMENT RATE AFTER THE AGE OF 65, AS A PROPORTION OF DANISH AND UNITED STATES EMPLOYMENT

Age Group	DENMARK	UNITED STATES
65–66	64	98
67–69	71	88
70–74	77	83
75–79	83	79
80 and over	67	67

Denmark. Great Britain's special position regarding low labor force participation by men after the age of 67 is probably attributable to one or more of the following factors: agriculture's limited role in the total economic structure, the large number of blue collar workers in the economy, and the relatively few independent and/or self-employed persons in the British labor force.

There seems to be no doubt at this point that the differences in retirement patterns between the United States and Great Britain on the one side, and Denmark on the other, can be explained to a great extent by the higher pension age in Denmark. This is seen from the fact that the labor force rates in all three countries are on a par in the periods immediately following that age at which the public pension can be obtained—ages 65–66 in the United States and in Great Britain, ages 67–69 in Denmark. After these age groups, the United States and Denmark are on a par, while Great Britain has a clearly lower labor force share during all remaining ages. This lower rate of employment in Great Britain must apparently be explained by special features in the British economic and social structure.

Labor Force Participation by Occupational Groups[2]

In Table X–8 all men within the three samples are distributed according to the occupational group they belonged to in their former or present occupation. Great Britain is characterized by a very large proportion of men belonging to the blue collar group, and correspondingly, a small group of farmers, both owners and laborers. In Denmark, on the other hand, farmers constitute a relatively large group, and the blue collar

Table X-8: PROPORTION OF MEN AGED 65 AND OVER IN EACH OCCUPATIONAL GROUP AND IN THE LABOR FORCE[a] (*Percentage Distribution*)

Occupational Group	In Occupational Group			In Labor Force		
	Denmark	Britain	United States	Denmark	Britain	United States
White collar	34	28	28	42	27	43
Blue collar	36	55	42	33	25	20
Service worker	2	11	11	[32][b]	44	38
Agricultural	28	5	18	42	27	38
Farm owners	21	2	14	39	[35]	38
Farm laborers	7	3	4	51	[21]	37
Total	100	100	100	38	28	32

[a] The number of men in each occupational group in each country is:
Denmark—white collar, 389; blue collar, 415; service workers, 28; agricultural workers, 310.
Britain—white collar, 280; blue collar, 553; service workers, 113; agricultural workers, 51.
United States—white collar, 300; blue collar, 454; service workers, 117; agricultural workers, 203.

[b] Numbers in brackets are computed on base of less than 50 cases.

group is rather small. Service workers are also small in Denmark compared to the corresponding group in the other two countries.

It may be argued that the differences in the total proportion of older men in the labor force in the three countries are the result of the differing structure of the labor force in each country. This is apparently not the case insofar as a comparison between the United States and Denmark is concerned. If the proportion of older men in the labor force in Denmark is computed using the occupational distribution of the older American work force, the total proportion of older men in the Danish work force is reduced by only 2 per cent to 37 per cent, chiefly because farm owners and laborers are less important in the United States than in Denmark.

Table X-9: STANDARD CALCULATION OF LABOR FORCE PERCENTAGES BY OCCUPATIONAL GROUPS IN THE THREE COUNTRIES

Country	Labor Force Percentage Weighed Proportional to		
	DENMARK	BRITAIN	UNITED STATES
Britain	28	28	29
Denmark	38	36	37
United States	33	29	32

As a consequence of the extremely small farm group in Great Britain, there will be a more distinct shift in the total American and Danish labor force participation rates if the British distribution in occupational groups is combined with the American and the Danish labor force rates as in the second column in Table X–9. The total American labor force percentage is then reduced to 29 per cent, which is close to the English rate, and the Danish labor force rate is reduced to 36 per cent. In other words, part of the explanation of the low labor force participation by older men in Great Britain, especially when compared with the somewhat higher rate in the United States, is found in the fact that the farm group which has a large number of older workers is very small in Great Britain.

Despite these standardizations, however, when one compares national differences in labor force participation within each occupational group, certain characteristic differences remain. If one wants to know whether such differences within the same occupational group are due to different patterns of retirement from country to country, one confronts certain difficulties. The level of labor force participation within a certain group partly reflects the extent to which the members of the group retire early or late in life. But it also reflects the life span of the members of this occupation, as well as shifts in the occupational grouping of the country as a whole. For example, if the labor force participation of older blue collar workers is low, this may be due to the fact that blue collar workers retire early in life. But it might also be explained by the fact that retired blue collar workers generally have long lives and that there are more among them in the population. And part of the explanation could be that there are more blue collar workers among the cohorts of men reaching normal pension ages, say, 10 to 20 years ago than among men reaching normal pension ages, say, 2 to 5 years ago. For example, if in one country the number of blue collar workers reaching normal pension ages 10 to 20 years ago was considerably larger than the number of blue collar workers reaching normal pension ages 2 to 5 years ago, this will cause relatively large proportions of blue collar workers in that country to be found in the oldest age brackets. Since labor force participation decreases with age, this would result in a lower labor force participation rate among all blue collar workers over 65 years of age in that country, compared to participation in another country in which there has been no such shift in the size of cohorts reaching pension ages.

However, most of the effects of possible shifting occupational groupings through time will be eliminated when one compares labor force participation in smaller age groups within each occupational group from country to country.

Labor Force Participation in Age Groups within Each Occupational Group

The three countries vary in the labor force participation of occupational groups. When Denmark is compared with the two other countries, what emerges is the relatively high labor force participation for older blue collar workers and farm labor. A comparison between Great Britain and the other two countries shows a very low labor force participation for older British men of white collar background. On the other hand, the labor force participation for older men in the service group is higher in Britain than in Denmark and in the United States. It is noteworthy too that the percentage of blue collar workers still in the labor force is greater in Britain than in the United States. What has been said to this point implicitly indicates that the most characteristic feature of labor force participation of older men in the United States compared with the other countries is a very low labor force participation of older blue collar workers.

WHITE COLLAR WORKERS

The more or less uniform total labor force participation of white collar workers in the United States and Denmark obscures the fact that actually there are relatively more persons aged 65 and 66 years in the labor force in Denmark than in the United States. On the other hand, labor force participation is relatively larger in the United States in the higher age groups after age 75 years.

Table X-10: PROPORTION OF WHITE COLLAR WORKERS IN LABOR FORCE, BY AGE GROUPS[a]

Age Group	DENMARK	BRITAIN	UNITED STATES
65–66	79	[42][b]	67
67–69	54	39	52
70–74	38	16	34
75 and over	22	22	29
Total	42	27	43
N=	389	280	300

[a] See footnote *a*, Table X–8.

[b] See footnote *b*, Table X–8.

The relatively high Danish labor force participation in the younger age groups is probably due to the higher Danish pension age, particularly for civil servants. The lower Danish employment in the higher age groups is presumably because there are fewer self-employed white collar workers in Denmark than in the United States. Self-employed white collar workers, as has been indicated earlier, constitute a group for which it is easier than for most others to go on working later in life. Such persons very often employ younger assistants, some of whom may be their relatives, and the older man is often able to fill a working role by being present, giving advice from long experience, and so forth.

British white collar workers, like most other occupational groups in that country, apparently retire rather early in life. It is interesting to note, however, that even in Great Britain some white collar workers go on working late in life, so that actually the labor force participation among British white collar workers is raised a bit between the age groups 70–74 and 75 years and over. This underlines again that self-employed white collar workers constitute a group with special possibilities for staying in the labor force until late in life.

AGRICULTURE

The older farm group (owners and laborers) is a group with relatively large labor force participation in all three countries (Table XI–11). Again here is a group—like self-employed white collar workers—for whom it is rather easy to go on working because farm work is adjustable to a person's working capacity. If a farm owner's working capacity or, perhaps more important, his ability for management functions is decreasing, he may give up certain productions on his farm and concentrate on those remaining. Or he may stick to the production methods he is used to, even if they are becoming old-fashioned, and still he will be able to earn a living. This often means that an old farmer, instead of specializing in certain productions (a process that calls for new investments and management ability) will, on the contrary, continue to raise his usual variety of crops. Even if a farm owner feels his ability for keeping up with progress in agricultural productivity is declining, he may still be able to earn a living at a level comparable to the pension level. One of the reasons for this is that a farmer has many of his basic necessities covered through his very occupation. Further, it must be pointed out that the borderline between being a farm owner and a farm laborer very often is quite vague. A farm owner running a small farm may more and more concentrate on assisting others, or alternatively, he may let out his own fields to others, he may turn over the management of his farm to relatives, and so forth.

Summing up, it may be said that independent farmers and agricultural laborers are able to continue to live in the country and to maintain a certain amount of employment from which they would be cut off in a town. But this is often connected with an old-fashioned lifelong attachment to the work one had in one's prime, an attachment which depends on association with a local community. Such an attachment is to some extent caused by the fact that agriculture's technique of production and its structure have, as a whole, not yet fully adjusted to modern possibilities. Assuming the continued modernization of the structure of agriculture and the dissolution of the village milieu, the agricultural sector with an especially high employment rate of older men will presumably disappear in the years to come.

Broadly speaking, these observations apply to the farm population in all three countries, Denmark, Britain, and the United States. Furthermore, it must be understood that they particularly apply the older the farmers are. In other words, it is likely, when the older men stay on in the labor force, that their work, their management, and so forth, may be out of step with the more advanced methods. Particularly with respect to the very oldest agricultural workers, there is a vague limit between being a farm owner and a farm laborer—and perhaps also between being inside and outside the labor force. If this is true, we may offer the following interpretation of the differences in labor force participation in the various age groups in the United States and Denmark.[3] In the United States, where

Table X-11: PROPORTIONS OF ALL WORKERS IN AGRICULTURE AND OF FARM OWNERS IN LABOR FORCE, BY AGE GROUPS[a]

Age Group	DENMARK		BRITAIN		UNITED STATES	
	All Agricultural	Farm Owners	All Agricultural	Farm Owners	All Agricultural	Farm Owners
65–66	[67][b]	[70]	[67]	[100]	[41]	[33]
67–69	62	[65]	[30]	[33]	[49]	[48]
70–74	48	44	[38]	[50]	45	[52]
75 and over	18	11	[5]	[13]	28	27
Total	42	39	27	[35]	38	38
N=	310	233	51	23	203	157

[a] See footnote *a*, Table X-8.
[b] See footnote *b*, Table X-8.

labor force participation is relatively low in the 65–69 year age group and relatively high after 70 years, the high labor force participation in the farm population is a clear expression of the fact that the oldest living generations of the male farm population wish to stay on in the country. When these men do so, they also maintain a certain contact with work; but this contact does not have to be very intensive. In Denmark the total labor force participation among older farmers is equally as high as in the United States. But it is the result of high participation rates in the youngest age groups, which may indicate that more than in the United States, in Denmark there is an actual association with farm work as such. This again may be explained by the fact that in the United States, where the agricultural area is abundant and where there are many different ways of running a farm, old-fashioned and ineffective farms can exist along with highly modernized agriculture. This is more difficult to achieve in Denmark, where land is scarce, the agricultural structure rather one-sided, and the demand for effectiveness strong, owing to the importance of export production in the agricultural sector.

BLUE COLLAR WORKERS

The group of blue collar workers is the largest group of older men in all three countries. Within this group we find important national differences in labor force participation from country to country. First, the Danish labor force participation is higher than both the American and the English. Second, and even more remarkable, the labor force participation among blue collar workers in Great Britain is greater than among American blue collar workers. The general tendency of rather low labor force participation among the British aged population as compared to the United States thus does not apply to this group.

In interpreting this important national difference, one has to realize that it is not directly explainable through varying levels of unemployment. The men in the labor force in our sample also include some unemployed— and indeed a greater number of unemployed in the United States than in the other two countries. Indirectly, however, the general higher level of unemployment in the United States may influence the proportion of aged in the labor force. If the general level of unemployment is relatively high, a man who loses his job after the age of 50 will often be without a job for a long time. This may well result in his finally giving up looking for a job; in other words, according to our definition, he leaves the labor force. This particularly will be the case when the unemployment is of a structural nature, that is, caused by labor-saving technical changes in the means of production. As the element of such structural unemployment is likely to be notably great in the American unemployment figures, this may explain in some measure why older American blue collar workers have left the labor force.

The retirement patterns within each age group, as well as the high labor force participation among Danish blue collar workers and the low percentage among American workers, are shown in Table X–12. As expected, the higher rate of employment in Denmark is again most pronounced in the 65–66 year age group, and again owing to the higher pension age in that country. A comparison between the United States and Great Britain shows that there are no important national differences in the labor force participation among blue collar workers in the age groups

Table X–12: PROPORTION OF BLUE COLLAR WORKERS IN THE LABOR FORCE, BY AGE GROUPS[a]

Age Group	DENMARK	BRITAIN	UNITED STATES
65–66	79	46	42
67–69	44	34	31
70–74	16	23	17
75–79	10	12	5
80 and over	[9][b]	6	4
Total	33	25	20
N=	415	553	454

[a] See footnote *a*, Table X–8.

[b] See footnote *b*, Table X–8.

65–69 years. The decisive factor is that the English labor force participation in the years after 70 is greater than the American labor force participation (and than the Danish until 80 years of age).

Seeing that the age at which a man is entitled to his full old age pension is 65 years in the United States and Great Britain, and 67 in Denmark, there is some indication that labor force participation of 40 to 45 per cent among blue collar workers during the first years after reaching the pension age is a common feature of modern industrialized countries. After that, the labor force participation rates are about 33 per cent in the United States and Great Britain, compared to only 16 per cent in Denmark. The low Danish percentage is perhaps explainable by the fact that the later the pension can be obtained, the faster it is accepted. The fact that Great Britain has quite high labor force participation in the age groups 70–80 years is more difficult to explain. Is it that owing to the structural element in American unemployment, more of those who would potentially have worked till late in life have left the labor force in the United States than in Great Britain? Or is it that the very high level of employment in Britain means that there are greater employment opportunities for the old there than in the United States? In comparing Britain with Denmark it must be kept in mind that although Denmark too has full employment, the lower pension levels in Britain vis-à-vis Denmark may also result in more pressure on the aged in Britain to take part-time jobs. (See Chapters 12 and 13, *infra*.) The inclination to do so may be strengthened by the fact that in Britain the retirement test for a pension is no longer effective after the age of 70.

Labor Force Participation by Marital Status

Many investigations show a tendency for a greater proportion of married than unmarried men inside the same career and occupational group to go on working. Among various reasons suggested to explain this, the most important presumably is that unmarried men (especially the never married men) on the average will have poorer health and, moreover, will often be less well socially adjusted than married men. Another reason may be that a married man generally is the breadwinner and as such prefers to go on working so long as his income from work is larger than that from any pension to which he may be entitled. Of course, this is especially the case when a man's wife is so much younger than he that she cannot get a pension at the time her husband may be entitled to one.

On the whole, the supposition that married men continue to work seems to be confirmed in all three countries. It is interesting and in accordance with the findings mentioned earlier that there is a notable drop in the labor force participation among unmarried men in Denmark when one passes from the age group 65–66 years to the 67–69 age group. As pointed out earlier, in all three countries there is a general tendency for around 50 per cent of all men to remain in the labor force in the years immediately after the age entitling them to full old age benefits. This is also the case as far as married men are concerned. But among unmarried

Table X–13: PROPORTION OF MEN IN THE LABOR FORCE, BY MARITAL
STATUS AND AGE

Age Group	Married			Unmarried		
	Denmark	Britain	United States	Denmark	Britain	United States
65–66	76	50	51	[73][a]	[43]	[48]
67–69	54	39	43	42	32	[37]
70–74	34	26	30	22	20	28
75 and over	19	11	22	14	11	9
Total	44	32	35	26	21	23
N=	799	701	825	342	303	256

[a] Numbers in brackets are computed on base of less than 50 cases.

men in Denmark in the age group 67–69 years, only about 42 per cent are
still in the labor force. This indicates that once a man has reached the
pension age he is more inclined to give up work when he is widowed or
single than if he has a wife.

The Pattern of Labor Force Participation

The following conclusions can be drawn about labor force participation
by older men.

1. The higher rate of labor force participation in Denmark is first and
   foremost due to the higher pension age in that country. The lower
   labor force participation rate in Great Britain is partly explainable
   through specific features of British economic and social structure.
   Among these can be mentioned the relatively few self-employed
   persons in Great Britain, especially among white collar workers, and
   the unimportance of agriculture.
2. The standard calculations for occupational groups show that the very
   moderate size of the farm group in Great Britain contributes to the
   small labor force participation of older men in that country.
3. A comparison between labor force participation in age groups within
   each occupational group shows that there are a number of common
   features in patterns of retirement in the three countries, particularly
   among the white collar and farm populations. In the blue collar group
   one finds again that, to a great extent, the different pension ages among
   the countries account for the differences in labor force participation.
   Yet, generally speaking, there seems to be more room for older blue
   collar workers in both Britain and Denmark than in the United States.
   Probably this is attributable to the higher rate of structural unemployment among blue collar workers and the more widespread automation
   in the United States.

4. There seem to be the same differences in labor force participation for married and unmarried men from country to country.
5. All this points to the fact that institutional conditions—such as pension age, occupational group, distribution of workers into employees and self-employed, the extent and nature of unemployment, automation, and marital status—probably play a greater role in old men's participation in work than do differences in the social value systems in the three countries and differences in national character, tradition, and so on.

Number of Working Hours

As may be seen from the findings, in Denmark and the United States farmers generally work more hours each week than men in all other occupations.[4] Blue collar workers as a whole work more weekly hours than white collar workers. Although there is no doubt that farmers' very

Table X-14: CUMULATIVE PROPORTIONS OF BLUE COLLAR AND WHITE COLLAR MEN AND OF FARM OWNERS WORKING A GIVEN NUMBER OF HOURS PER WEEK[a]

Hours Worked per Week	Blue Collar			White Collar			Farm Owners		
	Denmark	Britain	United States	Denmark	Britain	United States	Denmark	Britain	United States
Over 44	62	21	34	50	21	28	72	[71][b]	50
Over 39	73	57	61	57	45	52	82	[71]	61
Over 34	79	59	64	65	55	59	88	[71]	66
Over 29	82	65	72	68	63	63	90	[71]	70
Over 14	94	83	95	85	79	87	99	[100]	83
Over 1	100	100	100	100	100	100	100	[100]	100
N=	111	125	64	130	66	101	83	7	54

[a] The proportions of eligible respondents who answered this question in each country were: blue collar—Denmark, 90; Britain, 91; United States, 73. White collar—Denmark, 83; Britain, 88; United States, 79. Farm owners—Denmark, 92; Britain, 87; United States, 89.

[b] Numbers in brackets are computed on base of less than 50 cases.

extended working week is somewhat the result of the necessity of being present, rather than of working hard, in all the hours counted as working hours, nevertheless it is probably a general rule that farming claims more working hours than most other occupations. As far as blue and white collar workers are concerned, it is generally a rule that the work weeks at factories are longer than work weeks at offices. Nevertheless it is noteworthy that so many elderly blue collar workers in all three countries work more hours per week than is customary in each of the three countries. When the three countries are compared we find a clear tendency for old men in Denmark to have a longer working week than in the two other countries.

The above briefly mentioned differences between working hours in different occupational groups and from country to country will be further analyzed below. This will be done in connection with a series of calculations that are an attempt to estimate how much the labor force participation of older men, as previously reported, would be reduced when the number of hours the individual *actually* works per week is taken into consideration. This calculation uses the total number of working hours achieved per week by 100 men over 65 years of age in each of the three countries.

The data for the blue collar group shown below in Table X–15 illustrate the method of calculation. The proportion of workers who work 44 hours

Table X–15: PER CENT OF BLUE COLLAR WORKERS WORKING GIVEN HOURS, AND TOTAL HOURS WORKED BY 100 OLDER BLUE COLLAR WORKERS

DENMARK			BRITAIN			UNITED STATES		
Average No. of Hours per Wk.	Percentage Distribution of Workers	Total Hours (1 x 2)	Average No. of Hours per Wk.	Percentage Distribution of Workers	Total Hours (1 x 2)	Average No. of Hours per Wk.	Percentage Distribution of Workers	Total Hours (1 x 2)
46	62	2,852	49	21	1,029	48	34	1,632
42	11	462	42	36	1,512	42	27	1,134
37	6	222	37	2	74	37	3	111
32	3	96	32	6	192	32	8	256
22	12	264	22	18	396	22	23	506
10	6	60	10	17	170	10	5	50
Total	100	3,956		100	3,373		100	3,689
N=	111			125			64	

or more per week, or 35–39 hours per week, and so forth, is computed, using data taken from Table X–14. An arbitrary number of hours within each interval has been chosen as the average number of hours persons in each group work each week. The official labor market statistics for the United States show that quite notable proportions of older blue collar workers who work more than 44 hours per week have weekly schedules of 50–59 hours or of 60 hours and more, in spite of the fact that the normal weekly hours in the United States are now at 40 hours for younger persons. The average weekly hours for those in the sample working more than 44 hours have therefore been put at 48 hours for the United States.

Data from a special tabulation in Denmark show that a considerable proportion of people with weekly hours of more than 44 hours, work exactly 45 hours. This is partly due to the fact that the 45 hour week is established as the normal work week in Denmark, and it should be recalled that Danish workers, aged 65 and 66, are below the normal pension age for that country and therefore will likely work whatever hours are usual for persons not pensioned. Consequently, the average week for those in the Danish sample working more than 44 hours per week has been put at 46 hours. In Great Britain the normal weekly hours are 44, but in 1962 the average weekly hours for adult males in manufacturing, transport, et cetera, were 47 hours. Accordingly, in the British sample an average work week of 49 hours has been used for those workers who said they worked more than 44 hours. Each of the average hour-figures is multiplied by the percentage of all workers, working the number of hours in question. By summing up, the number of hours that 100 workers achieve per week in the three countries is then estimated as shown in Table X–15.

To interpret Table X–15, one must assume that the actual number of working hours accomplished is measured by the normal working week in the individual country per 100 workers; that is, 40 hours per 100 workers in the United States, or 4,000 hours; 44 hours per 100 workers in Great Britain, or 4,400 hours; and 45 hours per 100 workers in Denmark, or 4,500 hours. One hundred older workers in the United States who work 3,689 hours in a week, therefore, work 92 per cent of the normal working hours; in Britain 100 workers who work 3,373 hours, work 77 per cent of the normal working hours; in Denmark 100 workers who work 3,956 hours work 88 per cent of the normal working hours.

Many assumptions enter into this comparison of the amount of work carried out by older workers compared to younger workers. The problem of the unemployed in the labor force, previously mentioned, has not been considered. Likewise, no corrections have been made for the possibility that more old than young men are temporarily absent from work owing to holidays, illness, and so on. However, temporarily absent persons are found in all age groups. As the calculations include all persons in the labor force, they are based on the assumption that people who are in the labor force, but who are not working for the time being, for whatever reason, will distribute themselves according to weekly working hours similar to those whose working hours are known.

In summary, one finds that although in the United States 20 per cent of blue collar workers over the age of 65 are working, they accomplish only 92 per cent of the current working hours. If one assumes that everyone under the age of 65 works a full normal week, this means that in the United States older blue collar workers achieve only 18 per cent of the total number of working hours that a full-time employed younger age group accomplish. For Great Britain, the equivalent percentage is 19 per cent, and for Denmark, 29 per cent. It is obvious that a calculation based on these broad assumptions has illustrative rather than analytical value. It gives a picture of the number of hours that old men put in at work as compared with the ideal work week of men in a young age group. No doubt, there will also be some in the latter group who work more or less than the normal working week, and some who are unemployed.

If one wants a clearer picture of the decrease in work caused by old age as such, one has to compare the hours worked by older men with a younger age group's actual amount of work within a week. On the basis of official labor market statistics for the United States, one is able to calculate the actual number of working hours accomplished by 100 employed blue collar workers in the age group 40–44 years as 4,248 hours per week, that is, 106 per cent of the normal week of 4,000 hours. Of these 100 workers, 98 per cent were employed. Thus, the 40–44-year-olds who were employed did 104 per cent (98 × 106) of the practicable full work of the normal work week. Compared with this, older blue collar workers in the United States performed 17 per cent $\left(\frac{18}{104} \times 100 \right)$ of the total work accomplished by blue collar workers in the prime of life.

Another method of illustrating the decrease in work follows. This method, however, can be used only with the Danish material. To what extent do men aged 65 and 66 work less than men aged 62–64, despite the fact that the full old age pension is not obtainable until the age of 67? Data from the Danish sample, which included men aged 62–64, indicate that 81 per cent of these blue collar men are working and that a typical 100 of these men worked 4,236 hours weekly or 94 per cent of the usual work week. Thus, 62- through 64-year-olds altogether accomplished 76 per cent (94 × 81) of the normal work hours. According to a similar calculation for 65- and 66-year-olds, these men accomplished 73 per cent of the normal work hours. The reduction from 76 to 73 per cent implies that these men have started to live on their own resources, unemployment pensions, invalid pensions, or have been granted exemption from the normal pension age, or have reduced the number of weekly working hours mainly as a consequence of actually failing working capacity and/or zeal. This percentage reduction, which also reflects sampling variance, must be considered very small.

Because the higher Danish age limit for public pension apparently plays a large part in explaining the later retirement among blue collar workers in Denmark as compared to the United States and Britain, it is of interest to determine whether, once allowances are made for the differences in pension ages, the differences between the amount of work performed by blue collar workers over 65 in the three countries are decisive. In other words, do the workers of the three countries react similarly after having reached the age limit at which workers can claim the old age pension?

Several different possible sets of assumptions may be used in the discussion of this problem. It is first assumed that if the pension age in Denmark were 65, the same proportion of 65- and 66-year-olds would be working as in the United States—that is, 42 per cent. It is then assumed that three-fourths of those employed in Denmark would be working full-time and one-fourth would be working nearly full-time. That is, it is assumed that the difference between Denmark's 79 per cent employed of 65- and 66-year-olds and the United States' 42 per cent is composed of blue collar workers who—because they are still in what is in Denmark considered normal working age—are working full-time or nearly full-time. On the basis of these assumptions, the following figures are estimated for Denmark:

1. Number of blue collar workers, aged 65–66   71
2. Actual number employed   56
3. Denmark's percentage of employed blue collar workers   79
4. United States' percentage of employed blue collar workers   42
5. United States' percentage of employed transferred to Denmark gives number of employed   20
6. Calculated reduction in Denmark   26
7. Of this number, the following are deducted from working weeks of 45 hours and more   20
8. And the following from 40–44 hour working weeks   6

Based on this statement, Table X–16 gives the number of hours the reduced number of Danish blue collar workers who work will accomplish per week per 100 men.

Table X–16: REDUCED NUMBER OF WORKING HOURS OF 100 BLUE COLLAR WORKERS IN DENMARK, STANDARDIZED BY PERCENTAGE OF EMPLOYED IN THE UNITED STATES

Hours per Week	Actual Number of Workers (1)	Reduced Number of Workers (2)	Percentage Distribution (3)	Working Week in Average Hours (4)	Number of Working Hours per 100 Workers (3 x 4)
45	83	63	58	46	2,668
40–44	15	9	8	42	336
35–39	8	8	7	37	259
30–34	4	4	4	32	128
15–29	17	17	16	22	352
1–14	8	8	7	10	70
Total	135	109	100	—	3,813

The calculated working week of these men would be 85 per cent $\left(\frac{3,813}{4,500} \times 100 \right)$ of the amount of work to be accomplished by the reduced number of Danish blue collar workers if they all worked a full normal working week.

Earlier, we had pointed out that actually 33 per cent of all older blue collar workers in Denmark are still employed. If we deduct from this group the number who would be pensioned if the pension age in Denmark were 65 years rather than 67 years, a working participation rate of 26 per cent results. The blue collar workers here concerned have a work week that is 85 per cent of the normal. Consequently, if blue collar workers in Denmark retired at age 65, the total work week contribution of old people would go from 29 per cent (as presented earlier) to 22 per cent (0.26 × 0.85).

Table X–17 summarizes retirement/work relations of blue collar workers in the United States, Great Britain, and Denmark, comparing working hours lost due to old age with the situation of a younger age

Table X–17: WORKING HOURS LOST DUE TO OLD AGE, 100 BLUE COLLAR WORKERS

Working Hours Lost	UNITED STATES	BRITAIN	DENMARK Actual	DENMARK Calculated with Same Pension Age as United States
All full employed	100	100	100	100
Less: lost on account of complete retirement	80	75	67	74
Remainder	20	25	33	26
Less: lost by reduced weekly working hours[a]	2	6	4	4

[a] United States—8 per cent of 20; Britain—23 per cent of 25; Actual—12 per cent of 33; Denmark, Calculated—15 per cent of 26.

group whose members all work full-time. Table X–17 shows that the directly observed higher rate of employment among older blue collar workers in Great Britain as compared to the United States, 25 per cent $\left(\frac{25}{20} \times 100\right)$, is reduced by 6 per cent $\left(\frac{19}{18} \times 100\right)$ when the number of hours of a normal working week worked by the old is taken into account. Considering the many assumptions of the calculation, one can conclude that the reduction of work due to old age is approximately the same in the United States and Great Britain, with a resulting rate of 18 per 100 older blue collar workers employed in the United States and 19 per 100 in Britain.

On the other hand, Denmark has an exceptional position. Even though the "loss of work" caused by decrease in number of working hours (in proportion to the normal 45 hour week) is relatively greater than in the United States, Denmark has, measured in normal working weeks per 100 fully employed blue collar workers, a higher rate of employment of 60 per cent $\left(\frac{29}{18} \times 100\right)$ in proportion to the United States and 53 per cent $\left(\frac{29}{19} \times 100\right)$ in proportion to Great Britain. The main part of this, however, is attributable to the higher pension age in Denmark. Thus the stated higher rate of employment percentage in Denmark would be reduced to 22 per cent $\left(\frac{22}{18} \times 100\right)$ in proportion to the United States, and 15 per cent $\left(\frac{22}{19} \times 100\right)$ in proportion to Great Britain, if the Danish pension age were 65 years. American blue collar workers seem to be at the lower end and Danish blue collar workers at the upper end with regard to the total reduction in work (owing to complete discontinuance on the one hand, and reduced working hours for the remainder) setting in after the age at which one is entitled to a public pension. It should be added that the difference between the United States and Denmark is probably less than this calculation shows. As has been mentioned, the calculation is based on a comparison between those over 65 years of age who are actually employed, and a full-time employed younger age group. Since employment among, say, 40–50-year-olds in the United States is lower than in Denmark, the level from which to reduce the employment of the elderly is in fact lower in the United States than in Denmark. When this is remembered (it cannot be demonstrated in precise figures owing to the lack of labor market statistics in Denmark), the main part of the Danish higher rate of employment among blue collar workers is once more explainable by correction for the different pension ages.

Calculations along similar lines for white collar workers show that 100 employed white collar workers accomplish a working week of 3,453 hours in the United States, 3,246 hours in Great Britain, and 3,860 hours in Denmark.

If one takes the point of view that white collar workers to a certain extent have adjusted their working hours to the standard set by the

Table X–18: PER CENT OF WHITE COLLAR WORKERS WORKING GIVEN HOURS, AND TOTAL HOURS WORKED BY 100 WHITE COLLAR WORKERS

Average Hours per Week	DENMARK		BRITAIN		UNITED STATES	
	Percentage Distribution of Workers	Total Hours	Percentage Distribution of Workers	Total Hours	Percentage Distribution of Workers	Total Hours
50 hours	50	2,650	21	1,050	28	1,400
42 hours	7	294	24	1,008	24	1,008
37 hours	8	296	10	370	7	259
32 hours	3	96	8	256	4	128
22 hours	17	374	16	352	24	528
10 hours	15	150	21	210	13	130
Total	100	3,860	100	3,246	100	3,453
N=	130		66		101	

normal week for blue collar workers, one finds that in the United States white collar workers over 65 years of age accomplish a working week of 86 per cent of the normal week; in Great Britain they accomplish 74 per cent; and in Denmark, 86 per cent. If labor force participation rates for white collar workers are reduced by these percentages for a cut-down working week, one finds that white collar workers, in terms of the work that would be accomplished by a full-time employed younger age group, accomplish 37 per cent in the United States, 20 per cent in Britain, and 36 per cent in Denmark.

There is no point in making a calculation for white collar workers that would show the importance of the higher pension age in Denmark. As already mentioned, the white collar group includes many self-employed who may feel independent of the normal current pension age.

The following working hour calculation for farm owners, which omits the few British farmers, seems to confirm what has previously been said

Table X-19: PER CENT OF FARM OWNERS WORKING GIVEN HOURS, AND TOTAL HOURS WORKED BY 100 FARM OWNERS

Average Hours per Week	DENMARK		UNITED STATES	
	Percentage Distribution of Workers	Total Hours	Percentage Distribution of Workers	Total Hours
50 hours	72	3,888	50	2,700
42 hours	10	420	11	462
37 hours	6	222	5	185
32 hours	2	64	4	128
22 hours	9	198	13	286
10 hours	1	10	17	170
Total	100	4,802	100	3,931
N=	83		54	

about farming in Denmark and in the United States. The Danish farmers certainly work longer hours than their American counterparts, whether because of economic necessity or because there is no place for the marginal farm—in the American sense—in Denmark.

Reasons for Retirement

We have analyzed work and retirement among older men by studying labor force participation by age groups, by occupational groups, by the married and unmarried, and we have extended this analysis by calculating how extensive the work of the elderly is, as measured by their number of actual working hours. The conclusions drawn from these analyses were that national differences in labor force participation as a whole could probably be explained by differences in pension ages, self-employment, occupational grouping, et cetera, rather than by differences in the social value systems. Labor force participation, of course, is closely related to the question "Why do men stop work?" There is good reason for extending the study of work and retirement by taking a look at the reasons for retirement given by the retired men in our three samples. The setting of the problem will naturally be the following: do reasons for retirement within the same age groups and social groups differ from country to country? If they do, this may indicate national differences in men's attitudes towards continuing to work. If the reasons do not vary, this may indicate—in line with the previous conclusions—that institutional frames and economic and social structures are more important for patterns of retirement than social value systems. (A further detailed analysis of the reasons for retirement appears in Chapter 11, where a distinction is made between reasons for retirement among long- and short-term retirees.)

There are a series of obstacles to making relevant comparisons between reasons for retirement in different countries. Even inside a single country it may be difficult to study in detail the part played by different reasons for retirement. Very often when a person decides to retire, a whole complex of factors is at work at the same time. Even if at the time of the interview a person can state more than one reason—as he actually could in this survey—he will often give only that reason that seems the most obvious to him. If a person is forced to retire—that is, if there is a compulsory retirement age—he will often go on working in spite of declining health until he reaches this age limit. Then, he will probably give compulsory retirement as his reason for retirement, whereas a self-employed man with the same state of health may retire one year earlier, and give bad health as his reason.

The stated reason or reasons may well include attempts at justification. Such justification is likely to vary from one social class to the other, because the choice of motivation is clearly affected by different sets of social values. If it is considered immoral not to work, "health" is likely to be the reason given for retirement. If, on the other hand, it is considered mean to work, the reason given will more likely be "could afford to retire." Furthermore, since the answers concern the reason for an act that lies years—and for the oldest men, often many years—back in life, they no doubt include rationalizations after the fact. These rationalizations may be influenced both by the personal development of the individual and by any social developments in his own country since he stopped working.

Along with the difficulties in attaching the proper importance to each of the various reasons for retirement inside one country, there are a series of other difficulties when one wants to make comparisons from country to country. For example, differences in social values among various social classes will make themselves felt in different strengths according to the social composition in each of the three countries. Along with class differences there may be national differences in the reasons for retirement, so that people consider some reasons more morally acceptable than others.

The nature of the after-rationalization may well be influenced by a difference in the social development in each country. Differences in institutional conditions may influence the reasons stated, so that where a health test is needed to obtain a pension, bad health becomes a more predominant reason.

Finally, a difference in the organization of the present material complicates comparisons. As mentioned earlier, the respondent could state more than one reason for retirement. In Great Britain the number of answers have been summed and there has been no accounting for multiple reasons for retirement by the individual person. In the United States and in Denmark, the number of persons have been summed. The three tables (Tables X–20, X–21, and X–22) where the British answers and the American and Danish individuals are distributed in percentages according to the reason for retirement, must therefore be read with certain reservations. In Great Britain, 38 per cent of the stated reasons for retirement are "bad health." In the United States 22 per cent of the retired gave up work solely on account of "bad health," and another 25 per cent gave up working owing to "bad health" combined with other reasons. Undoubtedly, some Englishmen also retired owing to a combination of bad health and other reasons. Therefore, the following general instruction is given in interpreting the comparisons of the tables: If a reason is less frequent in Great Britain than in the other two countries, then this reason for retirement is even less important in Great Britain as compared to the other two countries than the figures directly show. Conversely, a reason has to be much more predominant in Great Britain than in the two other countries before one can conclude that it is actually more important in Great Britain than in either the United States or Denmark.

Table X–20 shows all retired men in the sample distributed according to their reason for retirement. "Bad health" and "work too tiring" seem to play a remarkably greater part in reasons for retirement in Denmark than in either Great Britain or the United States. Conversely, compulsory retirement, compulsory age limits, closing up of jobs, et cetera, seem to play more important parts in both Great Britain and the United States than in Denmark.

In interpreting the Danish material, it is probable that many interviewed persons stated that they retired for "bad health" only, in instances where other reasons were perhaps important. This may be deduced from the fact that a notable share of those who retired owing to bad health were automatically entitled to public old age pension and so could have stated "could afford to retire" or, alternatively, "reached pension age."

Thus, there is some reason to compare the influence of health on retirement in our three countries on a basis of putting together all those answers that include health in some way or other. Put together this way, for a population of survivors who are recalling their health at some past period, the British appear least likely and the Danes most likely to have retired because of bad health. To some extent this result is in accordance with the finding that men in Denmark are more incapacitated than men in either Britain or the United States as measured by their present ability

to function. (See Chapter 2. Present state of health versus bad health as a reason for retirement is further discussed in Chapter 11.) The reports of bad health, however, undoubtedly also reflect institutional conditions. The high pension age in Denmark means that pensions from former places of work up to the ages of 67–70 years are only available when retirement is due to failing health. The old age pension can first be claimed in the 68th year. (Some in the sample, however, were able to claim it in their 66th and 67th years—as the pension age limits were gradually changed in the

Table X–20: RETIRED MEN, AGED 65 AND OVER, BY REASONS FOR RETIREMENT[a] *(Percentage Distribution)*

Reasons for Retirement	DENMARK	BRITAIN	UNITED STATES
Bad health as only reason	42	38	22
Bad health combined with other reasons	7	—	25
Work too tiring, felt too old	12	6	3
Health, work too tiring, etc.	61	44	50
Compulsory retirement	17	26	24
Firm closed/job ended	—	6	5
Forced to retire	17	32	29
Could afford to retire, no need to work,	14[c]	11	19[b]
did not want to work	2	5	2
Family reasons (needed at home)	6[c]	7	—
Other reasons			
Total	100	100	100

[a] For Great Britain, number of answers. A slightly **different** percentage distribution, based only on those eligible to answer this question **and** excluding non-respondents, appears in Chapter 11.

[b] Excluding 5 cases, "with poor health and could afford to retire."

[c] Excluding those who had "reached public pension age."

year preceding the interview.) The access to invalid pensions (available by permanent reduction of ability to work) is probably easier in Denmark than in the two other countries. The economic consequences of these two factors are that the possibility of retiring in Denmark before the 68th year is dependent either upon one's being in poor health, or upon one's having private means.

Of course, there is a close connection between the rather high proportion of American and British retired men who have been forced to retire, owing to compulsory age limits, closing up of firms and jobs, and so forth, and the corresponding lesser proportion who have retired because of bad health. Failing health may lie behind many retirements caused by "job ended." And many men who stop working because they reach a compulsory age limit would probably have stopped at nearly the same time on account of failing health, although this information is not known to us. The fact that compulsory retirement is less usual in Denmark than in either the United States or Great Britain is partly explained by the fact that the compulsory age limits are rather high (70 years of age, among civil servants) and partly by the high proportion of the Danish sample belonging to the farm group. Further, job-termination was not tabulated separately among the reasons given for retirement in Denmark. The justification for this is that very few retirees said that they had retired because their job ended. This is due to the fact that the period during which one may draw unemployment benefits is a long one. If it is interrupted by shorter periods of employment, it can be drawn out over a period of many years. In order to claim unemployment benefits the recipient must be searching for work. Often he will remain in this position until he reaches the age for old age pension or, if his health is poor, until he can receive an invalid pension. *De facto* job-termination will therefore in Denmark most often give rise to retirement motivated by "bad health," "work too tiring," et cetera.

Finally it may be noted that retirement motivated by "could afford to retire," "did not want or need to work," et cetera, is relatively more frequent in the United States than in Great Britain or in Denmark. In Denmark, 8 per cent, those who reached the age limit for drawing public pension and by this could afford to retire, are classed in this category. For the United States and Great Britain we do not know why people thought they could afford to retire. In the United States, some 25 per cent in all mentioned "could afford to" as a reason, against 14 per cent in Denmark and about 15 per cent in Britain. These differences probably reflect the fact that there are more asset holders in the United States than in Denmark or Britain who have incomes from assets large enough to exist upon.

A provisional summing up thus indicates that, compared to the two other countries, the United States has a remarkably high percentage of people who retire because in some way or other they were capable of living on their own resources, that "bad health" plays a greater part in retirement in Denmark than in the other two countries, and that compulsory retirement is more common in the United States and Great Britain than in Denmark. These differences, on the whole, are explainable by differences in the economic and institutional structure of the three countries—for example, there is a somewhat higher rate of unemployment in the United States and Great Britain than in Denmark, there are many asset holders in the United States with assets big enough to exist on, and to these factors may be added a tendency to a higher level of incapacity among Danish than among British and American men. From this population of survivors it does not seem possible to trace important national differences in choice of reasons for retirement among the citizens of the three countries. If the rate of employment is raised in the United States, if the Danish farm owner's share of employment goes down, and if pension ages become more similar in the three countries, future cohorts of retirees may distribute themselves in a more similar fashion in the three countries. Since this conclusion is drawn from summary material, perhaps a closer analysis of these data will be appropriate.

In Table X–21 all retired men within the three samples are distributed according to their reasons for retirement and the age at which they stopped working. Bearing in mind that our respondents represent survivors, the figures show that reasons for retirement vary with the age at which men retired.

The great majority of men in all three countries who stopped working before reaching the 66th year did so owing to a reason that in one way or another implies "bad health." This simply serves to underline that the standard in all three countries is that a healthy man goes on working until about 65 years of age. For those retiring in the age group 65–69 years,

Table X–21: RETIRED MEN, AGED 65 AND OVER, BY AGE AT RETIREMENT AND BY REASONS FOR RETIREMENT[a] (*Percentage Distribution*)

Reasons for Retirement	DENMARK			BRITAIN			UNITED STATES		
	Under 65 Years	65–69 Years	70 Years and Over	Under 65 Years	65–69 Years	70 Years and Over	Under 65 Years	65–69 Years	70 Years and Over
Bad health as only reason	62	33	35	55	31	40	39	14	19
Bad health combined with other reasons	6	10	5	—	—	—	24	20	32
Work too tiring, felt too old	8	8	21	1	7	9	2	2	5
Health, work too tiring, etc.	76	51	61	56	38	49	65	36	56
Compulsory retirement	9	22	16	14	36	10	12	35	17
	—	—	—	6	7	6	6	5	4
Firm closed/job ended Forced to retire	9	22	16	20	43	16	18	40	21
Could afford to retire, no need to work, did not want to work	7[c] [4][d]	18[c] [5][d]	14[c] [7][d]	9	9	19	14[b]	22[b]	18[b]
Family reasons (needed at home)	1	3	1	6	5	4	3	2	3
Other reasons	7	6	6	8	5	11	—	—	1
Total	100	100	100	100	100	100	100	100	100
N=	204	291	211	159	438	175	192	346	193

[a] See footnote *a*, Table X–20.

[b] Excluding 5 cases, "with poor health *and* could afford to."

[c] Including "reached public pension age."

[d] Excluding "reached public pension age."

however, "bad health" is far less frequent among the reasons for retirement. This again is due to the fact that in all three countries the main part of the normal pension age limits (both the age entitling a person to public pension and the age for compulsory retirement) is found within this age group. The only important exception is that in Denmark compulsory retirement for civil servants is at the age of 70 years, but a Danish civil servant in poor health may draw a full pension from his 68th year. For this reason, and because the age entitling people to public pension is 67 years in Denmark against 65 years in the United States, the decrease of the importance of "bad health" in reasons for retirement for those who retired before the age 65 compared to those who retired between the ages of 65 to 69 is less marked in Denmark than in the United States. In other words, as pension ages are high in Denmark, "bad health" remains a predominant reason for retiring for some time after the age of 65. In all three countries "bad health" again becomes an important reason for retirement when one considers the group that did not stop working until after the age of 70. Probably the main part of this group were self-employed men who are independent of compulsory retirement and who will often go on working till declining health forces them to stop. In this connection it may be pointed out that the importance of retirement owing to the fact that work is felt to be tiring and the person feels to old to work increases in all three countries among those who stopped working after the 70th year as compared to those who stopped before this age.

In all three countries compulsory retirement means most to the person who stopped working in the age group 65–69 years. In Great Britain there are considerably more who could afford to retire among those who stopped working after the 70th year than among those who stopped working earlier. The same is true for Denmark (at a lower level), if one omits those who could afford to retire because they reached the public pension age. In the United States retirement because a man "could afford to" already plays a great part among those who stopped working before the 65th year. Unfortunately, we do not know for either the United States or Britain how many men in the age group 65–69 years who said they could afford to retire, were really able to do so only because they were now receiving public pensions.

Table X–22 shows the reasons for retirement reported by retired persons according to their social class at the time of retirement. The figures serve to illustrate the part played by these occupational groupings in the reciprocal importance of the reasons for retirement from country to country—that is, the greater proportion who "could afford to retire" in the United States than in the other two countries, the remarkably great proportion who retired owing to "bad health" in Denmark, and the rather modest proportion who retired owing to "compulsory retirement" in Denmark.

In each of the occupational groups, except the service category, a relatively high proportion of Americans said they retired because "they could afford to." However, this reason for retirement is most likely to be given by persons of white collar background. In all of the occupational

Table X-22: RETIRED MEN, AGED 65 AND OVER, BY OCCUPATIONAL GROUPS AND BY REASONS FOR RETIREMENT[a]
(Percentage Distribution)

Reasons for Retirement	DENMARK				BRITAIN				UNITED STATES			
	Blue Collar Worker	White Collar Worker	Service Worker	Agricultural Worker	Blue Collar Worker	White Collar Worker	Service Worker	Agricultural Worker	Blue Collar Worker	White Collar Worker	Service Worker	Agricultural Worker
Bad health as only reason	40	41	[21]	49	36	35	42	[60]	19	18	22	35
Bad health combined with other reasons	8	5	[16]	7	—	—	—	—	25	21	22	33
Work too tiring, felt too old	6	12	—	24	6	5	7	[12]	1	1	6	7
Health, work too tiring, etc.	54	58	[37]	80	42	40	49	[72]	45	40	50	75
Compulsory retirement	21	22	[37]	1	27	27	28	[7]	31	21	36	1
Firm closed/job ended	—	—	—	—	7	7	5	[2]	7	4	5	2
Forced to retire	21	22	[37]	1	34	34	33	[9]	38	25	41	3
Could afford to retire, no need to work, did not want to work	17[f] [5][g]	11[f] [8][g]	[21][f] [16][g]	12 [6][g]	11	13	10	[12]	16[b]	31[c]	8[d]	18[e]
Family reasons (needed at home)	2	2	—	2	6	6	4	—	1	4	1	3
Other reasons	6	7	[5]	5	7	7	4	[7]	—	—	—	1
Total	100	100	[100]	100	100	100	100	[100]	100	100	100	100
N=	280	222	19	179	456ª	200ª	72ª	42ª	360	171	73	124

a See footnote a, Table X–20.
b Excluding 5 "poor health and could afford to."
c Excluding 6 "poor health and could afford to."
d Excluding 2 "poor health and could afford to."
e Excluding 8 "poor health and could afford to."
f Including "reached public pension age."
g Excluding "reached public pension age."

groups in Denmark, "poor health" is a major reason for retirement. However, this reason is most often given by persons with agricultural backgrounds. Finally, "compulsory retirement" is mentioned more often by both Americans and British than by Danes in each occupational group (excluding the small service group).

The main cross-national differences in reasons for retirement, therefore, also appear when these retirement reasons are analyzed within the different occupational groups.

This may be seen very clearly when the retirement patterns of blue collar workers are analyzed. Danish blue collar workers—to a higher extent than American and British workers—retire owing to bad health, and to a lesser extent they are forced out of work owing to compulsory retirement. For the white collar group, the same cross-national differences are not quite so pronounced. Primarily this is due to the fact that such an extremely great proportion of American white collar workers give as a reason for their retirement the fact that they can afford to stop working. They can afford to, perhaps, because of the larger asset holdings among American white collar workers (a result, in part, of the fact that a larger number of American than of the British and especially the Danish white collar workers are self-employed). Compulsory retirement, which is applicable only to employees, is consequently less frequent among white collar workers in the United States than might be expected.

Finally, with regard to agriculture, it is a general feature of all three countries that persons employed in agriculture are more inclined than other workers to remain active until illness forces them out of work. Therefore, in all three countries it is among agricultural workers that "work too tiring, feeling too old," et cetera, is the most frequent reason for retirement.

If one ignores the fact that in the United States there are relatively more in the agricultural group who retired because they could afford to do so, there is a very striking resemblance in the distribution of retired farmers according to their reasons for retirement in the three countries. In spite of the difference in pension ages, in spite of different agricultural structures, and in spite of the great differences in the importance of agriculture to the general economy, there are no essential differences in the general farmers' desire to go on working in old age in the three countries. In other words, in all three countries about three-fourths of the older agricultural group, as compared to considerably lower proportions of the other groups, said that they continued to work until they could no longer do so. Apparently the attachment to agriculture seems to be more decisive for the way one withdraws from work than the attachment to a particular nation or culture.

A further examination of the reasons for retirement by individual age groups and by blue and white collar workers has not revealed other cross-national differences than those explainable by differences in pension ages, trade structure, perhaps size of asset holdings, and perhaps a somewhat higher level of incapacity in Denmark than in the two other countries. It is not possible to trace any important national differences in the choice of reasons for retirement among the citizens of the three countries and thus in their attitudes towards work in old age. The differences actually found seem to depend mostly on national differences in economic and institutional structure.

The conclusion of this chapter thus is that the cross-national differences both in labor force participation and in the reasons for retirement are the result of differences in the institutional frames and the economic and social structure of our three countries rather than of differences in the citizens' attitudes. However, logically, this main conclusion must be understood with the following reservation: the institutional frames we have created independently of each other may very well reflect differences in national attitudes and social value systems.

NOTES

1 Some of the calculations in this chapter have been made by cand. oecon Ole Asmussen in connection with his analysis of old people's retirement in Denmark. This analysis has been published in the series of The Danish National Institute of Social Research. *De aeldre aldersklasser II. Arbejdalivet* (Copenhagen: DNISR).

2 The grouping used distinguished between white collar workers, blue collar workers, farm owners and farm laborers, and service and household workers. White collar workers comprise: managers and proprietors who do not work in farming, clerical workers, sales workers, and professionals and technicians. Blue collar workers comprise: craftsmen, foremen, operatives, and laborers, who do not work in farming. Service workers include private household workers and other service persons.

3 As the number of farmers in Great Britain is very small, no comparisons are made between that country and the two other countries at this point.

4 Again, because of the very small number of cases British farmers are not included in these comparisons.

11 : *The Meaning of Work*

Work has meaning for the worker apart from its purely economic function. A job gives structure to the worker's day: the demands of his work determine the time a man rises in the morning and when he goes to bed at night. Work fills the day: the man who is working is unlikely to be concerned each day with how to dispose of leisure time. Work provides the worker with associates: few persons work in complete isolation. "Once work is organized," says an astute observer, "it is social."[1] For many persons work is the source of their sense of self-worth. Men in particular, in Western societies, find the role of the worker central to their self-conceptions. Those young and middle-aged who do not work are seen as "playboys"—persons adult in years but childish in that they lack occupation. The job determines who a man is and how a man feels.[2]

A man is never as aware of his work and its meaning to him as at that time when he anticipates retirement. Persons normally reticent may become quite volatile when they speak of their work. Such a preoccupation with work is illustrated in interviews with a 69-year-old man in the eastern United States and a 77-year-old man in Denmark.

Mr. Sterling, the American respondent, is married. He and his wife have four married children. All of their children but one live within ten minutes distance of the Sterlings.

The interviewer made three calls before she found Mr. Sterling at home. He was always "at work," since his hours of work are irregular. Mr. Sterling is a self-employed wholesale merchant. He has been in the "leather business" for fifty-three years. When the interviewer asked Mr. Sterling when he expected to stop working, Mr. Sterling said: "I hope I never have to stop." When Mr. Sterling was asked whether he would enjoy anything about retirement he replied: "I have no hobbies, although I like to fish sometimes. I'd still like to work. That's the only enjoyment I know." Mr. Sterling felt that if he ever should retire from work he would miss most "the feeling of being useful."

After the interview was over, the interviewer wrote: "Mr. Sterling enjoyed this interview so much he was sorry to see it end, because there was so much more he could tell me, about his early life, his start in business. . . ."

Mr. Hansen, the Danish respondent, is also married. He too, like Mr. Sterling, has four children. Mr. Hansen owns a factory. Two years ago he turned over the active direction of his factory to his son. Yet he continues to go to work each day because, as he told the interviewer, he would find it "terrible" not to go to the factory each morning.

As these brief descriptions of Mr. Sterling and Mr. Hansen illustrate, retirement from work means more for many men than adjusting to a different level of income. The man who retires must adapt a new way of behavior and often a new way of viewing himself. Since he is no longer a "worker"—an active person with a defined place in society—the retired man often begins to think of himself as useless, as "only an old man."

There is considerable evidence from American studies that men with different sorts of jobs find different meanings in their work. These reports state that professional and white collar workers tend to be greatly involved with their work and to find it a source of psychic satisfaction. Workers at the lower economic and skill levels, however, are more likely to see their work primarily as a source of income.[3] These findings, although limited to a single country, suggest an important series of questions for our analysis. Do men of the same occupational-class backgrounds, irrespective of country, share common attitudes towards work and towards retirement? Or are there country-by-country differences in the meaning of work for the worker? That is, do men view work and retirement differently in Denmark, Britain, and the United States? Based on the studies previously reported, we would hypothesize that older men who have comparable work and social backgrounds, irrespective of country, will have similar attitudes towards retirement or towards continuing in work.

To explore this hypothesis fully, several lines of analyses are necessary. We shall first summarize briefly the characteristics of older retired men and of older working men in the three countries to see whether from country to country there are marked differences in the background and occupational composition of those in the work force and of those retired. If such marked differences exist between the countries they may be expected to affect over-all attitudes towards work and retirement. We shall then describe retired men in greater detail and report on the satisfactions and dissatisfactions that they find in retirement and on their desire for further work. Following this discussion of the retired, we will consider older men who are still working, and for each country we will analyze the anticipations these men have about retirement. Then, we shall reconsider our original question: do similar work backgrounds in Denmark, Britain, and the United States have similar effects on the attitudes of older men towards retirement and work?

Older Men: The Retired and the Working

In each of the countries studied, Denmark, Britain, and the United States, the majority of men over 65 years of age are no longer at work or seeking work. The numbers of men still in the labor force, however, are substantial. Men over 65 in the labor force range from 4 of every 10 in Denmark

(38 per cent) to 3 of every 10 in Britain (28 per cent). (A detailed discussion of the nature of the older labor force in the three countries is given in Chapter 10, *supra*.)

Age-specific labor force rates for older men follow the same patterns in the three countries: men aged 65–70 are most likely of all older men to be working; men over 75 are the least likely to be working. Occupation-specific labor force rates, however, differ between Denmark and the United States on the one hand and Britain on the other. In the first two countries older men of blue collar background have the least chance of being employed. In Britain, however, the chances of employment for the older man of blue collar background are about the same as those for the older white collar and agricultural worker.[4]

The occupational composition of both the older work force and of the group of retired men varies from country to country. In Britain both the older work force and the retired are predominantly blue collar in origin. In Denmark and in the United States, the older work force is more equally divided among white collar, blue collar, and agricultural workers. Although the older work force is similar in these two countries, the occupational background of retired men in these countries differs. In the United States, a majority of the retired are former blue collar workers, while in Denmark retired blue collar, white collar, and agricultural workers are found in almost equal proportions.

The level of retirement income, as well as occupational background, may be expected to play a major role in affecting men's attitudes towards retirement. Men with higher incomes may have different attitudes towards their retirement than men with less adequate incomes. Income from employment is more important in Britain than in either Denmark or the United States in maintaining the level of income of older men. (A discussion of income levels in old age is given in Chapters 12 and 13, *infra*.) The man who continues to work in Britain is more likely than his counterpart in either Denmark or in the United States to have an income level that is above the middle income for men of his age. The economic situation of retired men in the three countries, however, is markedly similar. In each country, most retired men are found among the poorest in the elderly population.

These summary comparisons of older men who are working and older men who are retired in the three countries point up certain similarities and differences both in the work force and among the retired that may well affect the satisfactions and dissatisfactions men report in work and retirement. The main similarities found in the three countries are demographic: men who are working are younger and more likely to be married than retired men. A further finding in all three countries: while employment is the major way men maintain income levels in old age, work is especially important in Britain in maintaining levels of income. The major differences found in the three countries are in the occupational make-up of the older work force and of the group in retirement. In Britain, the largest group both in the older work force and among the retired are blue collar workers. In the United States, white collar workers are the largest group among those working, while blue collar workers are the largest group among the retired. In Denmark, white collar workers are the largest group among those working; blue collar workers, however, comprise less than half of all retired men.

The Satisfactions and Dissatisfactions of Retirement

It is generally assumed that older retired men will differ in their attitudes from older working men. It is also often assumed that all retired men are alike in their wants and desires. Retired men are not, however, a homogeneous entity. The retired include the younger and the older aged; those in good health and those in poor health; those who have been retired for a short time and those retired for longer periods. Further, as we have already indicated, retired men have various occupational backgrounds—white collar, blue collar, and agricultural.

Retirement in and of itself does not create a common bond among men. To some men retirement brings satisfactions; to others, retirement means unhappiness and distress.

Mr. Wilkins in the United States and Mr. Anderson in Denmark are each satisfied in his retirement. Mr. Wilkins is a 70-year-old married man. He and his wife live in Florida. They have three married children "back home in Chicago." Mr. Wilkins was a railroad worker who retired voluntarily when he reached the age of 62. Mr. Wilkins told the interviewer: "I did not have to retire, but my health wasn't too good and I could afford to retire." Mr. Wilkins misses the money he received when he was working, but he says: "We still continue with old friends from work through the railroad club." Mr. Wilkins enjoys not working. He describes his satisfaction in retirement as, "The old rocking chair and a book. . . . Now we do a little traveling when we couldn't before."

Mr. Anderson is a 67-year-old former factory worker. Like Mr. Wilkins he, too, is married with two adult children. Mr. Anderson left his job in a brewery when he was 65. He could have continued to work until he was 70 but his health bothered him a little. Mr. Anderson says his health has improved in retirement. He likes the freedom of not working, of not being obliged to turn up at the factory each day. Like Mr. Wilkins, Mr. Anderson keeps himself occupied in his retirement. He is an avid gardener.

To Mr. Corey, unlike Mr. Wilkins or Mr. Anderson, retirement means frustration.

Mr. Corey is an American, 71 years old. He and his wife live only a short distance from their two married sons and see them almost daily. Mr. Corey was a supervisor in a factory. He worked for 32 years at his job, and then, "I had to quit at 65. It's compulsory. I could have kept on—my work wasn't strenuous."

Mr. Corey enjoys nothing about his retirement. He says: "I'd sooner be working. The job I had I could still be doing if they'd leave me be. My job wasn't anything physical that you couldn't be doing it. It took me a long time to get used to not working." Mr. Corey misses many things about not working but "the fellows the most of anything—the association. The first year or two I was lost. Now I'm getting used to it."

Mr. Corey has been retired for six years. His "getting used to retirement" points up another major factor contributing to the heterogeneity of the retired. Men who are recently retired may hold very different attitudes from men who have been retired for long time periods. Recently retired men are more likely than men retired for longer time-periods to be undergoing a period of transition, a period when they are ceasing to think of themselves as workers and are beginning to think of themselves as retired.[5] If retired men in the three countries differ significantly in the number of years they have spent in retirement, this may well affect the satisfactions and dissatisfactions with retirement reported in the interviews.

LONG-TIME AND SHORT-TERM RETIREES

We shall now further describe the characteristics of retired men in the three countries. In this description of the retired we shall be seeking for background factors, other than occupation, which may affect attitudes in retirement. Therefore, in addition to the length of time these men have been retired, we shall consider how old they were when they stopped work,

Table XI-1: YEARS IN RETIREMENT, MEN AGED 65 AND OVER
(*Percentage Distribution*)

Number of Years in Retirement	DENMARK	BRITAIN	UNITED STATES
Less than 3 years	27	29	32
From 3 to 8 years	41	36	40
From 9 to 13 years	18	19	18
From 14 to 18 years	8	12	6
More than 18 years	6	3	4
Total	100	100	100
Average number of years in retirement	7.6	7.4	6.8
N=[a]	687	719	731

[a] The percentages of eligible respondents who answered this question are: Denmark, 97.3; Britain, 98.9; United States, 99.2.

and their degree of incapacity. In every instance we shall compare men in the three countries to see whether these background characteristics are similar or different from country to country.

In each of the three countries roughly the same proportion of retired men are recently retired—that is, retired less than 3 years. Among the total group of retired about 3 of every 10 are classified as recent retirees. Since some men have been retired for long periods, however, the average number of years men have been retired is 7.6 in Denmark, 7.4 in Britain, and 6.8 in the United States. Although the average number of years men

Table XI-2: AGE AT STOPPING WORK, MEN RETIRED FOR LONG AND SHORT PERIODS[a] (*Percentage Distribution*)

Age Stopped Working	Long-Term Retirees			Short-Term Retirees			All Retired Men		
	Denmark[b]	Britain	United States	Denmark[b]	Britain	United States	Denmark[b]	Britain	United States
60 years and under	19	14	12	1	—	—	14	10	8
61–64 years	18	13	21	8	8	12	15	11	18
65 years	13	30	21	9	34	25	12	31	22
66–69 years	26	25	24	44	31	27	31	26	25
70 years and over	25	19	22	38	26	35	28	21	26
Total	100	100	100	100	100	100	100	100	100
Average age	66.5	66.4	66.6	70.0	68.4	69.1	67.4	67.0	67.4
N=[c]	504	508	499	183	211	232	687	719	731

[a] Long-term retirees are defined as those who retired December 31, 1958, or before, and short-term retirees are those who retired January 1, 1959, or later.

[b] The Danish materials are for ages "61 and under" and "62–64 years." All other codes are identical.

[c] The percentages of eligible respondents who answered this question are: Denmark, 97.3; Britain, 98.9; United States, 99.2.

have been retired is similar in the three countries, both Denmark and Britain, compared to the United States, have a greater number of men who have been retired for 14 years or more.

How old were the men who are now retired when they stopped working? In all three countries, the average age at retirement of recent retirees clusters within the period of a year—70 years in Denmark, 68.4 years in Britain, and 69.1 years in the United States. Since the age at which men are entitled to pension benefits varies in the three countries—with Denmark having the highest pensionable age, 67—this similarity in average retirement age for recent retirees is somewhat unexpected. The average age at retirement of long-time retirees is also the same in all three countries, some time in the sixty-seventh year. This similarity in average retirement age for long-time retirees is undoubtedly accidental, since many men retired at the same time as our respondents have undoubtedly died.[6] An interesting phenomenon in all the countries, however, is the high proportion of men retired for more than three years who say they stopped working before reaching the age of 65. These early retirees make up 37 per cent of all long-time retirees in Denmark, 27 per cent in Great Britain, and 33 per cent in the United States.

Why did the men now in retirement retire? Furthermore, do the reasons given for retirement among either long- or short-term retirees vary greatly from country to country? In all three countries the majority of both long-term and short-term retirees say they retired voluntarily because they wanted to stop working. The majority of men who are now retired, then, claim that their retirement was by choice rather than a result of arbitrary work laws. The major reason for the retirement of recent retirees in all three countries is poor health. Sometimes, the respondent said directly that his health was too poor for him to continue working. At other times the respondent expressed this same feeling indirectly by attributing the reason for retirement to some characteristic of the job. Such men said they retired because the job was "too tiring" or "too exhausting." If the proportions of men who give either "poor health" or its indirect manifestation, "job too tiring," as their reason for retirement are combined, then 56 per cent of the short-term retirees among the Danes, 44 per cent among the British, and 41 per cent of the Americans say they retired for health reasons. About one-fourth of recent retirees in the United States say that they retired because they did not want to work any longer. When questioned further, most of these men did not refer to their health when explaining why they retired. Instead they said they thought they had adequate retirement incomes so that they could manage to get along without attempting to meet the demands of the job. Undoubtedly, some (but not all) of these men would have continued at work if their jobs were physically less demanding. If the men who said "I didn't want to work any more" are added to those who said that they retired for reasons of health, we find that 70 per cent of short-term retirees in Denmark, 59 per cent in Britain, and 66 per cent in the United States retired voluntarily either because of poor health or because they preferred leisure to work.

Men retired at least three years at the time they were interviewed were

Table XI-3: MEN RETIRED FOR LONG AND SHORT PERIODS, BY REASONS FOR RETIREMENT[a] (*Percentage Distribution*)

Reasons for Retirement	Long-Term Retirees			Short-Term Retirees			All Retired		
	Denmark	Britain	United States	Denmark	Britain	United States	Denmark	Britain	United States
Compulsory	21	33	33	21	39	31	21	35	33
Reached retirement age	21	26	28	21	33	27	21	28	28
Job eliminated[b]	—	7	5	—	6	4	—	7	5
Voluntary	78	77	66	78	70	69	79	75	67
Poor health[b]	45	42	45	45	39	38	45	41	43
Too tiring	12	7	3	11	5	3	12	7	3
Did not want to work any longer	14	15	16	14	15	25	14	15	19
Needed at home	1	6	2	3	3	3	2	5	2
Other	6	7	*	5	7	*	6	7	*
Total	100	c	100	100	c	100	100	c	100
N=	503	508	497	185	209	231	688	717	728

[a] See footnote a, Table XI-2.

[b] "Job eliminated" was not tabulated separately in Denmark; no differentiation between compulsory and voluntary retirement for "poor health" given in Britain.

[c] "Reasons for retirement" were multiply coded in Britain, so that the totals may add up to more than 100 per cent. Detailed information on non-respondents is not given in this or subsequent tables if 98 per cent or more of all eligible respondents have answered the question.

* Less than one per cent.

classified as long-time retirees. Many of these men had stopped work 10 years or more before they were interviewed. It is questionable whether in every instance these men could recall exactly the reasons why they had retired. Yet, from country to country there was general agreement among these long-time retired men. Poor health—or its variant, "the job was too tiring"—were said to be the major reasons for retirement. Fifty-seven per cent of the Danes, 49 per cent of the British, and 48 per cent of the Americans said that they had retired because of poor health or because the job was too tiring for them. If those men who said "I didn't want to work any more" are added to those who retired for reasons of health, 71 per cent of long-time retirees in Denmark, 64 per cent in Britain, and 64 per cent in the United States say that either health or their preference for leisure was the major reason for their retirement.

In each country, then, whether men have been retired for short or long periods the reasons they give for retirement are similar. Men say that they retire because their health makes it impossible or difficult for them to continue to work.[7] In comparing the three countries, there is some indication that the Danes are more likely than either the British or the Americans to say that they retired because of poor health. In part, this answer may reflect the organization of the Danish pension scheme. A Dane who retires because of poor health can receive full benefits on retirement even if he has not reached pensionable age. However, it may be that there is actually greater impairment among the Danes than among men in the other two countries in the years before retirement.

In this survey, our only objective measure of health is the index of incapacity computed for each respondent. When the countries are compared, each with the other, men in Denmark, whether retired for short or long periods, are more incapacitated than men in either Britain or

Table XI-4: MEN RETIRED FOR LONG AND SHORT PERIODS, BY LEVEL OF INCAPACITY[a] (*Percentage Distribution*)

Index Scores	Long-Term Retirees			Short-Term Retirees			All Retired		
	Denmark	Britain	United States	Denmark	Britain	United States	Denmark	Britain	United States
0	44	53	60	59	66	68	48	57	63
1–2	30	27	25	22	24	22	28	26	24
3–4	10	11	9	9	6	6	10	10	8
5 and over	15	9	6	10	4	5	14	7	6
Total	100	100	100	100	100	100	100	100	100
N=[b]	500	497	498	183	206	232	683	703	730

[a] See footnote *a*, Table XI–2.

[b] The percentages of eligible respondents who answered this question are: Denmark, 98.7; Britain, 96.7; United States, 99.2.

the United States. Therefore, it may be that more Danes than British or Americans really retired because their health was bad. Present health, however, has a direct relationship to the reasons men give for retirement. Men now in poor health are more likely than those now in good health to report poor health as having been the reason for their retirement. In other words, an alternative explanation for the greater proportion of Danes than of British or Americans who give poor health as a reason for retirement may be the present higher level of incapacity reported by the Danes.

In general, retired men in all three countries are functioning well as measured by the index of incapacity. About two-thirds of the short-term retirees in each country report no limitation whatsoever on their mobility. They can go outdoors without help and walk stairs without difficulty.

Table XI–5: PROPORTION OF RETIRED MEN, BY DEGREE OF INCAPACITY, WHO RETIRED BECAUSE OF POOR HEALTH[a]

Degree of Incapacity	DENMARK	BRITAIN	UNITED STATES
0	31	29	31
1–2	49	53	53
3 and over	71	68	77

[a] The total number of retired men with each incapacity score is: Denmark—0, 330; 1–2, 193; 3 and over, 160; Britain—0, 401; 1–2, 182; 3 and over, 120; United States—0, 455; 1–2, 173; 3 and over, 99. The percentages of eligible respondents who answered this question are: Denmark, 98.7; Britain, 96.3; United States, 98.6.

Although somewhat lesser proportions of long-term than of short-term retirees report no limitation on their capacities as measured by the index, these men too seem to be functioning fairly well. A basic question then becomes: Why should the incapacity levels of these men be so low when so many of these same men said that they gave up working because of poor health? There are several explanations for this apparent contradiction between the scores of retired men on the index of incapacity and their reasons for retirement. First, it should be stressed again that the index of incapacity measures function rather than pathology. In the answers to the questions that make up the index a man may say that he is able to go outdoors without help and that he is able to walk stairs. On the basis of the index of incapacity, this man is able to function—he is well. This same man, however, may have a heart condition which makes it impossible for him to work at his usual job. He may be unable to work outdoors if he is an outdoor worker, or unable to do heavy physical work if he is a laborer. He may therefore choose or have to retire for reasons of "health." His score on the index of incapacity and his reason for retirement would apparently contradict one another; yet his answers to the questions on both capacity and retirement would be essentially honest ones. Thompson and Streib in their study of retirement offer a clear explanation of this apparent contradiction: ". . . the *same state of health* for the worker might be incapacitating while for the retiree realization of goals is affected not at all. . . ."[8]

A second factor to be considered in reconciling reasons given for retirement and reports of functioning is that both subjective evaluations of health status as well as objective health may improve in retirement. In the Thompson and Streib study referred to above, the subjects were interviewed and had physical examinations both before and after retirement. The findings caused Thompson and Streib to relate retirement and health in the following manner: "If any general effect at all can be discerned, it is that retirement leads to an *improvement* in health."[9] It may be that some among our respondents who retired for reasons of health may have had improvements in their health during retirement. For these men, their physical capacities indeed may be greater now than at the time they retired.

Our survey, unlike that of Thompson and Streib, is cross-sectional not longitudinal. Our respondents are being studied only at a single point in time. Therefore, we are unable to say whether the health of our respondents improved during their retirement. We can say, however, that although most retired men named poor health as the major reason for their retirement, most men who are retired function quite well as measured by a scale of incapacity.

Our detailed analysis of the characteristics of retired men in the three countries indicates that in each country roughly the same proportion of retired men are recent retirees. Both short-term and long-term retirees give poor health as the major reason for their retirement. Short-term retirees, however, are less incapacitated than long-time retirees. But there is a difference in the level of incapacity of retired men in the three countries: the Danes, whether retired for short or long periods, are more incapacitated than either the British or the Americans.

ATTITUDES IN RETIREMENT

Retired men in the three countries are similar in age, in marital status, in income level, in their average number of years in retirement, and in the reasons why they retired. Retired men in the three countries differ in only two characteristics: past occupation and—for Denmark, compared with Britain and the United States—reported incapacity. Our analysis of what men in the three countries both enjoy and miss in retirement therefore must give separate consideration to men in specific occupational groups, and, wherever feasible, to men at different levels of incapacity. It is only through controlling these factors that we can determine whether retired men in the three countries have similar attitudes in retirement.

What do men say they enjoy in retirement? The answers to this question can be divided into three main categories: nothing, rest, and free time. In each of the countries some men mentioned specific leisure-time activities that they enjoyed. Such uses of leisure time are grouped into the

Table XI-6: THINGS ENJOYED IN RETIREMENT, MEN AGED 65 AND OVER, BY SOCIAL CLASS (*Percentage Distribution*)

Things Enjoyed in Retirement	White Collar			Working Class—Blue Collar and Service Workers			Agricultural Workers			All Classes		
	Denmark	Britain	United States	Denmark	Britain	United States	Denmark	Britain	United States	Denmark	Britain	United States
Nothing	49	29	28	49	45	33	54	a	52	50	42	35
Rest	24	52	11	23	37	18	27	a	21	25	41	17
Free time	15	}19	29	15	}18	14	11	}a	2	14	}17	16
Other	12		32	12		35	8	a	24	11		32
Total	100	100	100	100	100	100	100		100	100	100	100
N=b	203	177	170	286	475	428	170	37	121	659	689	719

a Per cents are not computed when base is less than 50.

b The percentages of eligible respondents who answered this question are: Denmark, 93.3; Britain, 94.8; United States, 97.5.

category "other" in Denmark and the United States, and directly into the category "free time" in Britain.

We expected that men of the same occupational categories would enjoy the same things in retirement. Contrary to our expectations, however, there are marked differences between retired men in the three countries in the things they enjoy in retirement. To begin with, the Danes show no occupational differences in the sorts of things they say they enjoy in retirement. Half the Danes, whether they are white collar, working class, or agricultural workers, say there is nothing about their retirement that is enjoyable. About a quarter of the Danes, irrespective of occupation, say they enjoy "resting," and about a quarter enjoy free time and leisure. In Britain, unlike Denmark, there are class differences between white collar and working class men in their answers to the question "What sort of things do you enjoy about not working?" Five of every 10 working class men, compared to about 3 of every 10 white collar men, enjoy "nothing" about their retirement. Half of all white collar men, however, compared to about 4 of every 10 working class men, enjoy "resting." Equal proportions of white collar and working class men enjoy "free time." In Britain, apparently, white collar workers are more likely than blue collar workers to find something agreeable in their retirement.

It is in the United States, rather than in Denmark or Britain, that many men report that they enjoy retirement. Among all occupational groups in Denmark and for blue collar workers in Britain, a high proportion of men say they like "nothing" in retirement. In the United States, only among agricultural workers do as many as half of all men find "nothing" to enjoy in their retirement. Among white collar and working class men the proportion who say that they like nothing about retirement drops to about 3 in every 10. Americans do not stress "rest" as a feature of their retirement. On the contrary, 61 per cent of all retired white collar men in the United States, 49 per cent of all blue collar workers, and 26 per cent of all agricultural workers report that they enjoy "free time" and "leisure." The findings suggest that a new leisure class made up of retired men who enjoy being retired may be developing among the elderly in the United States. Similar findings are reported from another American survey of the aged. The analyst here commenting on the obvious pleasure which many men say they find in retirement says:

> There seem to be more and more men who are well enough to work and who might get some kind of job if they were interested, but they prefer the leisure of retirement.[10]

Our earlier hypothesis that retired men in the three countries with the same occupational background will enjoy the same things in retirement is not verified by the data. Half of the Danes, irrespective of occupational background, like "nothing" about retirement; in Britain the majority of blue collar workers like "nothing" about retirement, while white collar workers like "rest"; in the United States, although half of all agricultural workers like "nothing" about retirement, the majority of both white collar and blue collar workers enjoy "free time" and "leisure." Occupational class differences are apparently not as important as specific country-by-country attitudes in determining what men enjoy about their retirement.

Earlier in this volume we have stressed the important role of health as an explanation of the behavior and attitudes of older men. We may now raise another question: will men in the three countries with similar levels of incapacity report that they enjoy the same things in retirement? Our findings indicate that, irrespective of country, the greater the degree of incapacity reported by retired men, the more likely these men are to say that there is nothing they enjoy in retirement. Further, as might be expected, the greater the degree of their incapacity, the less likely these

Table XI-7: THINGS ENJOYED IN RETIREMENT, MEN AGED 65 AND OVER, CLASSIFIED BY INCAPACITY (*Percentage Distribution*)

Things Enjoyed in Retirement	Score 0			Score 1–2			Score 3 or More		
	Denmark	Britain	United States	Denmark	Britain	United States	Denmark	Britain	United States
Nothing	41	33	28	53	44	41	62	65	55
Rest	23	45	17	25	43	17	26	27	18
Free time	20	}22	19	12	}13	14	7	}8	5
Other	16		36	9		28	5		22
Total	100	100	100	100	100	100	100	100	100
N=a	318	394	454	178	173	169	140	115	101

[a] The percentages of eligible respondents who answered this question are: Denmark, 90.7; Britain, 93.8; United States, 98.2.

men are to say that they enjoy their free time in retirement. In light of these findings, one might anticipate that the greater the incapacity of retired men, the more they would report that they enjoy resting in retirement. The proportion of men in both Denmark and the United States who say they enjoy resting, however, remains virtually unchanged with rises in incapacity level, and, in Britain, declines as the level of incapacity rises. The findings clearly indicate that in every country retired men respond in much the same way to their limitations in capacity. The more an old man is physically limited, the more likely he is to find nothing in retirement that pleases him, and thus to report that neither free time nor the opportunity for rest have any value to him. It is not so much their occupational backgrounds that determine what men enjoy in retirement. Rather, it is their degree of capacity, their ability to get about, that influence their retirement attitudes.

Let us now consider those things about their work that men say they miss most in their retirement. Earlier we would have hypothesized that men in the same occupational class, irrespective of country, would report

Table XI–8: MAJOR ITEM MISSED IN RETIREMENT, MEN AGED 65 AND OVER, BY SOCIAL CLASS (*Percentage Distribution*)

Major Item Missed	White Collar			Working Class—Blue Collar and Service Workers			Agricultural Workers			All Classes		
	Denmark	Britain	United States	Denmark	Britain	United States	Denmark	Britain	United States	Denmark	Britain	United States
Nothing	53	62	13	46	54	8	45	b	7	48	56	9
People at work	10	7	26	9	12	16	5	b	3	8	10	16
Feeling useful	5	6	7	4	5	6	8	b	16	5	5	8
Things happening around one	4	a	4	7	a	2	2	b	5	5	a	3
Work itself	19	8	14	11	3	16	30	b	31	18	4	18
Money	9	16	35	22	26	51	7	b	37	14	24	45
Other	*	1	1	1	*	1	3	b	—	1	*	1
Total	100	100	100	100	100	100	100	b	100	100	100	100
N=c	214	186	167	278	489	408	170	38	115	662	713	690

a British data combine categories "nothing" and "no answer"; and "things happening around one" with "other."

b Per cents are not computed when base is less than 50.

c The percentages of eligible respondents who answered this question are: Denmark, 93.8; Britain, 98.1; United States, 93.6.

* Less than one per cent.

that they miss the same things about their work when they retire. The findings about the country-by-country differences in the things men say they enjoy about retirement make this hypothesis untenable. A more useful hypothesis may be that irrespective of social class there are marked country-by-country differences in what men say they miss in retirement. And, as a related hypothesis, men of similar levels of physical functioning irrespective of country will miss the same things in retirement.

In substantiation of our revised hypothesis there are country-by-country differences in what men say they miss most about their work. The British and the Danes, unlike the Americans, report that they miss "nothing" about their past work. Of those who do miss something about their past work, the Danes primarily say that they miss the work itself, the British that they miss "the money." In both Denmark and Britain blue collar workers, who are usually at the lower end of the income scale, are more likely than white collar workers to report that they miss "money." In contrast to the Europeans, only about one in every eleven retired Americans missed "nothing" about his work. Although half of all American blue collar workers say that they miss the money the job brought them, substantial numbers report they miss "the people at work" and "the work itself." Both white collar and agricultural workers in the United States are less likely than blue collar workers to say that they miss "money." White collar workers also missed "the people at work," and numbers of both white collar and agricultural workers also missed "the work itself."

Other American studies have reported class differences in the meaning of work for older men. These findings are validated by our American survey. In the United States men of differing occupational levels tend to miss different things about their jobs when they retire. In both Denmark and Britain, however, retired men tend to say that they miss nothing about their work.

Our comparative data may be interpreted in one of two ways: either Danes and Britons, unlike Americans, are reluctant to speak of the values work may have for them, or, alternatively, there is a country-by-country difference in what men miss about their work. Americans are usually described as gregarious. This description would seem to explain some of our findings. Americans, whether of white or blue collar backgrounds, regularly report that they miss the people on the job and the work itself. The data, however, raise other questions. Why are the Americans in each occupational group more likely than the Europeans of similar occupations to report that what they miss most in retirement is their past income? Actually the ratio of retirement income to work income is higher in the United States than it is in Britain, so that retired Americans are better off than the retired British. It may be that those Europeans who miss income from employment say that they miss "nothing," while Americans straight out say that they miss money. Or instead, it may be that the Americans, accustomed to a higher level of living than the Europeans, once their income is reduced feel their deprivations more keenly.

The revised hypothesis that there will be country-by-country differences in what men say they miss about their work is validated by the findings.

Table XI-9: MAJOR ITEM MISSED IN RETIREMENT, MEN AGED 65 AND OVER, BY LEVEL OF INCAPACITY
(Percentage Distribution)

Major Item Missed	Score 0			Score 1-2			Score 3 and Over		
	Denmark	Britain	United States	Denmark	Britain	United States	Denmark	Britain	United States
Nothing	57	61	11	42	51	6	38	44	2
People at work	7	9	17	8	12	16	11	15	16
Feeling of being useful	5	3	7	6	7	7	4	7	12
Things happening around one	4	a	3	5	a	2	6	a	6
Work itself	15	4	17	17	6	19	26	7	19
Money	11	23	44	20	24	50	12	25	45
Other	*	—	1	2	—	1	2	2	—
Total	100	100	100	100	100	100	100	100	100
N=b	319	401	436	185	182	163	157	120	96

a British data combine categories "nothing" and "no answer"; and "things happening around one" with "other."

b The percentages of eligible respondents who answered this question are: Denmark, 93.6; Britain, 96.7; United States, 94.4.

* Less than one per cent.

Let us now consider the second hypothesis: in the three countries men of the same level of physical functioning will miss the same things in retirement. For each country there is a correlation between the level of incapacity of the respondent and the likelihood that he will report that he does miss something about his job now that he is retired. As incapacity scores rise, the proportion of men who say they miss "nothing" in retirement declines. As incapacity scores rise, so do the proportions of retired men who say that what they miss most about their jobs are the people at work, the feeling of being useful, and the work itself. The more incapacitated the man, the more likely he is to be nostalgic for the world of work. We may recall that the more incapacitated men were also the least likely of all men to report that they enjoyed their retirement. Incapacity limits the activity of the old man. As he recalls his working career he remembers himself as physically well, as a worker, a useful member of society. He now sees himself as physically limited and sick. He tends then to miss those aspects of the job that are related to activity.

It has been shown previously that feelings of loneliness are related to incapacity scores. We may then hypothesize that in all three countries those retired men who report that they are lonely, like incapacitated men, will say that what they miss most in retirement are the people at work or the work itself. This hypothesis is validated by our findings. Retired men who say that they are often or occasionally lonely are more likely to miss something about their work than are retired men who say they are never

Table XI-10: MAJOR ITEM MISSED IN RETIREMENT, MEN AGED 65 AND OVER, CLASSIFIED BY FEELINGS OF LONELINESS (*Percentage Distribution*)

Major Item Missed	Often and Sometimes Lonely			Never Lonely		
	Denmark	Britain	United States	Denmark	Britain	United States
Nothing	32	44	5	55	60	11
People at work	15	19	16	6	8	18
Feeling of being useful	7	4	10	4	5	6
Things happening around one	7	a	3	4	a	3
Work itself	25	6	22	16	4	14
Money	13	26	43	14	23	47
Other	1	1	1	1	*	2
Total	100	100	100	100	100	100
N=b	178	176	301	483	547	385

a British data combine categories "nothing" and "no answers"; and "things happening around one" with "other."

b The percentages of eligible respondents who answered this question are: Denmark, 93.6; Britain, 99.4; United States, 93.1.

* Less than one per cent.

lonely. These lonely men miss the people at work and the work itself. Irrespective of country, lonely men miss the comradeship of their fellow workers.

Many retired men miss some aspect of their careers as workers. It is generally believed that most retired men want to continue at work or would return to work if a job was available to them. This does not seem to be the case. Only a minority of retired men want to work: 1 of every 10 in Denmark, 1 of every 5 in Britain, and 1 of every 4 in the United States. Who are the men who want to work? Are they the men who earlier reported that they missed their jobs? The findings show that although the more lonely and incapacitated men were the most likely of all men to say that they missed their work, reported loneliness has no effect on whether a man wants another job. Retired men who say they are never lonely are as likely as lonely men to say they want to work. In Denmark 10 per cent, in Britain 23 per cent, and in the United States 22 per cent of those who are never lonely, compared with 10, 20, and 23 per cent respectively of those who are often lonely, want a job.

What then of incapacity? Does degree of incapacity affect whether or not a man wants to work? The less incapacitated a man is, the more likely he is to want a job. While the most incapacitated men are most likely to miss their work, it is the least incapacitated men who actually want to work.

Another factor that affects the desire for a job is the length of time men have been retired. Men retired for shorter periods are more likely to want work than men retired for longer periods. In Denmark 14 per cent, in Britain 39 per cent, and in the United States 33 per cent of recent retirees, compared to 9, 15, and 19 per cent respectively of long-term retirees, want a job. The findings indicate that it is not necessarily the man who misses his job mates who wants to return to work. The man who wants to work is the recently retired man who feels physically able to hold a job; such men believe that there is no reason why they should not work. They have recently been workers. If their skills were marketable a few years ago, why are they redundant now?

The analysis of retired men in Denmark, Britain, and the United States shows that country-by-country differences in the meaning of work for retired men are more important than cross-country differences for various occupational groups. Most retired men in Denmark and Britain enjoy nothing about their retirement and miss nothing in particular about their past work. In the United States, however, retired men report that they enjoy the free time and the leisure of retirement. What they especially miss about not working is their past salary. It is almost as though the American respondents feel that if they had more money retirement would be a desirable state.

In each country men who are in poor health are less likely than men in good health to report that there is anything at all pleasant in retirement. Men in poor health are most likely to say that they are lonely and that they miss their past jobs and their work mates. The analysis of the men who want to return to work, however, indicates that retired men in all three

Table XI-11: DESIRE FOR WORK OF RETIRED MEN AGED 65 AND OVER, BY INCAPACITY (*Percentage Distribution*)

Desire for Work	Score 0			Score 1–2			Score 3 and Over		
	Denmark	Britain	United States	Denmark	Britain	United States	Denmark	Britain	United States
Want work	13	29	27	9	15	22	6	11	11
Do not want work	60	71	44	38	85	25	20	89	8
Health too poor	27	a	29	53	a	53	74	a	81
Total	100	100	100	100	100	100	100	100	100
N=b	332	401	460	192	183	173	159	120	102

a The British tabulations do not include the category "health too poor."

b The percentages of eligible respondents who answered this question are: Denmark, 98.3; Britain, 97.6; United States, 99.9.

countries apparently make a realistic assessment of their capacity for work. Men with no incapacity who are recently retired are the most likely of all men to say that they want to work. These men are younger than the long-time retirees. Many still retain their work skills. If jobs were available these men probably could still be adequate workers.

The Satisfactions of Work

Not all older men are retired. In each country a substantial number of men over 65 are still working or are seeking work. The proportion of men over 65 in the labor force is greatest in Denmark, 38 per cent, compared to 28 per cent in Britain and 32 per cent in the United States. In part, this country-by-country difference in the participation by older men in the labor force is the result of the different retirement ages in the three countries, the usual age of retirement being 67 in Denmark and 65 in Britain and in the United States.

Men over 65 who are working differ from men who are retired. The working men are younger than the retired men, they are more likely to be married, and they are more likely to be in good health. Seven of every 10 older employed men in Denmark, and 8 of every 10 in Britain and in the United States, report no incapacity whatever on the incapacity scale. These men may be presumed to be in good physical condition for their age.

Men who continue to work past the usual retirement age do so for a variety of reasons, not all of which are mutually exclusive. Some men work because their incomes are so low that any income-producing work is preferable to retirement. Other men work because jobs are available to them, and they cannot conceive of a life in retirement. Still other men work because work has positive values for them which cannot be met in retirement. Unfortunately, the survey data do not permit the full exploration of each of these possible explanations of why older men continue to work. We do know, however, when these men expect to retire and what these men will both enjoy and miss in their retirement.

In the analysis of the satisfactions and dissatisfactions of retired men, we found that there were country-by-country differences in the meaning of work for these men. However, when retired men of roughly the same health status were compared from country to country, we found that these men reported the same reactions to retirement. In other words, comparable health resulted in comparable reactions to retirement irrespective of country. Older men still in the work force in the three countries, however, are almost uniformly in good health, just as they are almost always married and somewhat younger than the retired. The chief difference between the respective older work forces of the three countries is an occupational one. In Britain the greatest proportion of older men who are working hold blue collar jobs, while in Denmark and in the United States the greatest proportion of older working men have white collar jobs.

Differences between the three countries in the occupational make-up of the older labor force suggest that we might again wish to test our original hypothesis that, irrespective of country, men of the same occupational level will have similar attitudes towards work. White collar workers and self-employed farmers usually have more control over their work than blue collar workers.[11] We may postulate that older men in white collar and in agricultural work compared to men in blue collar occupations will want to continue work for a longer time period. We may also expect that men in white collar and in agricultural work will be more likely than men in blue collar work to say that work has more than an economic meaning for them.

Older men who are now working can be divided into two groups: those who expect to stop work within some foreseeable future period, say within the next ten years, and those who say they will never stop work. White collar workers and workers in agriculture in each country are the most likely of all employed men to say that they will never stop work, and blue collar working class men are the most likely of all men to say there is some definite time when they think they will retire. These findings are consistent for all three countries. What is surprising, however, is the over-all

Table XI–12: PROPORTION OF EMPLOYED MEN AGED 65 AND OVER IN EACH SOCIAL CLASS WHO SAY THEY WILL NEVER STOP WORK[a]

Social Class	DENMARK	BRITAIN	UNITED STATES
White collar	77	81	80
Working class	57	74	71
Agricultural workers	86	b	84
All classes	73	77	78

[a] The number of men in each occupational group in each country is: Denmark—white collar, 164; working class, 144; agricultural workers, 128; all classes, 436; Britain—white collar, 67; working class, 175; agricultural workers, 22; all classes, 264; United States—white collar, 126; working class, 132; agricultural workers, 77; all classes, 335. The percentages of eligible respondents who answered this question are: Denmark, 99.3; Britain, 95.3; United States, 97.4.

[b] Per cents are not computed when base is less than 50.

high proportion of older employed men in each country who say they will never retire. About 7 of every 10 of those over 65 who are still working apparently expect to work until they die. The findings suggest that, irrespective of occupation, those men who continue to work past the middle 60's are so work-oriented that they are literally unable to visualize any future that precludes their working.

Despite the fact that the majority of employed men say they will never retire, half of the men still working say there are some things they would enjoy in retirement. The general hypothesis, however, that there will be cross-country occupational differences in what men say they will enjoy in retirement is not substantiated by the data available for Britain and the United States. In Britain, working class men are more likely than white collar men to say they would enjoy "nothing" in retirement, while in the United States there were no differences between the proportions of blue collar and of white collar men who would enjoy "nothing" in retirement. Men engaged in agricultural work in the United States were the most likely of all men to say that there was nothing to enjoy in retirement.

Although the hypothesis that working men of similar occupational levels would enjoy the same things in retirement is not proven, what of the related hypothesis that working men of similar occupational levels would miss the same things in retirement? This hypothesis is only partly verified by the data. The differences in the meaning of work in each country.

Table XI-13: THINGS LIKELY TO BE ENJOYED IN RETIREMENT, EMPLOYED MEN AGED 65 AND OVER, BY SOCIAL CLASS[a] (*Percentage Distribution*)

Things Likely to be Enjoyed in Retirement	White Collar		Working Class— Blue Collar and Service Workers		Agricultural Workers		All Classes	
	Britain	United States	Britain	United States	Britain	United States	Britain	United States
Nothing	48	42	53	42	b	57	54	45
Rest	24	19	20	10	b	15	21	15
Other	28	39	27	48	b	28	25	40
Total	100	100	100	100	b	100	100	100
N=c	67	124	177	135	23	75	267	334

[a] Danish data were not available for this cross-tabulation.

[b] Per cents are not computed when base is less than 50.

[c] The percentages of eligible respondents who answered this question are: Britain, 96.4; United States, 97.1.

which were previously noted among retired men in Denmark, Britain, and the United States, do not disappear in the analysis of the older work force. In the European countries, in contrast to the United States, even among men who had previously said they would never retire, some men say they would miss "nothing" about their jobs were they to give up working. In both Denmark and Britain, 1 of every 5 working men says he would miss "nothing" about his job. In the United States, however, only 1 of every 50 working men would miss "nothing" if he were to retire. Of those who say they would miss something about their work, the Danes primarily miss the work itself; the British miss the money. The Americans who are still working are much like the British in saying that what they would primarily miss in retirement is work income.

Men of the same occupational level who are still working, irrespective of country, do show certain similarities, however. Blue collar workers are

Table XI–14: MAJOR ITEM LIKELY TO BE MISSED IN RETIREMENT, EMPLOYED MEN AGED 65 AND OVER, BY SOCIAL CLASS

(*Percentage Distribution*)

Major Item Likely To Be Missed	White Collar			Working Class—Blue Collar and Service Workers			Agricultural Workers			All Classes		
	Denmark	Britain	United States	Denmark	Britain	United States	Denmark	Britain	United States	Denmark	Britain	United States
Nothing	20	21	3	20	22	2	11	b	1	17	21	2
People at work	15	20	20	6	15	14	6	b	—	9	17	13
Feeling of being useful	7	10	25	10	7	11	15	b	21	11	7	19
Things happening around one	6	a	6	6	a	4	6	b	4	6	a	5
Work itself	37	22	20	20	10	13	58	b	39	38	14	21
Money	14	27	25	36	46	52	3	b	32	18	41	38
Other	1	—	2	2	—	3	1	b	1	1	—	2
Total	100	100	100	100	100	100	100	100	100	100	100	100
N=c	144	71	122	124	181	134	119	23	71	387	275	327

a British data combine categories "nothing" and "no answer"; and "things happening around one" with "other."

b Per cents are not computed when base is less than 50.

c The percentages of eligible respondents who answered this question are: Denmark, 88.2; Britain, 99.3; United States, 95.1.

more likely than white collar workers to say that they would miss "money" were they to retire. Men who have some control over their work—white collar workers and workers in agriculture—are more likely than blue collar workers to want to work indefinitely and to report that they would miss the work itself, "the job," were they to give up working.

In every country work is important in maintaining the morale of older men. Men who are working, compared to men who are retired, are more likely to say that they are never lonely or that time never passes slowly for them. In the two European countries (but not in the United States), men who are still working are more likely than retired men to say they are

Table XI–15: ATTITUDES OF EMPLOYED AND RETIRED MEN AGED 65 AND OVER

Attitudes	Employed			Retired		
	Denmark	Britain	United States	Denmark	Britain	United States
Proportion who say:						
"Never lonely"	87	94	70	72	76	56
"Never alone"	82	58	38	70	46	37
"Time never passes slowly"	94	89	78	77	60	55
N=	437	274	341	702	724	731

never alone. The role of work in maintaining morale among older men, however, can be overestimated. Those men who are still working are somewhat younger and in better health than those men who have retired. The major causes of the observed differences in morale between the working and the retired may be age and health rather than employment.

The Meaning of Work

There are differences between older men in Denmark, Britain, and the United States in what they enjoy and expect in their retirement and in what they miss about their work. These differences between the men of the three countries are so striking that they overshadow differences in the meaning of work for men of various occupations in any one country.

In both Denmark and Britain men see the period of retirement as a time when one does nothing or when one rests after a lifetime of work. In the United States men see the retirement period as a time for activity, and Americans in retirement enjoy their "free-time" activities or various leisure-time pursuits. In fact, the data suggest that activity is so highly valued by older Americans that the pastimes of retirement take on the aspects of work.

In both Denmark and Britain, once men have retired they say that they miss nothing about their work. Among those who do miss their former jobs the Danes tend to miss the work itself, while the British miss the income they received for working. Retired American men, unlike the Europeans, miss many things about their work. What they miss especially, once retired, is "money," the income the job brought them. Although work has other than economic meanings for the American worker, such non-economic meanings are more likely to be reported by white collar workers and workers in agriculture than by blue collar workers. Older blue collar workers in all three countries, and particularly in the United States, are likely to see their work as a source of income, not as an end in itself.

In all three countries a man's health status plays a major role in the attitudes he expresses towards work and retirement. While there are country-by-country differences in what men think about work, these differences vanish once men in each country are separated by their various health levels. In every country retired men in poor health are both the least satisfied of all retired men, and the most likely of all retired men to say that they miss something about their past work. It appears that the more a man complains about his health, the more likely he is to be nostalgic about his career as a worker. Despite the many memories men in poor health have about their work, however, these men do not want to return to paid employment. Their past work is associated with a state of good health and vitality. It is seen as part of a "golden age," now vanished.

In every country some retired men want to return to work. Men in Britain and in the United States, compared to Denmark, are more likely to say they want to work. These would-be workers are usually recently retired men in good health who feel they can still do "a day's work" if they had the opportunity. The longer the time men are retired, the less likely they are to want to return to work. This disinterest in work cannot be attributed solely to lessening strength associated with advanced age. Rather, there would seem to be a critical turning point, at which a man ceases to think of himself as a potential worker and instead accepts his role as one who is retired.

Older men who are still working have the same attitudes towards work and retirement as the retired men in their respective countries. The man who continues to work past the usual retirement age, however, is more work-oriented than his fellows. Many of these men say that they never want to stop work. It may be that, once retired, these men will come to accept retirement. On the other hand, it can be suggested that men who have worked for some years past the usual retirement age, once they have to stop working, are the least contented of all older men.

NOTES

1 Sebastian de Grazia, "The Uses of Time," in Robert W. Kleemeier, ed., *Aging and Leisure* (New York: Oxford University Press, 1961), p. 129.
2 Eugene A. Friedmann, Robert J. Havighurst, and associates, *The Meaning of Work and Retirement* (Chicago: University of Chicago Press, 1954), is a stimulating and pioneering report on the meaning of work for older persons. A historical discussion of the meaning of work is found in A. Tilgher, *Work: What It Has Meant to Man Through the Ages* (Homo Faber), trans. Dorothy Canfield Fisher (New York: Harcourt, Brace and Company, 1930). A brief summary of Tilgher's analysis is given in Robert J. Havighurst and Ethel Shanas, "Retirement and the Professional Worker," *Journal of Gerontology*, VIII (January, 1953), 81–85. Sigmund Nosow and William H. Form, *Man, Work and Society* (New York: Basic Books, Inc., 1962), points up the central role of work in Western society.
3 Friedmann and Havighurst, *op. cit.*, Chap. VIII, pp. 170–186.
4 For comparative rates of unemployment in Britain and the United States see Arthur F. Neef, "International Unemployment Rates, 1960–64," *Monthly Labor Review*, XXXVIII (March, 1965), 256–259.
5 See Harold L. Wilensky, "Life Cycle, Work Situation and Participation in Formal Associations," in R. W. Kleemeier, ed., *op. cit.*, esp. pp. 227–229.
6 Both short-term and long-term retirees in the sample are a population of survivors. For an assessment of the losses in the work force through retirement and through death see Stuart Garfinkle, "Table of Working Life for Men, 1960," *Monthly Labor Review*, LXXXVI (July, 1963), 820–823.
7 Poor health was the major reason why men said they had retired in a 1954 survey in Britain and in both 1952 and 1957 national surveys of the aged in the United States. For Great Britain, see Ministry of Pensions and National Insurance, *Reasons for Retiring or Continuing Work* (London: HMSO, 1954). For the United States, see Ethel Shanas, *The Health of Older People: A Social Survey* (Cambridge, Mass.: Harvard University Press, 1962), pp. 55–56; Peter O. Steiner and Robert Dorfman, *The Economic Status of the Aged* (Berkeley: University of California Press, 1957), Chaps. III and V. For an analysis of reasons for retirement reported by self-employed men and for other workers see Erdman Palmore, "Retirement Patterns Among Aged Men: Findings of the 1963 Survey of the Aged," *Social Security Bulletin*, XXVII, No. 8 (August, 1964), Table 4, p. 5.
8 Wayne E. Thompson and Gordon F. Streib, "Situational Determinants: Health and Economic Deprivation in Retirement," *Journal of Social Issues*, XIV, No. 2 (1958), 21.
9 *Ibid.*, p. 25.
10 Palmore, *op. cit.*, p. 7.
11 Blauner and others believe that job satisfaction is related to the degree of control that the worker has over his employment. Robert Blauner, "Work Satisfaction and Industrial Trends in Modern Society," in Walter Galenson and Seymour M. Lipset, eds., *Labor and Trade Unionism: An Interdisciplinary Reader* (New York: John Wiley and Sons, Inc., 1960), p. 346.

12 : *The Financial Resources of Older People: A General Review*

Despite the very differing institutional backgrounds of the three countries, a substantial proportion of the welfare budgets of Britain, Denmark, and the United States are absorbed by the payment of pensions to the aged. With the increase in the numbers of people over retirement age, expenditure on such pensions has also been rising in all three countries and has sometimes been called the increasing "burden" of government pensions.

On the other hand, there has also been growing concern about the adequacy of the standard of living provided by such pensions. There can be no doubt that some among the aged are relatively well off, but they are probably a minority. Recent studies of poverty in the United States and in Britain have suggested that certain groups among the aged—some of them quite sizeable—are extremely vulnerable.[1] Estimates of the actual numbers involved vary according to the poverty standard adopted. It appears that the aged in Britain form a higher proportion of the total number of individuals or families in poverty than they do in the United States, where unemployment and low earnings are also important factors associated with poverty. In any case, the evidence in both countries has been such as to cast some doubt about the adequacy of public financial provision for the aged and has intensified interest in studies of the sources and levels of the financial resources available to those in the population over 65. In Denmark, on the other hand, the view that there is much poverty among the aged has not been so widespread, although the need for more information about the financial position of the old has long been recognized.

These considerations alone would have led us to include a study of financial problems in our cross-national survey, even had we not been convinced that information about the economic resources of the aged was essential background data for an understanding of the other problems with which we have been concerned. At the same time there was some difference of emphasis in the three countries, which may be reflected in the results described in these chapters. The United States cross-national study was carried out only shortly before a nation-wide survey of the aged conducted by the Social Security Administration. The latter was in fact primarily concerned with a detailed study of finance.[2] It was clearly sensible to have some degree of division of labor between this study and the cross-national study. In Britain one major inquiry into the economic circumstances of old people had been conducted in 1959–60,[3] although this was not completely national in scope since it had been confined to a random sample of older people in seven selected areas. In Denmark, the cross-national survey itself was the first major study of the financial position of older people to be undertaken and more attention was therefore focused on the financial aspect of the survey by our Danish colleagues.[4]

The research workers in all three countries, however, addressed themselves to the same questions, of which the following are some examples: What is the relative importance of various sources of financial support for the aged—government benefits, the family, employment income, investment income, the running down of capital assets—and to what degree does the importance of these sources vary from country to country; what is the level of income available to the aged, and how does this vary? To what extent can any differences in sources or levels be attributed to the differing institutions of support for the aged in the three countries? Can we identify particular problem groups among the old? Can we speak of the old as a homogeneous group? Are there significant changes in the economic position of people once they are past retirement age? The concepts and definitions used in the collection and analysis of this financial material are described in Appendix B.

The Institutional Framework

To the student concerned with the development of the "welfare state" in modern industrial society, it is interesting to note how the economic dependency of old age was almost everywhere the first state of dependency to be recognized as legitimately requiring government provision. Pension legislation of some kind was usually the first, or very nearly the first, income maintenance legislation to find its way onto the statute books. To take one example, we find that the United States has lagged far behind Western Europe in other fields of government social security and welfare provisions, such as sickness and unemployment benefits, family allowances, and so on. But even the United States has a federally operated scheme of old age pensions.

In 1962, at the time of our field work, there were certain important differences in the form of government provision of pensions in Denmark, Britain, and the United States. Moreover, our study was carried out at a point in time when major modifications of the existing systems were under discussion or agreed upon in at least two of the countries. To provide a background both for our findings and for such discussions, therefore, we must begin by outlining the differing institutional frameworks in the three countries. In the following description we are concerned primarily with coverage, eligibility, and the method of calculating benefits under the government schemes, not so much with the way in which the schemes are financed.

THE DANISH PENSION SYSTEM

The Danish pension system has the oldest history, the first law providing state benefits for poor elderly people having been passed in 1891. At present it covers all resident citizens, and pensionable age is 67 for men (62 for women)[5] or age 60 if failing health or other exceptional circumstances warrant. There is a small minimum pension payable to all above the age of 67 irrespective of the amount of any other income, but this is no more than a token payment. In April, 1962, for instance, it was 1,380 Danish kroner a year for couples and 924 kroner for a single person. The minimum pension is linked to the average income level and represents about 10 per cent of the average gross income of family breadwinners.

The full pension, on the other hand, is linked to a cost of living index, and is intended to provide a subsistence income after an income test. The method of administering this income test is complicated and the following description is intended to serve only as a general guide. First, the full amount of the basic pension in April, 1962, was 6,456 Danish kroner a year for a married couple, and 4,284 Danish kroner for single and widowed men and women, in the Copenhagen area.[6] (It was slightly lower outside the capital at that time, but the geographical differences have since been abolished.) Income received in addition to the pension is ignored up to a specified deduction-free amount—which in 1962 was 3,300 Danish kroner a year for a couple, and 2,200 kroner for single and widowed people. Personal taxes paid, and contributions to health and life insurances, are also ignored. Different sources of income are treated differently in calculating the deduction-free amount. For instance, income from property is discriminated against and the actual income is increased by 25 per cent in calculating the amount of property income to be set against the deduction-free amount. On the other hand, one-third of wage and salary income, and 30 per cent, or not less than 2,500 Danish kroner, from private employers' pensions are ignored in calculating the amount from these sources to be set against the deduction-free amount. Over and above the deduction-free amount, calculated in this way, the pension is reduced by 60 kroner for every 100 kroner of other income. If the calculated "other" income exceeds 140 per cent of the deduction-free amount, the pension is reduced by 72 kroner for every 100 kroner of income over and above 140 per cent. Finally, if the "other" income exceeds 180 per cent of the deduction-free amount, the pension is reduced by 84 kroner for every 100 kroner of other income. Because of the special treatment accorded to such sources of income, the actual income from employment and private pensions that the aged are allowed to have over and above the full old age pension is considerably higher than the deduction-free amount. For instance, a couple in Copenhagen in 1962 could have about 6,500 kroner a year in income from wages, salary, or self-employment before the full old age pension was reduced at all.

There are no contribution conditions for the payment of either the full, or the minimum, pension. Both are financed out of general taxation. The pensioner himself makes an application for payment. Increments to the full pension may be earned by postponing retirement beyond 67, and special supplements are payable to pensioners over 80. Supplements are also given to invalids, to persons requiring assistance from others, and to persons requiring nursing. Over and above the stated supplements, which are available to all according to fixed rules, a special supplement can be granted to pensioners whose circumstances are particularly difficult.[7] The total effect of the regulations was that, at the time of our field work, 67 per cent of pensioners were receiving a full or supplemented pension, 13 per cent a reduced pension, and 20 per cent only the minimum pension.

The method of financing pensions out of general taxation in Denmark is in contrast, as we shall see, to practices in Britain and the United States. It is interesting to note, therefore, that the most recent change in the Danish system has been the introduction of a supplementary contributory pension scheme. In March, 1964, the Labor Market Supplementary Pensions Act was passed. This set up a fund into which flat-rate contributions are paid by employees (one-third) and employers (two-thirds). From this fund, supplementary pensions are payable to wage and salary earners. The maximum pension payable is 2,400 Danish kroner a year after twenty-seven years membership, although the relationship between benefits and contributions is set in a way very favorable to late entrants to the scheme. The other development of interest is new legislation that has been enacted which will gradually abolish the deduction rules for the full pension during the period 1965–70. By 1970 all aged persons will be entitled to the full pension irrespective of their other income.[8] Both of these pieces of legislation, however, came after our survey, and do not affect the position of the Danish sample. They are commented upon here because, as we shall see, they represent a move in the form of financial provision for old age which brings Denmark rather closer to Britain and the United States.

THE BRITISH PENSION SYSTEM

In Britain the first legislation in the pension field was in 1908. It allowed for a payment which made no pretense at providing a subsistence income, was subject to an income test, and was paid out of general taxation. Although three years later the contributory principle was introduced for sickness and unemployment benefits, it was not until 1925 that pensions became contributory. A scheme of old age pensions was then introduced for the working class only, based on contributions from employer, employee, and from the state. The 1948 National Insurance Act retained the tri-partite contributory framework but extended coverage to everyone (all income groups and employed and self-employed alike). The scheme provides a flat-rate pension, with supplements for dependents, to all who have satisfied certain contribution conditions. In 1962, 90 per cent of individuals over retirement age (65 for men and 60 for women) were qualified to receive a pension and 84 per cent were actually receiving one. Failure to satisfy full contribution conditions will mean a reduction in the rate of pension; but continuation of employment and payment of contributions past retirement age can earn increments.[9] Between the ages of 65 and 70, payment of the full pension is conditional upon retirement; otherwise the pension is reduced by any earnings above a minimum. At the time of our field work up to £3 10s. a week could be earned without deduction. Above that amount the pension was reduced by 6d. a week for every one shilling of earnings between £3 10s. and £4 10s. a week, and by one shilling for every one shilling earned above £4 10s.[10] After 70 the pension is paid in full, and apart from this special treatment of earned income between 65 and 70, the pension is not otherwise subject to an income test. In 1962 the full flat-rate pension was £4 12s. 6d. a week, or £240 a year, for a couple, and £2 17s. 6d. a week, or £150 a year, for a single person. Five per cent of the pensions then in payment were at reduced rates; 69 per cent were at the full flat-rate; and 26 per cent were incremented, the average value of the increments being £21 a year.[11]

In 1959 new legislation grafted onto the flat-rate contribution and benefit a small degree of graduation, but few of the retired today are yet affected by these provisions.[12] Together these contributions build up increments to the flat-rate retirement pension at the rate of 6d. a week for every £7 10s. of contributions paid. A man paying these graduated contributions on the maximum income throughout his working life would, after 40 years, earn increments that in 1965 would less than double his flat-rate pension. In 1962 only just over 100,000 pensioners were receiving such increments and no one was receiving an increment of more than £4 a year.

When the 1948 legislation was first introduced it was stated that the pension was intended to provide a minimum subsistence income. But this is no longer claimed. Most pensioners without other sources of income, as well as those pensioners having other resources but whose total income still falls below "needs" as defined, become entitled, after an investigation of their means, to supplementation of their pension by the National Assistance Board. At the beginning of 1962 this supplementation would bring a couple up to an income of £234, and a single person up to £139 a year, with rent usually paid in full in addition.[13] Official estimates suggest that some 24 per cent of all retirement pensioners are receiving supplementation of this kind, and that the proportion has fluctuated between a fifth and a quarter over the whole of the post-war period.

THE UNITED STATES PENSION SYSTEM

Government provision of old age pensions came latest in the United States. The Old Age, Survivors, and Disability Insurance Act of 1935

(O.A.S.D.I.), as amended, is still the effective legislation. Originally only about 60 per cent of the labor force were included, but coverage has been greatly extended in recent years and today it is about 91 per cent. In 1950 only 26 per cent of the population over 65 were eligible for benefits; by 1962 the percentage had risen to 78 per cent, and by 1964 to 83 per cent. In 1962, 72 per cent of the population over 65 were actually receiving benefits. This means, however, that among today's aged there are still more in the United States than in Britain who were excluded from coverage when they were in employment and therefore have no right to benefit.

Full benefits are payable at age 65 for workers and at age 62 for widows, although actuarially reduced benefits are available for workers from age 62. The benefits are payable subject to the satisfaction of certain minimum contributions, and between the ages of 65 and 72 are subject to reduction for earnings above a certain level. In 1962 this level was $1,200 a year. Above this the pension was reduced by one dollar for every 2 dollars earned between $1,200 and $1,700; above $1,700 it was reduced by one dollar for every dollar earned. This is very similar to the British earnings rule. A minimum and maximum pension are laid down, but between those limits the level of benefit to which an individual is entitled is based on the worker's average monthly wage in covered employment, heavily weighted in favor of those with low earnings. Dependents' allowances are also payable. From time to time general increases in benefits have been enacted. That of 1961 raised the level of the minimum pension and increased a widow's benefit from 75 per cent to 82.5 per cent of her husband's retirement benefit. That legislation also raised the maximum amount of annual earnings used as a base for the computation of benefits.

Thus there is a range of pension levels which in 1962 stretched from the minimum of $40 a month to a maximum of $127 for a single worker who retired at age 65; and from $58 to $190 for a retired worker with a dependent wife.[14] Average benefits in payment at the time of the field work were $128 a month to a couple, $73 a month to a retired worker without dependents, and $66 a month to an aged widow. In addition to these federal pensions, public assistance, subject to an income test, is also available to the aged on a state basis, the precise form of means test varying from state to state.[15] As the coverage of the O.A.S.D.I. scheme has increased, so the proportions of the elderly receiving assistance has declined. In 1952, 22 per cent of people over 65 were receiving old age assistance payments, but the percentage was down to 13 per cent by 1962.

One difference between the three countries that should be remembered in studying the cross-national data, is the treatment of public employees. In both the United States and Denmark certain groups, such as public and railroad employees, were for a long time excluded from the general social security program because they were covered by special pension provisions of their own. The situation has been changing, however, and some of these groups are now within the O.A.S.D.I. or the Danish old-age pension schemes. But those of the aged in our samples who had been in these occupational groups before these changes in the law would not have been so covered. In Britain such classes of worker also have their own pension schemes, but at least since 1948, and sometimes earlier, they have also been covered by the general government scheme.

Denmark, Britain, and the United States do, between them, provide an interesting spectrum of the main types of social security arrangements at present operating in advanced countries. In Denmark the basic scheme is non-contributory, financed entirely from general taxation, and available to all. With the small exception of the minimum pension, the scheme is basically income tested. This type of pension provision is today rather the exception, and, as we have seen, the most recent legislation in Denmark has involved at least some move towards the contributory principle and away from the income test. In the other two countries the schemes are contributory and benefits are available as of right, except that the benefits are reduced in respect of income from earnings within a certain age range.

In Britain the contributions come from employer, employee, and the government; in the United States they come from employer and employee only. The British program has been comprehensive for longer than its American counterpart, with the result that benefits are, at the moment, available to a higher proportion of those over retirement age in Britain than in the United States—although there again the situation is changing. But contributions and benefits in the United States have always been wage-related to some degree, whereas in Britain the recent move towards a small degree of graduation has not changed the basically flat-rate character of both contributions and benefits. In Denmark pensionable age is 67, compared with 65 in Britain and the United States; and in the latter country there has been a recent move towards an even earlier age, when actuarially reduced benefits became available from age 62. Finally, in both Britain and the United States the contributory pension scheme is supplemented by fairly extensive use of public assistance for the aged, available only after a test of means.

THE LEVEL OF SOCIAL SECURITY BENEFITS

It is tempting to make a comparison of benefit levels provided by the social security schemes of the three countries, in order to provide a benchmark for our examination of the total financial resources available to the aged. One difficulty is that in all three countries there is some variation in the level of benefit in payment. In Britain it is small and the flat-rate pension in 1962 can be taken as representing the level of benefit. In the United States we shall use the average level of benefit in payment; and in the case of Denmark we shall use the full pension, which is the minimum level of income guaranteed by the scheme in the absence of other income sources.

A much greater difficulty is to decide on the appropriate standard for comparison. In order to allow for differences in the general standard of living between the three countries, we want to compare the relative value of the three benefits. A standard frequently used in exercises of this kind is average adult male earnings in manufacturing industry. In Denmark the full pension for a couple in 1962 was 40 per cent of such earnings, but in Britain it was only 29 per cent. Average earnings data for the United States are available only for males and females combined—which would seriously affect the comparison with Britain and Denmark. We have used instead for the United States, therefore, the median total money income in 1962 of male operatives and kindred workers who were year-round, full-time workers. The average O.A.S.D.I. benefit in payment to a couple was then 29 per cent of this amount. Two interesting points emerge from this comparison, rough as it is. The first is how far the level of benefit is below the level of earnings in all three countries. The second is that the Danish pension level is relatively much more generous than in the other two countries.

In attempting international comparisons of this kind, where the economic structure of the countries varies so much (as, for instance, between Britain on the one hand, and Denmark and the United States on the other, in the importance of the agricultural sector), it is arguable that a better standard to take for comparison is the gross national product per head of the total labor force or per head of total population. By the first of such measures the full Danish pension for a couple was 29 per cent of the gross national product per head of the labor force; the average O.A.S.D.I. payment to a couple was 21 per cent; and the British pension for a couple was 22 per cent. As a percentage of gross national product per head of the total population the relevant figures were: Denmark 59 per cent, Britain 46 per cent, and the United States 52 per cent. The Danish pension level still appears relatively higher than in the other two countries, although how much higher does depend on the particular standard of comparison being used. Such international comparisons can be made only with the greatest caution. But in real terms it appears that the United States pension levels are higher than those in Britain by about the same amount as the general standard of living in the United States is higher than that in Britain. Danish pension levels are relatively higher than in either Britain or the United States and, since the general standard of living in Denmark and Britain is very comparable, it follows that the real pension levels in Denmark are also higher than those in Britain, although still below those in the United States. Other aspects of the social security schemes, however, such as the age of retirement, the role of public assistance, of other sources of income, and so forth, may also be important in relation to the total financial resources available to older people. We turn now, therefore, to an examination of the survey data itself.

A General Description of Sources of Income

Throughout this discussion we shall distinguish between married couples, women and men, the latter two groups being single, widowed, or divorced people.[16] These are the three basic kinds of income unit that we have used in our analysis, and the most superficial examination of the data reveals that the differences in the financial position of these three groups *within* countries is often as great as differences in the over-all position *between* countries. Since the proportions of the three types of income unit vary between the three countries, it can be misleading to discuss the over-all

Table XII–1: NUMBERS AND PERCENTAGE OF EACH OF THREE TYPES OF INCOME UNIT AGED 65 AND OVER PROVIDING FINANCIAL INFORMATION

Type of Income Unit	DENMARK		BRITAIN		UNITED STATES	
	Number	Per Cent	Number	Per Cent	Number	Per Cent
Couples	818	43	1,099	35	825	43
Men	331	18	495	16	256	13
Women	743	39	1,552	49	851	44
Number of cases[a]	1,892	100	3,146	100	1,932	100

[a] The percentages of eligible income units located who gave sufficient income information to be included in the analysis of income are: Denmark, couples 87, men 84, women 81; Britain, couples 77, men 82, women 80; United States, couples 88, men 89, women 90.

The financial tables that follow are based upon the information supplied by these co-operating income units. In this chapter the convention adopted for dealing with cases where a particular piece of information was missing for any of these cooperating income units differs from the convention adopted in the rest of this report. Here the "no answer" cases are, wherever possible, shown in a separate category in the financial tables. This is because there is reason to believe that they are not in all respects like these income units providing full income information (see Appendix B). Where the "no answers" are excluded, the percentage of cooperating income units on which the table is based is shown in a footnote.

position. The predominance of unmarried and widowed women in the population of 65 and over in Britain (already discussed in Chapter 6) has the result of giving Britain, in terms of income units, a relatively lower proportion of couples and a higher proportion of women than either Denmark or the United States. What are the sources of income available to these three kinds of income units in our three countries?

GOVERNMENT BENEFITS

In Table XII–2 the row described as "government benefits combined" shows the percentage of elderly income units who are receiving any kind of government benefit, that is retirement or war pensions or assistance. (See Appendix B for a full definition.) Some units may combine income from more than one kind of government benefit. For instance, we have already seen that in Britain and the United States some old age pensioners will be combining both pensions and assistance. In this comprehensive sense, government benefits are the most frequently received income source in all countries, the percentage of units receiving such income ranging

Table XII–2: PERCENTAGE OF COUPLES, MEN AND WOMEN WITH VARIOUS SOURCES OF INCOME

Type of Income Unit and Country

Source of Income	DENMARK			BRITAIN			UNITED STATES		
	Couples	Men	Women	Couples	Men	Women	Couples	Men	Women
Government benefits combined	83	89	95	88	87	94	78	86	75
Social security benefit	a	a	a	85	81	78	68	70	54
Public assistance	a	a	a	16	20	36	9	16	23
Other government benefits	a	a	a	a	a	a	18	19	8
Wages and salaries	36	19	10	34	21	10	37	18	15
Business, farm, or professional	21	13	4	a	a	a	23	16	10
Pension from previous employer	16	17	22	43	36	11	19	14	7
Rent, dividends, interest, and annuities	54	56	54	25	24	23	42	27	35
Other income	8	9	7	11	9	14	6	5	9
Source unknown	—	—	—	—	—	—	—	—	1
No income	—	—	—	*	*	*	*	1	7
N=	813	330	739	1,099	459	1,552	825	256	851

a Not available separately.

* Less than one per cent.

from 78 per cent of the couples in the United States to 95 per cent of the women in Denmark. The different features of the national schemes can be seen at work, however. In the United States only 78 per cent of the couples received government benefits because of the tendency, which we will examine later, for them more often to be working; at the same time women (who in our analysis, it will be recalled, are unmarried and widowed women) in the United States less often draw government benefits because of the comparatively recent extension of pension coverage. Indeed, only 54 per cent of them actually receive O.A.S.D.I. benefits; their total receipt of government benefits is increased because they are more frequently recipients of public old age assistance than are the other types of income unit. In both Britain and Denmark well over 80 per cent of the couples are receiving government benefits but they are receiving them less often than are the men and women in those countries—mainly, it would seem, because of the couples' continued employment.

EMPLOYMENT INCOME

Perhaps one of the most remarkable features of the structure of the income of the aged is the frequency with which income from employment —that is, wages and salaries or farm or business—is received. This is the corollary of the employment position described in Chapter 10. There we saw that the over-65's are certainly not coterminous with the retired. That chapter was concerned with the employment position of individuals, and primarily of men. Here we are interested in the employment income of income units. In the case of married couples, for instance, the husband, the wife, or both partners could be working but it will simply be reflected as one source of income from employment for that income unit. We shall also find, paradoxically, that some income units, when classified according to their employment status, still receive employment income even when retired. This results from certain difficulties of definition and methodology.

First, the classification of employment status is based upon the respondent's replies to questions about whether or not he worked last week. A man may describe himself as retired, but still have income from an odd day's gardening or some other casual activity. Secondly, the Danish and United States financial data relate to income received during the year preceding the interview (see Appendix B). Any person who retired during the course of that year will appear in our tables as receiving employment income. This does not apply to the British data. But in all three countries the couples are classified according to the employment status of the husband, whereas the wife may well have employment income. The result is that a fifth of the *retired* couples in the United States have wage and salary income, and 14 per cent have some self-employment income; in Denmark 17 per cent have wage and salary income, and 9 per cent have self-employment income; and in Britain, 10 per cent of the retired couples have some sort of employment income. A small proportion, even, of retired women have some income from employment.

Looking at the position for all income units, however, we find that on less than a third of the couples in all three countries have income from wages and salaries. So few people in Britain were receiving business or farm income that the category was merged with wages and salaries. But in Denmark and the United States between another fifth and a quarter of the couples have business or farm income. Some couples in these countries may have income from both these sources, but it would probably not be overstating the position to say that 50 to 55 per cent of all the aged couples in Denmark and the United States receive employment income, compared with only a third in Britain. We would expect to find that the women less often have employment income of any kind, and this is in fact the case in all three countries (only 10–15 per cent of women receive wages and salaries). But although employment income is much less important generally as an income source for women in all three countries, the differences between the countries remain. As for the men, between 18 and 21 per cent of them have wage and salary income; and in Denmark and the United States another 13 to 16 per cent have business or farm income.

These differences between the countries parallel the differences in the labor force position described in Chapter 10. There we saw that the crucial difference lay in the greater tendency of the self-employed to go on working past normal retirement age. Self-employment is far more common in the United States and Denmark than in Britain. This is due partly to the greater importance of agriculture in the economic structure of the first two countries. But in the white collar occupations too, self-employment is more common in Denmark and the United States than in Britain. This will emerge clearly when we come to examine the sources of income for various occupational groups. Some of the greater frequency of receipt of employment income in Denmark might be expected to be due to the later age of retirement in that country. (See this chapter, p. 353.) In fact, as we have seen, over-all there is very little difference between Denmark and the United States in the proportions receiving employment income. But in the first two years after 65 a difference does emerge. In the age group 65–66, 68 per cent of the couples in the United States have wage and salary income and 16 per cent have self-employment income. The corresponding percentages for couples in the same age groups in Denmark, where the pension is not yet payable, are 58 per cent with wage and salary income and 33 per cent with self-employment income. In the age group 67–69, 41 per cent of the couples in the United States have wage and salary income and 25 per cent have self-employment income. In Denmark 49 per cent of the couples in the corresponding age group have wage and salary income and 19 per cent have self-employment income. Since, as we saw in Chapter 10, the labor force participation of men is in fact higher in Denmark than in the United States between the ages of 65 and 69, the absence of marked differences in the frequency of receipt of employment income must in part be due to the higher labor force participation of elderly women in the United States and to more casual or intermittent employment activity not reflected in employment status figures of that country.

PROPERTY INCOME

Income from rent, dividends, interest, and annuities (or property income) is interesting for two reasons.[17] First, this is an income source for which the women in all three countries are relatively well placed compared with other income sources. But second, the differences between countries are again very marked. Denmark and the United States are more similar to each other than either is to Britain. In America 42 per cent of the couples, 35 per cent of the women, and 27 per cent of the men have this type of income. In Denmark over a half, but in Britain only a quarter, of all three types of income unit receive property income. We shall return to a discussion of these differences when we look at the asset position of the aged.

EMPLOYERS' PENSIONS

The type of income more common in Britain than elsewhere is a pension from a former employer. In Britain for couples and men this source of income is the one most often received after state benefits, more often even than employment income. Whereas in Denmark and the United States the proportion receiving such pensions varies between income units, it is (with the single exception of Danish women) a half or less of the corresponding proportions in Britain. For women in all three countries, however, most of such pensions are paid in respect of former husbands' employment.

"OTHER INCOME"

As Appendix B shows, the category of "other income" includes a number of miscellaneous income sources, like help from the family, from charities, and so on. None of them is very important on its own. There is no very marked variation between countries or between types of income unit. But the category "no income" requires comment. Among the couples and men in both Britain and the United States, there were one or two isolated cases who reported that they had no income at all. This, too, was the case among the women in Britain. But no less than 7 per cent of the women in the United States have no income from any source. This is a minority, but nonetheless it is a highly significant group, which certainly reflects the days when the coverage of federal pension provision was less extensive than it is now.

COMBINATIONS OF SOURCES OF INCOME

Old people frequently combine different sources of income. Considering the five income sources just discussed, we find that in Britain and the United States only 27–28 per cent of the couples have a single income source; 40–50 per cent have two, and a quarter to 30 per cent combine three or more sources. In both these countries the men and women are more often dependent upon a single source, but even then well over a

Table XII-3: PERCENTAGE OF COUPLES AND WOMEN WITH EACH NUMBER OF INCOME SOURCES, BY INCOME GROUP (Percentage Distribution)

Sources of Income	DENMARK								BRITAIN								UNITED STATES							
Median Income Groups[a] and Country	−21	−20	±5	+20	+50	+100	+101	All Income Groups	−21	−20	±5	+20	+50	+100	+101	All Income Groups	−21	−20	±5	+20	+50	+100	+101	All Income Groups
Percentage of couples with:																								
One source only	52	16	6		9	12	21	21	61	29	12	14	11	16	15	27	47	23		17	15	16	12	28
Wages or salary	2	2	—		6	12	21	1	—	*	1	8	9	13	14	5	3	1		10	8	15	10	6
Business, farm, or professional	—	—	—		—	—	—	—	—	—	—	—	—	—	—	—	1	1		3	3	1	—	2
Government benefits	50	13	6		—	—	—	19	59	29	9	5	1	1	—	21	42	16		3	4	—	—	18
Rent, dividends, interest, and annuities	—	—	—		—	—	—	*	—	—	—	—	—	—	—	—	—	—		—	—	—	—	—
All other	—	1	—		3	—	—	*	2	—	1	1	1	2	1	1	*	5		1	—	—	1	2
Two sources of income	43	57	46		41	35	30	42	35	56	64	62	50	49	39	49	40	56		51	37	35	42	42
With government benefits	41	55	44		36	24	11	36	34	56	64	60	44	37	25	45	38	46		45	32	20	17	33
Without government benefits	2	2	2		5	11	19	6	1	—	—	2	6	12	14	4	3	10		6	5	15	26	9
Three or more sources of income	5	28	48		50	54	49	35	4	15	24	24	38	36	47	25	12	21		32	47	49	45	29
With government benefits	5	28	48		49	51	44	33	4	15	24	23	34	34	45	24	11	21		30	47	47	40	28
Without government benefits	—	—	—		1	3	5	2	*	—	—	1	4	2	2	1	*	—		1	—	2	6	1
No source of income	—	—	—		—	—	—	—	—	—	—	—	—	—	—	—	—	—		—	—	—	—	*
No answer	—	—	—		—	—	—	2	—	—	—	—	—	—	—	*	1	—		—	—	—	—	—
Total	100	100	100	100	100	100	100	100	100	100	100	100	100	100	100	100	100	100	100	100	100	100	100	100
N[b]	206	116	52	46	78	97	113	813	256	216	82	99	138	108	122	1,099	280	81	43	69	78	86	139	825
Percentage of women with:																								
One source only	80	52	33	3	8	9	—	30	92	72	64	53	40	20	13	58	64	75	71		39	24	17	50
Wages or salary	—	—	—	3	2	2	—	*	—	—	—	—	—	1	—	*	2	5	2		5	1	1	2
Business, farm, or professional	—	—	—	—	—	—	—	—	—	—	—	—	—	—	—	—	2	1	—		—	—	—	1
Government benefits	80	52	33	—	6	7	—	29	88	71	63	51	36	10	—	53	53	69	60		31	23	16	38
Rent, dividends, interest, and annuities	—	—	—	—	—	—	—	—	—	—	—	—	—	—	—	—	—	—	—		—	—	—	—
All other	—	—	—	—	—	—	—	—	3	—	1	2	4	11	13	3	7	—	9		3	—	—	9
Two sources of income	18	44	57	81	67	38	46	48	7	25	36	40	49	59	42	34	14	22	23		44	54	46	31
With government benefits	18	44	57	81	66	33	31	45	7	25	35	38	42	56	36	33	13	19	18		40	50	40	28
Without government benefits	—	—	—	—	1	5	15	3	—	—	1	2	7	3	6	1	1	3	5		4	4	6	3
Three or more sources of income	2	4	10	16	25	53	54	20	1	3	—	7	11	21	45	8	1	3	3		7	4	15	6
With government benefits	2	4	10	16	25	53	52	20	1	3	—	7	11	20	43	8	1	3	3		7	4	13	6
Without government benefits	—	—	—	—	—	—	2	*	—	—	—	—	—	1	2	*	—	—	—		—	—	2	*
No source of income	—	—	—	—	—	—	—	—	—	—	—	—	—	—	—	—	21	—	3		10	18	22	13
No answer	—	—	—	—	—	—	—	2	—	—	—	—	—	—	—	*	—	—	—		—	—	—	—
Total	100	100	100	100	100	100	100	100	100	100	100	100	100	100	100	100	100	100	100		100	100	100	100
N[d]	91	194	82	64	99	57	85	743	350	278	207	188	202	135	94	1,552	272	95	62	41	70	70	174	851

a For the key to the median income groups in this and other tables, see Appendix B.

b The percentages of units providing sufficient income details to be allocated to an income group are: Denmark 87, Britain 93, United States 95. But "all income groups" includes all cooperating income units.

c Percentages not computed on a base of less than 50.

d The percentages of units providing sufficient income details to be allocated to an income group are: Denmark 90, Britain 94, United States 92. But "all income groups" includes all cooperating income units.

* Less than one per cent.

third of the men and about half of the women combine two or more sources. Denmark is rather apart. Not only are all three types of income unit very alike with respect to combinations of income sources, but old people in Denmark are even less dependent upon a single source than in the other two countries. This is due in part to the universality of some receipt of a government pension (that is, the minimum pension) in Denmark after age 67. But for men and women, in particular, it is the frequency with which they combine three sources of income which is so marked.

THE IMPORTANCE OF DIFFERENT SOURCES

A description of the frequency with which older people derive income from different sources tells us only a limited amount about the relative importance of these sources. In the analysis so far, a receipt of 10 dollars from any source has equal weight with one for ten thousand dollars. We already know that certain kinds of income (like full-time wage and salary income) will, on average, be at a much higher level than benefits under the social security schemes in the various countries. Such difference in the average level of receipt from the different sources can be illustrated with data from Britain and Denmark. Table XII–4 shows the median income from each income source for units receiving such income in Britain; while the Danish data show the mean income from each income source, again for those units receiving such income.

In general, income from employment (wage and salaries or business) is up to twice as high as the income from the next largest source—income from government benefits; and government benefits in turn provide an income up to twice as high as the income received from property or from other sources. The exception here is income from employers' pensions in Denmark, the level of which is dictated by the fact that most are the pensions of former civil servants or other white collar workers. In Britain there was little variation around the median of income from government benefits. But the amount of income received from the other sources varied very considerably—from only a few shillings to many pounds a week, with a heavy concentration around the few shillings.

One useful method of measuring the relative importance of different sources of income is to consider what percentage of the aggregate income of the whole sample is derived from each income source. This cannot be done from the cross-national material for the United States. But the Social Security Administration, in the first report of its survey (where, in other ways, the results agree closely with our cross-national results), shows that, in 1962, 30 per cent of the aggregate income of persons over 65 came from O.A.S.D.I. benefits, and another 15 per cent from other public benefits, veterans pensions, and public assistance. This is a total of 45 per cent from items which together make up a category a little wider than the government benefits of our cross-national survey because it includes railroad and public employees' pensions.[18] But employment income (which is our abbreviation for wages, salaries, business, and farm income) supplied no

Table XII–4: AVERAGE INCOME FROM DIFFERENT SOURCES FOR THOSE
INCOME UNITS WITH SUCH INCOME IN BRITAIN AND DENMARK[a]

| Source of Income | Type of Income Unit and Country Average Annual Income | | | | | |
| | DENMARK Danish Kroner | | | BRITAIN British Pounds | | |
	Couples	Men	Women	Couples	Men	Women
Government benefits	4,362	3,349	3,468	257	159	153
N=	593	268	644	970	431	1,459
Wages and salaries[b]	10,695	6,800	4,284			
N=	255	55	64	400	390	195
Business, farm, professional[b]	11,158	7,419	4,986	350	87	146
N=	139	39	18			
Pension from former employer	9,021	9,047	6,628	114	96	99
N=	117	52	143	436	168	155
Rent, dividends, interest, and annuities	2,345	1,443	1,513	39	39	47
N=	381	162	346	242	97	296
Other income	3,014	2,015	1,332	42	31	52
N=	89	43	94	120	39	206

[a] The Danish figures show the mean annual income; the British figures show the median annual income. In both cases the averages are based upon the number of cases where the amount of income from that source was known. The number of such cases is shown as N.

[b] In the case of couples, employment income of wife and husband is combined.

less than 32 per cent of the aggregate income of the sample. Interest, dividends, and rents were the next most important source, but they supplied only 15 per cent of aggregate money income. Private pensions (excluding those of federal and railroad employees) provided 3 per cent and "other income" 4 per cent of the total.

Table XII–5 provides similar information from the cross-national material for Britain and Denmark. Britain emerges as the country where the elderly are most heavily dependent upon government benefits for their income. Over a half of aggregate money income comes from this source, and in the case of the women no less than 70 per cent of their income is supplied in this way. It is interesting to see how, despite the generally greater frequency of receipt of employers' pensions in Britain, this is outweighed by the higher level of such pensions in Denmark. The result is that in Denmark 16 per cent of aggregate money income, compared with 12 per cent in Britain, comes from that source. On the other hand the percentages received from rent, dividends, and interest are very similar in the two countries, despite the fact that far more Danish old people have some property income.

Table XII–5: PERCENTAGE OF AGGREGATE MONEY INCOME SUPPLIED BY
EACH SOURCE OF INCOME FOR ALL INCOME UNITS IN DENMARK AND BRITAIN

| Source of Income | Type of Income Unit and Country | | | | | | | |
| | DENMARK | | | | BRITAIN | | | |
	Couples	Men	Women	All	Couples	Men	Women	All
Government benefits	28	38	53	37	48	51	71	56
Wages and salaries	30	16	7	22				
Business, farm, profes-sional	17	12	2	12	29	22	7	20
Employers' pension	12	20	23	16	15	16	6	12
Rent, dividends, interest, and annuities	10	10	12	10	7	10	10	10
Other income	3	4	3	3	2	2	5	3
Total	100	100	100	100	100	100	100	100
N=a	708	294	672	1,691	1,023	456	1,460	2,939

a The percentages of cooperating income units who supplied sufficient income information
to be included in this table are: Denmark, couples 87, men 89, women 90; Britain,
couples 93, men 92, women 94.

To the extent that our material may understate income from non-government sources and in particular from rent, dividends, and interest, the absolute level of these percentages should be treated with some caution. (For a discussion of this problem, see Appendix B.) But the amount of understatement is not large enough to affect fundamentally the order of importance of the different income sources.

Government benefits are important as an income source because they are so widely received by the old; employment income is important because after government benefits it is the next most widely received income source, but also because the average receipt from employment income is high. Other income sources tend to be less widely received and on average to be lower. In Denmark and Britain the survey material was analyzed to show what proportion of the sample was receiving its largest receipt from each of the different sources. The patterns are very similar in the two countries, despite the fact that the old in Denmark are more often receiving employment income. In both countries around two-thirds of the men and couples have their single largest income source from government benefits. For women the percentage rises to 75–80 per cent. Income from employment comes next, but it is a long way behind. It supplies between 12 and 18 per cent of the men and couples in the two countries with their largest income source, but only 3 or 4 per cent of the women.

To summarize this discussion of the sources from which older people derive their income, we can first say that the predominance of government benefits in all three countries is established. But somewhat more surprising is the emergence of employment income as such an important income source. Here two important differences must be noted. First, there is a major difference between Britain and the other two countries in that employment income is less often received in Britain by older people—principally, it would seem, because self-employment activities, not only in agriculture but also in other areas like the professions, are less important in Britain. Denmark and the United States are surprisingly similar in respect to employment income when the difference in the age at which the pension becomes payable in the two countries is remembered. Second, there is a major difference in respect to employment income between women on the one hand and men and couples on the other hand in all three countries.

The corollary is that in all three countries women are especially dependent upon government benefits. One other interesting cross-national difference has also emerged. Property income (rents, dividends, and interest) is received twice as frequently by older people in Denmark as in Britain; and in this respect the United States is more like Denmark than it is Britain. But particularly in Denmark and Britain the amounts of property income are small, as is shown by the fact that only about 10 per cent of aggregate money income is received from this source.

Income Levels

What kind of income levels are provided by these sources of income which we have just described? Meaningful discussions of income levels are difficult enough within a single country because of the problem of comprehending the complexities of an income distribution within a few simple statistics. They become even more difficult when one is concerned to describe and compare differences in income levels within and between three different countries. Very early on in our investigations it became clear that the income distribution of the elderly in all three countries was so skew that, if we wished to use a single statistic to compare average income levels, the median income level would be the most appropriate.

MEDIAN INCOMES

In Table XII–6 we show the median income for each of the three types of income unit in the three countries. In every case it is well above the corresponding level of social security benefit paid. But in Denmark the medians tend to be closer to the levels of benefit than in the other two countries. This is what one would expect to find as the result of an income-tested system of benefit payment. In the United States the couples are as much as 83 per cent and the men 61 per cent above their corresponding benefit levels. In Britain the couples and the men are 60 per cent above. In Denmark the couples are only 31 per cent and the men 21 per cent above. In all three countries, however, the median incomes of the women are close to the levels of social security payments—in Britain being 29 per cent, in the United States 25 per cent, and in Denmark only 13 per cent above.

Table XII-6: MEDIAN TOTAL MONEY INCOME AND SOCIAL SECURITY BENEFIT LEVELS IN 1962, COMPARED FOR THREE TYPES OF INCOME UNIT

Benefit Level and Median Income	DENMARK Danish Kroner per Annum			BRITAIN British Pounds per Annum			UNITED STATES U.S. Dollars per Annum		
	Couples	Men	Women	Couples	Men	Women	Couples	Men	Women
Social security benefit level, 1962	6,458	4,284		240		150	1,536	876	782
Median total money income[a]	8,419	5,222	4,851	390	239	192	2,804	1,406	982
Median total money income of men and women as a percentage of couples	100	62	58	100	61	49	100	50	35

[a] These are the medians of those cooperating income units who supplied information about total money income. The percentages of eligible respondents who answered this question are: Denmark, couples 87, men 89, women 90; Britain, couples 93, men 92, women 94; United States, couples 95, men 97, women 92.

We can now draw one tentative conclusion about the economic position of elderly women. Each of the three systems of social security recognizes that the income of a couple has to support two people. In Britain and Denmark the full pension for a single person is 62 per cent and 67 per cent respectively of the pension of a man with a dependent wife. In the United States the average benefits in payment to single persons are between 50 and 57 per cent of those paid to a couple. Estimates made in the United States of the ratio of the *requirements* of a single elderly person to those of an elderly couple range from 59 to 70–75 per cent.[19] The gap between the median total income of the women and of the couples in all three countries is much greater than one would expect from these figures. In the United States the median income of the women in the sample is only 35 per cent of that of the couples, and in Britain, although a little higher, is still only 49 per cent. Denmark, however, is once more the exception. The median income of the women there is 58 per cent of that of the couples—which must be the result of the income-tested pension compensating the women, to some extent, for their relative disadvantage with respect to other sources of income. In Britain and the United States, however, although (as we have seen earlier) women are more often receiving public assistance than are the couples or men, this compensates them to only a very limited extent for their deficiency of other sources of income. On any basis we must conclude that in these two countries elderly women are badly off compared with elderly men and couples.

But how do the median incomes available to all income units compare with the income levels available generally in the three countries? We express them, as we did for social security benefits, as percentages of average earnings in manufacturing industry and then as percentages of gross national product, first per head of total labor force and then per head of total population (Table XII-7).

It is interesting to note how, as in the comparison of social security benefits, gross national product per head of total population shifts the comparison in favor of the United States. (See this chapter, p. 354.) This is because the ratio of the dependent (young and old together) to the total population is higher in the United States than in Britain and Denmark. With the exception of the United States on this particular measure, there is considerable similarity in the relative position of the couples in all three countries. Their median income is a little over one-third of the gross national product per head of the labor force, and about half of average earnings in manufacturing industry. But the medium income of the elderly in Britain appears to be relatively lower than in Denmark (although in the case of the couples the differences are rather small). Except in the case of women, however, the very marked lead which the Danish pension levels have over Britain is not maintained in the levels of total income. Again, this is what one would expect from the way in which the pension scheme works in Denmark. The Danish advantage is greatest for those income units that are most heavily dependent upon government benefits in both countries, that is, the women. In the case of men and couples, however, other non-government sources of income, which in

Table XII-7: MEDIAN TOTAL MONEY INCOME OF THE ELDERLY IN 1962
IN RELATION TO GROSS NATIONAL PRODUCT PER HEAD OF THE LABOR
FORCE, GROSS NATIONAL PRODUCT PER HEAD OF TOTAL POPULATION, AND
AVERAGE EARNINGS IN MANUFACTURING INDUSTRY[a]

	Column 1	Column 2		
Country		Median Total Money Income of the Elderly as Percentage of Column 1		
	Gross National Product per Head of Labor Force	Couples	Men	Women
Denmark D. kr.	22,601	37	23	22
Britain £	1,106	35	22	17
United States $	7,448	38	19	13
	Gross National Product per Head of Total Population			
Denmark D. kr.	10,927	77	48	44
Britain £	527	74	45	36
United States $	2,981	94	47	33
	Average Earnings in Manufacturing Industry per Annum			
Denmark D. kr.	16,356	52	32	30
Britain £	824	47	29	23
United States $	5,368	52	26	18

[a] *Sources:* Gross National Products, 1962, from United Nations, Department of Economic and Social Affairs, Statistical Office, *Statistical Yearbook, 1963* (New York, 1964), Table 172, p. 523.

Total labor force and total population from Organization for Economic Co-operation and Development, *Manpower Statistics 1950–1962* (Paris: Statistical Division, 1963).

Average earnings in manufacturing industry:

Denmark—Hourly earnings of all male workers in manufacturing industry, 1961, from United Nations, Department of Economic and Social Affairs, Statistical Office, *Statistical Yearbook, 1963* (New York, 1964) Table 166, p. 499.

Britain—Males 21 and over in manufacturing industry, weekly earnings in October 1962, from Great Britain, Central Statistical Office, *Annual Abstract of Statistics No. 100* (London: HMSO, 1963) Table 148, p. 123.

United States—Median total money income of all male year round, full-time operatives and kindred workers, 1962, from U.S. Bureau of the Census, *Current Population Report* (Washington: Bureau of the Census, October 1963), Table 19.

Britain are not income-tested, serve in part to compensate for the lowness of the level of government benefits in that country.

In order to complete this comparison of the income levels available to the elderly in the three countries we converted the median income for each type of unit to a common currency—the United States dollar. There are well-known arguments against using the official exchange rates for doing this. But the O.E.C.D. have produced estimates of what they have called "purchasing power equivalent" exchange rates as between the United States and a selection of European countries.[20] The exchange rate we have used is, in effect, the measure of the amount of European currency required to purchase a basket of consumption goods which in the United States would cost one dollar. As is always the case with the construction of index numbers, the composition of the basket of goods is crucial in determining the answer obtained, and there is rarely one "correct" basket of goods. The O.E.C.D. (Organization for Economic Cooperation and Development) has published two estimates, the first using weights that reflect the pattern of consumption in each of the European countries; the second using weights that reflect the pattern of consumption in the United States. There are arguments in favor of using the European weighting system since the consumption pattern in countries with the lower standard of living might reasonably be available in the country with the higher standard, but not necessarily vice versa. On the other hand, using the Danish weights for the Danish purchasing power equivalent exchange rates, and the British for the British purchasing power equivalent exchange rates, may distort somewhat the comparison between Britain and Denmark. Indeed, it is probably the case that the best exchange rate to use in a comparison between the two European countries is the official one. To do so gives a result mid-way between that yielded by the use of the European and the United States weighting systems. In any case, however, such comparisons as we are making here can at best be extremely rough; all the more so, since it can be argued that the consumption pattern of the elderly will diverge as much from the average consumption pattern in their own country, as that average will diverge between the different countries themselves.

In Table XII–8 we present estimates using both European and United States weighting systems, taking the 1955 exchange equivalent as published by O.E.C.D. and corrected only for price increases in the three countries between 1955 and 1962. It should be noted that the use of the European countries' weights improves their position vis-à-vis the United States, particularly in the case of Denmark. Two points of interest emerge from the comparison. The first is that, as one would expect, the income of the elderly in the United States in absolute terms is higher than in the two European countries, but the margin by which it is higher for the elderly women—especially over elderly women in Denmark—is very slender indeed. Second, this comparison confirms that not only are the elderly worse off in Britain than in Denmark relative to the standard of living generally in their countries, but that they are also somewhat worse off absolutely. On the most conservative estimate, Danish couples have

Table XII-8: MEDIAN TOTAL MONEY INCOMES FOR THREE TYPES OF
INCOME UNITS IN 1962 EXPRESSED IN UNITED STATES DOLLARS PER ANNUM,
USING PURCHASING POWER EQUIVALENT EXCHANGE RATES[a]

	COUPLES	MEN	WOMEN
Exchange Rate Based on European Country Weights:			
Denmark	1,581	980	911
Britain	1,439	882	708
United States	2,804	1,406	982
Exchange Rate Based on United States Weights:			
Denmark	1,258	781	725
Britain	1,092	669	538
United States	2,804	1,406	982

[a] 1955 Purchasing Power Equivalent Exchange Rates for consumption from Milton Gilbert, *et al.*, *Comparative National Products and Price Levels* (Paris: Organization for Economic Cooperation and Development, 1958), Table 8, p. 40, corrected for price changes 1955–62 to yield:

European weights—5.325 Danish kroner = 1 U.S. $
0.271 £ sterling = 1 U.S. $
American weights—6.690 Danish kroner = 1 U.S. $
0.357 £ sterling = 1 U.S. $

income levels about 10 per cent higher than British couples and Danish women some 28 per cent higher than British women.

DISTRIBUTION OF INCOME

So far we have been discussing only levels of median income. The general economic position of the elderly will also be dictated by the distribution of income among the old within the three countries. In order to study these distributions we wished to group the data into intervals. But there were problems of interpreting intervals fixed in terms of the units of currency of three different countries. This problem also arises to a certain extent with the use of quartiles of the income distribution, although in fact we have made use of these from time to time. For a general description, however, we have grouped the data into intervals expressed as percentages of the median total income of each of the three types of income unit in each country. (For a full description, see Appendix B.)

There are disadvantages with this method. One consequence of choosing our income intervals in this fashion is that the absolute span of the income intervals varies considerably. The lower the value of the median, the smaller is the income interval in absolute terms. For instance, the smallest interval for women in Britain is only £20 a year, in the United States it is $100 a year, and in Denmark 489 kroner a year. The absolute values of the income intervals must therefore be kept in mind in the following discussion. The top income group (corresponding to more than twice the

Table XII-9: INCOME INTERVALS IN THE CURRENCY OF THE THREE COUNTRIES EQUIVALENT TO MEDIAN INCOME GROUPS

Median Income Group	COUPLES			MEN			WOMEN		
	Denmark, Danish Kroner per Annum	Britain, Pounds per Annum	United States, U.S. Dollars per Annum	Denmark, Danish Kroner per Annum	Britain, Pounds per Annum	United States, U.S. Dollars per Annum	Denmark, Danish Kroner per Annum	Britain, Pounds per Annum	United States, U.S. Dollars per Annum
21% or more below median	0–6,651	0 up to 311	0–2,240	0–4,178	0 up to 189	0–1,167	0–3,881	0 up to 155	0–785
6–20% below median	6,652–7,914	312 up to 371	2,241–2,661	4,179–4,910	190 up to 225	1,168–1,386	3,882–4,606	156 up to 184	786–932
Up to 5% above and below median	7,915–8,840	372 up to 410	2,662–2,944	4,911–5,483	226 up to 249	1,387–1,533	4,607–5,096	185 up to 204	933–1,031
6–20% above median	8,841–10,103	411 up to 470	2,945–3,365	5,484–6,266	250 up to 282	1,534–1,752	5,097–5,821	205 up to 228	1,032–1,178
21–50% above median	10,104–12,629	471 up to 587	3,366–4,206	6,267–7,833	283 up to 353	1,753–2,190	5,822–7,277	229 up to 290	1,179–1,473
51–100% above median	12,630–16,838	588 up to 782	4,207–5,608	7,834–10,444	354 up to 478	2,191–2,920	7,278–9,702	291 up to 386	1,474–1,964
101% and over, above median	16,839 and above	783 and above	5,609 and above	10,445 and above	479 and above	2,921 and above	9,703 and above	387 and above	1,965 and above
Median total money income	8,419	390	2,804	5,222	239	1,406	4,851	192	982

median income) for the couples in the United States is $5,609 or more a year which, in equivalent purchasing power, represents about £1,500 a year.[21] That is about twice the corresponding top income group for British couples, which begins at £783 a year. On the other hand the highest income group for U.S. women, $1,965 a year and over, falls within the lowest income group for the United States couples, underlining once again the disparity between women and couples in the United States. The highest income group for British women, £387 a year and above, is only marginally below the median income of the British couples; and the highest income group for Danish women, 9,703 Danish kroner a year and above, is only 15 per cent above the median income of the Danish couples.

In Britain every type of income unit is bunched more closely around the median than is its counterpart in the United States, where the extremes predominate. In the United States, for instance, about a third of all types of income unit are to be found with incomes 21 per cent or more below the median. In Britain, around a quarter are 21 per cent or more below. At the other end of the income scale some 28 per cent of all units in the United States have incomes more than 50 per cent above the median, whereas in Britain, where the percentage varies considerably for different income units, it is still only in the range 15–23 per cent. If these are the extremes of equality and inequality, we find Denmark in the middle. Compared with both the United States and Britain there are fewer old people in Denmark with incomes more than 21 per cent below the median; but there are perhaps rather more men and couples with incomes more than 50 per cent above the median than in Britain, although the percentages in both cases are very similar to those in the United States.

As another way of comparing the degree of inequality in the distribution of income among the old, concentration ratios were calculated for the three types of income unit in the three countries. The lower the concentration ratio, the less the inequality. For couples they were 0.28 in Britain, 0.31 in Denmark, and 0.33 in the United States; for men they were 0.31 in Britain, 0.32 in Denmark, and 0.33 in the United States; for women they were 0.26 in Britain, 0.27 in Denmark, and 0.34 in the United States.[22] These ratios confirm the general impression gained from what we call the median income distributions, namely, that the incomes of the aged are more equally distributed in Britain than in the United States. That they are also rather more equal in Britain than in Denmark is surprising in view of the income-tested nature of the pension in the latter country. But the greater inequality in Denmark is almost certainly due to the greater importance of employment income there than in Britain. The fact that the concentration ratios are similar for women in Denmark and Britain would support this hypothesis.

It is not easy to summarize the variety in the distribution of income in the three countries and combine it with our discussion about average income levels. However, there is nothing in our analysis that seriously affects our earlier conclusion that the aged in Denmark are relatively and absolutely better off than their counterparts in Britain. It also remains true

Table XII-10:   DISTRIBUTION OF COUPLES, MEN, AND WOMEN IN MEDIAN INCOME GROUPS
(Percentage Distribution)

Median Income Group	COUPLES			MEN			WOMEN		
	Denmark	Britain	United States	Denmark	Britain	United States	Denmark	Britain	United States
Percentage of units with incomes:[a]									
21% or more below median	25	23	34	18	29	36	12	23	32
6–20% below median	14	20	10	21	13	11	26	18	11
Up to 5% above and below median	6	7	5	10	6	3	11	12	8
6–20% above median	6	9	8	8	10	15	9	12	5
21–50% above median	10	13	10	8	11	5	13	13	8
51–100% above median	12	10	10	6	9	13	8	9	8
101% and over, above median	14	11	17	19	14	15	11	6	20
No answer[b]	13	7	6	11	8	3	10	6	8
Total	100	100	100	100	100	100	100	100	100
N=	818	1,099	825	331	495	256	743	1,552	851

Type of Income Unit and Country

[a] Units reporting "no income" are included in the lowest interval.

[b] Cooperating income units providing insufficient income information to be allocated to an income group.

that the aged in the United States are absolutely better off than their European counterparts. But there is also much greater diversity of economic position among the old in the United States, so that averages for that country do have to be treated with particular caution.

THE POOREST AND THE CONCEPT OF SUBSISTENCE

Is there any way of identifying the size of the groups in the three countries who might be said to have serious financial problems by their own country's standards? We are perhaps on dangerous ground in attempting to relate income levels to estimates of "need." But the exercise is illuminating even though it has to be hedged with qualifications. In the United States estimates have been made of the cost of a "modest but adequate" level of living for a retired elderly couple which in 1959 gave a budget of $2,500 a year.[23] For a single person the corresponding budget was $1,800. These budgets are in no sense "subsistence" budgets; they assume for instance that one-fifth of the couples would own an automobile, that there is some regular replacement of clothing and some allowance (although, it is argued, an inadequate one) for medical costs. An alternative approach to a "poverty" level budget suggested by Miss Epstein gives a minimum budget for couples of $1,800 and for single people of $1,300.[24] These minimum levels do not correspond exactly to the income intervals used in our analysis. But by interpolation we can say that just under 30 per cent of the couples, 47 per cent of the men, and no less than 60 per cent of the women in the United States have incomes below this minimum "poverty" level.[25]

For the British standard we must use the National Assistance Board scale rate which is intended to be a contemporary measure of a subsistence income, used in the administration of public assistance. In 1962 these rates were £234 a year for a couple and £139 a year for a single person; and although these rates have been increased in real terms since then, few people would argue that in 1962 this represented an overgenerous definition of "needs."[26] Since this scale rate is for needs excluding rent we must add to it the average rent allowance paid to retired persons in receipt of assistance by the National Assistance Board in 1962. The minimum budget then becomes £291 a year for a couple and £196 a year for a single person. On this basis nearly 23 per cent of the couples, 29 per cent of the men, and about half of the aged women in Britain had incomes below this poverty level. No such poverty standards are available for Denmark because in that country there has been widespread criticism of their meaningfulness. But in view of the general similarity of living standards in Britain and Denmark we thought that it would be interesting to apply the British National Assistance standards to the Danish income data. In every case the British standards are lower than the interval for the lowest income group in Denmark. By interpolation we can say that at the most a fifth of the Danish couples, 16 per cent of the men, and 12 per cent of the women fall below these standards.

It would be unwise to attach too much significance to the fact that the percentages below the minimum are somewhat higher in the United States than in Britain. Certainly no scientific study is required to see that the "modest but adequate" budget used in the former country represents a more generous absolute standard than a British "scale rate." But the minimum poverty level budget used here for our calculation represents, if anything, a slightly lower percentage of United States gross domestic product per head of the labor force than does the National Assistance scale rate of British gross domestic product per head of the labor force. The point we wish to make, however, is that in these two countries, at least, applying contemporary and minimum standards that are reputable, we find significant proportions of all types of income unit, but particularly of the women, falling below such standards. As for Denmark, if in the absence of a Danish standard we use the equivalent in Danish kroner of the British National Assistance scale rate plus rent, we find a very small proportion of the elderly with incomes below such a level. Once again the position of elderly women, in particular, in Denmark appears to be markedly better than in the other two countries.

THE ASSOCIATION BETWEEN SOURCES OF INCOME AND INCOME LEVELS

Is there any association between income levels and income sources? We have already seen that the median income received from different sources varies considerably, so we would expect such an association. But in fact the picture is a little complicated. It is true that in the lowest income groups in all three countries government benefits do predominate, that is, social security, public assistance, or the two combined; and in Britain it may be possible to say that the poor aged women are those with government benefits and very little else, as we have shown earlier. But in the United States and Denmark, significant percentages of the women and couples in the lowest income groups have property income. Among the couples in the lowest income groups, too, in Denmark and the United States, between a fifth and a quarter have wage and salary income, and 15 to 22 per cent have income from self-employment. As we shall see later, much of this self-employment income is the income of farm owners and as such may well be an understatement of their true real income because it takes no account of home consumption of farm produce.

Generally, however, we find that most people in full-time employment are in the middle or upper end of the income distribution. In all three countries the percentage of units receiving employment income either as wages or salaries or as business income rises steadily as the total income level rises. For instance, in both the United States and Denmark, over 60 per cent of the couples in the highest income group (that is, with more than twice the median income) have wages and salaries, and between a quarter and a third, income from self-employment. In the corresponding top income group for couples in Britain, 76 per cent have employment income. In the lowest income groups of the couples in the United States and Denmark, about a fifth to a third have employment income; but only

6 per cent in Britain. It seems that employment income may be relatively more important in Britain than in the United States in accounting for higher incomes among the couples.

Income from rent, dividends, and interest is another income source that increases in frequency as total income level rises. Among the couples in Denmark the percentage receiving this kind of income nearly doubles between the lowest and the highest income groups; in the United States it rises from 21 per cent to over 70 per cent. In Britain the corresponding percentages are 14 per cent and 47 per cent. In all three countries 70 per cent or more of the women in the top income group receive some income from rent, dividends, and interest, but in the bottom income groups the corresponding figures are: Denmark, 19 per cent; United States, 15 per cent; and only 8 per cent in Britain.

But people are in the highest income groups not only because they may sometimes have a relatively large income from a single source, most often employment, but also (as Table XII–3 shows) because they combine income from several different sources. The percentage of units in the highest income group with only one income source rarely exceeds 12 to 17 per cent of the total. On the other hand, 40–50 per cent of all units in the top income group in all three countries have three or more sources of income. The very lowest income group, on the other hand, contains predominantly the aged men and women with a single source of income. For instance, 80 to 90 per cent of the women in Denmark and Britain in the lowest income group have one source of income only.

Income Sources and Levels by Age

The people we are studying, between them, cover an age span of more than 30 years, and it would be surprising if we were not to find significant differences in the sources and levels of income between different age groups within the population of older people. Even if no other influence were at work, the decline in employment with advancing age would alone have the effect of reducing the level of income available to, say, the over-70's, as compared with that available to people between the ages of 65 and 70. In Table XII–11 we see how the sources of income change with age. It must be remembered that in Denmark the pension is not generally payable until age 67. Moreover, in Britain below the age of 70, and in the United States below age 72, earnings above a certain level can wipe out the government pension completely. But the trend is very similar and represents a movement in all three countries away from employment income towards government benefits for all types of income unit. It is perhaps worth noting, however, that the decline in the receipt of employment income, although marked in all countries, is less marked in the United States and Denmark than in Britain—mainly, it would seem, because of the stability of self-employment income among various age groups in the two former countries.

The trend towards government benefits with increasing age needs to be examined a little more closely, for in both the United States and Britain

Table XII–11: PERCENTAGE OF COUPLES, MEN, AND WOMEN IN DIFFERENT AGE GROUPS WITH INCOME FROM DIFFERENT SOURCES

Sources of Income	DENMARK			BRITAIN			UNITED STATES		
	Age Group			Age Group			Age Group		
	65–69	70–74	75+	65–69	70–74	75+	65–69	70–74	75+
Percentage of couples with:									
Public assistance	a	a	a	11	16	23	5	7	17
Social security benefit	65	98	99	74	96	90	55	79	75
Other government benefit	a	a	a	10	11	13	25	16	10
Wages and salary	53	30	14				52	30	20
Business, farm, or professional	25	19	17	47	30	17	21	25	25
Employer's pension	9	25	19	45	42	38	16	25	16
Rent, dividends, interest, and annuities	49	61	57	24	22	28	43	40	43
Other	10	8	5	10	12	12	8	4	7
Source unknown	—	—	—	*	—	—	2	—	1
No income	—	—	—	—	*	—	—	—	1
N=	372	218	223	471	332	296	343	271	211
Percentage of men with:									
Public assistance	a	a	a	14	14	27	14	12	21
Social security benefit	62	97	98	66	92	85	60	76	72
Other government benefit	a	a	a	16	14	11	32	17	15
Wages and salary	37	20	9				33	20	9
Business, farm, or professional	23	13	8	40	21	8	21	25	8
Employer's pension	13	16	19	39	36	34	11	17	13
Rent, dividends, interest, and annuities	53	56	57	19	27	25	22	29	29
Other	10	11	6	9	10	8	11	1	4
Source unknown	—	—	—	—	—	*	—	—	—
No income	—	—	—	*	—	—	*	—	1
N=	78	90	162	141	124	230	63	76	117
Percentage of women with:									
Public assistance	a	a	a	27	36	41	16	23	29
Social security benefit	88	97	99	85	80	72	64	63	40
Other government benefit	a	a	a	11	19	21	11	7	7
Wages and salary	20	8	4				29	12	4
Business, farm, or professional	6	2	3	18	12	4	9	10	11
Employer's pension	22	26	20	16	12	7	5	12	5
Rent, dividends, interest, and annuities	56	57	50	25	21	24	38	30	37
Other	10	6	6	18	14	12	11	9	7
Source unknown	—	—	—	—	*	—	1	1	1
No income	—	—	—	—	*	1	2	6	11
N=b	213	225	301	400	477	675	256	253	333

a Not available separately for Denmark.

b Nine women in the United States sample whose ages were unknown are excluded from this table.

* Less than one per cent.

there is a tendency for receipts of pensions from the social insurance schemes to fall over the age of 75 because coverage is less complete among the older age groups. The position of women over 75 in the United States, in particular, calls for comment because only 40 per cent of them are receiving O.A.S.D.I. benefits. But in part this decline is compensated for by the increased frequency of assistance payments (that is, income-tested payments) in both countries. Over age 75, 17 to 23 per cent of the couples, 21 to 27 per cent of the men, and 29 to 41 per cent of the women in the United States and Britain are receiving public assistance. In Denmark, on the other hand, the percentage with government benefits is relatively low in the age group 65–69 because of the later age of retirement. But after 70 it is very stable. There is some tendency in Britain for the percentage of old people receiving employers' pensions to decline over the age groups. This is because there has been a fairly continuous extension of the coverage of such schemes in the postwar period. Other income sources, in all countries, show remarkable stability with age.

We must beware, however, of drawing any conclusions from this cross-sectional data about what happens to the financial resources of *individuals* as they age. What we can say, however, is that the fact that the older among our sample population, in all three countries, are more dependent upon government benefits, and are less likely to have employment income, will almost certainly mean that the older are poorer. This is illustrated by an examination of income distribution by age in Table XII–12. Because employment income is relatively more important for couples and men than for women, the change is most marked for the former groups. The proportions of elderly couples falling in the lowest income group doubles or more than doubles between the ages of 65–69 and 75 and over; and, correspondingly, the proportions in the two highest groups fall by a half to a third. More than half of couples and men aged 75 and over in the United States have median incomes more than 20 per cent below the median income of all elderly men and couples. But even among the elderly women there is still some shift towards the lower income groups. It is most marked in the United States. The percentage of women with incomes more than 20 per cent below the median increases from 24 per cent in the age group 65–69, to 42 per cent in the age group 75 and over; and the percentage in the top income group decreases from 29 per cent to 16 per cent.

The median total money income in each age group underlines once again that in all three countries it is the very old who are the poorest. As between income units this is most true of the couples; the income levels of the women appear less affected by age. As between countries the United States stands out as the country with the biggest gulf between the age groups. For example, couples aged 75 and over in the United States have a median income only a little over a third of that of couples in the age group 67–69, and a little over a fifth of that of couples in the age group 65–66. In Britain, on the other hand, couples in the age group 75 and over have a median income 73 per cent of that of couples in the age group 65–69 (Table XII–13).

Table XII–12: PERCENTAGE OF COUPLES, MEN, AND WOMEN, ACCORDING TO AGE GROUP AND MEDIAN INCOME GROUP (*Percentage Distribution*)

Median Income Group	DENMARK			BRITAIN			UNITED STATES		
	Age Group			Age Group			Age Group		
	65–69	70–74	75+	65–69	70–74	75+	65–69	70–74	75+
Couples									
21% or more below median	23	24	44	16	27	37	26	34	55
6–20% below median	12	20	19	16	21	28	8	14	10
Up to 5% above and below median	6	10	7	9	8	7	5	7	5
6–20% above median	6	7	7	11	12	6	6	12	9
21–50% above median	12	11	9	16	14	9	11	10	7
51–100% above median	19	10	9	16	8	6	17	9	4
101% and over, above median	22	17	5	16	10	7	27	13	10
Total	100	100	100	100	100	100	100	100	100
N=a	318	197	193	441	307	275	320	260	196
Men									
21% or more below median	12	21	18	20	28	40	13	30	54
6–20% below median	17	20	34	13	16	15	8	9	14
Up to 5% above and below median	5	13	13	3	8	8	—	5	3
6–20% above median	11	9	7	9	8	15	10	3	5
21–50% above median	9	9	8	12	17	10	23	20	8
51–100% above median	6	13	3	17	8	6	20	16	7
101% and over, above median	40	13	17	27	16	7	25	16	9
Total	100	100	100	100	100	100	100	100	100
N=a	65	75	154	128	116	212	60	74	115
Women									
21% or more below median	11	16	13	18	23	29	24	36	42
6–20% below median	23	27	35	16	20	20	9	14	13
Up to 5% above and below median	9	11	15	14	15	13	8	8	8
6–20% above median	9	10	9	12	12	14	6	4	6
21–50% above median	19	14	12	16	12	14	12	7	7
51–100% above median	12	9	5	12	11	7	12	7	8
101% and over, above median	16	11	11	12	7	3	29	24	16
Total	100	100	100	100	100	100	100	100	100
N=a	201	202	269	372	452	636	234	238	304

a For percentages of cooperating income units supplying sufficient income information to be allocated to an income group, see footnote *a*, Table XII–5.

Is this relative poverty of the oldest to be attributed entirely to their eventual withdrawal from the labor force? Can a similar pattern be found in the income levels of different age groups among those who are completely retired? Relevant data are available only for Denmark and Britain. Table XII–14 shows the income distribution of those units who are wholly retired (in the case of couples, the classification is based upon

Table XII–13: MEDIAN TOTAL MONEY INCOME FOR INCOME UNITS
GROUPED BY AGE

Age Group	DENMARK D. Kr. per Annum			BRITAIN £ per Annum			UNITED STATES $ per Annum		
	Couples	Men	Women	Couples	Men	Women	Couples	Men	Women
65–66	12,500	11,000	5,243	} 458	330	208	4,908	b	1,327
67–69	9,000	6,000	5,784				3,155	b	1,327
70–74	8,369	5,345	4,780	382	237	192	2,804	1,972	982
75+	7,080	4,844	4,627	335	213	185	1,121	584	860
N=a	708	294	672	1,021	454	1,454	776	249	776

a Medians of the cases where total money income was known for the percentage of cases
reporting total money income; see footnote *a*, Table XII–6.

b Medians were not computed where the number of cases was less than 50.

the employment position of the husband); it gives three age groups. In
every case the percentage falling in the very lowest income group increases
as we move from ages 65–69 to the age group 75 and over.

There is no reason to doubt that the United States would show a similar
pattern. In societies that have been exposed to inflation and where at the
same time the real income levels of the active population have also been
rising, it is not surprising to find that the very old have benefited least.
They will have had less opportunity to accumulate savings, and the real
value of savings they have will have been reduced. But it is interesting to
see that in the United States the government pension scheme itself serves
to accentuate such differences. Since pensions are wage-related, the more
recently retired will have pensions based upon higher levels of earnings.
In Denmark, on the other hand, the income test serves to reduce such
differences. Moreover, the level of pensions is linked to the cost of living
index and special supplements are payable to the over-80's. (See this
chapter, p. 349.) However, one important point has to be made. Although
the older retired people do have lower incomes than the younger retired,
the difference is very small when compared with the dramatic difference
between the income distribution of those who are working and those who
are not. The age factor is indeed principally an employment factor, and
we shall return to a further examination of the income position of the
wholly retired in the next chapter.

The Ownership of Assets

To complete this general review of the financial resources available to
older people we turn now to examine the extent and nature of asset
ownership. For practical reasons the amount of information collected
about assets was rather limited, and cross-national comparisons are not

Median Income Group	Country and Age Group							
	DENMARK				BRITAIN			
	65–69	70–74	75+	All Retired	65–69	70–74	75+	All Retired
Percentage of retired couples:								
21% or more below median	39	32	46	39	26	31	41	33
6–20% below median	21	22	21	21	24	27	31	27
Up to 5% above and below median	11	9	5	8	12	7	7	9
6–20% above median	3	9	8	7	8	11	5	8
21–50% above median	13	9	8	10	13	12	9	11
51–100% above median	8	9	9	8	10	6	4	7
101% and over, above median	5	9	3	6	8	5	4	6
Total	100	100	100	100	100	100	100	100
N=	125	137	151	413	255	229	230	714
Percentage of retired men:								
21% or more below median	a	26	19	24	28	34	42	37
6–20% below median	a	23	34	26	19	19	14	17
Up to 5% above and below median	a	14	14	13	4	10	8	7
6–20% above median	a	11	6	8	13	10	15	13
21–50% above median	a	9	7	9	9	14	9	11
51–100% above median	a	5	3	3	17	7	5	8
101% and over, above median	a	12	17	17	10	6	6	7
Total	100	100	100	100	100	100	100	100
N=a	34	57	136	227	78	94	191	363
Percentage of retired women:								
21% or more below median	13	16	14	14	21	24	30	26
6–20% below median	27	28	35	31	19	22	20	20
Up to 5% above and below median	10	11	15	12	15	16	14	15
6–20% above median	9	11	9	9	12	12	14	13
21–50% above median	17	13	11	13	16	12	13	13
51–100% above median	10	10	5	8	8	9	6	7
101% and over, above median	15	12	12	12	9	5	2	5
Total	100	100	100	100	100	100	100	100
N=	165	189	264	618	303	405	608	1,316

a Percentages not computed on a base of less than 50.

always easy. For instance, details of amounts of assets in Britain and the United States were obtained by asking the old person interviewed to indicate into which of a number of groups his or her assets fell. The intervals had to be decided upon in advance of the field work and have not always turned out to be the most useful for cross-national purposes.

However, the first important point to note is that asset ownership is generally more widespread among the old in Denmark and the United States than in Britain. This was already foreshadowed by the finding that property income was more often an income source for the aged in Denmark and the United States than in Britain. But in all three countries there are more people reporting asset ownership than income from property. (For a discussion of this problem, see Appendix B.) The discrepancy is largest in Britain, but allowing for this does not alter the general picture. In Britain 58 per cent of the women, 63 per cent of the men, and 66 per cent of the couples reported ownership of some assets of which the value was known; in Denmark the corresponding percentages were 66 per cent of the women, 72 per cent of the men, and 75 per cent of the couples. (Data for total assets are not available for the United States.)

If we consider the different components of assets we find that the main difference lies in the much less frequent ownership, by the aged in Britain, of income-producing real estate or stocks and shares. The percentages having some liquid assets (that is, money in commercial or savings banks, et cetera) are similar in the three countries, albeit a little higher in Denmark. But in Britain only around 10 per cent of each of the three types of income unit own stocks and shares and about 5 per cent own income-producing property. The corresponding percentages in the United States are between 17 to 28 per cent owning stocks and shares and 18 to 26 per cent owning income-producing property; while in Denmark the percentage with stocks and shares is 26 per cent of couples, 18 per cent of men, and 16 per cent of women. Unfortunately, the data on income-producing property is not available for Denmark. But it appears that in Denmark it is very common for elderly people to own houses that contain two apartments, one of which is occupied by the old person, and the other of which is let out for rent. On our definition the value of the apartment let would appear as income-producing property. Farm ownership is also important in Denmark.

Although owner-occupied homes were excluded from the definition of total assets, we collected information about them, and we found exactly the same situation, except that home ownership was rather more common in the United States than in Denmark. It was twice as common in the United States as in Britain, and Denmark came in between. The paid-up value of life insurance policies too was excluded from the definition of total assets, but the information we collected shows that in this respect the United States and Britain were close together in the frequency with which the aged had some insurance—65–70 per cent of the couples, 46–53 per cent of the men, and 41–55 per cent of the women. But here Denmark was different; life insurance appeared to be practically non-existent; most insurance is of an endowment kind which is withdrawn

Table XII–15: OWNERSHIP OF LIQUID ASSETS, STOCKS AND SHARES, INCOME-PRODUCING PROPERTY, AND TOTAL ASSET HOLDINGS, BY INCOME UNITS, IN THREE COUNTRIES (*Percentage Distribution*)

Asset Holdings	Country and Income Unit								
	DENMARK			BRITAIN			UNITED STATES		
	Couples	Men	Women	Couples	Men	Women	Couples	Men	Women
Liquid assets									
Percentage with:									
No liquid assets	23	23	28	31	36	43	30	43	45
With liquid assets									
Worth less than:									
2,000 kroner (Denmark) or £100 (Britain); or $500 (U.S.)	12	9	18	17	17	20	8	11	10
Worth more than:									
2,000 kroner (Denmark); or £100 (Britain); or $500 (U.S.)	58	62	49	49	45	35	58	44	43
Total with liquid assets known	70	71	67	66	62	55	66	55	53
No answer, or value unknown	7	6	5	2	2	2	4	2	3
Total	100	100	100	100	100	100	100	100	100
N=	818	331	743	1,099	495	1,552	825	256	851
Stocks and shares									
Percentage with:									
No stocks and shares	71	81	81	87	88	86	66	77	75
With stocks and shares									
Worth less than:									
2,000 kroner (Denmark); or £100 (Britain); or $1,000 (U.S.)	16	11	8	1	1	2	6	5	4
Worth more than:									
2,000 kroner (Denmark); or £100 (Britain); or $1,000 (U.S.)	10	7	8	9	11	11	22	12	14
Total with stocks and shares known	26	18	16	10	12	13	28	17	18
No answer, or with amount unknown	3	1	3	2	*	1	6	6	7
Total	100	100	100	100	100	100	100	100	100
N=	818	331	743	1,099	495	1,552	825	256	851
Income-producing property									
Percentage with:									
No income-producing property	a	a	a	93	94	95	69	73	75
With income-producing property									
Worth less than:									
2,000 kroner (Denmark); or £500 (Britain); or $5,000 (U.S.)	a	a	a	1	1	1	4	5	4
Worth more than:									
2,000 kroner (Denmark); or £500 (Britain); or $5,000 (U.S.)	a	a	a	4	4	3	22	15	14
Total with property known	a	a	a	5	5	4	26	20	18
No answer, or with amount unknown	a	a	a	2	1	1	5	7	7
Total	a	a	a	100	100	100	100	100	100
N=	a	a	a	1,099	495	1,552	825	256	851
Total assets									
Percentage with:									
No assets	16	20	26	30	35	41	b	b	b
With assets worth less than:									
2,000 kroner (Denmark); or £100 (Britain)	7	9	15	16	15	18	b	b	b
With assets worth more than:									
2,000 kroner (Denmark); or £100 (Britain)	68	63	51	51	48	40	b	b	b
Total with assets known	75	72	66	66	63	58	b	b	b
No answer, or with amount unknown	9	8	8	2	2	1	b	b	b
Total	100	100	100	100	100	100	b	b	b
N=	818	331	743	1,099	495	1,552	b	b	b

a Information not available for Denmark.

b Information not available for United States.

* Less than one per cent.

before retirement age. This could be another factor helping to account for the greater frequency of asset-holding in that country, that is, if the matured policies had been invested. But the differences of the order of magnitude which we have found in asset ownership levels might lead us to suspect that differences of method in collecting the information had played their part. This possibility cannot be ruled out entirely, for in Denmark a more detailed investigation of asset ownership was made than in Britain and the United States; but it is unlikely to account for the whole of the difference.

For Britain and the United States, at least, a comparable picture to the one we have described for the elderly has been found in a comparison of the ownership of wealth among the general population in the two countries (in which survey data was used).[27] The authors concluded that assets are much more widely distributed in America than in Britain, and, moreover, that the differences are greatest for real estate, owner-occupied homes, farm, business, or professional practice, and, to a lesser extent, stocks and shares. The position with regard to the ownership of liquid assets and life insurance in the two countries, on the other hand, is similar. Although some of these differences can be accounted for by the great importance of farm owners and the self-employed generally in the United States, Lydall and Lansing concluded:

> Property is more widely held in America than in Britain, not because the higher-paid occupations have more property in America, but because more manual workers, more clerical and sales workers, and more retired and un-occupied persons have property in America.[28]

THE LEVEL OF ASSET HOLDING

The information from our survey about the value of the various asset holdings is scanty. We can say, however, that between two-thirds and 80 per cent of all those with liquid assets in the three countries own amounts worth more than £100, 2,000 Danish kroner, or 500 U.S. dollars. In the United States the values of holdings, where they exist, of stocks and shares, or of income-producing property, tend to be higher than in the other countries. For instance, a half to two-thirds of those with stocks and shares have holdings worth more than 1,000 U.S. dollars, while those with property, have property worth more than $5,000. In Denmark, on the other hand, substantial proportions of old people with stocks and shares have holdings worth less than 2,000 Danish kroner.

There is a significant difference, too, between Britain and the United States in the value of life insurance. In the former country, the percentage of units with insurance worth more than £500 is insignificant and the bulk of the policies are small, intended to cover burial expenses when the time comes. Despite the provision of some death benefits in the social security scheme in Britain, the value of such benefits is not enough to cover funeral expenses.[29] In the United States, women are badly off with respect to insurance; but about 40 per cent of the couples and men have policies worth more than $2,000.

In all three countries, but more particularly in Britain, there remain considerable numbers of old people with no assets of any kind, or assets worth very little. It is important to know whether the more substantial asset holdings compensate for low incomes. We can only give the most general answer to this question. In both Britain and the United States there does appear to be a high correlation between asset ownership and income level. For instance, in the lowest income groups in Britain, 40–50 per cent of all old people have no assets at all, and another 20 per cent have assets worth less than £100; in the highest income groups rather less than a quarter have no assets, or assets worth less than £100. Similarly, in the United States a half or more of the income units in the lowest income groups have no liquid assets, while the percentage without liquid assets in the highest income groups is only 10–15 per cent. So, although there will be some old people with low incomes who will have capital to draw upon, higher incomes tend to go with some, or with higher, asset holdings. But this is not so true of Denmark. Not only does asset-holding tend in general to be more widespread in that country; it also appears to be spread more evenly over the income groups.

Conclusions

in this chapter we have attempted to survey the general characteristics of the financial resources available to older people in the three countries. In the course of our discussion certain important differences between countries and between different groups within countries have emerged which we shall explore further in Chapter 13. We have, however, established the basic importance in all countries of income derived from the government, either through the social security schemes or public assistance. At the same time, certain features of the Danish situation—for instance, the smaller disparity there as compared with Britain between the income levels of women on the one hand, and men on the other, or between the income levels available to different age groups among the old who are completely retired—seem only explicable in terms of the basic features of the Danish pension at this time—namely, that it was income tested and linked to a cost of living index.

The continued importance of employment income in old age emerged at all stages. It very largely (although not entirely) accounted for the differences in income levels observable between those just over retirement age and those over 70. It also helped to account for the disparity between the financial position of women in all three countries compared with men and couples. At the same time, one of the major inter-country differences to emerge was the greater importance of employment income in the United States and Denmark compared with Britain, largely due, it appears, to the greater importance in the former countries of farming and self-employment activities generally.

Our attempts at international comparison have led us to conclude that on any measure the aged in Denmark are both absolutely and relatively rather better off than the aged in Britain. The high level of the full pension in Denmark more than compensates for the fact that it is income tested, that is, reduced according to certain amounts and kinds of other income. Not only are median incomes higher in Denmark than in Britain, but there are fewer of the old with incomes a long way below the median. Relatively, the aged in the United States are in about the same position vis-à-vis the younger active sections of the population as are the aged in Britain, but the higher standard of living in the United States means that the aged there are absolutely better off than in both Britain and Denmark. At the same time, income among the aged is more unevenly distributed in the United States than in either of the two European countries. Applying contemporary minimum standards appropriate to the United States and to Britain, we find significant proportions of all types of income unit, but particularly of women, to be in "need" in both countries.

Finally, the significance of wider asset ownership in the United States and Denmark compared with Britain remains to be assessed in the light of what we have found out about how older people use their assets, and the contingencies that they have to meet from their own financial resources. This we shall do in the next chapter. Nor have we so far considered the extent to which the picture painted here might be modified if account were taken of whether old people carry the burden of maintaining independent households, or whether they are in fact sharing their houses with their children. This, too, is a question for the next chapter.

NOTES

1 Dorothy Wedderburn, "Poverty in Britain Today: The Evidence," *The Sociological Review*, X (November, 1962), 257–282. Peter Townsend, "The Meaning of Poverty," *British Journal of Sociology*, XIII (September, 1962), 210–227. *Economic Report of the President to the Congress* (Washington, D.C.: GPO, 1964).

2 Some findings have already been published. The first article was by Lenore A. Epstein, "Income of the Aged in 1962: First Findings of the 1963 Survey of the Aged," *Social Security Bulletin*, XXVII (March, 1964), 3–24, 28. Subsequent numbers of the *Social Security Bulletin* have carried reports on other aspects of the survey.

3 Dorothy Cole with John Utting, *The Economic Circumstances of Old People* (Welwyn, Herts: Codicote Press, 1962).

4 The additional investigation of financial resources in Denmark was financed by the Danish National Institute of Social Research.

5 In all three pensions systems discussed here, the pensionable age for women refers to the age at which women, other than dependent wives, become eligible for a pension.

6 The rates of the full pension have been considerably increased since 1962; in April, 1965, they were 9,144 kroner a year for couples and 6,156 kroner a year for single and widowed persons (including a supplement of 444 kroner a year for couples and for single and widowed persons with less than 1,500 kroner a year from other sources).

7 It is believed that at least one half of all pensioners with the income-tested pension had one or more additions to their pension, ranging from some hundreds to more than 2,000 kroner a year in 1962.

8 There will remain a small income test in the form of an increment to the pension of those people who have very small receipts from sources other than the government pension.

9 *Systems of Social Security in Great Britain* (Geneva: International Labour Office, 1957).

10 There have been subsequent relaxations of the earnings rule. See Great Britain, *Report of the Ministry of Pensions and National Insurance for the Year 1963*, Cmnd. 2392 (London: HMSO, 1964), p. 39.

11 There have been two increases in the flat-rate pension since 1962. In March, 1965, the rates became £4 a week (£208 a year) for a single person, and £6. 10s. (£338 a year) for a couple.

12 "The Evolution of State Pension Schemes in Great Britain," *International Labour Review*, LXXXI (May, 1960), 456–479.

13 At the end of 1962, before the beginning of the second stage of the British fieldwork, the scale rates were raised by £14 and £10 a year respectively for couples and single people. They have been increased twice since then—the last increase being in March, 1965, when the scale rates became £326 and £198 a year respectively.

14 Lenore A. Epstein, "Income Security Standards in Old Age" (Paper read to the International Social Science Research Seminar in Gerontology, Markaryd, Sweden, 1963).

15 Wilbur J. Cohen, "Recent Developments in American Income Security Programs for Older Persons" (Paper read to the Sixth International Congress of Gerontology, Copenhagen, 1963). Margaret S. Gordon, *The Economics of Welfare Policies* (New York: Columbia University Press, 1963).

16 Henceforth to be referred to simply as men and women.

17 It should be noted that in the Danish and United States analysis, rent from lodgers and boarders is included in property income. In the British data it is shown as "other income." But its exclusion in Britain could not account for the marked differences commented on, on p. 359, because the numbers with such income are small. Women most often receive it—8 per cent in Denmark, 7 per cent in Britain, and 4 per cent in the United States have some income from lodgers and boarders. For couples and men the percentages range from 1 or 2 per cent in the United States to 2–5 per cent in Denmark and Britain.

18 Lenore A. Epstein, "Income of the Aged in 1962: First Findings of the 1963 Survey of the Aged," *op. cit.* There are differences in the definitions used in the Social Security Administration and cross-national surveys which are discussed in Appendix B. But they are unlikely to alter this picture substantially.

19 Lenore A. Epstein, "Income Security Standards in Old Age," *op. cit.*

20 For a discussion of the justification for this particular approach and the method of calculation, see Milton Gilbert and Associates, *Comparative National Products and Price Levels* (Paris: Organization for European Economic Cooperation, 1958).

21 Using the adjusted exchange rate based on British weights (see Table XII–8).

22 The concentration ratio is illustrated by Lorenz curves which show the percentage of aggregate income received by a given percentage of recipients arrayed by the size of their income. Inequality in the distribution is then measured by the ratio of the area between the Lorenz curve and the diagonal of equal distribution to the area of the whole triangle under the diagonal. As a measure of inequality the concentration ratio has a number of shortcomings. For a brief description of these and some examples of concentration ratios for the total population in a number of countries, see United Nations, Department of Economic and Social Affairs, *Economic Survey of Europe in 1956*, Part III, 278 (March, 1957). (Geneva, 1957.)

23 Helen Lamale, "Budgets of Older Persons" (Paper read to Fifteenth Annual University of Michigan Conference on Aging, Ann Arbor, Michigan, 1962).

24 Lenore A. Epstein, "Retirement Income and Measure of Need," *Research and Statistics Note 2* (Washington, D.C.: Social Security Administration, Division of Program Research, 1964). For a more sophisticated analysis of poverty lines, which gives roughly the same income standard for the non-farm aged, see Mollie Orshansky, "Counting the Poor: Another Look at the Poverty Profile," *Social Security Bulletin*, XXVIII (January, 1965).

25 Miss Epstein finds a higher percentage below the poverty line when she applies the Bureau of Labor Statistics, "modest but adequate standard" to the data from the Social Security Administration survey. See Lenore A. Epstein, "Income of the Aged in 1962: First Findings of the 1963 Survey of the Aged," *op. cit.*

26 Great Britain, *Report of the National Assistance Board for the Year Ended December 31, 1963,* Cmnd. 2386 (London: HMSO, 1964).
27 Harold Lydall and John B. Lansing, "A Comparison of the Distribution of Personal Income and Wealth in the United States and Great Britain," *American Economic Review,* XLIX (March, 1959), 43–67.
28 *Ibid.,* p. 62.
29 There are also social security death benefits in Denmark and the United States.

13 : *The Characteristics of Low Income Receivers and the Role of Government*

In the last chapter we described, in general terms, the sources and levels of money income available to the aged in our three countries. We must begin this chapter with an examination of the extent to which that picture should be modified if some of the mainly non-monetary resources available to the elderly are also taken into account. To what extent, for instance, do the old draw on their savings to maintain living standards? What is the effect of income in kind given by the family? To what extent should our comparisons of the position of the elderly between countries be modified in the light of these non-monetary factors? After examining these matters, we shall consider whether it is possible to identify certain basic determinants of the level of living of the aged in our countries irrespective of the differences in their over-all economic structure. How far, for example, does economic experience during working life influence the position of the individual in old age? What exactly is the role of government? Then we shall examine the characteristics of the major problem groups among the aged. Finally, we shall attempt to relate the difference and similarities in the position of the aged in the different countries to those differences in the institutional framework which we described in the previous chapter.

The Use of Savings and Non-Monetary Sources of Income

This analysis can be conducted only in the most general terms because a very much more detailed financial investigation than we were able to undertake would be required in order to put a money measure upon the consequences of, say, dissaving or consumption of farm produce. The main purpose of the discussion is to remind readers of the different factors and to give some indication of their likely impact upon the over-all picture.

THE USE OF ASSETS AND WINDFALL INCOME

In the last chapter we found that from a quarter of the aged in Denmark, and 30–40 per cent in Britain, possess no assets or income-producing property. For a sizable group, therefore, the question of drawing on their savings does not arise. But do those who own assets use them to supplement their income? The data for Britain and the United States do not provide a detailed study of change in the asset position of the aged because the question asked was simply "Did you use any of your savings in the last year to meet expenses?" The following figures should be regarded as indicating broad trends only.

Of those with any kind of assets, 20–30 per cent in Denmark, 30 per cent in the United States and 40–50 per cent in Britain dissaved. As percentages of *all* the elderly, these become 13–20 per cent in Denmark, 17–18 per cent in the United States, and 27–34 per cent in Britain. In Britain the amounts of dissaving were small, about a half being sums of less than £50. In Denmark, on the other hand, when people did dissave the amounts tended to be larger: 79 per cent of the couples and 64 per cent of the women who used assets, drew amounts of more than 1,000 kr. (roughly £50).

There is an interesting contrast between Britain and America in the use to which the withdrawals of savings are put (the information is not available for Denmark). Between 40 and 50 per cent of the elderly in both countries who drew on their savings did so, as they put it, for "general living expenses." But between 40 and 50 per cent in the United States also used savings to meet medical bills, an item of expenditure that scarcely figured in the British classification. In Britain, clothes, house repairs, holidays, and rates and taxes, in that order, were the other important items.

Those people in the lower income groups who possessed assets, in all countries, were more likely to draw on them than were those in the higher income groups. Differences in income levels might also help to explain the differences in savings behavior between countries. For it is noticeable that it is in Britain, where the aged have the lowest incomes and therefore the greatest need to use assets, that assets are in fact most frequently drawn upon. On the other hand there are other relevant considerations. It is possible that more of the assets of the aged in Denmark are held in the form of income-producing property linked to a dwelling or farm. (Chapter 12, p. 381.) Such assets are difficult to realize for the occasional supplementation of present income. In the United States, too, there is the ever-present worry of being involved in large medical expenditure. (See below, this chapter, p. 394.) This might well account for a certain reluctance to use up assets.

Table XIII–1: PURPOSES FOR WHICH PEOPLE HAD DRAWN ON THEIR
ASSETS IN THE YEAR PRECEDING THE INTERVIEW

Use to Which Dissaving Was Put	*Percentage of Each Type of Income Unit Who Had Drawn on Assets*[b]					
	BRITAIN			UNITED STATES		
	Couples	Men	Women	Couples	Men	Women
General living expenses	51	45	40	}46	c	50
Clothing	26	35	29			
Rates/taxes	18	11	16	9	c	12
Durable goods	11	11	7	7	c	3
Vacations	16	17	18	7	c	4
House repairs	26	13	30	12	c	11
Medical/funeral expenses	6	4	5	44	c	51
Other	8	8	9	2	c	1
N=[a]	370	133	449	138	46	144

[a] Percentages are of those persons who had drawn on their assets; that is, in Britain: couples 34 per cent, men 27 per cent, women 29 per cent; in the United States: couples 17 per cent, men 18 per cent, women 17 per cent.

[b] The dissaving could be used for more than one purpose, so the percentages do not add to 100.

[c] Percentages not computed on a base of less than 50.

Some information was also collected about windfall income—that is, lump sums received during the course of the preceding twelve months from an inheritance, betting wins, maturing of an insurance policy, and so forth. Windfall income proved to be an unimportant source of finance for the elderly in all three countries. Only 7–12 per cent of income units had received such sums and, although the amount received was not known in rather a large number of cases, those about which we do know were small in value. There is some indication that the British elderly who received such windfall income more often tended to spend it than did their elderly counterparts in the United States—which would be consistent with the general savings behavior of the elderly British.

NON-FAMILY INCOME IN KIND

There are three main sources of income in kind other than that received from the family. They are (i) through home ownership, (ii) through the consumption of home-produced food, and (iii) through the public provision of services and commodities free or subsidized.

Home owners among older people tend more often to own their homes outright and free of mortgage than do their younger counterparts. Out of a given income an older person may, therefore, have lower financial commitments in respect of housing than a younger person. Not only would this fact affect comparisons between the standard of living of the old and the young in one country; but variations in the extent of home ownership would also affect our inter-country comparisons. There are more elderly home owners in the United States and Denmark than in Britain. (Chapter 12, p. 381.) On the other hand, more of the elderly in Britain than in the other two countries are keeping house with younger people and to that extent are likely to be sharing housing expenses. It is difficult to say what the net effect of differences in housing tenure between countries will be. But probably it is quite small.

In Denmark and Britain, and to a lesser extent in the United States, public housing policy also enters the picture. In the first two countries there have been measures of rent control; and in all three countries there are programs to provide special subsidized housing for the elderly. Rent control has in the main affected older housing—which elderly income units living alone are most likely to occupy. Lower rents in such cases tend to mean poorer quality and lower standards of housing, so that again the net effect of rent control upon the standard of living of the elderly is, to say the least, ambiguous. Denmark is the country that has the most consistent policy to provide subsidized housing for elderly people. In so far as public housing policy would affect our picture of the standard of living of older people, it is probably in the direction of reinforcing the relative advantage of the elderly in Denmark, and of improving marginally the position of the elderly in all three countries in relation to the position of younger groups.

One important source of income in kind in an agricultural country could be the consumption of home-grown produce. For instance, in the calculation of appropriate poverty lines in the United States it has been assumed, on the basis of data supplied by the U.S. Department of Agriculture, that a farm family would need 40 per cent less cash than a non-farm family of the same size and composition in order to achieve a given standard of living.[1]

As we have already explained, the number of farmers in the British sample is so small, and their economic position so much closer to the position of other occupational groups, that allowing for the value of consumption of home produce would not affect the over-all picture of income levels in that country. In Denmark and the United States, it is a different matter. In both countries, as we shall see, there are significantly more farm owners and workers, than other social class groups, who are at the bottom, and fewer who are at the top, of the income distribution. The poverty of the farm group in the United States is particularly underlined by the fact that no less than 40 per cent of the women and 20 per cent of the men and couples in the rural group are receiving old age assistance. Although only 20 per cent of all aged income units in the United States are classified as farm owners and workers, they make up one-third of all the units receiving public assistance.

The overrepresentation of farm owners and workers in the bottom income groups is summarized in Table XIII–2. For instance, farm owners or workers are 18 per cent of all elderly couples in the United States but they are 30 per cent of the couples with income more than 20 per cent below the median. In Denmark farm owners or workers are 25 per cent of all elderly couples, but they are 36 per cent of all couples with incomes more than 20 per cent below the median.

The position of farm groups would certainly be improved if we were able to make full allowance for their income in kind.[2] Yet their weight in the total picture is not so great that it would change it completely. Table XIII–3 gives the income distribution of the elderly in the three

Table XIII–2: THE REPRESENTATION OF FARM OWNERS AND WORKERS AMONG ALL ELDERLY INCOME UNITS AND AMONG INCOME UNITS WITH INCOMES MORE THAN 20 PER CENT BELOW THE MEDIAN IN DENMARK AND THE UNITED STATES

	DENMARK			UNITED STATES		
	Couples	Men	Women	Couples	Men	Women
Percentage of all elderly income units who are farm owners and workers	25	29	17	18	21	23
Percentage in the bottom income group who are farm owners and workers	36	50	27	30	27	30

countries, excluding the farm population altogether in Denmark and the United States. A comparison with the findings reported in the previous chapter shows, at the very most, a reduction in those two countries of 5 percentage points in the size of the group with incomes more than 20 per cent below the median, and smaller percentage increases mainly in the income groups immediately above the median. In the United States there is other evidence to suggest that allowance for income in kind would not reduce substantially the numbers of the old in poverty. In her recent study Mollie Orshansky uses a lower income level as her indicator of poverty for farm than for non-farm families. But she still concludes that 40 per cent of all persons over 65 not in institutions are in poverty. In Denmark, on the other hand, it seems possible that the much smaller percentage found with incomes below the equivalent of the British national assistance scale rate consists largely of old people in rural areas.

There is one final major source of income in kind from outside the family. In Denmark and Britain there tends to be greater provision of welfare services for the aged by public authorities than in the United States. Of these services by far the most important is the health service. In these two countries medical care and medicines are available, very

Table XIII-3: PERCENTAGE OF THREE TYPES OF INCOME UNITS IN MEDIAN INCOME GROUPS, BUT EXCLUDING FARM OWNERS AND WORKERS IN DENMARK AND THE UNITED STATES (*Percentage Distribution*)

Types of Income Unit and Country

Median Income Group	COUPLES			MEN			WOMEN		
	Denmark	Britain	United States	Denmark	Britain	United States	Denmark	Britain	United States
Percentage of units with income:									
21% or more below median	21	23	29	12	29	33	11	23	30
6–20% below median	13	20	11	22	13	12	25	18	10
Up to 5% above and below median	6	7	6	11	6	3	11	12	7
6–20% above median	6	9	9	7	10	5	9	12	7
21–50% above median	10	13	9	9	11	15	13	13	8
51–100% above median	14	10	11	6	9	14	9	9	9
101% and over, above median	17	11	18	25	14	16	13	6	21
No answer	13	7	7	10	8	3	9	6	8
Total	100	100	100	100	100	100	100	100	100
N=	623	1,099	671	235	495	200	618	1,552	585

largely free, to all sections of the population, including the elderly. In the United States persons receiving old age assistance can obtain medical care as part of that program but the quality and extent of that care vary widely. The recent Kerr-Mills bill was designed to pay the medical bills of those persons not receiving assistance, but who were "medically indigent." Its effect, however, has not always been to increase the number of the aged receiving some help with their medical expenses. There is no doubt that, whatever happens at the bottom of the scale, other elderly people not eligible for assistance are substantially affected financially by the medical expenses which they have to incur. In this respect, therefore, our money income figures will understate the real income of the aged in Britain and Denmark compared to that of the aged in the United States.

FAMILY INCOME IN KIND

Regular money allowances from children to their elderly parents not living in the same household have been included as part of total money income. But only a small minority—1 or 2 per cent of income units in all three countries—received family help of this kind. Earlier, however, (Chapter 7, p. 206), we saw that many more elderly people receive occasional cash gifts from their children. Of all individuals, with and without children, 5 per cent in Denmark, 15 per cent in Britain, and 28 per cent in the United States reported receiving a gift from a child in the month preceding the interview. We have no means of judging what constituted a "gift" or what its value would be. But the British and United States' findings in the present study agree in general terms with the picture that has emerged from more detailed investigations of family help to older people. As a result of such help from the family outside the household, the real standard of living of the old may be a little higher than the money income figures would suggest, but the differences are likely to be quite small for two reasons. First, in the United States, much of the help from the family takes the form of assistance with bills for medical care. In other words it is channeled to meeting the special needs of the elderly. Second, in all three countries, as Chapter 7 shows, because of the value placed upon independence and the part that the old person plays in a complex system of family exchange, the elderly are to be found giving help as well as receiving it. So that the *net* value of all help received in kind is often small. To the extent that net help is received it tends to be received by the poorest among the elderly, particularly elderly widows living alone.

A more important source of family help in terms of living standards is probably derived from the fact that many old people actually live *with* their children. In the first place, if there are other income receivers in the household, the basic expenses of housing, fuel, and light—even food to some extent—can be shared. In the second place, if the other members of the household are higher income receivers than the old person there might be some further support and the old person might well share indirectly in a generally higher standard of living. We could not measure the economic value of such household sharing directly, but, as we have already shown,

Table XIII-4: PERCENTAGE OF COUPLES, MEN, AND WOMEN, IN EACH QUARTILE OF THE INCOME DISTRIBUTION, LIVING ALONE OR WITH OTHERS *(Percentage Distribution)*

	Income Quartile and Country											
Household Type	DENMARK				BRITAIN				UNITED STATES			
	Lowest	2nd Lowest	2nd Highest	Highest	Lowest	2nd Lowest	2nd Highest	Highest	Lowest	2nd Lowest	2nd Highest	Highest
Couples:												
Living alone	82	81	81	78	66	73	67	73	75	78	78	79
Sharing with relatives	16	18	15	19	32	25	31	25	23	22	20	19
Sharing with non-relatives	2	1	4	3	1	2	2	2	2	1	2	2
Total	100	100	100	100	100	100	100	100	100	100	100	100
N=[a]	177	177	177	177	256	255	255	255	194	194	194	194
Men:												
Living alone	50	67	61	62	24	41	40	37	45	53	61	47
Sharing with relatives	41	26	26	16	68	53	50	49	48	41	29	50
Sharing with non-relatives	9	7	13	22	8	6	10	15	6	5	10	3
Total	100	100	100	100	100	100	100	100	100	100	100	100
N=[b]	74	73	74	73	114	114	113	113	62	63	62	62
Women:												
Living alone	59	72	57	67	25	42	60	53	26	47	56	52
Sharing with relatives	39	24	31	19	73	56	34	39	72	49	37	40
Sharing with non-relatives	2	4	12	14	2	2	6	8	2	4	7	8
Total	100	100	100	100	100	100	100	100	100	100	100	100
N=[c]	168	168	168	168	364	364	363	363	196	196	196	196

[a] The percentages of units providing sufficient income details to be allocated to a quartile income group are: Denmark 87; Britain 93; United States 95.

[b] The percentages of units providing sufficient income details to be allocated to a quartile income group are: Denmark 89; Britain 92; United States 97.

[c] The percentages of units providing sufficient income details to be allocated to a quartile income group are: Denmark 90; Britain 94; United States 92.

the pattern of living arrangements of the elderly does vary with social class. In this chapter, therefore, we must consider to what extent the poorer among the old are to be found sharing households with relatives and are to that extent, at least, potentially recipients of help of the kind described above.

The fact is, of course, that the great majority of couples live alone and there is only a very slight tendency for those with the lowest incomes to be more often living with relatives than alone. There is, however, a marked, and very similar, tendency in both Britain and the United States for elderly women in the lowest income groups to be more often sharing a home with relatives. More than 70 per cent of the women in the lowest quartile of the income distribution are living with relatives; in the highest income quartile it is only 40 per cent. Another way of looking at the same phenomenon is that in the United States 44 per cent, and in Britain 33 per cent, of those elderly women living with relatives have money incomes more than 20 per cent below the median income of all elderly women. The corresponding percentages for elderly women alone are only 21 per cent and 12 per cent. A much higher proportion of women in all income groups live alone in Denmark than in the other two countries, but even so the percentage of women in Denmark who live with relatives is twice as high in the lowest as in the highest quartile. As for men, the quartile income distribution suggests that in all three countries there may be some tendency for those in the lowest quartile of the income distribution more often to live with relatives and for those higher up the income distribution more often to live alone or with non-relatives (which in economic terms is probably nearer to living alone than to living with relatives).

Living arrangements are likely to make a difference, therefore, only to the standard of living of elderly women and possibly marginally for elderly men; and it is mainly in Britain and the United States that the difference will be made. But it was precisely in these two countries that we found the elderly women to be so much worse off compared with men and couples. Should we then modify the conclusions of Chapter 12 to say that, if account is taken of subsidies obtained from other members of the household and from sharing household expenses, then the economic position of the women would be closer to that of other elderly income units?

There are two reasons for proceeding with caution. First, certainly in Britain, and to some extent also in the United States, the way in which public assistance is administered will help to raise the money incomes of elderly people living alone above those of comparable elderly people sharing house. This is because in Britain the scale rates that measure "need" are higher for householders than for non-householders and in the United States elderly people sharing with relatives are less likely to receive public assistance. Our figure of total money income of course includes assistance allowances. More of the men and women living alone are receiving public assistance. In the United States 18 per cent and 26 per cent of the men and women living alone have public assistance, compared with only 15 per cent and 20 per cent of those living with others. In Britain, of those living alone, 25 per cent of the men and 46 per cent of the

Table XIII–5: PERCENTAGE OF COUPLES, MEN, AND WOMEN, BY MEDIAN INCOME GROUPS, LIVING ALONE OR WITH RELATIVES (*Percentage Distribution*)

Median Income Group	DENMARK		BRITAIN		UNITED STATES	
	Alone	With Relatives	Alone	With Relatives	Alone	With Relatives
Couples:						
21% or more below median	26	24	22	27	33	37
6–20% below median	15	13	21	16	10	11
Up to 5% above and below median	6	10	7	9	6	3
6–20% above median	5	6	8	11	9	6
21–50% above median	10	8	13	10	9	13
51–100% above median	12	10	10	8	12	6
101% and over, above median	14	15	11	11	16	18
No answer	13	14	7	8	6	6
Total	100	100	100	100	100	100
N=ᵃ	655	138	765	314	639	174
Men:						
21% or more below median	15	28	23	35	32	42
6–20% below median	22	26	14	13	14	8
Up to 5% above and below median	14	5	6	6	2	5
6–20% above median	6	9	10	11	5	6
21–50% above median	7	9	13	9	20	7
51–100% above median	6	6	11	6	11	14
101% and over, above median	20	10	12	13	14	17
No answer	11	7	11	6	3	2
Total	100	100	100	100	100	100
N=ᵇ	197	86	182	266	133	107
Women:						
21% or more below median	11	18	12	33	21	44
6–20% below median	28	29	18	19	12	11
Up to 5% above and below median	13	10	14	13	8	7
6–20% above median	8	10	16	9	5	5
21–50% above median	12	13	17	8	11	5
51–100% above median	8	6	10	8	10	6
101% and over, above median	13	5	7	5	24	16
No answer	8	10	6	5	10	5
Total	100	100	100	100	100	100
N=ᶜ	466	190	693	783	393	412

[a] The following percentages of couples living with non-relatives are excluded from this table: Denmark 3; Britain 1; United States 1.

[b] The following percentages of men living with non-relatives are excluded from this table: Denmark 14; Britain 10; United States 6.

[c] The following percentages of women living with non-relatives are excluded from this table: Denmark 9; Britain 5; United States 5.

women have national assistance compared with 16 per cent and 28 per cent of those living with others. In Denmark, on the other hand, the income test for the pension does not take any account of living arrangements and in Denmark we found that the difference in the income levels of the old living alone and sharing house was much smaller (Table XIII-5).

The second factor to be considered is the financial position of the rest of the old person's household. This we were not able to investigate directly. But we know that, particularly in Britain, and to some extent in the United States, significant proportions of the elderly women living with relatives were living with unmarried children (often daughters) or with siblings (see Chapter 7). It also appears from other survey data that in Britain at least, these daughters and sisters themselves quite often have low incomes and are not in a position to subsidize the old mother or sister with whom they are keeping house.[3] It would therefore be a mistake to assume that a joint household automatically means a subsidy to the old person or a major improvement in her standard of living.

To some extent, however, the picture of *poverty* among elderly women must be modified to take account of their living arrangements. But does the judgment of the *adequacy* or otherwise of their financial resources have to be so modified? Here, as with definitions of poverty, the criteria to be used in judging "adequate" have to be defined, and are bound to be heavily overlaid with value judgments. In the last half century public opinion in most industrialized countries has moved away from a system that compels relatives to support their aged parents. Denmark has never had such a system—a fact that is, in itself, significant in the light of the apparently much lower level of family economic support in that country. Britain has already moved further in the direction of non-support by relatives than has the United States, where some individual states still retain an obligation for children to give financial support to their aged parents before public assistance will be considered. Insofar as the goals and objectives set for the social security system in each country are to enable old people to maintain independent households, "because this is what they want" (see Chapter 7, p. 193), then this must also be the criterion for judging the adequacy of old peoples' incomes. As for the differences between countries, it is interesting to note that in the country where, on our evidence so far, the aged are best off relative to the younger section of the population—namely, Denmark—direct or indirect economic support from the family appears to be least important.

To summarize this discussion of non-monetary sources of income available to the elderly, the three most important factors that might lead us to modify the conclusions of Chapter 12 are: first, the importance of home consumption of farm produce in Denmark and the United States, which would have the effect of reducing somewhat the percentage with very low incomes in those two countries; second, the existence of a national health service in Britain and Denmark, which has the effect of raising real income in those two countries relative to the United States; third, the nature and extent of family economic support, which probably raises the real income of elderly women mainly in the United States and Britain. The fact that different factors can be operating in the same country in different directions itself suggests that if quantitative estimates were available the net effect upon the general income picture of Chapter 12 would be small. Certainly none of these factors is sufficiently important to change our conclusions about the main determinants of income levels in old age.

The Basic Determinants of Income Levels in Old Age

There are four basic determinants of income levels in old age: (i) retirement and the contrast between work and no work; (ii) previous economic status during working life; (iii) for women, widowhood; and, finally (iv), the role of government.

RETIREMENT

The first thing to note is that "retirement" for people after the age of 65 is principally a phenomenon affecting couples—that is, only some 35 to 43 per cent of income units. Most of the men and women who have ever worked are already retired by that age. Social security benefits become payable to women in all countries before age 65. About 90 per cent of the single and widowed women in our sample were already completely retired. So, too, were 80 per cent of elderly men in Britain and in the United States; in Denmark, partly because of the later pensionable age, only 76 per cent were retired in that country. In contrast, however, only 60 per cent of Danish couples, 66 per cent of United States couples, and 71 per cent of British couples were completely retired.

Retirement, as we saw earlier, is not necessarily an abrupt process. A certain percentage of the elderly, particularly again of the couples, were working part-time; and, as we explained in the last chapter, a certain number of those people classified by us as completely retired were still receiving income from employment. This was either because they had ceased to work sometime during the year before the interview; because they had some very casual income; or because, in the case of couples, they had a wife who was working.

But, as Table XIII-6 shows, the main difference between the structure of income of the employed and the retired is the shift from employment income to government benefits. Virtually all of the retired in Britain and Denmark are receiving government benefits. Because of the less extensive coverage of O.A.S.D.I. only three-quarters of the retired couples in United States have such benefits and this might help to explain why casual employment was more important for the retired there. As many as 23 per cent of retired couples were receiving wage and salary income in the United States. But once again we must note that this source of income is very much less frequently received in Britain than in the other two countries. Nearly a half of the retired couples in Britain, compared with only a quarter in Denmark and in the United States, are receiving an employer's pension. Corresponding figures for retired men are: Britain 41 per cent, Denmark 22 per cent, and the United States 16 per cent. For retired

Table XIII–6: PERCENTAGE OF COUPLES, BY EMPLOYMENT STATUS WITH VARIOUS SOURCES OF INCOME

Sources of Income	DENMARK			BRITAIN			UNITED STATES		
	Full-Time Work	Part-Time Work	Retired	Full-Time Work	Part-Time Work	Retired	Full-Time Work	Part-Time Work	Retired
Wages or salary	61	75	17	} 97	96	10	62	66	23
Business, farm, and professional practice	43	30	9				40	36	14
Old age assistance	} 55						1	13	10
Social security		80	96	49	97	98	38	74	75
Other government benefits	1	18	23	19	41	49	3	11	24
Pension from previous employer	53	52	55	30	20	23	5	14	24
Rent, dividends, interest, and annuity	6	11	8	7	10	13	43	44	41
Other	—	—	—	—	—	—	7	6	6
Unknown source	—	—	—	*	—	*	1	2	*
No income							—	—	*
N=	211	97	489	204	101	770	151	126	541

* Less than one per cent.

women they are: Britain 11 per cent, Denmark 24 per cent, and the United States 7 per cent.[4]

The data on the percentages of aggregate money income supplied by employers' pensions indicate that the level of such pensions received in Denmark is higher than in Britain. (See Chapter 12, p. 362.) But the more widespread coverage of such schemes in Britain (and they have been growing apace in recent years)[5] is quite striking. Part of the difference between Britain and Denmark on the one hand, and the United States on the other, will be due to the greater weight, in the first two countries, of the public sector—where employers' pensions are almost universal. About one-half of all the private pensions being received by the British sample, and about two-thirds of those received by the Danish sample, were in respect of some public sector employment. But in private industry pension schemes are apparently more widespread in Britain than in the United States or Denmark, despite the British trade unions' relative lack of interest (compared with some, at least, of their American counterparts) in bargaining for such fringe benefits.

Other income sources appear to change little with retirement, except possibly in Britain. There receipts from miscellaneous sources—which include a number of items, such as trade union pensions, or allowances from charities, which are payable only to retired persons—are rather more frequent for the retired than for the employed. On the other hand, receipts of property income are rather less frequent for the retired in Britain, whereas they remain stable in the other two countries.

The effect of these changes upon income levels is considerable. There is a marked shift from the upper to the lower income groups. Only for women is the contrast not so marked. This is because, although women's earnings are lower during employment than those of men, nevertheless, when they retire they become entitled, in Denmark and Britain at least, to the same level of pension as men. If we concentrate upon the couples, where the number in the sample in employment is reasonably large, we find that in Denmark and Britain the contrast between the income distribution of the retired and the employed is very similar. Only 5–7 per cent of the couples working full time, but over a third of the retired, are in the income group that is more than 20 per cent below the median. On the other hand, over a third of the employed, but only 6 per cent of the retired, have incomes more than twice the median. The pattern is similar in the United States but the decline in the percentage of retired couples in the top income group is less marked. This could be because continued employment is a more important factor accounting for relative wealth in Britain and Denmark than it is in the United States.

The gap between the income levels of the elderly who continue to work full time and those who have ceased to work is summarized in a comparison of the median incomes of the two groups. In all three countries the retired couples have a median income roughly one half that of the couples still working full time. This is not, of course, a measure of the drop in income which an individual suffers when he retires. But it is an indication of the distance between the income levels of the elderly in work and those

Table XIII-7: PERCENTAGE OF COUPLES IN MEDIAN INCOME GROUPS, BY EMPLOYMENT STATUS (*Percentage Distribution*)

Median Income Group	DENMARK			BRITAIN			UNITED STATES		
	Full-Time Work	Part-Time Work	Retired	Full-Time Work	Part-Time Work	Retired	Full-Time Work	Part-Time Work	Retired
21% or more below median	7	21	39	5	7	33	11	33	43
6–20% below median	6	14	21	2	14	27	6	9	12
Up to 5% below and above median	3	11	8	5	9	9	5	4	6
6–20% above median	6	7	7	9	24	8	7	12	9
21–50% above median	12	15	10	16	24	11	14	13	9
51–100% above median	27	14	8	25	13	7	18	10	10
101% and over, above median	39	17	6	39	8	6	39	18	12
Total	100	100	100	100	100	100	100	100	100
N=[a]	117	84	413	190	77	714	140	117	513

[a] See footnote *a*, Table XIII-4.

Table XIII–8: MEDIAN TOTAL MONEY INCOME OF COUPLES WHO ARE
EMPLOYED FULL-TIME AND OF COUPLES WHO ARE COMPLETELY RETIRED

	DENMARK D. Kr. per Annum	BRITAIN £ per Annum	UNITED STATES $ per Annum
Employed full-time[a]	15,125	676	4,770
Retired[a]	7,313	348	2,481
All couples[b]	8,419	390	2,804

[a] The medians for the United States and Denmark have been obtained by interpolation
from the income distributions—excluding cases where total income was not known.

[b] Including couples employed part time.

not in work at a single point of time. In Chapter 12 we compared the
level of median incomes of the whole sample with the levels of government
pensions. Not unnaturally we now find that the income levels of the
retired are closer to pension levels than were the median incomes of the
whole sample. But there is still considerable variation between countries.
In Denmark the retired couples are no more than 20 per cent above the
full pension for a couple; in Britain they are 45 per cent above. This is yet
another illustration of the effect of the Danish income-tested pension.

Although the most noticeable contrast is between the income levels of
the elderly in full-time employment and those retired, the median total
income available to full-time workers over 65 is still lower, in all three
countries, than average adult male earnings in manufacturing industry.
This is not a strict comparison of like with like. It is a comparison of total
income (that is, all sources) with earnings only, and it is of employment
income in any sector, including agriculture, with earnings in manufacturing only. However, it does suggest that the elderly person who continues to
work past retirement age is less well placed—from an earnings viewpoint
—than his younger counterpart.[6]

THE EFFECT OF SOCIAL CLASS

The only indicator we have of economic status during working life is
the classification called, in this report, "social class." (For a discussion of
the definition, see Chapter 8.) For a number of reasons it is only an
approximate indicator. It is a classification of occupations, which of
necessity has to be made in rather crude groupings. In the United States
and Denmark the sample was classified on the basis of the respondents'
description of their last or present occupation. If there had been much
job-changing in the years just before retirement, then the last job would
not necessarily be a reliable guide to economic status during working life

Table XIII–9a: PERCENTAGE OF COUPLES AND MEN, BY SOCIAL CLASS, WITH VARIOUS SOURCES OF INCOME

Percentage of couples with:

Source of Income	DENMARK				BRITAIN			UNITED STATES			
	White Collar	Blue Collar	Service	Farm Owner and Worker	White Collar	Blue Collar	Service	White Collar	Blue Collar	Service	Farm Owner and Worker
Wages and salary	34	48	b	18	}35	}33	}49	35	44	45	17
Business, farm, or professional practice	32	2	b	37				29	12	6	47
Old age assistance	}81	}81	}b	}88	}85	}90	}90	5	8	6	19
Social security								64	74	67	62
Other government benefits	24	19	b	—	53	37	49	18	20	23	12
Pension from previous employer	62	43	b	60	40	17	21	18	22	31	3
Rent, dividends, interest, and annuity	6	14	b	3	8	13	13	60	32	31	39
Other income	—	—	—	—	—	—	—	8	7	5	2
Unknown source	—	—	—	—	—	—	—	2	1	—	—
No income	—	—	—	—	*	*	—	—	—	—	2
N=a	272	295	17	195	342	669	71	250	330	82	148

Percentage of men with:

Source of Income	DENMARK				BRITAIN			UNITED STATES			
	White Collar	Blue Collar	Service	Farm Owner and Worker	White Collar	Blue Collar	Service	White Collar	Blue Collar	Service	Farm Owner and Worker
Wages and salary	16	24	b	13	}31	}17	b	22	15	b	14
Business, farm, or professional practice	19	1	b	23			b	26	7	b	33
Old age assistance	}89	}89	}b	}90	}73	}92	b	4	17	b	24
Social security							b	70	75	b	56
Other government benefits	26	20	b	1	36	36	b	18	24	b	13
Pension from previous employer	67	49	b	53	43	19	b	26	16	b	4
Rent, dividends, interest, and annuity	3	17	b	5	5	9	b	54	20	b	27
Other income	—	—	—	—	—	—	b	2	7	b	4
Unknown source	—	—	—	—	—	—	b	*	—	b	—
No income	—	—	—	—	1	*	b	—	—	b	2
N=a	106	112	10	96	109	333	44	50	115	35	55

a See footnote a, Table XIII–11a.

b Percentages not computed on a base of less than 50.

* Less than one per cent.

Table XIII-9b: PERCENTAGE OF WOMEN, BY SOCIAL CLASS, WITH VARIOUS SOURCES OF INCOME

Source of Income	DENMARK White Collar	DENMARK Blue Collar	DENMARK Service	DENMARK Farm Owner and Worker	DENMARK Unclassifiable	BRITAIN White Collar	BRITAIN Blue Collar	BRITAIN Service	BRITAIN Unclassifiable	UNITED STATES White Collar	UNITED STATES Blue Collar	UNITED STATES Service	UNITED STATES Farm Owner and Worker	UNITED STATES Unclassifiable
Percentage of women with:														
Wages and salary	10	9	22	1	b	11	9	17	6	13	14	27	8	21
Business, farm, and professional practice	5	1	1	6	b	(11)				11	2	2	23	11
Old age assistance						(88)				12	19	22	41	26
Social security benefit	93	97	97	97	b	88	98	96	90	56	63	66	39	40
Other government benefits	(93)									10	10	6	5	6
Pension from previous employer	30	28	19	2	b	17	8	9	3	11	5	5	2	18
Rent, dividends, interest, and annuity	65	37	44	60	b	40	13	23	32	54	26	31	23	48
Other income	9	8	7	2	b	15	13	17	18	11	9	10	5	7
Unknown source	—	—	—	—	b	*	—	—	—	2	*	—	—	1
No income	—	—	—	—	b	1	—	1	—	4	9	4	10	1
N=a	277	172	135	127	20	457	855	126	114	231	259	95	193	73

(Note: In the original, braces combine certain rows. For Denmark the values 93, 97, 97, 97 span "Old age assistance," "Social security benefit," and "Other government benefits." For Britain the white-collar value 11 spans "Wages and salary" and "Business, farm, and professional practice," and the values 88, 98, 96, 90 span "Old age assistance," "Social security benefit," and "Other government benefits.")

a See footnote a, Table XIII-11b.

b Percentages not computed on a base of less than 50.

* Less than one per cent.

as a whole. In this respect the system used for the British material was rather more satisfactory since the classification was of the occupation followed during most of the working life.

Some association between past economic status and financial position in old age is to be expected. Income sources in old age will often depend upon the former occupation of the old person. In the United States the O.A.S.D.I. scheme was extended only comparatively recently to cover farmers and farm workers; therefore, the proportions in that occupational group who are receiving social security benefits will be lower than in some others. In Britain and Denmark pensions from former employers have, in the past at least, been far more common for white collar employed (not self-employed) than for blue collar groups. In addition, the higher the income level (which will be associated with occupation) during working life, the more likely is the individual to have been able to put some money aside for his old age, and therefore to have property income. The higher the social class group to which the old person belongs, too, the more likely he is to have inherited capital.

Elderly women, are, however, in a rather special position with regard to some of these factors. Except for some single women who will have had a normal working life in paid employment, most women will have had their economic position determined foremostly by that of their husbands. This is the reason for classifying widows in social class groups on the basis of their husband's former occupation. But a second variable, which could affect their economic position considerably, is the length of time for which they have been widowed. Extreme examples are the elderly widows in Britain who lost their husbands in the First World War—so long ago, in fact, as to make their marriage of little relevance to their economic position in old age today. We would therefore expect the association between social class and economic position in old age to be much less close for elderly women than for the men and couples. Indeed, we found there were a number of elderly women in all three countries who could not be classified in any social class grouping, because the information they could give about their husband's occupation was inadequate. They appear in the tables described simply as "unclassifiable."

Tables XIII–9a and XIII–9b show that the white collar group in Britain and the United States, together with the farm group in the United States, less often receive social security benefits than any of the other groups. In Britain and the United States the white collar groups are roughly twice to three times more likely to receive income from rent, dividends, and interest, than are the blue collar groups. In Denmark and the United States the white collar and farm groups are particularly likely to receive some sort of employment income. For instance, in the United States as many as a quarter of the elderly women who are classified as farm workers are recorded as receiving self-employment income; and of the white collar couples in Denmark 34 per cent have wage and salary income and another 32 per cent self-employment income, compared with 48 per cent of the blue collar group with wage and salary income and 2 per cent with self-employment income. In Britain and Denmark there is some

Table XIII-10: PERCENTAGE OF COUPLES, MEN, AND WOMEN, IN EACH QUARTILE OF THE INCOME DISTRIBUTION AND BY SOCIAL CLASS (*Percentage Distribution*)

	Income Quartile											
	DENMARK				BRITAIN				UNITED STATES			
Social Class	Lowest	2nd Lowest	2nd Highest	Highest	Lowest	2nd Lowest	2nd Highest	Highest	Lowest	2nd Lowest	2nd Highest	Highest
Couples:												
White collar	21	24	37	50	18	18	35	51	14	16	33	53
Blue collar	37	37	41	39	76	71	57	41	39	55	40	33
Service	—	2	1	3	4	8	8	7	11	14	12	3
Farm owner and worker	38	30	19	6	—	—	—	—	34	15	14	10
Not known or unclassifiable	4	7	2	2	2	2	1	1	2	*	*	*
Total	100	100	100	100	100	100	100	100	100	100	100	100
N=[a]	177	177	177	177	256	255	255	255	194	194	194	194
Men:												
White collar	20	29	27	54	21	11	18	34	10	13	21	31
Blue collar	35	41	39	29	71	79	68	53	47	52	42	42
Service	1	—	3	5	9	8	11	10	14	14	11	16
Farm owner and worker	45	30	28	8	—	—	—	—	29	19	26	11
Not known or unclassifiable	*	—	3	4	—	2	3	3	—	2	—	—
Total	100	100	100	100	100	100	100	100	100	100	100	100
N=[b]	74	73	74	73	114	114	113	113	62	63	62	62
Women:												
White collar	25	33	24	56	26	20	24	46	16	19	27	40
Blue collar	27	27	26	18	59	67	62	38	37	29	36	22
Service	20	17	22	17	9	7	7	8	10	14	14	9
Farm owner and worker	23	18	21	5	—	—	—	—	29	33	16	15
Not known or unclassifiable	5	5	7	4	6	6	8	8	8	5	7	13
Total	100	100	100	100	100	100	100	100	100	100	100	100
N=[c]	168	168	168	168	364	364	363	363	196	196	196	196

a See footnote a, Table XIII-4.
b See footnote b, Table XIII-4.
c See footnote c, Table XIII-4.
* Less than one per cent.

Table XIII–11a: PERCENTAGE OF COUPLES AND MEN IN MEDIAN INCOME GROUPS, BY SOCIAL CLASS (*Percentage Distribution*)

Median Income Group	DENMARK				BRITAIN			UNITED STATES			
	White Collar	Blue Collar	Service	Farm Owner and Worker	White Collar	Blue Collar	Service	White Collar	Blue Collar	Service	Farm Owner and Worker
Couples:											
21% or more below median	15	26	b	38	13	29	14	18	35	35	56
6–20% below median	10	16	b	17	11	24	21	5	13	20	6
Up to 5% above and below median	7	5	b	8	6	8	13	3	8	5	3
6–20% above median	6	7	b	5	8	9	14	10	8	10	5
21–50% above median	12	7	b	9	17	10	13	8	10	11	9
51–100% above median	12	17	b	5	16	7	13	16	9	7	7
101% and over, above median	23	14	b	3	20	7	8	30	13	6	10
No answer	15	8	b	15	9	6	4	10	4	6	3
Total	100	100	100	100	100	100	100	100	100	100	100
N=a	272	295	17	195	342	669	71	250	339	82	148
Men:											
21% or more below median	11	13	b	31	24	31	b	18	39	b	45
6–20% below median	18	29	b	20	6	16	b	8	12	b	9
Up to 5% above and below median	8	14	b	8	3	6	b	2	4	b	2
6–20% above median	6	8	b	9	8	11	b	8	3	b	7
21–50% above median	8	8	b	6	11	11	b	16	17	b	16
51–100% above median	8	4	b	6	10	8	b	6	17	b	7
101% and over, above median	31	17	b	4	25	9	b	34	9	b	9
No answer	10	7	b	15	11	8	b	8	1	b	4
Total	100	100	100	100	100	100	100	100	100	100	100
N=c	106	112	10	96	109	333	44	50	115	35	55

a The following percentages of couples whose social class grouping was not known are excluded from this table: Denmark 5; Britain 2.

b Percentages not computed on a base of less than 50.

c The following percentages of men whose social class grouping was not known are excluded from this table: Denmark 2; Britain 2.

Table XIII–1b: PERCENTAGE OF WOMEN IN MEDIAN INCOME GROUPS, BY SOCIAL CLASS (*Percentage Distribution*)

Median Income Group	DENMARK					BRITAIN				UNITED STATES				
	White Collar	Blue Collar	Service	Farm Owner and Worker	Unclassifiable	White Collar	Blue Collar	Service	Unclassifiable	White Collar	Blue Collar	Service	Farm Owner and Worker	Unclassifiable
21% or more below median	7	11	16	20	b	20	24	26	18	20	38	33	42	25
6–20% below median	22	33	23	32	b	12	22	17	13	10	10	12	16	7
Up to 5% above and below median	9	14	13	10	b	9	15	12	15	7	7	8	7	8
6–20% above median	5	11	9	9	b	9	13	11	16	5	7	10	2	—
21–50% above median	14	12	15	13	b	14	13	8	14	7	9	10	7	11
51–100% above median	8	9	10	2	b	14	6	13	7	10	9	11	6	4
101% and over, above median	21	6	9	2	b	12	3	4	6	30	14	16	15	34
No answer	14	4	6	12	b	10	4	9	10	13	6	2	6	11
Total	100	100	100	100	100	100	100	100	100	100	100	100	100	100
N=a	272	170	135	125	41	457	855	126	114	231	259	95	193	73

a The following percentages of women whose social class grouping was not known are excluded from this table: Denmark 2; Britain 7.

b Percentages not computed on a base of less than 50.

tendency for the white collar groups more often to have a pension from a previous employer than the blue collar or service groups, but this is not so generally the case in the United States.

Since the white collar group is well placed with respect to those income sources that we know, from the previous chapter, to be associated with high levels of income, it is not surprising to find that it is the wealthiest group in all three countries. In general a fifth or less of all the income units in the lowest income quartile belong to the white collar group (the exceptions are women in Denmark and Britain, where a quarter of the lowest quartile belong to the white collar group). But between 40 and 50 per cent of all income units in the top income quartile (with the exception of men in Britain and the United States) are in the white collar group. This picture is also supported by the evidence on asset ownership and social class, which is available only for Britain and Denmark. The white collar groups are more likely both to have assets and to have assets of a relatively substantial amount, than are the blue collar groups. Once again Danish farm owners are like the white collar groups in the matter of asset ownership.

On the other hand, the income distributions of the various social class groups also show that there is considerable diversity of economic position within all social class groupings. Although in most cases a fifth to 30 per cent of the white collar income units are in the highest income groups, in some cases as many as a fifth are also to be found in the lowest income group. In Denmark and the United States, too, as many as 13–14 per cent of the blue collar couples have incomes more than twice the median income for all couples. The diversity is particularly marked in the case of the farm groups in the United States. More of them than of any other social class grouping are to be found in the lowest income group (for instance, 56 per cent of the couples), but there are still some 10 per cent in the highest income group. However, the effect of income in kind in modifying the picture at the bottom end of the farm income distribution must be borne in mind.

Because of the importance of the farming sector in Denmark and the United States and the very heavy concentration of low incomes among the aged in that sector, it is worth asking how the over-all income distribution in these two countries would compare with that of Britain if the farming sector were to be excluded. In other words, how far are differences in the distribution of income among the aged in the three countries to be attributed to differences in their economic structure? With the exception of Danish men where, as we have seen, 45 per cent of all income units in the bottom income group are farm workers and owners, the couples are the most affected. The exclusion of the agricultural sector brings the income distribution in the three countries closer together. It remains the case, however, that there are fewer very poor couples in Denmark than in Britain and the United States, and that there are more rich couples in Denmark and the United States than in Britain (Table XIII–3).

The data on income distribution and on sources of income suggest that there may be some difference of composition within our broad social class groupings in different countries. For instance, service workers in Britain appear to be closer to the white than to the blue collar groups in their economic position, whereas in the United States it is the other way around. There may also be differences among the white collar workers. It seems that the white collar group in Britain contains a higher proportion of public service "bureaucrat" workers than in the United States and Denmark, and a correspondingly lower percentage of entrepreneurial and managerial workers.

Differences in income level between the social groups in the three countries, although all in the same direction, are more marked in some than in others. The data on income distribution, for instance, suggest that there is a relatively heavier concentration of blue collar workers in the lower income groups and fewer in the top income groups, as compared with the white collar groups, in the United States than in Denmark. In Britain there appears to be less contrast than in the United States, but more than in Denmark. This is also true of social class differences in asset ownership in Britain and Denmark. This view is confirmed by Table XIII–12 which

Table XIII–12:   MEDIAN TOTAL MONEY INCOME OF COUPLES AND WOMEN, BY SOCIAL CLASS GROUP

	DENMARK D. Kr. per Annum	BRITAIN £ per Annum	UNITED STATES[a] $ per Annum
Couples			
White collar	11,367	515	4,262
Blue collar	8,687	351	2,658
Farm owner	7,020	} N.A.	} 1,908
Farm worker	6,458		
Women			
White collar	5,826	218	1,326
Blue collar	4,740	186	919
Farm owner	4,500	} N.A.	} 834
Farm worker	4,200		
Unclassifiable	4,950	200	1,290

[a] Medians for the United States have been obtained by interpolation from the income distribution, excluding cases where total income was not known.

shows the median income of income units in the three main social class groups in the three countries. We find that in the United States the median income of the blue collar couples is only 62 per cent, and that of the farming group only 44 per cent, of that of the white collar group. In Britain the median of the blue collar group is 68 per cent of that of the white collar group. In Denmark the gap is even narrower. The median income of the blue collar couples is 76 per cent of that of the white collar group; and the median of the farm workers is 48 per cent, and that of the

farm owners 60 per cent, of that of the white collar group. The same trend
is shown in the median incomes of the women. The median income of the
United States women classified as blue collar is 69 per cent of that of the
white collar group; but in Denmark and Britain it is 81 and 85 per cent
respectively.

When studying concentration ratios we saw that the income of the
elderly in Denmark appeared to be somewhat more unequally distributed
than in Britain, and we then posed the question—was this because of the
greater importance of employment income in Denmark? We are not in a
position to carry out any sophisticated analysis. But the fact that the social
class groups are at least as homogeneous in their economic position in

Table XIII–13: PERCENTAGE OF WOMEN IN MEDIAN INCOME GROUPS,
BY MARITAL STATUS (*Percentage Distribution*)

Median Income Group	BRITAIN		UNITED STATES	
	Single	Widowed/Divorced/Separated	Single	Widowed/Divorced/Separated
21% or more below median	20	23	19	33
6–20% below median	17	18	2	12
Up to 5% above and below median	11	14	2	8
6–20% above median	10	13	—	5
21–50% above median	12	13	8	8
51–100% above median	11	8	6	8
101% and over, above median	11	5	44	18
No answer	8	6	18	7
Total	100	100	100	100
N=	316	1,236	84	767

Denmark as in Britain, if not more so, would lend added support to the
view that the main contribution to inequality in the incomes of the old in
Denmark comes from the contrast between the position of those in and
those not in employment, which is particularly affected by the later
pensionable age in that country and by the rather special position of the
agricultural community. The differences between the economic position
of the social class groups in any one country are less marked than between
the employed and the completely retired. That these differences are not
independent variables can be seen from the greater tendency of the white
collar income units to have employment income. But they are still sufficiently great to conclude that in all three countries the economic experiences of working life truly shape life chances.

Further interesting light is shed on the relationship between sex,
marital status, and economic position in old age by examining the
economic position of the single (that is, never married) elderly women on

the one hand and the elderly widows on the other. Data are only available for Britain and the United States. In both countries, but particularly in the United States, single women in old age are better off than the widowed. No less than a third of the widows in the United States have incomes more than 20 per cent below the median but only a fifth of the single women are in this position. On the other hand 11 per cent of the single women compared with 5 per cent of the widowed in Britain, and as many as 44 per cent of the single compared with 18 per cent of the widowed in the United States, have incomes of more than twice the median.

Single women in both countries are more likely to have employment income, or pensions from their previous employers. They are also almost twice as likely in both countries to have incomes from rent, dividends, and interest, as the widows. The income levels of the single women in both countries still remain much lower than those of men. Moreover, we must remember that widows are more likely than are the single women to be sharing the homes of their children and therefore possibly receiving some subsidy. But the financial problem of the poor elderly woman appears to be particularly a problem of the elderly widow and especially so in the United States.

The Role of Government

The exploration of the economic position of the elderly in the three countries continually brings us back to the differences that exist between Britain on the one hand, and Denmark and the United States on the other, in the importance of the agricultural sector and in the importance of employment income generally for the aged. Yet we have also seen that in all three countries the most important source of income, measured both in terms of frequency of receipt and in terms of the contribution it makes to the aggregate income of the aged, is income from the government. The coverage and the level of government income must therefore be a basic determinant of the level of living in old age. In total 56 per cent of the aggregate money income of the aged comes from government benefits in Britain, 45 per cent in the United States, and 37 per cent in Denmark. We return therefore to a further examination of whether there are any significant differences in the extent to which the aged in the three countries are dependent upon government income. One important meaning of dependency is the extent to which an individual relies for his income upon government sources. Table XIII-14 shows "dependence" as measured by the percentage of an income unit's total money income that is derived from government sources as we have defined them (not only pensions but old age assistance, and so forth.) (See Appendix B.) Income units have been grouped into ranges of dependence; there are those who are completely dependent, that is, receive 100 per cent of their income from the government. Then we have distinguished a group that receive between three-quarters and 99 per cent of their income from the government, and so on.

There is a marked difference between government dependence in

Denmark on the one hand, and in Britain and the United States on the other. Many more income units—in some cases up to twice as many—in the two latter countries compared with Denmark receive *all* of their income from the government. On the other hand, a rather higher proportion in Denmark than in the other two countries receive the bulk—that is, between 75 and 99 per cent—of their income from the government. Earlier we commented upon the greater frequency with which the aged in Denmark were receiving two or more sources of income and suggested that this might be attributable to the existence of the universal minimum pension. It now appears, however, that there are also relatively more of the elderly in Denmark who have small amounts of non-government income to combine with their government pension.

Since the retirement age in Denmark is two years later than in the other two countries we might have expected to find significantly more of the elderly couples and men there with no government benefits at all. But this situation in Denmark is counterbalanced in the United States by the limitations of coverage in the past, together with the marked tendency, in certain occupations, to go on working past retirement age.

Another interesting fact, revealed by Table XIII–14, is the high proportion—over a fifth—of elderly women in the United States who have no government income. These are the elderly women, particularly widows, who were not covered by the provisions of the O.A.S.D.I. scheme and who are not receiving any public assistance or other benefit. In Britain, on the other hand, elderly women are particularly dependent upon government income. Over a half receive all of their income from this source. Yet we have found that in both countries it is the elderly women, particularly the widows, who are badly off. Here is an interesting contrast: in the United States it is the absence of government provision which helps to account for the low incomes of elderly women, whereas in Britain it is dependence upon the government which means relative poverty. Another contrast is between the position of elderly men and women on the one hand, and couples on the other, in both Britain and the United States. Despite the group of women in the United States without government benefits, somewhere between a third to a half of all men and women in these two countries rely entirely upon the government for their income. But no more than a fifth of the couples are in this position.

Lastly, and most important of all, it becomes clear from Table XIII–14 that despite the very different systems of government support for the aged in Denmark, Britain, and the United States the level of benefits provided by these systems is crucial in determining the standard of living of the majority of the elderly in all three countries. One-half to two-thirds of all income units in the three countries receive more than one-half of their total income from government sources. To this extent, therefore, the relative levels of pensions and of public assistance payments could be all-important in explaining the relative financial position of the aged in the three countries.

At this point it is important to recall the differences in the structure of the government systems in the three countries. In Denmark the significant

Table XIII–14: THREE TYPES OF INCOME UNIT AND THEIR DEPENDENCE ON GOVERNMENT BENEFITS (*Percentage Distribution*)

Type of Income Unit and Country

Percentage of Total Money Income Coming from Government Benefits	DENMARK			BRITAIN			UNITED STATES		
	Couples	Men	Women	Couples	Men	Women	Couples	Men	Women
100%	13	20	26	21	33	53	19	43	39
75–99%	20	27	28	21	15	15	11	7	5
50–74%	11	11	13	20	18	12	19	16	9
25–49%	8	4	5	14	11	8	15	12	11
1–24%	20	19	15	6	3	2	9	5	5
No government benefits	16	10	4	10	11	5	18	12	21
Government benefits not known	—	—	—	—	—	—	2	2	2
Total income not known	12	9	9	7	8	6	6	3	8
Total	100	100	100	100	100	100	100	100	100
N=	818	331	743	1,099	495	1,552	825	256	851

level of government benefit is the full pension, for that provides a basic floor below which the level of an old person's income will, in most cases, not fall. In Britain, however, such a floor is provided in general not by the level of the retirement pension, but by the level of the national assistance scale rate and rent allowances. Any old person with no income other than a retirement pension (or the few cases without entitlement to a retirement pension but with income from other sources below the level of the scale rate) would, in theory, receive supplementation from the National Assistance Board. In practice there are holes in this floor. Perhaps as many as one in three of the aged in Britain with entitlement do not apply for supplementation.[7] The reasons are complex, but in essence are a mixture of ignorance and pride springing from a determination to remain independent and to manage without "charity." In the United States it is even less easy to speak of a floor. The *minimum* O.A.S.D.I. payment is not a universal floor because of some of the limitations of coverage among today's old. As for public assistance, this is administered on a state-to-state basis with variations in the rules for determining eligibility and need. It may be that the aged in the United States are also sometimes reluctant to apply for assistance that involves a means test. The effect of government operations in providing a minimum income level of the aged is likely, therefore, to be most uniform in Denmark, followed by Britain, and least uniform of all in the United States.

THE CHARACTERISTICS OF LOW INCOME RECEIVERS

The chief characteristics of the low income receivers are very similar in all three countries. The main problem group is undoubtedly elderly women and in particular elderly widows. Their position is serious in Britain but even more so in the United States. To some extent, the position of elderly women is only another aspect of the problem of the absence of employment income in old age. The financial difficulties of elderly women spring from the fact that they are far less likely to be working than men, even in the same age groups; and from the fact that, because few of them have in the past worked regularly, and full-time, they less often have income from sources like employers' pensions.

The result is that in Britain, where property income is not very common, elderly women are principally dependent upon government benefits. In the United States their position with regard to employment income and employers' pensions is the same as in Britain, but American elderly women are rather more likely to have property income. What they lack is social security provision. We find that in both Britain and the United States elderly women are the main recipients of public assistance. True, relatively more of them are living with relatives and so may receive help from those with whom they are sharing households. But as we have argued above, the effect upon their standard of living will not always be great.

In Denmark, however, the main pattern of incomes for women appears to be the combination of government benefits with small amounts of property income or employers' pensions. But because of the operation of the income test in the administration of the pension, government benefits in Denmark serve to compensate elderly women for their deficiency with respect to those other income sources that are available to couples and men. Hence the gap between elderly women and the rest of the elderly population, although it still exists, is smaller in Denmark than elsewhere.

The second characteristic of those at the bottom of the income distribution is that they are very old. There is, of course, overlap: most of the very old are old women. But the older among the couples and men in all three countries are also worse off than their younger counterparts because the older people are less likely to be working. Furthermore, we have found some evidence to support the view that the elderly retired are rather worse off than the younger retired.

Chapter 2 showed that the most incapacitated among the old were elderly women and the very old. These are now seen to be the poorest groups in Britain and the United States. Hence we would also expect to find an association between low income and incapacity in those countries. The data are not available for Britain but those for the United States do confirm this expectation. The problems of old age do not come singly— bereavement, failing health, incapacity, and low income are all likely to come together.

The last characteristic of some at the bottom of the income distribution is special for Denmark and the United States. It is the tendency for a disproportionate number of them to be farm workers and owners. In the United States their poverty is due to a combination of low farm incomes and of the low coverage of the agricultural population by social security benefits. In Denmark the year of the survey was a particularly bad one for the farming community. Moreover, although well covered by government pensions, farm owners and workers less frequently receive income from non-government sources than do the other groups.

The single exception is property income, where the farm groups in Denmark are well placed. We have argued above that the position of the rural old might be improved if we could take account of their non-money income, but that is unlikely to alter the picture very much.

A Summary of the Economic Position of the Aged

It is perhaps surprising to find that, despite the differences that exist in the over-all standard of living between the United States on the one hand, and Britain and Denmark on the other, the basic determinants of the standard of living of the aged are the same in all three countries. They are, first, whether or not the old person goes on working, and, second, the availability, the level, and the form of government benefits that are provided when working life begins to decline.

The old person's own resources, in the form of assets or pensions from private employers, are useful supplements to other income sources but in no sense are they genuine substitutes for government provision in any of the countries we have studied. In cases (such as that of some elderly women in the United States) where the old person has to rely on these other sources without government support, the result is often considerable poverty.

It is sometimes argued that as general income levels rise people will more and more be able to make their own provision for old age. The assumption appears to be that savings will be accumulated during working life either directly, or through insurance and the membership of private pension schemes. In view of such arguments, the evidence of the similarity between the United States, with its higher living standards, and the other countries is particularly interesting. Moreover it would be in the United States, where there are still strong ideological pressures against public provision for meeting states of dependency, that one would expect "self-provision" to be most developed. But this is not the case. Dependence upon government provision, by whatever measure, whether it be the percentage of income units largely dependent on government or the percentage of aggregate money income derived from government sources, is very similar in the United States and Britain. It is greater in the United States than in Denmark. Indeed, there is an expectation that dependence, in these two senses, will increase in the United States over the next few years because of the increased coverage of today's working population by the O.A.S.D.I. scheme.

Property income supplies only 15 per cent of the aggregate money income of the aged in the United States, private pensions rather less; and there are still very substantial groups of the elderly without any such income. As income levels have risen in the United States so have standards of consumption, and hence wants and needs. In old age government provision is still required, and to a large extent increasingly relied upon, to ensure that needs are met at these higher contemporary levels.

THE ROLE OF THE FAMILY

The role of the family in supplying economic support for the aged is generally of minor importance in all these countries. So great appears to be the desire for independence among the old that family help is rather to be seen as part of a network of mutual help and exchange, more closely related to the nature of family structure and interaction than to economic considerations. But such considerations are not entirely absent. There is a good deal of agreement that the living arrangements of a number of elderly women in the United States are dictated by economic necessity; and this must certainly be true of the small group who have no income at all.[8] In Britain economic factors also play their part, but on their own they are not enough to explain the living arrangements of elderly women, not least because a high proportion have always lived with their children. In Denmark the absence of as clear a pattern of family support as in the other two countries appears to be as much related to the historical roots of Danish family structure as to the contemporary economic position of the Danish aged.

It is certainly not the case that the existence of government schemes of economic support undermines family support. Where those government schemes leave holes in the net of support, and where parts of their administration carry overtones of "charity," they fail to prevent the emergence of identifiable, and relatively deprived, groups among the aged. It is here that family help is most apparent.

BETTER OR WORSE OFF?

Taken as a whole the aged in the United States are absolutely better off than in the European countries, although the poverty of some of the elderly women in the United States is underlined by the fact that they come perilously near, in real terms, to having European income levels. The Danish aged are better off absolutely than the British. The Danish aged are also probably better off than both the British and the United States aged, relative to the standard of living of other groups of the population in each country. Another possible frame of reference by which the position of the aged might be judged is their own immediate past experience. The sample was asked to say how their present financial position compared with that when they were 60.[9] Such a question can be little more than an indicator of subjective feelings. It is improbable that a realistic comparison could be made by people of 70 or 80 with a situation 20 years earlier when prices and real income levels generally will have changed so much.

Less than 20 per cent of the people over the official retirement age in Denmark considered themselves to be worse off now than before retirement. A good 40 per cent said about the same, but as many as 30 per cent said they were better off. In Britain on the other hand, over a half, and 30 per cent in the United States, considered themselves worse off. Only 11 per cent in Britain and 14 per cent in the United States said they were better off. The subjective judgment by the old people of their economic position

Table XIII–15: REPLIES TO "HOW WOULD YOU SAY YOU ARE GETTING ALONG FINANCIALLY NOW, COMPARED WITH WHEN YOU WERE 55–60?"[a]

	Percentage of All Income Units Replying					
	About the Same	Better	Worse	Can't Make Comparison	No Reply, etc.	Total
Denmark	44	28	17	10	1	100
Britain	34	12	51	3	1	100
United States	47	14	34	3	1	100

[a] Age 55 was used for this question in Denmark and age 60 in Britain and the United States.

agreed with our ranking of their position according to the economic evidence from the survey.

HETEROGENEITY AMONG THE OLD

Diversity of circumstances among the aged has been a recurrent theme of this book. What is true of health, for instance, is also true of financial resources. There are wide differences in economic circumstance between different groups among the aged population in any one country. But one fact that has emerged is that these differences are greater in the United States than in the European countries. There are greater extremes of wealth and poverty among the aged in the United States; there are greater differences between the agricultural and the non-agricultural sectors; between the elderly white collar and the blue collar groups; between elderly couples and men on the one hand and women on the other. Yet another dimension of inequality, which we did not investigate specifically in this survey because it was not relevant to international comparisons, is that of race. It is clear that differences between white and non-white will also affect the aged in the United States.[10]

The greater economic inequalities in the United States is a finding at least partially foreshadowed by some studies of the over-all distribution of income in Britain and the United States.[11] In studying inequality among the aged we are studying what is predominantly a low income group. Recently published data on estimates of the numbers and conditions of people with incomes at or below relevant poverty lines in Britain and the United States suggest there are real differences between the two countries.[12] Many more of the poor in the United States are to be found with incomes a long way below the poverty line in that country, in contrast to Britain, where national assistance acts as a net through which some may fall, but if they do fall it is not too far. It is significant that not only is the uniformity of British national assistance missing from the United States, but in addition the United States pension system itself contributes to heterogeneity. The fact that the social security system is wage-related serves to re-emphasize inequalities. Those with the highest O.A.S.D.I. benefits will, because they were the highest earners, tend to have the highest assets and other resources.[13]

Were it not for the later age of retirement and the greater importance of employment among the elderly in Denmark we should probably find that the elderly in Denmark were the most homogeneous of all in financial terms. There is probably less difference in income levels in Denmark than in Britain between the elderly men and couples and the women. This is mainly the result of the particular form of government pension scheme in Denmark. Because it is income tested and pays supplements to the very old it serves to iron out some of the grosser differences that still exist in Britain with its basically flat-rate scheme.

Earlier in this volume we saw that the elderly in Denmark are more homogeneous in their patterns of family interaction and living arrangements. The differences that do exist are not so much class differences as difference between white and blue collar on the one hand, and agricultural workers on the other. The fascinating question for the sociologist interested in the development of social policy is whether the form of pension provision in Denmark, with its egalitarian consequences, has its roots in a society less class-divided in other ways. To answer such a question requires a detailed historical analysis, but it is not without significance that the original pressure for pension legislation in Denmark came from an alliance of farmers and urban working class, and that the "means test" approach never seems to have carried with it the overtones of charity and pauperism which even today attach, albeit in a modified form, to the operations of the National Assistance Board in Britain or to the public assistance agencies in the United States. The fact, however, that the pressures behind the introduction of O.A.S.D.I. in the United States in 1935 could be broadly described in the same way as in Denmark shows that this cannot hope to be the full explanation.

In Britain the opposition to the means test undoubtedly contributed to the emphasis eventually placed in the 1948 pension legislation upon equality of treatment. Every citizen who had paid his contributions was to be entitled, as of right, to the same flat-rate pension. This is to give priority to equality of status rather than economic equality.[14] From the beginning, the O.A.S.D.I. scheme in the United States, which links contributions and benefits to the level of earnings, has been furthest from economic egalitarianism.

The issue here is not economic egalitarianism and certainly not its application in old age. But the question raised by the survey data is not whether equality is desirable, but whether the emphasis placed in Britain and the United States upon equality of status in the pension schemes may have been at the expense of meeting, as adequately as in Denmark, some of the economic needs of vulnerable groups among the aged.

There are three features of the Danish pension system that account for the relatively better financial position of the aged in Denmark. The first is the high level, relative to other incomes (such as earnings), at which the full pension is set. In this connection it must be asked how far this high level has been maintained *because* the system is income tested. This becomes an issue of crucial importance now that Denmark is introducing a system of basically full flat-rate pensions for all. The second feature is that this full pension is linked to the cost of living.

The third is the income test, which enables those resources that are available for pensions to be devoted to those who need help most—the aged women, the very old—in other words, to those who for any reason have little in the way of non-state income.

Up to the present the different systems supplying government financial support for the aged have not produced very wide differences in the allocation of total resources to the aged. Total payments of cash benefits under social security schemes and public assistance expressed as a percentage of gross national product show only small variations. They were highest, 3.3 per cent, in Britain where the percentage of the total population aged 65 and over is highest. They were lowest in the United States,

Table XIII–16: TOTAL CASH PAYMENTS UNDER SOCIAL SECURITY AND
PUBLIC ASSISTANCE SCHEMES TO THE ELDERLY, AS A PERCENTAGE OF
GROSS NATIONAL PRODUCT IN THREE COUNTRIES, 1962

	Total payments in 1962	As Percentages of G.N.P.[a]
Denmark Danish Kr. (million)[b]	1,298.6	2.9
Britain £ (million)[c]	928.0	3.3
United States U.S. $ (million)[d]	13,029.2	2.3

Sources: [a] Gross national product. United Nations, Department of Economic and Social
Affairs, Statistical Office, *Statistical Yearbook, 1963* (New York, 1964), Table 172,
p. 523. United Nations, Department of Economic and Social Affairs, Statistical
Office, *Statistical Yearbook, 1962* (New York, 1963), Table 165, p. 498.

[b] Danish data relate to 1961. *Social Welfare Statistics of the Northern Countries, 1960*
(*1960/61*) (Stockholm: Nordisk Statistisk Skriftserie, 1964), Table 2a, p. 16.

[c] Great Britain, Central Statistical Office, *National Income and Expenditure, 1964*
(London: HMSO, 1964), Table 39, p. 43. Great Britain, Ministry of Pensions
and National Insurance on behalf of the National Assistance Board, *Report of
the National Assistance Board, 1962,* Cmnd. 2078 (London: HMSO, 1963),
Table, p. 30 (expenditure on retirement pensions, non-contributory old-age
pensions, and national assistance to persons aged 65 and over).

[d] United States, Department of Health, Education, and Welfare, Social Security
Administration, *Social Security Bulletin, Annual Statistical Supplement, 1962*
(Washington, D.C.: U.S. GPO, 1964), Table 6, p. 5; Table 7, pp. 6–7.

2.3 per cent, where, too, the percentage of the population aged 65 and
over was lowest. In Denmark the percentage was nearer to that in Britain,
being 2.9 per cent. These figures would confirm that it is not only the total
amount of resources allocated, but also the way in which those resources
are distributed among the old, which is very important in shaping the
final outcome in terms of the adequacy or otherwise of income levels for
the individual old person.

The contributory principle has a long history in both Britain and the
United States and there seems little likelihood that it will be abandoned.
But since in neither country are contributions and benefits linked in a
strict actuarial way, both countries could seek to modify the system of
social security provision along lines that would improve relatively the
position of the problem groups as we have identified them. The position of
elderly women will be automatically somewhat improved in the United
States as the coverage of the elderly population by O.A.S.D.I. provisions
improves. But relatively higher benefits for the single and widowed, and
some linking of benefits to price indices, if not to an index of average real
income, would help a great deal in both Britain and the United States.

NOTES

1 Mollie Orshansky, "Counting the Poor: Another Look at the Poverty Profile," *Social Security Bulletin*, XXVIII (January, 1965).

2 In Denmark interviewers were instructed to include the value of home consumption in the income of the self-employed, but there is doubt about how effectively this instruction was followed.

3 Dorothy Cole with John Utting, *The Economic Circumstances of Old People* (Welwyn, Herts: The Codicote Press, 1962), pp. 85–86.

4 The fact that women in Denmark are relatively well off with respect to private pensions suggests that it is more common in that country than in Britain or the United States for the widow to retain rights to her husband's pension when he dies.

5 *Occupational Pension Schemes—A New Survey by the Government Actuary* (London: HMSO, 1966), pp. 10–11.

6 Unfortunately we cannot say whether this is because of declining individual earning capacity in a given job; because of shifts in later life to lower paid jobs; or because the elderly in employment will be overrepresented in declining industries—or a combination of all three reasons.

7 Dorothy Cole with John Utting, *op. cit.*, pp. 95, 104; also Peter Townsend and Dorothy Wedderburn, *The Aged in the Welfare State* (London: Bell and Sons, Ltd., 1965), pp. 117–118.

8 Mollie Orshansky, *op. cit.*, p. 17.

9 In Denmark the age chosen was 55.

10 It is estimated that 28 per cent of all families in poverty in the United States are non-white. Mollie Orshansky, *op. cit.*, Table 2.

11 Lydall and Lansing conclude: ". . . it appears that pre-tax income per spending unit is, in general, very similarly distributed in the two countries. The only significant discrepancy is that the United States contains more relatively low-income spending units." Harold Lydall and John B. Lansing, "A Comparison of the Distribution of Personal Income and Wealth in the United States and Great Britain," *American Economic Review*, XLIX (March, 1959), 43–67.

12 Mollie Orshansky, *op. cit.*

13 Lenore A. Epstein, "Income Security Standards in Old Age" (Paper read to the International Social Science Research Seminar in Gerontology, Markaryd, Sweden, August, 1965), pp. 10–11.

14 T. H. Marshall, "Citizenship and Social Class," *Sociology at the Crossroads* (London: Heinemann, 1963), p. 107. Professor Marshall argues that the extension of the social services is not primarily a means of equalizing incomes. "What matters is that there is a general enrichment of the concrete substance of civilized life. . . . Equality of status is more important than equality of incomes."

14 : *Summary and Conclusion*

Aims of Research :   This study has aimed in very broad outline to establish what are the present capacities of the elderly populations of industrial societies in relation to their social and economic circumstances. Are they integrated into society or not? By collecting data on a national scale in three countries the investigators believed that an exceptionally firm basis for an advance in knowledge would be laid. By submitting the collection of these data to rigorous control and coordination of a kind not so far equalled in any cross-national or comparative study, the investigators further believed that better constructed theories, particularly of the middle range, about the aged and aging were likely to be developed. Much of the existing knowledge about old people was not only fragmented and localized, but was tenuous or uncertain because the different perspectives, values, definitions, and interests of research workers in different countries had led either to conflicting results or at least to results that varied widely in emphasis and precision. Cross-national collaboration in applying the techniques of the sample survey seemed to offer a rare and yet a most attractive opportunity. The particular contribution of this study is therefore felt to lie chiefly in its scope and in the systematic approach adopted towards the theoretical framework, hypotheses, and definitions.

Principles of Approach :   The study has important interdisciplinary features in that certain of the approaches of sociology, economics, social administration, and social history are reflected and interrelated. Persons aged 65 and over represent a major stratum of the populations of industrial society and have come to comprise an integral part of such society. They also straddle productive and dependent roles and epitomize (if any age-group or generation can be said to epitomize) the typical problems attributed to contemporary industrial society—of alienation, anomie, isolation, and loneliness. This is what lends the study of the aged its particular fascination and gives it wider relevance. The integration of this age-group into society could be said to depend on their functional capacity, employment status, social status, the structure of their families, family contacts, social "aloneness" or isolation, relative income level, and access to organized social services. All these concepts or variables were investigated. An attempt was made to define each of them operationally. Some have been taken over from other work. Others have been developed as new instruments of research. It was of course impossible in these social surveys to explore some matters very far, but, even if the data collected fall a long way short of what would be ideal, some attempt has been made to show how important it is to look at peoples' lives "in the round" (and therefore to indicate the great value of correlating or combining different sociological and economic variables) if any special aspect of their lives is to be really understood. Equally, an attempt has been made to show how important it is to develop sociological generalizations in the context of information obtained about cross-sections of entire populations.

A Dual Thesis—Integration: The chief conclusion of this report has a dual, and what will seem to some a paradoxical, emphasis. First, persons aged 65 and over are more strongly integrated into industrial society than is often assumed either by the general public or by sociological theorists. Certain commonly accepted parts of the general theory of industrialization or modernization, which have been increasingly criticized in recent years, are not consistent with such facts as are reported here about old peoples' family and social relationships. By their general health or, more specifically, the personal and household functions they perform, in the services they receive from their families, and in the frequency of their contacts with children and other relatives, most old people are fairly securely knitted into the social structure. Physical activity is largely self-sustaining. Integration with the family and the local community is maintained by the immediate network of personal, or "privatized," relationships, based on reciprocity, common interests, inculcated loyalties, and affection.

A Dual Thesis—Separation: Second, major problems are nonetheless to be found among the elderly. To a varying extent we found poverty, isolation, lack of adequate care in infirmity, and insufficient meaningful occupation among them. In some respects the elderly could be said to be kept at arm's length from the social structure. Many of their problems, though by no means all, arise as the consequence of formal actions on the part of mass society that confirm their separate retired status. Political actions are taken to introduce social security legislation, permit cheap travel on public transport, and build special types of housing. Public services, private corporations, and large firms adopt fixed ages of retirement. The public increasingly identifies "the old," "pensioners," or "the retired" as a special category in society. Many of the elderly themselves tend to resist such identification and reveal their uneasiness about it. They say they are not old in any real sense of that word or they describe their activities in terms that suggest they like to think they have altered their occupational pattern rather than "retired." Far more belong to clubs and organizations for people of all ages rather than of specific ages, and in most industrial societies few of them concert their actions on behalf, say, of higher pensions. So while society itself tends increasingly to typify the elderly as a distinct social stratum or category, the latter do not display many features of collective organization or self-consciousness. They therefore comprise a kind of potential or embryonic "class" accommodated uneasily in the present class structure.

Balance Between Formal and Informal Relationships : This dual relationship of the elderly to the rest of industrial society has been touched on at frequent points in this report. It is revealed even in the choice of the subject matter of chapters. In some ways it can be represented as a balance between the integrative impulses of informal primary relationships and the segregative impulses of formal industrial society or, more crudely, as a balance between the private and public aspects of the life of the elderly in modern society. Because industrial society is formally committed to the objectives of greater prosperity, higher productivity, and accelerating technological change, it tends to give precedence to the values of youth, innovation, and achievement and therefore to develop means of *accommodating* rather than *integrating* the elderly. But the informal aspects of social relationships are by no means consistently integrative nor the formal aspects consistently segregative. For example, some old people lack or lose primary relations; some social services deliberately bring old and young together. The two juxtaposed processes are changing in speed and strength over time. The disjunction of the facts of integration and those of segregation have to be understood before deductions or inductions can be inferred about the course of individual aging or the likely changes that have been and are taking place in the position of the old in society. We will now summarize the data leading to these conclusions.

Integration and Health

Capacities : We started by asking how incapacitated old people are. In the three countries the average man of 65 can expect to live for another 12–14 years and the average women of 65 for another 15–16 years (Table I–2). Only a tiny minority of 4 or 5 per cent of all old people are living in hospitals and other institutions (Table II–1). Around another tenth are bedfast or housebound (Table II–2). A special index of incapacity was used to measure the broad ability of the old people to perform those minimal tasks which make them independent of others for personal care. Excluding the bedfast, around 5 per cent of the non-institutionalized are seriously incapacitated (scoring 7 or more on the index) and from another 11–16 per cent moderately incapacitated (scoring 3–6) (Table II–3). So far as certain specific disabilities are concerned, we found that from 3–6 per cent are blind or nearly so (Table II–6); around 15 per cent experience giddiness, and 1–2 per cent actually experience a fall during a week (Table II–13). Again, these figures exclude the elderly in institutions. Altogether from 1 in 4 to 1 in 3 are ill during the year and altogether about 1 in 10 enter the hospital for at least a day during the year (Table II–14). Relatively more of the very old (those over 80), of women, of the single and widowed, and of those with the lowest incomes are seriously incapacitated.

Minority Incapacitated :   To express these facts in the most general terms, about 1 in 10 of the elderly population of the three countries are in hospitals and other institutions or are bedfast or seriously incapacitated at home. Another 1–2 in 10 are moderately incapacitated or restricted in mobility.

Majority Active :   By contrast, a majority of the elderly in the three countries maintain good health and are still active. Plainly, they are *physically* able to continue to participate in social relationships. From a half to three-fifths are able to function without limitation, as measured by the incapacity index. From two-thirds to three-quarters are not ill in bed during the year; and from a third to two-fifths do not see a physician during this period (Chapter 2).

Attitudes to Health :   In their attitudes towards their health, too, the majority of old people are relatively equable. They say their health is good for their age (Table III–1). The minority saying their health is poor tend to be people with some or severe incapacity, though in all countries there are interesting exceptions (Tables III–2 and III–4). Some people with poor health say their health is good, and vice versa. These are health "optimists" and "pessimists." (Those who take attitudes that seem to correspond with their objective condition might be described as "health realists.") Those rating their health as poor or fair tend to respond negatively to other questions about their subjective moods and feelings. Irrespective of living arrangements they are far more likely to say that time often passes slowly and to say that they are often or sometimes lonely (Tables III–7 and III–8). Old people who say their health is poor, however, are a minority. In all three countries *most* old people think their health is at least as good as or even better than that of their contemporaries. Far more think it is better than think it is poorer (Tables III–9 and III–10).

Integration and Family

Sharing a Household :   A large part of this report is concerned with contacts between old people and their families. Are old people isolated or integrated? What are the tests of involvement with family—in the sense that they participate in the activities of the extended family? These seem to be sharing a household, geographical proximity, frequency of family contacts, and the exchange of services. First, sharing a household. From a fifth to a quarter of the elderly in the three countries live alone, and another one-third to one-half live as married couples on their own. But substantial minorities—27 per cent in Denmark, 45 per cent in Britain, and 35 per cent in the United States—live with others, mostly with unmarried or married children and brothers or sisters (Table VII–1). Of those with children 20 per cent in Denmark, 42 per cent in Britain, and 28 per cent in the United States live with at least one of them (Table VII–7). Rather more than half of these are living with unmarried children.

Family Proximity : Second, geographical propinquity. Of those with children there are, in addition to those who live with them, another 55 per cent in Denmark, 40 per cent in Britain, and 49 per cent in the United States who live within 30 minutes journey of one or more of their children (Table VII–7). Altogether, three-quarters or more of old people with children live with, or within 30 minutes journey of, at least one of their children.

Frequency of Family Contacts : Third, frequency of contacts within the family. The number of old people with children who report seeing a child the same day or the previous day is 62 per cent in Denmark, 69 per cent in Britain, and 65 per cent in the United States. Around another fifth report seeing a child within the previous week. In all three countries the great majority even of old people living alone have frequent contacts with their children; more than half report seeing a child the same day or the previous day and more than another quarter within the previous week (Table VII–10). Again, from a third to nearly two-thirds of those living alone report staying with children overnight during the previous year; and rather smaller proportions report children staying overnight with them (Table VII–15). Altogether more than a third of old people with brothers and sisters report seeing at last one within the previous week (Table VII–11). Contacts with siblings are more frequent among those persons who lack children or who do not see their children weekly or daily (Table VII–13).

Exchange of Family Services: Fourth, exchange of services. Our data take two forms—answers to general questions about patterns and kinds of help and answers to specific questions about source of help during a previous illness and with certain everyday personal and household tasks. From rather less than a half to substantially more than a half of old people in Britain and the United States report giving help to their children and grandchildren, including money gifts as well as such types of help as housekeeping services. Around two-thirds report receiving help from their families, including regular and occasional money allowances or gifts. Considerably fewer old people in Denmark, though still a substantial minority, report such services (Table VII–17). In illness from a third to two-fifths rely for help with housework, meals, and shopping upon husbands or wives and a similar proportion upon children or other relatives. In all countries a considerable minority rely on children or other relatives outside the household as the main source of help. Only from a fifth to rather more than a quarter of the old people in the three countries rely on persons or agencies outside the family, such as social services, or have no source of help (Table V–4 and Chapter 5). Over a range of everyday personal and household tasks—for example, housework, meals, shopping, bathing, and dressing—the great majority of those old people who experience difficulty rely on husbands and wives, children, and other relatives for assistance (Tables V–5 and V–8). Between 8 and 9 in every 10 of the bedfast at home depend primarily on members of their families for meals, housework, personal aid, and so on (Table V–9).

Modifications of Theory : These were the principal measures of family involvement that we developed. We would not pretend that they are comprehensive. In various respects the data are limited. We are unable, for example, to explore the content or quality of family "contacts" and the total role and extent of extra-familial activities in relation to familial activities. We believe, however, that the statistical evidence cross-nationally of "integration" is sufficiently formidable to demand modification of much existing theory about the extended family and the relations between generations in industrial society. It also provides a useful framework for theories about the social processes of aging.

Family Structure : Integration, however, is neither universal nor consistent. There is great variety among the aged. A major thesis of this report is that family structure influences the organization and geographical distribution of the extended family and its sub-groups, and the character and intensity of different types of individual relationships. How could the family structure of the elderly be described? The survey showed that nearly a fifth of the elderly in Denmark and the United States and nearly a quarter in Britain are single or otherwise childless (Table VI–2). Yet between a fifth and a seventh of those with surviving children have six or more (Table VI–3). Around 90 per cent of those with children have grandchildren; and 23 per cent in Denmark and Britain, and 40 per cent in the United States, have great-grandchildren (Table VI–6). Around 80 per cent of the elderly have surviving brothers and sisters, some of them five or more (Table VI–7).

Diversity of Structure : One important feature of the family structure of the aged in industrial society therefore is its diversity. At one extreme there are from 3–5 per cent of the elderly, most of whom are single or widowed, who lack children and brothers and sisters. At the other extreme there is a large minority who have grandchildren and great-grandchildren as well as at least two children (Table VI–8). Most of these old people also have surviving brothers and sisters. In Britain, for example, as many as 5 per cent of old people have five or more brothers or sisters *and* five or more children. The old person may therefore have no kin at all, or he may be knitted into a complex network of surviving kin spanning several generations.

Four Generations : A second important feature of family structure is its frequent extension to the fourth generation. That the four-generation family is already a *common* phenomenon in industrialized societies is one of the more surprising facts to emerge from the cross-national survey. From a half to three-fifths of all old people in the three countries belong to an immediate family structure of three or four generations and also have more than one surviving child. These persons might be said to have good potential family resources for help in old age. Another fifth have resources in depth over two, three, or four generations, but either they have only one child, or, if they have two or more children, they lack grandchildren.

Sons or Daughters : A third feature of family structure that we found to be important was the large proportion of "families" of children who are males only or females only. From a fifth to a quarter of the elderly have a single child. Around another fifth have families consisting of two or more sons or two or more daughters only (Table VI–4).

Structure and Organization : How does family structure affect household composition? For example, we found that compared with widowed persons those who are married more commonly maintain households independent of married children (Tables VI–16 and VII–2). Single persons more often share a household with a brother or sister than do widowed persons—even than widowed persons who are childless (Table VI–17). Widowed persons with sons only are more likely to be found living alone than widowed persons with daughters only (Table VI–18a). Divorced persons compared with widowed persons are less often found living with their children.

Structure and Geographical Distribution of the Family : Fewer widowed than married persons live at considerable distances from their children. The fewer the children, the more likely it is for old persons to be found living further than 30 minutes journey from their nearest child (Table VI–21). This is much as one might expect. But the distribution by family size is by no means random. Children in small families tend to compensate. The chances of an only child's living with or near an old person, for example, are found to be much greater than those of an eldest or youngest or, at least for Britain, of any other child ranked in age-order. The sex of children has some but not a marked effect on family proximity. Although a higher proportion of nearest daughters than of nearest sons in Britain and the United States are to be found living in the same household as a parent, the difference is largely canceled out by the higher proportion of nearest sons than of nearest daughters who are living within 30 minutes journey of the old people. And in Denmark the differences in geographical distribution between sons and daughters are small. On a broad cross-national basis, then, there is no evidence of marked matrilocal family organization.

Structure and Individual Relationships Within the Family : More of the widowed than the married, more of those with several children than with one child only, and more of those with daughters than with sons only, are found to have seen at least *one* child the previous day (Table VI–23). Even when children live at comparable distances, contacts with daughters are found to be more frequent than contacts with sons. However, the difference between sons and daughters in their contact with parents is less marked than previously anticipated, and a large proportion of old people clearly have frequent contacts with at least one of their sons.

Structural Compensation : One important finding was the operation of a principle of compensation or substitution in family organization, distribution, and relationships. More widowed than married old people of comparable age live with single children (Table VI–25). We would suggest that children sometimes postpone marriage if a father or mother, particularly a father, dies during their adolescence or early adulthood. Children in small families tend to live closer to and see more of their parents than do children in large families. Again, people without children see more of their siblings than do people with both children and siblings (Table VII–13). Finally, those who do not share a household with a child tend to live near at least one of their children. This form of family compensation is particularly noticeable in Denmark, the country tha thas the lowest proportion of older persons living with children (Table VII–8).

Structure and Social Norms : Such findings suggest a structural explanation for inconsistencies between existing patterns of family organization (including household composition), family "distribution" or family contacts, and social norms. The integrity of marriage is respected, partly by recognizing the right of a married couple to live in an independent household. Social distance between the adult generations is also observed. But it is the responsibility of adult children to provide comfort and care during a parent's infirmity or upon his or her bereavement. Preferment is given in family organization and management to relations with daughters over relations with sons. Preferment is given in relations with children over relations with siblings but if people do not marry, or if they marry and do not have children, relations with siblings can be maintained throughout life—especially if these siblings are childless or single.

Social Class and Family Relations : What effect has social class on family structure and relations? In this survey occupation was used as a rough indicator of class position and the elderly population was divided into four categories: white collar, blue collar, service workers, and agricultural workers. Compared with the elderly belonging to working class groups ("blue collar" and "service workers"), fewer belonging to middle class (or "white collar") occupations share a household with children or live within 10 minutes journey of them, and more of these middle class persons live further than one hour's journey distant (Table VIII–6). In Britain and the United States fewer middle class persons report seeing a child the same day or the previous day and slightly more report not seeing any child for more than a month (Table VIII–9).

Class Differences in Family Structure : The above statements of differences between middle class and working class elderly in their family relations have to be strongly qualified for two reasons. First, there are differences in marital status and size and *structure* of family between the classes, which to some extent "explain" differences in family relationships. Compared with working class old people (that is, those formerly belonging to "blue collar" and "service worker" categories), more middle class old people are single or childless or have only one or two children. Fewer have a surviving daughter and fewer have several surviving children. Fewer in Britain and the United States, but not in Denmark, are widowed (Table VIII–1). All this suggests why fewer of the middle class than of the working class elderly share households with children. Fewer among the middle class have a fourth, a fifth, or a sixth child who was born late in life and who is only now reaching the usual marrying age, and fewer are widowed and therefore fewer are likely to live with a married child in old age. These differences also suggest why the interdependence of the elderly middle class man and wife tends to be contrasted in sociological studies of family and community with the close relationship between daughter and elderly working class parent, particularly mother (Tables VIII–4 and VIII–5).

Similarity Between Classes in Family Relations : Second, the difference between middle class and working class elderly in their family relations is far smaller than is generally supposed—at least in terms of the rough indices adopted in this study. Although there is a tendency for more working class than middle class elderly to live with or near at least one of their children, nevertheless the over-all differences between the classes in frequency of contact and patterns of help are small. For example, the percentages of persons of "white collar" background who share a household with a child or report seeing one the same or the previous day are 60 in Denmark, 62 in Britain, and 61 in the United States. The comparable percentages for persons of "blue collar" background are 59, 71, and 65 respectively (Table VIII–9). There are, indeed, indications that more of the elderly from "white collar" than "blue collar" backgrounds have certain kinds of relationships with their children. For example, more stay overnight with their children and more have children to stay with them during a year (Table VIII–11). In Britain and the United States more give help to their children and grandchildren, though about the same proportions *receive* help from their children (Table VIII–13).

The Family Relations of Farmers and Farm Workers : In all three countries more persons from a background of agricultural work than from a background of "blue collar" or "white collar" work are likely to report seeing their children the same or the previous day (Table VIII–9). This class difference is fairly pronounced for Denmark, where a much larger proportion of the former category than of the latter two either live in the same household with children or have seen them the same or the previous day. The difference between those with agricultural and other backgrounds is not so pronounced in Britain and the United States, however, and is certainly not as pronounced as is commonly assumed.

Integration, Social Services, and Formal Associations

Functions of Social Services : It is often supposed that in the course of time social services and other formal organizations and associations have "taken over" the functions previously performed by the family and the local community and that as a result many of the elderly live in a kind of comfortable seclusion provided by the health and welfare services, special housing services, and clubs and centers—or, in short, by "the Welfare State." This is a misrepresentation of social change. In some important respects these services and associations integrate the elderly into society by supplementing, or substituting for, the informal services and activities of the family. They may, for example, furnish expert professional help which the family cannot supply, or help persons who lack families altogether. Theorists who have postulated the loss of functions by the family, the dispersion of the extended family, and the segregation of the aged during urbanization and industrialization tend to discount such positive developments.

Services for Those Without Families : The information about aid that was collected in the cross-national survey had to be limited in scope, but we found that the community social services are concentrated overs whelmingly among those who have neither the capacities nor the resource- to undertake the relevant functions alone and that these services primarily reach those people who lack relatives or who have only slender family resources. Of the 4–6 per cent in institutions in the three countries, from a third to over a half are in a hospital (Table IV–5). Institutionalized persons tend to be people of advanced age, many of whom are 80 and over (Table V–3). In the United States and Britain, for example, about two-fifths are aged 80 and over. A disproportionately large number of them are single or widowed (Table V–2). Of those receiving domiciliary services we also found, at least in Britain, that a disproportionately large number are moderately or severely incapacitated, live alone, and are single or, if married or widowed, childless. The evidence therefore suggests that the social services tend to complement rather than replace informal community and family associations and that they tend to reach those in genuine "need." But the total role of the domiciliary and residential social services is small. The number of old people actually helped in their housework, provision of meals, and care during illness is dwarfed by the numbers being helped by husbands and wives and relatives (Tables V–4 and V–10). The services are also generally acknowledged to be functionally inadequate (see Chapter 5, particularly pp. 103–107).

Social Isolation and Loneliness

Few in Extreme Isolation : We sought to establish how many old people in the three countries have little contact or relationship, by comparison with other persons of the same age, with family, local community, and society. Only a very small minority (4 per cent or fewer) live in extreme isolation in the sense that a week or even a day can pass without human contact (Table IX-1). Few people lack meaningful every day relationships and social activities. A larger proportion, amounting to a quarter in each country, say they are often alone (Table IX-1). There are relatively more women than men among them. Around half of all those who actually live alone see children or other relatives every day and this is why a large proportion deny they are often alone (Tables IX-3 and IX-5).

Characteristics of the Isolated: Those who are isolated tend to be persons who are older than average, single or widowed, lacking children and other relatives in the immediate vicinity, retired, and infirm. It is the interaction of three or more of these factors—rather than any single factor—which tends to produce isolation.

Loneliness and Desolation : Only a minority of the elderly say they are often or sometimes lonely, varying from 17 per cent in Denmark to 28 per cent in Britain and 30 per cent in the United States (Table IX-9). Isolation as such does not appear to explain loneliness. There are old people in all three countries who live in extreme seclusion but deny they are ever lonely. In exploring the facts we drew a distinction between *peer-contrasted isolation*, or having few social activities and relationships by comparison with age-contemporaries, and *desolation*, or having been deprived of former social activities and relationships, usually through the loss of a social intimate such as a spouse or another close relative by death, admission to a hospital, or migration. Peer-contrasted isolation and desolation tend to be interrelated, of course, but do not coincide. The data broadly support the hypothesis that desolation rather than peer-contrasted isolation is the causal antecedent of loneliness and may be important in helping to explain the propensity to suicide among older people (Tables IX-10 and IX-13). For example, more of those who have been widowed recently than 10 to 20 years previously say they are lonely, irrespective of living arrangements. The data also suggest that the feelings of those who experience severe social loss are relieved by remaining or substitute relationships (Tables IX-14 and IX-15). The concept of "structural compensation" has emerged in this cross-national study as of critical importance in explaining social and psychological diversity.

Integration and Occupation

Proportions in Employment : To what extent are the elderly integrated into the employment structure? About a third of the men in the three countries are still in employment—varying from 28 per cent in Britain to 32 per cent in the United States and 38 per cent in Denmark (Table X-1). Among those at work there are a substantial number who are working fewer than 30 hours a week—about a third of the white collar workers and a fifth to a third of the industrial manual workers in all three countries (Table X-14). The number of elderly women who are employed is 8 per cent in Britain, 13 per cent in the United States, and 8 per cent in

Denmark. For relatively few women, then, is employment customary over the pensionable ages.

Employment and Health : What explains the relatively low proportions of elderly men who are employed? Clearly one important factor is health. A minority of men, especially among the older age-groups, are too infirm to take any form of employment, whatever the economic and social conditions. For example, from 14 per cent to 24 per cent of those who are retired have scores of 3 or more according to our index of incapacity (Table XI–4). But this leaves a large gap between the number who appear to be active and the number actually employed. A substantial majority of all men over the age of 65, probably around two-thirds, are active and have little or no incapacity. From 58 per cent to 68 per cent of all men in the three countries, for example, score 0 according to our index of incapacity (Table II–9). The general evidence about the activity and capacities of men over 65, together with historical evidence from advanced industrial societies about proportions employed and the relatively high proportions of elderly men currently in the labor force of some emerging industrial societies, suggests that while infirmity and ill-health are important in explaining a part of current retirement rates they are by no means predominant. Social, industrial, and economic factors may be more important. Thus, only 44 per cent of retired men in Britain, 50 per cent in the United States, and 61 per cent in Denmark give ill-health or strain of work, whether alone or in combination with other factors, as the reason for their retirement (Tables X–20 and XI–3). Interestingly enough, the country with fewest men giving ill-health as the reason for retirement is also the country with the fewest men actually employed, and vice versa.

Influence of Pensionable Age upon Retirement: Also important in explaining the proportions retired are state and occupational pension arrangements. The cross-national data show that the proportions working are affected by the minimum statutory pension age. In Denmark, for example, the "normal" age at which the state pension can be drawn is 67, compared with 65 in Britain and the United States. As a consequence over three-quarters of Danish men aged 65 and 66, compared with only a half in the other two countries, are still in employment. Moreover, employment among older age-groups may also be affected by pension arrangements. In Britain, for example, the pension of those aged 70 and over is not reduced if they have substantial earnings. This may help to explain why in that country, compared with the others, a relatively larger number of men in their 70's with an industrial manual background continue to work (Table X–12). The earnings rule in the United States does not cease to operate until the age of 72.

But absolute size of income expected in retirement does not seem, by itself, to be correlated with retirement rates. In all three countries (though only marginally so in Britain) more of the men categorized as being in, or having been in, white collar occupations and agriculture than in industrial "blue collar" occupations are still at work past the age of 65 (Table X–8).

Further data on the relationship between the pre-retirement incomes and expected retirement incomes need to be studied. In general, in addition to the occupational pattern, there are other internal structural effects on the proportions of elderly men at work. When age is held constant more married than widowed men are found to be at work (Table X–13).

Variable Age of Retirement :   The availability of a pension at a fixed age does not of itself determine retirement. In all three countries half the men who are up to two years older than the normal pension age are still at work (Table X–4). Moreover, substantial numbers retire *before* this age, most of them because of bad health (Table X–21). Only from a fifth to a third of retired men in the three countries report stopping work at the statutory pension age (Table XI–2). However, it is striking that the proportion of men at work two years after the "normal" pension age is nearly the same in all three countries. Retirement rates and attitudes to retirement seem to be determined by the interaction of the following factors: health, living standards during work and after retirement, the expectations people have of men in their roles in family and society, the level of general demand for workers, as well as the formal conventions about retirement which are differentially adopted by industry, the trade unions, and the state. The pension age adopted by an industrial society tends in fact to symbolize the agreed balance that is struck between different social institutions and groups about the exact relationship of the elderly to the work force. The age at which men retire may have only a distant relationship to the "approved" age and will in practice depend considerably on individual opportunities as well as individual capacities and wishes. The self-employed, for example, have much more freedom than do wage earners.

Compulsory Retirement :   The statutory or "approved" pension age and the availability of a state pension, or perhaps an occupational pension too, are often reinforced by compulsory termination of employment as a factor in causing complete retirement from work. As many as one-fifth of the retired men in Denmark and one-third in Britain and in the United States give compulsory retirement or the winding-up of a firm as the reason for their retirement (Tables X–20 and XI–3). Most of the rest, as already stated above, give ill-health or heaviness of work load as the reason for retirement and only between a fifth and a quarter give miscellaneous reasons, such as being needed at home and not wanting to work any longer (Table X–20). The evidence that men *choose* to retire is not therefore, on this showing, substantial—although rather more men in the United States than in Britain and Denmark, one-fifth of all retired men in that country, say they no longer want to work or can afford to retire. There may be others in all three countries who in fact have preferred to retire but who offer ill-health as a reason for their retirement. Further detailed exploration of the question of choice at the point of retirement is greatly needed.

Attitudes to Retirement of Those Still Employed :   Despite the existence of a statutory state pension age and arrangements for pensions, around a third of men over the pension age are still at work. About three-quarters of them say they do not want to stop working. Fewer than a quarter say they look forward to stopping. Irrespective of occupation, those men who continue to work until they are past the middle-60's are so work-oriented that they are literally unable to visualize any future that precludes their working. Many make the assumption both that their health will not deteriorate and that they will not be obliged by their employers to give up working. Relatively more of those with a background of white collar and agricultural than of the blue collar employment want to continue (Table XI-12). About half of these employed men are unable to specify anything that they are likely to enjoy if and when retired (Table XI-13). On the other hand, all but a small minority, about a fifth in Denmark and Britain and just a few in the United States, specify various things that they will miss— money, the work itself, the feeling of being useful, and the people they meet at work (Table XI-14).

Attitudes of the Retired to Retirement :   A substantial proportion of those in Britain and the United States who have been retired for less than three years (39 per cent and 33 per cent respectively), but a smaller proportion in Denmark (14 per cent), say they want work (Chapter 11, p. 338). About half the remaining men say their health is too poor to work. Fewer of those who have been retired for more than three years want work— 9 per cent in Denmark, 15 per cent in Britain, and 19 per cent in the United States. It seems that substantial numbers of active men, particularly among the recently retired, would like to continue to work.

From a third to a half of all men say there is nothing they particularly enjoy about retirement—although, on the other hand, from a half to three-quarters say there is nothing that they particularly miss, except, in some instances in the European countries and in many instances in the United States, money (Tables XI-6 and XI-8). More retired than employed men are lonely and more, too, find that time passes slowly (Table XI-15). To some extent this is because more of the retired are old, widowed, and infirm. The cross-national survey needs to be followed up by more intensive inquiry. Positive as well as negative attitudes to retirement are common. Adjustment to retirement varies. Some people appreciate the rest and the opportunity to spend their time as they please. More than half of all retired men in the United States and Britain and half of all retired men in Denmark specify that they enjoy rest and other things in retirement (Table IX-6). Others resent the loss not only of money but the feeling of being useful, the respect of others, and the enjoyment of the work itself. The cross-national study suggests that the statutory pension age and the level of incapacity of older men are important in shaping attitudes but that the satisfactions, customs, and roles associated with a lifetime's work have a continuing influence.

Integration and Income

Approach to the Study of Living Standards :   The relationship of the elderly to society depends not only on the expectations and demands of the family, the community, and industry, but also upon the financial resources that are made available to old people. The inequalities between different groups of the elderly and also between the elderly and other sections of the population have to be explored. Trends in individual living standards during the latter stages of the life cycle have to be studied. Over-all comparisons of the sources and level of incomes and assets have to be made.

Sources of Income: Among the elderly population there are three broad types of income unit: (i) married couples, (ii) women, and (iii) men—the latter two being single, widowed, or divorced people. Between three-quarters and nine-tenths of the units in all three countries receive state benefits of one kind or another, including public assistance as well as pensions. Around a third of the couples and between 10 per cent and 20 per cent of the men and women have income from wages and salaries. Over half the units in Denmark, and from a quarter to two-fifths of the units in the other countries, have some income from rent, dividends, interest, and annuities. Substantial minorities also have an occupational pension of some kind (Table XII–2).

Lower Incomes of the Elderly :   The average pensions payment to an elderly couple in Denmark is about 40 per cent, and in Britain and the United States 29 per cent, of the average level of industrial earnings. The median total money income from all sources of elderly couples in Denmark and the United States is 52 per cent and in Britain 47 per cent of the average level of industrial earnings. The best standard of comparison to use for the income of the elderly is arguable, but whichever standard is adopted the same conclusion holds: that in all three countries incomes are well below the levels available to the younger population. Moreover, in Britain and the United States there are between a fifth and a third of all income units with incomes more than 20 per cent below the median so that, at least in these two countries and to some (though lesser) extent in Denmark, it may be said that there are important groups of the elderly whose incomes are very small. (See Chapter 12, pp. 353–354 and Tables XII–7 and XII–10.) The median earnings of elderly couples and men and women still in full-time employment are considerably below average industrial earnings, just as the total income of the retired elderly is, in turn, well below that of the employed elderly. Retired couples in all three countries, for example, have about half the income of couples receiving earnings from full-time employment (Table XIII–8).

Inequalities of Income Among the Elderly :   There are marked inequalities between types of income unit as well as between the retired and those remaining at work. Widowed and single men and women, particularly women, have low incomes by comparison with married couples, even allowing for the fact that the couples' income has to support two people. Expressed in relation to the median income of couples, the median income of widowed and single women is 58 per cent in Denmark, 49 per cent in Britain, and as low as 35 per cent in the United States (Table XII–6). This is partly explained by the higher proportion of couples who have income from earnings but also by the higher proportion who have income from occupational pensions and also, because they are younger and tend therefore to have better "qualifications," from marginally higher social security benefits. Higher proportions of the couples than of the men and women also tend to have some assets (Table XII–15).

Inequalities Within Types of Income Units :   There are great differences in level of income among income units of the same type. For example, between a quarter and a third of the couples have a gross money income of more than 20 per cent below the median income but between another tenth and a fifth have money incomes more than 100 per cent above the median income (Table XII–10). In the United States a third of the women have an income more than 20 per cent below the median, but another fifth have incomes more than 100 per cent above the median (Table XII–10).

Inequalities of Income and Assets: The three forms of inequality that have been described—the lower incomes of the elderly, the inequalities between couples, single men, and women, and the difference within income units—relate primarily to money incomes. To go further and explore inequalities in *living standards* means taking account also of assets, dissaving, and income in kind. Around two-fifths of the men and women in Britain, and around a quarter in Denmark, have no assets; and a further substantial minority have only a few (Table XII–15). Between a half and two-thirds of the income units in the three countries have liquid assets, though some of these, particularly in Britain, have assets that are worth very little. From a tenth to a quarter have holdings of stocks and shares and a substantial minority in the United States own income-producing property (Table XII–15). But substantial asset holdings do not in general appear to compensate for low incomes in Britain and the United States, though they do to a modest extent in Denmark.

Dissaving, Home Ownership, and Income in Kind: A minority of the elderly with liquid assets who dissave do so to meet general living expenses and, in the United States, medical bills (Table XIII–1). A substantial group, and more in the United States than in the European countries, own their own homes. The home consumption of farm produce, particularly in Denmark and the United States, helps to offset the low incomes of some of the elderly. There is a substantial amount of help in kind and cash gifts from the family, particularly in Britain and the United

States, sometimes by virtue of joint living arrangements these indirect subsidies can be very important; and, finally, the existence of strong public health and welfare services in Britain and Denmark has the effect of raising the real incomes of the elderly in those countries (Chapter 13, pp. 391–394).

Income "Severance" Rather than Adjustment upon Retirement : Despite qualifications that have to be made with respect to assets and income in kind, the evidence suggests that the change in the income of persons from employment to retirement in these three industrial countries might properly be described as "severance" rather than as a process of income "maintenance" or of gradual income "reduction." For some the transition is eased by part-time earnings, by the continued employment of a spouse, and by the existence of an occupational pension as well as a state pension. But these are haphazard and fortuitous rather than socially planned contingencies. And the circumstances of the retired are not homogeneous. For widows and for those who have been retired for considerable periods, income levels tend to be lower than for married couples, widowers, and recent retirees. The problems of integrating into the economic structure the growing number of older people who are outside the ordinary operations of the labor market do not appear to be adequately met by current institutional provisions.

Changes with Age

Advancing Age and Incapacity : It is not surprising that more people in their 80's than in their 60's are found to be incapacitated. What is surprising is that the increase in incapacity with age is less marked than might be expected. For example, the number who are seriously incapacitated (scoring 7 or more on the index) rises from 3 per cent, 4 per cent, and 4 per cent respectively of those aged 65–69 in Denmark, Britain, and the United States—to 6 per cent, 17 per cent, and 12 per cent respectively of those aged 80 and over. The proportion of those in their 80's, compared with those in their late 60's, who report illness during the previous year is only marginally higher in Denmark and Britain and remains about the same in the United States (Chapter 2). The process of institutionalization and death throughout the period between the 60's and the 80's must of course be remembered. But the data tend to suggest that physical decrescence may be swift for many older people in the terminal stage of life and also that the majority of those who do survive to the 80's can in no sense be described as persons who are in a state of "medicated survival." Indeed, there is some evidence suggesting that those in their 80's and 90's feel they have joined a biological and psychological "elite." More of them than of those in their 70's, for example, are found to be health optimists (Chapter 3).

Disability in Extreme Old Age : It would be wrong, however, to lose sight of the fact that substantial proportions of those in their 80's do experience major difficulties and an important minority account for a very large share of the health and welfare services provided in each country. From a third to a half have difficulty in climbing or descending stairs, and in cutting their toenails, for example. Substantial proportions have trouble in washing, bathing, and dressing, and about one in four report giddiness (Chapter 2). Moreover, large proportions of persons of advanced age are in institutions, which means that comparisons between older and younger people in private households are distorted to a certain extent. In both Britain and the United States, for example, the proportion of the population who are inmates of institutions rises slowly with age from about 2 per cent of those aged 65–69 to 4–5 per cent of those aged 75–79, until it increases sharply to 10–11 per cent of those aged 80 and over (Table IV–6).

Extremes of Isolation and Integration : Family and social activities are found to change in character with advancing age. There seem to be contacts with fewer people but such contacts as there are seem to be of longer duration and they may be of emotionally greater significance to older people, though this remains to be demonstrated. Social involvement is largely maintained. The family status of old people in their 80's is different from that of those in their 60's. At the age of 65–66 over half the women in all three countries, but at 80 or over from only a tenth to a fifth, have a husband alive (Table VI–12). Again, in the late 60's, six in seven, but after the age of 75 only two in three, have brothers or sisters alive (Table VI–13). The proportions having children and grandchildren change little between the 60's and 80's (though the average *number* of their grandchildren certainly increases). Contrasting with the losses are increases in the proportions having great-grandchildren. At the age of 80 or over nearly half the old people with children in Britain, over half in Denmark, and over two-thirds in the United States have great-grand-children (Table VI–15). With increasing age, therefore, structural developments make it likely that slightly more old people run the risk of social isolation. More of those who are childless become detached from an extended family through the death of husbands or wives and close relatives such as siblings. But the birth and marriage of grandchildren and great-grandchildren tend for many to replenish the circle of relatives from whom attention, affection, and care can be expected. At one extreme are the old people with no descendents and no surviving siblings or in-laws. At the other are the old people who belong to a loose-knit structure of four generations of direct descendants.

Advancing Age and Family Contacts : With advancing age proportion-ately fewer *widowed* old people live alone; slightly more live with married children (Table VII–18). To some extent these findings are associated with the larger proportion of older people in their 70's and 80's who are incapacitated (Table VII–25). Rather more *married* people live as couples on their own; slightly fewer live with single children (Table VII–19). The number of old people reporting that they have seen one of their children the same day or the previous day tends actually to increase and the number reporting they have not seen a child for more than 30 days marginally to decrease (Table VII–21). The number having frequent contacts with siblings declines from around two-fifths to about a quarter or a third; but the number having frequent contact with other relatives is maintained (Table VII–23). The proportion giving help declines and the proportion receiving help rises but the changes are by no means dramatic. Between a quarter and a half of those aged 75 and over report helping their children (Table VII–24). These data also suggest that while there is little substantial change with age in the *frequency* of contacts with children, there is a change in the *direction* of contacts: fewer are outgoing.

Little Evidence of Increasing Isolation: Let us sum up the evidence about social isolation and advancing age. Because more people in their 80's than in their 60's are widowed, proportionately more of them are found to be living alone. More too say they are often alone (Tables IX–16 and IX–18). But the trend with age is not marked. On none of the rather general measures of isolation that are considered in Chapter 9 are more than two-fifths of those in their 80's "isolated" or alone (Table IX–1). The small minority of extreme isolates increases marginally in Britain and the United States, and rather more sharply in Denmark, but still only to 6 per cent (Table IX–16). The great majority of those living alone have a number of daily social activities and relationships (Tables IX–4 and IX–7), and although there is some falling off with increasing age the fall is not sharp. Moreover, much of it is attributable to the higher prevalence of infirmity. It seems likely that while there may be a contraction in the number of "peripheral" social relationships there is little change in the number of "central" (that is, household, familial, and immediately local) relationships.

Little Evidence of Objective Disengagement : While the data collected have had to be restricted they do not suggest that, *independent of growing infirmity,* social disengagement is a widespread phenomenon. Bereavement is perhaps the most important isolating experience in old age and yet even this experience, as at other ages, draws a chain of "reintegrating" responses from family and community. Old people who are widowed, for example, sometimes move to join their married children. Once they overcome their initial grief the elderly find that compensating relationships provided by family and friends mitigate their sense of loneliness.

Little Evidence of Subjective Disengagement : The evidence on attitudes is sparse but does not in general suggest that as old people get older they disengage *subjectively.* Feelings of loneliness, for example, are expressed more and not less commonly by people at the more advanced ages, though when increased widowhood and infirmity are taken into account, there is in fact little difference, statistically speaking, between persons in their 60's and those in their 80's and 90's (Tables IX–16 and IX–18).

Disengagement and Employment : Much the same is true of the attitudes to retirement of men who remain fairly active. In all three countries the majority of men now over 65 report work beyond the normal pension age. Half the men aged up to two years older than the normal state pension age are still in employment. Among those in their late 70's fewer than a fifth are employed and among those aged 80 and over there are still from 10 per cent to 15 per cent employed (Table X–4). The decrease with age in the proportions employed, while corresponding to some extent with the statutory pension ages, is therefore more gradual than is commonly supposed. The majority of those still employed expect to go on working all their lives (Table XI–12). Many of the retired have worked beyond the normal pension age (Table XI–2). Some would prefer to return to some form of employment (Table XI–11).

Disengagement and Retirement :   Over half of the men who retire at or before the normal pension age do so for reasons of ill-health or strain or heaviness of work (Table X–21). Among those retiring subsequently, this reason is less prominent but still important. A substantial proportion of men who have recently retired but are not incapacitated would prefer some form of work but this proportion becomes smaller with increasing age, higher level of incapacity, and length of time from the point of retirement (Table XI–11).

Changes in Income with Age :   In all three countries people in their 70's and 80's tend to have smaller incomes than people in their 60's (Table XII–12). Largely this is because more of the younger people have full-time or part-time earnings but also because more of each successive wave of people who reach retirement age have an occupational as well as a state pension, and more of the younger cohorts tend to have some assets. When the employed are discounted the incomes of those who are retired still tend to be higher for the younger than for the older persons in the elderly population—though differences are more marked in Britain than in Denmark (Table XII–14). In the latter country the fact that the pension is income tested, is related to a cost of living index, and is supplemented by an additional payment once individuals are aged 80 helps to reduce the differences that might otherwise arise between older and younger persons. Altogether, in societies in which real incomes are rising and which have also been exposed to inflation there is a problem of devising an institutional framework that will protect the economic interests of the non-active population.

Differences Between Men and Women

Capacity :   Differences in condition and reaction between the sexes have been reported at many points in this book. Some of the more important must be emphasized here. First, there is some evidence from all three countries that, although more women than men survive to advanced ages, fewer of them are in good health. *In all age-groups* (with the exception of one group in Denmark) more women than men are moderately or severely incapacitated—scoring 3 or more in the index of capacity

(Table II–10). More report giddiness (Table II–13); and more report illness during the previous year (Table II–14). Reflecting this general finding is the finding that fewer women than men in each country say their health is good for their age (Table III–1).

Involvement in Family: More women than men have frequent contacts with their families but the difference is not marked. Slightly more women then men are isolated. There is a big difference in marital status. Roughly twice as many men as women—around three-quarters compared with a third to two-fifths—are married. Roughly half as many are widowed or single (Table VI–1). Together with the fact that there are more women than men in the elderly population, this difference in marital status suggests why most of the elderly persons found to be living alone are women. But the actual *proportion* of widowers and bachelors living alone is not markedly different from that of widows and spinsters (Table VII–1). Slightly fewer women than men live further than 30 minutes journey from their nearest child (Table VII–7) and rather more report seeing a child the same or the previous day (Table VII–9). More women than men report staying with children or having them to stay (Table VII–15). More also report seeing brothers and sisters recently (Tables VII–11 and VII–12). More tend to be involved in the exchange of services within the family (Tables VII–17 and VII–24). Some of these statements apply less strongly to Denmark than to Britain and the United States, and some comparisons between the sexes reveal no differences at all. For example, for both Britain and the United States old women in each occupational class are much more likely than old men to live with a married daughter. In Denmark, on the contrary, old men and women in each occupational class are equally likely to live with a married daughter and, in fact, few of either sex report this sort of living arrangement (Table VIII–8).

Involvement in Occupation :   One reason why women tend to be slightly more integrated than men are with their families is that more of the men continue in employment. Around a third of the men over 65, compared with about a tenth of the women, are still at work (Chapter 11). Women retire from paid employment less reluctantly than men, usually because they are expected to play a bigger role in the home and family. Substantial numbers of men do not retire at the pensionable ages; many of the men who do retire express a wish to return to work; and many too talk more emphatically about the losses instead of the gains of retirement (Chapter 11).

Inequality of Income :   Finally, men and women tend to differ in economic independence. Either because of employment income or more favourable pensions, single and widowed men tend to have higher living standards than single and widowed women. The discrepancy is particularly marked in Britain and in the United States, where the relatively poor pension provisions for elderly widows probably reinforce their material dependence upon their families (Chapter 13).

Differences Between the Three Elderly Populations

Differences in Incapacity: In this summary we have concentrated so far on those features of aging and the circumstances of the aged that are common to the three countries. Some of the differences should also be emphasized. Up to age 75 there are few differences between the elderly populations of the three countries in their capacities. The proportions of each sex reporting various impairments and illness in the year are broadly similar. But among the older age-groups relatively more old people in Britain and (though to a lesser extent) in Denmark than in the United States report impairments. Thirty per cent of the men and 46 per cent of the women in Britain aged 80 and over report moderate or severe incapacity (scoring 3 or more on the index), compared with 18 per cent and 32 per cent in the United States. In the former country, compared with the latter, more men and women aged 80 and over report difficulty with a series of physical tasks, with one exception (Table II-11). More report illness during the year (Table II-16). This tendency in Britain is worth further inquiry and no doubt has a complex explanation. Future investigations in Britain are likely to attach importance to the high incidence of chronic conditions such as bronchitis and arthritis, the poor condition of a substantial minority of housing, and the relatively large proportion of persons who are widowed.

Attitudes to Health : Paradoxically the incapacitated in Britain more often say their health is good than in either of the other two countries. For example, twice as great a proportion of those in Britain who are severely incapacitated as in Denmark and the United States continue to rate their health as "good" (Table III-4). At the other extreme, substantially more elderly Americans than either the Danes or the British whose incapacity or impairment is negligible say their health is poor. Elderly Americans set such high standards of "wellness" for themselves that any restriction on functioning is interpreted as a sign of poor health. As argued earlier (Chapter 3), observers from de Tocqueville onwards have frequently noted that Americans place stress on physical well-being, independent activity, and achievement, so much so that to be ill is widely regarded as "inherently undesirable." Age and physical decrescence, however slight, tend therefore, it is suggested, to be interpreted pessimistically. But, as this thesis is followed up, a number of complicating factors will have to be taken into account—for example, the evidence that some Americans with limited capacity say they are in good health (Table III-4).

Family Relations : In their family relationships the elderly in Denmark tend to differ from those in Britain and the United States. Relationships with children tend to be more loose-knit than in the other two countries. For example, fewer elderly Danes share a household (Table VII-1)—a situation perhaps partly associated with there being fewer houses with a large number of rooms (Tables VII-4 and VII-5); fewer give to and receive help from children (Table VII–17); and fewer stay overnight with children or have children to stay (Table VII–15). Relations between the generations are functionally more independent. Relationships with children are also bilateral (for example, contacts with sons are nearly as frequent as with daughters). In Britain and the United States there is more stress on the mother-daughter relationships (for instance, three times as many widowed persons live with married daughters as with married sons). However, this difference between Denmark and Britain and the United States is not extremely pronounced and tends to be overshadowed by certain similarities in patterns of family contacts. As emphasized in Chapter 7 there is more variation in the relationships between generations *within* each country than there is *between* the three countries involved. In Denmark the proportion of males to females, and of male deaths to female deaths, at advanced ages is higher than in Britain and the United States, and a larger proportion of the elderly still have husbands or wives alive. This greater "equality" between the sexes may partly explain our findings. But, as also hypothesized in Chapter 7, the slightly greater independence of the generations in Denmark may be attributable, in part, to the early development in that country of certain extra-familial associations, such as cooperative movements and voluntary associations, and to the relative absence of the principle of "family responsibility" from social security and tax legislation.

Agricultural and Other Occupations : In all three countries more persons from a background of agricultural work than from urban middle class or working class backgrounds have several children and fewer are single or childless (Table IV–2). Yet between occupational backgrounds the differences in living arrangements and frequency of contact with children are marked only in Denmark. In Denmark twice as many of the elderly from agricultural than from other backgrounds share a household with children (Table VIII–4 and 5). Including those sharing a household more report seeing one of their children the same or the previous day (Table VIII–9). Patterns of living arrangements and of family contacts for those from agricultural backgrounds are rather similar in the three countries. It is the elderly from non-agricultural occupations in Denmark—whether middle or working class, but particularly the working class—who tend to differ in living arrangements and family relationships from their counterparts in the other two countries.

Differences in Proportions Employed : The proportion of elderly men who are employed is higher in Denmark (38 per cent) than in Britain (28 per cent) and the United States (32 per cent) (Table X–1). The relative excess is concentrated among those aged 65–67. The later pension age in that country seems to be the primary determinant. There is an even later customary retirement age for some white collar workers, such as civil servants who work until 70. Proportionately more men in their seventies are still at work in Britain, partly because the pension can be retained in full.

White Collar Employment : In both Denmark and the United States markedly more people with a background in white collar than in blue collar occupations are still at work. In the United States two factors in particular seem to account for this. A large proportion of white collar workers—particularly teachers and civil servants—can still find work, despite the development of pension schemes and the practice of early retirement. On the other hand, structural unemployment greatly restricts the opportunities for many unskilled and semi-skilled manual workers to maintain employment throughout their 60's, and still less their 70's. In both Denmark and the United States there are substantial numbers of self-employed, and since more of them are included among the white collar workers this accounts for part of the difference between the classes in the proportions employed. Britain would appear to be making less use of white collar skills among the elderly than the other two countries. Not only are fewer with such a background still in employment, they also tend to work fewer hours (Table X–14).

Differences in Retirement Patterns : Differences between the three countries in the reasons offered for retirement are not striking. Rather more men in Denmark than in the other two countries say ill-health caused their retirement—but since fewer men in that country are retired, and more retire in the late 60's and 70's than in the mid 60's, this is understandable. So too is the finding that fewer in Denmark are retired compulsorily. Fewer men in that country than in the others are employed in large-scale industry and more in agriculture. The formal retirement ages of the state and the civil service are later in Denmark. Fewer of the men in Denmark than in Britain and the United States who are retired say they want work (Table XI–13). This seems to be explained by the fact that more are satisfied with their level of income (Table XIII–15). Fewer men who are still employed say that money will be the particular item they will miss (Table XI–8). However, in the United States there are signs that a significant sub-stratum of the men who are retired enjoy retirement. (Chapter 11, pp. 332–340.) All in all, the cross-national study suggests that at this time different patterns of employment and retirement seem to be more explicable in terms of differences in pension ages, economic and social structure, relative size of incomes and asset holdings, and disability rates than in terms of individual attitudes and national personality traits or value systems.

Absolute Incomes Higher in the United States : There are a number of important differences in living standards between the three countries. First, the absolute living standards of old people in the United States, on average, are higher than in the European countries. If the different currencies are translated into roughly equivalent purchasing power the incomes of married couples are about double, of men half as much again, and even of women still very slightly higher in the United States than in the two European countries (Table XII–8). This reflects the higher levels of living generally of the United States population as compared with those of European countries. When Denmark is compared with Britain, the Danish aged are better off absolutely than the British.

Income Inequalities Among the Aged Greater in the United States : Second, income inequalities *within* the elderly population, as between the employed and the retired, the married and the widowed, and the older and the younger persons, tend to be greater in the United States than in Denmark and Britain (Tables XII-10, XII-11, and XIII-12). When contemporary minimum "needs" standards are applied to the elderly in the three countries it would seem that in Britain and the United States there are substantial proportions of all types of income units who are living at levels below these standards, particularly women. The proportions in Denmark are much smaller, but still significant. But in the United States many of those in poverty are a long way below the poverty line, in contrast to the poor in Britain, where the uniformity of national assistance and the greater scope of the pension scheme prevent the great majority from falling far below it. In the United States public assistance varies widely in coverage and amount from state to state.

Elderly Relatively More Prosperous in Denmark: Third, income inequalities as between the elderly *retired* and the rest of the population are smaller in Denmark than in Britain and the United States. The Danish pension is relatively more generous than in the other two countries. Despite approximately the same general living standards in the two countries, Danish couples have income levels about 10 per cent higher than British couples and Danish women some 28 per cent higher than British women. Subjectively, more of the elderly in Denmark than in the United States, and more in the United States than in Britain, say they are as well off or better off now than before the age of 60. Compared with Britain the Danish income levels are explicable in terms of the basic features of the Danish pension system—namely, that it is income tested, is linked to the cost of living index, and involves supplements for persons over 80.

Income Distribution and Class Structure : Except for the wide difference between the employed and the retired the elderly in Denmark are financially more homogeneous than in the other two countries. There are fewer in "subsistence" poverty and fewer at the extremes of wealth and of income. The differences in income that do exist are not so much class differences as differences between urban and rural groups. The fascinating question for the sociologist interested in social policy is whether the form of pension provision in Denmark, with its egalitarian consequences, has its roots in a society less class-divided in other ways. It is likely, for example, that the large numbers of small holders and independent craftsmen in that country have continued to modify the "typical" class structure of industrial societies (Chapter 13, pp. 403–413, 420–422).

Social Policy

Theoretical Standpoint : One of the chief aims of the cross-national survey was to derive knowledge that could be of value in the evolution of social policy. We have tended to assume that the continued expansion of social services is necessary for social and economic development, whether in the "functional" sense of maintaining social equilibrium and institutionalizing conflict, or in the more dynamic sense of reinforcing morale and security and setting limits to emerging inequalities so that technological and organizational changes may be introduced. The growing role of publicly organized social services is a universal and, we would argue, an inevitable phenomenon in industrial countries. Human needs grow and change in societies that themselves are rapidly becoming more complex. First, populations become hungry for goods and services that neither the individual nor the family but only technology and the modern professions, can supply. Second, neither the market alone nor the market and charity in conjunction can cope with the acceleration of public demand for services and with the problems of efficient and equitable distribution. From time to time some, though not necessarily all, of the deficiencies of the market are made good in the public sector. The widespread assumption that the Welfare State threatens the individual and the family because it undermines their self-sufficiency is fundamentally false. As we have seen, the Welfare State tends to serve the ends of the individual, the family, and the community as a whole, and largely complements their resources. The real problem is how *efficiently* in different countries the state adjusts resources to need, and "distributes" social justice. Our theoretical standpoint is a "relativist" one, of insisting on viewing the condition of the aged or the poor in relation to that of the rest of the society in which they live, and also of comparing social services cross-nationally and relating them to appropriate stages of economic evolution.

Health Services : In all three countries the formal organization of social services has become increasingly thoroughgoing and complex in recent years. We will consider medical care, welfare services, and income security. We find that in general the United States spends a higher proportion than Britain and a much higher proportion than Denmark of its gross national product on health services (Table IV–1 and Chapter 4). But in most industrial countries expenditure on health has been rising faster than real national income (Table IV–2), and in real terms national income per head is much higher in the United States than in the two European countries. It is possible therefore to argue that the latter countries may be spending as much of their resources on health as the United States did when it was at a comparable point in its economic evolution—or they may be spending even more.

Physicians and Nurses : Despite relatively higher expenditures on health, the United States does not have a marked advantage in sheer numbers of staff. When compared with other Western countries, Denmark,

Britain, and the United States have broadly similar numbers per 1,000 population of physicians, nurses, and hospital beds (Table IV–4). However, Britain has slightly fewer health personnel than the other two countries, and fewer of her nurses are qualified. Britain has relatively more old people too, and slightly more of them are incapacitated. Yet fewer old people enter a hospital during a year than in the other two countries and, on average, they have rather more medical consultations (Table IV–11 and Chapter 4, pp. 83–87). More of them are visited by a doctor when ill in bed at home (Table IV–9) and more of the housebound and of the bedfast are visited regularly by a doctor (Tables IV–15 and IV–16). In relation to the average number of medical consultations with young adults, the number with persons 65 years of age and over is much higher in Britain than in the United States. Moreover, in relation to expenditure on general hospitals, expenditure on chronic disease and mental hospitals is higher (Table IV–3).

Inequalities of Utilization : In the United States illness is treated at home less often than in Britain and Denmark (Table IV–9). Short stays in the hospital and consultations in an office or surgery are more common. A large proportion of the elderly who are incapacitated have low incomes (Table II–9) and fewer of the "blue collar" than of the "white collar" classes use hospital services (Table IV–13). Generally, the evidence from the survey and elsewhere suggests that fewer medical resources are devoted to the aged, and among them the services are utilized more unequally, than in the two European countries.

Community Care : Community care services are found to be unevenly developed within each of the three countries and are relatively smaller in the United States than in the European countries. There is much less home nursing in the United States. Meals services do not exist, except experimentally in a few areas. Home-help services reach less than one in a thousand of those aged 65 and over, compared with around 30 or 40 in a thousand in Denmark and Britain (Table V–1). Proportionately less specially designed and "sheltered" forms of housing have been built, though legislation has recently been passed and it seems that building rates might quickly improve. On the other hand, the American public's interest in the problems of the aged has been rapidly mobilized in the last few years, the average purchasing power of the elderly is higher, and fewer of them, at least than in Britain, occupy poor quality housing.

The Shortcomings of the Health and Welfare Services in All Three Countries : Many of the statements that can be made on the basis of the cross-national data are in themselves incomplete but, when taken with other research studies, they point to a general situation of inadequate social services for the elderly. In all countries, but particularly in Denmark and the United States, a substantial number of the bedfast living at home are not visited regularly or occasionally by a doctor (Chapter 4 and Table IV–16). Of those with severe incapacity but who are not bedfast (that is, those scoring

7 or more on the index of incapacity), from two-fifths to three-fifths are not visited during a month by a doctor (Table II–7). In Denmark and the United States there are more than twice as many bedfast living at home, and in Britain more than four times as many, as there are people (not all of whom are bedfast) in all institutions (Chapters 2 and 4). Not all these people may be in need of medical and other services, of course, but many are likely to be. The large number of bedfast old people living at home is one of the most striking new facts to have emerged from this survey, and requires more investigation. Prima facie there seems to be a strong case for reviewing the role of the physician and the possible development of community nursing and health care in relation to the bedfast and housebound elderly.

In all three countries new and additional needs—partly attributable to an increase in numbers of the elderly population (particularly those aged 75 and over), and partly to rising standards of personal care and greater awareness of the problems of the elderly—have outstripped the growth of many services. There is wide agreement that community care services, especially home-help services, need to be greatly expanded (Chapter 5). In Britain 4 per cent are receiving home help and another 6 per cent say they need it; many of the latter appear to justify it in terms of their level of incapacity, the numbers living alone, and the lack of relatives available to help. In Denmark nearly the same proportion as in Britain are receiving home help (Table V–1), and other research has suggested that this figure too is a long way short of true requirements. In other ways the cross-national survey suggests that home-help services need to be developed for a substantial minority, say at least 1 in 10, of the population aged 65 and over. For example, 8 per cent of the Danes and 6 per cent of the Americans and British have difficulty in doing heavy housework or cannot do it at all and have no help (Table V–10).

Isolation and Visiting Services : The survey showed how untrue are some gloomy generalizations that the majority of the elderly in industrial societies lead lonely and isolated lives. Although around a quarter of the elderly say they are often alone and from a fifth to a third say they are lonely, yet fewer than 1 in 20 live in extreme isolation. But the survey also showed that for these persons it is not so much for want of a gesture from members of their families or from their neighbors that they are isolated as that they lack human and financial resources altogether. In all countries the development of a substitute network of visiting services and day centers, for example, is a pressing need.

Need for Occupation : Two alternative assumptions are often made about the retirement of men in industrial societies. One is that retired men want to continue to work and would return to work if jobs were available. The other is that the great majority of men look forward to retirement and, when once retired, enjoy it. Our evidence shows that the truth is more complex. Certainly there is a substantial number of retired men who say they do not want work and there are many, particularly in the United

States, who refer specifically to the enjoyment of rest and leisure. On the other hand, around a third in all three countries remain at work after the normal pensionable age. The great majority of them expect to go on working all their lives. Moreover, a third of the men in the United States and well over a third of the men in Britain who have been retired for less than three years say they want some form of work. The data show that all but a few of these men have little or no incapacity (Table XI–11). They represent nearly 200,000 in Britain and nearly 500,000 in the United States. In addition there are substantial numbers of men in Britain and the United States who have been retired for longer than three years who say they want work. In Denmark, partly because of the later retirement ages but also because of the greater degree of satisfaction with pension levels, the number is relatively smaller but still big enough to justify further investigation. There may be a difference between society's provisions for retirement and the extent to which the elderly find these provisions acceptable, although the effects of disability make it difficult sometimes to assess both the true attitudes of the elderly and whether or not these attitudes are realistic. Altogether, despite the undoubtedly successful adjustment of some to retirement, there is evidence here for more alternative forms of employment and sheltered employment for older men, and for forms of occupation in occupational therapy units, day centers, and (especially for the housebound) at home.

Income and Government Intervention :   Despite the very different systems of government support in the three countries, the *level* of benefits provided by these systems is crucial in all three in determining the standard of living of the majority of the elderly. From a half to two-thirds of all income units receive more than half their total income from government sources. This fact is important in relation to future policy. It is sometimes assumed that in the "growth" societies savings can be accumulated during working life or through insurance and membership of private pension schemes and that dependence on publicly sponsored schemes will diminish. But, despite higher absolute standards of living than in the other two countries and the strong ideological pressures against public and in favor of "self" provision, the dependence of the elderly in the United States on government benefits is little different from, and is potentially heavier than, that in the two European countries. The problems in "affluent" societies of state action to overcome relative poverty may be growing rather than diminishing.

The Principles of Schemes of Income Support :   The results of the cross-national survey direct attention to the need to develop schemes of income-support that relate incomes in retirement more closely to (i) the incomes of the employed section of the community and (ii) increases from year to year in real earnings and national income. The basic or minimum benefit needs to be higher; and benefits need to be linked to an earnings index. Particularly in Britain and the United States there is strong evidence, too, for redistributing resources to people of more advanced age among the

elderly, particularly to those among them who are disabled and to widows
—categories which overlap to a marked extent.

The Cross-National Approach to Social Policy :   This is a pioneering cross-
national study. Others will improve on our techniques of inquiry and
analysis. But we hope we have shown how the gap between sociological
analysis and the formulation of principles for social policy might be
bridged. At the same time, we have tried to indicate the kind of insights
into the adequacy of government provision for the elderly that can be
obtained by cross-national study. Certainly we have shown that sections
of the elderly population are not integrated into society and that they
experience problems of isolation, ill-health, privation, and lack of adequate
care. But we have also demonstrated many positive features of family and
community support, continued good health, activity, and adjustment to
old age. Perhaps this is the single most optimistic theme of the report.
There are serious problems of the elderly in all three societies, but they do
not assume dimensions that are inherently unmanageable, given imagina-
tive leadership and the accelerated development of social services.

Appendix A: Sample Design and Response

The universe sampled was the total population of the continental United States, of England, Wales, and Scotland, and of Denmark, aged 65 and over, living in private households.

SAMPLE DESIGN

In all three countries the sample was a stratified multi-stage probability sample, similar in design to many other surveys carried out in each country concerned.

In Denmark a three-stage sample design was used.

(i)   The primary sampling units were formed on the basis of local administrative districts. These sampling districts, 2,833 in all, were stratified according to degree of urbanization, occupation and industrial structure. A random sample of 222 districts, each containing approximately 500 households, was selected from these strata with probability proportional to the number of households in the districts.

(ii) Within the selected districts area clusters were designated containing approximately 5 households. A sample of area clusters was then selected, within each district, with unit probability.

(iii) All households in the selected clusters were visited and all persons aged 65 and over resident in the households were included in the sample.

In Britain a three-stage sample design was also used.

(i)   Local authority administrative areas were the primary sampling units. These primary units, of which there are about 2,000, were grouped into standard administrative regions, and then within regions were stratified by degree of urbanization and by economic status. Eighty primary sampling units were then selected with probability proportional to their parliamentary electorate (that is, total population aged 21 and over).

(ii) At the second stage, addresses were selected with unit probability from the electoral registers for the selected primary units.

(iii) At the selected addresses all persons aged 65 and over were included in the sample.

In the United States a five-stage sample design was used.
(i) At the first stage all standard metropolitan areas and individual counties outside these areas were grouped into 68 strata according to the following criteria: geographic region, size, size of largest community; median family income, economic characteristics, availability of certain medical facilities; racial characteristics. One primary sampling unit was drawn from each of these strata with probability proportional to its estimated 1960 population.

(ii) The second stage was a selection of localities from within these primary sampling units. Within each primary sampling unit localities were ordered according to cities with block statistics, other urban places, urbanized minor civil divisions, and non-urbanized minor civil divisions. Within each of these categories localities were ordered by the 1960 population. The final selection was then of localities with probability proportional to size.

(iii) The third stage was a selection of area clusters or segments. The number of such segments to be selected from any one locality was determined by (a) the desired sampling ratio for the entire United States, (b) the probability of the particular locality, and (c) the estimated number of households it was desired to interview to yield 2.5 interviews with persons 65 and over per segment (this being the number of interviews it was decided would provide a suitable balance of precision and economy). In localities with recent city directories the segments were selected by sampling columns of addresses. In other localities census tracts and block units were used. The final selection of segments was made with probability proportional to the number of households in them.

(iv) The fourth stage consisted of a listing of households in each selected segment or block. Households were selected from these listing sheets with probability determined by the ratio of the final sampling ratio of households to the probability with which the segment had been selected.

(v) At the selected households all members aged 65 or over were included in the sample.

THE FIELD WORK

Investigation in the field took place at approximately the same time in the three countries—mid-April to August, 1962 (see Chapter 1, p. 14).

RESPONSE

Appendix Table A–1 summarizes the number of households or addresses designated for screening in Britain and the United States.

There was a higher completion rate for the screening interviews in Britain, possibly because no information other than the age and sex of persons resident at the address was asked for. In the United States the screening interview lasted about 20 minutes and information about adult education activities in the household, as well as demographic characteristics, was obtained.

In Denmark it was possible to obtain, from the municipal registers, information about the age and sex of the members of households where screening interviews were not successfully completed (that is, at 1,743 or 16.9 per cent of the original sample of 10,377 households). This was done and all selected households containing people aged 65 and over were revisited. In this way there was no loss of information specifically attributable to the screening interview as was the case in Britain and the United States.

Table A–1: SCREENING SAMPLE: BRITAIN AND THE UNITED STATES

	BRITAIN	UNITED STATES
Number of addresses or households selected	8,160 (100.0%)	13,293 (100.0%)
Number of screening interviews completed	8,098 (99.2%)	12,005 (90.3%)
Number of refusals, not at home, etc.	62 (0.8%)	1,288[a] (9.7%)

[a] A few segments, including an Indian reservation, were not assigned for screening.

Table A-2 summarizes the number of persons aged 65 and over resident at the selected addresses or households in the three countries, and the number of interviews successfully completed. Where persons in the sample were at home but too sick to be interviewed, an interview was, wherever possible, conducted with the person responsible for the sick older person. These are "proxy" interviews.

If the households or addresses not enumerated at the screening stage in Britain and the United States are assumed to contain the same proportion of individuals aged 65 and over as those successfully enumerated, the over-all completion rate, excluding proxy interviews, would be reduced to 83.6 per cent in the United States and 83.0 per cent in Britain. The reasons for refusal and for non-contact were diverse. They ranged from

Table A–2: PROPORTION OF INTERVIEWS COMPLETED

	DENMARK	BRITAIN	UNITED STATES
Total individuals aged 65 and over	2,912 (100.0%)	3,008 (100.0%)	2,739 (100.0%)
Interviews completed	2,445 (83.8%)	2,518 (83.8%)	2,442 (89.8%)
Proxy interviews	75 (2.5%)	73 (2.4%)	97 (3.5%)
Refusals, non-contacts, etc.	392 (13.7%)	417 (13.8%)	200 (7.3%)

"not interested," "opposed to surveys," to "too nervous" or "too tired" to be interviewed. A few older people were away at the time of the interviewer's visit; others were too ill or confused and no proxy respondent was available.

THE CHARACTERISTICS OF RESPONDENTS AND NON-RESPONDENTS

Comparing certain key characteristics of the respondents and, where known, of the non-respondents suggests that the differences between the two groups are quite small.

There is close agreement between the respondents and the full sample in respect of sex. There may be some slight overrepresentation of the younger age groups among the respondents in both Britain and the United States. This would largely disappear, however, if we assume that those individuals whose ages are not known, had the same age distribution as the rest of the sample. There also appears to be some slight overrepresentation among the respondents, again in both of these countries, of older people living quite alone and an underrepresentation of married couples (Table A–3).

THE CHARACTERISTICS OF RESPONDENTS COMPARED WITH OFFICIAL DATA

Comparisons of the respondent sample can be made with only one or two independent estimates of the characteristics of the universe. These are summarized in Table A–4. Again the agreement is very close. The British responding sample may be slightly deficient in females and in persons over 85. But the official estimates with which the comparison is being made include the institutional population aged 65 and over, which will contain a higher proportion of the older age groups. There may be some deficiency of women in the responding Danish sample, and a small age deficiency in the range 65–69. The balance of the sexes is extremely close in the United States, but there is the possibility of some small deficiency in the older age groups (although, again, this could be explained by the inclusion in the official estimates of the institutional population).

Table A-3: CHARACTERISTICS OF RESPONDENTS AND NON-RESPONDENTS

Characteristics	DENMARK Total Located N	Per Cent	Respondents Including Proxy N	Per Cent	Non-Respondents N	Per Cent	BRITAIN Total Located N	Per Cent	Respondents Including Proxy N	Per Cent	Non-Respondents N	Per Cent	UNITED STATES Total Located N	Per Cent	Respondentsᵃ N	Per Cent	Non-Respondents N	Per Cent
Sex																		
Male	1,353	46	1,184	47	169	43	1,196	40	1,035	40	161	39	1,220	45	1,081	44	139	47
Female	1,559	54	1,336	53	223	57	1,811	60	1,556	60	255	61	1,519	55	1,361	56	158	53
No answer	—	—	—	—	—	—	1	*	—	—	1	*	—	—	—	—	—	—
Marital Status																		
Single	235	8	191	8	44	11	318	11	287	11	31	7	126	5	116	5	10	3
Married	1,577	54	1,374	55	203	52	1,418	47	1,244	48	174	42	1,487	54	1,335	55	152	51
Widowed, etc.	1,089	37	951	37	138	35	1,136	38	1,059	41	77	19	1,096	40	991	40	105	36
No answer	11	1	4	0	7	2	198	4	—	—	135	32	30	1	—	—	30	10
Age																		
65–69	1,127	39	945	38	182	46	999	33	903	35	96	23	973	36	914	37	59	20
70–74	850	29	730	29	120	31	825	27	742	29	83	20	825	30	770	32	55	19
75–79	545	19	491	19	54	14	568	19	517	20	51	12	441	16	408	17	33	11
80–84	390	13	354	14	36	9	325	11	290	11	35	8	270	10	233	10	37	12
85 and over							157	5	136	5	21	5	140	5	104	4	36	12
No answer but 65+	—	—	—	—	—	—	134	5	3	*	131	32	90	3	13	*	77	26
Household composition																		
Alone	809	28	693	28	116	30	596	20	561	22	35	8	553	20	526	22	27	9
With others, including spouse	2,102	72	1,826	72	276	70	2,342	78	2,028	78	314	75	2,157	79	1,916	78	241	81
No answer	1	0	1	0	—	—	70	2	2	*	68	16	29	1	—	—	29	10
N=	2,912	—	2,520	—	392	—	3,008	—	2,591	—	417	—	2,739	—	2,442	—	297	—

ᵃ Excluding proxy interviews.   * Less than one per cent.

Table A-4: COMPARISON OF RESPONDENTS AND OFFICIAL ESTIMATES OF THE POPULATION

Characteristics	DENMARK		BRITAIN		UNITED STATES	
	Responding Sample	Official Estimates[a]	Responding Sample	Official Estimates[b]	Responding Sample	Official Estimates[c]
Sex						
Male	47.0	46.6	39.8	38.4	44.3	44.6
Female	53.0	53.4	60.2	61.6	55.7	55.4
Age						
65–69	37.5	38.4	34.6	36.4	37.4	36.2
70–74	29.0	} 61.6	29.4	27.8	31.5	28.9
75–79	19.5		20.1	19.6	16.7	19.1
80–84	} 14.0		10.9	10.8	9.6	10.1
85 and over			4.9	5.4	4.3	5.7
No answer			0.1	—	0.5	—
Total	100.0	100.0	100.0	100.0	100.0	100.0
N=	2,520	453,000	4,209	6,151,000	2,442	17,308,000

Source: [a] Population in private households only. *Statistiske Efterretninger*, No. 45 (Copenhagen: Det Statistiske Departement, 1964).

[b] Great Britain, The General Register Office, *The Registrar-General's Quarterly Return for England and Wales, Quarter ended 30th September, 1962* (London: HMSO, 1962). Great Britain, The General Register Office, *Quarterly Return of the Registrar-General—Scotland* (London: HMSO, 1963).

[c] U.S. Bureau of the Census, Current Population Reports, *Population Estimates, Estimates of the Population of the United States by Age, Color and Sex, July 1, 1950 to 1962*, Series P–25, No. 265 (May, 1963). (Washington, D.C.: U.S. GPO, 1963), Table 1, p. 11.

RELIABILITY AND SAMPLING ERRORS

The samples appear to provide a good representation of the universe sampled in respect of age and sex. Nor is it likely that the non-interviewed cases will materially affect the estimates of most of the variables discussed in the report. The major exception is the financial material, where there was further non-response from some units who completed the rest of the questionnaire. This problem and the direction in which bias may be expected is discussed in Appendix B. One of the most striking features of the samples is the great similarity of response in the three countries.

As in all sample surveys the estimates in this report are subject not only to possible error arising from non-response, but also to sampling error, or the variations that arise by chance through studying only a sample and not the whole population. Most of the estimates in the text are of percentages of the universe possessing various characteristics. As a guide for the reader, we have prepared a table showing the sampling error of various percentages in random samples of different sizes. Table A–5

Table A–5: ESTIMATED ADDITIONS AND SUBTRACTIONS FOR THE ESTABLISHMENT OF 95 PER CENT CONFIDENCE LIMIT

Estimated Percentage	All Persons Aged 65 or over; Sample Size Approx. 2,400		Sex-Specific: Aged 65 or Over		Size of Sub-Sample					
					100		250		500	
					Lower and Upper Limits[a]					
	A	*B*	*A*	*B*	*A*	*B*	*A*	*B*	*A*	*B*
2 or 98	1	1	1	1	—	—	—	1	1	2
5 or 95	1	1	1	2	—	—	3	4	2	3
10 or 90	1	2	2	2	6	10	4	6	3	4
20 or 80	2	2	3	3	9	11	6	7	4	5
30 or 70	2	2	3	3	11	12	7	8	5	5
50		2		4		13		8		6

[a] For estimates of less than 50 per cent the appropriate figure from the A column should be subtracted from the estimate and the appropriate figure from the B column should be added. For example, suppose a sub-group estimate based on 500 interviews were 10 per cent. The range would be 7–14 per cent (i.e., 10 per cent minus 3 and plus 4). For estimates of more than 50 per cent, the figure from the A column should be added and the figure from the B column subtracted. For estimates of 50 per cent the upper and lower limits are the same distance from the estimate.

gives a rough idea of the allowance that should be made.* For practical purposes the reader may assume that there is only a one in 20 chance that the true proportion will lie outside the range of the estimate given in the text, plus or minus the sampling error shown in Table A–5.

* For a discussion of the problems and the method of calculating the limits in Table A–7, see Jacob J. Feldman and James S. Coleman, "Appendix B, Methodology," in Ethel Shanas, *The Health of Older People: A Social Survey* (Cambridge, Mass.: Harvard University Press, 1962), pp. 193–206.

Appendix B: Methodological Appendix to Chapters 12 and 13

A number of methodological problems arise in the collection and analysis of financial data from individuals or families. In this survey we have tried to follow the practices most generally adopted by statisticians concerned with collecting such data for social accounting purposes.

Total Money Income is defined to *exclude* capital gains and any windfall receipts of a capital nature from betting, from occasional gifts or loans, from matured insurance policies, or from the sale of capital assets. Income is defined net of any expenses that are incurred in connection with business activity, with the management of property, or with the letting of rooms to boarders or lodgers.

We have worked with a concept of *gross* income, before payment of any direct taxes or social security contributions. There are three reasons for this. First, analysis of the relative importance of different income sources is only possible using a gross income concept. Second, although differing tax structures in the three countries could well affect the real income of the aged differently, we were in no position to estimate the total effect of the incidence of direct and *indirect* taxes, or of indirect benefits (for instance, the real value of the free health service in Denmark and Great Britain). In many cases indirect taxes and benefits will be just as important as direct taxes in changing the initial distribution of income. Third, this is the easiest way in which to collect income information from respondents who tend more often to know the gross rather than the net figure.

We have also worked with a concept of total *money* income. Income in kind may be of three types. The first is gifts received from friends or relatives. It is arguable how far these constitute "income" rather than "windfall" receipts. Some general questions about such gifts were included in the questionnaire and they are discussed in the text. But we were unable, in any case, had we even wished to do so, to treat such receipts as income by putting a money value upon them. As for the second income in kind— non-money income derived from farm activity, from owner-occupation, or from rent-free accommodation—in this particular study we could not explore it in the detail necessary to impute a value to such receipts. The effect of such imputation is known to be insignificant in Great Britain. Unfortunately, it may not be so in Denmark or the United States, with their much larger agricultural populations. This problem is again discussed in the text. The third sort of income in kind is, perhaps, one of the most important for the aged. It is that arising in the form of subsidy from other members of the household with whom the aged may be living. Again, however, this survey was not one in which the effect of such transfers could be pursued in detail. There is, however, a general discussion of this problem in the text of Chapter 13.

Assets : Assets were defined to include cash and deposits in commercial and saving banks (together called liquid assets); holdings of stocks and shares, which in the United States would include Savings bonds; and income-producing property other than "owner-occupied" houses. Again, because of limitations imposed by an already over-lengthy interview schedule we did not measure assets net of liabilities, but there is little reason to suppose that this makes any significant difference to the findings. We established the estimated value of any owner-occupied home, but in Denmark and Britain, where we have an estimate of "total assets," the home is not regarded as being part of the total assets of the aged. Similarly, the capital value of other durable consumer goods and of life assurance is also excluded from our concept of total assets, although, again, data on life assurance was collected. The arguments for making these exclusions are twofold. First, the valuation of these assets is difficult to achieve in the interview situation. Second, there are often difficulties in the way of the old person's realizing such assets. In Britain, for instance, it is very difficult for an old person to obtain a mortgage on an existing owner-occupied property. For those readers who are unhappy about our treatment of total assets, the data is presented so that they can make the allowance.

Dissaving : We have estimated the net reduction of assets by asking respondents for net withdrawals from the bank, about the net sale of property, or the net sale of stocks or shares. We also collected information about windfall receipts through betting wins, inheritance, tax refunds, and so forth.

The Period Covered : Income is a flow over time and if it is to be measured the reference period must be defined. Unfortunately there is often conflict between the period convenient for analysis (usually a year) and that which is most convenient from the point of view of the respondent's memory (which may vary with the source of income). Wages may be received each week or each month, interest on stocks every six months; the self-employed may not know the total of their income until well after the end of their trading year. In both the United States and Denmark it proved possible to use a year as the reference period. Many of the respondents were, or had been, preparing their annual income tax return shortly before the time of field work. The Danish income data has been checked by their Inland Revenue Department.

In Britain a shorter reference period was necessary. The amount received and the number of receipts in the previous 12 months were recorded for each income source. Where these were not weekly receipts they were converted to a weekly basis and the analysis was first carried out in terms of total gross weekly income and subsequently converted to annual equivalents. The income data for Britain is, however, derived not only from the cross-national round of interviews conducted in mid-May–July, 1962, but also from a second round conducted in November–December, 1962. This takes care of any possible seasonal variation in income (which, in fact, turns out to be negligible)[1] but does mean that the British figures are an amalgam of the period mid-May, 1961 to December, 1962, whereas the Danish and United States material relates to the calendar year 1961. It also means that the total size of the British sample for financial data is much larger than that of the other two countries.

Definition of Sources of Income :   In defining the main sources of income that we wished to distinguish for purposes of analysis, some flexibility between the three countries had to be allowed.

I. *Government Benefits*—These include any transfer income from central or local government other than payments of pensions to former employees of the central or local government. They include pensions paid from government schemes of social security; income derived from public assistance (local and national), war, disability pensions, or sickness benefits.

In Denmark, government benefits are almost exclusively old age pensions, and no further breakdown is meaningful. In Britain and the United States some sub-totals are available:

Social Security
    (i) In the United States this means payments under the Federal Old Age, Survivors, and Disability Insurance Program.
    (ii) In Britain this means payments under the National Insurance Acts.
Assistance
    (i) In the United States payments by the states under state assistance programs.
    (ii) In Britain, payments by the National Assistance Board.
Other Government Benefits
    All other public benefits, such as veterans' or disability pensions, but excluding unemployment benefits.

II. *Wages and Salaries*—All payments to employees, full- or part-time, or for casual or irregular work. In the case of couples, wage and salaries refer to income from these sources for both the husband and wife (where the latter has any such income).

III. *Business, Farm, or Professional Practice*—Income from self-employment net of business expenses. In Britain there were so few cases of such income that they have been included with wages and salaries.

IV. *Employers' Pension*—All pensions being paid by or in respect of previous employment, including central and local government employment.

V. *Rent, Dividends, Interest, and Annuities*—All income from real estate, from stocks, shares, and other investment, or from purchased life annuities (other than those arising from previous employment, which are included as employer's pension). Net income from lodgers and boarders is included here in the Danish and United States figures. The total is sometimes referred to in the text as *property* income.

VI. *Other Income*—Includes such items as alimony, regular cash allowances from children and relatives outside the household, income from charity, and (in the case of the United States) unemployment benefit, and (in the case of Britain) income from lodgers and boarders.

The Unit of Analysis : Analysis of income and assets in terms of individuals is meaningless for married couples. We have therefore made our analysis in terms of "income units"—single, widowed, or divorced men, single, widowed, or divorced women, and married couples. Only married couples where the husband is 65 or over have been included in the financial analysis because we felt that the financial status of the couple would be largely determined by the position of the husband. By the same argument all couples where the husband is 65 or over, irrespective of the age of the wife, have been included in the analysis.

Cross-National Comparison of Financial Data : For much of the analysis we wished to group the income data into intervals, but we were faced with the problem of interpreting intervals fixed in terms of the unit of currency of three different countries. It was therefore agreed to consider distributions of income in terms of intervals expressed as percentages of the median total income of each of the three types of income unit in each of the three countries. The percentages are:

> 21 per cent or more below the median
> 6 per cent up to 20 per cent below the median
> Up to 5 per cent above and below the median
> 6 per cent up to 20 per cent above the median
> 21 per cent up to 50 per cent above the median
> 51 per cent up to 100 per cent above the median
> 101 per cent and over, above the median.

It should be noted that where the median income for a particular type of income unit in a country is low, the absolute size of the income interval will be small. Details of the intervals measured in the currency of each of the three countries are shown in Table XII–9.

Response and the Reliability of the Data : The general problems of sampling error, and possible bias in the information collected arising from non-response are discussed in Appendix A. But a special word needs to be said about these difficulties in relation to the financial data because in Denmark and Britain there was additional non-response to the financial questions. It is interesting that such additional non-response was negligible in the United States. In total, no financial data is available for 17 per cent of the income units approached in the original sample in Denmark. It is also lacking for 20 per cent in Britain but for only 11 per cent of income units in the United States.

Is there any reason to believe that the non-respondents form a special group in so far as their financial position is concerned? The trouble is that, except for Denmark, little is known about the financial position of those who did not cooperate; and in so far as we do have data about age, sex, and marital status—factors that might indirectly be correlated with financial position—the evidence is inconclusive. In Britain reweighting of the final cooperating sample to allow for some overrepresentation of certain classes of income unit has little effect on the final estimate of, for instance, the percentage of old people with assets. In financial surveys of the general population there is a good deal of evidence to suggest that non-response tends to be highest among the higher income groups. But we know that in the cross-national surveys we lost information from the sick, the infirm, and the mentally confused, who, as a group, may well be among the poorest.

Those income units who gave some financial information form the basis of the analysis in Chapters 12 and 13. They have been called "cooperating income units" (see Table XII–1). Even some of them, however, failed to provide complete financial information. Sources of income might be known, but not the amount of income from every source. There is some evidence that the units giving incomplete information in this way tend to be among the better-off old people. For instance, a higher proportion of them tend to belong to the white collar social class group. These cases are shown, therefore, where it is likely to be important, in a "no answer" category so that the reader may make some allowances for possible bias in the material if he wishes.

We must also ask whether the information given by respondents is reliable. There is evidence that there may be some underreporting of income and assets in surveys of the kind we have conducted. The best check on the reliability of the cross-national data is therefore to compare it with other estimates of key variables. We have selected one comparison for each country in order to give some indication of the nature and extent of bias, if any, in our financial material.

Denmark is able to provide the best check because the cross-national

Table B-1: RESPONSE BY INCOME UNIT

	DENMARK			BRITAIN			UNITED STATES		
	Couples	Men	Women	Couples	Men	Women	Couples	Men	Women
I. Income units located in the sample	946	395	914	1,422	603	1,931	933	287	946
II. Income units supplying no income information	128	64	171	323	108	379	108	31	95
III. Income units supplying some income information	818	331	743	1,099	495	1,552	825	256	851
IV. Percentage cooperating of total number located, i.e. (III) as percentage of (I)	87	84	81	77	82	80	88	89	90
V. Income units supplying total income information	708	294	672	1,023	456	1,460	776	249	784
VI. Percentage supplying total income information of total number located, i.e. (IV) as percentage of (I)	75	74	74	72	76	76	83	87	83

income data for that country was compared individually against income tax returns. It was found that the mean annual taxable income of the non-respondents was 9,676 Danish kroner compared with 8,964 Danish kroner for the respondents. Since the non-respondents are 17 per cent of all units, reweighting would give a mean annual income of 9,085 Danish kroner. This would suggest an underestimate of about one per cent in the sample material. The over-all Danish picture of income sources and levels is probably therefore very reasonable.

The British material is possibly rather more understated. The comparison, in Table B–2, with data from an earlier British study is remarkably close. But allowing for the fact that the cross-national field work was carried out two years later, after there had been increases in the level of governments benefits, one might have expected the levels of income shown by the cross-national survey to be higher than those shown by the earlier survey. Possibly the earlier survey overstated the position, but in any

Table B–2: COMPARISON OF THE BRITISH CROSS-NATIONAL INCOME DATA AS OF 1962 WITH THE DATA FROM THE 1959–60 SURVEY OF OLD PEOPLE[a]

Weekly Income Grouped	COUPLES		MEN		WOMEN	
	1959–60	Cross-National	1959–60	Cross-National	1959–60	Cross-National
Percentage of units with:						
No income and up to £3	—	} 8	17	13	32	23
£3 up to £4	—		30	23	31	33
£4 up to £5	12		15	15	13	18
£5 up to £6	21	16	7	12	8	8
£6 up to £8	22	28	13	11	6	6
£8 up to £10	13	14	3	7	3	2
£10 up to £15	14	17	7	6	3	2
£15 up to £20	7	6	1	3	2	1
£20 and over	10	5	7	2	2	1
No answer	—	7	—	8	—	6
Total	100	100	100	100	100	100
N=	298	1,099	141	495	607	1,552
Median income per week	£7 10s.	£7 10s.	£4 8s.	£4 11s.	£3 10s.	£3 14s.

[a] The 1959–60 data are reported in Dorothy Cole with John Utting, *The Economic Circumstances of Old People* (Welwyn, Herts: Codicote Press, 1962). The material differs from the cross-national data for Britain in a number of ways:

(i) The period covered relates to July, 1959–March, 1960.
(ii) The sampling method differed in that the 1959–60 survey had a random sample of income units within seven areas selected to represent the national picture.
(iii) More detailed prompting for income sources and assets was used in the 1959–60 survey.
(iv) Where assets but no asset income were reported, income was imputed at an appropriate rate of interest in the 1959–60 survey.

case it, too, is survey material and subject to error. But other comparisons, for instance with official figures, of the percentage of old people receiving national assistance, and of the numbers of tax units above the exemption limit for the elderly[2] confirm that the cross-national income data in Britain may be a little understated and that certainly "no answer" cases should be assumed to belong to higher income groups.

In Table B–3 we compare the United States cross-national data with data from the Social Security Administration survey of 1962.[3] There are

Table B–3: COMPARISON OF THE UNITED STATES CROSS-NATIONAL INCOME DATA WITH THE SOCIAL SECURITY ADMINISTRATION SURVEY DATA[a]

Yearly Income Grouped	DISTRIBUTION OF TOTAL MONEY INCOME					
	Couples		Men		Women	
	Cross-National	Social Security	Cross-National	Social Security	Cross-National	Social Security
Percentage of units with income of:						
Less than $1,000			36	32	51	49
$1,000–1,499	34	35	14	25	13	21
$1,500–1,999c			13	12	8	13
$2,000–2,499b			20	16		
$2,500–2,999	15	19				
$3,000–3,999c	13	16			20	17
$4,000–4,999	10	11	15	16		
$5,000 and over	17	20				
No answer	6	—	3	—	8	—
Median income	$2,804	$2,875	$1,406	$1,365	$982	$1,015

[a] The Social Security Administration data differ from the cross-national data for the United States in a number of ways:

  (i) The period covered relates to the calendar year 1962.
  (ii) Persons resident in institutions were included in the Social Security Coverage.
  (iii) The Social Security Administration sample was reweighted to allow for non-response on financial items from accepted schedules. This was done by matching respondents giving incomplete with those giving complete information. No adjustment was made where there was complete non-response.
  (iv) More detailed prompting for income sources and assets was used by the Social Security Administration.
  (v) Receipts from O.A.S.D.I. benefits were checked against Social Security records and corrected if wrong outside of a given margin.
  (vi) When an asset was reported and no asset income, the latter was imputed at a rate of 4 per cent by the Social Security Administration.

[b] The percentages of couples falling in the income interval $2,000–2,499 in the Social Security Administration data have been split to correspond to the cross-national data. The true interval here is therefore $0–2,240 and the next interval is $2,240–2,999.

[c] The percentages of units falling in intervals in the cross-national distribution at these points have been split to correspond with the intervals shown in these tables.

some differences, but generally the picture is one of remarkably close agreement, particularly when it is remembered that the Social Security Administration sample was four times as large as that used in the cross-national survey. Again, however, the comparison is with other survey material—which could itself be subject to some error.

One final piece of evidence, which would suggest some understatement of income in all three countries, comes from an examination for internal consistency of our data. We find a large discrepancy, in all three countries, between the percentage of units reporting the ownership of assets, and the percentage reporting income from rent, dividends, and interest. It is largest in Britain, well over a half of all units with assets failing to report asset income. However, the British data (for instance, comparison with the

Table B–4: COMPARISON OF THE PERCENTAGE OF INCOME UNITS REPORTING INCOME FROM RENT, DIVIDENDS, INTEREST, AND ANNUITIES, AND THOSE REPORTING OWNERSHIP OF ASSETS

Type of Income Unit	Receipt of Income from Rent, Dividends, Interest, and Annuities	PERCENTAGE OF UNITS REPORTING			
		Ownership of Known Amounts of			
		Total Assets	Liquid Assets	Stocks[a]	Property
Denmark					
Couples	54	75	70	8	b
Men	56	72	71	7	b
Women	54	66	67	8	b
Britain					
Couples	25	66	66	10	5
Men	24	63	62	12	5
Women	23	58	55	13	4
United States					
Couples	42	b	66	34	26
Men	27	b	55	23	20
Women	35	b	53	25	18

[a] Includes United States Savings Bonds, usually reported as stocks and bonds.

[b] Not available for the United States and Denmark.

1959–60 survey) suggest that for the most part this discrepancy represents a failure to report very small amounts of asset income which frequently are left to accumulate in the savings bank.

To summarize this necessarily brief examination of the reliability of the financial information, we can say that there is reasonable agreement in all three countries between the cross-national and other independent data relating to the financial position of older people. The cross-national estimates of income levels and distribution may be biased downwards somewhat, but the amount of such bias is relatively small and will not seriously affect the general picture described in Chapters 12 and 13, nor invalidate the conclusions drawn.

NOTES

1 Myra Woolf, "Older People in Great Britain Technical Report—Cross-National Survey" (SS. 343, SS. 343A) (unpublished report) (London: The Social Survey, n.d.).
2 Peter Townsend and Dorothy Wedderburn, *The Aged in the Welfare State* (London: Bell & Sons, Ltd., 1965).
3 Lenore A. Epstein, "Income of the Aged in 1962: First Findings of the 1963 Survey of the Aged," *Social Security Bulletin*, XXVII (March, 1964), 8, Table 2.

Index

As this book is a comparative study of the elderly in Britain, Denmark, and the United States, there are no major headings in this index for each country separately. Persons interested in special topics in any one country are asked to refer to that topic in the index.